NORWEGIAN MIGRATION TO AMERICA

THE AMERICAN TRANSITION

by

Theodore C. Blegen
Dean of the Graduate School in the
University of Minnesota

The Norwegian-American Historical Association
Northfield, Minnesota, 1940

PUBLICATIONS OF THE

NORWEGIAN-AMERICAN HISTORICAL ASSOCIATION

To

Arthur Andersen and Birger Osland

PREFACE

IN THE FOREWORD to my *Norwegian Migration to America, 1825–1860,* I suggested that the immigrant has been the focal point for the interplay of two creative forces in our national life, the European heritage and the American environment. That volume traces the genesis and early expansion of Norwegian immigration, explores the European backgrounds, and interprets the movement in a setting of international history. The present work — a companion volume — pictures the American transition of the Norwegian immigrant as the dynamic process it was, with the same creative forces in constant interplay.

In interpreting immigrant transition, I do not lose sight of backgrounds, but the major emphasis is given to the merging of the immigrant with the life of the New World. This embraces the whole experience of an immigrant people and invites a generous chronological and topical sweep. In grappling with social history on so broad a scale I encountered many difficult problems of research and used some unusual sources, including the findings of linguists who have probed immigrant speech and the writings of novelists who have probed immigrant souls.

It is my hope that this book will be read both for the story that it tells of one immigrant element and for the approach that it makes to an understanding of social forces which have not yet been sufficiently scrutinized by historians. The history of American life — portrayed realistically, as a never-ending process of transition, and with understanding of all the peoples who have participated in the making of America —

still remains to be written. If the present book marks even a step toward such a synthesis, I shall feel more than repaid for the effort of writing it.

I am deeply grateful for aid given me by many persons and institutions, and I offer them my sincere thanks. In this volume, as in the first, I made use of materials collected in Norway as a fellow of the John Simon Guggenheim Foundation; and a research fellowship awarded by the Norwegian-American Historical Association enabled me to devote the entire year of 1939–40 to writing. Mr. Arthur Andersen, Mr. Birger Osland, Mr. Frederic Schaefer, and Mr. O. M. Oleson took a cordial interest in my work and gave me substantial encouragement. Dr. Carlton C. Qualey helped me to assemble material on immigrant settlement. I owe a special debt of gratitude to Dr. Gertrude Ann Jacobsen, who aided me in collecting and arranging data on the social aspects of immigrant pioneering and on the role of the Norwegian sailors in America. Mrs. Ingrid Gaustad Semmingsen of Oslo kindly acquainted me with the results of her studies of the emigrant voyage. Dr. George M. Stephenson read the entire manuscript and gave me many valuable suggestions. Professor Einar I. Haugen examined several chapters, as did the Reverend Clarence J. Carlsen, and I profited by their criticisms. Two research assistants, Miss Margrethe Jorgensen and Mr. J. A. Fagereng, gave me help some years ago in my studies of immigrant pioneering and of the immigrant press. My sister Martha read carefully my chapter on aspects of everyday life. The drawings at the heads of the chapters are the work of Mr. John L. Ellingboe of Minneapolis. Miss Bertha L. Heilbron, Miss Sarah A. Davidson, and Mrs. Arthur J. Larsen undertook the final editorial revision and piloted the book through the press; Miss Jane McCarthy designed the title page; and Mrs. Helen Katz compiled the index. Finally, my wife's interest, advice, and encouragement were fundamental in the writing of the book from first to last.

THEODORE C. BLEGEN

CONTENTS

ILLUSTRATIONS

THE AMERICAN TRANSITION

I. FROM OLD WORLD TO NEW

"IN THESE DAYS," reads a Norwegian newspaper of the early 1850's, "one continually meets the so-called Americans . . . who are on their way to the Norwegian colonies in the West." These "Americans" had not yet seen America. They were Norwegian emigrants just out of their home valleys, making their way to seaports where vessels were waiting to carry them overseas. They had a look of "earnestness and decision," and if asked whether they did not find it hard to leave their home valleys, they were likely to reply, "Oh, yes, but we have made up our minds and will hold to our decision."[1]

The Norwegian writer Alexander Kielland tells of a German tourist, many years later, who while making his way to the interior of Norway met a stream of people journeying toward the coast. "Was sind das für Leute?" he asked. "Emigrants," was the reply. "They were earnest men and women in new homespun clothes," continues Kielland. They were accompanied by swarms of healthy, red-cheeked chil-

[1] *Christiania-posten,* May 8, 1851.

dren, some led by the hand, others carried in arms or on backs. There were traveling chests with names and addresses inscribed on them. "Over everything there was an air of well considered, slowly ripened resolution — the scanty but solid baggage, the new strong clothes, no unnecessary sentimental small things in their hands." The novelist tried to read the faces of these people in passage from Old World to New. No joy, scarcely a sign of what one would call hope, "only a firm, sorrowful resolution and a heavy pain lay in the depths of these eyes, which wept or were unable to weep."[2]

Such sights were as familiar to the people of Norway throughout the nineteenth century as were caravans of covered wagons to the people of the American West. Prospective emigrants had read the letters of their relatives and friends in America. They had studied the problems that faced them in the old country, and felt the pull of the New World. Not a few of them had talked with "returned Americans" in such scenes as that described by Bojer in his novel of emigration: "Outside the church next day the returned American, Erik Foss, had gathered a little crowd around him. The men stood there with their heads thrown well back, asking him questions, listening and staring. The newcomer was tall and fair, with a brown mustache; and he wore, like the gentlefolks, a collar and tie, a brown frock-coat, and a top-hat and shiny boots. But you could see from his hands that he knew what work meant. Seven years he'd been out there; and though he was only the son of Scraggy Olina, he was a big man now."[3] The emigrants had conned the pages of Ole Rynning's *True Account of America,* of Johan R. Reiersen's *Pathfinder for Norwegian Emigrants to the United North American States and Texas,* or of some other emigrant guidebook. They had talked with neighbors and friends and

[2] Alexander Kielland, *Samlede værker,* 2:117 (Copenhagen, 1903). The passage occurs in the novel *Arbeidsfolk,* published in 1881.

[3] Johan Bojer, *The Emigrants,* 23 (New York, 1925).

listened to praise and condemnation of America. Many of them had been visited by captains or other agents of vessels that specialized in the emigrant traffic. Some had received tickets or money from America. The prospects and problems of the New World venture had been threshed over in family circles on winter nights. Out of it all had come the decision to follow the trail of Cleng Peerson and Ole Rynning and thousands of other "Americans."[4]

"The best time to leave Norway," advised Rynning, "is so early in the spring as to be able to reach the place of settlement by midsummer or shortly after that time. In that way something can be raised even the first year; namely, buckwheat, which is planted in the last days of June; turnips, which are planted in the latter part of July; and potatoes. It is very unfortunate to go too late in the year to gather fodder for one or two cows and build a house for the winter."[5] This was sage advice that nearly every "America letter" reinforced, and the prospective emigrants took it seriously, as did the captains and owners of emigrant vessels. The advantages of an early start in the spring coincided with those attendant upon the breakup of winter as a favorable time for the vessels to set out. The result was that the spring months of March, April, and May became the gala season for emigration. Year after year, though total numbers might vary, the movement had the same seasonal rhythm. After a lull during the winter months, there was a considerable rise in March, then full tide in April, a somewhat less heavy migration in May, and a gradual decline during the later summer months.[6]

During the long and dark winter the victims of that disease

[4] The basic causes of Norwegian emigration to America are discussed in the writer's *Norwegian Migration to America, 1825–1860,* ch. 2 (Northfield, Minnesota, 1931); and in ch. 15 of the present volume.

[5] Theodore C. Blegen, ed., *Ole Rynning's True Account of America,* 98 (Norwegian-American Historical Association, *Travel and Description Series,* vol. 1 — Northfield, 1926).

[6] See table 9 in Udvandringskomiteen, *Foreløbig indstilling* (Christiania, 1913).

which Norwegians called "America fever" were busy getting ready for their departure in the early spring. The immediate practical question was what to take with them; and Rynning, typical of the emigrant guides, gave them specific answers. They must have provisions to take care of their needs for twelve weeks, particularly foods that could be "kept a long time without being spoiled." He suggested "pork, dried meat, salted meat, dried herring, smoked herring, dried fish, butter, cheese, primost, milk, beer, flour, peas, cereals, potatoes, rye rusks, coffee, tea, sugar." There was danger of sickness on the voyage, and Rynning therefore advised "a little brandy, vinegar, and a couple of bottles of wine, as well as raisins and prunes to make soup for the seasick"; a cathartic; sulphur powder and ointment "for the itch"; Hoffman's drops; and spirits of camphor. Cleanliness was important, and he urged the emigrants to be supplied with "linen for change, salt-water soap for washing, and good fine combs."

The captain, Rynning pointed out, must supply wood and water for twelve weeks. He urged all emigrants to have formal contracts, drafted in both Norwegian and English, with the captains or owners of the vessels in which they sailed. Make sure, he said, that the water is kept in good casks and that there is enough to supply each person with three quarts a day. If "the water in some casks is spoiled," he added, "the good water is to be used up before beginning with the bad, and the captain shall take water for his own use from the same barrel as the passengers." The captain should also be obligated to make certain that everyone had enough provisions to last for twelve weeks. Incidentally, the "passengers must also furnish their own light." All this was formidable enough, but it by no means exhausted Rynning's list of essentials. The emigrant must take with him bedclothes, clothing of fur and homespun, an iron plate for baking flat bread, a spinning wheel, if possible a hand mill, silverware, and tobacco pipes to sell in America. A mechanic must have his tools. Good rifles with percussion locks, Rynning said, would prove useful and, if sold in the United States, profitable. He also mentioned the need of books and of materials to use for busy work during the long voyage.[7]

One writer, telling of his grandfather's journey to America, relates that the women of the family spun, wove, and sewed throughout the winter, making dresses, suits, underclothing, and other garments as if there would be no clothes to get once the family had left their old home. Since there were twelve persons in the family, one can readily understand that their task was no small one, particularly since they also had to prepare food for twelve mouths on what might turn out to be a three-month journey. The men had to turn to carpentry, sawing, planing, and hammering as they made a dozen traveling chests, all with homemade iron bands, locks, and huge keys. They were painted red, with blue corners, and each bore, in large letters, the inscription "Syver Guttormsen, Inmansville, Rock Co., Wisconsin, U. S. A."[8] A Norwegian-American woman, recalling scenes from her childhood, wrote, "All through the winter I helped mother with the preparations. In the evening darkness my brother and I often sat and built air castles, dreaming of what we should do when we got to America."[9] Another writer recalls that the loom and spinning wheel were busy throughout the winter; some of the cattle were sold, the others slaughtered; and meat was salted for the journey, flat bread baked, and the chests made ready.[10] Butter was usually packed in spe-

[7] See Rynning's chapter, "Guiding Advice for Those Who Wish to Go to America," in *True Account of America,* 96–100.

[8] J. S. Johnson, "Bedstefars reise til Amerika," quoted in *Norsk-amerikaneren,* 291 (Seattle, 1928).

[9] Siri Lee, "Amerikareise i 1866," in *Samband* (Minneapolis), no. 69, p. 130–134 (January, 1914).

[10] Andrew L. Lien, "En Amerikareise i '49," in *Samband,* no. 52, p. 374–384 (August, 1912).

cial kegs, sometimes large enough to hold a hundred pounds, and often it would spoil long before the voyage was over. Cheeses, such as brown primost or *pultost,* were also subject to the uncertainties of weather and time; and an observer recalled that in spoiling they gave off first a great odor, then an intolerable stench, and sometimes were found to be filled with maggots. The flat bread, the same writer remembers, was placed in wooden barrels or casks. "A large part of this bread was made of oatmeal; part of it was oat and barley flour mixed. The finest was made of bolted rye, but only a small quantity of this was in use by ordinary emigrants." For the earlier stages of the trip the emigrants might have *lefse*—"folded up like an ironed handkerchief."[11]

Usually an auction was held before the departure. "The cow, the calf, and the sheep, as well as the odds and ends, went under the auctioneer's hammer," one immigrant recalled.[12] The *gaard* was disposed of, an auction held, and everything sold, relates Clara Jacobson, who pictured migration in terms of two small children who unhappily failed to take their rag dolls with them and who had some concern about prevalent reports of Turks who smelled the blood and liked the flesh of Christians, especially plump *bonde* girls.[13] Bojer gives a vivid picture of an emigrant auction: "Here there was a sledge upon which Kai had dragged home so many loads of wood, a wheelbarrow, a spade and a fork, a calf, two sheep, a griddle, a coffee-kettle and two saucepans, two beds and some bedclothes, some tables, and a trough in which Karen had mixed cakes on the rare occasions when she had any flour. Some one bid twelve cents for the lot. 'Too little,' said Ebbe. 'Fourteen cents . . . that's better . . .

[11] Karl E. Erickson, "The Emigrant Journey in the Fifties," edited by Albert O. Barton, in *Studies and Records,* 8:88–90. Johnson mentions a butter keg holding a hundred pounds, in *Norsk-amerikaneren,* 291.

[12] Johan Gran, "En Amerikareise i 1872," in *Samband,* no. 103, p. 49, 50 (November, 1916).

[13] Clara Jacobson, "En Amerika-reise for seksti aar siden," in *Symra,* 9:120–137 (1913).

The Departure from a Norwegian Farm Home
[From a lithograph of a painting by Adolph Tidemand.]

NORWEGIAN EMIGRANTS IN THE STEERAGE OF A SAILING VESSEL
[From a contemporary view of 1866, reproduced in Fredrik Scheel and Jacob S. Worm-Müller, *Den norske sjøfarts historie,* 609 (Oslo, 1935).]

twenty-four . . . ah, that's more like! thirty . . . bid up, good folks!"[14] Kari, in Wergeland's emigrant song, was obliged to give up her spinning wheel, and to it, symbol of familiar and cherished things, she addressed her good-by:

Good-by, my old comrade,
As now I must leave thee,
My heart, it is breaking,
My going will grieve thee.
No longer at night
By the glow of the fire
Shall we sit and gossip
And know heart's desire.[15]

So the people set out for such ports as Stavanger, Bergen, Christiania, Porsgrund, Langesund, Drammen, and Kragerø. From many an inland valley the journey meant several stages: first a trip by sleigh, then a transfer to wagons, then perhaps a long wait for a boat sailing one of the fjords, and finally the arrival at the seaport, where not infrequently the travelers found the emigrant vessel not ready to sail and were delayed many days, and even weeks, perhaps camping at the pier or finding the most inexpensive lodgings, eating their precious food, spending their money.[16]

An old emigrant ballad tells of Bergen in the gala days of emigration: "So we rowed up the bay; and there lay the mighty ships, with masts hewn of the tallest trees in the forest — all ready to sail for America. It was a wondrous sight to see: the decks swarmed like an ant heap, kerchiefs and caps of every color — and all were bent on leaving the country."[17] In the earlier years, however, neither Bergen nor any other Norwegian port witnessed such scenes, and the emigrants were obliged either to buy a vessel themselves, as

[14] *The Emigrants,* 54, 55.

[15] The original is printed in Theodore C. Blegen and Martin B. Ruud, eds., *Norwegian Emigrant Songs and Ballads,* 85–87 (Minneapolis, 1936).

[16] G. J. Anderson, "Beretning om amerikareisen i sekstiaarene," in *Samband,* no. 32, p. 57, 58 (December, 1910). See also the previously cited narratives by Jacobson, Gran, Johnson, and Lee.

[17] Blegen and Ruud, *Norwegian Emigrant Songs and Ballads,* 321.

the sloop folk did in 1825, or to find passage to Göteborg, Hamburg, Havre, or some other European port from which they could hope to sail for America.[18] From the middle 1830's Norwegian captains and shipowners began to appreciate the possibilities of the emigrant trade, and gradually a fleet of sailing vessels became available, nearly all of them attempting to combine the emigrant traffic with the carrying of iron or of other products and with trade out of American and Canadian ports. Thus emigration is intimately related to the development of the Norwegian merchant marine.

A Norwegian historian rightly points out that, whereas lumber, coal, and grain were of fundamental importance in the general growth of the merchant marine of the world, there was a fourth factor, namely, the transportation of "living goods." The "emigrant traffic," he declares, "was the backbone of transatlantic commerce." And he exclaims, "What would it have been, indeed, without the modern gigantic folk migration, without the ceaseless stream of emigrants who sought their fortune in the New World from the time of the 1820's, but especially from the 1840's, with a great culmination about 1850 because of the gold discoveries in California and Australia, and then onward through the century with a steadily rising rhythm!" The emigrant traffic was important not only because of the vast number of persons carried across the seas but also because it stimulated the opening of new markets for European goods and the carrying of American products to the Old World. For Norway, the regularity of the emigrant trade was of special significance, for it encouraged the flow of capital into the building of larger and better vessels and it meant regular enterprise by Norwegian vessels in world trade.[19]

Toward the mid-century Norway was becoming aware

[18] Blegen, *Norwegian Migration,* 58, 87.

[19] Jacob S. Worm-Müller, in Worm-Müller and Fredrik Scheel, *Den norske sjøfarts historie,* vol. 2, pt. 1, p. 547–550 (Oslo, 1935).

of the importance of the direct connections that emigration had established between itself and the United States. In 1845 a newspaper argued for a "livelier trade connection with America" and spoke appreciatively of three shiploads of American products received that summer from New York. An expanding American trade, it believed, meant increased respect for the Norwegian flag, profitable employment for the country's merchant marine, and the obvious economy of firsthand importation of American products.[20] In 1848 another newspaper wrote in similar vein, pointing out that a decade earlier it had been an exception for a Norwegian ship, not to speak of a Norwegian tradesman, to establish any contact whatsoever with the United States, whereas now there was a fairly regular connection between that rich country and Norway. In 1847 alone, it said, twenty-nine Norwegian vessels arrived in New York, ten direct from Norway with emigrants and iron; and the year had witnessed the direct importation from America of cotton, wheat, flour, rice, tobacco, rye, logwood, rosin, and other products.[21]

The Norwegian ship captains were alert to the possibilities in trade that offered themselves in North American ports. One Norwegian vessel carried emigrants to New York, there took a cargo for Jamaica, then loaded for London, and finally returned to Norway.[22] In 1849 the bark "Hebe" took cotton, tobacco, and flour direct to Norway from New Orleans.[23] The "Ebenezer" in 1851, after an emigrant voyage to New York, carried freight to the West Indies, then returned to New York for a cargo that it took to Norway.[24] Another

[20] *Nordlyset* (Trondhjem), October 27, 1845.

[21] *Correspondenten* (Skien), May 28, 1848. The list included 450 bales of cotton and 40 of hops, 540 barrels of wheat flour, 300 of rosin and 200 of potash, 3,000 bushels of wheat and 10,500 of rye, 20 casks of rice and 20 of tobacco, and 26 tons of logwood. The total amount of Norwegian iron taken to New York was 8,500 ship pounds. A ship pound was about 350 pounds.

[22] The "Incognito," a brig. *Christiania-posten,* May 24, 1851.

[23] A newspaper said, "This is presumably the first cargo which up to the present has been imported directly from New Orleans." *Christiania-posten,* April 28, 1849.

[24] *Stavanger amtstidende og adresseavis,* July 11, 1851.

vessel of 1851 landed immigrants and then made several trips carrying freight between New York and Venezuela. In the same period a whaling vessel carried emigrants and iron to New York before setting out for the whaling grounds.[25]

Late in 1849 a Norwegian newspaper surveyed Norway's commerce with North America in the period from 1836 to 1849.[26] It is significant that this survey took its starting point with 1836, the year of the departure of two emigrant vessels from Stavanger for New York. Though it is true that Norwegian vessels were rarely seen in American harbors before 1836, one can find occasional and interesting exceptions. These include, for example, the "Eucharis," which sailed for America late in 1815 with fifty cases of Norwegian glassware;[27] the "Prima" of Larvik, which in 1818 carried from Bergen to Baltimore a party of 273 German emigrants who had been stranded in the Norwegian seaport after leaving Germany in a Dutch vessel;[28] the "George," which appeared at Charleston in 1824 from Rotterdam to take on a cargo of tobacco, rice, and cotton;[29] and of course the "Restoration," which a year later carried the pioneer band of Norwegian immigrants to America, with a small cargo of iron that was disposed of in New York. But these were exceptional instances, and for certain years, even in the early 1830's — 1830 and 1831, for example — consular reports indicate that no Norwegian vessels docked at New York.[30] The survey of 1849 showed a great change for the period from 1836 to 1849, when no fewer than 107 Norwegian vessels made

[25] Worm-Müller, *Den norske sjøfarts historie,* vol. 2, pt. 1, p. 559, 563.

[26] "Oversigt over Norges direkte forbindelse med Nordamerika i aarene 1836 til 1849 begge inklusive," in *Christiania-posten,* November 19, 1849; reprinted in *Den frimodige* (Trondhjem), January 5, 1850, and various other Norwegian newspapers. I have had a photostat made.

[27] Scheel, in *Den norske sjøfarts historie,* vol. 2, pt. 1, p. 112.

[28] Bergens udgaaende toldbog, 1818, in Riksarkiv, Oslo; and Scheel, in *Den norske sjøfarts historie,* vol. 2, pt. 1, p. 138, 139.

[29] Riksarkiv, Oslo: F. D. Journalsaker, F, 1825/114.

[30] See the consular reports in Riksarkiv, Oslo: Journalsaker, F, for the years mentioned.

trips to America, the majority of them as emigrant carriers, though some carried only iron. The survey disclosed a growing interest in America based upon the rising volume of emigration, the emergence of the United States as the chief market for Norwegian iron, and increasing imports from the United States, including considerable cotton and rice. "The export of iron to the United States," writes a Norwegian economic historian, "was a result of emigration." He points out that by 1846 Norway was exporting nearly twice as much iron to America as to Denmark, hitherto its chief market for that product.[31]

Meanwhile, emigration was mounting, and the number of vessels making contact with North America was increasing, not only through the carrying of passengers direct from Norway, but also through the enterprise of Norwegian captains who entered the general European commercial and emigrant trade. In 1851, for example, Norwegian vessels brought emigrants to America from Galway, Dublin, Limerick, Antwerp, and Havre de Grace.[32] One Norwegian shipowner, it was reported in 1855, had built six vessels for the transatlantic trade.[33] The possibilities in the lumber-carrying trade from Quebec, opened at the mid-century by the change in the British navigation laws, soon turned Norwegian ocean shipping largely toward Canada. The almost certain prospect of taking on a cargo in Canada made it possible to reduce emigrant fares from $25.00 or $30.00 to $15.00 or under; and during the 1850's Quebec became the objective of most of the emigrant-carrying vessels that left Norway. The trade was of course broader than merely an emigrant

[31] Worm-Müller, vol. 2, pt. 1, p. 560. The export of Norwegian iron went from 157 ship pounds in 1841 to 175 in 1842, 4,229 in 1843, and 9,898 in 1846. The total for the period 1841–49 was 52,660. Later there was a marked decline.

[32] Worm-Müller, vol. 2, pt. 1, p. 562.

[33] This shipowner was Chr. Stephansen. See *Stavanger amtstidende og adresseavis,* May 21, 1855. This magnate of the trade sent the "Amerika" of Arendal to New Orleans in the fall of 1850 with a party of emigrants, including some bound for California. *Den vestlandske tidende* (Arendal), September 10, 1850.

trade, for not a few vessels left Norway outside the usual emigrant season, perhaps carrying cargoes first to England or Ireland and then going on to Canada, or making their way in ballast direct to Canada, there to pick up cargoes for the British Isles. The great increase in the traffic, however, was bound up with the emigrant trade; and Norwegian vessels were numerous at Quebec — 77 in 1859, 100 in 1860 (and 107 at other British-American ports), and 130 in 1861. Fifty-nine Norwegian vessels arrived in ports of the United States in 1852, including 16 direct to New York from Norway; two years later the number was down to 45, with only 4 direct from Norway to New York; and in 1856 the total number was 30.[34]

Fair they were, the brigs, schooners, sloops, barks, clippers, that lay in Norwegian harbors awaiting the emigrants; and they were proudly named — the "Viking," "Valhalla," and "Washington"; the "Emilie," "Ebenezer," and "Emigrant"; the "Favorite," "Fortuna," "Superb," "Preciosa," "Flora," and "Harmony"; the "Achilles," "Herkules," "Juno," "Sirius," "Salvator," "Ægir," "Tegner," and "Peder Tordenskjold"; the "Ellida," "Drafna," "Fædres Minde," "Den Norske Klippe," "Incognito," "Laurvig," and "Duo Fratres."[35] But neither proud names nor gallant lines and sails meant much to the emigrants who were crowded into the steerage for the long ocean journey. "Away! away! Draw up the gangway! We'll pack you bumpkins like herring in a barrel," sang Wergeland in a satirical emigrant song, "'tis only an interlude twixt barrel and palace."[36]

[34] Worm-Müller, vol. 2, pt. 1, p. 566 ff.; Blegen, *Norwegian Migration*, 351. The Quebec route, according to a newspaper of 1852, had brought the fares down from 22 specie dollars for adults and 12 for children to 14 and 7 respectively. *Morgenbladet* (Christiania), June 1, 1852.

[35] The best account of the emigrant traffic is that by Worm-Müller, in *Den norske sjøfarts historie*, vol. 2, pt. 1, p. 547–635. This scholarly and intensely interesting study is accompanied by many illustrations showing emigrant vessels and scenes. A brief treatment is A. Ragnv. Brækhus, *Fra "Restaurationen" til "Stavangerfjord"* (Bergen, 1925).

[36] Blegen and Ruud, *Norwegian Emigrant Songs and Ballads*, 90.

The setting of this interlude has been described by a contemporary observer. "On a temporary floor built in the hold of a vessel," writes Karl E. Erickson, "a two-story row of spaces for beds was constructed along the whole length of both sides of the ship, usually wide enough for four persons to sleep in. On deck a moderately-sized shed fitted up with a number of fireplaces for cooking was erected, also an outbuilding on each side near the rail. This completed the alterations necessary for the comforts of passengers, who always had to furnish their own bedding as well as their food. Below the floor was a large room reserved for the multitude of large heavy chests packed to the brim with clothing, bedding, and other trappings belonging to the emigrants. . . . In another part of the hold were stowed away many large casks of fresh water, enough to last for three months in case the voyage should require that length of time. . . . The provision boxes and smaller chests belonging to the passengers were placed in rows in front of their beds and made fast to prevent sliding off."[37] A ship captain recalled the arrangements as "very primitive and inadequate"—a deck of planks "with hatchways down into the hold, where all the baggage was stowed away on top of the cargo. Two rows of bunks of rough boards were built up, one above the other, the whole length of the ship from fore to aft." There were "no separate rooms for men and women. Light was admitted through open hatchways and partly through skylights in the deck." But when storms came, no light at all was admitted. "One can imagine the sufferings of the wretched creatures who were shut up in the dark room night and day, for the hatches were battened as the waves went over the deck continually. The room of the emigrants was lighted by two or three lamps that were burning night

[37] Erickson, in *Studies and Records,* 8:80. "The bunks are so low that we cannot sit up in them," wrote an immigrant of the "Sjofna" in 1853. *Christiania-posten,* June 8, 1853.

and day down there in the poisoned air and amid all the filth."[38]

But the emigrants, as they stood on the crowded wharf, did not yet know about the misery of storm and closed hatches. Their chests were rowed out to the vessel, which was anchored in the harbor, and these stout wooden containers were hoisted carelessly on deck by means of rope and hooks thrust into the handles.[39] Then, amid the stir and bustle of the crowds, the emigrants said good-by to their friends and relatives and were ferried out to the sail-driven home where they were to live for the next two months or more. Customarily a minister came on board to hold a farewell service and to preach a solemn sermon admonishing the emigrants to live the good life and not to forget their fathers' god.[40] Finally the anchor was lifted, and, in the words of an emigrant song, "The winds swell the flapping sails, and the ship glides majestically out to sea. The groves fade away, and the deep valley and the mountain peaks are lost in the mists."[41] "After we had lifted the anchor," wrote one emigrant, "our captain gave us a talk, explaining our duties, urging us to be cleanly, obedient, alert, and helpful to one another, and advising us to observe the rules posted in several places on the boat. He then asked God's blessing on us all. And so our journey was started in God's name."[42] There

[38] H. Cock-Jensen, "An Emigrant Voyage in the Fifties," translated by Karen Larsen, in *Studies and Records,* 1: 127–130.

[39] Erickson, in *Studies and Records,* 8: 82, 83.

[40] See Gran, in *Samband,* no. 103, p. 51; Erickson, in *Studies and Records,* 8: 83, 84; and Blegen, *Norwegian Migration,* 120. "As we passed out through Drammensfjord," wrote Knud Knudsen in telling of the sailing of the "Emilie" in 1839, "Candidate Valeur, who accompanied us to Gothenburg, gave a touching address, which was admirably adapted to the circumstances of our journey and in which, with evident spiritual earnestness, he encouraged us all to live moral lives and always to have God in our thoughts." O. M. Norlie, ed., *Knud Knudsen's beretning om en reise fra Drammen til New York,* 9, 10 (Decorah, Iowa, 1926).

[41] From "Emigrantskibet," written by Christian Olsen in 1861. Blegen and Ruud, *Norwegian Emigrant Songs and Ballads,* 246–254.

[42] Henrietta Larson, ed., "An Immigration Journey to America in 1854," in *Studies and Records,* 3: 62. Miss Larson translates and edits a letter written on June 21, 1854, by Ole O. Østerud.

was much to do: the supplies of smoked and salted meat and flat bread to be attended to and the first meals to be prepared; bedding to be placed on the straw heaped into the bunks; children to be cared for; and chores of various kinds to be performed. "In order to maintain cleanliness below deck and preserve healthy conditions among the passengers," writes Erickson, "it was customary with some captains to divide off all the adult males in the steerage into seven gangs, one for each day in the week. . . . They would sweep, scrub, and clean out all dirt, both on deck and below, early in the morning when they were called out."[43]

Sometimes one and occasionally two galleys, or cook-houses, were set up on deck, and there, using wood supplied by the vessel, the emigrants took turns in making fires, boiling coffee and tea, cooking porridge and soup, and making ready other foods. With as many as a hundred persons waiting for a chance to use these poor conveniences, however, the process was irregular and slow at best; the shanties, with fires running all day long, were filled with smoke and grime and the penetrating smell of old fat fried over and over again; and often the less aggressive people were cheated out of their turn or were pushed out when their food was only half cooked. When the weather turned stormy, it was difficult for anybody to use the cooking facilities.[44] The results were bad enough even if the food supplies held out, but on long journeys they frequently ran low; and the physical discomfort and suffering caused by inadequate and improperly cooked foods were increased when the daily allotment of water was cut down or when the water spoiled. Be sure to have a carefully drawn contract, advised an immigrant in 1844. He explained that he himself, on the vessel that he crossed on, got only two pots of water a day. Worse, it was ill-tasting and ill-smelling, and he was "nearly ready to die

[43] *Studies and Records,* 8:76, 77.

[44] Jacobson, in *Symra,* 9:123–125; Cock-Jensen, in *Studies and Records,* 1:127.

of thirst" before he landed. And in prolonged storms the passengers in the steerage could not even get on deck. Down in their quarters "pails, cans, pots, kettles, and everything else left unlashed would rattle about and create a perfect pandemonium. All that the poor occupants could do was to cling fast to the nearest post or bed rail and stay there until the rolling ceased somewhat. Oftentimes this was in intense darkness, as the hatches had to be closed to exclude the furious sea and save the passengers from drowning. All this created a confusion and chaos that naturally tried new souls, and bodies too." The emigrants as a rule were not sea folk. They were unaccustomed to the roll of a ship, and of course there was a vast amount of seasickness, especially among the women. After a storm, when the hatches were opened, people came stumbling out, gasping for air, and the steerage was "most frightful and sickening to behold."[45]

Many of the Norwegian captains made valiant efforts to combat disease on board the emigrant vessels, urging the passengers to exercise on deck, using chlorine and vinegar in desperate attempts at fumigation, and employing household remedies of various kinds. The "Hector" of Kragerø, built in 1853, even had a special room with eight beds for sick people, an early approach to isolation for contagious diseases. But it was rare indeed that a doctor accompanied the passengers; usually there was no medical inspection before sailing, or, if the captain arranged for one, it was likely to be perfunctory; and, what with crowding, bad air, inadequate food, and the filth of the steerage when closed for days at a time, it often happened that terrible diseases would break out and spread with appalling speed. An old ship captain

[45] See Erickson, in *Studies and Records,* 8:79; a letter of Guttorm R. Thistel, in *Tiden* (Drammen), November 29, 1844; and a discussion of conditions on the emigrant packets, in *Bergens stiftstidende,* September 22, 1842. Gunder J. Heisholt in 1844 told of a trip in which the passengers had to make use of salt water, and had to break up some of their chests and casks for firewood. The letter, written from Pine Lake, Wisconsin, on October 21, 1844, is in Riksarkiv, Oslo: Finans- og Tolddept., Kontor D, Journalsaker, 1844, no. 1915.

tells of a voyage in 1854 on which a scourge of dysentery added to the torment of the emigrants. "It began in the upper bunk aft and continued regularly on starboard until it jumped over to larboard and there spread in the same manner." A woman was the first victim, and in the midst of her sufferings she gave birth to a baby. Three days later the mother died. The ship was belayed, the flag flew at half mast, a ceremony was held, and the body was buried in the sea. This was only the beginning. The captain relates that the misery increased with each day. "The symptoms of the illness were a violent diarrhea and profuse discharge of blood followed by exhaustion" and a gross swelling of the body. One death after another occurred, until thirteen passengers had been lowered into the sea. Food supplies began to run low, and the captain and his passengers rejoiced when they came to the Newfoundland banks and there caught eighty-six "unusually large codfish." As a last resort the captain gave all the sick people a laxative oil, and he reports that there were no deaths after that. Many years later he recalled that the "poor unfortunates were gentle and resigned and bore their crosses with great patience." At last, after eleven weeks and three days, the vessel reached the quarantine station near Quebec, where a medical inspection was held and twenty sick persons were left behind.[46]

Cholera, typhus, smallpox, typhoid fever, and measles were some of the diseases that raged on board emigrant vessels. The "Ellida" docked at New York in 1842 with nine passengers dead and some thirty who were sent to the hospital "half dead." Three children born on the voyage were among the victims of the disease, which an immigrant described as a "kind of cholera or typhus."[47] In 1861 a ship from Arendal arrived at Quebec with forty-seven pas-

[46] The captain of the "Laurvig" was H. Cock-Jensen who tells the story in *Studies and Records,* 1:130–132. The "Hector" is described in *Morgenbladet,* July 28, 1853.

[47] See an emigrant narrative in *Skiensposten,* September 5, 1842.

sengers dead and sixty sick; another had thirty-three dead, mostly children under six who had been attacked by measles; and yet another reported forty-six dead and sent eighty-four to the hospital. At the quarantine at one time there were nearly four hundred sick emigrants, most of them Norwegians.[48] "God be thanked, I was well and active on the voyage," wrote an emigrant in 1851, "everything went well and satisfactorily among the passengers, with the exception that we had seven deaths on our journey to this place."[49] In 1853 another wrote, "The journey to America took a long time, nine and a half weeks, but was very lucky; we had good weather and much calm, not much seasickness, but four small children died during the voyage."[50] Good weather and pleasant sailing conditions were reported for a voyage in 1855, but all were "quiet and sorrowful" when a boy of fourteen died of typhoid fever.[51] Ole Nielsen, in a diary kept on a voyage in 1866, makes the reader feel his terrible anxiety for his wife and a small son, both ill during much of the journey. One day he chronicled the death of a man in the bunk below his who was well and robust only the day before. A woman, Olaug Ruspergaarden, died and was buried at sea, a heavy stone tied to her ankles. But Nielsen's wife got well and soon his boy was much better. And so he wrote that his pride was centered upon the betterment of his son — and his whiskers, "which grow and increase in beauty." After reaching Quebec he wrote thankfully, "God keeps His hand over me."[52]

As one reads the America letters, with their reports of death at sea, their accounts of the "sad and solemn cere-

[48] *Stavanger amtstidende og adresseavis,* July 30, 1862.

[49] Hans O. Thorud, January 27, 1851, in *Drammens tidende,* April 23, 1851.

[50] Jacob O. Wollaug, April 10, 1853, in *Christiania-posten,* May 25, 1853.

[51] An emigrant letter of August 6, 1855, in *Stavanger amtstidende og adresseavis,* September 10, 1855.

[52] Ole Nielsen's diary of his journey runs from April 27 to July 19, 1866. The original diary is in the Ole Nielsen Papers at Gudmunsrud, Aal, Hallingdal, Norway. A transcript of this remarkably interesting document is owned by the Minnesota Historical Society.

mony" of burials in mid-ocean — bodies placed in wooden boxes or wrapped in canvas and weighted with rocks, to "sink slowly with a spiral motion into the trackless deep"[53] — one recalls the words of Friedrich Kapp: "If crosses and tomb stones could be erected on the water as on the western deserts, where they indicate the resting-places of white men killed by savages or by the elements, the routes of the emigrant vessels from Europe to America would long since have assumed the appearance of crowded cemeteries."[54] And Carl Wittke, looking at the general migration from Europe, writes, "Many did not survive the ordeal; others survived it only to fall victims in American ports to disease or to some of the worst exploiters of helpless humanity that any generation has ever seen; and many no doubt cursed the day they ever left their native firesides."[55]

Yet, bad as conditions were on many of the Norwegian emigrant vessels, those on the English packets in the same period seem to have been worse. Fourteen Norwegian emigrants who crossed on such a packet in 1853 wrote a joint letter telling of bruised heads, broken ribs, a broken collarbone, and teeth knocked out as a result of brutal treatment by seamen whose orders, given in English, they could not understand; of food thrown to the emigrants as if they were dogs and of the emigrants fighting for it like wild animals; of bunks full of lice; of dangers of assault upon wives, sisters, and daughters; of passengers so weak when they arrived in New York that they could hardly walk. "If we were to tell all the bloody events we saw, it would fill several volumes," they said.[56] Another report told of the "law of the fist"

[53] Erickson, in *Studies and Records*, 8:86.

[54] Quoted in George M. Stephenson, *History of American Immigration, 1820–1924*, 248 (Boston, 1926).

[55] *We Who Built America*, 113 (New York, 1939).

[56] A letter written in New York on November 30, 1853, in *Morgenbladet*, January 14, 1854. Wittke compares the conditions on some of the immigrant ships with the "suffering of the middle passage during the African slave traffic." *We Who Built America*, 113 ff.

prevailing in the cookhouse, of constant fighting and quarreling, and of a storm in which water rushed into the steerage, with chests, trunks, sacks, and other objects plunging against the bunks and the sides of the vessels.[57] Halvor Johansen Nymoen, who crossed on an American ship in 1839, told of passengers who were kicked and struck while the crew called them "devils" and laughed at their agonies.[58]

In many countries there was a humanitarian concern about the emigrants. The traffic was seriously discussed in the Norwegian parliament from 1843 to 1845 and a law was proposed to regulate ship conditions, but unfortunately the parliament was not convinced of the necessity of action, and the measure failed to pass. In 1847 the United States government abandoned the old limitation of two passengers to each five tons of a vessel, and decreed instead a minimum of fourteen square feet of space for each passenger and a minimum height of six and a half feet for each deck. That year the state of New York established Castle Garden as the regular place of landing for arriving immigrants and also set up a state board of commissioners of emigration. The United States, meanwhile, investigated the problem of typhus, cholera, and other diseases prevalent on emigrant vessels, and in 1855 ordained more air space between decks as a measure to combat such scourges. All this did relatively little good, however, for the emigrant traffic shifted to Quebec in the early 1850's, and the English laws were more lenient than the American in permitting large numbers of passengers. The situation at Quebec, as it developed during the 1850's and 1860's, naturally gave great concern to the Norwegian consular officials stationed there, as indeed it also did to Canadian officials, and it was consular reports of crowding, sickness, wretchedness, and death that finally moved the

[57] *Christiania-posten,* February 12, 1854.

[58] Nymoen sailed from Göteborg on a voyage that lasted from May 25 to September 4. *Tiden,* January 7, 1840.

Norwegian government to take action in 1863. A passenger act required medical inspection of crew and passengers before departure from a Norwegian port, regulated the permissible maximum number of passengers in relation to the space available for each one, and established basic standards of light, water supply, and the seaworthy condition of the vessels. The law was admirably conceived and its terms were evolved after careful study of similar legislation in other countries. Had it been passed in 1845, it doubtless would have proved effective. Now it came too late. It grew out of the conditions of the traffic in the era of the sailing vessels owned and manned by Norwegians. But only a few years after the law was passed, that era came to an end. The sailing vessels gave way to steam vessels; and there was a trend away from Norwegian vessels to English and other foreign carriers.[59]

The emigrant voyage in the earlier period was marked by suffering, sickness, and death; but human nature is fortunately a resilient thing, and the story of the crossing from Old World to New has its bright side, too. "In spite of the absence of comforts," writes the same captain who buried thirteen of his passengers at sea, "life on board such an emigrant vessel might be quite gay. When the weather was fine and the Atlantic lay clear and smooth, the deck at times rang with merriment in the evenings. The accordion was brought out and to its tones the couples whirled about. Games were played — in wooden shoes and wadmal skirt many a time —

[59] See Blegen, *Norwegian Migration,* ch. 10; Socialdepartementet, *Ot. prp. nr. 24: Om forandring i lov om kontroll med befordring av utvandrere,* 16 (1921); Einar J. Anderson, "The Voyage of the Immigrant and How It Has Changed," in *Swedish-American Historical Bulletin* (St. Peter, Minnesota), 2:86 ff. (August, 1929); and Stephenson, *American Immigration,* ch. 19. In 1853 the "Argo," 184½ commercial lasts, carried 250 passengers to Quebec; the "Tegner," 221½ lasts, 265 passengers; and the "Deodata," 171½ lasts, 220 passengers. *Christiania-posten,* May 7, 1853. Johan Gasmann, captain of the "Salvator," gives his views on the entire problem of conditions on board emigrant vessels in a letter of December 18, 1843, in Socialdept., Oslo: Lovkontor, Utvandringen, Kong. Prop. 1845, folder 3.

and here life-long connections were formed."[60] On the "Washington" in 1842 many of the passengers were from Telemark, lovers of song and dance. On a Sunday they would wash and dress up, have prayers and devotions, sing hymns to the accompaniment of flute and violin. On evenings frequently there was dancing, with four passengers and four members of the crew playing the violin and one seaman, a flute. A typical daytime scene was that of younger women knitting and sewing, old women reading or singing songs, men staring out at the sea.[61] The country people, writes Clara Jacobson, liked to dance spring and Halling dances, the townspeople waltzes and schottisches. The mountain folk had their traditional costumes. Some of the older women smoked pipes. There was a friendly spirit on board notwithstanding some class differences and a considerable difficulty in understanding dialects from other parts of the country than one's own valley.[62]

"When the weather was pleasant," writes an immigrant, "we often had a good time, for all kinds of games and amusement were allowed. We frequently danced. Even the captain, himself, was often with us, entertaining us with adventure and hunting stories and the like. On the evening of the day after Pentecost we had a ball. We each gave twelve cents and the captain contributed the rest."[63] The young folk, Erickson recalls, climbed, wrestled, danced, played "back-hitting," hanging the culprit, and barber of Seville. The latter was a game involving a four-foot piece of pine board sharpened as a razor, soapsuds, and the shaving of a victim. It seemed so funny to the emigrants that "a number laughed themselves black, while others tumbled over on deck wriggling and squirming like eels." Sometimes one individ-

[60] Cock-Jensen, in *Studies and Records,* 1: 128.

[61] *Skiensposten,* July 22, 1842. The newspaper gives a summary of a diary kept from June 3 to 9, 1842.

[62] Jacobson, in *Symra,* 9: 125–128.

[63] Østerud, in *Studies and Records,* 3: 63.

ual made special contributions to the good spirits of the company. Of one such person Erickson writes, "He was *par excellence* the funny man of the voyage and passengers on that vessel yet living remember his jokes and pleasantries, pranks and tricks. . . . Everyone was his friend, he offended nobody, and he always displayed a kind disposition." [64]

A pleasant interlude in the customary voyage was a stop on the Newfoundland banks, where the passengers tried to catch codfish — and usually, to their unbounded delight, succeeded. They "cast out big baited hooks attached to strong lines, and before many minutes one after another of the big finny tribe was landed on deck." And then there was a feast on "savory and delicious fish" the joy of which is perhaps not understandable by anybody who has not lived for weeks on dried and salted meats and hard bread.[65]

Sometimes there was a Seventeenth of May celebration held in mid-ocean, while emigrants sang songs and listened to toasts to the country they had left.[66] The imminence of childbirth rarely prevented a family from setting out from Norway on the adventure of emigration, and there were many births and christenings on the vessels. The captain conducted the baptismal service; and one hears of Anne Tegneria, an infant born on the "Tegner"; Sirius, a child of the "Sirius"; Nora Atlanta, who first saw the light on the north Atlantic; and Anna Pauline, who was born on the "Lynne" and whose second name, therefore, is the record of an emigrant pun.[67] "There were no deaths on the whole trip," wrote an immigrant, "but a child was born while we lay in

[64] Erickson, in *Studies and Records,* 8: 77–79, 85.

[65] Erickson, in *Studies and Records,* 8: 86. Knudsen tells of good luck on the banks in 1839 — "the largest and richest fishing grounds in the world." To those grounds, he said, came Frenchmen, Spaniards, Englishmen, Irishmen, and Americans. The catch made by the emigrants represented, he said, a combination of fresh supplies and enjoyable sport. *Beretning,* 17, 18.

[66] See "The Seventeenth of May in Mid-Atlantic," in Blegen and Ruud, *Norwegian Emigrant Songs and Ballads,* 24–29.

[67] See, for example, Lien and Lee, in *Samband,* no. 52, p. 374–384; no. 69, p. 130–134.

the Bay of St. Lawrence. Two days later the child was baptized by the captain. A woman from Gjærdrum gave birth to twins during the night when we were between Quebec and Montreal. Our captain baptized these babies, also, the next day in Montreal."[68] After the "Washington" reached New York in 1842, Anders Larsen Folseland and Ollaug Olsdatter were married on board ship. An American minister performed the ceremony, the captain translating his words into Norwegian, with the quarantine doctor and a port official standing at the right and left of the couple. The bride had a crown of flowers on her head. She and the bridegroom, as well as the crew and passengers, were dressed in their best clothes. After the ceremony the doctor solemnly gave the couple rules for healthful living, and in the evening the company danced until midnight.[69]

When at last the vessels reached Grosse Isle, the quarantine station some miles below Quebec, rowboats swarmed about them offering to sell milk, bread, butter, fish, and other foods to the immigrants at small prices. Many, writes Erickson, here "saw and enjoyed the first wheat bread in loaves that they had ever eaten." The scene left a deep impression on his mind, for he exclaimed, "How the immigrants feasted and enjoyed a change from the everlasting dry and salt to fresh food was a caution." But to many there was no joy in this arrival, for a doctor came on board, isolated the sick from the well, and ordered the former ashore while his assistants proceeded to fumigate the ship. Soon it would push on to Quebec, leaving the sick to die or, if they got well, to come on later. Many never rejoined their families. Cholera and other diseases would pursue the emigrants into Quebec and on their way to the American interior. Sometimes both parents would die and the children would be left in houses of mercy. "Verily," writes Karl E. Erickson, "the lot of

[68] Østerud, in *Studies and Records*, 3:64.
[69] *Skiensposten*, September 5, 1842.

many an emigrant was hard, especially so when exposed to attacks of pestilence among strangers in a strange land, with no home, no means, and no friends to assist" them.[70]

Often the Norwegian captains would accompany the emigrants from New York to Albany or some other town on the way to Buffalo, or from Quebec to Montreal, and their kindly interest and help were remembered with deep gratitude. "Our captain was a fine man," wrote one immigrant. "He maintained a strict discipline and kept everything clean and in as good order as it was possible for him to do. Because of this his passengers were always comfortable. He was like a father to us all." They presented a gift to this friendly seaman, who accompanied his passengers from Quebec to Montreal: "We each contributed a little money and bought a gold watch chain for our captain. It cost fifteen dollars."[71] In 1839 a party of immigrants paused in Albany to write a letter of thanks to Captain Anchersen of the "Emilie," and they asserted that it was as touching to say good-by to him as it was to leave their fatherland.[72] In 1849 many passengers paid public tribute to Captain Westergaard of the brig "Favorite," who had journeyed on to Troy with them. Another group in the same year wrote a testimonial to the humanity, good will, sympathy, and prudence of Captain Stranger of the "Vesta."[73] Two officers of the "Herkules," Captain Overvien and Skipper Hans Friis, were similarly praised by the passengers they had guided across the Atlantic. These officers, the passengers said, had never ceased

[70] *Studies and Records,* 8:74–76, 87, 88.

[71] Østerud, in *Studies and Records,* 3:62–64.

[72] *Tiden,* December 31, 1839; and Knudsen, *Beretning,* 22–24. Anchersen treated all the passengers to fresh meat in Göteborg; to fish in Udøefjord and twice in the English Channel as well as on the Newfoundland banks; and in Albany they were his guests at a meal in a large hotel. Anchersen believed in getting good accommodations on the journey west even if the price was higher than that for poor accommodations. A letter in which he defends himself against criticism is in *Tiden,* January 13, 1843.

[73] *Stavanger amtstidende og adresseavis,* August 10, 1849; *Morgenbladet,* August 17, 1849.

to take an interest in their welfare, and, among other things, had held a prayer and song service for them each evening during the voyage.[74] Sometimes a captain won the admiration of his passengers by the skill with which he sailed his vessel. Captain Clausen of the "Ebenezer" made the trip in record time in 1850, leaving Stavanger on April 19 and arriving in New York on the evening of May 14.[75] If many of the emigrants praised their officers, there were some who wrote in a different tone. One, in 1854, advised people not to trust their captain too much. "Many look more to the dollar," he wrote, "than to the good of their countrymen."[76]

When the sloop folk arrived in New York in 1825, they were hailed as a "Novel Sight," and a reporter described their appearance, stating that those from the farms were dressed "in coarse cloths of domestic manufacture, of a fashion different from the American," and that the people from the Norwegian towns wore "calicoes, ginghams, and gay shawls."[77] In the late 1830's, an immigrant recalled, people in Boston marveled at the "foreign language of the emigrants, their clothes, and their customs," and were "even more astonished to find that people who came from a land so near the ice region as Norway looked like other human beings."[78] By the 1840's, however, such initial surprises had worn off; the arrival of immigrants had become a routine thing; and the processes of exploitation of the incoming throngs, who were unfamiliar with the language and conditions of America, were in full swing. The immigrants, perhaps after a stop at quarantine and a wait of a few days while they scrubbed their clothing, landed in New York amid great excitement, exposed to the clamor and machina-

[74] *Den norske rigstidende* (Christiania), November 22, 1843.

[75] *Stavanger amtstidende og adresseavis,* June 18, 1850. See also a tribute to Captain Clausen in the issue for February 14, 1852.

[76] Tønnes Fladestøl, in *Stavanger amtstidende og adresseavis,* October 26, 1854.

[77] *New York Daily Advertiser,* October 15, 1825.

[78] *Billed-magazin,* 1:7 (October, 1868).

CASTLE GARDEN

[From Commissioners of Emigration of the State of New York, *Annual Report*, 1868, p. 18.]

INTERIOR OF CASTLE GARDEN

[From Commissioners of Emigration of the State of New York, *Annual Report*, 1868, p. 20.]

tions of runners and agents, though somewhat protected after Castle Garden in the late 1840's became the regular place of debarkation. Then, having purchased tickets for the interior, they set out by steamboat on the Hudson for Albany, where they transferred to canalboats for Buffalo. There, in turn, they customarily got passage on Great Lakes vessels for Chicago or Milwaukee. It took Hans O. Thorud in 1851 "ten hard and long days" to make the trip on the Erie Canal, where he and his friends were crowded into small space and "treated like swine."[79] Not a few of the immigrants reported that the crowding on canal and lake boats was so intense that they were shoved in like baggage and would lay down their children and have to stand beside them. Many died on the journey west, wrote an immigrant who believed that the chief cause was the fact that they were wedged into "rotten boats." Yet another immigrant said that the trip on the canal and the lakes was the worst part of the entire journey.[80] Interpreters and guides were sometimes available, but there was always danger of fraud at their hands. Not all the Norwegian immigrants went by steamboat and canalboat from New York to Buffalo. In 1845, for example, some three hundred Norwegians were transported by railroad, paying $3.50 for adults from the eastern metropolis to the port on Lake Erie. One of the passengers described the train as a row of "wonderful closed wagons with windows," with an engine hauling fifteen cars loaded with passengers and baggage. "The first night," he writes, "we were in a town Jutikka [*Utica*] and the next in a town Rochester. Since the nights were dark we stood still."[81]

"When you land in America," wrote a Swedish immigrant, "you will find many who will offer their services, but beware

[79] *Drammens tidende,* April 23, 1851.

[80] *Morgenbladet,* January 29, 1846; *Drammens tidende,* January 28, 1851; undated letter of Jacob O. Østern, in Historiografisk Samling, Oslo.

[81] Salve Tallaksen and others, March 3, 1845, in *Norge og Amerika* (Arendal), 1:38–43 (September, 1845).

of them because there are so many rascals who make it their business to cheat the immigrants."[82] Ole Munch Ræder in 1851 described the methods by which immigrants were fleeced, including the printing of elaborate fraudulent tickets; and he told of swarms of agents active in New York and Albany throughout the season.[83] The immigrants were cheated on every side — by runners and agents, by the keepers of boardinghouses, even by guides and interpreters who spoke their own language and offered their services in the seeming spirit of kindness to fellow countrymen. In the early 1850's a man who said that he was the Reverend Jakob Ottesen fell in with a party of immigrants who were making their way to Buffalo by canalboat. He was very kind to them, helped them in various ways, held prayers, and finally offered to change their gold, which he said had lost value because of the great production of California gold. Then, with more than three hundred dollars of their precious money, this liar and thief, who had masqueraded under the name of a respected pioneer clergyman, disappeared.[84] Many immigrants who had come to America with only small margins of money to use in meeting the expenses of getting out to the western settlements found themselves stranded in New York, Albany, Buffalo, or other eastern cities, and were obliged to seek work. Year after year Lars Larsen and other kindly Norwegians in Rochester took penniless immigrants into their homes, fed them, and helped them to find jobs or to go on their way to the West. Similarly, at Muskego, Even Heg made his capacious barn available as a temporary home for people who somehow had managed to make their way to Wisconsin and were ready to look for land, many of them sick and without funds. The establishment of the state board of commis-

[82] Quoted in Stephenson, *American Immigration,* 249.

[83] *Drammens tidende,* March 11, 1851.

[84] G. F. Dietrichson, "Et frækt bedrageri af en Norsk paa en canalbaad," in *Stavanger amtstidende og adresseavis,* September 2, 1853, from *Emigranten,* July 29, 1853.

sioners of emigration in New York and the designation of Castle Garden as a landing depot for immigrants represented one attempt to protect the arriving foreigners; and not a few agencies throughout the country, including states and towns as well as special societies and churches, attempted in various ways to mitigate the many evils to which the people were exposed. Scandinavian societies were formed in Boston, Chicago, La Crosse, and elsewhere to advise and help them, but at best their efforts touched only a small portion of the mass.[85]

Meanwhile, the stream of migration shifted from New York to Quebec; and many thousands made their way to the interior from the Canadian port. "When the immigrants arrived at Quebec," writes Erickson, "they were transferred without much delay to large river steamers that carried them to Montreal, which is at the head of ocean navigation on that river. Then passage was taken on canal steamers some twenty-five miles to a place called La Chine; sometimes this journey was made by railroad. The canal has a number of locks, and the passage through them was a novel experience to newcomers. At La Chine passengers boarded large lake steamers that carried them through the Thousand Islands and Lake Ontario, in the western part of which liners were running to different landing points. One of these liners took the passengers to the city of Lewiston, and from there both passengers and luggage were carried about seven miles to Niagara Falls on large stagecoaches drawn by horses, thence to Buffalo by rail, and then on steamers over the Great Lakes to Milwaukee or Chicago." The entire trip, he said, took

[85] Blegen, *Norwegian Migration*, 109, 130; Stephenson, *American Immigration*, 250, 251. On the Massachusetts emigration protection society, see *Christiania-posten*, October 20, 1853, and January 6, 1854, and *Stavanger amtstidende og adresseavis*, March 4, 1854; and on the La Crosse society, *Morgenbladet*, August 3, 1866. An interesting account of Castle Garden, taken from *Emigranten*, is in *Aftenposten* (Christiania), September 24, 1855. In 1864 the federal government established the office of superintendent of immigration with a view to giving advice and protection to immigrants, but the law making this provision was repealed four years later.

about seven days.[86] Other records tell of immigrants taking the railroad to Port Sarnia, then crossing to Port Huron, and there catching steamboats for the western cities.

On the Canadian, as on the American, route, the immigrants had sickness, fraud, and poverty as traveling companions. As early as 1854 the general agent for emigration at Quebec announced that the government had been obliged to aid poor emigrants in getting on from Quebec to Milwaukee or Chicago. In fact, as many as eight hundred had been given free passage on the Great Western Railway in a single summer. He said that thereafter the fund at the disposal of his department would be used to help only the sick; and his announcement was made public in a Christiania newspaper.[87] But conditions got worse rather than better, and the consular reports from the 1850's and 1860's are filled with details about the problems occasioned by poverty and disease among the Norwegian immigrants.

The journey to the West was not without hazards other than those of fraud and sickness; and in 1852 a great disaster occurred when the "Atlantic," with a load of more than five hundred people, chiefly Norwegian and German immigrants, was rammed and went to the bottom in Lake Erie. Among those drowned were at least sixty-eight Norwegians. They had crossed the ocean on the "Argo." Their captain, writes Erik Thorstad, one of the survivors, "contracted with a company to carry us and our baggage to Milwaukee for seven dollars for each adult and half fare for the children." They made their way to Montreal and Toronto, were taken to Niagara Falls, and then were conveyed to Kingston, from which steamers took them to Buffalo. "Buffalo," wrote Thorstad, "is a very large town and has about 50,000 inhabitants, but I did not think it was really a pleasant place.

[86] Erickson, in *Studies and Records,* 8: 68.

[87] An announcement by A. C. Buchanan, in *Aftenbladet* (Christiania), January 10, 1855.

Along the wharves, especially, it was quite unwholesome." The party included many people who were without funds: "From Quebec to Buffalo some seventy-five poor people from Valders had free transportation. But here they had to remain as they did not have enough money to pay passage across the lakes." He goes on to relate how the immigrants left Buffalo in a large steamer, the "Atlantic." He made a bed of his chest, covered it with bedclothes, and went to sleep; but at two o'clock in the morning was wakened by a "heavy shock." The "Atlantic" had been rammed by the "Ogdensburg" and quickly sank. "The misery and the cries of distress which I witnessed and heard that night are indescribable," wrote Thorstad, "and I shall never forget it all as long as I live." He and sixty-three other Norwegians were among the rescued. They were transported to Milwaukee, where a public subscription was taken up for them. With the money that Thorstad received he bought "two coats, a pair of trousers, a pair of shoes, two shirts, and a bag." At the end of his letter, written from the "Town of Ixonia," Jefferson County, Wisconsin, a few months later, he said, "Although I have lost all my possessions, I have not lost my courage. The same God who has helped me in the time of danger will, I hope, continue to be my protector."[88]

The physical transition from Old World to New was, as Professor Wittke suggests, an ordeal, but, as he also says, "it must not be forgotten that thousands upon thousands survived and that these counted the cost lightly, in view of the new opportunities open to them in America."[89] Decade after decade, notwithstanding hardships and suffering, the stream of migration increased in volume. Many of the tor-

[88] Henrietta Larson, ed., "The Sinking of the 'Atlantic' on Lake Erie," in *Studies and Records*, 4:92–98; letters from George Pemberton, acting consul at Quebec, December 21, 1852, and C. E. Habicht, acting consul general at New York, October 27, 1852, in Riksarkiv, Oslo: Indredept., Kontor D, Journalsaker, 1852/2058, 2336; and *Skandinaven* (New York), October 27, 1852. A copy of the latter paper is in the Royal Library, Stockholm.

[89] *We Who Built America*, 118.

tures of the earlier period were mitigated in the age of steam-driven liners and of railroads; but the modern migration also had its quota of problems and difficulties. Meanwhile, the immigrants went west, looked for jobs, spread out from Chicago and Milwaukee to the Norwegian settlements at Fox River, Muskego, Koshkonong, Rock Prairie, and elsewhere in the quest for fertile land and all that it meant in terms of prosperity and happiness. From the older settlements they struck out for new frontiers, becoming a part of the American westward movement. Clara Jacobson tells of a stop of two weeks in Muskego, where the immigrant family found haven in the barn of the hospitable Even Heg. Then they set out for Galena, there caught a steamboat for Lansing in northeastern Iowa, and finally walked thirty miles to the ultimate destination, where they arrived so tired that they dropped in a heap.[90] So the immigrants reached journey's end. It was the end of one ordeal and the beginning of another — the ordeal of American frontier life and of the transition, to be worked out over years and decades, to the life of the New World. The promise of that life had sustained and strengthened them in the many hardships which, as the ocean captain said, they bore "with great patience."

[90] *Symra*, 9:128–133.

II. FRONTIER ORDEAL

OFTEN THE IMMIGRANT pioneer did not succeed in getting established on his own land during the summer of his arrival in America. He and his family might depend upon the bounty of friends and relatives or upon the kindly aid of fellow Norwegians with whom they had no previous acquaintance. Meanwhile, the problem of the man of the family was to get work somewhere — as a harvester on a near-by farm or as a laborer in town, in the woods as a lumberjack or in a sawmill as a sawyer, on a railroad in whatever rough work offered, or elsewhere. The land problem was eased after the Homestead Act was passed in 1862, but before that it was necessary to raise some ready cash in anticipation of the payment of $1.25 an acre for government land. Immigrants did, indeed, squat on open lands, but many sought work in order to lay aside enough funds to buy a farm.

Lars Davidson Reque in the autumn of 1840 walked from Chicago to the Koshkonong area in Wisconsin, selected land, walked on to Milwaukee to the land office, where he paid a hundred dollars for eighty acres, and then trudged back to

Chicago to find work. This ambitious pioneer had come to America in 1839, but it was not until the spring of 1842 that he began farming. In the meantime he had worked on the Illinois Canal and as a fireman on a Great Lakes steamboat; he had been a lumberjack in the pine woods of Michigan and Wisconsin, floated logs on the Muskegon River, and held a job in a sawmill. Even after beginning his career as a farmer, he worked winters in the Wisconsin lead mines. He became very prosperous, lived four years in the first log cabin that he built — its roof made of planks that he had shaped with a broadax — then put up a larger cabin, and by the 1850's had a frame house — " one of the finest places in the community." His farm grew to nearly three hundred acres and boasted an orchard of more than seven hundred apple trees.[1]

Once an immigrant family arrived upon the land of its choice, the immediate problem was to cultivate some ground and plant a crop as soon as possible, perhaps of potatoes and other vegetables, in order to assure a food supply during the first winter.[2] Reque, for example, began by clearing a small bit of land and planting two bushels of potatoes, using the only tools he owned — a spade and an ax.[3] Some kind of shelter was, of course, necessary, but a house was secondary in importance to the business of planting. In the days of covered wagons, weeks might pass with the family residing in the wagon boxes before cabins were made ready; sometimes tents were used. Frequently the first building was hastily improvised from any materials that happened to be handy — a mere shed or perhaps an underground habitation with dirt walls on three sides. Søren Bache and a companion at Muskego in the fall of 1840 built a house in the side of an Indian mound, making an excavation measuring twenty-four by eighteen feet, with a depth of seven feet. They put

[1] A. Sophie Bøe, "Lars Davidson Reque: Pioneer," in *Studies and Records,* 6:37–39.

[2] T. Helgeson, *Fra "Indianernes lande,"* 195 (1913).

[3] Bøe, in *Studies and Records,* 6:39.

in supports for a roof, covered the room securely, and then paneled the sides with boards. They were so pleased with the job that they then proceeded to build a separate kitchen in the same fashion. They were not disturbed in their pleasure by the fact that the mound was an old Indian grave: at the bottom of their excavation they dug out a dozen or more skulls, with a mass of bones, and Bache, recording the find in his diary, compared the grave with the ancient royal mounds of Norway.[4]

Hans Gasmann, who settled at Pine Lake, Wisconsin, in the early 1840's, had means far in excess of those of the average immigrant, but he, too, gave his first attention to cultivating a small piece of land. He built, not a log house, but a frame structure consisting of a living room, kitchen, and pantry, with two small bedrooms and a loft on the floor above. Unlike most immigrants he at once put up a barn for his horses and cattle.[5] Even Heg at Muskego also built a commodious barn in the early years of that colony. Many farmers, however, went without such buildings for some years. Swine rambled through the woods at will and their owners gave little attention to the business of feeding them. On some frontiers there might be improvised structures offering some manner of shelter for farm animals at night. As grain was threshed, the straw was used to cover frames of poles for the temporary shelter of stock. Occasionally the immigrants built houses large enough to serve both as cabins and as barns. A farmer in Goodhue County, Minnesota, for example, put up a cabin sixteen by twenty-six feet in size, using bark-covered logs, and divided the structure into two

[4] Bache Diary, September 2, 1840. For a description of this manuscript diary, the original of which is in the library of St. Olaf College, Northfield, see Blegen, *Norwegian Migration*, 119. O. S. Johnson, "Lidt nybyggerhistorie fra Spring Grove og omegn," in *Samband*, no. 88, p. 570 (August, 1915). This article appears in installments from March, 1915, to October, 1916. Bache regarded the Indian burial at Muskego as very old, for on the mound, he says, were growing the largest oak trees of the vicinity.

[5] See a letter of Hans Gasmann, October 18, 1843, in *Christianssandsposten*, December 22, 1843.

parts by means of a log partition. On one side of this cabin lived the farmer and his family, on the other, pigs, calves, and chickens; and on one occasion a church service was held in the building to the accompaniment of a barnyard choir.[6] With the passing years the farmers — especially in the upper Northwest — added barns, stables, corn cribs, granaries, chicken coops, wagon houses, and other buildings — and thus created clusters of houses that were to some extent reminiscent of the village-like character of a Norwegian *gaard*.

A controversy was raging in Norway in the 1840's with reference to conditions among the immigrants in America, and the pioneer minister J. W. C. Dietrichson bluntly compared the frontier houses with barns in the mother country. It was a common assertion in the press of Norway that no immigrant was able to build a decent house for himself. The immigrants themselves were forced to admit that the houses in the Muskego colony were inadequate, but they pointed out that those at Pine Lake were good, some of them comparable with *bonde* houses in Norway. One enterprising Norwegian actually made a trip to America in 1846 to satisfy himself as to the truth about immigrant living conditions. He found that a well-to-do immigrant like Gasmann was in a position very different from that of poor people, who as a rule had hurriedly built houses usually consisting of only one room, with a loft, and sometimes with a shed, or lean-to, at one side, serving as a kitchen.[7] Captain Gasmann, when he visited his brother at Pine Lake in 1844, found that the houses were "quite small, but . . . good enough to protect" against the weather — and in fact better than many of the houses of the mountain folk in Norway. Some of the settlers, he said, had already built "good and roomy houses."[8]

[6] O. M. Norlie, ed., *Fra pioner-presternes saga*, 175 (Decorah, 1931).

[7] See a letter written by Hans Evensen, in *Morgenbladet*, January 7, 1847.

[8] Johan Gasmann, "From New York to Wisconsin in 1844," in *Studies and Records*, 5:48. The document appeared originally in Norwegian in Norwegian newspapers of 1845. It is here translated and edited by Carlton C. Qualey.

Some immigrants wrote in a defensive tone about their houses. One, in 1842, said, "Here everyone builds so that he can remain within his house when it is finished, and improve it as his wealth increases, while in Norway many 'build themselves out.' When the buildings are completed, they have nothing in them. Both I and my Norwegian neighbors have now just as good houses as we had in Norway."[9] Occasionally a newcomer misrepresented the situation although using language that had a certain literal accuracy. One writer of an America letter, for example, maintained that he was living in a three-story building — but he meant a cellar, a single main-floor room, and a loft.[10] Another spoke emphatically about the excellence of the western building materials, oak and maple, and insisted that they would not readily decay.[11] It remained for the critical Søren Bache to note in his diary that a friend of his lived in a house that resembled the little black drying-house of a Norwegian *gaard*, its roof and back side made of bark, the interior blackened by smoke from the chimney.[12] In later years, when the immigrant communities bore the marks of prosperity — sturdy frame houses, large barns, and other buildings — there was a cheerful willingness to recall the disadvantages of the early housing. One pioneer spoke of the necessary hurry with which the very first buildings were erected, the lack of light, the unsubstantial construction, and the difficulty of keeping warm in winter.[13] Crevices in the log walls were usually chinked with mud, clay, or plaster, but often the chinking would crack, with unpleasant results in cold or wet weather. Bache said that some people "were about ready to die of frost inside as well as outside" their houses on cruel

[9] A letter of Gjert G. Hovland, in *Christianssandsposten,* February 23, 1843. The letter is dated July 9, 1842, and is written from the Fox River settlement.

[10] Helgeson, *Fra "Indianernes lande,"* 221.

[11] Ellef B. Tangen to relatives, January 14, 1844, in *Bratsbergs-amts correspondent,* April 1, 1844.

[12] Bache Diary, September 28, 1844.

[13] Helgeson, *Fra "Indianernes lande,"* 221.

A PAGE FROM THE DIARY OF SØREN BACHE,
MARCH 26 TO APRIL 1, 1847

[From the original in the possession of St. Olaf College, Northfield, Minnesota.]

winter days at Muskego.[14] And Munch Ræder, writing in 1847, said, "Very few Norwegians have yet built comfortable houses. The great majority live in log cabins of the sort that can be erected in one day."[15]

Log houses were the typical dwellings in all wooded areas where the Norwegian immigrants settled. Their size ranged from twelve by twelve to twelve by fourteen feet, and occasionally they measured fourteen by twenty, with a height usually running from seven or eight to fourteen feet. After occupying the first temporary shanty, hastily erected, it was no uncustomary thing for the immigrants to build substantial log houses. To some extent they used building techniques learned in the old country, especially in shaping and fitting logs and adjusting corners, but the cabins tended to conform to the frontier American styles. Windows were narrow; roofs were normally covered by shakes or shingles, though in the initial stages of pioneering they were often sod-covered; and ornamentation of any kind was rare — the Norwegian second-floor veranda, for example, was most unusual in the West, if indeed it ever was used.

A house measuring twenty-four by fourteen or sixteen feet, and fourteen feet in height, was considered unusually large. It normally would contain three rooms downstairs — a living room, bedroom, and kitchen. Usually the stairs to the loft were on one side of the kitchen, with the cellar entrance below it. Houses of the more normal width of twelve or fourteen feet had only one room, though frequently the loft — low and dark and reached by a rough ladder — was perforce used as a sleeping chamber. Ordinarily a bed or bunk was built in the main room against an end wall, sometimes across the entire wall space, with a center post as a brace, thus affording two bed spaces; and often another

[14] See, among scattered entries, that for April, 1840, in the Bache Diary.

[15] Gunnar J. Malmin, ed., *America in the Forties: The Letters of Ole Munch Ræder*, 68 (Norwegian-American Historical Association, *Travel and Description Series*, vol. 3 — Minneapolis, 1929).

bunk was built above the first, after the manner of berths in the steerage of an emigrant packet. With a dozen people crowded into one small cabin, however, such bunks and the loft were not enough — the puncheon floor was also used for sleeping purposes. Usually after a year or two a lean-to was added. It was sadly needed in most instances. Mrs. Reque insisted that in order to turn around in her first cabin, she had to go outside. As the initial mud or clay filling fell out from the crevices between the logs, the walls might be rechinked. Sometimes they were covered with boards and plastered on the inside. In the Christmas season in the old Wisconsin settlements the cabins were usually given a whitewashing.

Ultimately a new and larger cabin was built, and this, in turn, soon gave way to a frame house. The old cabin was then made available to newcomers, or used as firewood, or turned into a granary or pigpen. On many a western farm of a later period, the original cabin remained in place alongside a farmhouse that would have been regarded as a mansion by the settlers of the log-cabin era. Economic progress was reflected in the advance to a more adequate housing. Dr. William J. Petersen views the log cabin as a symbol of frontier life — a rough-hewn habitation, generally a sturdy shelter, wrought from virgin timber by independent settlers with their own hands, though sometimes with the friendly co-operation of log-raisings, and always offering hospitable haven to visitors. The symbolism should make room for other aspects and interpretations, however. For example, the crowding and discomforts of the log cabins of the initial stages of western pioneering may serve as symbols of the frontier ordeal itself. Among the Norwegians, it may be added, pioneer co-operation in special jobs, such as building cabins or felling trees, was a social institution and was dignified by the name *dugnad*. Apart from a common job done by neighbors, this meant an occasion at which ample supplies of food and home-brewed beer or whisky were served, with evenings devoted to storytelling. In *Peder Victorious*, Beret Holm entertains her neighbors at a shingling party and the day closes with food, punch, and tales out of the past.[16]

The immigrants used as building materials the supplies natural to a particular region. In much of the Middle West logs were easily secured, whereas lumber was both expensive and — before the day of railroads and convenient lumber-yards — had to be hauled long distances. Some immigrants insisted, with entire justice, that a log cabin was less likely to be blown away than a board shanty.[17] In the Beloit region of Wisconsin, limestone was available, and the settlers of an early day erected houses, barns, and churches of stone. Bache visited one home in 1846 which boasted a stone basement and an outside chimney from which, in the American manner, the owner intended to heat another room — his brewhouse, as it happened.[18] As the settlers pushed westward, they used logs as building materials as long as they were within striking distance of woods; but on the plains they built dugouts and sod houses, or, if they used wood, they were obliged to employ the quickly warping cottonwood. The dugouts, built in hillsides in the fashion employed by Bache at the Muskego Indian mound, usually had roofs of split poles covered with hay and sod. At the front a doorway was built, sometimes a window. The sod houses were made of large chunks of hard sod piled up in layers like bricks, with roofs of poles covered by miscellany with a substantial layer of sod at the top. Professor Dick points out that with all its disadvantages — and they were many,

[16] See "De første nybyggerboliger," in Helgeson, *Fra "Indianernes lande,"* 222; Elisabeth Koren, *Fra pioneertiden*, 95, 148 (Decorah, 1914); Bøe, in *Studies and Records*, 6:42, 46; Johnson, in *Samband*, no. 88, p. 570–576; and William J. Petersen, "The Pioneer Cabin," in *Iowa Journal of History and Politics*, 36:387–389 (October, 1938). On the institution of *dugnad*, see *Decorah-posten*, September 25, 1936.

[17] Helgeson, *Fra "Indianernes lande,"* 221.

[18] A letter written at Beloit on November 29, 1851, in *Stavanger amtstidende og adresseavis*, June 12, 1852; Bache Diary, March 22, 1846.

especially for the housewife — the sod house was "cool in summer and warm in winter," safe from fire, and substantial enough to last for a half dozen years. Dr. Petersen, speaking of the Iowa sod dwellings, says that they were "snug and warm; water did not freeze in them in the coldest weather."[19] A pioneer minister in the Dakota country writes, "We went down in a cellar three feet below the surface of the ground with some sod above so as to form one room with the height of a man. In this two families with a total number of six people were to cook, eat, sleep." There the minister also held church services. Ultimately he built a frame house, but, he reports, "we had to use cottonwood for everything, even for the shingles on the roof." The members of his congregation cut logs, hauled them to a sawmill, and transported the lumber to his land.[20]

If the houses of the early frontiersmen were primitive, their furniture was no less so. At first chairs were a rarity. Log stumps served as stools. An immigrant chest made a sufficiently solid dining table, with the advantage that it served at the same time as a safe storage place for clothing and household articles. Sometimes boxes were turned bottoms up, provided with four legs, and thus made to function as chairs or tables. The bunks were usually supplied with straw or hay mattresses over hard boards or springs of taut cords, with sheepskin bedcovers. The prize piece of furniture in one pastor's home was a sofa made of young aspen trunks. A Dakota house had a cottonwood dining table, a bed of the same wood, and some small cottonwood stumps and benches. Some of the pioneer families at first built genuine Norwegian hearths, but the American stove was highly prized by all the immigrants, and an effort was made

[19] "Jordkjældere og torvhytter," in *Telesoga* (Minneapolis), no. 47, p. 6–10 (September, 1921); Gustav O. Sandro, *The Immigrant's Trek,* 19 (Sioux Falls, South Dakota, 1929); Everett Dick, *The Sod-house Frontier 1854–1890,* 115 (New York, 1937); Petersen, in *Iowa Journal of History and Politics,* 36: 402.

[20] Norlie, *Fra pioner-presternes saga,* 130.

to install one as soon as the family could afford to buy it. American rocking chairs found their way into the cabins of the humblest pioneers.

Mrs. Elisabeth Koren describes in detail the interior of one pioneer house: "This is a very large room, which includes the entire house, with an ordinary small stove in the middle of the floor. This is far from able to create a suitable temperature for the large room, which, although new, is wretched enough. The floor consists of unplaned boards which bob up and down when one walks on them. The entry to the cellar is in the one end and is covered with a pair of loose boards laid an inch apart. The ceiling consists likewise of unplaned boards through which one can look up into the loft and glimpse the sky through the roof. Near the trap door of the cellar stands a bed and under this a box, which is pulled out at night and serves as a bed for the youngest members of the family. On the other side of the windows are shelves full of tools. In the lower end of the room Ingeborg has her milk shelves and other kitchen articles. Near the stove stands the table by which I now sit, and around it usually stands a circle of chairs, which are distinguished by their variety of form and material. On these Sivert and his sons, as many as can find places, have their seats. Ingeborg, the mistress of the house, a pretty and attractive woman who always wears a white cap, is working with the dinner with the help of her two small daughters and is at this moment baking biscuits for us." [21]

The human touch in Mrs. Koren's picture serves to remind one that, however small and lacking in comforts, the log cabins and sod houses were homes where human beings lived. In these houses were the smells of cooking, the lusty eating of food by tired and hungry folk, the clatter of housework,

[21] Koren, *Fra pioneertiden,* 95, 106, 145; C. K. Preus, "Minder fra Spring Prairie prestegaard," in *Symra,* 2:18–30 (1906); Norlie, *Fra pioner-presternes saga,* 130; Johnson, in *Samband,* no. 88, p. 570 ff.

the tumult of children, the give and take of family talk, the murmur of traditional devotions, the peace of darkness and rest at night. Here were spinning wheel, loom, copper kettles, bowls, pots, pans, dishes, and other paraphernalia of the housewife.[22] In the morning the husband, after his breakfast, went to the fields to do the day's work, sometimes using tools and implements that he had brought with him from Norway — scythe and broadax, for example — but more frequently employing the mechanical products of American ingenuity and rejoicing with each new advance in the realm of farm machinery. The farmer worked hard, but his wife worked even harder. She did the housework, cared for the children, prepared the meals, helped to care for the cattle, pigs, sheep, and chickens, milked the cows, churned the butter, made the soap, did the canning in summer and fall, prepared cheese, carded and spun the wool, wove cloth, dyed it with homemade dyes, knitted and sewed clothing, mended mittens and socks.[23] On occasion she pitched in and helped to rake hay or bind the grain after it had been cut with the cradle. She bore children year after year; and she cared for the sick when her home was struck by disease. She got little leisure or relaxation. Mrs. Gro Svendsen, who loved to read, evidently was obliged to get in most of her reading during her confinements. For most of the pioneer women there was the diversion of going to church of a Sunday or of spending a part of an evening before the fireplace or in the dim light of a tallow candle. Probably the housewife knitted while stories out of long ago were told. She or her husband, or perchance a grandmother, would spin tales of wood nymphs, hobgoblins, trolls, and ghosts, hair-raising stories from the Norwegian "Black Book," told in a hushed voice, or accounts of the heroic struggles of supermen.[24]

[22] See Johnson, in *Samband,* no. 88, p. 571.

[23] I have in part paraphrased an admirable statement by Johnson of the work of the pioneer women. See his article in *Samband,* no. 88, p. 572.

[24] Johnson describes frontier winter evenings, in *Samband,* no. 88, p. 573.

The early Norwegian settlers were reluctant to venture out on the prairie, but even in the 1840's Munch Ræder concluded that those who had done so in Wisconsin — at Rock Prairie, for example — "as a rule were more successful than those who had cut their way into the woods." He found that "one or two years will generally suffice to fill the barns out on the prairies," whereas the woods people worked for three or four years and even then had difficulty in raising "enough food for their own use." He granted that it often was hard to find water on the prairies and that getting wood for fences, fuel, and buildings offered difficulties, particularly since speculators often bought up near-by woods. But he still thought it wiser to take prairie lands than to go into the woods. "I think capital can be invested more profitably than in felling trees," he said, and he brushed aside the difficulty of getting necessary wood. Even the price demanded by speculators for woodlands held on the edge of the prairies usually was "only two or three dollars an acre." Munch Ræ-

S. R. Fox's

Avertissement.

Den norske Befolkning i Central-Wiskonsin og fornemmelig den i Madison og Omegn indbydes herved ärbödigst til at besöge Fox's Butik og undersöge fölgende Sorter Varer, bestaaende af amerikanske, engelske og tydske Isenkramvarer, Säle- og Vognbeslag, hvilke udsälges i Huset udenfor hvilket er anbragt den store Hängelaas i Morris-Street
Madison . . . . Wiskonsin

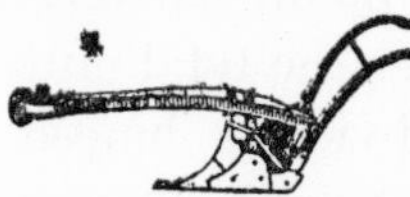

Grand de Tour, Whitewater og Janesville Plouge, Horse Powers, Horse Rakes, Grain Cradles, Liar, Orve, Hö- og Halmknive, Hyppere, Hö- og Halmgafle, Gjödselgreber, Oreaag med Klaver og Kramper; med et Ord: Alle Slags Agerdyrkningsredskaber kunne forefindes hos

S. R. Fox.

Down's og Cowen's Brönd-, Cisterne- og Länke-Pumper med Trä- og Zink-Vandhävere; Bröndkister af Jern og Trä, Bröndhjul, samt Havesprøiter med Tougverk af alle Slags, sälges af S. R. Fox.

Tömmermands-, Bygnings- og Murervärktöi af ethvert Slags, saasom Hövle, Sauge, Hammere, Hammerörer, Huggejern, Strikmaader, rette og skraa Vinkler, Vaterpas &c. &c.,
tilligemed
Bygningsbeslag af alle Slags, Blyhvidt Olie, Kit samt Vinduesglas af forskjellige Störrelser, hvilket Alt forefindes hos S. R. Fox.

De som behöve et Sät gode Bordknive, gode Barberknive eller andre fine Knive, kunne finde det bedste Udvalg deraf tilligemed Saxe, og et Parti smukke Fuglebure, hos S. R. Fox.

Smede kunne finde et godt Udvalg af Värktöi for sit Haandvärk, bestaaende af Bälge, Ambolter, Skruestikker, Slägger, Hammer Tänger, Raspe, File &c. &c., tilligemed et godt Parti Jern og Staal i alle Störrelser hos

S. R. Fox.

A NEWSPAPER ADVERTISEMENT

[From *Den norske Amerikaner*, March 1, 1856.]

der called attention to the possibilities in buying up prairie lands, dividing them into farms, building a cabin on each farm, plowing an acre or two, then selling to incoming immigrants who were eager to get established quickly. "I know many Norwegians who have made good profits in this way," he said; and he quoted figures to show that it was also theoretically possible to buy land and, using hired labor, to clear, plant, harrow, and harvest, and thus regain in a single year the total outlay plus some profit.[25] Such a procedure obviously hinged upon the possession of a certain amount of capital for investment, and the ordinary immigrant had no surplus. He went the long way, did the pioneer job from beginning to end with his own hands and the help of his children, and gradually built up reserves. Once the wooded lands were cleared, the problem was to break the soil. "Did you ever see one of those huge breaking plows?" asks R. B. Anderson. "On its beam, which was from eight to twelve feet long, there was framed an axle, on each end of which was a wheel, sawed from an oak log. This wheel held the plow upright. It was a sight worth seeing, when a ten or twelve year old boy drove an ox team of six to ten yoke, and the heavy queer-looking plow, with its coulter and broad share was turning the virgin soil in black furrows two to three feet wide."[26]

For many of the immigrants there was, as has been suggested, a considerable element of time involved in establishing themselves as independent farm owners. Sometimes they would claim and improve lands and then sell the improvements and set out for new and more favorable frontiers. The usual story, according to Kendric C. Babcock, exhibits a preliminary period of one to five years in the older settlements of Illinois or Wisconsin, then a hunt for good lands

[25] Ræder, *America in the Forties*, 73 ff.

[26] Rasmus B. Anderson, *First Chapter of Norwegian Immigration (1821–1840)*, 435 (Madison, 1895).

farther west. He tells of Levor Timanson, who settled in Rock County with his father in 1848 and for some years was a farm hand, a mason, and a carpenter, then trekked in 1853 to Iowa and Minnesota, and finally selected land in the Spring Grove region of Minnesota, where by 1882 he was the prosperous owner of 840 acres. Of the immigrant farmers generally, Babcock writes, "They were in turn apprentices and journeymen, and finally attained to the full dignity of masters of their own estates." He quotes an early account of the Norwegian settlers in Dakota, "Most of them came with just enough to get on Government land and build a shack. . . . Now they are loaning money to their less fortunate neighbors."[27]

The immigrants accepted the frontier doctrine of land for the actual settlers and were generally hostile to speculators. Sometimes they joined land claim associations to protect actual settlers from the machinations of buyers who attempted to secure the ownership of lands which had been occupied and improved by others. Sometimes they took steps against speculators without benefit of claim associations. According to Munch Ræder, the Norwegians had much to learn from the Yankees, who were very clever about introducing "a certain appearance of law and order even into a practice which in the nature of the case is the direct opposite of law and order." Had the Norwegian settlers at Koshkonong late in 1846 operated through a regularly organized land claim association, they probably would have been more effective than they were in dealing with a certain speculator from Milwaukee. An immigrant had occupied forty acres of land without purchasing it or even entering a claim. He put up a cabin and a stable, fenced the land, and began to cultivate some fifteen acres. Meanwhile the specu-

[27] Kendric C. Babcock, *Scandinavian Element in the United States*, 95–98, 101 (University of Illinois, *Studies in the Social Sciences*, vol. 3, no. 3 — Urbana, 1914).

lator, also a Norwegian, proceeded to buy the land and attempted to take it over in midwinter without compensating the squatter for the improvements he had made. Friends of the squatter intervened and attempted to persuade the buyer to sell the farm to the actual settler at the original purchase price. This he refused to do. The result was that a crowd of some twenty or thirty Norwegians, their faces blackened, appeared one night at the house where the speculator was stopping, dragged him out of bed, put a halter around his neck, probably struck him, and forced him to sign a document promising to sell the land and to make out a deed to the actual settler.

This seems to have been a casual raid, without the authority of a claim association behind it. The buyer promptly appealed to the Norwegian pastor, J. W. C. Dietrichson, insisted that he had been nearly murdered, and accused certain members of the minister's congregation of being the culprits. The pastor gave him little sympathy. He said that if the man wanted to prove that he was indeed a man of honor, as he maintained, he would fulfill the contract he had signed and thus at one stroke show that he was not a coward who signed under duress or a dishonorable scoundrel who chose to live on the labor of others. He had only himself to thank for the treatment he had received. This ministerial argument did not carry conviction, the man promptly appealed to the justice of the peace for redress, and the case was brought to court. Dietrichson, after refusing to serve as an interpreter, was called as a witness, though he explained in court that he knew nothing about the Milwaukee man save that he was a liar and a deceiver. The upshot was that the speculator won his case, and a fine of $150.00 was assessed against the men accused of mistreating him, including the poor farmer who had cultivated the land. Munch Ræder believed that if the matter had been handled by a regular claim association and under its formal rules, the speculator would not have succeeded in his scheme.[28]

In 1870, when A. Lewenhaupt, the chargé d'affaires attached to the Swedish-Norwegian legation at Washington, investigated the general problem of the migration of Norwegians and Swedes to America, he gave much attention to their houses and economic status. By that time the early settlements had grown prosperous. A typical one, he found, was "situated at the edge of a little forest, and consists of many beautiful farmhouses surrounded by luxuriant corn and wheat fields." The dwellings, white frame houses with four windows in the lower story and two in the upper, reminded him of "the small country dwellings near Stockholm." He took note of "the little shanty inhabited by the immigrant during his early years" standing near the newer frame house. Barns were still not very common, he said, in the Illinois region, where he found that "the cattle and horses are placed in large sheds covered with straw but open on the sides." Not uncommonly the immigrant who upon his arrival twenty years earlier had been obliged to mortgage his trunk "is now the owner of a fine, well-developed farm of 360 acres, of which the greater part is open field, and of seven cattle and nine horses, besides valuable farm implements and machinery." Such an establishment Lewenhaupt judged to be worth from fifteen to seventeen thousand Norwegian specie dollars. The advance to prosperity was closely related, he believed, to the general rise in land values. "Once the land had been bought, its value rose from year to year with the approach of the railroad and the accessibility of a labor supply." It was of course no longer possible for a poor immigrant to buy land in Illinois, but if he went to western Min-

[28] A detailed and highly interesting account of this episode is given by Dietrichson in a letter from Koshkonong dated January 29, 1847, and published in *Stavanger amtstidende og adresseavis,* April 10, 1847. Ræder's comments on the case are in *America in the Forties,* 76, 77. Some interesting information about "claim jumpers" and claim associations is in Helgeson, *Fra "Indianernes lande,"* 163–168.

nesota and Kansas, he might find circumstances similar to those from which the Illinois pioneers had so richly profited. All this did not mean that the immigrants uniformly were prosperous. Some lived in shanties on five-acre tracts; often a recently arrived family inhabited the original cabin of the prosperous farmer and had no other furniture than "a bed, one chair, one cradle, and the big chest." Lewenhaupt, after extensive observations of the Scandinavian immigrants, both new and old, said, however, "It is impossible to travel in the West without reaching the conviction that the principal motive for immigration is fundamentally the hope of bettering the conditions of life, and that this hope may actually become a reality for the majority."[29]

The Swedish official of 1870 spoke of the perils of disease on the emigrant voyage, but he did not consider it necessary to discuss the problem of health in the western settlements. Had he made his trip in an earlier period, he doubtless would have felt obliged to analyze the health conditions among the immigrant settlers. Pioneering, with its problems of adjustment in both social and economic respects, was an ordeal even for those immigrants who retained their health and strength. Unhappily, however, circumstances added ordeal by fever to the many other hardships that the pioneers had to undergo. Many factors let down the defenses against the attack of disease on the American frontiers of the earlier period. The water supply of the settlers was often uncertain, sometimes polluted. Houses were often terribly crowded. New immigrants, recently disembarked from festering emigrant packets, poured into the communities, frequently poverty stricken and germ laden. Sewage facilities were completely primitive. The concept of public health was still

[29] The Lewenhaupt report was printed as a sixteen-page pamphlet entitled *Indberetning fra hans majestæts chargé d'affaires i Washington angaaende udvandringen fra de forende riger til de nordamerikanske Forenede Stater,* without indication of date and place of publication. I have had a photostat made of a copy which I found in the Norwegian archives.

a thing of the future. The wonder is not that many died, but that so many survived.

Usually the sites of Norwegian settlements were fairly well chosen, and their rating from the point of view of health was relatively good; but sometimes the pioneers made hasty and ill-advised selections. The area of the Beaver Creek colony in Illinois, selected in the late summer of 1837, turned out to be swampy the following spring, with malaria lurking in the mosquito-infested stagnant water that flooded much of the ground. Muskego, too, was low, a popular breeding spot for anopheles; and the disadvantages of its site were made the more acute when hundreds of new immigrants descended each season upon the settlement, with their quota of germs and infection gathered up on the crossing and the inland journey. In Chicago many of the pioneer Norwegians lived along the river or the lake shore amid nauseating sanitary conditions and reaped the inevitable crop of disease.

Privations on board ship; the use of contaminated food and water; exposure to typhoid fever, typhus, and cholera; and the hazards of the inland journey by people who often were nearly penniless — these things constituted something less than an ideal introduction to American pioneering. The challenge of the West was to buoyant strength, to vitality in making adjustments to new conditions of work and climate. Many immigrants went as far as their money carried them — and then were dependent upon assistance in some form. Even if they were able to buy land or ventured, without funds, to squat on the public domain, they often were so reduced in their reserves that they started out with inadequate equipment. Thus they faced difficulties even without encountering ordeal by fever. The psychic adjustment was made harder by such circumstances as the arrival of parties in the burning heat of July or August, or, if they came in the autumn, a quick plunge into the cold of winter. The strangeness of American food, the difficulties of the English language, and nostalgia sometimes contributed a final touch of initial disillusionment. But human beings are not easily defeated by circumstances. They manage to emerge from their trials, often scarred and hurt, but not beaten. Many individuals, it is true, could not weather them and went down, but by and large the immigrants who came to America triumphed over the hardships into which they were plunged. The story of the ordeal by fever is revealed in hundreds of America letters and other contemporary records, and in modern times an illuminating and scholarly monographic study of the subject has been made by the distinguished American pathologist, Dr. Ludvig Hektoen, in collaboration with the historian, Dr. Knut Gjerset — both sons of Norwegian pioneers.[30]

The pioneers were not blind to the danger of sickness. Rynning in 1838 warned of "an unaccustomed climate" and said that "diarrhea or the ague afflicts almost every one." He advised cautious treatment. "Nature helps herself best without medicine," he said, and he urged immigrants not to try "quack medical treatment."[31] Søren Bache at Muskego in the winter of 1843–44 analyzed the causes of the prevalent diseases with considerable insight. One party after another of new immigrants had arrived, most of them without funds, and they were taken into the homes of the older settlers "with the result that there were sometimes fifteen to twenty persons in each house." They had nothing to drink except "the brown lake water," and the American food did not agree with them. "The hazards of the long journey and the unwonted climate lowered their resistance." Furthermore, "those who were well had to nurse the sick both day and night" and consequently "their vitality was sapped and it was not long before they, too, succumbed to the disease."

[30] "Health Conditions and the Practice of Medicine among the Early Norwegian Settlers, 1825–1865," in *Studies and Records,* 1: 1–59.

[31] Rynning himself died in the autumn of 1838 and at the time there was only one person in the settlement who was well. *True Account of America,* 11–14, 90.

Sometimes there was nobody to look after the sick "and the houses became contaminated." This analysis was recorded in a Muskego diary early in December, 1843.[32] A Chicago immigrant in 1841 wrote that he and a neighbor rowed far out in Lake Michigan to get pure water.[33] Olaus F. Duus of Waupaca, Wisconsin, was disturbed about the possible contamination of the public water supply when he visited a large city.[34]

"Practically all the Norwegians have been sick, some of them as much as a year at a time," wrote Munch Ræder in 1847.[35] "Fever and ague," or malaria, seems in particular to have taken toll of the settlers in nearly all the early Middle Western colonies. It was not alone the toll in lives — Bache said that seventy persons died at Muskego in the fall of 1843 — but the recurrence of the disease, its pernicious inroads upon strength and energy, that made it a cruel enemy of success and happiness. The contemporary records are filled with allusions to malaria, and foes of emigration in Norway made capital of the wretchedness reflected in America letters that told of the incursions of this disease. An American minister, Milton Wells of Burlington, Wisconsin, visited the Muskego settlement during the winter of 1843–44 — the same year that occasioned Bache's analysis — and wrote an account of his observations which drives home as does no other single document the misery that the settlers endured. "The amount of wretchedness and suffering which prevailed" at Muskego during the winter, he said, "was such as abso-

[32] Bache Diary, December 4, 1843.

[33] Knut A. Rene, *Historie om udvandringen fra Voss og vossingerne i Amerika*, 177 (Madison, 1930). This immigrant, Arne Vinje, attributed his own sickness to unaccustomed hard work, hot weather, and "filthy drinking water."

[34] Olaus F. Duus to his parents, May 14, 1858, in the Duus Papers, preserved in the Historiografisk Samling, Oslo. This is a series of manuscript letters written by Duus to his parents in Norway from the Waupaca parsonage in Wisconsin in the period from 1855 to 1858. The writer had typewritten transcripts, totaling 115 pages, made for the Norwegian-American Historical Association. Duus took note of the fact that the people of St. Louis used Mississippi River water for drinking and cooking purposes.

[35] *America in the Forties*, 66.

lutely to mock all description." He visited one family in which he "found every individual, eight in number, prostrated with disease. Two of them, the father and a daughter of some sixteen years of age, were then shaking violently with the ague. The daughter shoeless, and both nearly destitute of all clothing, stood hovering over a few live coals, by the side of which stood an old filthy looking copper teakettle, from the spout of which they would take turns in drinking. The others were huddled together into bunks filled with prairie hay, with nothing over them to shelter them from the rigorous cold of a December day, save a few sheepskins sewed together." The only sign of food that Wells saw in the house was a "wooden bowl, partly filled with what I took to be shorts, kneaded and prepared for baking." His wife accompanied a physician to another Norwegian cabin and there found "the sick mother in bed with her dying husband, with no one to administer to their necessities, or even to speak a word of consolation to them, save two little girls of some seven and nine years of age." Before the fire was a "little naked child, reduced to a skeleton." Wells tells of another hut where the doctor called and "found a dead man lying upon a bench out of doors, and ten sick ones, some of whom were dying, indoors." The clergyman reported that a hundred deaths had occurred in the settlement. He wrote the story in detail, gave it the pleasant title of "Wisconsin Antique — A Norwegian Settlement — A Tale of Distress," and sent it to the American Home Missionary Society.[36] Drs. Hektoen and Gjerset give many examples of the disastrous consequences of malaria in the pioneer settlements which enable one to understand why "even the fatal inroads of the dreaded cholera seem to have

[36] I found the original of this letter, or report, dated August 20, 1844, in the archives of the American Home Missionary Society at the Chicago Theological Seminary, University of Chicago. It appears in printed form in the *Home Missionary* (New York), 17:129, 130 (October, 1844).

been regarded by the settlers as a less serious affliction than the fever and the ague."[37]

Cholera was a scourge that killed with appalling swiftness, visiting its fury upon the settlements in the 1840's, and 1850's. An attack more than decimated the Norwegian colony in Chicago. "About one hundred of our countrymen died during the Epidemic, here last summer, 25 of whom were of our churchmembers, some of the ablest among us to sustain the Gospel," wrote the council of Paul Andersen's Chicago church in December, 1849.[38] The disease ravaged the Fox River settlement. Many of the settlers were well one day and dead the next. A Muskego man reported 1849 as the "awfullest summer I have ever experienced in my life." Three or four persons died every day and only a few families were well. "Hans Tweito and myself," writes John E. Molee, "had all we could do to carry the dead out of the houses and haul them to the grave with our oxen, while others dug the graves." Koshkonong, Rock Prairie, Bonnet Prairie, and Spring Prairie were among other Norwegian settlements that knew the fury of cholera — a visitation that made people think of the Black Death of a bygone age. A Norwegian minister, typical of his kind in braving the cholera areas, lost his way, with a companion, in the Bonnet Prairie settlement, and decided to spend the night in a farmhouse. "In the first house which they found all were dead. In the next house nearly all were sick with the cholera, and so they continued from house to house, until they came home. Sickness and death they found everywhere." This dread disease, brought inland from the seaboard, west from Atlantic ports, and up river from New Orleans, played havoc in many American communities; and its spread, as Drs. Hektoen and Gjerset make clear, was advanced by the insanitary condi-

[37] In *Studies and Records*, 1:19-21.

[38] This letter, dated December 25, 1849, is in the archives of the American Home Missionary Society.

tions and practices of many of the pioneer settlements, where "nothing was done to disinfect or properly dispose of the highly infectious discharges of cholera patients." Not even outhouse toilets were in use in the early days on the frontier; windows were not screened; few of the pioneers dug wells, and those who did, ordinarily made very shallow ones; water was taken from streams, springs, or lakes, stored in barrels, and often contaminated.[39]

In view of these conditions it is not surprising to learn from the researches of Drs. Hektoen and Gjerset that not only malaria and cholera but many other kinds of diseases were prevalent in the pioneer settlements, including pneumonia, typhoid fever, and tuberculosis. One of the most interesting of their generalizations is that "Fewer persons seem to have died of tuberculosis in those early days than later," and they attribute this to the fact that generally the people who came from Norway "were healthy and had robust constitutions." They conclude that the "high rate of mortality resulting from tuberculosis among the Norwegian people in America, even up to our own day, is probably the heavy penalty they have had to pay for the poverty, squalor, and hardships of pioneer times."[40] That smallpox had comparatively little prevalence among the settlers was doubtless due to the fact that the adults ordinarily had been vaccinated in Norway. "Yesterday evening," wrote Bache at Muskego on a day in August, 1846, "there arrived three loads of immigrants from Hallingdal, who remained overnight and proceeded westward today. Two families, however, remained behind because one had a child with smallpox

[39] Gjerset and Hektoen, in *Studies and Records,* 1:13–19. For comparative purposes see an interesting article by Dr. John M. Armstrong, "The Asiatic Cholera in St. Paul," in *Minnesota History,* 14:288–302 (September, 1933).

[40] *Studies and Records,* 1:25, 26. Several Norwegian-American doctors in 1878 reported that consumption was "very common among the Norwegian immigrants." A Decorah doctor offered the opinion that one of the causes was "coffee and similar gifts" of civilization. See Ch. Gronvald, "The Effects of Immigration on the Immigrated Norwegians," in Minnesota State Board of Health, *Sixth Annual Report,* 31–37 (Minneapolis, 1878).

which died this forenoon, and in the other the wife was ill and this evening at sunset gave birth to a boy. Thus up in the loft where they spent the day one child was born into the world and another departed in less than six hours."[41] The fear of smallpox sometimes led pioneer mothers to write to relatives in Norway for vaccine.[42]

Typhoid fever was often taken west from the ships where it had raged during the crossing from Europe to America. It was difficult to prevent its spread once it struck, for in the cramped cabins there could be no real isolation. The sick and well would occupy the same beds and eat with the same utensils. The resistance to typhoid fever, however, appears to have been strong. Dr. J. W. Magelssen, in an Iowa community, once had seven typhoid patients in one settler's cabin, and all recovered.[43] In general, the settlements on high land and considerably to the west of the Lake Michigan area, particularly in the period after the 1840's and 1850's, do not reveal such disastrous conditions as those which prevailed at Muskego and other colonies of the first pioneer era. Measles and whooping cough and sometimes other diseases did indeed appear, but one can find lengthy series of America letters or long diaries which have comparatively little mention of disease. Mrs. Gro Svendsen, who wrote letters from an Iowa community in the 1860's and 1870's, had a family of ten children, and of these only one died up to 1878 — a

[41] Bache Diary, August 30, 1846.

[42] Gro Nielsdatter Svendsen to her parents, June 3, 1864, Nielsen Papers. This series of remarkable letters written by Mrs. Svendsen in the 1860's and 1870's to her parents at Aal tells of her emigration in 1862 and of her experiences on a farm near Estherville, Iowa. There are also some letters by her husband and — toward the end of the series — a few by her children. Transcripts in the possession of the Minnesota Historical Society have been used by the writer.

[43] Gjerset and Hektoen, in *Studies and Records,* 1:31. A few cases of leprosy, it may be noted, were brought by emigrants from Norway to America. In the 1860's a Norwegian doctor, J. A. Holmboe, made a special investigation of such cases among the immigrants and wrote a report on the subject for a Norwegian scientific journal. See Gjerset and Hektoen, in *Studies and Records,* 1:24. Somewhat earlier, in 1857, another Norwegian doctor, Joachim A. Voss, made a trip to America to study medical conditions and published an elaborate report. See Blegen, *Norwegian Migration,* 347.

small girl from measles. Olaus Duus at Waupaca in the 1850's worried about the water supply and made some reference to measles and "Spanish flu," but, apart from presenting a pathetic story of an immigrant family just arrived from the seaboard in which two boys died, he rarely mentioned disease.[44] Of the St. Ansgar colony it has been said, "There was no cholera in the new settlement, and no fever, except ague, which troubled us some. The people were well, and very few died during the early years."[45] Rølvaag's *Giants in the Earth* suggests fairly good health conditions in the prairie settlements, and the suggestion is paralleled by Mrs. R. O. Brandt's historical account of "Social Aspects of Prairie Pioneering," which deals primarily with the 1880's.[46]

The pioneer ministers, perhaps because of the very rigors of their life, seem to have been robustly resistant to disease. Duus, after driving about on long journeys and frequently being entertained in cabins in comparison with which "our woodsheds at home, if only they had a stove, would be infinitely more comfortable," was astonished at his own health and strength. "I swear I believe I have been able to endure more here than I ever could have endured at home," he said. Over a period of some years he complained only once of sickness. He reported in 1857 that he was a "victim of Spanish flu," which "has certainly done its work with great thoroughness." He described his condition in a vivid line: "Here I sit as stiff and uncomfortable as if I had swallowed a meat spit."[47] Mrs. Elisabeth Koren watched faithfully

[44] Nielsen Papers; Duus Papers.

[45] Quoted by Gjerset and Hektoen, in *Studies and Records*, 1:11.

[46] In *Studies and Records*, 7:1–46. Dr. Gronvald in the 1870's said that the "most common chronic complaint among the Norwegians is, in America as it was in Norway, chronic gastritis and dyspepsia." Among the various causes that he suggests is the common fare in America — pork and meat instead of "voluminous farinaceous dishes," wheat bread, "commonly not well baked, and eaten warm," instead of "the easily digestible flat-bread," and too much coffee. In view of Dr. Gronvald's phrase "in America as it was in Norway," his discussion of causes seems hardly convincing. Minnesota State Board of Health, *Sixth Annual Report*, 24–26.

[47] Duus to his parents, December 29, 1857, Duus Papers.

over the health of her husband and recorded his every cold in her diary. He held a service in a cabin where it was "unbearably hot" and then went home, where it was very cold, and the result was a cold. He treated such an affliction, complicated by a lame back, by "going out to chop wood." An attack of "bilious fever," with no doctor available to care for him, kept the pioneer minister in bed for some time. But in general his health was good and both he and Mrs. Koren lived to enjoy a sturdy old age.[48]

The sufferings of women do not often get recorded in the immigrant letters, perhaps because it was thought indelicate to speak of gynecological disorders. Most of the housewives had many children and were usually attended, not by doctors, but by midwives. "I had thought of writing you," Gro Svendsen said after the birth of her fifth child, "just as soon as I was strong enough, but the first two weeks after my son's birth I was in no position either to write or to read because my eyes were so sore. I think I must have strained my eyes by reading too much both now and in my former confinements, because I have never been able to restrain myself when it came to reading. It is my greatest pleasure and I snatch every available moment for it." After the birth of her seventh baby, this pioneer woman wrote, "My health is not always of the best, but God has spared us thus far from any illnesses of long duration, so it seems to me I should not complain but rather thank God for all his goodness." She died after her tenth child was born. Incidentally, this woman took note of a case of tuberculosis in 1871: Lars Sando, sick all winter, died in the spring, leaving his wife Guri with eight little children in poor circumstances. "People have helped them a great deal already," wrote Mrs. Svendsen, "and there will be no let-up now."[49]

[48] Koren, *Fra pioneertiden,* 113–115, 165.

[49] See Mrs. Svendsen's letters to her parents, including those of August 1, 1869, and May 18, 1871, Nielsen Papers.

Mrs. Svendsen also observed a case of insanity that occurred in her community: "Tollef Medgaarden left this part of the country with his family last fall. No one knows where he went. Debt was the explanation for their sudden departure; his daughter Thuri with her two children went with them; it was over a year since she came back to her family; her husband Tosten went insane last fall and went to the asylum."[50] There can be no doubt that the attrition of immigrant woes — loneliness, death, calamities, plagues, economic reverses — left deep marks on the minds of people, not a few of whom were naturally introspective, and that insanity sometimes appeared in the train of such experiences. A modern scientific investigator, Dr. Ørnulv Ødegaard, concludes that "the ratio of insanity among the Norwegianborn of Minnesota is higher than in Norway," and he attributes this to "a very high incidence of senile and arteriosclerotic psychoses" which in turn spring from "the physical and mental strain of immigrant life."[51] Dr. Ødegaard believes that "insanity seems to be especially frequent among immigrant women — probably because they have less power of resistance" to that strain. He goes on to offer various possible explanations of the "relative prevalence of insanity in the immigrant women." He speaks of the "lonely life in poorly settled districts" as something felt more acutely by the women than by the men; and of the "primitive state of midwifery and obstetrics under pioneer conditions." This situation made "infections, bleeding and death of the child" common happenings; and there was also the "feeling of being without adequate help and assistance" — a sense of insecurity that added to the pressure of mental strain. One of the chief difficulties of the newcomer was, as Dr. Ødegaard suggests, that of adapting himself to "entirely new conditions of life," and here he finds that the problem on the whole was

[50] Mrs. Svendsen to her parents, February 11, 1877, Nielsen Papers.

[51] Ørnulv Ødegaard, *Emigration and Insanity: A Study of Mental Disease among the Norwegianborn Population of Minnesota*, 192 (Copenhagen, 1932).

more difficult for the women than for the men — the women interested in the concrete and the "familiar details of every day life," the men generally content with their work and stimulated by the American democracy in which they soon found themselves playing an active part.[52] The scientist's explanations undoubtedly come near the truth, but the realistic story of pioneering suggests that probably it was not that women had "less power of resistance" to its strain, but simply that the strain itself was greater for the women than for the men — the day's work, the unrelenting attrition of chores and duties, the carrying on of innumerable bleak activities amid child-bearing, loneliness, anxiety, and primitive conditions of medical care and treatment.

Given the conditions of health that prevailed in the early frontier West, a system of expert medical and hospital care would certainly have gone far toward restoring the balance of things, but unfortunately such a system was lacking. Doctors did indeed come to the communities, but usually after the first critical ordeal of pioneering had passed. Even then it was no easy thing to establish a remunerative practice, and the doctors found themselves obliged to handle circuits comparable in extent to those of the pioneer clergymen. Meanwhile, settlers did their best with home remedies; relied upon laymen who for one reason or another were believed to have curative powers or to be skilled in treating disease; used the patent medicines that flaunted their all-embracing claims in the press or weighed down the shelves of stores;

[52] *Emigration and Insanity*, 88. Dr. Ødegaard's scholarly monograph includes a valuable bibliography. See also Gronvald, in Minnesota State Board of Health, *Sixth Annual Report*, 26–31. Dr. Gronvald, a physician in the Holden community of Goodhue County and a member of the state board of health, wrote in this report of 1878: "Of the disorders of the nervous system Hypochondriasis and Hysteria seem to be very common among the immigrated Norwegians, and are supposed to be more frequent here than in Norway." He also suggests that among women such disorders are influenced by "early and frequent child-birth, from which they rise too early." He accepts the view that there is more acquired insanity among the Norwegians in Minnesota than among the people in Norway, in proportion to population totals, and suggests, by way of explanation, "the excitement and cares of an immigrant's life, and the acknowledged frequency of hypochondriasis."

and sometimes turned for help to books of medicine published for family use and wide commercial sale. The care of the sick was well intentioned, but, apart from the fact that medical science itself was a world away from what it became in a later epoch, that care was unscientific, haphazard, inadequate, compounded of good common lay sense and a bundle of superstitions, of traditional methods and alleged remedies, of stimulants, applications, rubbing, and sundry preparations.[53]

There were usually certain women in a community who had local reputations as midwives or as helpers in emergencies of all kinds; and sometimes they knew about herbs and concoctions of one sort or another. The best of them combined shrewd sense with strong and cheer-giving personalities and were practical physicians of genuine service to their communities. "My mother had no regular education as doctor, but had a handy way in taking care of the sick," wrote a daughter of Kari Veblen. "Doctors were far away; Northfield, twelve miles; Faribault, fourteen. Home remedies were generally used in those days. Pretty soon my mother got such a reputation that neighbors thought she could help in any kind of sickness. Her practice was successful, I believe for the reason that if she had no medicine on hand, she usually gave some advice that seemed to make them well again."[54] Sometimes, however, the lay medical advisers were charlatans and mountebanks, and Drs. Hektoen and Gjerset publish records of one midwife in a Wisconsin Norwegian settlement who gained a reputation for "miraculous cures" and as a "Necromancer on a large scale," but whose deceptions were found out and who ultimately was written down as a "humbugger" preying upon a "gullible and ignorant public."[55]

[53] Gjerset and Hektoen, in *Studies and Records,* 1:38.

[54] Erling Ylvisaker, *Eminent Pioneers,* 11 (Minneapolis, 1934).

[55] *Studies and Records,* 1:33. Drs. Gjerset and Hektoen mention several women "who labored heroically in these important fields of medical work."

Mrs. Koren was dismayed when she found that her parishioners came to the parsonage to be cured of physical, as well as of spiritual ailments. The trouble began when people discovered that she had both a "doctor book" and a small medical supply chest. Someone came to her about a sore eye; she suggested a search for more expert advice than she was able to offer, but was told "there was no use going to anyone else if we knew nothing about it." Mrs. Koren, always honest and clear-eyed, confessed in her diary that the patient "truly could not have turned to anyone less experienced" in such matters than herself. But she tried to be of service. She gave advice, doled out medicines, and was gratified when her friend C. L. Clausen presented her with a copy of Samuel Warren's *Passages from the Diary of a Late Physician*.[56] R. O. Brandt in Dakota found himself forced into a temporary medical practice when smallpox threatened his parish in the 1880's. "My husband had a talk with the doctor at Estelline," writes Mrs. Brandt, "and brought back a supply of vaccine points. Many people, old and young, came to the parsonage for free vaccination."[57] Probably many of the Norwegian-American homes toward the end of the century had "doctor books," sometimes combined with cookery recipes; and some of the women owned maternity books, such as Mrs. Prudence B. Saur's *Maternity: A Book for Every Wife and Mother*.[58] Peddlers and country stores reinforced the influence of newspaper advertisements in spreading the habit of swallowing patent medicines, many of them alcoholic in content — and innocently prized in hundreds of temperance homes.[59]

[56] Koren, *Fra pioneertiden,* 131, 170, 171, 180, 193.

[57] Brandt, in *Studies and Records,* 7:6, 7.

[58] Information received from Dr. Gertrude Ann Jacobsen of Minneapolis.

[59] See the discussion of patent medicines in Gjerset and Hektoen, *Studies and Records,* 1:35 ff. Ræder remarked in the 1840's, "I do not believe there is any other country on earth where sound, healthy people use as much medicine as here for the prevention of disease." *America in the Forties,* 67.

Meanwhile, however, doctors from the old country were establishing practices in the West and Norwegian Americans were beginning to seek medical educations in American colleges. Trained men like Hans C. Brandt, Johan Dundas, Gerhard Paoli, Søren J. Hansen, and Stephen O. Himoe appeared on the scene to introduce professional standards that led to marked advances in the care of the sick.[60] The Norwegians began to patronize these physicians and also to turn to American doctors in the various western settlements. And so there came a transition from the improvised and crude medical conditions that characterized the early frontier to the higher standards and trained professional skills that marked a more firmly established society. As in so many aspects of American life, specialization of function replaced the lay approach. The doctor pioneered on the frontiers of human service, an advance guard of the professional men who were to play an increasingly important role in many domains of western civilization as it emerged from its log-cabin and sod-house stage. The coming of professional medicine synchronized with a gradual widening of the frontiers of the science of medicine and a deepening of lay understanding of the importance of safeguarding health. And so new barriers were built against the onslaught of sickness and new ways devised to check its ravages.

[60] A series of informing biographical sketches of pioneer Norwegian-American doctors concludes the invaluable monograph by Drs. Gjerset and Hektoen, in *Studies and Records*, 1:41–59.

III. LANGUAGE AND IMMIGRANT TRANSITION

"WE HAVE BECOME strangers — strangers to the people we forsook and strangers to the people we came to," wrote Professor Rølvaag in 1911. "The people we forsook, we remain apart from, and the people we came to, we also remain apart from. We have thus ceased to be an integral part of a larger whole; we have become something by ourselves, something torn off, without any organic connection either here or there."[1] This concept played a large role in Rølvaag's thinking, from his portrayal of the two worlds of Paal Mørck to the prairie trilogy inaugurated by *Giants in the Earth,* and it is clear that language was close to the heart of the matter — language not in the sense of "just picking up words and phrases used in trade and travel," but as a medium in which "one's emotional life can move . . . freely and naturally."[2] To Rølvaag's mind, the immigrant faced an insoluble dilemma. "The giving up of one language and the

[1] Theodore Jorgenson and Nora O. Solum, *Ole Edvart Rölvaag: A Biography,* 155 (New York, 1939).

[2] Jorgenson and Solum, *Rölvaag,* 168, 169.

acquiring of a new," he wrote in 1929, "requires a spiritual adjustment which forever will be beyond the power of the average man, because it requires a re-making of soul. He cannot give up the old because that would mean death to him, and he cannot master the new—the process is simply beyond his power."[3] Rølvaag believed that the Middle West, with its vast immigrant population, has harbored two Americas—one hidden, and one on the surface; one represented by immigrant memories, traditions, language, and cultural complexities, the other by the institutions and customs of English-speaking America. The solution of the problem would involve two tendencies working toward each other: "The hidden would have to work its way gradually through the crust of a new language, and the surface institutions would have to send their roots deeper and deeper into the soil beneath."[4]

Many other students of American cultural forces have taken note of the dual personality of the immigrant. Thus Kristian Prestgard, the noted editor of the Norwegian-American newspaper *Decorah-posten,* has interpreted it as "The Tragedy of the Immigrant." The Norwegian American, to him, is Norwegian "by birth and training," by memory and cultural heritage. He is at the same time American by virtue of his work and achievement, his sacrifice and patriotic service, his attachment rooted in long and patient participation in the task of building America. Prestgard believes that a "disaster" has taken place in "the mind and the soul of the individual"; and this he symbolizes by the sentimental return of an immigrant to his homeland. The immigrant finds, however, that it is not his home, that its people are not his people, that his eyes do not see things as they did before he went away; whereupon the restlessness

[3] A letter to Professor Percy Boynton. Jorgenson and Solum, *Rölvaag,* 168.

[4] The quotation is from a passage in which Professors Jorgenson and Solum interpret Rølvaag's position. *Rölvaag,* 159.

that made him return drives him to catch the first steamboat for America again. Once more in his adopted country he finds that his children do not enter readily into the world of his own mind. The immigrant apparently has not made that "spiritual adjustment" that Rølvaag considered beyond the average man's power. Though Prestgard says little about language, he is never far away from the realities that it represents for the individual.[5]

That there was in fact such a dualism in the immigrant soul no one can deny. The immigrant, as Professor Einar Haugen strikingly puts it, "straddles two cultures" and from "his first day in the new land a tug of war between his old and his new self was going on."[6] But out of this very struggle emerges an aspect of the problem that gives a different color both to the dilemma of Rølvaag and the tragedy of Prestgard. For the struggle was a struggle of adjustment by large groups of people; and by its very nature it implied contacts at innumerable points with the new American world into which they were projected. The immigrants did not remain wholly apart from the people they came to; they were not wholly torn off from those they forsook. What happened needs to be interpreted by linguist and historian as well as by novelist and editor; and the totality of the picture that is emerging is somewhat different from what has been suggested. For one thing, the immigrant neither gave up his old language nor, though he learned some English, did he master the new, but he was nevertheless not left helpless or frustrated. What he did was to create, by gradual and normal processes of change, adaptation, and growth, something like an intermediate language—Norwegian-American, which combined both languages, broke the shock

[5] Kristian Prestgard, "The Tragedy of the Immigrant," in *Scandinavia* (Grand Forks, North Dakota), vol. 1, no. 5, p. 38–49 (May, 1924). The article is translated into English by Dr. Knut Gjerset.

[6] Einar I. Haugen, "Language and Immigration," in *Studies and Records*, 10:1, 2.

of his new-world plunge, and on the whole served his needs effectively. In the second place, while residing in this half-way linguistic house, he enjoyed the security of a fairly solid, though temporary, foundation of what may be described as a Norwegian-American way of life. It was not exactly Norwegian nor was it wholly American, but it had contact with both and was colored by both. At the same time it possessed many inner bonds — of custom, speech, social life, institutions, the propinquity that was the reward of group settlement, and, perhaps above all, the bond of mutual sharing in processes of change. For no description of dilemma or tragedy, in terms of status, must close one's eyes to the fact that immigrant life was not static. It was dynamic, changing, growing; and, considering the group as a whole, it discloses no finalities. Immigrants, too, were always human beings; and in interpreting them one must never forget the human base. Prestgard's returned emigrant, for example, does indeed typify the individual of dual personality, the victim of an inner struggle for some kind of unity, but he is also in some sense an Everyman trying unconsciously to recapture a vanished past, and his tragedy to a certain extent is that of the cleavage of generations, a cleavage accentuated by the pace of modern life and by no means limited to immigrant families.

The immigrants from the first were aware of the need of learning English. English was all about them, and before many compact Norwegian settlements were built up there was an ever-present practical need of acquiring a knowledge of the language. "My son attends an English school and speaks English as well as a native," wrote Gjert G. Hovland in 1835.[7] Another immigrant, in 1836, pointing out the difficulties of American pioneering, added, "I write that he who is free and unoccupied can get ahead here, if he will take

[7] *Christianssandsposten,* February 23, 1843. The letter, to Niels Sivertsen, was written in 1835 from the New York Kendall settlement.

care of himself and learn the language."[8] One of the chapters in Rynning's famous "America Book" was headed "What language is spoken in America? Is it difficult to learn?" He pointed out that there were as many languages spoken in America as there were different nationalities streaming into the country, but the English language, he said, "predominates everywhere." Ignorance of it was a handicap to the Norwegian immigrants, felt "especially on the trip to the interior of the country." He did not look upon the language problem as a major difficulty, however, for "by daily association with Americans one will learn enough in two or three months to get along well. Some half-grown children who came over last summer already speak very good English. Before having learned the language fairly well, one must not expect to receive so large daily or yearly wages as the native-born American."[9]

Children were sent to the common schools to learn the language, and even some of the older immigrants joined them. An immigrant letter from the forties, written at Chicago, reports that "Nils Vike, Nils Lie, and Nils Andersen Flage have attended school in order to learn how to 'reckon' and to write English"; and Søren Bache, one of the leaders of the Muskego settlement, spent a winter in Milwaukee attending an English school.[10] Johan R. Reiersen noted in 1844 that the Norwegians in the Fox River settlement had schools "in common with the neighboring Americans," and he added that the majority of the settlers understood English and usually attended the "American churches in the vicinity." An immigrant the next year wrote that English was "spoken everywhere" — but he made an exception of the more compact settlements of Norwegians, Swedes, Germans, or French, "where they generally continue

[8] A letter of Ole Østensaa Helland, October 12, 1836, in Socialdept., Oslo: Lovkontor, Utvandringen, Kong. Prop. 1845, folder 1.

[9] Rynning, *True Account of America,* 89, 90.

[10] Rene, *Historie om udvandringen fra Voss,* 370; Bache Diary, 1841–42.

to speak their native tongue among themselves." It is typical of pioneer opinion that he believed the use of the native tongue would "die out in the second generation."[11] The urge to learn the English language was one of the potent factors in the support and patronage of the common schools by the immigrants, notwithstanding the prolonged controversy that centered about that institution. Many of the immigrants themselves had begun to study English even before reaching America, using convenient manuals that were issued in Norway for their benefit.[12] As a result of conscious effort, coupled with the stimulus of American associations, many learned to speak English with a fair degree of effectiveness. A language is not learned in a day, however, and there unquestionably was a considerable period of transition marked by relatively slow progress. A pioneer Wisconsin minister tells of a Norwegian settler who was asked by a Yankee whether or not he had any hay for sale. "Yes Sir, I have," replied the immigrant, "de price is 4 Dollars, naar ye take it paa de slough." The Yankee inquirer undoubtedly grasped the meaning of this answer, and the observer remarked, "Yes, we Norwegians talk an extraordinary American, and still the Yankees say that there is no other foreign nationality that speaks it so well as we."[13]

Meanwhile, as thousands of immigrants sought the lands of the Middle West, there was a natural, indeed an inevitable, tendency for the Norwegians to develop compact settlements—communities of neighbors of like origins. This tendency has been exhibited in greater or less degree by every immigrant people—English, German, Dutch, Scandinavian, and others. It is rooted in the magnetic attraction

[11] Reiersen's comment on the situation at Fox River has been translated and edited by Theodore C. Blegen and published under the title "Norwegians in the West in 1844," in *Studies and Records,* 1:113, 114. See also Nils H. Nærum to J. H. Nærum, November 16, 1845, in *Bratsbergs-amts correspondent,* March 5, 1846.

[12] See Blegen, *Norwegian Migration,* 255.

[13] Duus to his father, July 8, 1856, Duus Papers.

of understanding and friendliness in a new environment—the assumptions that accompany familiar speech, accepted social ideas and institutions, common traditions, and shared history. For the Norwegians this meant a transfer to the West of a *bonde* group society marked by the *bonde* culture bred in the valleys of Norway. A remarkable aspect of the tendency of the Norwegian immigrants to flock together was that it was not enough for them to seek out fellow Norwegians. They went further and associated themselves with people who had come out of the very valley, the very *bygd*, from which they themselves hailed in the old country. This district aspect of Norwegian settlement was influenced by the general course of the migration movement, which began in southwestern Norway and spread, wave-like, over other areas, so that people from a given district might normally be expected to be brought within its scope at one time. Sometimes entire shiploads of folk from a given district would sail together, seek lands jointly in the New World, and settle as a compact unit. If the earlier history of the movement as a whole thus helps to explain the initiation of *bygd* settlement groups, there is no doubt that, as time went on, people from a given *bygd* found themselves drawn to settlements of folk native to their own districts—often encouraged by letters and even prepaid tickets.

It is not sufficient, therefore, in suggesting the special flavor or color of a given Norwegian settlement in America, to say that it was Norwegian. Notwithstanding an inevitable intermingling and jostling, the distinguishing marks of a settlement ordinarily were furnished by the particular customs of some particular valley or area of old Norway. "Almost everywhere," writes Holand of the Wisconsin Coon Prairie settlement, "there were natives of Gudbrandsdal, with an occasional Biring or Telemarking."[14] Professor

[14] Hjalmar R. Holand, *Den sidste folkevandring,* 136 (Oslo, 1930). Holand heads his chapter on this settlement "America's Gudbrandsdal."

George T. Flom has taken particular note of the *bygd* phase of the Norwegian-American settlements—the strength of the Numedal group at Jefferson Prairie and eastern Koshkonong; of the "Valdriser" at Blue Mounds and Manitowoc, Wisconsin; of the Sogn people in Goodhue County, Minnesota, and certain particular areas in Illinois and Wisconsin; of the Stavanger element in the Fox River settlement in Illinois and the Story City region of Iowa; of the Upper Telemark folk at Muskego and Pleasant Springs; of the Haring element in Lee County, Illinois; of the Vossing group in Chicago and various other places of the Middle West; of the Hallingdal group at Rock Prairie; of Solør, Ringebu, Landing, and many other groups at special places in the Middle West. Sometimes in one large settlement there were several *bygd* elements, but it is interesting to note that often within these settlements there were clearly defined areas of *bygd* groups, as in Koshkonong, where the Telemark element was strong in one township, the Sogn in another, and the Numedal in still another. This does not, of course, mean that there was no intermingling of groups. Munch Ræder, after attending a pioneer Wisconsin church service, said, "One thing which distinguished this gathering from an average country congregation in Norway was the fact that there were people here from all parts of Norway—upcountrymen, northerners, easterners, westerners, and *Nordmænd*." Such a mingling, he noted, was regarded as beneficial in softening many local prejudices imported from Norway; but he found that by no means had all such prejudices been removed. The folk from the Bergen vicinity in Norway, for example, were "regarded as a people by themselves"; and the *Nordmænd* rarely intermarried with Norwegians from other parts of Norway.[15]

[15] Ræder, *America in the Forties,* 135, 136. "In the mountain districts of Valders, Hallingdal, and Telemark," Mr. Malmin explains, "those who live beyond the mountains are called *Nordmænd,* or 'Northerners.'" See George T. Flom's *History of Norwegian Immigration to the United States, passim* (Iowa

The distinguishing marks of the various *bygd* groups were many, including the lore of history and tradition accumulated through a thousand years or more in a Norwegian district that by geography and by isolation had been definitely marked as different from other *bygds* and people. Each district had its own wealth of ballad and folk story, of custom and dress, even of temperamental characteristics.[16] But the most conspicuous distinguishing mark was dialect. For each district, through the sweep of years, had developed its own vernacular, and it was the dialects of the common people that were carried to America and heard in the everyday life of the western settlements. The dialects were authentic speech, shaped by local development through the sweep of centuries, and they were vastly different from the literary Norwegian-Danish, the book language, the language of the church and press and written literature of Norway. The language problem of the immigrant, therefore, was complex. It involved the dialect that was his spoken speech; and it also involved a much closer contact with other Norwegian dialects than he had known in the Old World. These dialects he understood, for their basic elements were not unlike, but the dialect of another valley of the homeland marked a person off as not, in an intimate sense, belonging to one's own people. The language problem also involved the literary Norwegian, which was employed in the Norwegian-American church and in the immigrant press — a language that the immigrants from all the various Norwegian districts understood well enough, for they had read the Bible and catechism in Norwegian-Danish, had been confirmed in that

City, 1909); also his essay "Det norske sprogs bruk og utvikling i Amerika," in *Nordmands-forbundet* (Christiania), 5:243 (May, 1912). Hjalmar R. Holand, in *De norske settlementers historie* (Ephraim, Wisconsin, 1909), gives a wealth of detail on the *bygd* aspect of Norwegian immigration and settlement.

[16] How deeply the *bygd* and its associations were imbedded in the immigrant mind may be indicated by the fact that at present there are approximately a half hundred *bygdelags* in the United States, societies made up of immigrants, and of the descendants of immigrants, who originated in particular districts in the old country.

language, and had heard it from the pulpit in Norway, but they did not, save in exceptional instances, speak it. It involved, finally, the English language, which, however compact the Norwegian-American settlements, impinged upon them in a score of ways — through the common schools to which their children were sent, through local government and politics, and through their business dealings with reference to land, markets for their crops, and many other objects and undertakings.[17]

The literary language of the Norwegian-American church and press reached out to all the dialect groups and undoubtedly served as a cohesive force, setting up common interests that traversed dialectal boundaries. But it did not afford a bridge to the American speech of the strange world of the immigrant. As a consequence he had to build that for himself, and he did it normally, easily, skillfully, demonstrating once more what a pliable thing language is on the lips of people faced by new circumstance. Group settlement freed him from the necessity of suddenly putting away his native dialect like a worn garment. It also saved him from being impaled upon the other horn of the Rølvaagian dilemma — an abrupt and complete shift into the intricacies of English. But he was obliged nonetheless to take linguistic account of the fact that he was living in contact with an American world marked at a hundred points by customs, practices, and objects which the experience and linguistic usage he was familiar with in a distant Norwegian valley did not fit.

He therefore created a Norwegian-American speech, not consciously, not artificially, not as a written language, but unconsciously, naturally, and as an instrument for everyday oral use. This language employed the Norwegian dialect as

[17] The most comprehensive and illuminating work on the entire subject of Norwegian speech in the United States is Einar I. Haugen, *Norsk i Amerika* (Oslo, 1939). This consists of six lectures delivered in 1938 at the University of Oslo: "Det store landnåm," "Bondemål og bygdefolk," "Fra bygdemål til verdenssprog," "Navneskikk i nybygden," "Skrift og tale," and "Diktende trang."

[illegible]
Rasin County 1842.

Da her gives Leilig-
hed vil ieg Skrive
nogle Ord angaaende
de mit her befindende
og saa vil ieg bekient-
giøre Eder en enfoldelig Efterret-
ning om Amerika Jeg er nu forsi-
den med Kone og Børen vel med
Hilsen ogsaa fornøied, Jeg flyttede
fra Illinois til Wesconsine hvor
De meste af Norske have Bosat sig
og ieg kiøbte der 81 Aker med
Land for Regieringens Priis, og
dette Landstykke holder ieg bedre
end en Kaup Jordegods i Norge,
Min Formue bestaar af 15 Kreatu-
re med smaat og stort, og 6 Sauer

[illegible]
meget let, I forleden Aar havde ieg
11 Stykker og samlede Høi for dem
i en Tid af 3 Ugger allene ~~hielpe~~
foruden min Kone hialp mig imil-
lemstunder, De faar saa mange
forskillige Berethninger om Amerika kommer tildeels af uerfaren-
hed deels af Menneskers Siebne
her saavel som i andre Deeler i
Verden, sandt er det at de som
vil reise hertil maa udstaa forskillige Prøver for det første
men især hvad Opholdet angaar
er ~~forskillig~~ Forskielen millem Amerika og Norge meget Stor, Dag-
lønnen er høi og Livnetsmid-
lerne billige, en Arbeider har
her 10 a: 14 Daler Maanen en
Pige 6 Daler Maanen, 1 [illegible]

An America Letter of 1842

[From a manuscript volume of immigrant letters copied in Norway in the 1840's by an unknown compiler. Bequeathed to the present writer by the late I. D. Hustvedt of Cannon Falls, Minnesota.]

its base and frame, but it amalgamated into that dialect, organically, words and expressions drawn out of the English language which precisely fitted new objects, situations, and meanings presented by the American environment. It was an achievement that warrants unqualified respect and careful study both by linguists and by historians, and to the former, notably such scholars as Professors Flaten, Flom, and Haugen, who have recorded, analyzed, and interpreted this Norwegian-American speech, historians owe a debt of gratitude. In according the Norwegian-American speech scientific analysis, they have illuminated the processes not only of an interesting linguistic transition, but also of that broader social and cultural re-orientation of immigrant life which the adaptations of language reflect.

The issues, as Professor Rølvaag discerned, have a deeper meaning than mere words and phrases, for they center about the adjustment of the mind of the immigrant to the two worlds that his experience encompassed. Language opens the door to an understanding of the subtle inner struggle that was going on. He was a hewer of wood and a carrier of water. He started at the bottom rung of the ladder. His mind was sensitive to the pain and loss inseparable from migration; and as he mulled over his experience he thought much about the land he had come from. He wrote letters home; he looked forward with pleasure to greeting friends and relatives who later joined in the mighty emigration; the press kept him informed about events in Norway; he devoted a corner of his mind to a romantic idealization of his old fatherland; and, as Professor Haugen shrewdly points out, he found himself deeply interested in historical parallels that linked his own adventure with the migrations of the Vikings.[18] Having the opportunity, owing to the magnitude of the immigration and the compactness of the Norwegian settle-

[18] *Norsk i Amerika,* 20; see also Blegen and Ruud, *Norwegian Emigrant Songs and Ballads,* 24–29.

ments, to go on using his native speech, he was caught up in the swirl of Norwegian-American life, went to a Norwegian-American church, read Norwegian-American newspapers, joined Norwegian-American societies, perhaps sent his son to a Norwegian-American college. On all sides he found cultural transfers from his homeland. He thus made himself a part of an institutionalized Norwegian-American life. But all the time he was living in an American world, too. He took out citizenship papers; he became a voter. Often he got a chance to serve in some local office. Now and then one of his countrymen was elected to the legislature or some other state office. The immigrant enlisted in the army when Lincoln called for soldiers. He rubbed shoulders with Americans at the store, in the land office, at political meetings, in camp, and on the march. He learned some English, sometimes became effectively bilingual, but in any case he saw his children bilingual, often advancing with startling — and to some contemporary observers even dismaying — rapidity along the road of transition.

So the immigrant lived in a Norwegian-American domain, not quite forsaking the people he came from, not quite a stranger to the people he came to. He was on the bridge of transition. He was making his way into American life. In short, he was a Norwegian American. He took the English language into his system, not in a mighty gulp, but bite by bite. He adjusted himself to American ways, not by some instantaneous and magical transformation, but idea by idea. Meanwhile he moved in a Norwegian-American world that was not lacking in compensations, a world in which he was not so frustrated as Rølvaag suggests, not so tragic as Prestgard thinks. Life was not easy for him — he faced difficulties, knew hardship, suffered, made sacrifices, experienced cultural loss; but his life was far from an unrelieved round of unhappiness. Sometimes his hope blossomed into triumph; he was not without genial relationships;

he had land and work, he made material advance, he was drawn into church and social life, and his world even furnished a certain excitement in the rumble of controversy and traditional combativeness that found voice in newspapers, church councils, and laymen's discussions in the churchyard. Sometimes his existence was so normal in its ways, so generous in its opportunity for self-expression, that he was hardly conscious of being an immigrant. This, of course, was more likely to be the case among the everyday folk than among the educated minority who were steeped in the intellectual and literary traditions of the old country. The latter were sometimes sharply conscious of the linguistic changes that were taking place and hostile to their progress. But for the majority the transitions both in their universe of ideas and in their language were synchronous. Of the language itself, after the linguistic processes got well under way, Professor Haugen has said, "The shell is still Norwegian, but the inward pattern, the spirit of the thing, is American. This is Norwegian-American, the language of the Norwegian immigrant."[19]

The adaptation of language started very early among the Norwegian immigrants. When Munch Ræder, a keenly observant Norwegian traveler, visited the Wisconsin settlements in the summer of 1847, he quickly noted this tendency, and his contemporary analysis of it is possibly the earliest available, and certainly one of the most penetrating.[20] The immigrants, he said, "do not bother about keeping the two languages separate, so that they may speak Norwegian to their own countrymen and English to others; instead, they eliminate one word after the other from their Norwegian and substitute English words in such a way that the Norwegian will soon be quickly forgotten." Such a tendency, he realized, was common among emigrants of all national-

[19] In *Studies and Records,* 10:39.
[20] *America in the Forties,* 33–35.

ities, but the Norwegians, he thought, "seem to have a special knack at it." They begin by adopting the English words "yes" and "no" in place of "ja" and "nei." "Gradually other English words, pertaining to their daily environment, are added." He offers illustrations: "They have a 'fæns' about their 'farm' and have probably 'digget' a well near the house so that they need not go so far to get water to use on their 'stoven.'" He goes on to explain that such a well is needed even if there is a "læk" or a "river" near by. Frequently the settlers have small gardens in which they grow, among other things, "pompuser" (pumpkins), and beyond the garden is "fila." Munch Ræder was one of the few Norwegian observers who sensed the true character of the amalgamation of English. He points out, for example, in explaining "fila," that it is the English word "field" used "with the genuine Norwegian feminine article 'a.'"[21] In continuing his examples, he follows the settler to town, where he sells his wheat or "flour," and goes to the "store" to buy various articles; and he comments on "ægeren" (the ague) as one of the "worst troubles he has in this strange country."

If Munch Ræder thus anticipated the modern linguists in noting and analyzing this process, he also anticipated Rølvaag in his comments on some of the larger issues. He especially urged the importance of maintaining cultural links between the settlers and their mother country. "Every one, indeed," he wrote, "who would like to see them preserve their national characteristics and their memories of their native land as long as possible must, first and foremost, turn his attention to the problem of preserving their language by

[21] Many Norwegian observers have looked upon Norwegian-American as a lawless mixture of Norwegian and English and, lacking understanding of the normal and orderly linguistic processes that were at work, have ridiculed the speech. Novelists in Norway, attempting to put Norwegian-American into the mouths of their characters, have failed to capture the authentic speech of the immigrants, and instead have offered an absurd, fabricated jargon. Haugen gives a few examples in *Norsk i Amerika,* 40 ff.

keeping it constantly before their eyes and ears."[22] He recognized the importance of group settlement as a factor in the problem, for the very fact of a group protected them "against influences foreign to themselves, because their relationship to one another is stronger than their relationship to other races." The pioneer minister Dietrichson had been asked to preach in English occasionally, but Munch Ræder expressed the hope that he would not do so, though he realized that the establishment of an American congregation alongside the Norwegian might have some good results. He believed, however, that it "would tend to Americanize our countrymen too soon," and he desired to use both church and language as instruments for preserving the Norwegian nationality in America as long as possible.[23]

Pioneer immigrant letters from the 1840's abound in American expressions woven into the Norwegian speech, such as the following: holes that *gufferotten* (the gopher rat) always keeps open; ran *røvern* (the river) year after year; *grubbe* en *acre* (grub an acre); to *tripper* (two trips); lægge *sidewalk* (lay a sidewalk); *digge* kobber (to dig copper); en svær *fiver æger* (a high ague-fever); *opbræke* nogle *æker* (break some acres); paa *printing officin* for *congress-medlem* John Wentworth (at the printing office of Congressman John Wentworth).[24] In the 1850's the pioneer minister, Duus, observed the process and complained that one never heard such a Norwegian word as *hvedemeel,* but in its place *flour;* as *gjerde,* but *fence;* as *lade,* but *barn;* as *stald,* but *stable;* and he quoted as Norwegian-American

[22] *America in the Forties,* 18.

[23] *America in the Forties,* 55. Ræder was impressed by the "great ease" with which the Norwegian immigrants "learn the English language and, unfortunately, the equal facility they have in forgetting their own as soon as they cease to use it every day," and he went on to compare them with their ancestors who settled in Normandy. *America in the Forties,* 33, 34.

[24] The examples are drawn from immigrant letters printed in Rene, *Historie om udvandringen fra Voss,* 193–212, 368–375, and *passim.* The normal form for "office" would be "officen," not "officin."

The little American.

Den lille Amerikaner.

En letfattelig Veileder

for Emigranter og Andre, som i kort Tid ville lære at forstaae, og at gjøre sig forstaaelige

i det engelske Sprog.

Af

F. W. Günther.

Oversat efter 7de Original-Udgave.

2det forøgede Oplag.

Christiania.
Trykt paa Feilberg & Landmarks Forlag
hos Werner & Comp.
1851.

THE TITLE PAGE OF A MANUAL OF ENGLISH FOR NORWEGIAN EMIGRANTS
[From a copy in the library of the Royal Fredrik University, Oslo.]

the phrase, about a horse, that "den jomper fence" (it jumps the fence).[25] Duus, like many educated Norwegians who came to America, looked upon Norwegian-American as a defiling of linguistic purity, yet even he, in his later letters, fell into some of the new ways of speech. An ironical writer of the 1850's, publishing an entire letter, or essay, composed in the mixed Norwegian-American speech, asked whether one could *dile* (make a deal), *seine* en *not* (sign a note), or *rekorde* en *dyd* (record a deed) in Norwegian. The ministers *edikœta* (educated) in this country *pritja* (preach) occasionally in English, he said. On the general problem he concluded that for the Norwegian there was no "*isiere* way than to *mixa* the language."[26] Many persons noted the emergence of a Norwegian-American speech. "Naa er *Feieren* like in paa *Fila* vaar" (Now the fire has come right up to our field), someone called to Mrs. Elisabeth Koren, who recorded the phrase in her diary for March 15, 1854. Sometimes the observers were obviously city-bred folk who had no liking for the Norwegian vernacular and whose attempts to quote Norwegian-American usually betrayed their own ignorance. Johan Schrøder in the 1860's, for example, took note of the emerging speech and gave several alleged examples of it, but in each instance made manifest his lack of understanding both of the basic dialect and of the orderly rules governing the American-Norwegian linguistic union. One sentence that he recorded was "Smaagutten sætter *Bridelen* paa *Kolten* for at *starte* ud i *Prœia* og *fetche* Kua heim" (The small boy is putting the bridle on the colt to

[25] Duus to his father, July 8, 1856, Duus Papers. Didrik Arup Seip quotes much of the letter of July 8, 1856, in his "Nordmenn og norsk språk i Amerika," printed as a separate from *Ord och bild* (Stockholm, 1932).

[26] *Emigranten,* December 27, 1859. A translation which attempts to preserve the characteristic touches of amalgamated English appears in Arthur C. Paulson and Kenneth Bjørk, eds., "A School and Language Controversy in 1858," in *Studies and Records,* 10:100–106. At some points the original document, however, is not authentic Norwegian-American. In his ironical zeal the author went too far and in some instances simply seized American phrases without incorporating them into the Norwegian dialect.

start out for the prairie to fetch the cows home).[27] But the farmer whose speech Schrøder purports to quote would scarcely have turned the masculine "prærien" into the feminine — and mutilated — "præia."

Not the least significant aspect of the history of Norwegian-American speech is the searching analysis that has been accorded it by linguists, most of them descendants of the pioneers who originally fashioned it. This field of scholarship was pioneered in 1897 by Peter Groth, a scholar in New York, and three years later Professor Flaten of St. Olaf College published a Norwegian-American vocabulary of 561 words, all drawn from the speech of Norwegians in Goodhue and Rice counties, Minnesota.[28] He himself was brought up in a community where this language was spoken and he explains, "I was ten or twelve years old before I found out that such words as *paatikkelé* (particular), *stæbel* (stable), *fens* (fence), were not Norse but mutilated English words. I had often wondered that *poleit, trubbel, söpperéter* were so much like the English words *polite, trouble, separator.* So common is this practice of borrowing that no English word is refused admittance into this vocabulary provided it can stand the treatment it is apt to get. Some words are, indeed, used without any appreciable difference in pronunciation, but more generally the root, or stem, is taken and Norse inflections are added as required by the rules of the language."[29] In 1939 Professor Flaten printed a series of eight true stories in "Minnesota-Valdris," that is, Norwegian-American as spoken by people of the Valdris dialect in Minnesota, and he pointed out the interesting fact that children of the third or fourth generation can still talk this

[27] Johan Schrøder, *Skandinaverne i de Forenede Stater og Canada,* 223, 234 (La Crosse, Wisconsin, 1867). Schrøder attributed the story to some earlier tourist who visited a Norwegian-American country home.

[28] Peter Groth, *Nogle eiendommeligheder ved de til Amerika udvandrede Nordmænds sprog* (Christiania, 1897); Nils Flaten, "Notes on American-Norwegian with a Vocabulary," in *Dialect Notes* (New Haven), 2:115–126 (1900).

[29] Flaten, in *Dialect Notes,* 2:115.

mixed language.[30] Some characteristic Norwegian-American phrases from Professor Flaten's earlier study are: "E ha *pruva up klémen* min" (I have proved up my claim); "I aar *lusa* je hele *kroppen* min" (This year I lost my entire crop); "Je *fila* saa *bæd;* je ha *kætscha kold*" (I feel so bad, I have caught cold); "Je kunde ikke faa *resa* saa mye *kaes* at je fik betalt *morgesen* i *farmen* min" (I could not raise enough cash to pay the mortgage on my farm).[31]

In Professor Flaten's more recent study he offers two Norwegian-American sentences which, though artificial in the sense that they are not quoted from actual parlance but have been put together by himself as an illustration, suggest the lengths to which the substitution of English words for Norwegian might go. A porter at a hotel in Norway was bewildered when a Norwegian-American visitor asked him, "Er det *ålreit* om je *liva sætkjelen* min på *seidvåka* mens je *rønna upp* på *romme* mitt?" (Is it all right for me to leave my satchel on the sidewalk while I run up to my room?). His second example relates to travel: "Per, *hitsj* upp *timø* før *boggen rett av,* kjøyr *tronken* på *dipon,* kjøp mig ein *raundtripp tikkett* te Chicago, o få *tronken kjekka*" (Per, hitch the team to the buggy right off, take the trunk to the depot, buy me a round-trip ticket to Chicago, and have the trunk checked). In both instances Norwegian supplies the frame, but the substance, including every noun, is American-English.[32]

Meanwhile, Professor Flom, the dean of Norwegian-American philologists, made a series of illuminating studies of Norwegian-American based upon scholarly observation of the speech of the Koshkonong settlement in Wisconsin, presenting one contribution after another over a period of

[30] Flaten, "Valdris-rispo. Sannferdiga skrøno på Minnesota-Valdris," in *Maal og minne: Norske studier* (Oslo), pt. 1, p. 30–48 (1939).
[31] Flaten, in *Dialect Notes,* 2:118, 119.
[32] Flaten, in *Maal og minne,* pt. 1, p. 31 (1939).

more than a quarter of a century.[33] By 1926 he was able to publish a Norwegian-American vocabulary of 1,025 words, with the interesting information that 735 were nouns, 235 verbs, 43 adjectives, 7 adverbs, and that the list included no conjunctions or pronouns.[34] He has explored the phonology of the words, classified them in respect to the various interests and enterprises of the immigrants, and interpreted the speech in the setting of immigrant life.

More recently Professor Einar Haugen of the University of Wisconsin has worked out an elaborate questionnaire for a vast inquiry into the nature of Norwegian speech in America, dividing it into such categories as personal and family history, home and family life, the human constitution, household life, buildings and grounds, farming, weather, and topography, travel and communication, business, trade and government, social affairs and institutions, and human relationships — a classification that is of suggestive interest to the social historian.[35] He has made use of the phonograph in his effort to record and preserve examples of current Norwegian-American speech, and he has revealed, in several searching essays and a broad-ranging scholarly book, the possibilities of the linguistic approach to an understanding of the "immigrant's psychological and cultural development."[36]

[33] George T. Flom, "English Elements in Norse Dialects of Utica, Wisconsin," in *Dialect Notes*, 2:257–268 (1902); "The Gender of English Loan-nouns in Norse Dialects in America," in *Journal of English and Germanic Philology* (Baltimore), 5:1–31 (1903); "Det norske sprogs bruk og utvikling i Amerika," in *Nordmands-forbundet*, 5:233–250 (May, 1912); "On the Phonology of English Loan-words in the Norwegian Dialects of Koshkonong in Wisconsin," in *Studier tillägnade Axel Kock*, 178–189 (Lund, 1929); "English Loanwords in American Norwegian as Spoken in the Koshkonong Settlement, Wisconsin," in *American Speech* (Baltimore), 1:541–558 (July, 1926); "Um det norske målet i Amerika," in *Norsk årbok*, 1931, p. 113–124 (Bergen, Norway).

[34] Flom, in *American Speech*, 1:541–558.

[35] The *Questionnaire for an Inquiry into Norwegian Speech in America* was issued in mimeograph form in 1936. Dr. Haugen has kindly furnished me with a copy.

[36] See his recent book *Norsk i Amerika*, and his article, as previously cited, in *Studies and Records*, 10:1–43. The value of the article is greatly enhanced by five "authentic samples of American Norwegian speech," four of them transcribed

These vocabularies and analyses mirror the intellectual transition that the immigrants went through in the face of new conditions, concepts, and practices. All the *bygd* dialects exhibit a similar development: they changed gradually into Norwegian-American while retaining much of their own particular flavor; and there was, at least to the extent that they took over English words, a certain leveling of dialects. Professor Haugen points out that there were two main stages in the linguistic process. The first, typical of the first generation, was that of amalgamating English words into the Norwegian dialects, invariably giving them the Norwegian flavor of sound and ending and gender, in effect making Norwegian words of them. The second, characteristic of the bilingual second generation, was built upon the first but unlike it in the tendency to take over additional English words and phrases without clothing them in the garments of Norwegian grammar and pronunciation. The linguistic road to Americanization, in other words, was nearing an end.[37]

For the social historian, it is not so much the technical aspects of the linguistic process that invite attention as the procession of words with its attendant transition in outlook. The immigrant vocabulary, he learns from the linguist, was "being constantly atrophied" at the Norwegian end and "renewed" at the American end, and as one views the process — old words going out, new words coming in — it is like a moving picture of the interior of the immigrant mind. His old language, perfectly shaped to fit the economy and culture of an ancient Norwegian *bygd,* is being reshaped to fit a new world; and the process reflects a re-orientation of the mind

from phonograph recordings. Mr. Haugen has set forth the general problem of the study of Norwegian-American, with full bibliographical references, in his *Om en samlet fremstilling av norsk-amerikansk sprogutvikling,* issued in 1939 by the Norwegian Academy of Science in Oslo; and he has dealt with a special aspect of the problem in his "Phonological Shifting in American Norwegian," in *Language* (Philadelphia), 14:112–120 (April, 1938).

[37] Haugen, *Norsk i Amerika,* 47, 48.

itself. Professor Haugen offers, for example, a linguistic interpretation of the adjustment of the immigrant mind to the American harvest. Of thirty-two key words brought to America out of the old environment, only seventeen proved useful here, and two of these were charged with meanings quite different from their old. Some of the American words that were slipped into place in the Norwegian's changing vocabulary were *kridl* (cradle), *ryper* (reaper), *harvistar* (harvester), *katta* (cut), *sjakkar* (shocks), and *treskjarkru* (threshing crew). The language changes suggest that approximately fifty per cent of American agriculture was new to the immigrant.[38]

If one glances at the Norwegian-American word lists, one finds a variety of terms having to do with American farming in all its aspects. Consider, for example, such items as *farmar* (farmer), *höi-ræk* (hayrack), *hyppel-tré* (whippletree), *fæning-mölle* (fanning mill), *drægge* (drag), *fid* (feed), *grönri* (granary), *grubbe* (grub), *söpperéter* (separator), *stæbel* (stable), *sjante* (shanty), *nekk-jogg* (neckyoke), *pitsfork* (pitchfork), *kjors* (chores), *hitsche* (hitch), *haske* (husk), *paster* (pasture), *haa* (hoe), *fens* (fence), *busel* (bushel), *bins* (beans), *barlé* (barley), and *kjæns-bogg* (chinch bug).[39] It was natural that farming, with its new methods and problems, should have made large contributions to the immigrant vocabulary, but one finds various other large fields, too, in which new words and ideas crowded upon the immigrant mind. Professor Flom calls attention, among other things, to the necessity of taking over into Norwegian-American new terms for money, measures, and weights in order to accommodate such items as *yard, gallon, acre, section, quarter, dollar,* and *peck;* of making room for new official and administrative names, such as *governor, Congress, township, poll*

[38] *Studies and Records,* 10: 30–34.
[39] These words are selected from Flaten's vocabulary in *Dialect Notes,* 2: 120–126.

tax, courthouse, nominate, county, register of deeds, assessor, school superintendent; of introducing new words having to do with business and land, such as *hardware store, retail store,* and many other kinds of stores, *saloon, saloonkeeper, værhus* (warehouse), *clerk, settlement,* and *claim;* and of giving place to new words for foods and drinks of various kinds, such as *ais krim* (ice cream), *bifsteak* (beefsteak), *pie, biscuit, bacon, ham, cider,* and *whisky.* Dr. Flom has gathered many words that are not easy to classify, but are nevertheless of interest from the point of view of American transition, such as *barrgin* (bargain), *banfair* (bonfire), *laibræri* (library), *sörpraisparti* (surprise party), *sörkis* (circus), *risk, humbug,* and *svindla* (swindle); and he has also taken note of various phraseological loans, such as to *find out,* to *give up,* to be *interested in,* and to *draw out one's money,* which the Norwegian American frequently translated into Norwegian, giving to his speech, in addition to its actual loan words, a flavor of American idiom.[40] Professor Haugen has taken a sharp interest in the classification of loan words, and he mentions, among others, such fields as games and play, sickness, geography (with *creek* and *river* taken into Norwegian-American because the American creek and river were quite different from streams and rivers in Norway), transportation, tools and implements, and certain phases of household economy. In all these fields he finds extensive borrowing, but it is significant that the linguists have also found certain realms little touched by the invasion of American terms. This is notably true of the realms of abstract ideas, church and religion, and intimate home life.[41] Even these, in the long sweep of time, were destined to be profoundly influenced by the change from the Old World to the New, but the process was slower and more subtle than the

[40] Flom, in *Nordmands-forbundet,* 5: 247–250. Compare his list of loan words, in *American Speech,* 1: 545–558.

[41] Haugen, in *Studies and Records,* 10: 22–30.

shift in outward circumstance; and by the time it began to show itself in obvious ways, the heyday of the Norwegian-American speech had passed.

While the Norwegian Americans were thus bridging the distance between their native tongue and the speech of the American West, they were also coping with the problem of American place names. Munch Ræder, as early as 1847, took note of the Norwegian flavor that these names acquired on the lips of the immigrants. The Wisconsin Ashippun settlement, for example, was called *Espen;* the Indian name Koshkonong was given a genial Norwegian adoption by its transformation to *Koskeland;* and Oconomowoc became *Kolmiwok.*[42] The immigrants spoke easily of such places as *Aiovai* (Iowa), *Viskonsn* (Wisconsin), *Sy Dakota* (South Dakota), *Kalleforni* (California), and *Minniaplis* (Minneapolis).[43]

As for family names, there was confusion, rooted, on the one side, in the problem of accepting as a surname the old *gaard,* or farm, name from Norway, or a " son " name derived from the first name of the father. On the other side was the problem of American pronunciation and deciphering of complicated Norwegian *gaard* names. Professor Haugen illustrates the confusion by citing the case of a settler named Johannes Opstedal, one of whose sons called himself Johnson, a second Dal, a third Opdal, and a fourth Opstedal.[44] Such names as Hansen, Olsen, Petersen, Johnson, and Anderson, derived from the first name of the father, were of course easy for Americans to pronounce and to spell, and because they offered so little difficulty they became widespread. There was a tendency to adopt one name as a surname to be passed on from generation to generation, so that Peter, the son of Hans Johnson, was definitely Peter Johnson, not

[42] Ræder, *America in the Forties,* 35. The usual form was " Kaskeland," not " Koskeland." Some of the pioneers said " Kaskenang."

[43] Flom, in *American Speech,* 1:558.

[44] Haugen, *Norsk i Amerika,* 74.

Peter Hansen. As time went on, however, the old *gaard* names from Norway, which had come down through long ages, tended more and more to be adopted and preserved, though in some instances they lost their identity through Americanization, Braaten turning into Barton, Vetleson into Wilson, and Prestgard into Prescott.[45] Sometimes they were translated literally into English, Tordendal becoming Thundervalley and Bakke, Hill; and sometimes, as Professor Flom points out, the clerk in a land office would casually change a Norwegian name, Knutson to Newton, for example.[46] In many rural communities the custom of attaching some distinguishing mark to a first name, derived either from work or location, was not uncommon, and one hears of Ola by the Spring, Ola in the Cellar, Knut in the Grove, Aslak the Digger, Nils by the River, John on the Bottom, and Hans by the Lake.[47] Martha and Lars Larsen of sloop fame gave their children such names as Martha Allen, Lydia Glazier, George Marion, Clara Elizabeth, and Georgiana Henrietta. This was not typical, though there was a tendency among the pioneers, as time went on, to use names of a less pronounced Norwegian character than those of the earlier pioneer children; and this tendency may have been forwarded by the Americanizing of many of the traditional first names — Synnøve to Susie, Gunnhild to Julia, Tjøstøl to Chester, and Birgit to Betsy.[48]

"The various farms," wrote Munch Ræder in the 1840's, "do not, as a rule, have special names, except occasionally to indicate the owner's old home in Norway, and such a name applies not so much to the farm as to its owner so that it is not retained in case he sells his farm." Probably Ræder

[45] Haugen, *Norsk i Amerika,* 76. His chapter on "Navneskikk i nybygden" is a contribution of unusual interest and value.

[46] Flom, *Norwegian Immigration,* 352. See also his interesting study of "Norwegian Surnames with Special Reference to Orthography and Foreign Influence," in *Scandinavian Studies and Notes* (Urbana, Illinois), 5:139–154 (1920).

[47] O. Jorgens, "Emigranter," in *Samband,* no. 37, p. 212 (May, 1911).

[48] See Haugen, *Norsk i Amerika,* 70, 71.

was too early a visitor to give a correct general picture of the tendency with respect to farm names. It appears that the Norwegian customs were rather widely copied by the immigrants, and there are even instances of later owners of farms taking over the family names of the earlier owners — an indication that the names had been attached to the farms. Naturally, the rapidity of change in American farm ownership broke down such customs. Munch Ræder relished the old Norwegian family names that "are met everywhere as one travels through the settlements," and, he added, they "contribute not a little toward leading one's fancy back to the valleys up among the mountains at home, five thousand miles away, in spite of the considerable differences in landscape between Wisconsin and Telemarken."[49] A modern historian of Norway, glancing at the story of Norwegian emigration to America, asserts that with scarcely more than a single exception the Norwegian immigrants did not leave a record of place names on the American map. He believes that they merely took over Indian names or accepted geographic names chosen by Americans.[50] In many areas to which the Norwegians came, the basic nomenclature, it is true, had already been established before their arrival; but where they pioneered considerable areas of land, they left characteristic marks on the map. How seriously the Norwegian historian erred may be understood by looking at the map of Minnesota, which reveals no fewer than two hundred Norwegian geographic names. They apply for the most part, as one would expect from the fact that the immigrant pioneering was largely agricultural, to townships, villages, and lakes — particularly to townships in the western counties of the state.

These place names are of several different classes. Not a

[49] Ræder, *America in the Forties*, 35.
[50] Wilhelm Keilhau, *Det norske folks liv og historie gjennem tidene*, 10:366 (Oslo, 1935).

few of them recall towns and districts in Norway. Some of these are Oslo, Bergen, Drammen, Stavanger, Christiania, Trondhjem, Numedal, Helgeland, Aurdal, Hitterdal, New Solum, Nerstrand, Fossum, Arendal, Hovland, Bygland, Soler, Dovre, Sandnes, Winger, Wang, Nordland, Sundahl, and Foldahl. Another class is that of family names, usually derived from early or prominent pioneers, and these have been estimated to constitute sixty-five per cent of all the Norwegian place names in Minnesota. In not a few instances they are also identical with the names of towns or valleys in Norway, but research has disclosed that they are derived for the Minnesota map from family names. Their genuine Norwegian tang is fully caught in a list prepared by Mr. Roy W. Swanson in his study of "Scandinavian Place-names in the American Danelaw."[51] For here are Haugen, Arnesen, Barsness, Breda, Torgerson, Sorlien, Jerne, Myhre, Tansem, Ulen, Storden, Lien, Inger, Arveson, Teien, Ness, Aastad, Brandsvold, Grimstad, Hereim, Neresen, Glesne, Bredeson, Kjorstad, Harstad, Frovold, Fedje, Hegg, Thorstad, Fossen, Granrud, and many others. Sometimes a personal name is given an American ending, for example, Dalton, named for the pioneer Ole C. Dahl;[52] occasionally a name is curiously changed, for example, Tynsid, derived from Tønset; and now and then one encounters a woman's name, like Gudrid. The map also discloses a "poetic-patriotic" group of names which includes Tordenskjold, Wergeland, Eidsvold, St. Olaf, Nidaros, Normanna, Nora, Walhalla, Vineland, and Viking. Sverdrup Township in Otter Tail County may re-

[51] This excellent article appears in the *Swedish-American Historical Bulletin*, 2:5–17 (August, 1929). In commenting on the Minnesota names I have also used Warren Upham's *Minnesota Geographic Names: Their Origin and Historic Significance* (*Minnesota Historical Collections*, vol. 17 — St. Paul, 1917). Haugen deals with the subject in *Norsk i Amerika*, 67, 68.

[52] A Wisconsin pioneer named Iver Kleven had a farm along a newly built branch line of a railroad. He lost no time in starting a lumberyard, and the road established a station. It was at first called Pine Bluffs, but the name was soon changed to Klevenville in honor of the farmer. See "Optegnelser af Iver Kleven, Klevenville, Wis., om hans liv og virke," in *Samband*, no. 37, p. 205 (May, 1911).

call to some either the Norwegian statesman-professor of 1814 or the famous liberal parliamentarian of the nineteenth century, but it is in fact named in honor of the Norwegian-American Georg Sverdrup, the president of Augsburg Seminary in Minneapolis. A fortunately small class of place names includes those fabricated by settlers, occasionally in combination with other Scandinavians — the most melancholy example is Swenoda, a compound from "Swedes," "Norwegians," and "Danes." And there are some Norwegian names that appear to have been given by Yankees, rather than by Norwegians, such as Norway Grove and Norwegian Lake. Wisconsin, North Dakota, and other states reveal a certain amount of Norwegian village and township nomenclature which is rooted in immigrant settlement. But it is probably true, as Professor Haugen suggests, that the freest play of Norwegian-American interest in nomenclature has been exhibited in the naming of their more than seven thousand churches or congregations.[53] There the classification is on the whole similar to that for Minnesota place names, the principal difference being the appearance of vast numbers of names drawn from the Bible and the history of the church, and the inclusion of church heroes, like Landstad, Hauge, and Pontoppidan, among the personal names. Many of the churches derived their names from the particular towns or communities where they were located; some were named for Norwegian places or on the poetic-patriotic principle.

Meanwhile, the Norwegian-American speech flourished in the compact Norwegian settlements throughout the Northwest. The first pioneering generation gave way to the second — the more generally bilingual — generation. The second grew up to a triple accompaniment of language. First, there were the *bygd* dialects turned into Norwegian-American and even more rapid strides than before toward English.

[53] Haugen, *Norsk i Amerika,* 65–67.

Next, there was English itself, learned in the common school, in association with neighbors, and under the impact of American institutions. Finally, there was the more formal Norwegian of the pulpit and press, of books and pamphlets, of parochial schools, academies, and colleges. And on all sides Norwegian-American social and institutional life expressed itself in a variety of ways. With the additional factor of large waves of new immigrants pouring into the West in the decades following the Civil War, it is not surprising that bilingualism lasted with stubborn tenacity, even to the third generation. A scholar of language believes that today Norwegian is understood by more than a million people in the United States; and the figure may be compared with those of the federal census for 1930, which reported 347,852 persons in the American population who were born in Norway, 476,663 of Norwegian parentage, and 275,583 of part-Norwegian parentage — a total of 1,100,098.[54]

The story of language and transition sweeps over a long period — from the days of Ole Rynning and the early pioneers down to the changed world of today. It discloses not only the intimacy of language with the fundamentals of immigrant social and economic life, but also something of the spirit of immigrant transition — a thing that often eludes the student who confines his attention to the more formal documents of history. The linguistic halfway house has served its essential purposes; the pioneer Norwegian-American speech is now primarily a matter of historical interest. But that interest has an unusual vitality, for it runs athwart a basic problem of American life which has engaged the con-

[54] See *Norsk i Amerika*, 58, 59. H. L. Mencken gives some attention to Norwegian as spoken in the United States in his *American Language*, 627–631 (New York, 1938). "A Study of Norwegian Dialect in Minnesota," by Anne Simley, in *American Speech*, 5:469–474 (August, 1930), tells of an examination of the speech of 115 students of college age in a western Minnesota school, about half of them representing the third or fourth generation, only twenty-three having both parents born in Norway. Of the 115, only eleven had no discernible Norwegian accent or coloring in their English speech. Of the eleven, six reported that they had learned Norwegian before English.

cern of many thinkers and writers. It is the problem of immigrant success or failure in the attempt to achieve a "unified cultural personality." It appears that what, upon superficial retrospect, has the character of linguistic confusion was in reality a struggle of large numbers of people toward some kind of intellectual, or cultural, unity; in this struggle Norwegian-American played a mediating role. The struggle is an unconscious attempt of Rølvaag's "hidden America" to break through the linguistic crust to the surface. It is only as such attempts are recorded, as linguists, historians, and novelists interpret the immigrant saga, and as popular understanding of American life deepens, that the hidden and surface forces of American culture can be expected to meet and to coalesce.

IV. THE RELIGIOUS IMPULSE AND THE AMERICAN CHURCHES

THE NORWEGIAN IMMIGRANTS who came to America in the earlier years of the migration movement carried with them a deep religious impulse, whether their basic motives for emigration were economic or social and religious or both. Many were followers of Hans Nielsen Hauge, the great Norwegian pietistic leader who became the apostle of a "living faith." These followers were familiar with the struggles of Hauge, his travels up and down the country, and his persecution by the state under an eighteenth-century law against conventicles, which had been lifeless for decades. They shared his spirit of pietism. They thought of themselves as "awakened." They had a stubborn belief in the rightness of lay preaching. And they felt the glow of the religious revival that had moved the common folk of Norway under Hauge's leadership.

The Haugeans set up no independent church organization of their own. They were not separatists. But they were instinctively critical of high-church and aristocratic tendencies. They came out of a Norway that was seething with interest in religion and in which the spirit engendered by Hauge was broadening from a matter purely of Godly zeal to a broad-gauged struggle of the common people against the aristocracy. The fight for the repeal of the Conventicle Act was but one phase of a fight of the *bønder* against the official classes, and in this struggle the laity tended to be on one side, the state-church clergy on the other. There was little separatism in Norway, but it was not a coincidence that the Quakers, who were persecuted because of their way of worshiping God, figured prominently in the early migration to America.

The Haugean conventicle was superimposed upon the formal establishment of the state church. It was an informal gathering, devoted to evangelism and edification,[1] leaving to the state such matters as churches, pastors, salaries, and the symbols of organized religion. The props of the conventicle were not external, but rather the earnest piety of the "awakened" in conjunction with the basic faith of Christianity as they interpreted it under the orthodox Lutheran doctrine.[2] When the Haugeans went to America, it was these things that they took with them. The state church did not go with them. In fact, no clergyman of the state church went with them until nearly two decades after the emigration was launched by the "Restoration" and its band of sloop folk.

The formal organization of the Norwegian Lutheran church in America might have taken place several years earlier than it did. In 1839—fourteen years after the voyage of the "Restoration"—a party of emigrants leaving Drammen made a valiant attempt to take with them a spirit-

[1] Clarence J. Carlsen, "Elling Eielsen, Pioneer Lay Preacher and First Norwegian Lutheran Pastor in America," 72–74. This master's thesis, prepared at the University of Minnesota in 1932, is a work of careful scholarship. The Minnesota Historical Society has a copy.

[2] Laurence M. Larson, in *The Changing West and Other Essays*, 154, 155 (Northfield, Minnesota, 1937), gives a good analysis of the Haugean tradition.

ual leader who had been trained in theology at the national university, but their efforts were unavailing. They wanted assurance that their children would be brought up in their own faith. More than a week before they sailed on the "Emilie," they petitioned the Norwegian church department to authorize the ordination of one Peter Valeur for ministerial service with them in the New World. This was a "call"— but the church department was disturbed because it did not originate in an organized congregation, and the department properly concluded that it could undertake no control over a minister in America. After much cogitation, it did indeed grant the petition, but not until December—and the "Emilie" had sailed in June. Before departing, the emigrants had listened to a farewell sermon by Valeur. Crossing the Atlantic, these pious people closed each day with prayer and religious songs under the direction of lay leaders.[3]

In America the early immigrants were obliged to depend upon lay leadership in religious matters. It was not just that most of them believed in lay preaching, but that no ordained ministers of their own Norwegian Lutheran church were among them. In 1838 Ole Rynning said that they "do not as yet have ministers and churches. Every man who is somewhat earnest in his belief holds devotional exercises in his own home, or else together with his neighbors."[4] It is an evidence of the vitality of the religious impulse among the immigrants that, notwithstanding the absence of ministers and churches, they were active in religious worship. In the western settlements a phalanx of some seventeen lay preachers, nearly all of them Haugean in their views, kept the religious fires burning. The very informality of the

[3] The records relating to this attempt to induce a Norwegian clergyman to go to America four years before the arrival of Clausen and five years before Dietrichson are in Riksarkiv, Oslo: Kirkedept., Referatprotokoller, 1839, no. 64, res. 244. Blegen, *Norwegian Migration,* 120, 121; and Gunnar J. Malmin, "Litt norsk-amerikansk kirkehistorie fra de norske arkiver," in *Lutheraneren* (Minneapolis), 8:75 (January 16, 1924).

[4] *True Account of America,* 86, 87.

religious scene, however, invited what some historians have characterized as "confusion," but which, from another viewpoint, was a move toward the clarification of belief. The immigrants of the Fox River area in Illinois have been described as "unstable Haugeans" and followers of will-o'-the-wisps, and they have been compared unfavorably with the Norwegians of the Wisconsin settlements.[5] It is probable that the difference was not very substantial, however. In all parts of the frontier, Norwegian immigrants were influenced to a greater or less degree by the powerful, friendly, and aggressively zealous American churches. If there was a difference, it may be remembered that the Illinois settlements date from the middle 1830's and that there was a smaller gap of time between the founding of the Wisconsin settlements and the appearance of clerical Lutheran leadership than was the case in Illinois. Moreover, while the religious life centered about lay leadership and home devotions, the Illinois settlements were the scene of the pioneer impact of American churches and American religious tendencies upon the immigrants. In the absence of an organized Norwegian Lutheran church, and amid the hardships and loneliness of frontier life, together with the initial stimulation of American religious liberty, the wonder is that there was so relatively little affiliation with the American churches. Most of it, as a matter of historical fact, developed, not in the very earliest period of western pioneering, but after Lutheran church organization was under way among the immigrants.

"Every one can believe as he wishes, and worship God in the manner which he believes to be right," wrote Rynning from Illinois, "but he must not persecute any one for hold-

[5] See J. Magnus Rohne, *Norwegian American Lutheranism up to 1872*, 34–42 (New York, 1926). Dr. Rohne advances the view that the Numedal, Vossing, and Telemark group in Wisconsin were a "decided advance over the Fox River type," which had a Stavanger background. The former, he believes, had "a profound respect for the clergy and their work" (p. 42).

ing another faith. The government takes it for granted that a compulsory belief is no belief at all, and it will be best shown who has religion or who has not if there is complete religious liberty."[6] Sometimes a note of bitterness entered the writings of the immigrants. Thus an immigrant of 1843 declared that the Americans were active in the worship of God and that anyone who feared and loved God could do so just as well in America as in Norway where he was "surrounded by covetous ministers who often gave more annoyance than edification to the common people."[7] The kindly and philosophical Ole Nattestad wrote, "As far as religious sects are concerned, there are many kinds, and I have as yet little knowledge of their teachings; but as far as I can understand them, they almost all believe in one true God."[8]

Elling Eielsen, a Lutheran lay preacher who towered above all the other pioneer lay leaders in force and ability, was to appear on the midwestern scene in 1839 and to work with unexampled energy to preserve the immigrant allegiance to Lutheranism. In 1843–44, with the ordination of Eielsen and the coming of Clausen and Dietrichson, the era of ordained Lutheran preachers and of formal organization of Norwegian-American Lutheranism was to begin. Both before and after the beginning of that era, however, the immigrants were constantly coming into contact with American religious ideas and institutions. On the American side, the general period was one of fervor and missionary zeal. The American churches were reaching out to the frontier with contagious enthusiasm and organized power.[9] In viewing the contacts of the Norwegians with the American churches,

[6] *True Account of America*, 86.

[7] Ellev B. Tungen to relatives, January 6, 1843, in *Christianssandsposten*, May 15, 1843. Tungen wrote from a settlement in Wisconsin.

[8] Ole Knudsen Nattestad, *Beskrivelse over en reise til Nordamerica i 1837*, 28.

[9] Colin B. Goodykoontz, *Home Missions on the American Frontier* (Caldwell, Idaho, 1939), and Gunnar Westin, *Protestantismens historia i Amerikas Förenta Stater* (Stockholm, 1931). The latter, the best treatment of its subject, has a searching analysis of "Den sociala orons tid (1830–1865)."

therefore, one expects to find an interesting chapter in immigrant transition. It is a chapter that involves, among others, the Quakers, the Baptists, the Mormons, the Methodists, and the Episcopalians.

Immigration served as a bridge between Norwegian and American Quakerism. The importance of the Quaker factor in the Norwegian-American saga hinges, however, not upon large numbers or upon any great growth of Norwegian Quakerism in the United States — for only a small minority of the immigrants have affiliated with the American Friends. It is derived rather from the priority and quality of Quaker leadership in the early migration and, not least, from the quiet sincerity and friendliness that characterized the adherents of the Quaker faith. The initiation of modern Norwegian migration to America was bound up with the story of the Norwegian Friends in Stavanger; and Quaker influences were many and significant in the development of the emigration movement from 1825 to the middle 1830's.[10]

The leader of the sloop folk, Lars Larsen, with his wife and family, quickly joined the Rochester Monthly Meeting of Friends after reaching western New York in 1825. His action emphasizes the international scope of Quakerism: the Stavanger Quakers, whose society he had helped to found, received their initial impulse from Friends in England; now, in 1825, Larsen, armed with a certificate from the Stavanger Friends, aligned himself with the American Quakers, who on their part had lent ready aid to the pioneer Norwegian immigrants and given them a friendly welcome to the New World.[11]

Larsen's home in Rochester became not only a center for Quaker influence but also a major station, a temporary sanctuary, for Norwegian immigrants on their way to the West.

[10] Blegen, *Norwegian Migration,* ch. 2.

[11] John Cox, Jr., "Norwegian Quakers in Western New York," in *Friends' Intelligencer* (Philadelphia), 82:848 (November 24, 1925); Henry J. Cadbury, "De første norske Kvækere i Amerika," in *Decorah-posten,* November 20, 1925.

In relation to both, Larsen's wife, Martha, shares with the leader of the sloop folk a place of honor and historical importance. "Twelve Norwegians came here today," she wrote on one occasion in 1837, "and are now sitting at the table eating their supper. About two weeks ago there arrived from ninety to a hundred people. They stayed at our house and my brother's house about a week, and we furnished meals for nearly all of them." Martha Larsen thus did a work of mercy and kindness, but she did much more than supply the newly arrived immigrants with shelter and food. "I have gone around town looking for work for them," she wrote, "and Lars has taken many of them out into the country." She had a deep concern about religion, as is apparent in a comment that she made about her husband: "He is greatly interested in church work, is diligent in his work, and we live together with great happiness, for God has blessed us with both temporal and spiritual gifts."[12] After attending a Quaker Yearly Meeting in Philadelphia, Martha Larsen wrote to Elias Tastad, the staunch leader of the Friends in Stavanger, "O my dear Friend Elias, thou cannot have any idea what a good meting the yearly metings are. It has felt to me as a kingdom on the earth, and if I may express myself, the friends has piered to me like angels for thier love and chareity are very great towards each others."[13] No immigrant better exemplified the religious impulse than this pioneer Martha.

That Quaker historians have been able to trace American Quaker affiliations for several early Norwegian immigrants should occasion no surprise, for from 1818 to 1873, of the 230 members of the Stavanger Quaker group, 72 emigrated to America; and not a few Quakers from other Norwegian com-

[12] Martha Larsen to Elias Tastad, October 11, 1837, in Tastad Papers, in the archives of the Society of Friends, Stavanger, Norway, translated in "Letters from the Sloop-folk," in *American-Scandinavian Review* (New York), 13:361, 362 (June, 1925).

[13] *American-Scandinavian Review*, 13:363, 364.

munities joined the westward migration.[14] The natural thing for them to do in the earlier years was to seek membership in an American society. Ole Johnson, a member of the sloop party of 1825, affiliated with the Quakers at Farmington, New York, in 1826, and transferred to the Rochester meeting, where the Larsens were members, two years later. In 1828 he married the widow of one of the leading Stavanger Quakers and took her and her son, Peter Olson Frank, to Rochester. Other sloopers who established American Quaker affiliations were Halvor Iverson and Knud Anderson Slogvig, the latter prominent in Norwegian-American history as an immigrant leader in 1836. Of Daniel Rossadal and his wife, sloopers who pioneered in the Fox River settlement, Rasmus B. Anderson remarks that they were "zealous Quakers and remained faithful to the creed of their adoption to the end." Metha Trulsdatter, one of the Stavanger Quaker founders, lived at Farmington, New York, and was interested in, if not a member of, an American Quaker group. Ingebrigt Larson Narvig, an immigrant of 1831 who pioneered in Michigan, was himself a Quaker and his wife was of the western New York American Quakers. The Larsens on one occasion visited with a Philadelphia Quaker, Tormon Bournison, who undoubtedly was of Norwegian origin.[15]

These and other examples indicate that the Norwegian Quakers held fast to their Quakerism and placed themselves within the orbit of American Quakerism. In the West, however, there was some tendency toward setting up distinctively Norwegian-American Quaker societies. As early as 1842 a small group of Norwegian Quakers in the Iowa Sugar Creek settlement pushed northward from Lee to Henry County, and there, near Salem, "built a Norse meeting-house for their use." These Quakers of the West never lost

[14] Blegen, *Norwegian Migration*, 47 and note.

[15] Cox, in *Friends' Intelligencer*, 82: 848, 849; Cadbury, in *Decorah-posten*, November 20, 1925.

touch with their friends in Norway.[16] Erich Knudsen, for example, writing to A. Kloster of Stavanger in 1865 from Salem, gave advice, among other things, on emigration. "Thou art aware," he wrote, "that this is a better country and has some advantages over that but notwithstanding the human family have their trials in various ways here as well as other places." He speaks of the Civil War, "the dreadful and horrible war," as virtually over, and says that several Friends departed from their principles to the point of paying for substitutes. He himself would neither accept noncombatant service nor pay for a substitute to serve in his place. "For my part I would suffer the consequence rather than do either." [17]

Ultimately Marshall County, Iowa, blossomed out as the "largest center of Norwegian Quakerism in the United States." [18] The leaders of this development were Quakers from Stavanger, including Søren Olsen, an emigrant of 1854 who found congenial Quaker friends in the West and ten years later helped to establish a Norwegian Quaker meeting near LeGrand, at Stavanger, Iowa.[19] This meeting, or society, it is said, "became the asylum and received much of the strength of the parent meeting in the old country"—including Mathias Husebøe, one of the Stavanger leaders, and Tonnes Stangeland, a talented Quaker minister.[20] The Norwegian Quakers in Iowa were greatly strengthened when in 1869 a company of approximately fifty people from Roldal, Norway, thirty-six of them Friends, emigrated in a body

[16] Louis T. Jones, *The Quakers of Iowa,* 175 (Iowa City, 1914). This Quaker church preceded the historic Muskego church in Wisconsin by three years. The Muskego church is often described as "the first Norwegian church built in America."

[17] Erich Knudsen to A. Kloster, January 30, 1865, in Kloster Papers, archives of the Society of Friends.

[18] H. F. Swansen, "The Norwegian Quakers of Marshall County, Iowa," in *Studies and Records,* 10:127.

[19] Jones, *Quakers of Iowa,* 176, 177.

[20] John Frederick Hanson, *Light and Shade from the Land of the Midnight Sun,* 71–73 (Oskaloosa, Iowa, 1903).

and made their way to Iowa.[21] The American Stavanger Quaker group grew in numbers from a mere handful in pioneer days to 107 in 1874 and 222 in 1890, and it was strong enough to open a school, the Stavanger Boarding School, in the early 1890's.[22]

In the later, as in the earlier period, southwestern Norway was the dynamic center of Norwegian-American Quakerism. There seems to have been relatively little direct spread of Quaker ideas from Americans to Norwegian Americans. Curiously enough, however, the Norwegian Quakers of Iowa represent to a considerable extent American Quaker influences planted in Norway. An American Quaker leader, Lindley Murray Hoag of Iowa, had visited Norway in 1853 as one of a group of Quaker emissaries. While there he succeeded in arousing a deep interest in Quakerism among the people of Roldal. His influence led to the formation of a Quaker society and its affiliation with the Stavanger group; and ultimately these Roldal Quakers set out for Hoag's own state in the American West — a migration so inclusive that the Norwegian meetinghouse of these Friends was closed and sold.[23]

Norwegian-American Baptist beginnings are rooted in the socially fertile soil of the Fox River settlement. The story centers about the vigorous personality of Hans Valder, a layman of the Haugean school who had been a teacher in Norway before his emigration in 1837. He joined the Bap-

[21] Jones, *Quakers of Iowa,* 177, 321. A packet of "Epistler og breve" in the Kloster Papers, contains, among other items, a communication signed by Søren Olsen, April 8, 1869, from "Stavanger-Vennernes forberedende forsamling i Marshall County Iowa."

[22] Swansen, in *Studies and Records,* 10:131–134. Professor Swansen states that the Iowa "Stavanger Meeting was the only one in the United States which was Norwegian speaking."

[23] On Hoag's visit to Norway, see Hanson, *Light and Shade,* 129–142, 213; Jones, *Quakers of Iowa,* 177, 178; and John Marcussen, "A Remarkable Chapter in the History of the Friends," in *Friends' Intelligencer,* 64:548, 549, 563–565 (1907). Much information on the Norwegian Quakers in Iowa is to be found in the Kloster Papers, including letters from Søren Olsen, July 3, 1866, and March 3, 1869; from Thore Heggem, July 17, 1860, and March 17, 1869; and from Mathias M. Husebøe, March 21, 1868.

tist church in 1842, together with a handful of other Norwegian immigrants, and made his own home a place of assembly for those of Baptist leanings. In 1844 he became himself a Baptist minister — the first among his countrymen — commissioned to "work among the Norwegians in La Salle and surrounding counties" of Illinois. Four years later a Norwegian Baptist church was organized at Indian Creek, in the Fox River community, under his leadership; and its members petitioned for financial help from the American Baptist Home Missionary Society. Of unusual interest is a letter written by Valder in March, 1848, on behalf of this pioneer group of Norwegian Baptists.[24] His purpose was to explain the "destitute condition, and want of religious improvement" among his countrymen. He tells of his own conversion in 1841 and his baptism the following year. He and his friends held weekly meetings at which sometimes he himself, and occasionally a friendly American elder, preached. "It was a little heaven to us," he wrote.

He dwells upon the obstacles that he faced after his ordination as a Baptist minister. He was looked upon by many as a heretic; a society was formed in opposition to his group; and he was denied a meetinghouse. All this Valder summed up tersely: "I have had many trials and difficulties." Sixteen persons supported his application for aid from the missionary society, seven of them joining in a pledge amounting to the grand total of thirteen dollars for the year. Requesting a grant of fifty dollars, Valder said, "The gospel we will and must have preached to us." His zeal was unmistakable: "We are in great want, and we feel our unworthiness. We have no claims upon you or any other; but the commission is, 'Preach the Gospel to every creature,' and so 20,000 Norwegians must not be neglected in a Christian land." His

[24] The text of this letter, which is dated March 7, 1848, is printed under the title "The First Norwegian Baptist Minister and Church in the United States," in the *Baptist Home Mission Monthly* (New York), 5:131 (June, 1883).

friends explained that Valder was called upon to preach at three stations — Little Indian, East Side of Big Indian, and Crookleg Settlement.

The society granted the requested aid, and in the spring of 1848 Valder took up his appointment as a missionary. No considerable growth took place, but a year later he reported, "Our little church has increased since the 1st April from seven to nineteen, seven of the number by baptism and five by experience. We ask all to pray for the Norwegians in Illinois." Those converted, he explained, were people "who, for many years, were members of the Lutheran Church, unexperienced in a *change of heart,* and enemies to God and his truth."[25] That year Valder reported to the Ottawa Baptist Association that his church people were "poor in this world's goods, yet rejoice that the Lord has been present with them."[26] A few years later, in 1853, Valder joined the northward migration and founded the community of Newburg in Fillmore County, Minnesota.[27] His departure left the small Baptist group in Illinois without effective leadership. A report in 1861 stated that it numbered twenty-two members, but summed up the state of the church in these words: "Norwegian. — Are much discouraged, owing to being scattered, to spiritual declension, and limited means of grace. Have a flourishing Sabbath School and a small library."[28] Valder, meanwhile, seems to have migrated not only away from Illinois but also away from the Baptist faith. In Minnesota, where he won success as a farmer, innkeeper, and local politician, he was inactive in

[25] American Baptist Home Missionary Society, *Seventeenth Report,* 53 (New York, 1849). The report is dated March 14, 1849.

[26] Ottawa Baptist Association, *First Anniversary,* 5, 8 (Princeton, Illinois, 1849). In 1851 the Norwegian church had eighteen members. Its condition was thus reported: "Have no minister; are few and feeble." Ottawa Baptist Association, *Minutes,* 1851, p. 12 (Ottawa, Illinois, 1851). Copies of these rare pamphlets are in the library of the University of Chicago Divinity School.

[27] Holand, *De norske settlementers historie,* 362, 363.

[28] Ottawa Baptist Association, *Minutes,* 1861, p. 14 (Elgin, Illinois, 1861).

religious matters until, many years later, he joined the Methodist church.

The humble beginnings in which Valder had a part in Illinois were succeeded in the following decade by a considerable Norwegian-American Baptist development, the Norwegians co-operating with the Danes, who were active in Wisconsin and elsewhere from the 1850's on. The organization of the Danish Baptist Church of Raymond Township, Wisconsin, in 1856 has been termed the "birthday of permanent Danish Baptist missions in America." To this community came in 1858 a gifted Danish organizer and preacher, Lars Jorgensen (Hauge), who played a prominent role in spreading the Baptist faith among his own countrymen.[29] The Dano-Norwegian co-operation continued throughout a long period — in fact, into the twentieth century, for it was not until 1910 that the Norwegian Baptist Conference in America was formed.[30]

One of the channels for the religious impulse among the Norwegian settlers in the West was Mormonism.[31] Not only were Norwegian pioneers in the Illinois and Iowa colonies won over to the faith of the Latter-day Saints, but their affiliations were bound up with an intensive missionary program that carried Mormonism to the Scandinavian countries after 1850 and resulted in a considerable migration to the New Jerusalem of the West. It has been suggested that one reason for the remarkable attraction of Mormonism for the Swedes was the fact that many of them were powerfully drawn by things foreign. Distance, it is said, invested insti-

[29] *Seventy-five Years of Danish Baptist Missionary Work in America,* 6–16 (Philadelphia, 1931). This work was published by the Danish Baptist General Conference of America. See also Jonas O. Backlund, *Swedish Baptists in America* (Chicago, 1933).

[30] Nels S. Lawdahl, *De danske baptisters historie i Amerika* (Morgan Park, Illinois, 1909); S. J. M. P. Fogdall's master's thesis, "The Dano-Norwegian Baptists in America," prepared at the University of Chicago in 1915; and P. Stiansen, *History of the Norwegian Baptists in America* (Wheaton, Illinois, 1939). Dr. Stiansen's book is published by the Norwegian Baptist Conference of America and the American Baptist Publication Society.

[31] Blegen, *Norwegian Migration,* 181, 249, 254, 333–335, 362.

tutions and practices with a special enchantment for them.[32] This explanation probably carries some weight so far as the Norwegians are concerned, too, but it was, in the first instance, propinquity, not distance, that made a bridge between the immigrants and the followers of Joseph Smith. The Illinois and Iowa settlers were in the vicinity of the Mormon capital, Nauvoo, in the period before the Mormon migration to Utah. Nearness was reinforced by skillful Mormon missionary work; and the Mormon doctrine, emphasizing adult baptism and promising a special sanctuary to true believers after the anticipated second coming of Christ, made a strong appeal to many pietistic pioneers torn loose from their old environment and facing frontier difficulties. When the proselytism ultimately was carried to the Scandinavian countries, the enchantment of distance was coupled with that of free land, the promise of ideal conditions, and passage money to cover the costs of translation to the new-world Zion.[33] These were powerful inducements, indeed. Economics buttressed religion; and it is not an unrelated circumstance that the Mormon appeal evoked its greatest response from the very poor.

The Mormon methods were described by the early Lutheran minister, J. W. C. Dietrichson, who witnessed a Mormon meeting held on the banks of the Fox River. One of the seventy Mormon disciples mounted an ox-drawn wagon and preached to a throng which included many Norwegian settlers. He devoted his chief attention to baptism, emphasizing its need, not once, but again and again, for sinners. A second speaker described the Mormon church as the true church of Jesus Christ—the only road to grace.

[32] This is one of several interesting explanations suggested by Dr. George M. Stephenson in his *Religious Aspects of Swedish Immigration: A Study of Immigrant Churches*, 93 ff. (Minneapolis, 1932). His ch. 6 is an excellent account of the Swedish Mormons.

[33] This appeal was expressed powerfully in a *Voice from the Land of Zion* (Copenhagen, 1878), a propaganda pamphlet used by the Scandinavian mission. Stephenson, *Religious Aspects*, 95, 96.

Psalms were sung and the throng moved nearer the water to observe the baptism of several Norwegian immigrants. Dietrichson, no friendly observer, called a meeting of his own and delivered a head-on attack upon Mormonism in the presence of Norwegian spokesmen for the Mormon cause.[34]

This event took place in the spring of 1845, and Dietrichson then estimated that eighty persons in the Norwegian Fox River colony had accepted Mormonism. In his book of travels, published at Stavanger the next year, he said that, in all, a hundred and fifty Norwegians in the western settlements had become Mormons.[35] The leadership of this group was recruited in part from Haugean lay preachers, notably Jørgen Pedersen, who had been a schoolteacher in the old country; Ole Heier, an active Haugean from Telemark, who rose to high Mormon rank, though he ultimately withdrew from his Mormon affiliations to become a Baptist; and Gudmund Haugaas from Stavanger, one of the famous sloop folk of 1825, who attained the dignity of a Mormon bishop. Knud Pedersen, a native of Hardanger, went to the Fox River settlement in 1837 as a boy of thirteen, was baptized a Mormon six years later, worked as a Mormon missionary among his countrymen in Illinois and Wisconsin, and migrated in 1849 to Utah, where he rose to distinction as Bishop Canute Peterson.[36] E. G. M. Hogan, an emigrant of 1837 from Telemark, settled first in Illinois, later in Lee County, Iowa, where he was baptized by Haugaas in the early 1840's, and went on to Utah in 1848.[37] Both Peterson

[34] Dietrichson's letter, written at Koshkonong on May 10, 1845, is in *Stavanger amtstidende og adresseavis,* July 21, 24, 1845.

[35] J. W. C. Dietrichson, *Reise blandt de norske emigranter i "de Forenede Nordamerikanske Fristater,"* 102. Dietrichson gives a full account of his impressions of Mormonism on p. 92–108. The edition cited is a reprint issued at Madison in 1896 by R. B. Anderson.

[36] Anderson, *First Chapter,* ch. 30.

[37] "Missionaerer udsendt fra Zion til Skandinavien," in *Morgenstjernen: Et historisk-biografisk maanedsskrift,* 2:11, 12 (January, 1883). The editor of this Salt Lake City periodical was Andrew Jensen. A file of the first three volumes is in the possession of the Minnesota Historical Society.

and Hogan were later selected by the Mormon church to serve as special emissaries to Norway.

Late in 1844 Haugaas and Peterson visited the Muskego and Koshkonong settlements in Wisconsin, baptized four settlers at Muskego, and went on to hold several meetings in the Koshkonong area, where the Lutheran pastor, Dietrichson, thought of them as fishing in disturbed waters. He noted that Haugaas had become a "High Priest of the Order of Melchisedek." Dietrichson treated the Mormon missionaries with careful personal courtesy, seeking to avoid any act that would make martyrs of them, but he attended one of their meetings and publicly controverted their doctrines. He found that they represented themselves as holding strictly to Christian teachings. They rejected infant baptism, and they predicted the imminent return of Christ, the coming destruction of the world, and a thousand-year rule by Christ in the New Jerusalem, surrounded by the Mormon faithful.[38]

Notwithstanding such missionary efforts, the Mormons made relatively little headway among the Norwegian immigrants in Wisconsin, Iowa, and Illinois. The chief significance of the movement probably lies in its direct impact upon Norway through missionaries sent to that country after the great Mormon trek to Utah. No large number of Norwegians crossed the plains in that trek, but some of the Norwegian Mormon leaders, notably Peterson and Hogan, did. The establishment of a Mormon mission in Copenhagen in 1850, under the leadership of Erastus Snow, one of the twelve Mormon apostles, was the signal for an intensive and carefully organized proselytism in the Scandinavian countries. By 1883 this effort had enlisted the services of

[38] Dietrichson tells of this visit in a letter of December 28, 1844, in *Stavanger amtstidende og adresseavis,* April 3, 1845. The letter pictures a "disturbed life." Dietrichson remarks, "Just as we are surrounded by Irish, Scotch, English, German, American, and other nationalities, so we also have the most varied religious groups about us, and we are the only Lutherans among Baptists, Anabaptists, Methodists, Catholics, Presbyterians, and Sabbatarians."

289 missionaries, resulted in the baptism of nearly forty thousand converts, and led to the dispatching of more than twenty thousand people, in fifty-seven emigrant groups, to the West.[39] Using Copenhagen as a center, missionaries were active in Denmark, Sweden, and Norway; the *Book of Mormon* was made available to Scandinavian readers; tracts were printed; and a bimonthly organ known as *Skandinaviens stjerne* ("The Scandinavian Star") was issued. Bishop Canute Peterson was sent to Norway in 1852 and Hogan joined him the following year. As these and other Mormon emissaries spread their doctrines in Norway, Norwegian authorities exhibited grave concern; and the question arose as to whether the Mormons were entitled to inclusion under the Toleration Act of 1845. The church department rejected the view of the theological faculty of the national university that the Mormons were Christians in the historical meaning of the word and were therefore entitled to toleration.[40] It proceeded to arrest and impose fines upon Mormons, thereby adding the fuel of persecution to the religious fire. When Peterson set out for America late in December, 1855, he escorted a company of 510 Scandinavians. He returned to the northern scene later and in 1873 led the largest single group of Scandinavian Mormons sent to the West up to that time — a company of 872.[41]

By the middle 1880's a compact settlement of Scandinav-

[39] The most informing account of the Scandinavian Mormon mission is "Erindringer fra missionen i Skandinavien," in *Morgenstjernen,* beginning with vol. 1, January, 1882, and continuing regularly through three years of that periodical. A summary for the period 1852–1883 is "Emigration fra Skandinavien," also in *Morgenstjernen,* 3:371, 372 (December 15, 1884).

[40] Eilert Sundt, "Om Mormonerne i Christiania," in *Morgenbladet,* March 6, 7, 1855; Blegen, *Norwegian Migration,* 333–335.

[41] These figures are from "Emigration fra Skandinavien," in *Morgenstjernen,* 3:371. A statistical survey of the Mormon work in Norway, issued at Salt Lake City in 1884 and covering the period 1850–83, records a total of 4,274 persons who were baptized by the Mormons in that period, and 1,584 who emigrated. From this list it appears that of Peterson's group of 872 emigrants in 1873, relatively few were Norwegians. The Norwegian Mormon emigration total for 1873 was only 63. "Statistisk oversigt over den skandinaviske mission fra aaret 1850 til 1883: Norge," in *Morgenstjernen,* 3:368 (December 1, 1884).

ians, totaling not far from twenty thousand, was to be found in the San Pete Valley of Utah, south of Great Salt Lake. The Norwegian contingent, however, was numerically much less significant than the Danish and Swedish. In 1870, for example, there were only 301 Norwegian-born people in the "Land of Zion." It has been estimated that in 1910, out of approximately 60,000 Scandinavian Mormons, 30,000 were Danes, 20,000 Swedes, and 10,000 Norwegians; and Dr. Qualey points out that in 1930 the Norwegian element in Utah totaled only 6,198, as compared with 24,895 Danes and 15,838 Swedes.[42] Such figures suggest that the Mormon propaganda in the Scandinavian countries had its greatest effectiveness nearest its base in Copenhagen; and it is significant that much of the Swedish Mormon proselytism was centered in near-by Skåne. By the early 1880's the great Scandinavian Mormon migration was looked upon by the Mormons as an epic story, and a monthly "historical-biographical" periodical was founded at Salt Lake City which, employing the Danish language, devoted its columns for three years chiefly to a full-length historical study entitled "Recollections from the Mission in Scandinavia."[43]

The Mormon Scandinavian mission probably would have been carried on even if the early Scandinavian immigrants in the West had not come into contact with the forces centering at Nauvoo, for the Mormons established an ambitious bureau of emigration and planned a general European campaign. The fact remains that Mormon lines of sequence and of influence can be drawn from the Fox River and Sugar Creek Norwegian settlements to the Old World by way of Utah. The propaganda in Norway, as well as in Denmark and Sweden, was naturally the more effective because it was

[42] Stephenson, *Religious Aspects,* 97, citing A. O. Assar, *Mormonernas Zion* (Stockholm, 1911). Carlton C. Qualey, *Norwegian Settlement in the United States* (Northfield, 1938), has an informing section on "Norwegian Mormons," 196–198.

[43] *Morgenstjernen,* beginning with vol. 1, no. 1, January, 1882.

voiced by native sons of those countries. Meanwhile, at Norway, Illinois, a Mormon church, served by leaders of Norwegian descent, has continued to function through the years and is an institutional link between the pioneer era, when Nauvoo was in its glory, and the present.[44]

The historian of Methodism among the Norwegian and Danish immigrants writes that in America these immigrants "breathed the air of freedom, not least in the realm of church and religion. Here, in determining which church organization they should unite with, they could rely upon themselves or their conscience or their spiritual need." He points out that in the old country the Lutheran church "had played the role of persecutor" and that many immigrants, breathing the New World air, felt a desire to affiliate with some Protestant church other than the Lutheran. "And," he asks, "in that event, bearing in mind their spiritual nature and instinct, which church stood closer to them than the Methodist Episcopal Church, with its zeal, its practical interpretation of the gospels, and its popular form and manner?"[45]

Zeal and organization went together, and both in the East and in the West the two were brought to bear upon the problem of winning the immigrants to the Methodist faith. There were two centers, in particular, from which the Methodist influence was exerted upon the Scandinavians. One was the Scandinavian Seamen's Mission and the other the Methodist Home Missionary Society, both in New York City, but both having wide ramifications. The Seamen's Mission had been opened as early as 1845 by Olof G. Hedström, a Swedish immigrant, whose church was the Bethel

[44] O. M. Norlie, *History of the Norwegian People in America*, 211 (Minneapolis, 1925). Dr. Norlie states that Senator Reed Smoot was descended, on his mother's side, from the pioneer Norwegian Mormons, and that Dr. John A. Widtsoe, one of the council of twelve apostles and at one time president of the University of Utah, was born in Norway.

[45] A. Haagensen, *Den norsk-danske methodismes historie — paa begge sider havet*, 8 (Chicago, 1894).

ship "John Wesley," which served as a center of Christian influence among the throngs of Scandinavian sailors in New York. Hedström was also deeply interested in the unending stream of immigrants arriving at the eastern seaport and used every opportunity to meet them and to give them aid and spiritual comfort. His brother Jonas was an emissary of the Home Missionary Society in carrying Methodism to the Swedes in Illinois in the late 1840's.[46] It was a Danish missionary, however, who pioneered the Methodist cause among the western Norwegian settlers. Christian B. Willerup, also an emissary of the Methodist Home Missionary Society, appeared in Dane County, Wisconsin, in 1850. He had come to America as a boy of sixteen and had lived for many years in Georgia. Soon after beginning his work among the Norwegians he wrote that he had never before preached in his native language, had scarcely used it at all for twenty years, and found that his speech was a mixture of Danish and English. At first he made use of a schoolhouse for services, but after organizing a Methodist congregation at Cambridge in 1851 with ten initial members, he succeeded in getting a substantial stone church built.

"I left Milwaukee for a trip out into the country toward the west," wrote Willerup, recording his first impressions of the Norwegian settlements. "When I got out on the prairie to visit families, it was exactly as if I were in Norway. I heard no other language than the Norwegian — their dress, conduct, customs, and the like were just what they were in Norway. Since I found no church, I preached sometimes in the town schoolhouse and at other times in private homes out on the prairie." The church founded by Willerup at Cambridge, Wisconsin, has been called the first Scandinavian

[46] A good account of the work of Hedström in New York is given in J. M. Reid, *Missions and Missionary Society of the Methodist Episcopal Church,* 1:429–435 (New York, 1879). This account, written by the head of the Methodist missionary work, goes on to survey the Methodist missions among the Scandinavians in the West as well as in Norway, Sweden, and Denmark. A careful and illuminating study of "The Methodists in Sweden" is in Stephenson, *Religious Aspects,* ch. 8.

Methodist church in the world. In erecting a stone edifice for it, the minister and his congregation had many difficulties. Some of the problems of a frontier preacher are suggested by Willerup's account of how, on one occasion, he used his salary of a hundred and twenty-five dollars for a three-month period. He was obliged to pay ninety dollars of it for labor on the building and an additional thirty dollars for a wagon, leaving five dollars for his wife to use in meeting household expenses for the next three months.[47]

Willerup made the Wisconsin settlement a base for frequent missionary journeys, and in the next few years several other Norwegian Methodist churches were organized, among other places at Racine, Primrose, Viroqua, Highland, and Richland, Wisconsin. There were seven congregations by 1856, three of them with church buildings of their own; and the prospects appeared to be bright for a rapid spread of Methodism among the Norwegians. They were somewhat dimmed, however, when Willerup in 1856 was recalled by the missionary society for service in Norway as the director of Methodist activity in that country.[48]

Meanwhile the Norwegian-born O. P. Petersen, a sailor who had been won over to Methodism and had served as an assistant to Hedström on the Bethel ship, had taken up the work in the West. He had been sent first to Norway, where he spent the year 1849–50 introducing Methodism to his countrymen there. He returned to New York and in 1851 was commissioned to go to Iowa to work among the Norwegian settlers west of the Mississippi. At Washington

[47] Haagensen, *Den norsk-danske methodismes historie,* 11–16; *Danske i Amerika,* 1:227, 354 ff. (Minneapolis, 1907). An excellent account of Willerup, with extracts from his letters and reports to the Methodist Home Missionary Society, is in this work, 1:354–364.

[48] *Danske i Amerika,* 1:361–364. A report made in 1855 by Willerup to the head of the missionary society is summarized, with mention of Methodist missionary activity among the Norwegians and Danes at Racine, where Willerup established himself after leaving Cambridge, and at such places as Heart Prairie, Madison, Janesville, Whitewater, Sugar Creek, Primrose, Dodgeville, and Coon Prairie.

Prairie, in Winneshiek County, the heart of Norwegian Lutheranism in Iowa, he organized a Methodist church in 1852. Immigrant Methodism soon spread to other settlements in Iowa and also made its way into Minnesota, where, at St. Paul, the first Scandinavian Methodist church of Minnesota was organized early in 1854 under the Swedish minister C. P. Agrelius. The year 1853 had witnessed the beginning of a Methodist organization in the Fox River settlement — a congregation that evidently had a general Scandinavian character, for it was served successively by Danish, Norwegian, and Swedish preachers.[49]

Petersen, like Willerup, was looked upon as admirably suited for the mission of spreading Methodism in Norway, and in 1853 he was withdrawn from his enterprise in the West and asked to return to the mother country. Among the Norwegians, as among the Swedes and Danes, immigrant affiliations with the Methodist church resulted in the spread of Methodism in the mother country. Modern Methodism, in fact, took its rise in both Sweden and Norway as a direct result of Methodist contacts with immigrants in America — one of many emigrant influences that washed back upon the European world.[50] In Norway Petersen and Willerup were the pioneer missionaries; but as the work grew, Willerup was transferred to Denmark, and other missionaries joined Petersen in advancing the Methodist cause in Norway, which by 1877 had twenty-one Methodist churches, with 2,821 members. The Methodist historian of missions, Dr. J. M. Reid, calls attention to the role not only of missionaries but also of America letters in the spread of religious ideas from America to Europe. "The spirit of testimony that in America trem-

[49] Haagensen, *Den norsk-danske methodismes historie,* 16–21; Norlie, *Norwegian People in America,* 212. The original "Kyrko Book" for the Scandinavian Methodist Church in St. Paul gives the record of the organization meeting of this church, held on January 4, 1854. This manuscript record is in the possession of the Minnesota Historical Society.

[50] Stephenson, *Religious Aspects,* ch. 8.

bled upon the lips of Scandinavian Christians just born into the kingdom of God," he writes, "breathed itself in hundreds of letters that went back to Norway, Sweden, and Denmark." When he maintained that "Norway and Sweden were made all alive with correspondence of this sort," he undoubtedly indulged in exaggeration, but it is not unlikely that the immigrant letters were influential.[51]

Methodism made some progress among the Norwegian immigrants in the West, who reported nine congregations in 1857, with 258 members.[52] It did not, however, make the sweeping gains that some observers, conscious of the extraordinary power of Methodism on the American frontier, anticipated. Several reinforcing causes seem to account for this fact. One was the advancing organization and strength of the Lutheran church, which naturally limited the potentiality of Methodist gains among the immigrants. Another was perhaps the tendency of the Methodist immigrant churches toward an inclusively Scandinavian character, which encountered an obstacle that the American Methodists could not easily understand — the particularistic national-mindedness of the Norwegians. Neither the Swedes nor the Danes were untouched by this spirit, but it seemed to have an unusual efflorescence among the Norwegians. They were, of course, cousins of the Swedes and Danes, but they had not gone uninfluenced by the rising tide of nationalism, with waves of romanticism, in nineteenth-century Norway. In any event, it is plain that they did not readily adjust themselves to the idea of Scandinavian-American religious union. Probably the marked Americanism of the American Methodist church, which sometimes expressed itself in a distinctly nativistic spirit, tended also to check the advance of Methodism among the Norwegians. The institutionalized char-

[51] Reid, *Missions and Missionary Society,* 1:442–450; Haagensen, *Den norsk-danske methodismes historie,* 204 ff.

[52] Haagensen, *Den norsk-danske methodismes historie,* 22.

acter of the church, too, seems to have been an obstacle to a quick acceptance of it either in Norway or among the immigrants in America.[53] It must not be supposed that the progress of Methodism among the Scandinavians was inconsiderable, however, even if it was not sweeping. By 1870 the Norwegians, with the Danes, were ready to establish a theological seminary at Evanston, Illinois, and Scandinavian Methodism in America was on a fairly solid footing. On the whole Methodism appears to have been considerably stronger among the Swedes, however, than among the Norwegians.

The contact of the Norwegians with Episcopalianism was made in Wisconsin in the early 1840's. What happened is outlined in a sketch that appeared in the Episcopalian *Spirit of Missions* in 1846: "At Pine Lake there is a settlement, known as the 'Scandinavian Settlement,' composed of Swedes, Danes and Norwegians. A deputation from this body waited upon our Bishop in the winter of 1843–4, praying he would extend over them his spiritual jurisdiction. At the same time, they presented one of their own number, a Swede, as a person in whose piety, devotion, and talents, they had unbounded confidence, and whom they desired might be ordained, after due preparation as their minister. Mr. Gustaf Unonius, foregoing the endearments and comforts of home, became a resident student of Nashotah Mission, where he devoted himself to close application under the instruction of the Rev. Messrs Breck and Adams. The Rev. Gustaf Unonius is now in holy orders, and officiates for his countrymen in the Norse language, having 225 individuals under his spiritual charge, of whom 156 are communicants."[54]

Unonius, who founded the Pine Lake settlement in 1841, was a Swedish Ole Rynning, a man of university training and considerable intellectual stature, who not only led a colony of his countrymen to his "New Upsala" of the West, but also

[53] Stephenson, *Religious Aspects*, 256, 257.
[54] *Spirit of Missions* (New York), 11:332 (September, 1846).

wielded an able pen in making its attractions known in the Old World. A document written by him soon after he reached Wisconsin was published in Christiansand, Norway, in 1843 as a pamphlet entitled "Letter from a Swedish Emigrant, Containing Useful Information about North American Conditions," and undoubtedly influenced Norwegians to select Pine Lake as a suitable site for settlement.[55] It was that colony, in fact, that Hans Gasmann sought out when, in 1843, this former member of the Norwegian Storthing, with a family of thirteen children, emigrated to America.[56] During the summer of that year, according to Unonius, "the settlement was further increased by several Swedish and over fifty Norwegian families, and thus a little Scandinavia was created on the shores of Pine Lake." These families did not merge in one Scandinavian settlement, however, with all national barriers down. "On the east side," writes Unonius, "were the Swedes, on the west the Norwegians, and omitting occasional misunderstandings, the two nations lived happily together, and I must admit that in my future personal relations and contacts with the Scandinavians of the settlement, I was shown greater affection and more active support from the Norwegians than from my own countrymen."[57]

A few years later a Norwegian colony was developed to the northwest of Pine Lake, at Ashippun, where Adam Løvenskjold reported some thirty families, chiefly from Gjerpen in Sogn, in 1847.[58] A brother of Hans Gasmann, the ship cap-

[55] *Brev fra en svensk emigrant, indeholdende gavnlige oplysninger om de nordamericanske forholde* (12 p.). The letter by Unonius also appeared in the Swedish *Aftenbladet* for January 4 and 5, 1842, and is translated in George M. Stephenson, *Letters Relating to Gustaf Unonius*, 40–52 (Rock Island, 1937). In this volume Dr. Stephenson published a number of documents, with an introduction.

[56] Blegen, *Norwegian Migration*, 206–208.

[57] Filip A. Forsbeck, "New Upsala: The First Swedish Settlement in Wisconsin," in *Wisconsin Magazine of History*, 19: 312 (March, 1936). This is one in a series of three documentary articles which contain extensive translations from the reminiscences of Unonius published in 1861 and 1862 at Stockholm under the title *Minnen från en sjuttonårig vistelse i nordvestra Amerika*.

[58] Løvenskjold's "An Account of the Norwegian Settlers in North America," is in the *Wisconsin Magazine of History*, 8: 77–88 (September, 1924).

tain Johan Gasmann, visited Wisconsin in 1844 and wrote in terms of unqualified approval of the region. "The country about Pine Lake, where I found my brother living in a log house, he and his family well-satisfied," he said, "is very beautiful. . . . Many Swedes have settled about Pine Lake and are all very well established. Many Norwegians, of whom I knew several, are also living in this region, all, as far as I could find out, well satisfied with that which they have been able to accomplish. Their houses are still quite small, but are good enough to protect them from the winter." [59] Hans Gasmann, too, wrote appreciatively of the colony that Unonius had founded. He took out a claim for 160 acres of land and bought an additional thousand acres, always interested, as an ultimate purpose, in "a higher welfare for all my children." [60]

It was in this general settlement that Unonius, whose cabin was a community center, came under the influence of the brilliant young Episcopal leader, James Lloyd Breck, who was sent to the Wisconsin frontier by Bishop Jackson Kemper to try out his plan for restoring the unity of the church, for saving the West from sectarianism, and for achieving an effective "concert of action." Breck put Episcopalian literature in the hands of the Swedish immigrant and impressed him as a "true Christian and energetic minister of the Gospel." It was doubtless with great interest that Unonius learned from Breck that the Episcopalians were opening in 1842 their "associate mission," the Nashotah Episcopal Seminary, only a short distance from Pine Lake. The Episcopal minister made use of Unonius as an interpreter, encouraged him to call the settlers together in religious services, and urged upon his mind the similarity between the state church of Sweden and the Episcopal church. It seemed to Breck that the door of access was opened by similarity of

[59] *Studies and Records,* 5:46–48.
[60] Blegen, *Norwegian Migration,* 206, 207; Qualey, *Norwegian Settlement,* 55–57.

liturgy. The Scandinavians, he believed, "were themselves fully as ready to enter our door, opening into the American church, as we were to enter theirs, opening into their hearts."[61]

It was against this background, and in conformity with the wish of the settlers that Unonius should become their pastor, that he enrolled at the Nashotah institution. Meanwhile, the settlers proceeded with their religious devotions. In the summer of 1843 Breck wrote, "They have no chapel yet built; we had therefore to occupy a private house. Its front door was strewn with pine branches, whilst within was a table arranged altar-wise, and a chancel railing, all in pure white."[62] Early in 1844 he wrote that the bishop had "organized a parish among the Swedes, Norwegians, and Danes, called the 'Scandinavian Parish.'" Their burial grounds were consecrated in an impressive ceremony which led Breck to comment, "The miserable manner in which the dead are disposed of in these western lands almost overturns the doctrine of the belief in the Resurrection; and a solemn consecration of particular spots is loudly demanded."[63] The congregation organized at Ashippun was called St. Olaf's and the name is a clue to the Norwegian character of its constituency.

"In the humble chapel of the Nashotah Mission," wrote Bishop Jackson Kemper in 1845, "I ordained, on Wednesday, the 14th May last, Mr. Gustaf Unonius, a Native of Sweden, who had enjoyed many advantages in his own country, and whose sound judgment, studious habits, and unfeigned piety afford the promise of great usefulness. There

[61] Charles Breck, *Life of the Reverend James Lloyd Breck, D.D.*, 81 (New York, 1883). A study of Unonius and the Swedish Episcopalians is in Stephenson, *Religious Aspects*, 201 ff. and ch. 15. Breck said of Unonius, "He was bred a lawyer in Sweden, and is both a gentleman and a scholar." *James Lloyd Breck*, 46. Breck's ideas and the frontier work of the Episcopalians are discussed in Goodykoontz, *Home Missions*, 261–269.

[62] Breck to his sister, June 22, 1843, in *James Lloyd Breck*, 39.

[63] See a letter of February 24, 1844, in *James Lloyd Breck*, 43, 44.

are already four stations at which he officiates among the Norwegians, many thousands of whom have lately come into the Territory. He has organized two congregations, and will probably soon organize more." Kemper looked upon the admission of Unonius to the diaconate and "the bringing in of these Norwegians to all the privileges of the American Church" as "among the first fruits of the Nashotah Mission."[64] That this mission was deeply interested in the immigrants of the West may be seen by the fact that in 1847 its student body was made up of twelve Americans, one Englishman, one Irishman, two Swedes, one Dane, one Norwegian, one Jew, and three Oneida Indians — all intending to work among their own people.[65]

Dietrichson, the Norwegian state-church minister, visited the Pine Lake settlement in 1844, while Unonius was still a student in the Nashotah school. Unonius felt that there was no essential break from the Lutheranism of the Swedish state church in the step that he had taken. He "was satisfied in his own mind that he could enter the Episcopal church with his Lutheranism unblemished." He had even appealed to the archbishop of the Church of Sweden for approval of his action, but he failed to win the endorsement that he expected. To Unonius the situation was an emergency. He was on a distant frontier. No emissaries from the Swedish state church had sought out their countrymen in the West; and Lutheran organization among the Scandinavians was little developed. Dietrichson promptly set forth what he considered important differences in doctrine between the Lutherans and the Episcopalians in such matters as baptism, the Lord's Supper, predestination, and the episcopal succession. Later Unonius,

[64] Protestant Episcopal Church in the United States, Board of Missions, *Proceedings*, 1845, p. 52 (New York, 1845); *Spirit of Missions*, 9:277 (August, 1844), and 10:302 (September, 1845).

[65] *James Lloyd Breck*, 67. Breck wrote in 1848, "The Americans are found everywhere, and at the head of every enterprise; whilst the foreigners are, for the most part, settled in communities, according to the language or national habits of each" (p. 78).

with Breck, attended the dedication of the Norwegian Lutheran church at Muskego and there informed Dietrichson that he was intending to employ the Norwegian ritual in his services, but encountered serious objection from the Norwegian clergyman.[66]

After a period of service as a minister in an American congregation in Manitowoc, Wisconsin, Unonius went to Chicago, where he found his countrymen deeply concerned about "how they should best order" their religious matters. He had translated the Episcopal *Manual for Churchmen* into Norwegian and distributed copies of this document among the people. The upshot of his efforts was that Swedes and Norwegians joined hands in 1849 in forming in Chicago the St. Ansgarius congregation as part of the Illinois episcopal diocese. Unonius took note of the existence of a Norwegian Lutheran church in Chicago, but declared that it had laid aside the liturgy of Norway and "introduced an extemporaneous mode of worship." He also was aware of the existence of Eric-Jansonism and the dissension among the people who had followed its tenets, and he believed that he might do something toward bringing them back "into the universal Church of Christ."

The Scandinavian petitioners to the Episcopal Bishop of Illinois, Philander Chase, declared that they had considered how the "faith of our fathers could be best promoted and maintained among us and our children." They wished to preserve that faith and the church ceremonies and mode of worship "unto which we have been accustomed from our infancy." The Lutheran church, divided into groups and with-

[66] Dietrichson's account is in his *Reise*, 70–74. Unonius looked upon Dietrichson's criticisms as nothing more than a verbal battle among theologians. He invited the Norwegian to preach to his congregation, but Dietrichson declined. Dr. Stephenson, in *Religious Aspects*, 201, 202, analyzes the reasons for the action of Unonius in choosing the Episcopal church. See also Stephenson's *Letters Relating to Gustaf Unonius*, 31. A critical analysis of the problem of Unonius and the Episcopalians, made by a contemporary, is in Ræder's *America in the Forties*, 47–50.

out coherence, did not, they believed, meet their problem. "We have come to the conclusion," they wrote, "that in our present circumstances the only way by which we can secure to ourselves and our children the faith of our fathers, and continue faithful to that Church, into whose bosom we have been received, is to enter into communion with the Protestant Episcopal Church of this country." [67]

A turbulent period followed, in which Unonius was engaged in sharp controversy with Swedish Lutheran leaders; and in 1858 he returned to Sweden, feeling that his work in America had by no means been crowned with success.[68] The attempt to cling to the state-church tradition by way of American Episcopalianism did not win wide support from the immigrants. Dr. Norlie points out that both the Pine Lake and the Ashippun congregations ultimately became Lutheran, and he explains, in touching upon the Episcopal interest in possible amalgamation, that the Lutherans have not stressed episcopal succession.[69] Dr. Stephenson comes nearer the roots of the matter, however, when he says that Unonius did not understand the spirit of nonconformity among the immigrants, the spirit of the *läsare* and Haugeans.[70] In a word, the immigrants tended to shy away from the state church itself. Perhaps it was not so much the name of Episcopalianism or the precise differences between Episcopalian and state-church doctrine that defeated the project of Unonius as the fact that the Swedish and Norwegian immigrants

[67] "Organization of a Scandinavian Protestant Episcopal Church in Chicago, Illinois," in *Spirit of Missions,* 14:132–137 (May, 1849). This document opens with a statement by Unonius, and it presents the text, dated March 8, 1849, of the petition to Bishop Chase.

[68] The story is told by George M. Stephenson in an article on "The Stormy Years of the Swedish Colony in Chicago before the Great Fire," in Illinois State Historical Society, *Transactions,* 1929, p. 166–184. The Swedish Lutheran ministers looked upon Unonius as a proselyter and a traitor to the Lutheran cause. He was even sued for slander in the acrimonious feud that developed.

[69] Norlie, *Norwegian People in America,* 213. As early as 1851 the Norwegian Lutheran pastor, Nils Brandt, began work in the Pine Lake region.

[70] Stephenson, *Religious Aspects,* 202, and *Letters Relating to Gustaf Unonius,* 38, 39.

turned away from an actuality that came closer to the state church of Sweden than did their own Lutheran churches. In any event, the beginnings that center about Unonius do not appear to have led to any marked advance of the Episcopal faith among the Scandinavian immigrants, however interesting they may be as a chapter in the larger religious education of the immigrants.

V. THE EMERGING CHURCH

"THE LORD has brought me to this place safe and sound," wrote a Norwegian immigrant the day after his arrival in New York in the early autumn of 1839. "Our voyage lasted fifty days; a few storms occurred, but they seldom kept on for more than a day." This immigrant viewed the American metropolis with curious eyes: "I walked about in the city last night in order to see and hear, but in all the streets there was peace and quiet, and I observed neither games nor drinking nor dancing." He decided to depart for the interior, but left his ultimate destination to divine guidance: "I intend to set out for Rochester this evening or tomorrow; how God will then steer my way I cannot know." He voiced a deep piety: "My longing is now the same as before: to be a true child of God and that all my mistakes and weaknesses will serve to make me truly humble." He had a stern concept of the Christian life: "Freedom is good when it is not abused, but . . . we can stand little of the cup of joy — the goal of God's children is tribulation, for it leads to the kingdom of God." He asked his friends to keep themselves untainted by the world, "for the times are bad, and there are many bypaths that weaken our faith and love." He had certain forebodings: "What I fear most is that there will spring up sects and parties, and that each person will attach himself to his own party. Since various concepts of God's Word have already found expression, it is to be feared that a small spark will light a great fire."[1]

This immigrant of 1839 was Elling Eielsen, and these words, written upon the threshold of his American career, were in authentic tone. For Eielsen was a Haugean lay preacher. He was on his way to the settlements of his countrymen — a "crude but insistent force" destined to leave deep marks upon their religious history.[2] The coming of this restless, forceful, uncompromising lay chieftain of religion symbolizes in special degree the transfer from Norway to America of the Haugean spirit. For he represented in preeminent degree the Lutheran low-church point of view, pietism, puritanism, the concept of the congregation as a body of the "awakened," the belief in the rightness of lay preaching.

Eielsen was only thirty-five years old on that September day when he explored for the first time an American city, but he was already a lay preacher of wide experience — one of the most active and widely known in Norway after Hauge's death in 1824. He was born on an ancient *gaard* in Voss in 1804, the year the gentle Hauge was thrown into prison for violation of the Conventicle Act. His father, a schoolteacher, was a follower of Hauge, and the great religious leader had himself on several occasions visited the *gaard*. Eielsen had little formal education, but his training compared well with that of the best of the American circuit riders. He learned the Catechism and the Explanation; he "read" for confirma-

[1] Elling Eielsen to friends in Bergen and vicinity, September 4, 1839, in *Lutheraneren,* 15:489 (April 22, 1931). The letter, written in New York, is signed "Elling Eielsen Sundve." Usually, in after years, the Norwegian surname was not used.

[2] Larson, *Changing West,* 157.

tion; he unquestionably profited from the talk of his teacher father; and he acquired the trades of blacksmithing and carpentry, a potential bond of labor and skill between himself and frontier farmers in the day when he should trudge from settlement to settlement on missionary enterprises. Following his conversion in the 1820's, Eielsen traveled the country over, held conventicles, gained power and fluency as an impromptu preacher, defied the state authorities as no Norwegian lay preacher had dared to do since Hauge was put in jail, hammered home with fierce conviction what he considered the verities of sin and conversion and sanctification; struck out at the regular clergy and the state church; and, as the fruit of his effort, helped to revive the Haugean movement.[3]

Incessant travels, mainly on foot; incessant preaching; and incessant contacts with everyday people were part of the education of Elling Eielsen. "I believe that this man knows the Bible by heart," said an adversary who engaged him in argument.[4] He launched his missionary travels with a journey into the far North of Norway, accepting the challenge of remote places and hardship; but in the course of time he went east and south also, crisscrossing the land. "I must set fire to the whole country," he said. When in 1837, after spreading his activity into Sweden and Denmark, he collided with the Danish Conventicle Act and was briefly imprisoned, he rejoiced in his martyrdom. Soon he was looking for new frontiers. He was aware of the migration of his countrymen to the United States. He knew that the state church had sent no ministers to them. The Drammen Haugean, Tollef Bache, who was deeply interested in America and particu-

[3] Carlsen, "Elling Eielsen," ch. 2, 3. See also Christopher O. Brohaugh and J. Eisteinsen, *Kortfattet beretning om Elling Eielsens liv og virksomhed*, 5–57 (Chicago, 1883), and Erick O. Mørstad, *Elling Eielsen og den "evangelisk-lutherske kirke" i Amerika*, 17–70 (Minneapolis, 1917). A useful "Elling Eielsen bibliografi" by O. M. Norlie is in *Visergutten* (Canton, South Dakota), February 23, March 2, 9, 16, 23, 30, April 6, 13, 1939.

[4] Quoted in Mørstad, *Elling Eielsen*, 70.

larly the emigration of Haugeans to that country, encouraged him to carry his preaching to the emigrants. And in 1839 he made his decision. "I have no more room in these countries," he is reported to have said. "I will go to America."[5]

The natural objective for Eielsen was the Fox River settlement in Illinois, for it was then the largest Norwegian colony in the country. Whether divine guidance took place or not when he reached Rochester, there appears to have been no delay about his migration beyond that city to the West. He stopped in Chicago to preach to his countrymen there and then pushed on to the Fox River country. There, Haugean lay preachers like Ole Olsen Hetletvedt and Endre Aaragebø, who preceded Eielsen, had been active, but the time had obviously come for a more aggressive and effective leadership than they could supply. That, Eielsen was able to give. Some historians, picturing a state of utter religious confusion at Fox River, have asserted that Eielsen quickly "routed the sects" that he found there.[6] This does not quite picture the true situation, however. The settlers were undoubtedly feeling their way, learning about the American sects, and responding in some degree to the friendly interest that the American churches took in them, but plainly the American sects had made little advance among them. It will be recalled that Hans Valder did not join the Baptist church until 1842 and the Norwegian Baptist church at Fox River was not founded until 1848. The Mormon movement did not get well under way among the Norwegian settlers until some years after Eielsen arrived; the advance of Methodism among them did not come until the 1840's and 1850's; the Episcopalian movement, which did not touch the Scandinavian settlers until the early 1840's, was centered in Wisconsin; and it seems doubtful that Eielsen had any considerable

[5] Carlsen, "Elling Eielsen," ch. 3; H. G. Heggtveit, *Den norske kirke i det nittende aarhundrede*, 2:189 (Christiania, 1912–20).

[6] See Rohne, *Norwegian American Lutheranism*, 41.

influence upon the Quakers, who built a Norwegian church in a near-by Iowa settlement in 1842. The traditional picture clearly needs revision. What Eielsen did was simply to provide a focus that had hitherto been lacking for the basic Lutheran interests of the settlers, most of whom in the earlier period were Haugeans. The Fox River settlement was a strategic center for his work, though even during his first summer he took an active interest in Norwegians in other districts.

Although a man of Eielsen's extraordinary force was in himself a focus for the Lutheran religious impulse of the colonists, something more was needed — a meetinghouse, a church. And the evangelist who was also a carpenter built such an edifice himself, probably not long after he arrived. "Elling Eielsen Syndve has bought a piece of land in Fox River on which he has built himself a house," wrote a group of immigrants in a joint letter in the fall of 1840, adding that he had visited Chicago several times during the summer to give religious talks.[7] His house, the upper floor of which was fitted up as a place for religious services, was church and home combined. The next June an America letter from Fox River called attention to the fact that there were "no churches or houses of God" in the settlement until Eielsen came and "put up a house of prayer where services are held every Sunday." The letter described the workings of an immigrant church which depended upon lay leaders for its sermons: "There are several men who preach, one each Sunday. This gives me much more inspiration than I got from listening to the old minister at home, for one can neither hear nor understand what he says."[8]

[7] Anders L. Flage and others, Chicago, November 23, 1840, in *Vossingen* (Madison, Wisconsin), vol. 4, no. 3, p. 10 (1922). Earlier, on March 16, 1840, Jørgen Pedersen Tvedt wrote that Eielsen "has bought twenty acres a little ways from us and is thinking of building a large house where the Norwegians can gather every Sunday to consider God's Word." *Morgenbladet,* September 9, 1840.

[8] Mons Larssen Skutle to Anve Knudsen Skutle, June 22, 1841, in *Vossingen,* vol. 4, no. 3, p. 13, 14.

In 1841, convinced that it was necessary to provide basic Lutheran literature in English, Eielsen set out for New York City, walking the entire distance from Illinois. He arranged to have an English translation of Luther's Small Catechism put into print. This action was explained in a letter written in New York on August 20, 1841, some three weeks after his arrival. "The Norwegians are very widely scattered over the country," he wrote, "but nevertheless I have visited most of them." He was encouraged by a revival that had taken place in the winter and spring, and he wrote of the willingness of the settlers to assemble for religious services. Notwithstanding this, he believed that no immigrants were more indifferent than the Norwegians to religion, and he put the blame upon drinking and dancing. The children of the settlers had not been instructed in religion, and he had concluded that Luther's Catechism must be translated. With the help of a friend he had arranged to have the book turned into English and printed. As soon as it was ready he proposed to set out for Illinois again, where he would distribute the copies. Always curious about the life surrounding him, Eielsen attended an open-air meeting of Methodists in New York, a scene that led him to remark, "The ministers here exhibit a greater concern for the salvation of the people than do the ministers in Norway."[9] The next year, in 1842, Eielsen once more made the long trip to New York, this time to meet another pressing need in the field of religious instruction. He arranged to have printed in a single volume, in Norwegian, Pontoppidan's "Truth unto Godliness" and the Augsburg Confession. His errand accomplished, he trudged back to Illinois, probably equipped with his usual traveling paraphernalia — coffeepot, compass, rubber coat, and ax.[10]

[9] Eielsen to friends in Norway, August 20, 1841, in *Lutheraneren*, 15: 548, 549 (May 6, 1931). *Eielsen's Catechism Photographically Reproduced from the Original* (36 p.) was reprinted by Dr. Norlie in 1925. The original, the first book issued in the United States by a Norwegian, bore the title *Doctor Martin Luther's Small Catechism, with Plain Instruction for Children* (New York, 1841).

[10] Carlsen, "Elling Eielsen," 67–69.

As Lutheranism began to take form among the immigrants, it became apparent that lay leadership was not enough. Lacking ordained ministers, the religious life was essentially unorganized. In Norway the Haugeans naturally made use of the state-church organization; in the West, lacking such an institution, they discovered that certain functions could not well be handled through the more informal services of lay preachers. The immigrants, as Eielsen said later, were like sheep without a shepherd. The upshot of the matter was that Eielsen, responding to the wishes of his followers, was ordained as a minister on October 3, 1843, by a German Lutheran pastor, and so the lay leader emerged as the first Norwegian Lutheran minister in America. The validity of the ordination was later challenged by hostile critics of Eielsen, especially from within the camp of the Norwegian Synod, but historical investigation has completely sustained it. Eielsen responded to a call from his countrymen in a frontier emergency. Once a high-church clergyman complained bitterly to Eielsen about the alleged inadequacy of his examination, and Eielsen replied that he had been "tried as a Christian, under persecution, wakefulness, nakedness, and hunger."[11]

Meanwhile, in the Wisconsin Muskego settlement, which hitherto had been dependent, like the Fox River colony, upon lay preachers for its religious leadership, church organization was also emerging. The movement at Muskego centered about a twenty-three-year-old Dane, Claus L. Clausen, who arrived in America in the summer of 1843 with a party of Norwegian immigrants and made his way to Wisconsin with the hope of becoming a schoolteacher for the children of the Muskego pioneers. He had studied in Danish public schools, been confirmed, attended a German private school, enjoyed

[11] The phrase is in Dietrichson, *Reise,* 31; Dr. Rohne translates it in *Norwegian American Lutheranism,* 68. Mr. Carlsen fully establishes the validity of Eielsen's ordination in his "Elling Eielsen," ch. 5, with references to the voluminous writings that the controversy on this question occasioned. Interesting documents are in Brohaugh and Eisteinsen, *Kortfattet beretning,* 201–206; and a pertinent statement by Eielsen is in *Morgenbladet,* January 18, 1862.

the advantages of a ministerial tutor, interested himself in conventicles, blossomed out as a lay preacher, learned about the Haugean movement in Norway and about Eielsen's visit to Denmark in 1837, and become acquainted with Wexels, the noted antirationalist and Grundtvigian, as well as with the younger Hauge in Christiania. He considered for a time the possibility of going to Africa as a lay assistant to a Norwegian missionary, but in Drammen came under the influence of Tollef Bache, the noted Haugean who earlier had urged Eielsen to go to America. Bache's son had written from the Muskego settlement that there was need of a teacher who could instruct the children of the community in religion and who might perhaps become the pastor of the people. This prospect made a sharp appeal to Clausen, a democratic youth who liked people and took a practical interest in their problems. He therefore abandoned all thought of the African mission, returned to Denmark, married, and in the spring of 1843 set out for America with his bride. Before leaving he heard the famed Grundtvig preach in Copenhagen, visited Wexels in the Norwegian capital, and took under advisement the possibility of seeking ordination from the Church of Norway, but was told by Wexels that, since he was not trained in theology, he probably would not be successful in such a quest.[12]

Once Clausen arrived in Wisconsin, however, he encountered a sharp urgency on the part of the Muskego settlers to have him become at once a full-fledged minister. "My intention had been," he wrote in his diary, "to begin with

[12] Rasmus Andersen, *Pastor Claus Laurits Clausen*, 1–61 (Brooklyn, 1921); A. Margareth Jorgensen, "Claus L. Clausen, Pioneer Pastor and Settlement Promoter, 1843–1868," ch. 1–3. The latter, of which the Minnesota Historical Society has a copy, is an excellent master's thesis, prepared at the University of Minnesota in 1930. Clausen's first wife, Martha Clausen, died at Muskego only a few years after she went there. She is remembered for a farewell song composed when she left Denmark and now known among all Scandinavian Lutherans:

> And now we must bid one another farewell,
> The peace of our God keep you ever.

school instruction for the children submitted to my care, and not to enter upon church matters before I had myself learned through experience about the situation and the people. But all with whom I talked about this urged me emphatically not to carry this intention into effect, but on the contrary to seek ordination as quickly as possible so that as a regularly equipped minister I could assemble the scattered flock and feed them with God's true and undistorted word and the precious sacraments, for this need was more than great, while there were not a few who could undertake to teach the children."[13] So he acceded to the wishes of his constituents. Many reports unfavorable to Eielsen came to his ears and he seems to have been shocked in particular at the news that Eielsen had ventured to administer the Lord's Supper. The Muskego settlers petitioned a German Lutheran pastor in Milwaukee to ordain the young man, with the assurance that they would gladly accept him as their minister. On October 13, 1843, he was duly examined in German by the Milwaukee clergyman, with a committee of his Muskego friends as witnesses. "Here we sat," wrote one of them in his diary, "as stiff as wooden carvings and heard something that was going on, but what was it? I don't know, because I didn't understand."[14] On October 18, fifteen days after Eielsen had been ordained, Clausen was inducted into the ministry. "This morning," wrote Bache, "a great part of the Norwegian people gathered in our house to witness the ceremony of ordination, which was planned for today."

Thus Muskego, like Fox River, took the first steps in the transition from lay preachers and unorganized religion to ordained ministers and formal churches. In the autumn of 1843 the Muskego settlers launched a plan for building a church and at the same time authorized Clausen to reach out to other areas, regarding Muskego as a central station in a

[13] The diary is published in Andersen, *Clausen,* 58, 59.
[14] Bache Diary, October 13, 1843.

large field of missionary activity.[15] In December those who desired to be regarded as members of the congregation signed their names in a list.[16] Clausen, absorbed with missionary journeys and the burdens of caring for the spiritual needs of a community that was scourged by sickness and death, did not trouble to frame a formal constitution for the congregation; and the completion of its organization was left to the hand of a sterner and more systematic churchman than he.

Unhappily Clausen and Eielsen did not find it feasible to work together in harmony, notwithstanding the fact that Clausen had had friendly relations with the Haugeans in Norway and that many of the Muskego colonists were of the Haugean persuasion. Clausen did not accept the ordination of Eielsen as valid; it was at best, in his opinion, a license to preach; and he looked upon Eielsen as a disturbing influence among the immigrants. Eielsen, in turn, declined an invitation to speak on one occasion when he visited Muskego and suspected Clausen of Grundtvigian heresies.[17] As Professor Larson says, Eielsen "never learned how to travel comfortably on the highways of compromise and made little effort to come into agreement with his adversaries."[18] Perhaps both sensed the emergence of a basic church division — not then clear in outline — that would find Eielsen on one side and Clausen on another, with the one skeptical about an official clergy, even though, in the circumstances of immigrant pioneering, he accepted ordination; and with the other attaching a higher importance to the ministerial office and its symbols, even though he himself was primarily a layman, not a clergyman of formal theological training. Neither was a devotee of high organization; and with time they tended to come nearer one another rather than to move farther apart, chiefly

[15] Jorgensen, "Clausen," 25, 26.

[16] The total number of persons was 270. Bache Diary, December 14, 1843.

[17] Clausen Diary, in Andersen, *Clausen,* 59, 60; and Jorgensen, "Clausen," 28–31.

[18] *Changing West,* 157.

because both were acutely sensitive to lay thought, emotion, and action.

The lines of church division were sharply drawn with the advent in 1844 of J. W. C. Dietrichson, the first Norwegian university-trained clergyman to appear among the immigrants. A "call" had been dispatched early in 1844 from immigrants at Rock and Jefferson prairies and two other Wisconsin settlements to Bishop Sørenson of the Church of Norway asking that a minister be sent to the West. It so fell out, however, that young Dietrichson — he was then about twenty-nine years old — had been ordained before this call arrived and had been granted permission by the Norwegian church authorities to go to the United States to work among the immigrants. In the same year that he was thus commissioned, another theological candidate, Lagaard by name, who desired to be sent to America, was refused permission, since he had no call.[19] Like the Swedish state church, that of Norway exhibited no particular concern about the religious affairs of the immigrants. Dietrichson's decision, reinforced by a generous offer from a Norwegian citizen to shoulder all the expenses of his expedition, was personal in its inception. Its objectives, however, were broad-gauged, for he went to America not merely to serve a given congregation, but to produce ecclesiastical order out of what he considered disorder, to organize Norwegian-American Lutheranism according to the ritual of the Norwegian state church, to examine the religious needs of the immigrants. This self-chosen mission sprang from the mind of an uncompromising high-church divine, well-educated, touched by Grundtvigian influences, imperious of habit, and of a military family whose traditions, it is said, included a sharp temper, severity, and lordliness. This man proposed an ecclesiastical transfer from the valleys of Norway to the woods and prairies of the West. He intended to assure "to those who valued the Church of

[19] Malmin, in *Lutheraneren,* 8:76.

Norway, its ritual and history, an unbroken continuity of this Church upon American soil."[20]

"This morning as I went to my work," wrote Bache at Muskego early in August, 1844, "I met a young man with fresh and rosy cheeks, tall of stature, well-built, and looking like a hero from the old Norwegian mountains."[21] The young man was Dietrichson, just arrived and hunting for Clausen. He met the Muskego minister and preached to his people. "He prayed for the Swedish and Norwegian king," dryly commented Bache.[22] It probably was no coincidence that Clausen, before long, presented his congregation with a formidable document setting forth the conditions on which he would continue to serve the church and inviting those who did not agree to find themselves another pastor, a move that promptly met with a withdrawal from the congregation of the Haugean Even Heg and several other prominent members.[23] This episode signalized the domination of Clausen by his aggressive colleague. Dietrichson plunged into furious activity. He traveled about the settlements; made Koshkonong his headquarters; and promptly scrutinized the validity of the ordinations of Eielsen and Clausen, rejecting the one and accepting the other. But when he thus presumed to read Eielsen out of the ministry, he encountered no docile spirit. Eielsen not only proceeded serenely to function as a minister, to ride the circuit, and to organize congregations wherever he could, but he acknowledged no need of validating his status to Dietrichson. When Dietrichson

[20] A full account of Dietrichson's mission and objectives is in his own *Reise*. See my summary in *Norwegian Migration*, 250–255. "Dietrichson's powerful — I might almost say apostolic — character has most particularly qualified him for the task of establishing new congregations and arranging religious affairs," wrote the contemporary observer Ræder. "He is, perhaps, not quite so well qualified when it comes to dealing with the petty troubles which enter into every society and particularly among the lowly and uneducated, when their beliefs are shaken and their moral standard unbalanced as a result of important external changes which vitally influence their inner life." *America in the Forties*, 51.

[21] Bache Diary, August 7, 1844.

[22] Bache Diary, August 11, 1844; Dietrichson, in *Morgenbladet*, December 8, 1844.

[23] Bache Diary, October 16, 1844.

plainly asked him to abandon his activities, the forthright Eielsen said that he was the Norwegian emigrants' preacher, called by God and by man, and that he could do no other; apart from that, he said, Dietrichson's doctrine was false and papistical.[24] There was no compromise between the two, no recognition that there was room for both amid the broad and religiously untilled field of the immigrant population. Eielsen felt himself confirmed in his fears of high-church tyranny; and Dietrichson did not learn tolerance from the American frontier.

So Dietrichson went forward with his program, organized congregations in East and West Koshkonong, at Rock and Jefferson prairies, and at various other points, with Koshkonong and Muskego as central, or parent, bodies. He was satisfied with no mere listing of names, after the fashion of the easy-going Clausen, who was always more interested in the life of his congregation than in its form. He set up conditions that must be pledged and subscribed to by name: acceptance of church order under the ritual of the Norwegian state church; obedience to the minister; and an agreement not to install any minister not regularly ordained. Early in February, 1845, when 227 men of Koshkonong signed a formal call to Dietrichson to be their minister, they promised him forty acres of land, ten of which were to be plowed and fenced, a house, three hundred dollars a year for five years, voluntary fees for special services, and offerings at Christmas, Easter, and Pentecost.[25] Dietrichson accepted this call, but

[24] Dietrichson tells of this interview, which occurred in the Fox River settlement, in his *Reise,* 32. Eielsen dealt harshly with Dietrichson in a letter that he wrote in 1845 to Norwegian friends. Dietrichson, he believed, was interested solely in the "external acceptance of churchly forms" and interpreted pure Lutheran doctrine in terms of masses, gowns, and dead ceremonies. The letter, dated February 28, 1845, is printed in the Norwegian periodical *Grannen* for March, 1930, p. 1–4. Ræder listened to "a friendly conversation" between Eielsen and Dietrichson and was impressed by Eielsen's "free and at the same time modest bearing." He added, "The expression on his face is bold and yet not lacking in spiritual qualities." *America in the Forties,* 52.

[25] Dietrichson, *Reise,* 38–55; and his letter of December 28, 1844, in *Stavanger amtstidende og adresseavis,* March 30, April 3, 7, 10, 1845.

returned to Norway in 1845, leaving Clausen in charge of the congregation at Koshkonong.

Meanwhile, Dietrichson's energy had influenced the building of churches, particularly two in the Koshkonong area, both dedicated in the fall of 1844. The historic Muskego church, projected in 1843, occupied the next year, and dedicated on March 13, 1845, was built of oak logs "matched after the Norwegian fashion of building houses." It was dressed smooth on the interior, with doors, pulpit, and galleries of walnut.[26] On the gala day in 1845 it was filled with people eager to hear the services. An order soon came, however, that they must all go outside, where those who were members were asked to enter in pairs while the nonmembers should enter as they wished. Then, with the Episcopalians Unonius and Breck and the German pastor Krause present, Dietrichson and Clausen both spoke and the dedication took place. Bache records the sermon of Dietrichson with a note of irony. The Norwegian clergyman, he says, spoke largely of Norway in the spirit of one trying to make the people regret their emigration and to fill them with homesickness. He reminded them of how happy they had been among their native mountains; that only one religion flourished in their homeland; how toilsome the long voyage to America had been; and that now they were living in the American desert.[27]

The sum total of Dietrichson's influence before his departure for Norway was a definite move toward organization, high-church ritual, and discipline, coupled with a flinging down of the gage of theological battle to all adversaries. Within the church itself discipline was enforced with an iron hand by the young clergyman in black gown and fluted ruff. The Lutheran service, after tolling bells had summoned the worshipers, proceeded from the opening prayer of the sexton through the various hymns, creeds, prayers, text of the day,

[26] H. J. Ellertsen, quoted in Anderson, *First Chapter,* 419.
[27] Bache Diary, March 10, 13, 30, 1845.

THE INTERIOR OF THE OLD MUSKEGO CHURCH

[From a photograph made in October, 1940, by Mr. Paul Hamilton of the Minneapolis Institute of Arts. The building is preserved on the grounds of the Luther Theological Seminary, St. Paul, Minnesota.]

sermon, and on to the benediction and chants and closing prayer, with an ordered solemnity. The evangelical fervor of an Eielsen service might indeed be lacking, but this ceremony added an element of beauty and dignity and of the consoling security inherent in traditional forms to the lives of frontier men and women.[28]

It is only against the background of the state-church ritual that one can properly interpret the episode of Halvor Pedersen, alleged to have been a drunkard and an impious disturber, who, after being dropped from church membership as a result of his unbecoming conduct, was assigned to a particular place in the rear of the church. When this alcoholic individualist arrived, however, he rejected the assigned seat as an indignity and marched down to the very front, where he stationed himself near the altar. This was a challenge that Dietrichson could not and would not evade. He first invited strangers — meaning the worthy Halvor Pedersen — to leave, but the man refused to move. Then the pastor planted himself in front of him and addressed a personal rebuke to him, whereupon he had the sexton and two assistants throw him out of the church. Pedersen promptly sued Dietrichson for assault and battery. In the trial, Pedersen's attorney designated the clergyman as a "pope" whose authority needed to be limited by the state. He had, indeed, only ordered a man thrown out of the church, but what guarantee was there that another time he would not order someone beheaded? The defense replied that not only had Dietrichson not laid a hand upon Pedersen, but that the state, under American principles, should not intrude in church affairs, and that the pastor had merely followed the discipline of his church. The frontier jury sustained Pedersen; Dietrichson was found guilty and fined. This episode Professor Marcus L. Hansen interprets

[28] Dr. Rohne gives an admirable summary of Dietrichson's conception of church order and discipline and he analyzes the conduct of public worship in Norwegian Lutheran churches of the conservative wing in his *Norwegian American Lutheranism*, 80–88. Ræder commented on the "beautiful and dignified manner" in which Dietrichson conducted services. *America in the Forties*, 55.

as a "spontaneous immigrant Puritanism,"[29] but its true significance lies, not in the circumstantial chance that the case revolved about an alleged drunkard, but in the central question of the maintenance of high-church Lutheran discipline. Dietrichson took an appeal to a higher court, which rejected it on a technicality, but he was not greatly disturbed about the action of the American jury. What was important to him was that he had firmly upheld within his congregation the principle of church discipline.[30]

And so, with energy undiminished, Dietrichson set out for Norway in 1845, published there in 1846 a book of travels describing his adventures in America, appealed to young theologians to join him in the western world, denounced emigration, requested and received a subsidy from the Norwegian government with the virtual condition that he should use his pen actively to counteract "the disturbing and frivolous emigration desire," and in 1846 returned to the theological battleground of Wisconsin to take over the Koshkonong call, Clausen in turn assuming that of Luther Valley.[31]

Meanwhile, no less energetic than Dietrichson, his Haugean low-church rival, Elling Eielsen, continued his endeavors. He was, as Professor Larson has said, "pastor at large; his parish was wherever Norwegians lived and could be assembled in house or church." In his missionary enterprise he even extended his activity, shortly before the Civil War, to far-distant Texas, where there were several struggling Norwegian colonies. "He is, to be sure, a Haugean," wrote Elise Wærenskjold, a sensitive observer in Texas, "but an unusually able man who is a tireless worker." She was im-

[29] "Immigration and Puritanism," in *Studies and Records*, 9:19, 20. Professor Hansen improves the story by having the minister seize the sinner by the collar and hurl him through the door.

[30] Dietrichson tells the story very frankly in his *Reise*, 57–68.

[31] The matter of the governmental subsidy is revealed in Riksarkiv, Oslo: Kirkedept., Journalsaker, July–August, 1846, res. 1556. See Blegen, *Norwegian Migration*, 250 ff. A request by Dietrichson for additional pastoral assistance in America is in *Morgenbladet*, August 16, 1845.

pressed by his energy: "He visited all the Norwegians and preached every day and almost the entire day. Thus, on the day we had the Lord's Supper, he first gave an excellent sermon; then a very long textual exposition; in the afternoon he talked first with the people about starting a religious school and arranged matters so that we should have a Sunday school; then he took up the temperance cause, in which he is very active." At a near-by place he succeeded in reviving a temperance society that had been established some years earlier. Eielsen, Mrs. Wærenskjold said, made the long and difficult journey to Texas without any guarantee of funds; he asked nothing and would not accept a church offering. Nevertheless, the three Norwegian settlements that he visited raised about a hundred dollars with which to reimburse him for his expenditures. "There is a general wish," Mrs. Wærenskjold concluded, "that he would come here as our minister, and I do not believe that we could get anybody who would be better fitted than he to work here."[32]

In the middle 1840's, however, Eielsen had not yet swung out upon such wide missionary journeys as the Texas venture, but instead was grappling with the problem of synodical organization. "I have nowhere read that Christ kept a protocol when He journeyed about and held meetings for the people," he said on one occasion.[33] The remark is a clue to his lack of enthusiasm for the formalities of church organization. The unmistakable trend of Dietrichson toward the setting up of an organized front and the equally unmistakable determination of Eielsen and his friends not to be drawn within the orbit of that movement, coupled with the influence of such younger men as Paul Andersen and Ole Andrewson, help to explain why the Haugean leader was willing to turn to organization. Yet this is not the whole story. The

[32] A letter of Mrs. Elise Wærenskjold, dated Four-mile Prairie, Texas, March 24, 1860, in *Tønsbergs* [Norway] *blad,* May 16, 1925; Larson, *Changing West,* 160.

[33] Quoted by Thrond J. Bothne, in *Kort udsigt over det lutherske kirkearbeide blandt nordmændene i Amerika,* 834 (Chicago, 1898).

Eielsen followers were widely scattered; on every side in the frontier West were evidences of the compact organization of American religion; both environment and example pointed toward immigrant organization; and Eielsen could not close his eyes to the obvious need of binding his followers into a firmer brotherhood. On April 14 and 15, 1846, at Jefferson Prairie, Wisconsin, he and his associates formed the first synod among the Norwegian-American Lutherans — variously known as the Evangelical Lutheran Church of America, Elling Eielsen's Synod, Eielsen's Synod, the Ellingian Brotherhood, or the Ellingians.[34]

Paul Andersen, born at Vang in Norway in 1821, had arrived in America in 1843, and was possibly the first Norwegian American to matriculate at an American college. He entered Beloit College in 1844 and there came under Presbyterian influence while at the same time breathing the air of western American culture at its best. A dynamic young man, attracted by the American world, deeply religious, liberal, and sympathetic toward the needs of his fellow immigrants, Andersen found himself urged by his Presbyterian friends not to enter the Presbyterian ministry but to become instead a Lutheran minister and to serve his countrymen. No friend of state-church ceremonial, he was drawn to Eielsen and was present at the organization of the synod in 1846. There, too, among others, was Ole Andrewson, a native of Upper Telemark, a *seminarist* from Norway, who had had experience as a parochial school teacher before his emigration to the United States in 1841. He established himself on a Wisconsin farm, but also ventured out as a lay preacher; and he joined Eielsen in the move to organize a synod.[35]

The constitution of Eielsen's Synod, adopted in 1846 and

[34] Carlsen, "Elling Eielsen," ch. 6; Ole J. Hatlestad, *Historiske meddelelser om den norske Augustana-synode,* 37 ff. (Decorah, 1887).

[35] O. M. Norlie, *Norsk lutherske prester i Amerika, 1843–1913,* 96 (Minneapolis, 1914), gives brief biographies of Andrewson and Andersen, with portraits. See also George M. Stephenson, *The Founding of the Augustana Synod 1850–1860* 14–17 (Rock Island, Illinois, 1927).

reaffirmed four years later, is an interesting exposition of the Eielsen viewpoint. The ideal of a selected membership was set up: "No one ought to be accepted as a member of our body, except he has passed through a genuine conversion or is on the way to a conversion." The church body was to be "in conformity to the genuine Lutheran faith and doctrine, and built on God's Word in the Holy Scriptures in conjunction with the Apostolic and Augsburg Articles of Faith." This was no high-church organization: "With popish authority and also the common ministerial garb we henceforth have absolutely nothing to do." The synod was created against a background of lay preaching: "Those who are talented with aptitude for teaching must procure the necessary knowledge, as far as the circumstances permit; but this, as everything else, must be subject to the Lord in faith and obedience, that not ours but His Will be done." It was recalled that the founder of the Christian religion "chose lay and unlearned men to proclaim his Gospel." One provision authorized contributions in support of traveling lay preachers. In administering the sacraments, the ritual and altar book of the Church of Norway were to be employed; but there was to be no laying on of hands in absolution, and it was carefully provided that forgiveness of sins should be declared only to penitent souls. The constitution declared for the furtherance of schools and instruction, the securing of necessary books, and the education of the children in both languages; and it condemned slavery in scathing terms.

This constitution, in the theological wars that followed, was shelled with explosive criticism. One charge was that of Grundtvigianism, made, curiously enough, in the face of Eielsen's well-known opposition to that concept. Another was that of Donatism, based upon the attempt to transplant to America the Haugean congregational concept. The constitution revealed the traditional confessional basis of the Norwegian-American Lutherans generally. It did not define the relations of congregation to synod; perhaps experience had not enabled its architects to envisage the details of such a relationship. All in all, the constitution caught the spirit of the low-church group that it represented.[36]

Organization did not do away either with inner dissension or with external controversy. Eielsen and the young men associated with him did not see eye to eye. Andersen, in particular, was keenly alive to the spirit of transition all about him. He was more closely in touch with American Lutheranism than any other Norwegian Lutheran leader of his day. The liberal *Lutheran Observer,* for example, he found refreshing, its views "dear to his heart."[37] He was attracted by the Franckean Synod and was in fact ordained by that body in 1848. Andersen unquestionably sympathized with Eielsen in his combat with the high-church Dietrichson; but from the Franckean point of view Eielsen was an extremely conservative Lutheran, and ultra-Norwegian in his interests. The Franckeans were ranked as "the most liberal Lutheran body in the country." For Andersen the bridge to Franckeanism seems to have been friendly contacts with members of that synod in the West. Once he crossed it, the liberal and American tone of the synod, its outspoken hostility to slavery, and its pietism made a strong appeal to him. He and Andrewson, as well as Ole J. Hatlestad, a schoolteacher and lay preacher who had come to America in 1846, broke with Eielsen in 1848 at a meeting held in the Fox River settlement. Several charges, some evidently of a personal character, were read against Eielsen; he left the meet-

[36] Dr. Rohne has done a service to scholarship by translating the Eielsen Constitution in his *Norwegian American Lutheranism,* 107–110. He argues that the Eielsen Constitution was revised in 1850 and that in the process the original was "practically destroyed, and an entirely new, purely Ellingian, document was produced," and he suggests the possibility of dating the synod from 1850 instead of 1846 (p. 100). But Carlsen, analyzing the entire problem in his "Elling Eielsen," ch. 6, convincingly shows that this position is untenable, that the Constitution was reaffirmed in 1850, and that the synod unquestionably dates from 1846.

[37] Stephenson, *Augustana Synod,* 15. Andersen, writing to the *Lutheran Observer* (Baltimore), expressed the hope that "the paper might have a long life and carry its views of Christian union and brotherly love to its thousands of readers.'

ing; and those who remained proceeded to put through a resolution accepting the "ecclesiastical rule and discipline" of the Franckean Synod. In uniting with that synod, the Norwegian group reserved the right to continue to use Luther's Small Catechism and Pontoppidan's Explanation, and it specified that its affiliation should last only so long as the synod should "walk in agreement with the Word of God and rightly teach the ways of God." So one group of Norwegian immigrants moved tentatively toward liberal American Lutheranism.[38]

Eielsen now regarded himself as the sole orthodox minister among his countrymen in the New World, for to his mind Dietrichson and Clausen were tainted with Grundtvigianism, Andersen and Andrewson with anticonfessionalism.[39] He was heartened by the accession of the gifted Peter A. Rasmussen, a parochial school teacher fresh from Norway, in 1850. Rasmussen served in his fold for a half dozen years before turning to other church affiliations. In 1850 Eielsen took stock of the situation confronting him, called his followers together, and with some thirty-six associates reaccepted the constitution that had been made the basis of the synod four years earlier.[40]

Paul Andersen, meanwhile, had set in motion a Norwegian, or Scandinavian, Lutheran church in Chicago early in 1848, the first of its kind in the great Middle Western city. After three years he found himself ready to establish, if possible, a union synod of the West; he had in fact set up a preliminary

[38] The resolution of affiliation with the Franckean Synod is translated by Carlsen from the text as given in a letter dated April 7, 1849, and published in Rene, *Historie om udvandringen fra Voss.* "Elling Eielsen," 101. He also gives a good account of the relations between Andersen, Andrewson, and Eielsen. See also Brohaugh and Eisteinsen, *Kortfattet beretning,* 79 ff.; Mørstad, *Elling Eielsen,* 139–147; and Hatlestad, *Historiske meddelelser,* 42 ff.

[39] Rohne, *Norwegian American Lutheranism,* 104, 105.

[40] On Rasmussen, see Norlie, *Norsk lutherske prester,* 101, and Mørstad, *Elling Eielsen,* 174 ff. Johan A. Bergh gives the text of the Eielsen Constitution in *Den norsk lutherske kirkes historie i Amerika,* 27–33 (Minneapolis, 1914). See a statement by Eielsen, dated January 14, 1862, in *Morgenbladet,* January 18, 1862, of which the writer has a photostat.

"Scandinavian Conference" in 1850; and on September 18, 1851, he joined hands with Americans and Germans in organizing the Evangelical Lutheran Synod of Northern Illinois. This move brought, on the very next day, the adhesion of one of the great pioneer church leaders of Swedish America, Lars Paul Esbjörn. One historian has interpreted the founding of the Synod of Northern Illinois as a "direct protest against the loose confessionalism of the Franckean Synod," but Andersen declared that his participation in the new synod was motivated by no animus against the Franckeans. The Franckean connection he had regarded as informal and tentative.[41] What he considered essential was a special union synod in the West. So was launched a movement in Swedish and Norwegian Lutheranism that was destined to lead to the emergence in 1860 of the Scandinavian Augustana Synod and, ten years later, of the Norwegian Augustana Synod and the Conference of the Norwegian-Danish Evangelical Lutheran Church in America.

In the period of initial struggles, Andersen's Chicago congregation succeeded in getting financial aid for its pastor from the American Home Missionary Society, a national body sustained by the Congregationalists and Presbyterians but submerging denominational lines in its deep interest in the advancement of Christian work everywhere. From Andersen's reports, preserved in manuscript these many years, one can get a picture not only of a pioneer immigrant church but also of a leader who deserves to be better known than he is.[42]

Andersen looked to the day when laborers would be "raised up here on American soil" to work among the "mass of

[41] Stephenson, *Augustana Synod*, 17; Paul Andersen, *Om den lutherske kirke i Amerika*, 8–11 (Chicago, 1880); Rohne, *Norwegian American Lutheranism*, 104.

[42] Andersen's original letters are preserved in the American Home Missionary Society Archives. All citations that follow are to these manuscripts. It should be noted, however, that some of the Andersen letters, with a series by T. N. Hasselquist, have been published under the title "Reports to the American Home Missionary Society, 1849–1856," with a foreword by Dr. Conrad Bergendoff, in Augustana Historical Society, *Publications*, 5:35–84 (Rock Island, 1935).

foreign population," and he believed that evangelization would synchronize with the Americanization of the people.[43] His Sabbath school, he reported in the summer of 1849, was prosperous and well-attended. That year cholera ravaged Chicago and the Middle West and the church lost twenty-five of its most active members, the congregation reported in a request by its council for a subsidy for the year 1850. A "little house of Worship" had been built and a debt of five hundred dollars created. An American, endorsing this application, referred to Andersen as not only a faithful pastor but also as "missionary at large for the Evangelical Norwegians in the North West." Andersen himself reported that he had made five trips into the Northwest during the year. His own people, he found, were generous and willing, but they had few means and had to depend for food and shelter upon their labor from week to week.[44]

In the spring of 1850 Andersen said that he tried in season and out "to preach the Word with simplicity and plainness." The cloud left by the visitation of cholera had lifted. He worked on the principle of a selective membership and refused to admit to church membership a man who ran his shop on the Sabbath. His ministry, as explained in a later letter, included preaching services three times on Sunday, with three prayer meetings during the week.[45] Invited by twenty-five families in Dane County, Wisconsin, he had paid a visit to that Norwegian center. He urged the immigrants to send their children to English schools. He favored the establishment of temperance societies. Not so many church members had died during 1850 as the year before, he re-

[43] Andersen to the American Home Missionary Society, March 31, 1849.

[44] Andersen to the American Home Missionary Society, June 30, 1849, January 1, 1850; and a letter from his church council, signed by Iver Larson and three others, December 25, 1849.

[45] Andersen's letters of April 1, July 1, and October 1, 1850; and one from the church council, December 16, 1850. Andersen's observations on conditions at Koshkonong are in the *Home Missionary*, 23:119, 120 (September, 1850).

ported, but the seven lost were among the most valuable in the congregation.

In 1850 the eastern Lutheran leader, William A. Passavant, visited Chicago and wrote of Andersen's congregation: "They own a neat and comfortable frame church, and are evidently walking in the fear of the Lord and the comfort of the Holy Ghost." Andersen himself, he added, "firmly holds the doctrines of the church set forth in the Augsburg Confession; and . . . instructs his people in the Word of God as thus explained; likewise using Luther's Small Catechism and Pontoppidan's Exposition." Passavant was not wholly satisfied, however: "We could have wished that more of the usages of the Norwegian Church had been retained in their worship, but rejoice that we found so much to commend in their religious services." He found that there were 170 communicants, and a total congregation of about 300. The strategic position of Chicago impressed him. The church, he said, "stands at the door by which the great body of those taking up their residence in Illinois, enter the country. It at once extends to them the hand of brotherly love and Christian kindness; it gathers them in from the vessels by which they arrive; turns away their feet from the places of temptation to the house of God; and serves as a bond of connection between this place and the new home wherever they may be settled."[46]

Andersen served, he said in 1851, a fluctuating community; some of his people were there for only a few months of the year; many sailed on the Great Lakes in the summer or secured work on farms, while in the winter the Scandinavian sailors congregated in Chicago. All in all, it was not easy for the congregation to acquire stability. The immigrants, he said, were all poor, but some were beginning to get ahead. The *Prairie Herald* commented on the fact that Andersen

[46] George H. Gerberding, *Life and Letters of W. A. Passavant, D. D.*, 211, 212 (Greenville, Pennsylvania, 1906).

was making a Norwegian version of *Pilgrim's Progress* available to the American Tract Society, which had already issued several works in Norwegian and had two colporteurs at work among the Norwegians in Wisconsin. Andersen remarked in the spring of 1851 that he had only a small library, but that it included a copy of Dwight's *Theology.* Reporting a revival, he explained that he had made no effort to produce a "merely mechanical excitement." In addition to preaching twice in Norwegian and once in English each Sunday, he was presenting a series of lectures on church history, beginning with the Reformation.

Andersen carried on his work amid family affliction: sickness, the death of his only child, the death of a brother who was studying at Knox College, and other trials; but he did not lose courage. He was aware of the problems occasioned by rapid transition — "when situated as some of us are, in the midst of the most confused breaking up of old views and associations and yet without half time enough for new things to mature." The emigrants, accustomed to "proper subordination" in the Old World, suddenly found themselves in possession of "glorious American liberty," but hardly knew how to enjoy it or wherein real liberty consists. He himself defined liberty as full freedom to do right, without being molested or made afraid by anybody. In his Sabbath school, he said in 1852, were Norwegian, Danish, Swedish, German, English, American, French, and other children. He observed the rush of the westward movement: "The Lord has blessed us with a remarkable degree of health during the past quarter," he wrote on July 1, 1852; "our city is thronged with peopul and with business; and immigrants from Europe and elsewhere are flocking in by the thousand; our population has increased during the last twelv years from 4,853 to more than 40,000 inhabitance." All this soon brought on sickness: Andersen made a hospital of his own house; gave food and clothing to poverty-stricken transients; then broke down in health himself and was confined to his bed for three weeks.[47]

In the midst of such events and problems, Andersen's energy was devoted mainly to his church and its many difficulties, and theological controversy occupied relatively little of his attention. Yet his opposition to the "formalists" found repeated expression. He criticized the "ecclesiastics of the Norwegian State Church." It was not enough, he thought, merely to break some "branches of the ever-fruitful tree of superstition"; he wanted to "cut its very roots." His fight was directed mainly against the camp of Dietrichson and his associates; but he looked upon Unonius, the Episcopalian, as guilty of unchristian proselyting, and on one occasion he sponsored a debate in his own church, in which Unonius, Passavant, and others took part. Once in his reports to the American Home Missionary Society he made a sharp attack upon his old friend Eielsen and "his company of spiritual enthusiasts and impostures [*sic*]." In addition to his other activities, Andersen found time to issue translations of the Illinois state constitution in 1847 and the constitution of the United States in 1854.[48]

While Andersen was thus concentrating his efforts in Chicago, his colleague Ole Andrewson, for whom Franckeanism was similarly a bridge from Eielsen's Synod to the Synod of Northern Illinois, was working at several places, including Racine, in the vicinity of the Muskego settlement; the Fox River region; and, later in the 1850's, Rock County, Wisconsin. To the American Home Missionary Society, which extended support to him also, he described "Indifferentism, Formalism and Superstition" as his major difficulties. Telling of conflict with the Mormons, Baptists, and other sects,

[47] Andersen's letters of January 1, March 1, July 1, October 1, 1851; January 1, March 1, April 1, July 1, October 1, 1852; a letter of the church council, December 10, 1851; and a clipping, "Books in Norwegian," from the *Prairie Herald*, February 25, 1851.

[48] Andersen's letters of March 31, 1849, and April 1, 1851; Gerberding, *Passavant*, 216; Norlie, *Norsk lutherske prester*, 96.

he declared that he was between two extremes, the state church on the one side and American revivalism on the other. Mormonism and fanaticism in the Fox River region, he said, left a condition resembling that of a prairie after it has been swept by a fire. He brought out a hymnbook, edited a religious paper which he hoped "by the blessing of God" would "prove to be of some servise among my countrymen"; saw most of his Illinois congregation migrate to Iowa in a body; worked as a farmer to "make both ends meet" for the support of a family of twelve; was aghast at the prevalence of drunkenness, Sabbath breaking, and swearing in the settlements; agreed to have a two-month parochial school at Clinton, Wisconsin, "when not interfering with the District School"; and in the later 1850's served four stations in Wisconsin. In 1853 he wrote from Racine County, "We have also 8 poor Students in the Illinois University at Springfield, which demends our assistances & wich we from time to time must do something for."[49]

The university to which Andrewson referred was a central point in the activities of the Synod of Northern Illinois. Throughout the decade the Swedes and Norwegians cooperated with Americans and Germans in what Dr. Stephenson has termed a "polyglot Lutheran synod" and a "melting pot institution."[50] There was an obvious gap between the symbolism of men like Lars P. Esbjörn, who stood for the unaltered Augsburg Confession, and the views of their American associates; and the project in unionism bears the marks of a search for synodical connections by Scandinavian leaders imperatively in need of the stability that they seemed to promise. Illinois State University, an academy moved from

[49] This paragraph is based upon a series of some thirty manuscript letters, written in English by Andrewson, with a few from his church council, in the period from 1852 to 1858, all addressed to the American Home Missionary Society and preserved in its archives. The letter mentioning the students in Illinois is dated March 1, 1853, and is devoted principally to the activities of the Scandinavian Evangelical Lutheran church in Racine County. A letter of March 12, 1852, states that Andrewson was ordained on September 20, 1851.

[50] Stephenson, *Augustana Synod,* 149.

Hillsboro to Springfield and there given a new and impressive name, gave promise of solving one of the most pressing problems confronting both the Swedes and the Norwegians, that of raising up leaders for the church, as Andersen had suggested, from among the ranks of the Scandinavian immigrants.[51]

The promise seemed particularly bright when Esbjörn was established as professor at the college in 1858 after heroic efforts had been made to raise funds for this purpose. There were as many as twenty Norwegian and Swedish young men at the institution in the late 1850's, including Abraham Jacobson, who became a noted pioneer minister. Apart from the pinching poverty of both the Scandinavian teacher and his students, however, the road for the Scandinavians in the union project proved rough and difficult. Esbjörn felt that there was danger of the Scandinavians being engulfed in an American tide. Francis Springer, the president of the university in the early 1850's, spoke of thrusting "the leaven of American ecclesiasticism and evangelization among the immigrants bearing the Lutheran name."[52] This somewhat nativistic leader resigned in 1855 and two years later the more conservative William M. Reynolds took office, but a complex of circumstances led to the secession of the Scandinavians in 1860. There was dissension within the synod, a gulf between Esbjörn and his American colleagues, the one conservative, or "Old Lutheran," the other liberal, or "New Lutheran," and one faction among the Americans complained of the "hyper-orthodoxy" of the Norwegian and Swedish symbolists.[53] The Norwegian Synod and other critics on the outside thrust lances at the Scandinavian participants for

[51] Henry O. Evjen, "Illinois State University, 1852–1868," in Illinois State Historical Society, *Journal*, 31:54–71 (March, 1938); and "Scandinavian Students at Illinois State University," in *Studies and Records*, 11:17–29; Stephenson, *Religious Aspects*, ch. 13.

[52] Quoted in Stephenson, *Religious Aspects*, 182.

[53] Stephenson, "The Founding of the Augustana Synod: Illustrative Documents," in *Swedish-American Historical Bulletin*, 1:3 (March, 1928).

yielding to a "shameful trick of the devil" and entering the camp of a "dangerous enemy of the Lutheran Church."[54] There was a spirit of national particularism which resulted in the setting up of Swedish and Norwegian conferences and uniting both in the face of the Americans. Springfield was far away from the centers of the northward- and westward-moving Swedish and Norwegian immigrant population; and from Minnesota adherents came a threat of secession from the synod. And there was a web of personal, financial, and other complications within the college itself. The upshot was the spectacularly sudden resignation of Esbjörn in the spring of 1860, the withdrawal of nearly all the Scandinavian students, and the establishment in June, 1860, at the Norwegian Lutheran church at Jefferson Prairie, Wisconsin, of the Scandinavian Evangelical Lutheran Augustana Synod in North America, which took its confessional stand upon the historic creeds, the unaltered Augsburg Confession, and the symbolical books. There remained the unionism implicit in Norwegian and Swedish co-operation in the Augustana Synod, but at the end of a decade the Norwegian minority rose up to secede from their Swedish colleagues.[55] Secession is a familiar phenomenon among the Scandinavian Lutherans in America.

Meanwhile, important developments had taken place among the more conservative Norwegian Lutherans. The irrepressible Dietrichson plunged into activity at Koshkonong after his return from Norway in 1846. He had been aware of the need for a synodical organization even before his departure for Norway, but such a step seemed to wait upon new ministerial recruits.[56] Dietrichson, with Clausen, in 1847 even considered the possibility of launching a Lutheran

[54] Quoted from *Kirkelig maanedstidende* (Decorah) by A. A. Stomberg, in "Early Efforts at Scandinavian Church Union in America," in Swedish Historical Society of America, *Year-book,* 1923–24, p. 17, 18 (St. Paul).

[55] Stephenson, *Religious Aspects,* ch. 13; and *Augustana Synod.*

[56] Dietrichson, *Reise,* 118.

seminary for the training of ministers, Clausen offering to guarantee a salary of two hundred dollars a year and to make some land available for a trained man from Norway who would undertake the task of organizing the institution and giving instruction.[57] The plan did not materialize, but in 1848 another university-trained clergyman, Hans A. Stub, arrived in America to take over the ministry at Muskego, and he joined Dietrichson and Clausen in a call for a general meeting in the spring of 1849 to frame a constitution for the proposed synod.[58] A tinge of Grundtvigianism in the call, and a fear, evident particularly at Muskego, that Dietrichson had in mind the initiation of a state-church episcopal system occasioned a lay reluctance to participate in this move, and it proved abortive.[59]

In 1850 Dietrichson took his departure for Norway, never to return to the emigrant scene.[60] That year witnessed, however, the arrival in the West of yet another Norwegian university product, Adolph C. Preus, who became the minister at Koshkonong and was destined to become the president of the Norwegian Synod. Preus, Stub, and Clausen now launched a new effort to organize on an intercongregational scale. It is an evidence of the growth of Norwegian-American Lutheranism that this effort took concrete form in

[57] A letter by Dietrichson, August 23, 1847, discusses the plan for a theological seminary. *Nordlyset* (Trondhjem), November 19, 1847.

[58] Bergh, *Den norsk lutherske kirkes historie*, 63–65, gives the text of the call issued in April, 1849, by the three ministers. A letter by Stub, written from Muskego on August 21, 1848, tells of his first impressions of America, and more particularly of the situation at Muskego, where he found two divided parties. One group feared that the ministers were trying to set up a Catholic establishment among the Wisconsin Norwegians, and Stub therefore decided that the best policy was to set aside the Dietrichson congregational organization and make a new start in the hope of uniting both factions. His letter is in *Stavanger amtstidende og adresseavis*, October 24, 28, 1848. This letter occasioned a criticism by Clausen, and Stub therefore published a much fuller version of the story in a letter of April 16, 1851, in the same newspaper for July 18, 22, 25, 29, August 1, 5, 1851. Dietrichson, in turn, replied to Stub on September 16, 1851.

[59] Rohne, *Norwegian American Lutheranism*, 113.

[60] Dietrichson's *Nogle ord fra prædikestolen i Amerika og Norge*, published in Stavanger in 1851, includes the texts of three sermons that he delivered in the Middle West.

a meeting early in January, 1851, attended by delegates from some eighteen or nineteen congregations. Despite the agreement of these delegates upon a constitution for the "Norwegian Evangelical Lutheran Church in America," as they called the new body, the synodical seas were treacherous. The church's doctrine, taken over from the departed Dietrichson, was defined as that revealed through the Word of God "in our baptismal covenant," together with the canonical books of the Old and New Testaments interpreted in accordance with the historic creeds, the unaltered Augsburg Confession, and Luther's Small Catechism. This definition foundered, because of the phrase "in our baptismal covenant," upon the reef of Grundtvigianism. In the proceedings as a whole the lay group was wary of decisions that seemed to point toward clerical dominance, with the Muskego forces openly hostile. The shadow of Dietrichson lay over this frontier church convention. When Clausen, always intimate with lay feeling, later defended the constitution as adopted, he felt obliged to stress the point that, in his judgment, sufficient guards had been set up against pastoral arbitrariness. Historically, it is not so much the guards, as the fear of such arbitrariness on the part of laymen, that take on significance. Eielsen, viewing the development from the outside, naturally pounced upon the Grundtvigianism in the definition of doctrine.[61]

The decisive factor in undoing the labors of the convention of 1851 and reshaping the movement toward synodical organization was the arrival in the Norwegian-American world of three additional pastors from Norway, all trained at the Norwegian national university, all responsive to tendencies that had asserted themselves in the university under the leadership of such inspiring teachers as Gisle Johnson and

[61] *Democraten,* December 5, 1850; *Christiania-posten,* April 25, 1851; Bergh, *Den norsk lutherske kirkes historie,* ch. 11, 12; Rohne, *Norwegian American Lutheranism,* 112–116.

C. P. Caspari. These men, all immigrants of 1851, were Herman A. Preus, who went to a pastorate at Spring Prairie that lasted more than forty years; Nils O. Brandt, who established himself in the Pine Lake area of Wisconsin, and Gustav F. Dietrichson, who took over the Luther Valley call upon the withdrawal of Clausen.[62] Preus, "orthodox to the finger-tips," always concerned primarily about "pure doctrine," a grim debater and fighter to whom most things were either black or white, was to become the president of the Norwegian Synod for a generation after the retirement in 1862 of the gentler A. C. Preus. "We must rejoice when we are condemned as being hard-hearted, intolerant, and unchristian," H. A. Preus exclaimed in the late 1850's in a tone that reminds one of the belligerents in the theological wars of Puritan New England. He welcomed charges of intolerance and exclusiveness, for "truth must be exclusive over against falsehood and error, light over against darkness."[63]

The leadership of H. A. Preus emerged early in 1852, when the action of 1851 was reconsidered by a general church meeting held at Muskego. The newly arrived pastors, all anti-Grundtvigian, remained aloof until the meeting had accepted a motion to regard the action of 1851 as merely preliminary: in a word, to clear the road for a new start. Then they joined the deliberations, which now included a half dozen pastors and men from twenty-one congregations. The Grundtvigian phrase in the definition of doctrine was stricken; the problem of possible affiliation with the Joint Ohio Synod was examined but deferred; the school problem was briefly defined; resolutions looking toward the promotion of spirituality among the church members were adopted, one adjuring them to avoid "night-hawking, public dancing parties, gambling parties, drinking bouts, cursing, swearing,

[62] Norlie, *Norsk lutherske prester,* 97, 98. On Brandt, a remarkable "traveling missionary," see Ylvisaker, *Eminent Pioneers,* 53–64.

[63] Quoted from *Kirkelig maanedstidende* in Rohne, *Norwegian American Lutheranism,* 163.

sabbath breaking, etc." — a Puritan note that Eielsen himself might have sounded.[64] The completion of synodical organization, however, was left to the year 1853, when further changes in the constitution were adopted and the instrument was submitted to, and approved by, the congregations. Thus the Norwegian Synod officially dates its founding from 1853. It is of interest to note that Clausen in the 1852 meeting tried to promote the cause of a broad Norwegian-American Lutheran union and that subsequently a conference was held with Eielsen at which both sides agreed that the "suspicion, hate, and quarreling" that had taken place were unchristian and destructive. As neither side offered any compromise on basic matters of doctrine and religious viewpoint, such an agreement was little more than an amenity, and Eielsen had no compunctions about returning to the assault.[65]

Before the move toward organization reached its climax in 1853, yet another Norwegian university-trained clergyman cast his lot with the immigrants. This was Jakob Aall Ottesen, one of Brandt's contemporaries at the Christiania university from 1844 to 1849 and thereafter for three years a teacher in a Norwegian Latin school. Like H. A. Preus, he was a tenacious controversialist and grimly purposeful leader. He joined the two Preuses, Clausen, Stub, G. F. Dietrichson, and Brandt in the meeting beginning on February 5, 1853, at East Koshkonong to work out final changes in the synodical constitution. After its acceptance by the congregations, it was adopted at a meeting in the Luther Valley church held from October 3 to 7, 1853.

The basic enactments of the Norwegian Evangelical Lutheran Church in America — usually spoken of as the Norwegian Synod, or the Synod — reflect faithfully the general

[64] Rohne reviews the events of this meeting in *Norwegian American Lutheranism*, 118–124.

[65] According to Bergh, *Den norsk lutherske kirkes historie*, 90, Eielsen and his friends took the initiative in this effort of 1852 toward a better understanding. A second conference, in 1855, dealt more fundamentally with questions of differences in doctrine.

position of the high-church Lutheran orthodoxy. The confessional stand remains that of 1851, with the omission of the Grundtvigian phrase about the baptismal covenant. The Dano-Norwegian ritual and altar book are accepted. The polity is synodical-presbyterian, with a synod, the highest authority within the church, occurring every alternate year. No one not properly examined, rightly called, and ordained is a clergyman. The synod shall establish rules, general and special, in "religious-ecclesiastical matters," choose a president from the ranks of the pastors and a church council of six members, evenly divided between clergymen and laymen. The local congregations have the right to regulate their internal affairs with the condition that their acts shall not run counter to the synodical constitution and enactments. A pastor cannot admit anyone to a congregation save upon satisfactory testimonial from a former pastor, acceptance of the church doctrine, and submission to its order. The parish concept of the congregation is implied in a provision that a clergyman shall not administer the Lord's Supper to any newcomer if he has been a resident within the parish for more than a year without becoming a member of the congregation. It should be noted, however, that denial of communion was authorized in cases of persons "willingly and with delight" living "in one or more vices or sins of malice." Every congregation was enjoined to "establish and maintain religious schools." Baptism by persons not recognized as "properly examined, called, and ordained pastors" could not henceforth be acknowledged; and the doctrine of conversion after death — a Grundtvigian tenet — was branded as "erroneous and dangerous."[66]

The problem of lay preaching, which bulked so large in the ideology of Eielsen and his followers, was discussed through-

[66] Dr. Rohne translates the constitution, bylaws, and synodical decisions in his *Norwegian American Lutheranism,* 129–134. On the founding of the Norwegian Synod, see also Halvor Halvorsen, ed., *Festskrift til den norske synodes jubilæum 1853–1903,* 41–78 (Decorah, 1903).

out the decade within the Synod ranks, especially in the late 1850's, and resulted in a formulation of standpoint in 1862 in the characteristic fashion of a series of theses. These theses, which constituted a synodical decision, may be summed up briefly: the office of the public ministry is instituted by God, who has not instituted any other order for the "public edification" of Christians; the act of leading public edification is an exercise of the public ministry; it is "sin when anyone without a call or in the absence of need undertakes this"; in the case of real need, however, anyone who can exercise the office of public ministry in proper Christian order has both the right and the duty to do so. The Synod defined this need, or emergency, as the absence of a pastor; or the presence of a falsely teaching pastor or of a pastor who could not serve the people "sufficiently."[67]

While the Norwegian Synod thus was defining its doctrine and creating a compact organization, its strength was recruited by several additional ministers from Norway who made notable contributions to its leadership. One of these was Ulrik Vilhelm Koren, who was born in Bergen in 1826, studied at the university in Christiania from 1844 to 1852, taught briefly in a Latin school, and emigrated to America in 1853 to serve the Norwegian congregations in the vicinity of Decorah, in northeastern Iowa. It is a remarkable fact that three university-trained clerical immigrants who arrived in the United States from 1850 to 1853 gave the Norwegian Synod its presidents for the sweep of years from 1853 to 1910. They were A. C. Preus, the pioneer president, from 1853 to 1862; H. A. Preus, president in the critical generation from 1862 to 1894; and Koren, whose term ran from 1894 to 1910. Koren was urbane and scholarly, a church statesman, the "chief literary defender and expounder" of the Synod's "aims and ideals."[68] His wife, Elisabeth Koren, typified

[67] The theses, published in *Kirkelig maanedstidende* in 1862, are conveniently translated in Rohne, *Norwegian American Lutheranism,* 178.

[68] Rohne, *Norwegian American Lutheranism,* 128.

the contribution made to American life by the wives of the frontier Norwegian-American clergymen. She made a humble log-cabin parsonage a place of grace and beauty, a cultural center. Sensitive, gentle, deeply interested in the people her husband served, a lady of fine traditions and influence, she left a distinct mark upon immigrant life in the West.[69]

Other Norwegian university men who sought ministerial service in the West during the 1850's included Olaus F. Duus, stationed at Waupaca and Whitewater, Wisconsin, from 1854 to 1859; Johan Storm Munch, at Wiota and Dodgeville from 1855 to 1859; and Peter M. Brodahl, an immigrant of 1855 who served no fewer than twenty-one congregations radiating out from Black Earth, Wisconsin. All three, like Dietrichson, returned permanently to Norway after some years on the American frontier. There were also Fredrik C. Claussen, an immigrant of 1857 who went to Spring Grove, Minnesota, and with that community as a center served some thirteen congregations; Claus F. Magelssen, who assumed the Orfordville, Wisconsin, charge in 1859; and Bernt J. Muus, who established himself in Goodhue County, Minnesota, in 1859. Muus, a nephew of the famed Ole Rynning, attended the national university of Norway from 1849 to 1854, taught in his native country for two years, and for a time served as the editor of the important *Norsk kirketidende*. He was a man of extraordinary drive and energy, undertook to serve as many as twenty-eight congregations on the Minnesota frontier, interested himself deeply in the problem of religious education, and like so many of the pioneer ministers had a talent for the rough-and-tumble of controversy, in which he neither gave nor asked for quarter.[70]

[69] See Mrs. Koren's classic *Fra pioneertiden.*

[70] Brief biographies of these clergymen may be found in Norlie, *Norsk lutherske prester.*

None of the Norwegian university men of the 1850's possessed greater ability or exercised a deeper influence upon the Norwegian Americans than Laur. Larsen, who with a background of five years as a university student in the university at Christiania arrived in 1857 at the frontier pastorate of Rush River, Wisconsin. He and his wife, city-bred and of gentle traditions, adjusted themselves competently to the life of a pioneer rural community. Larsen developed a small farm about his parsonage; went on long missionary journeys; oriented himself to the New World by reading such papers and magazines as the *New York Tribune*, *Emigranten*, *Maanedstidende*, and the Missouri Synod's *Lehre und Wehre;* served his people with complete devotion; had a driving passion for purity of Lutheran doctrine; and inevitably became prominent in the councils of the Synod.

The vast growth of Norwegian-American life and the rapid spread of settlement presented a challenge to Norwegian-American church leadership. It was plainly not being met by efforts to persuade Norwegian university men to go to the West. It is true that some fifteen or more graduates of the Norwegian university had gone to America in the early period, and it is equally true that they had a remarkable influence upon Norwegian-American Lutheranism; but in general Norwegian theologians were reluctant to emigrate. Not a few of those who did returned to Norway; indeed, in the sweep of time, of sixty-one Norwegian Synod clergymen who got their training in the Christiania university, thirty returned to their native land after spending more or less time in American service. Those who remained were not enough. It was no uncommon thing for one minister to serve from a half dozen to twenty different congregations because of the shortage of clergymen. Pioneer leaders like Clausen, Dietrichson, Paul Andersen, and Elling Eielsen understood that some plan must be worked out for the training of a ministry in America if the challenge was to be met with effectiveness.

Laur. Larsen, too, grasped the problem with realistic understanding; and when the Norwegian Synod turned to the Missouri Synod for aid in solving it, it was Larsen who was selected by the Norwegian church body to be its representative on the faculty of Concordia Seminary in St. Louis, to aid in training Norwegian young men for leadership in the immigrant churches.

The hope of stimulating a migration of Norwegian-trained ministers to America was not abandoned. In fact, Larsen himself went to Norway in 1860 to try to recruit ministers, and one appeal after another was broadcast in Norway with the purpose of enlisting young men who had enjoyed the advantages of theological training in the national university of that country. But the Norwegian Americans, like the Swedish Americans, were coming to a realization of the patent fact that they would have to depend upon themselves not only for trained ministers but also for instrumentalities of higher education in general. When the move toward a system of higher education took form and Luther College was established, Larsen was the natural choice for president of that institution. That office, which he held from 1861 to 1902, was a strategic eminence from which he exerted leadership among the Norwegian Americans.[71]

So in the 1850's the Norwegian Synod, pioneered by educated leaders representing the best theological training available in the home country, presented to the western world the front of an organized and growing body. If Eielsen, in organizing his followers in 1846 caught faithfully the spirit of the low-church movement, the Synod leaders of 1853, not less faithfully, caught that of the high-church orthodoxy. Both represented transfers of ecclesiastical structure and

[71] Karen Larsen, *Laur. Larsen: Pioneer College President* (Northfield, 1936); and " The Adjustment of a Pioneer Pastor to American Conditions: Laur. Larsen, 1857–1880," in *Studies and Records,* 4:1–14. Halvorsen lists the sixty-one Norwegian Synod clergymen who were trained in the Christiania university. Halvorsen, *Festskrift,* 123, 124.

religious spirit from Norway to America. Both synods were rooted in tendencies that had developed in the Old World, but both inevitably represented a transition to the New. Like every other aspect of immigrant life in America, the migration of idea and spirit across the Atlantic led to subtle processes of change. The Norwegian Synod did indeed transfer the ritual and ceremonies of the state church of Norway; it set up a general organization which dominated the local; it staked out a parish concept of the congregation; it allotted a place of high importance and responsibility to the pastor; and it emphasized orthodoxy — pure doctrine — with a rigor that led an acute critic of a later time to suggest that it was in effect a substitute for the law that had accompanied the church in a state-church land.[72]

Yet, with the possible exception of zealots like Dietrichson, the Synod leaders and vigilant laymen well knew that they were not transferring the state church itself to America. They realized that in a country of separation between state and church and on a frontier whose watchwords were democracy and freedom, there would inevitably be changes, differences, modifications, new developments. What they sought was to combine the familiar liturgy and traditional principles of Norwegian Lutheranism with the development of a free church on American soil, retaining a high-church motif. Lay preaching was as nearly excluded as they felt it could be. Yet, facing the conditions of the frontier West, they could not wholly exclude it. They made a place for emergency, but they could not accept Eielsen's broad concept of emergency, which embraced the entire complex of conditions in which the Norwegian immigrants in America found themselves.

The Norwegian Americans witnessed a sharp issue between high- and low-church thinking, between the Norwegian

[72] Georg Sverdrup, "Den norsk lutherske kirke i Amerika," in Andreas Helland, ed., *Samlede skrifter i udvalg,* 1:223 (Minneapolis, 1909).

Synod and Eielsen's Synod, with a middle way opened by Paul Andersen and the Synod of Northern Illinois, and with a multitude of paths leading toward the American churches. In the controversies between the Norwegian and Eielsen's synods, the protagonists on both sides were sincere, devout, deadly in earnest, oftentimes bitter. What they could not grasp was the fact that the world of the Norwegian immigrant was big enough for both views. The one was both spur and check to the other. The lay fight against the state-church pastoral concept probably meant ultimately a more democratic clergy. The Synod emphasis upon education and a powerful clergy looked toward cultural leadership, a more civilized church. With the great union of Norwegian Lutheran forces in 1917, the right of lay preaching was vindicated; but in the long meantime a system of education for ministers, not in Norway but among the Norwegians in the United States, had become a reality. The milieu and emergency that lent contemporary force to Eielsen's contention had disappeared. Eielsen's theory triumphed as the Synod leaders' practice became virtually universal.[73]

Both the Haugean concept of the congregation and the geographical, or parish, idea have played roles in Norwegian-American Lutheranism, with modifications on both sides, though trends of historical development have perhaps moved in the general direction of the former. The persistent struggle for low-church ideals left deep marks upon the church, with the ultimate result that the Norwegian-American high church

[73] The right of lay preaching ultimately triumphed in Norway, also. See Mons O. Wee, *Haugeanism*, 64–66 (St. Paul, 1919). Eielsen, defender of the doctrine of lay preaching, was by no means opposed to the training of preachers. As early as 1854, in a meeting of his own synod, he moved "that a seminary be erected where young men who are gifted and Christian-minded could be trained to be parochial teachers as well as preachers, and where they could receive instruction in the branches most necessary for the proper performance of these offices." The seminary thus proposed was established at Lisbon, Illinois, in 1855, with Rasmussen at its head, and it ranks "as the first educational venture of its kind among Norwegians in America." J. Magnus Rohne, ed., "Report of the Annual Meeting of the Haugean Churches Held at Lisbon, Illinois, in June, 1854," in *Studies and Records*, 4:19, 24, 33.

was relatively low as compared with high-churchism in other Lutheran churches. There was a place in immigrant life for the dignity and beauty of the Synod service as well as for the personalism that sprang from the Haugean view. Both sides were Puritan; both struck sharply and persistently at the frivolities and vices of the times; but probably the Synod philosophy was more tolerant toward the transplanted traditional culture, the lore and music and folk custom brought from the Norwegian valleys to the Middle West, than was the Eielsen school. Immigrant life had need of all the cultural richness inherent in song and tale and dance and amusements fashioned through centuries of history, for the immigrant's struggle to subdue frontiers, like that of the native American, was carried on to the accompaniment of cultural loss.

If the most striking contrasts appear between the Norwegian and Eielsen's synods, the tendency represented by Paul Andersen, the Synod of Northern Illinois, and the Augustana Synod was not less important than either, pointing as it did toward a more moderate position which drew certain values from both sides and which at the same time made some contact with American Lutheranism. Lutheran unionism as tried under the leadership of such men as Esbjörn and Andersen, however, proved an empty dream. The experiment of a synodical union that rose above lines of nationality and language failed. The move in the direction of American Lutheran liberalism foundered. Not only did the Swedes and Norwegians secede from the general coalition, but even their effort at co-operation among themselves was defeated by the divisive force of nationality. The movement was foundational in Swedish-American Lutheranism, however, and it also projected itself significantly into Norwegian-American Lutheranism.

How deep the issues in the theological controversies and experiments in the 1840's and 1850's were is evidenced by the fact that most of the subsequent church development among the Norwegian Lutherans in America is rooted in this period. The tendency represented by Andersen led directly to the Norwegian-Danish Augustana Synod and the Conference of the Norwegian-Danish Evangelical Lutheran Church in America, both launched in 1870. Eielsen's Synod led to Hauge's Synod of 1875, though Eielsen himself continued the synod that bore his name. The Norwegian Synod continued as the church body of the majority for several decades, but it was divided in 1887, when the issue of predestination, largely generated by the affiliation with the German Missouri Synod, resulted in the secession of a group of fifty-five ministers known as the Anti-Missourian Brotherhood. The 1880's witnessed a notable union movement, and in 1890 the Anti-Missourians, the Conference, and the Norwegian Augustana Synod joined hands, forming the United Norwegian Lutheran Church in America. This union, in turn, was jolted when in 1897 one group organized the Lutheran Free Church, in principle a federation of free congregations. This resulted primarily from a clash between two viewpoints which had been held in the Conference — the so-called old tendency and the new, the latter led and interpreted by Georg Sverdrup and Sven Oftedal and centering in the Minneapolis theological school and college, Augsburg Seminary. Meanwhile a more inclusive movement of union slowly developed through two decades, eventuating in 1917 in a coalition of the Norwegian Synod, the United church, and Hauge's Synod. Thus many of the tendencies that had hitherto expressed themselves along separate lines were merged in one great body — the Norwegian Lutheran Church in America.[74]

The very storms and turbulence of Norwegian-American Lutheranism probably account for the fact that the Norwe-

[74] For brief reviews of Norwegian-American Lutheranism, see E. K. Johnsen, in O. M. Norlie, *Norsk lutherske menigheter i Amerika 1843–1916*, 1:28–40 (Minneapolis, 1918), and Andreas Helland, *Augsburg Seminar gjennem femti aar 1869–1919*, 9–23 (Minneapolis, 1920).

gians in greater degree than the Swedes have retained their Lutheran faith in America. The Swedish Americans greatly outnumber their Norwegian-American brethren, yet approximately twice as many Norwegians as Swedes are members of the Lutheran church in America. The Norwegians have had, from first to last, no fewer than fourteen separate Lutheran synods, whereas the Swedes, following the experimental stage of the Synod of Northern Illinois, have had only one — the Augustana Synod. The Norwegians broke into camps and factions; the Swedes, though they were by no means lacking in intrasynodical controversy, stood essentially united. Often within a single community a Norwegian immigrant could make his choice of church affiliation among three or four Norwegian Lutheran churches, whereas the Swede who did not find himself content to join an Augustana Synod congregation could not find any Lutheran alternative unless he crossed the boundaries of language. The theological contentiousness of the Norwegians created a diversity within the general framework of the organized Lutheran church which tended to accommodate a similar diversity of individual religious attitude and impulse and gave liberal scope to combative fervor.

The frontier era was marked by significant beginnings, the laying of foundations, rapid growth. Its atmosphere was that of flux, movement, transition. Both then and later there was no little crossing of church boundaries as men engaged in the quest for a churchly haven. The dynamic and eloquent Peter A. Rasmussen, for example, began as a follower of Elling Eielsen, crossed to the Norwegian Synod, seceded from that body as an Anti-Missourian, and ultimately found haven in the United Norwegian Lutheran church. The immigrant lived in a world of religious freedom, and this meant fundamentally freedom of choice. He was free to choose not only among the various tendencies and organizations that sought to interpret Lutheran Christianity, but also among Methodist, Baptist, Quaker, Mormon, Episcopalian, and other American churches that held out kindly hands, with offers of help and fellowship in meeting and solving the baffling problems of religion and life. He could travel the road to Rome if Catholicism answered his need. He could join the Norwegian colony of Moravians in Wisconsin, following the leadership of such men as Nils Otto Tank and A. M. Iverson, if he found himself in sympathy with the ideals that Count Zinzendorf had put into practice at Herrnhut.[75] He could go the way of Unitarianism, as did the brilliant preacher and writer, Kristofer Janson. He could turn away from the church, eschewing all connection with organized religion, as did Marcus Thrane, the pioneer labor leader of Norway, who after the collapse of his labor movement found haven in America, there as in his native land inspired by a vision of social justice. For one of the glories of the immigrant was that he shared in the American heritage of genuine religious freedom.

[75] A brief account of the Norwegian-American Moravian enterprise is presented in Blegen, *Norwegian Migration*, 335, 336. See also Hjalmar R. Holand's interesting account of "Ephraim: A Venture in Communism," in his *Old Peninsula Days*, 86–108 (Ephraim, Wisconsin, 1934).

VI. ASPECTS OF EVERYDAY LIFE

THE IRREPRESSIBLE Frithjof Meidell in the 1850's recorded the arrival at Springfield, Illinois, of "thirty pieces of Norwegian beef, enveloped in homespun and sacking." The shipment, he explained, consisted of "humans of both sexes, all very redolent of *gammelost, spegemat,* and other such national delicacies."[1] If the Norwegian immigrants thus presented a droll sight to a fellow Norwegian, they were even more droll to Americans. They themselves were quickly conscious of the differences between their garb and that of the people among whom they had cast their lot. The result was a combat between thrift and vanity, and usually vanity won. The immigrants faced what the ironical Thorstein Veblen was later to describe as "the need of conforming to established usage, and of living up to the accredited standard of taste and reputability."[2]

Many immigrants arrived in America well-provided with clothing, but innumerable letters from the New World ad-

[1] A letter dated June, 1853, in *Aftenbladet,* May 29, 1855. Though unsigned, it is clearly by Frithjof Meidell.

[2] *Theory of the Leisure Class,* 168 (New York, 1899).

vised them that they were facing an inevitable transition in their style of dress as well as in other matters. They were warned that American freight was expensive, trunks and boxes awkward to handle, and the American climate different from the Norwegian. "Cloth and clothes can be bought here just as well as in Norway," was the pithy comment of one letter; and another said, "A newcomer can immediately be detected by his garb, and since newcomers are regarded with very little esteem, all of them proceed at once to buy clothes of an American cut."[3]

The warning was particularly emphatic when addressed to women. "The women had better take as few of their clothes with them as possible, since they won't do here in America at all," wrote an immigrant in 1850. "Women's clothes are entirely different here. The men folks can bring their clothes with them; it is practicable for every adult to take a good chest with him and each grown woman would be wise in taking a spinning wheel with her."[4] In the 1840's another immigrant wrote that women who intended to go into domestic service should have only the clothes that were necessary for the trip, for upon entering American homes they would be required to wear American dress.[5]

For those who took such advice, the problem was quickly met if they had money with which to buy new clothes or if they immediately found work; but many fell upon hard times and soon regretted their lack of comfortable and warm Norwegian clothing. Some, in fact, suffered intensely from the cold of their first American winter, especially if that winter happened to be 1843–44 and if they lived at Muskego. There Americans of the vicinity took up a collection of food and

[3] Ole Olsen Johnsgaarden, January 28, 1853, in *Arbeider-foreningernes blad,* July 16, 1853; and *Aftenbladet,* May 29, 1855.

[4] Knut Bertelsen Skeie to his brother, 1850, an original manuscript in the possession of O. O. Stene, Norheimsund, Norway. The Norwegian-American Historical Association has a transcript.

[5] Trond Knutson Bakketun to his family, Chicago, January 23, 1844, quoted in Rene, *Historie om udvandringen fra Voss,* 256.

clothing for the relief of the needy. Søren Bache records that though many of the immigrants "had land aplenty, they lacked the necessities." Clausen, the minister, and a visiting artist whose name was Th. Lund supervised the distribution. "Some of the finest clothes," Bache remarks in his diary, "were sold for the money they would bring and the money then used to buy necessities like beef and pork, since such fine clothes were of no use to people of the working class; they need things that are more durable."[6]

As time went on the tone of many of the America letters changed with reference to Norwegian clothing. The hard times following the panic of 1857 and the stress of the Civil War undoubtedly had something to do with the shift of emphasis. A practical farmer's wife, Mrs. Ole Svendsen, gave some advice in 1863 to those contemplating emigration. "No one emigrating from Norway ought to sell everything he has, the way the majority do," she said, "because everything that is useful in Norway is also useful here. Women could well bring their clothes with them, with the exception of their headdress, bodices, jackets, and kerchiefs — those they might as well sell — but their other clothes can be made over and used here, for Norwegian things are much better than anything you can buy here."[7]

The feeling that American-made clothes were inferior to Norwegian was common in many Norwegian-American circles, especially in small towns and outlying rural sections, where the available local wares were of poor quality and offered almost no selection. In time the mail-order houses were to release the immigrants from their dependence upon the local store, but meanwhile there was much dissatisfaction and grumbling. The American habit of buying clothing ready-made did not at first commend itself to the immigrants,

[6] Bache Diary, January 10, 12, 1844.

[7] See a letter, probably written in 1863, from Mrs. Svendsen to her family, Nielsen Papers.

who preferred the Norwegian system of having things made to order at home. Olaus Duus, the Wisconsin frontier minister, sharply condemned the American system. "One rarely finds shoemakers here," he wrote, "since all shoes are bought ready-made in the shops and are seldom repaired because that is expensive and the material is often poor. Shoes are usually manufactured in the eastern states and always by machine. A pair of shoes that would cost three specie dollars at home costs from $4.00 to $4.50 here. Nineteen-twentieths of all men's clothing are also bought ready-made in the shops and they too are machine-made. A sewing machine in operation is a very interesting sight. All these clothes have a strong tendency to wear out in the course of a single summer, and ragged Yankees are therefore a very common sight. Go to a Yankee's house and you will be sure to see a tattered object working around, chopping wood, milking, or doing some such chores. Look at his clothes and you will rarely find him except out at the elbow and in rags and patches."[8]

Disapproval of the quality of American goods led many immigrants to order clothes direct from Norway. This practice was too expensive and time-consuming to be followed on a large scale, but often prospective emigrants were asked to take some extra baggage with them. Requests for woolen cloth and yarn were frequent, for American wool was regarded as shoddy. Immigrants especially wanted Norwegian socks, notwithstanding the patient industry with which immigrant wives plied their knitting needles. "Homespun is a very practical thing to take along," wrote an immigrant to his brother in Norway. "The price of homespun here is a half dollar an ell. Socks are a dollar and a half a pair. My dear brother, since it is a case of one for all and all for one, if you can possibly manage it, won't you bring us from twenty to thirty ells of homespun? I'll pay back whatever it costs you. I'd also like to have you bring us each four pairs of

[8] Duus to his parents, December 4, 1856, Duus Papers.

suspenders. I'll pay for those, too. You had better take enough homespun for yourselves also, as well as suspenders, if you can afford it."[9] Duus likewise appealed to his relatives in Norway: "I do hope you will find it possible to send me some black cloth for a coat and trousers as well as some duffel for an overcoat. I am buying myself out of house and home trying to keep in clothes here; the cloth is the worst shoddy and never lasts. Perhaps for thirty dollars I can buy a *bonjour* here that I could get for fourteen at home. Last fall I paid eighteen dollars for one, but I was convinced from the very start that the cloth was nothing more than a mixture of cotton and wool. The same thing was true of an overcoat that I bought which lasted only from six to eight months. The cloth was of blue thread which ran one way and some shoddy that ran the other. I also wish you would send me a good woolen dress for Sophie, for what you buy here is just trash."[10] When occasionally a box arrived from Norway, Duus and his family were delighted: "Many thanks for the lovely socks; they are 'indeed first rate' and my old ones were dangerously near to falling off. Mamma's dress fits beautifully and all the shoes as well, except mine, which are a little tight. The children's clothes fit very well, too, and do the Duuses credit. I must say that Olaf looks very fine in his velvet blouse."[11]

As time went on, however, most of the immigrants discontinued their orders to Norway and accepted the clothes they could get in America. Farmers and artisans wore jeans and work shirts in the summer. In the winter, corduroy pants and sheepskin coats, in conjunction with native red flannels, kept them warm. Their wardrobes might be rounded out by a suit of "store clothes" for Sundays and holidays. Occasionally they might have fur coats made from

[9] Skeie to his brother, 1850.

[10] Duus to his father, March 31, 1858, Duus Papers.

[11] Duus to his father, October 14, 1857. See also letters dated July 9 and December 29, 1857, Duus Papers.

Norwegian pelts. Thus Assor Naesbo " sewed black fur coats both for Ole and my brother out of the pelts Svend brought with him," reported Mrs. Svendsen in 1871.[12] Ulrik Koren, the pioneer minister, bought a large buffalo robe in Wisconsin for use on cold winter rides. Warm footgear for winter wear was a source of some worry. The Korens and their neighbors met the problem by drawing buffalo-skin boots over their shoes.[13]

Except in the larger cities, women's clothing tended to fall to a drab utilitarian level. Picturesque native costumes, with their touch of bright color, were largely abandoned. It was an unusual sight that led Mrs. Koren to observe that " Ingrid, a pretty, brisk peasant woman . . . has continued to wear a part of her national costume." [14] The elaborate and gay costumes, reminiscent of traditional folkways in Norwegian valleys, were laid aside in immigrant chests, to be brought out from the sanctity of moth balls on special occasions only. In later years, especially after the *bygdelags* became active, these costumes were donned for merry folk dances and gala entertainments. Some of them, in modern times, found their way into the collections of historical museums.

Native frocks were replaced by Mother Hubbard wrappers, protected by bountiful aprons tied around the waist. For festive occasions homemade dresses, not always well cut, rarely dainty, but usually carefully sewed, were the rule. Often they were the product of the women's own spinning wheels and looms, though gradually, manufactured materials tended to replace the handmade. The favorite materials were wool and linen, but cottons — ginghams, calicoes, percales — rapidly came into their own. The American tendency toward cotton was lamented by Mrs. Svendsen, who emphati-

[12] Mrs. Svendsen to her parents, May 18, 1871, Nielsen Papers.
[13] Koren, *Fra pioneertiden,* 206.
[14] *Fra pioneertiden,* 101.

cally preferred wool and linen. Sewing machines found their way into the immigrant homes shortly after they came on the market, and ready-made patterns were early adopted.

"Our women were rarely beautiful," wrote Laurence M. Larson, recalling pioneer scenes in Iowa. "What they might have been, with greater care given to the needs of the body and the selection of clothing, cannot be known; but economic and religious ideals forbade much attention to these matters. Cosmetics were regarded with horror, as they were by nearly all the 'decent' women throughout the land; in the old country they served as the trade-mark of commercial immorality. No doubt the women of our neighborhood loved beautiful clothes; but their taste was primitive; their dresses were badly made and badly worn. Moreover, the plainer the costume, the more pleasing it was to the Almighty. We believed with the Preacher that all is vanity, and strove manfully to suppress the promotings of pride and all its related sins, especially when it appeared in other households." Professor Larson also recalls another aspect of dress: "The question of the feminine hat was for some years a disturbing problem in our settlement. The older women wore the Shaker bonnet in full confidence that it could not possibly have a sinful taint; in this view they were doubtless correct. The younger women wanted something different. To some of the more strenuous spirits in our neighborhood this craving was clear evidence of sinful inclinations. And so the conflict went on."[15]

Mrs. Koren, who came to America as a bride, had an ample trousseau on her arrival in Iowa. She was a beautiful woman, with a normal degree of vanity; clothes interested her; and yet her diary contains few references to her wardrobe or to those of her feminine parishioners. She was concerned about finding warm clothing for her husband and herself — her husband's overcoat (unfortunately lost on one

[15] Laurence M. Larson, *Log Book of a Young Immigrant,* 127 (Northfield, 1939).

of his parochial visits), rough-weather footgear, her own old brown coat (generous in size and used by Vilhelm as well as by herself). When her parishioners admired her clothes, she was pleased, but she had little to say about their garb. Her allusions were rather to the physical beauty or freshness of the women she met or to their manner and personality. She liked the custom, then in vogue in Europe, of wearing white caps, and she continued to employ such headgear until she was an old and venerable lady. She described Mrs. Preus — her good friend "Linka" in the years to come — as a "plump little young woman in a blue dress and a little white cap."[16]

Some of the *bønder,* both men and women, brought their wedding costumes with them. These elaborate habits, beautifully designed and handsomely embroidered, with lofty and exquisitely wrought crowns for the brides, became family treasures and were handed down from one generation to another. Some immigrant marriages were undoubtedly solemnized in the authentic manner of the Norwegian *bygd,* but family photographs in immigrant albums suggest that American wedding costumes soon became the vogue. Not until the end of the century did bridal veils become the rule. A Norwegian American of the younger generation recalled that "the women never tired of describing mother's beautiful wedding dress of green and white striped delaine with garlands of roses."[17]

Many Norwegian immigrants seem to have been horrified by the manner in which American women dressed. When Mrs. Koren was in New York, her hostess regaled her with tales: "Fru M[ølbach] told me about American ladies, how many of them, even though their husbands earn no more than Mølbach and though they have no maids — for they work and scrub for themselves — dress up in velvets and

[16] *Fra pioneertiden,* 72.

[17] Anna R. Hilleboe Christensen, "Wife and Mother: Gjertrud Rumohr Haug Hilleboe, 1833–1909," in Alma A. Guttersen and Regina H. Christensen, eds., *Souvenir "Norse-American Women," 1825–1925,* 32 (St. Paul, 1926).

silks and then promenade up and down Broadway. Their husbands see them only for brief visits since they rarely have their meals at home. She knew some, she said, who spend a thousand dollars a year for clothes, although they often have bedding and table linen that is hardly presentable."[18] The aristocratic Norwegian bride looked about her curiously on the train from Chicago to Milwaukee in 1853: "There sits a young lady dressed in silk from top to toe, with white kid gloves, who appears to be very much taken with herself and her costume. Her husband, however, doesn't look like much. Next to her sits a woman with a number of children and quite unconcernedly she is beginning to take down her hair. And such a variety of shoes as one sees, some are very small, narrow and highly polished, made to tread on velvet and silk; others are quite large with thick soles, whose owners ought to be forbidden to walk on these lovely carpets."[19]

The critical note of Mrs. Koren is echoed by Duus, who pictured a scene in a Yankee log cabin, where he found "an elegant woman sitting in a rocking chair, with a coiffure so elaborate that you might think *Lieblein* had curled it." She was "swinging her feet in the direction of the stove," which occupied the center of the floor, and was sewing on a bedspread or an ornament. She invited the visiting pastor to have a chair, but did not rise to greet him. In the midst of their conversation, she belched nonchalantly, to the embarrassment of her guest.[20] Frithjof Meidell also drew an unfavorable picture of the American woman, who, in his opinion, had "no taste in dress" save for expensive clothes, was lazy and rude, affected illness as a matter of fashion, and used rouge. "I must admit," he said, "that American women do look like angels; it may well be that the resemblance is heightened by all this daubing, for after all, in all

[18] *Fra pioneertiden,* 63, 64. The entry is dated November 30, 1853.
[19] *Fra pioneertiden,* 70.
[20] Duus to his parents, December 4, 1856, Duus Papers.

these blessed years, who has ever seen any except painted angels?"[21] Such opinions must, of course, be treated with due caution, for they were obviously based upon limited observation and were tainted with a nationalistic bias.

Norwegian servant girls and seamstresses seem to have been the first to succumb to the prevalent American fashions. From the beginning, they were the despair of Norwegian bachelors because of their financial independence. Their wages, ranging from a dollar to a dollar and a half a week, were considered fabulous. Norwegian girls were always in demand in American families by virtue of their cleanliness and industry. The ironical Meidell mocked them in his usual fashion. "You should see our Norwegian peasant and servant girls here! You wouldn't recognize them or believe your own eyes—that these lovely creatures have been transplanted from Norway's mountain crags!" At home, he said, they were flat-heeled, round-shouldered, clumsy; here they "trip about, their backs arched, with their parasols and their fans and their heads all enveloped in veils. Aase, Birthe, and Siri in an unbelievably short time are converted to Aline, Betsy, and Sarah," and they take pride in having "a little 'miss' before their names."[22] A susceptible bachelor wrote home in a despairing request for some pretty, unspoiled Norwegian girls: "I am sure you will laugh but, believe it or not, the servant girls have certainly come into their own here. The first Sunday after their arrival in America they still wear their usual old Norwegian clothes; the next Sunday, it's a new dress; the third, a hat, a parasol, a silk shawl, new clothes from top to toe." Naturally there was "an avalanche of boys" visiting them "nearly every evening."[23] Some of the young men tried to keep up with the pace set by

[21] *Aftenbladet,* May 29, 1855.

[22] *Aftenbladet,* May 29, 1855.

[23] Enewald Grude to S. T. Halland, April 27, 1855. Transcripts of the Halland manuscripts are in the possession of the Norwegian-American Historical Association.

the young women. "It certainly costs to keep one's self in clothes and lodging here," lamented one. "I bought myself a hat for five dollars, a pair of shoes, three dollars, a coat, sixteen dollars, and for a fine shirt I have to pay one dollar out of my earnings, which I fancy you will think a high price."[24]

Immigrant infants were first put into the cumbersome swaddling paraphernalia of the mid-century. Christening frocks, a yard or more in length, were usually made of fine cotton, batiste and the like, and occasionally, but rarely in the early period, of silk. A Dakota girl had a frock of fine crepe de Chine, simply made, but of prodigious length. The dress of girls and boys was conspicuous mainly for its discomfort. Up to the age of three or four, boys in well-to-do families wore velvets and silks with lace collars, and were hardly distinguishable from girls. Sunday dresses were long-bodiced or fell in full folds from tiny yokes. Those worn everyday were simple and conveniently short. Many of the children received dresses or dress goods from fond relatives in Norway. An immigrant woman, acknowledging in 1850 a dress that had been presented to her daughter, said, "She still has it in good condition and when it can no longer be used it will be put away as a remembrance of Uncle Perneman and Aunt Dorea in Norway."[25]

Youngsters were supplied with new clothes at least once a year, usually at Christmas.[26] A girl delivering her "piece" in a Christmas program naturally did not feel very happy unless she wore a new dress. All this meant, of course, hard work for the mother, whose task it was to card, spin, weave, and sew the clothes for her brood. Time, invention, pros-

[24] Elling Halland to his family, November 9, 1855.

[25] Henrietta Jessen to her sister, Eleonore Williamsin, February 20, 1850. The Norwegian-American Historical Association has a transcript of this letter, which is translated in full in the writer's documentary article, "Immigrant Women and the American Frontier," in *Studies and Records*, 5:22–26.

[26] Ylvisaker, *Eminent Pioneers*, 6.

perity, and "stores" lightened the work, but stalwarts like Mrs. Kari Veblen (one of whose numerous children was a boy named Thorstein) never complained, even when there were no short cuts. Pioneer mothers had few idle moments. They knitted much of the time, occasionally even while walking; and knitting was one of the few employments permitted during the solemn Twelfth-night period.[27]

Mrs. Svendsen reported how overjoyed she was when her husband's parents presented her six boys with entire sets of new home-tailored clothes — but the records do not reveal any elation on the part of the boys.[28] Even new suits for confirmation seem to have given growing boys chiefly a feeling of acute discomfort. Many young girls, however, lived for the day when confirmation finery would become a reality. Some wore the traditional black confirmation dress; occasionally there might be a gift of a white lace dress.[29] Others had to be contented with ordinary homemade products. Mrs. Koren's lace collar and cuffs provoked the admiration of one of her parishioners, who expressed a wish that her daughter might have similar adornments for her confirmation dress. "I promised that I would teach them how to make them," wrote the gentle and wise lady, "whereupon they were very contented." [30]

For most Norwegian immigrants the exigencies of pioneer life afforded small opportunity for personal adornment, yet tucked away in the immigrant chests were many specimens of Norwegian arts and handicrafts. Norwegians were fond of jewelry; and beautiful specimens, both of gold and of silver, were not uncommon. Breastpins, in particular, were treasured, some of them wrought of gold inlaid with enamel, others set with fine cameos. The most interesting, however, were the intricate and large silver or gold filigree brooches

[27] Ylvisaker, *Eminent Pioneers,* 7.
[28] Mrs. Svendsen to her parents, August 16, 1870, Nielsen Papers.
[29] Ylvisaker, *Eminent Pioneers,* 42.
[30] Koren, *Fra pioneertiden,* 117.

with spangles, designed to be worn with native folk costumes. Duus, almost always harsh in his criticism of things American, reflected a common suspicion of American jewelry when he wrote to Norway, "I'd like a solid gold brooch of a pretty pattern for Sophie, one that costs from six to seven specie dollars, since everything here is mere trash and soon falls to pieces, even though one has to pay about twice as much for it as one would at home."[31] Some of the treasure-trove of the immigrants was later garnered by museums. In the Norwegian-American Historical Museum at Decorah, for example, there are displays of exquisite laces, beautifully embroidered belts, Hardanger work used for aprons and blouses and for household ornaments, wool embroideries of colorful and striking designs, tapestries, handmade shoes and gloves, snuffboxes, wallets, pipes, and handsome canes. Such articles testify to a certain appreciation of beauty and of integrity of workmanship which was among the intangibles that the Norwegian immigrants carried with them across the ocean.

The absence of official uniforms in America impressed the immigrants. One letter writer interpreted this as an expression of American democracy. He took particular note of the fact that even the ministers in the American churches did not wear clerical garb.[32] "The same thing," he continued, "applies to judicial and other government officials. I have yet to see an official in a garb different from the ordinary. This puts everyone on the same footing, equally free and equally respected, whether he be official or peasant, merchant or artisan." On the other hand, many of the immi-

[31] Duus to his parents, December 29, 1857, Duus Papers. A. Sophie Bøe relates that her grandmother, before emigrating to America, sold two bridal crowns, one silver, a "precious old heirloom," and the other beaded. Anna Reque, she says, was an expert in needlework, noted for her "fine tatting and embroidery." *The Story of Father's Life (Rev. N. E. Bøe)*, 3, 30. A copy of this mimeographed work is in the library of the Minnesota Historical Society.

[32] A letter written at Milwaukee, July 19, 1853, in *Morgenbladet,* November 28, 1853.

grants felt a certain affection, perhaps nostalgic, for the clerical garb of their own Lutheran ministers. In the Synod churches the clergymen were careful to wear the traditional gowns and collars of their estate. One of Mrs. Koren's perplexing problems was that of packing Vilhelm's "prestekjole," and she was dismayed by the necessity of tucking it into her old brown greatcoat and throwing it over the saddle.[33] Duus, facing a dilemma, wrote urgently to his father in Norway for advice. Neither he nor his precious Sophie had mastered the art of starch-making—and as a consequence his clerical collar either sagged limply or threatened to lacerate his neck—and dignity.[34]

In the case of the Norwegian-American pioneer, clothes assuredly did not "make the man," but they played a role of no little importance in his everyday life; and the story of how he clothed himself, viewed in its social and economic aspects, helps one to understand the very human person who wore the clothes. As in immigrant life generally, the keynote in this story is transition. The day came when few would have agreed with the early and emphatic pronouncement of Mrs. Svendsen: "Norwegian clothes are preferable to any others, you may be sure. No matter how much you are inclined to find fault with Norway and to praise America, the fact remains that the Norwegian are the best."[35]

In matters of food, as in clothing, the immigrants had to adjust themselves to new and different ways. "When we arrived," writes N. N. Rønning, "accustomed as we were from childhood to our milk and porridge, our flat bread, *lefse,* and dried meat, we found none of these familiar Norwegian dishes."[36] The departure from the daily fare to which they

[33] Koren, *Fra pioneertiden,* 142, 156.
[34] Duus to his parents, January 8, 1856, Duus Papers.
[35] A letter of 1863 from Mrs. Svendsen to her parents, Nielsen Papers.
[36] *Bare for moro,* 24, 25 (Minneapolis, 1913).

were accustomed caused the newcomers a certain amount of mental, if not dyspeptic, confusion — and its concomitant, grumbling. The Muskego settlers, defending America against hostile criticisms, branded such grumbling as childish. "The discontent which was expressed by some of the immigrants at the beginning would be more becoming to children than to adults," they declared in their famous manifesto of 1845. They ridiculed complaints that many immigrants had missed "the sort of food that they were used to" and that "this or that article of food did not taste the same as it did at home."[37]

Undoubtedly many immigrants, facing the American frontier diet, fell back on their old Norwegian recipes, time-tested and adjusted to frugal ways. On the other hand, the records indicate that many others, enjoying an unaccustomed abundance of food, were believed to be undermining their digestive systems and making themselves prey to the vendors of patent medicines. "One must be temperate in food and drink," solemnly warned Johan Gasmann, the ship captain who journeyed to Wisconsin in the 1840's to observe conditions. "The large amount of pork which the Americans use is not good for people unaccustomed to such a heavy diet, and it is hardly healthful for the natives. At least, I have heard several Americans maintain that biliousness is often caused by the excessive eating of pork. It is not surprising that the American farmer gives his employees plenty of pork, for it costs him little and is a substantial food. Our farmers from the uplands think it is a fine food, but in a warm climate, used in excess, it is very injurious, especially when eaten without an abundance of vegetables."[38] Several immigrants echoed this distrust of

[37] *Morgenbladet,* April 1, 1845; Bache Diary, March 30, April 1, 1845.

[38] Captain Gasmann's narrative is conveniently translated by Qualey, in *Studies and Records,* 5:30–49. In the passage cited the writer has made a small correction in the translation. The document is printed in two Norwegian newspapers for 1845, and the writer has a transcript of the original text.

the American diet. "Food here is not the right sort for the newcomers," said Søren Bache, "since the usual food here is pork, beef, and wheat bread, whereas in Norway they were accustomed to coarse rye bread, milk, and cheese."[39] And in the 1850's Frithjof Meidell declared that the "good food" in America was responsible for much sickness. "When a poor Norwegian mountaineer arrives here and stuffs his porridge-and-flatbread stomach with all the nourishing American food, it is not to be wondered at that he becomes sick." Nevertheless, he believed that the American superabundance of food was no occasion for alarm, but rather a constant delight. Even the fences, he said, were made of hams and tobacco.[40]

Not a few of the immigrants wrote with naive delight about the American food, and in fact presented it as yet another argument for emigration. "I want you to know, dear brother," wrote one, "that I am enthusiastic about America and that we are all flourishing here. . . . Every meal, I sit down to a table loaded with good things, as good, I may say, as any of the delicacies set before guests in Norway." Even if he were offered several hundred dollars, he would not go back to Norway, where he "simply could not feel at home" after his American experience.[41] "At every meal a lord's fare!" exclaimed another.[42] And yet another, urging his sister to come to America, said that she would have "good food, pork that is tempting to eat, and with it wheat bread, for there is plenty of that sort of food in America." He was thinking of sending some bacon home to Norway for Christmas.[43] There were notes of warning to offset such exuber-

[39] Bache Diary, December 4, 1843.

[40] *Aftenbladet*, May 29, 1855.

[41] Halvor Halvorsen, with Peder Halvorsen, to a brother, December 28, 1852, in *Arbeider-foreningernes blad*, March 5, 1853.

[42] Hovland, in *Christianssandsposten*, February 23, 1843.

[43] Elias Hansen Narjord to his family, January 26, December 26, 1856. Transcripts of Narjord's letters are in the possession of the Norwegian-American Historical Association.

ance, however. One immigrant hoped that the mere desire for bacon and cake would not make people emigrate. American cookery did indeed have its points, Elias H. Narjord admitted, but he noted that after the immigrants "live as they like, eating and drinking what they prefer," they tend to return to familiar Norwegian dishes.[44] Others agreed that there was likely to be a new desire for the flat bread, herring, porridge, and *surprim* (a cheese made from the whey of sour milk) for which they once had so gratefully said grace — even if the porridge was *vasgrøt*, "boiled, that is, in water instead of milk."[45]

It mattered little what the locale was, the diet of the earlier pioneers was, for the most part, simple and monotonous. Wealthy hosts like the Hegs at old Muskego could not offer much variety on the hospitable tables that they set for their many guests. But in some instances, before farms were well established, there was acute scarcity of food. An American clergyman visited a cabin at Muskego in 1844 and wrote, "Aside from the tea kettle we saw but one article of furniture, and that a wooden bowl, partly filled with what I took to be shorts, kneaded and prepared for baking. This, as near as I could learn, was all they had in the house with which to support life."[46] A ten-year-old boy in another settlement was left alone when his father went away for provisions. "While father was away," he wrote, "I had to stay alone on the claim to care for the cows, and I had to get along with the food supplies which were left in the house, a little bread, a piece of pork and a bit of sausage."[47] On these foods he lived for three weeks. Special circumstances might cause hardships. Mr. Holand tells of a farmer who

[44] Narjord to his family, March 30, 1855. See also a letter written from Waukesha County, Wisconsin, February 18, 1856, in *Morgenbladet*, May 5, 1856.

[45] J. S. Johnson, "Rock Prairie," in *Samband*, no. 46, p. 107 (February, 1912). This article appears in installments from November, 1911, to February, 1913.

[46] Wells, "Wisconsin Antique." See *ante*, p. 58.

[47] Helgeson, *Fra Indianernes land*, 232.

went away for a barrel of flour, but as a result of a clerk's mistake brought back, not flour, but a barrel of sugar. "There was no way out of it; they had to grind a little wheat in a coffee grinder."[48] On the Dakota plains an early blizzard caught the settlers unawares. "We had not dug our potatoes nor threshed our grain," a pioneer woman recalled. "This winter there was one storm after another, so people could not get anywhere, nor get to threshing. My brother, Ed. Rose, and my father walked to Goodwin, eighteen miles, with a little handsled in order to bring home some flour from a mill there. The flour was divided among the neighbors and relatives. Two such trips were made. However, after that we all had to grind wheat in our coffee mills for flour to make bread."[49]

Marketing was naturally an interesting and even exciting experience for the pioneers. As soon as their circumstances permitted, they bought food supplies on a large scale, and kegs, sacks, and barrels were crowded into the cramped cabins. The problem of storage undoubtedly caused many to lament the absence of the picturesque old *stabbur* which they had known in Norway. Smokehouses were indeed built on many Norwegian-American farms in time, but they usually were squat little buildings, devoid of the carving, paneling, and artistic beauty of the Norwegian food houses.

Pork, as the early America letters indicated, was one of the staples of the pioneer diet, and the immigrants cheerfully disregarded the warnings to be sparing in their use of it. Pigs were cheap, litters large, the meat savory. Dr. J. S. Johnson was moved to an apostrophe: "And then the pork! It is difficult to show how great a part pork has played in the development of civilization. It has constantly been the solid foundation upon which the pioneer has founded his

[48] Hjalmar R. Holand, *Coon Prairie*, 30 (Minneapolis, 1927).

[49] Mrs. Lou Norman of Brandt, South Dakota, quoted by Brandt, in *Studies and Records*, 7:9, 10.

cookery. The hog has always been his faithful follower and ally and has never shown the least tendency to forsake the unequal alliance." He closed by proposing a toast in honor of the hog.[50] Mrs. Koren complained that alive, the pigs invaded both church and cabin, and dead, they appeared on the pioneer's table three times a day. At first she found delightful the nutty fragrance of bacon which filled the houses. "Today too," she wrote on one occasion, "I wakened to the aroma of frying bacon and coffee, hurried to dress, fetched a bowl of water and went out in front of the house to brush my teeth, and then sat down to eat my bacon, which strangely enough tastes equally good to me every time I eat it and that is morning, noon, and night." Usually fried or boiled potatoes accompanied it. "Now we are to eat dinner," remarked Mrs. Koren one day, "and have both potatoes and onions with the bacon." In the end, however, she revolted against the unvarying fare. "I ate biscuits and drank coffee this noon, but begged to be excused from eating the bacon."[51] But pork was a versatile dish, with many forms, and even disguises, to vary the monotony. It was served fresh and salted, pickled and pressed. As *sylte,* or headcheese, a special Christmas dish, it was served cold; as *stek* (roasted or fried), it was served hot. Even hired men found its persistence a difficult problem, however. A hungry Dakota laborer managed to eat fried pork and half-cooked potatoes, but reminded himself of Peer Gynt, who spat and trusted to the power of custom.[52]

The economic advance of the immigrants is reflected in the story of their foods. As fortune smiled upon them, they began to emancipate themselves from the benevolent tyranny of the pig. Among other things, beef, veal, mutton, and lamb became a part of their menu. Slaughtering emerged

[50] Johnson, in *Samband,* no. 46, p. 107.

[51] *Fra pioneertiden,* 97, 124, 125.

[52] Thomas Sorby, "Erindringer fra mit første aar i Yankeeland," in *Vikværingen* (Minneapolis), 5:94 (November, 1920).

as one of the routine occasions on the farm, and there was always fresh meat for Christmas. Then the ingenuity of the housewives was centered upon preparing one Norwegian delicacy after another. *Kjøtboller,* or meat balls, were a great favorite. The meat, usually a mixture of beef and pork, was forced through a grinder or chopped until it was as fine as paste, then spiced, mixed with milk or cream and eggs, rolled into balls, fried to a deep brown, and served with a rich gravy. Sometimes very small meat balls were dropped into steaming beef soup. "Helene astounded me by serving beef soup with carrots and potatoes in it for supper," wrote Mrs. Koren one day in 1854. "It tasted delicious, for it was so long since I had tasted soup."[53] The less choice cuts of beef were boiled, or the sides smoked and dried for *spekekjøt.* "Boiled beef and meat soup constituted the usual dinner courses," recalled a St. Olaf College student who ate his meals in a boardinghouse—and who found the memory unpleasant.[54]

Mrs. Koren spurned veal roast after a somewhat too steady diet of it in American taverns on her journey inland in the early 1850's, but ultimately it regained its place as a great favorite of hers. Unfortunately it could not be served as it was in Norway, with the succulent *sukkererter* (tender and very sweet green pods of peas) as a fillip. A popular and nourishing dish was *faar i kaal*—mutton or lamb stew, cooked with cabbage and flavored with whole black peppercorns; and a favorite cold dish was *rull*—rolled, spiced, and pressed mutton, sliced very thin. Slaughtering meant, among other things, sausage-making, with a premium upon ingenuity—and sometimes a penalty upon digestion. *Rullepølse* of many kinds, including the hard and highly spiced *spekepølse,* or summer sausage, were concocted and draped

[53] *Fra pioneertiden,* 128.

[54] H. B. Kildahl, "Minder fra St. Olaf skolens ungdom," in *Symra,* 10:234 (1914).

the walls of the smokehouses. Blood sausage or pudding was a favorite, especially among the north Norwegians; and there were even *blodpannekaker,* blood pancakes, though they were disdained by the more squeamish.

Inevitably the Norwegians, especially those from western Norway, sadly missed their well-known salt-water fish—cod, herring, mackerel, salmon. Fresh-water fish they enjoyed, but often it was not available. Mrs. Koren rejoiced when, with guests in her home, a small boy presented her with a string of fresh trout.[55] But the wonderful Norwegian herring, smoked or pickled, was a rare luxury in the early years. Later it was imported from Norway and elsewhere, to the delight of the Norwegian Americans. For a considerable time they had to deny themselves even their much loved *lutefisk.* Salt cod, however, shipped out from Massachusetts, began regularly to reach their communities. They hastened to revive the art of *luting:* dried cod was first soaked in water, then in a solution of lye, then in water again, finally boiled, and served with melted butter. Fish soup, a milk and fish concoction flavored with parsley or leek, was a cherished dish, as were fish pudding or fish balls, served either fried or in a cream sauce. Great was the Norwegian-American appreciation when canned fish balls, packed at Stavanger, became available in the Middle West.

Fowl, domestic and wild, was welcomed on the immigrant tables. "Every man here has a large number of pigs and also chickens," wrote an immigrant in the early 1840's. "There are some who have as many as a thousand chickens."[56] Yet chicken, when served in the Duus and Koren homes, was a treat that called for comment in letter or diary. One of Mrs. Koren's early culinary triumphs was chicken soup, served with dumplings. The Norwegians soon learned

[55] *Fra pioneertiden,* 165, 168.

[56] From a letter written by Ole K. Trovatten in 1842. See Blegen, *Norwegian Migration,* 200.

how to prepare all manner of wild fowl — prairie chickens, turkeys, ducks, pheasants; and they liked the domestic varieties of turkey, goose, and duck. The passenger pigeon — now extinct — was at one time a leading food supply in a village of the Koshkonong settlement: "There was a large forest west of the Reque farm, and here thousands of pigeons would come for the night. . . . People came in large numbers to kill the birds for food. Farmers arrived with wagons and bushel baskets, which were quickly filled. . . . The meat from these birds was delicious, but people soon tired of pigeon steak."[57] In many parts of the frontier other foods furnished welcome variety — rabbit, venison, antelope, bear, even squirrel. Duus, an epicure, found turtle soup delicious. And of course eggs, though often more valuable to a skimping farmer's wife as "cash in trade," were part of the distinction of the American table. "We have lived like lords lately," wrote Mrs. Koren, "with soft boiled eggs for breakfast and game for dinner, but now that glory is past and pork again reigns supreme."[58]

Coffee was the most cherished of all drinks among the Norwegian immigrants, as among the Swedish, and both became famed as devotees of the coffee cup. Today Willmar, a little Minnesota town, almost solidly Scandinavian, observes "afternoon coffee" as an established social institution and advertises itself as the "coffee center of the United States." Milk, however, offered almost endless possibilities in the devising of food. It was socially less, but economically much more, significant than coffee. There were differences, however, between the Norwegian and American dairying scenes. Cattle herding lacked in America the romantic charm that it was invested with in Norway. There were no mountain *sæters* to which milkmaids took herds for summer grazing. The excessive heat of the midwestern summer in-

[57] Bøe, in *Studies and Records*, 6:46.
[58] *Fra pioneertiden*, 143.

terfered with the preservation of fresh milk. Milkhouses around wells or convenient springs were built wherever possible, and there were crude cellars and "caves," but they did not furnish the same atmosphere for the aging of cheeses that the cool mountain air of Norway afforded. Mrs. Svendsen had difficulties on the Iowa prairie. "I remember I used to wonder," she said, "when I heard that it would be impossible to use milk here as we did at home, but I certainly have discovered that it is true. It is so hot here in summer that it is impossible to work it into cheese; besides there is no way of protecting it from the flies and other pests. . . . It is futile to try to make cheese in the early summer; during the fall, however, it is possible to keep it. In summer if one has more milk than one can use while it is sweet, it simply has to be thrown to the hogs." She also speaks of the difficulty of keeping butter from getting rancid. It had to be sold at once, and she recorded that she received "from eight to ten cents a pound" for it.[59]

Fresh milk was used in a variety of ways. Heated and thickened with flour, it made milk porridge. It was also combined with various cereals. *Grøt,* or porridge, had endless possibilities. Combined with butter melted in flour, and flavored with sugar and cinnamon, it made *smørgrøt.* When cream was substituted for milk, the result was *fløtegrøt,* or *rømmegrøt,* a priceless delicacy that was frequently reserved for special occasions like weddings or holidays. *Risengrynsgrøt,* a rice porridge, sprinkled with sugar and cinnamon, and sometimes with raisins and currants, is said to have made the children shout with glee. Fortunately the Norwegians were fond of sour milk. *Fillebunk* or *hel melk* was popular. The milk was allowed to sour with the cream still on it and was eaten with sugar and sometimes cinnamon sprinkled over the top. The most common cheese was *surprim,* or primost, which was made by slowly heating sour

[59] From a letter of 1863 from Mrs. Svendsen to her parents, Nielsen Papers.

milk until the curd separated from the whey, and then cooking down the latter until it turned a light brown. It could be eaten at once or permitted to harden, whereupon it was pressed into a mold. It resembled the favorite *gjetost* in appearance, but not in taste. Since few Norwegian Americans kept goats, they rarely had *gjetost* in the period before that cheese began to be imported from Norway. Incidentally, the Norwegian-American farms did not present the sight, so familiar to the Norwegian countryside, of goats scrambling on turf-covered roofs or on distant crags. Other Norwegian cheeses that were not uncommon were *mysost* (a whey cheese), *pultost* (a soft strong curd cheese with caraway seeds), and *gammelost,* highly regarded but so odoriferous that it was considered diplomatic, and sometimes necessary, to serve it under glass.

Bread and breadmaking absorbed much of the housewife's interest. Many immigrants, especially on the farms, continued to make their native flat bread, potato cakes, and *lefse.* The first was easy enough to make, once crops of rye, barley, and oats were available. *Lefse* was an unleavened potato bread. Munch Ræder tells of dining in a Norwegian-American home in 1848, when his hosts, as soon as they were "confident that we were altogether Norwegian," served flat bread. The Yankees, it appeared, often made fun of this food. Munch Ræder persuaded a Yankee to try *fløtegrøt* and was gratified when he pronounced it "first rate."[60] American leavened bread became very popular among the Norwegian immigrants, and they found it simple to bake in the American cookstoves which, as the farmers began to attain a certain prosperity, graced their kitchens. At first yeast was made at home, a little of the leaven preserved from one baking to another. Dry yeast cakes, however, soon were obtainable at the stores. The Norwegians were fa-

[60] *America in the Forties,* 16.

miliar with leaven from Norway, for their favorite Christmas bread—*julekake*—was made with yeast, as were also their malts and ales. *Julekake* was a standard delicacy of the Norwegian-American Christmas—a rich sweetened white bread, much like coffeecake, flavored with cardamon and crammed with raisins and candied citron peel.

American bread was, in the early years, a novelty for the Norwegians, and breadmaking a great event. "It is very fortunate that Karen likes to bake, and only yesterday she said she would miss it if she returned to Norway," wrote Laur. Larsen to his parents in the 1850's. "We have laid a plan that some day we are to introduce American methods of baking and so bestow a blessing upon our mother country. Even in the towns here there are no bakeries, but they have some excellent stoves so that every housewife can bake her own bread at the same time she is cooking other food. And such bread! I don't believe I shall ever want to eat Norwegian bread again."[61] In Norwegian towns of the time it was not uncustomary for people to send their bread to the community baker to be baked. Immigrants who mastered the art of American breadmaking instructed later arrivals. Thus at Spring Prairie, Wisconsin, Mrs. Lars Reque taught Mrs. Sjur Reque how to make bread and other American dishes while members of the latter's family were preparing to settle on their own land.[62]

American cake, with its rich icings, was at first prohibitive in expense, but in time the abundance of butter, flour, eggs, and cream, and the inexpensiveness of sugar, made possible desserts that were unknown in Norway. In that country, according to Rønning, "the woman was most renowned who could spin the most yarn or weave the most cloth in a day. Here in the Norwegian settlements that woman was most

[61] Larsen, *Laur. Larsen,* 39; and Laur. Larsen, "Atter nogle gamle minder," in *Symra,* 9:241–250 (1913).

[62] Bøe, in *Studies and Records,* 6:42; and Rene, *Historie om udvandringen fra Voss,* 315.

Lærebog

i de forskjellige Grene af

Husholdningen

af

Hanna Winsnes.

11te Udgave,
gjennemseet og forøget af **Maren Vinsnes.**

Christiania.
I Kommission hos J. W. Cappelen.
Forlagt af Chr. A. Wulfsberg.

1880.

THE TITLE PAGE OF A POPULAR NORWEGIAN COOKBOOK BY HANNA WINSNES

renowned who could make the best 'cake.'"[63] American pie also met with a warm reception. Naive wonderment over this remarkable dish shines out in an America letter of 1851, which reports the abundance of fruits and berries in Wisconsin: "Strawberries, raspberries, and blackberries are common. From these they make a wonderful dish combined with syrup and sugar, which is called *Pai*. I can tell you that that is something that glides easily down your throat; they also make the same sort of *Pai* out of apples or finely ground meat, with syrup added, and that is really the most superb."[64] Pancakes and waffles were not precisely unknown in Norway, but the American versions of these dishes seemed different and they aroused genuine enthusiasm. Duus commented on pancakes, in particular: "These so-called pancakes are both to an American and also to our Norwegian-American taste wonderfully palatable for breakfast. They are fried in bacon fat and eaten with syrup." His boys, he reported, were "eating pancakes with great gusto."[65] Mrs. Koren mentioned the fact that "Vilhelm" had brought home with him an original thing—a "utensil for turning pancakes."[66]

Norwegian desserts, meanwhile, held their own against the American, and usually crowded the latter out on such special occasions as Christmas. Indeed, these desserts were almost a Christmas ritual, and they had a sanctity that would have been profaned had they been served commonly throughout the year. The range of Norwegian cakes was so wide as to defy description, but there were a few marked favorites, almost all of them small, more like cookies or pastries, but ordinarily without icings. *Sandbakkels* were perhaps the prime favorite, a dainty concoction, rich in butter, sugar, and

[63] *Bare for moro*, 25.

[64] An anonymous letter of November 29, 1851, in *Stavanger amtstidende og adresseavis*, June 12, 1852.

[65] Duus to his father, January 27, 1858, Duus Papers.

[66] *Fra pioneertiden*, 191.

eggs, sometimes flavored with finely chopped almonds, and baked in fluted tins. *Berlinerkranser* (Berlin wreaths) were made from a similar mixture, but shaped in wreath form and topped with egg white, sugar, and chopped nuts. *Fattigmand,* ironically called "poor man" because they were made from a dough rich in eggs, had a traditional popularity. The dough was rolled thin, cut into diamond or leaf shape with a little metal wheel, and fried in deep fat. Even in strictly temperance homes these cakes were often flavored with brandy bought for this special purpose; for other purposes it would, of course, have been considered immoral. *Krumkake* required a special skill: these cakes, fashioned into hollow cylindrical form, bore the delicate patterned imprint of the special iron on which they were baked. They broke at almost the slightest touch. *Pebernøtter* (pepper nuts) were a spicy cookie, shaped like a nugget—a favorite with children and an ideal instrument for comfortable adult dunking.

Puddings made from milk or fruit juices were common. *Rødgrøt* was a favorite, simple to make from any or all juices. Prunes, raisins, currants, apples, or lemons were added to the juice, which was always spiced, usually with stick cinnamon and cloves. The base was sago or tapioca, common in Norwegian-American larders. Mrs. Brandt records her dismay when her husband came home, in the Dakota country, with three pounds of sage instead of the sago he was asked to buy. Both Norwegian desserts and many other kinds of food were explained in a volume by Hanna Winsnes entitled "Textbook in the Various Branches of Housekeeping," originally published in Christiania in 1845 and brought out in edition after edition. Immigrants of the upper classes usually carried this handy book to America and found it of great practical value. It was comprehensive in treatment and gave information not only on cooking but also on gardening, caring for cattle and other domestic animals, slaughtering, soapmaking, ale brewing, and wine making. Probably few of the ordinary country housewives were familiar with this manual, however. Their knowledge of cooking came to them as a part of the traditional lore of the rural districts of Norway.[67]

The Norwegian women were highly skilled in canning and preserving fruits. "You will have to excuse the form of this letter," wrote Elise Wærenskjold from her Texan plantation. "I am having to watch a kettle of cherries which I am preserving, while I write."[68] Duus in 1857 apologized for the fact that his wife did not add a postscript to his letter: "She is in a great rush canning blueberries and Morten and Olaf are sitting beside her helping her out — by eating."[69] Many immigrants regretted the absence of such Norwegian favorites among berries as *Tytteber* (lingonberries) and *multeber* (cloudberries), but few American fruits, vegetables, or other products were novelties to them. American corn was an exception, and tomatoes were unknown to most of them. Nor had many known melons. "But I must tell you something about a fruit called watermelon," wrote Mrs. Svendsen in 1865. "We have a tremendous amount of that sort of fruit; I can't think of anything to compare with it in Norway. They are as big as a child's head, some larger, some smaller, round and green outside but either red or yellow inside as the case may be, very sweet and juicy. They are eaten just as they are taken from the field, provided they are ripe."[70] Tropical and semitropical fruits reached the immigrant frontier communities earlier than one might suppose. Bananas, it is true, were almost unknown until the end of the century in the Iowa settlement where Professor Laurence

[67] Brandt, in *Studies and Records*, 7:37. I have used the eleventh edition of Hanna Winsnes, *Lærebog i de forskjellige grene af husholdningen* (Christiania, 1880).

[68] Mrs. Wærenskjold to Thomine Dannevig, May 27, 1871, in *Tønsberg blad*, May 19, 1925.

[69] Duus to his parents, August 14, 1857, Duus Papers.

[70] Mrs. Svendsen to her parents, December 3, 1865, Nielsen Papers.

M. Larson grew up, but oranges were not uncommon, and lemons were evidently a customary part of the stock of the country store. Lemonade was a prized drink. In 1854 Mrs. Koren wrote, "I have been out to pick our first mignonette, so there we sat and thought we were very European and civilized with our lemonade and mignonette; but I wonder if lemonade would ever have tasted so good to us there."[71]

For many of the Norwegian immigrants home-brewed ales were a much more familiar drink than lemonade; and there was a large patronage of stores and saloons, where beer and whisky were available for purchase. The early immigrants, for the most part, carried with them to America the old Norwegian social concept of drinking. It was frequently, in Norway and also in the western settlements, a phase of such celebrations as weddings and baptisms and even of such ceremonies as funerals. According to O. S. Johnson, a careful student of one of the typical Norwegian communities in the West, the old drinking customs were also brought to America by the immigrants, including drinking songs and ballads with genial traditions behind them.[72] It was common to have ceremonial drinking at Christmas and at various other festive times. A writer on Norwegian-American temperance history suggests that in America, amid new conditions and with liquor easy of access, drinking became very common among the Norwegians; but the evidence indicates that, on the whole, it was less common among the immigrants than among the people in Norway. The use of liquor in that country was at its highest point in the 1830's, and in 1833 the average annual consumption of alcohol in Norway was estimated at approximately eighteen quarts per person.[73]

[71] *Fra pioneertiden*, 177.

[72] O. S. Johnson, in *Samband*, no. 90, p. 704 ff. (October, 1915).

[73] J. L. Nydahl, *Afholdssagens historie*, 249 (Minneapolis, 1896); Erling Tambs Wicklund, *Bøndene og brennevinsspørsmålet i Norge 1800–1850*, 62, 63 (Oslo, 1925).

There is no statistical evidence available on the use of liquor among the early immigrants, but many of the records from the frontier era indicate a fairly wide patronage of the agencies that dispensed strong drinks of one kind or another — usually one kind, whisky. On some farms a jug of whisky was placed in each corner of the field as a means of encouraging workmen to make their rounds swiftly.[74] For the Norwegian Americans in many communities throughout the Middle West, the frontier saloon served as a social club, where many went to visit and to drink with their neighbors and friends, occasionally to excess. In Scandinavian communities the Norwegians sometimes blossomed out as saloonkeepers, and even on the far frontier they tried their hand at the business. A missionary crossing the Dakota prairie in 1886 arrived in a town of a hundred inhabitants. Only one was a Norwegian, and the missionary was "pained and chagrined" to learn that he ran a saloon.[75] A protest against the use of liquor took form and grew in volume, but on the part of many there appears to have been a friendly tolerance of liquors. The liking for ale and wines among the clergy is well documented. Pastor Duus in the 1850's complained that in honoring the birthday of an aunt in Norway, he was obliged to drink to her, not in good wine, but in "tea or in home-brewed ale." This he briefly disposed of as fantastic — but American. On one occasion he sought to buy some port wine in a local store, but upon tasting it found that it was not fit to be used.[76]

Both the prevalence of the use of liquor among the immigrants and the force of the Puritan spirit among them are reflected in the protest that developed. The Norwegians felt

[74] Professor Einar Haugen has a record of this custom, received from Martin Midttun of Petersburg, North Dakota.

[75] John H. Blegen, "A Missionary Journey on the Dakota Prairies in 1886," translated and edited by Theodore C. Blegen, in *North Dakota Historical Quarterly*, vol. 1, no. 3, p. 20 (April, 1927).

[76] Duus to his parents, February 11, 1856, Duus Papers.

the impact of the prohibition movement that centered in the Maine Law agitation of the early 1850's; and one of the early Norwegian-American reformers was the churchman, A. C. Preus, who declared that after observing conditions among the Norwegians for eight months he felt impelled to call upon them to join the cause of temperance reform. He favored the Maine Law, urged the formation of abstinence societies, and witnessed the emergence of an organized movement among his countrymen. Such societies were launched in no fewer than nine congregations as early as 1851.[77] The next year a Norwegian-American temperance monthly, *Avholdenhedsvennen* ("The Friend of Abstinence"), was started at Racine, Wisconsin, with the avowed purpose of working "against the physical and moral evil of indulgence in alcoholic stimulants, which has ruined and poisoned our whole social life, an evil whose injurious and ruinous effects we can observe daily."[78] Thus began a temperance movement which grew rapidly after the Civil War, attracted to its ranks some able Norwegian-American leaders, and gained with time considerable support among the people.

[77] Nydahl, *Afholdssagens historie,* 249–253; *Emigranten,* March 11, 1859.
[78] See *post,* 326 n.

VII. PIONEER FOLKWAYS

Generous hospitality was characteristic of the Norwegian-American frontier homes. There were people who liked to be complimented for their "genuine old Norwegian hospitality,"[1] but the spirit was essentially that of the American frontier. The frontier rule was that no one should be turned away unfed and unwarmed, and this rule was followed by immigrants and native Americans alike. Even a house temporarily deserted might be occupied by strangers upon occasion. Søren Bache in 1839 tells of coming to a house where he and his companion hoped to secure lodging. They entered it, found no one at home, and made themselves comfortable. Presently the American housewife returned to find strangers in her house. She was surprised, but welcomed them as guests, explaining that she was not frightened, for she knew "that there had been no Indians in the vicinity that year."[2] Even the Indians, however, would stalk into a frontier home in the almost certain expectation that they would be given food.

[1] Rene, *Historie om udvandringen fra Voss,* 321.
[2] Bache Diary, November 9, 1839.

Usually the Norwegians had their own social nuclei, for friends and relatives tended to settle in compact groups, often with the pleasant bond of dialect among them. Even on the prairie complete isolation was rare. The first winter in a new settlement was often much like that of Per Hansa in *Giants in the Earth*. There might be house-to-house visits among the women, sometimes walks of miles, with small children trudging along with them. Organized activities usually waited upon the founding of a church, but the arrival of a visiting minister on his periodic rounds meant the assembling of scattered people. Even if the traveling parson arrived on a weekday, the news of his coming spread rapidly and the people flocked to some central cabin for a religious service.

Visitors were doubly welcome because ordinarily they brought news of the outside world from which many of the immigrants felt permanently cut off. The arrival of a Norwegian newcomer occasioned calls from people throughout the community who hoped for news of friends and relatives in the old country; and the arrival of letters from the older settlements or from Norway was similarly an inducement to community visiting. But the visitor *par excellence* was the minister. All homes were open to him and he was besieged with invitations. Mrs. Koren, in that charming diary of the 1850's which is one of the treasures of the social historian, describes the "royal progress" of her husband and herself into Iowa to the Washington Prairie community where they spent their first American winter. In Dodgeville, Wisconsin, the Korens expected to stay at a tavern, "but a Norwegian blacksmith asked us if we would not accompany him home." They were crowded into a little "cramped and suffocating" *stue*, or room, where presently the workman's wife arrived, "amazed to find company." On another occasion, in Iowa, they were ushered into "quite a large living room with a big stove in the center of it" and were greeted by their hosts, who "were overjoyed to have the minister they had been waiting for so long, actually in their midst." They "offered us the best the house could afford and were on the whole so friendly that we soon felt very much at home." The loft in which the Korens were given a bed also accommodated a mother and three children recently arrived from Norway. The next evening the hosts served cream porridge to the distinguished guests.[3]

Not long thereafter Mrs. Koren was meeting her parishioners in the crowded room of the largest house of the community in which her husband had just held his first service. "You are most welcome to America," was one of the customary greetings extended to her. Occasionally someone would say, "What a beautiful breastpin you have there!" Invited to a dinner, she found that her hostess eagerly wished her to remain not merely for the meal but overnight. She was treated with homemade wild grape wine and *fattigmand* and then sat down to a table "loaded down with fried pork, spareribs, sausages, bread and butter, cake, and excellent coffee." On yet another occasion, in a drab and miserable hut, she fell into a melancholy mood, but, she says, "my mood didn't last long. The people were so friendly; they gave us their bed and slept in the loft themselves." The next day she visited a near-by cabin filled with the smell of snuff and tobacco. There she found two old women in their native costumes, one of whom proffered snuff to the minister.[4]

Always the pastor's wife found herself regarded with friendly curiosity. One woman hoped that Mrs. Koren would allow her to drive her around in the community on some day when the minister was away. "It would be very nice if I could show off the minister's wife to them," she said.

[3] Koren, *Fra pioneertiden,* 79, 95.
[4] *Fra pioneertiden,* 99–102, 108 ff.

One day Mrs. Koren tramped through heavy snow to a neighbor's house, where she was invited to dinner and treated to *melkevelling*—milk porridge. If the minister's family was thus always welcome in the pioneer homes, it followed that the parsonage was a social center, a permanent open house. "Helene had no sooner cleared the table for one group than she would have to set it again," wrote Mrs. Koren on a winter day in 1854, "so that the entire day the house has been full of the delicious fragrance of fried pork." [5]

Once, making a Sunday call, Mrs. Koren found a family in the midst of its devotions: a man "in his rocking chair reading out loud from the Bible," a young wife with a child in her lap, a grandmother and great-aunt, "gray hair tucked up under their caps," seated on stools, and an old man lying on his bed. Occasionally such visiting within the parish was supplemented by the social pleasure of synodical meetings, to which wives accompanied the pastors. At one, held in Janesville in the autumn of 1854, Mrs. Koren recorded an invitation after dinner to Pastor Unonius' for "coffee in the evening." Once a meal was served in the open, with the "starry sky as a ceiling," and the ministers joined heartily in singing old familiar songs. Mrs. Preus recalled that there was a close fraternal bond among the ministers' families.[6]

Scenes on the Dakota prairies in a later period are reminiscent of those on the Iowa and Wisconsin frontiers of the 1850's. Mrs. Brandt, crossing the prairie with her husband, finally came to the one-room house of Mons Steensland. There the ministerial family was cordially greeted; and in the one room that night slept the farmer and his wife, a number of children, Pastor and Mrs. Brandt, and the driver. In the Dakota community the parsonage was the largest house and so it "served . . . as a community center for the activi-

[5] *Fra pioneertiden,* 111, 117, 130, 139.

[6] *Fra pioneertiden,* 157, 183; Lulla Preus, "Minder fra den gamle Paint Creek præstegaard," in *Symra,* 7:1–15 (1911).

at opleve noget mere Mærkværdigt. Om
Aftenen kom Knud og sagde at det var
bestemt at vi skulde bo hos Erik Egge og
at vi kunde flytte naar vi behagede. Som
blev her om Aftenen, da kom et Par andre
Bønder med en Stundgaa. Vil. vilde sat
oppe en Stund af Natten for at studere,
men det blev saa bidende koldt, at det ikke
lod sig gjøre. [illegible] hvor koldt det var
at ligge og den Aften paa det luftige Loft,
hvor foruden os, Nilsen Barnekone, Kari og hans
des tre Børn ligger, det Rum, som Sengene
lade tilbage, er opfyldt med Familiens Klæder,
Dagtøier, Melkebakker o.s.v. Saaledes saa vort
første Sovekammer i vort nye Hjem ud.

Juleaften 1853.

Det var en underlig Juleaften, [illegible], saa
forskjellig fra alle, jeg hidindtil har oplevet.
Her sad vi, Vilhelm og jeg, for første Gang
adskildt fra Slægtninge og Venner i en lille
Bondestue, langt inde i Amerika. Til Aften
har vi spist Ribbensteg og drukket Kaffe.
Nu sidder vi med en Blyskaal, hvori der er
Skraabtalg og lidt Tøi til Væge, stillet op
paa en Saltbøtte for at lyse lidt. Vilh.
studerende paa sin Prædiken til imorgen;
vi venter hvert Øieblik Erik tilbage fra
Decorah, hvorfra han formodentlig skal
bringe den Seng, vi skal ligge i. Da vi
havde spist Middag idag, spændte Nils fire Stude for
Sleden, og sagde vore venlige Værter [illegible]
[illegible] at besøge dem og [illegible] os
[illegible] Sleden. Vilh. paa den [illegible] jeg paa
[illegible] Kuffert, [illegible] os fast saa
godt vi kunde, for det var just ikke den
jevneste Vei, vi havde at passere. Nils gik

A Page from Mrs. Koren's Diary, Christmas Eve, 1853
[From the original in the possession of the Reverend Paul Koren, Decorah, Iowa.]

ties of the congregation." The choir met in the living room, the confirmation class in the kitchen, and bazaars and festivals were held in "the larger unfinished room upstairs."[7]

The hospitality of established settlers to newcomers was boundless. Lars Larsen in Rochester kept open house for the immigrant throngs moving westward, sometimes entertaining fifty or more people at one time.[8] Even Heg converted his Muskego barn into an immigrant receiving house and won fame in Norway and in America for his unfailing generosity.[9] Of Lars Davidson Reque of the Koshkonong settlement, R. B. Anderson writes, "He has done a great deal for newcomers from Norway. His house in Deerfield has been a sort of objective point for them. He has taken them into his home, fed them free of charge, taught them valuable things regarding American affairs, and sent them forth with hope and cheer to begin life in the 'new world.'"[10]

Even before churches were organized, the social combined with the religious instinct to bring about informal community gatherings. The neighbors, writes Elias H. Narjord, assembled on Sundays for the reading of books of sermons. A letter of 1857 reveals the social scene in one part of the Iowa country: "Our neighbors are for the most part from Holtaalen and often of a Sunday we gather together, sometimes for scriptural readings. Last Christmas during the holidays Bør Olsen from Holtaalen visited us and several neighbors; a month ago Jokom Nilsen Østus from Røraas and Elisabeth-Maria were here . . . last Easter we visited them and thus it goes. We are often visited by our neighbors from Røraas

[7] Brandt, in *Studies and Records*, 7: 4, 16–18.

[8] See Lars Larsen's letter, written in October, 1837, in *Stavanger amtstidende og adresseavis*, December 15, 1837.

[9] "His hospitable cabin," writes Albert O. Barton, "became the temporary home for hundreds of other immigrants, and was even known as the 'Heg Hotel.'" "Muskego, the Most Historic Norwegian Colony," in *Scandinavia*, vol. 1, no. 1, p. 23 (January, 1924).

[10] Quoted by Bøe, in *Studies and Records*, 6: 51.

because they have to pass by our place on the way to market."[11]

Occasionally there might be a picnic to enliven the outlook of the immigrants. On September 19, 1853, a number of Norwegians living in the Boston region carried picnic baskets to a lake called Fresh Pond. This place, wrote one of the campers, "had something so Norwegian about it that involuntarily we were reminded of our dear fatherland." Here they sang and made speeches, and one of the group composed a special song for the occasion. The practical outcome of the picnic was that they "decided to form a society for the purpose of helping Norwegian newcomers who did not know the language or the customs" of America.[12] More characteristic than such secular celebrations were the festivals of the church, scrupulously observed, though perhaps lacking some of the solemnity that clothed them in the old country. "In preaching to his various congregations," writes Mrs. Brandt, "my husband observed and made good use of all the church festivals during the year: first, second, and third day of Christmas, Maundy Thursday, Good Friday, first, second, and third day of Easter, Pentecost, prayer day, Thanksgiving, and so forth. Services were held in sod houses and in schoolhouses when they were available."[13] The adoption of American holidays came gradually, though Thanksgiving was observed in the 1850's by the Norwegians in Wisconsin, long before President Lincoln's historic call for a national day of thanks.[14]

The immigrants had not been long in America before they felt the contagion of the American Fourth of July. In 1846 Søren Bache participated in a July 4 celebration marked by a parade, speeches, a public dinner at noon, music and ora-

[11] Narjord to relatives in Norway, January 26, 1857.

[12] A letter from Massachusetts, October 20, 1853, in *Christiania-posten*, January 6, 1854.

[13] Brandt, in *Studies and Records*, 7:12.

[14] *Emigranten*, November 18, 1857.

tions at a near-by grove in the afternoon, and a torchlight parade in the evening.[15] Larson tells of the typical July 4 celebration in an Iowa community in the years after the Civil War — the "roar of something that was called artillery" in the morning; the rumble of farmers' wagons coming into town; the procession to a grove, where there was a program culminating in an oration; and then, later in the day, amusements, dancing, and a display of fireworks. In the 1870's, when Larson was a boy, Norwegians were occasionally represented among the speakers of the day. "Nothing so far in my life had impressed me like this gorgeous day in Forest City," Larson wrote many years later. "The crowding and jostling on the rickety sidewalks, the noise and din to which there was no lull, the blare of the band and the overpowering rhythm of the martial airs, the pageantry, the flags, and the bunting — all of these had a subtle power of fascination, even when they confused and almost distracted me."[16] One may safely think of Larson as the typical Norwegian-American boy in this reaction to the traditional American Fourth. As the Norwegian Americans developed their own community life, they began to plan and manage their own Fourth of July celebrations, sometimes including a sermon as well as the usual patriotic address, and singing both "America" and the national anthem of Norway.[17] As early as 1837 a party of immigrants celebrated the Norwegian national holiday in mid-ocean under the leadership of Ole Rynning, but there seems to be little evidence of an interest in the Seventeenth of May in the early Norwegian colonies of the West. By the 1860's Seventeenth of May celebrations were being held in some communities where there were many Norwegian immigrants; widespread observance of the Norwegian national holiday did not develop until

[15] Bache Diary, July 4, 1846. This early Fourth of July celebration was held in Madison, Wisconsin.

[16] Larson, *Log Book*, 114–117.

[17] Brandt, in *Studies and Records*, 7:23, 24.

somewhat later; and its vogue in America was influenced by the rise of the custom in Norway, which in turn was closely connected with Norwegian political currents of the 1860's. *Syttende Mai* became ultimately a recognized social institution among the Norwegian Americans — a part of their folkways — and many organizations gave it a large place in their activities.[18]

Christmas among the early immigrants was celebrated, as in Norway, for the entire Twelfth-night period. There was an attempt to reproduce the traditional Norwegian Christmas, but inevitably there were American innovations and as the settlers adjusted themselves to the American tempo, the celebration tended to be distinctly less protracted than it had been in the old country. In the early years Christmas was primarily a family occasion, though neighbors might drop in as guests. There seem to have been at first few presents, seldom a Christmas tree, no hanging of stockings, and no talk of Santa Claus. In time American customs were widely adopted and merged with the Norwegian. An authentic picture of Christmas customs on the frontier is given by a daughter of pioneers, Aaste Wilson, who writes, "They practiced the old customs from Norway. They invited one another to Christmas celebrations, and then they had home-brewed ale, made from malt or molasses or sugar cane. There were some who had whisky, too, but money was scarce and they couldn't have much of anything. . . . Nearly everybody slaughtered for Christmas so that they could have meat and sausages. Then they had potatoes and flat bread and doughnuts and sauce made from dried apples. And most of them had cream porridge. We youngsters liked to stay and listen to the old folks and thought it good fun when they told about old things from Norway. They would

[18] *Emigranten,* July 18, 1864; Carl G. O. Hansen, "Pressen til borgerkrigens slutning," in Johannes B. Wist, ed., *Norsk-amerikanernes festskrift 1914,* 34, 35 (Decorah, 1914).

talk about all kinds of things and even tell stories of trolls and ghosts. . . . Sometimes they would sing ballads and *stev*," or impromptu rhymes. "I heard father occasionally sing 'Sons of Norway, the age-old kingdom,'" she writes. "It was the women especially who sang *stev*, and sometimes they would have *stev* competitions." Before Christmas came, "everybody was terribly busy," for "then people had to whitewash their log houses and bake and slaughter." The children "longed desperately for Christmas to come"—it was a wonderful event to them "even if the houses were small and low." Then on Christmas Eve there was a great dinner, with cream porridge as the chief dish. There were songs before and after the meal, and there was a table prayer when "we held each other's hands and gave thanks for the food. Father said they always did that at home in Sauherad."[19]

Professor Laurence M. Larson reports that December 24—Little Christmas Day, as it was called—was essentially secular, a day for the children, whereas Christmas Day proper and the second and third Christmas days were church days, observed with special services, including an offering to the minister. Larson recalls that both the house and the children were scrubbed vigorously in preparation for the great day. The Yule meal was the Christmas Eve dinner, introduced by a hymn, the reading of the Christmas story, and a grace by one of the children. Then came a feast of rice pudding, bread, apples, and candies. "To have so many good things at the same meal was a real experience."[20] Lulla Preus remembers that in the Preus parsonage at Paint Creek the custom of using a Christmas tree was observed, with candles, paper ornaments, gilded nuts, and the like.

[19] Aaste Wilson, "Live blant nybyggjarane," in *Telesoga*, no. 33, p. 30–32 (September, 1917). See also, for Norwegian backgrounds, Ola Andreassen, "Lidt om juleskikkene i gamle dage," in *Telesoga*, no. 32, p. 24–29 (June, 1917).

[20] Larson, *Log Book*, 82–84.

There was dancing, singing, and playing around the tree, then a banquet to which *fattigmand* and *julekake* added the crowning touch.[21] In the Brandt parsonage on the Dakota prairie, many years later, a congregational Christmas festival was held, with gifts for all the children, a box-elder tree substituting for an evergreen.[22] In the Veblen home there was a special cake for each child, with his name inscribed in frosting. Each youngster was given a large, hand-dipped candle, and all the candles were lighted simultaneously "so that the sudden outburst of brightness would be a symbol of the Star of Bethlehem."[23] In many communities the fine old custom of putting out a sheaf of grain for the birds was carefully observed.

Besides the familiar hymns of the immigrants, sung both in church and in home, there was a wealth of folk song kept alive through use on many occasions. Some of the songs were rollicking and lusty, some plaintive and melancholy. There were cradlesongs like "Bissam, bissam baadne"; and love songs like "Oh, Ole, Ole, I loved you so dearly" or "Astri! Mi Astri!"—a charming ballad reminiscent of the English "Drink to Me Only with Thine Eyes." There were shepherd's calls that seemed to carry echoes within echoes, and there was a sad lament for "My Tulla," a favorite sheep traded to the wolf for a "bloody spot on my finger." Children joined with older folk in singing about the old lady from Hakkedalen:

> Here comes on crutches Sally
> Far up in Hakke Valley.

[21] Preus, in *Symra,* 7:8–11.

[22] Brandt, in *Studies and Records,* 7:18–20.

[23] A. A. Veblen, "Jul i Manitowoc-skogen," in *Samband,* no. 93, p. 134–148 (January, 1916). See also an article in the same issue of *Samband* by Eldrid Wæthing-Ringerud on "Gamle juleskikke." The quotation is from Ylvisaker, *Eminent Pioneers,* 5. Veblen, in his vivid description of early Christmas customs, recalls gifts as a part of the celebration. He mentions handkerchiefs, mouth organs, drums, books, dolls, and striped candy. Ale was brewed at home for Christmas, and Veblen also remembers that since whisky was then very inexpensive, those who liked liquor for the Christmas festivities had little difficulty in getting it.

And they liked the ballad of Paul and Reynard the Fox. At a frontier party, nearly everybody both could and would join heartily in singing to a lively tune the ancient song "Aa kjøre vatten, aa kjøre ve'":

Oh, carry water and carry wood,
And drive the timber o'er the line, Sir.
Oh, drive and carry whate'er you would,
I'll take my sweetheart every time, Sir.
With cheeks so red and with eyes so blue,
The lovely maidens they thrill me through.
For me alone
Give me my own,
And life will be a merry rhyme, Sir.[24]

It was no chance circumstance, but a natural development, that Auber Forestier and Rasmus B. Anderson in the early 1880's brought out a *Norway Music Album* which made available for home use the old Norwegian folk songs, spring dances, and hallings, with English translations of the original texts.[25]

The immigrants were familiar with the traditional lore of legend, superstition, riddles, and proverbs that came out of the long Norwegian past. For the most part, however, they were emancipated from belief in the ancient superstitions, as were the people of Norway in an age of rapid change in the national economy. Yet the superstitious beliefs, transmitted from one generation to another, were told and retold because they were entertaining, and witchcraft and trolls figured in the immigrant lore. There was little creation of new episode, however, in the realm of superhuman phenomena. Professor Haugen collected from Dane County, Wisconsin, a pioneer tale of a log-cabin household of some eight or nine persons who "lived and slept in the same room." The grandfather was sick, and one day near midnight the family

[24] My translation of this song is a free one. See the program of the St. Paul *Festival of Nations*, April 21, 22, 23, 1939, p. 24.

[25] Rasmus B. Anderson and Auber Forestier, eds., *The Norway Music Album* (Boston, 1881). This valuable work was published in a new edition in 1909.

heard an unseen power pick up the stove handle and drop it on the stove three times. This signified, according to the grandmother, that the sick man would die within three days; and — so goes the story — he did. Professor Haugen has also rescued the tale of a pioneer who believed that a neighbor woman employed witchcraft in producing better butter and getting higher prices for it than he did. In his efforts to counteract her special power he employed a traditional Norwegian remedy. He attempted to seal a curious fungus into a gun barrel, but in the process of forging, the barrel exploded — and the pioneer later said that the witch was on her way to the scene when the explosion occurred.

Riddles well-worn with use were always popular, such as "What is it that goes all day long but doesn't move from the spot?" — a clock; and "What tree grows with its root up and its top down?" — an icicle. And the old proverbs of Norway, many of them peculiarly applicable to the conditions of pioneer life, were transplanted to the immigrant West, such as "Little pitchers have big ears"; "When the need is greatest, help is nearest"; "He knows best how the shoe pinches who has it on"; and — a four-word condensation of the thought embodied in the saying about never crossing a bridge until you come to it — "That day, that sorrow."

Marriage was generally regarded as a sacrament of the church, and few immigrant couples felt that their union had been properly celebrated until the church had set its official stamp of approval upon it, even if the traditional religious ceremony postdated the actual marriage in common law. In frontier settlements where ministers appeared only on rare occasions, it was no uncustomary thing for the marriage to be performed by a lay preacher or perhaps a justice of the peace; but, whether such formalities had been observed or not, church sanction was likely to be requested and accorded later. When a clergyman arrived, couples came from many parts of the countryside to be married, sometimes a trifle hazy about the precise legal requirements, as is illustrated in the case of a young man who appeared with his bride before the Reverend Nils Brandt. When asked to produce his marriage license, he solemnly handed the minister his first citizenship papers.[26]

Weddings were sometimes sedate, and even severe, affairs, unattended by special celebrations;[27] but usually, and especially after the earlier difficulties of pioneering had been overcome, they occasioned much celebration and merrymaking, with everybody clad in his best clothes. At many parties there was a generous consumption of whisky. Often there were dances lasting far into the night. An interesting account of a frontier wedding in the Wisconsin Spring Prairie community tells of the bridegroom playing host in serving whisky to the guests, an elaborate wedding supper, and — after the minister had conveniently departed — a dance which continued until daylight. The dancing was interrupted by the traditional frontier charivari, and about midnight there was a "grand meal of lutefisk and smoked meats."[28]

A hasty remarriage by a widow or widower was looked upon with grave disapproval by most of the immigrants. When the pioneer minister C. L. Clausen, whose first wife died in November, 1847, remarried in February, Bache felt moved to make a severe entry in his diary: "People, especially Clausen's most loyal supporters have lost some of their wholehearted enthusiasm for him as a result of this precipitous remarriage" — and he took note of the fact that the

[26] The anecdote is told in an admirable sketch of the Reverend Nils O. Brandt by Ylvisaker, in *Eminent Pioneers,* 54–64.

[27] "Ugh! What a terrible way to be married!" was the eloquent exclamation of Elisabeth Koren after one prosaic wedding performed by her husband. *Fra pioneertiden,* 124.

[28] Ylvisaker, "The Funny Side of Things," in *Eminent Pioneers,* 109. It was the custom in pioneer days, writes A. Sophie Bøe, "for the prospective bridegroom to buy the material for the bride's dress, and for the bride to make the bridegroom's wedding shirt." *Story of Father's Life,* 29.

ceremony was performed, not by the Norwegian minister Dietrichson, but by an American clergyman. The implication seemed to be that Dietrichson would have nothing to do with the affair.[29] There was also grave suspicion of the wisdom, if not the morality, of marriage outside the Norwegian fold. There were indeed instances of intermarriage between Norwegians and Americans or people of other stock in the earlier frontier period, and with the passing years the practice became common, but the feeling of doubt about such a departure from a straight Norwegian alliance lingered long. It was particularly acute if the question of a Protestant-Catholic union was involved. The theme ultimately appeared in the realm of Norwegian-American fiction, for Rølvaag describes the marriage of the Norwegian Lutheran Peder Victorious and the Irish Catholic Susie, and he brings the traditional folkways into a clear focus by probing the troubled attitude of Peder's mother, Beret.

Notwithstanding a considerable amount of indulgence in liquor among the early Norwegian immigrants and the retention of many time-flavored amusements and festivities from the old country, there was a deeply rooted Puritan spirit among them, and particularly among those who shared the Haugean religious viewpoint. This spirit expressed itself not only in the movement for temperance reform but also in a severe disapproval of dancing, the theater, card playing, display in dress, and other practices and customs that for one reason or another were considered worldly and sinful. Alongside this Puritanism ran a more tolerant attitude which sprang from traditional ways in the old country and had not been bent by the Haugean philosophy. Professor Marcus L. Hansen believes that the immigrant Puritanism became progressively more pervasive with time. He cites the episode of a Norwegian picnic held on a Sabbath in Wisconsin in 1857. This outing resulted in considerable public criti-

[29] Bache Diary, March 6, 1847.

cism, and a clergyman ranged himself on the side of the critics. Some people asked why the clergy should frown upon practices which were not disapproved by the clergy in the old country, and the answer was that, if such practices brought the church "into disrepute," they should be abandoned. Hansen contends that church discipline tended to become "more and more strict," and he writes, "One after the other, social pleasures that were brought from the Old World fell under the ban. Temperance and Sunday observance were early enforced. Then card playing and dancing were prohibited. Simplicity in dress and manner of living were praised as virtues. The children of the immigrants were the subject of much concern." Ultimately, he says, the immigrant churches adopted "much of the New England atmosphere."[30]

That there was a pervasive Puritanism among the Norwegian immigrants is beyond all doubt, but its roots are deeper than Professor Hansen's essay suggests. The temperance movement among the immigrants certainly drew much strength, if not its original inspiration, from American sources; but in general the Norwegian-American Puritanism was independent of New England, or American, Puritanism. It was brought to the West from Norway by the immigrants themselves, particularly by those who accepted and followed the teachings of Hauge, Eielsen, and other apostles of pietism. The spirit was rooted in a sincere protest against the "worldly" practices that were associated in the popular mind with rationalism. It represented an alliance of Godliness with a profound distrust of human pleasures that tempted people away from the strait and narrow path. Eielsen had scarcely landed in New York in 1839 before he sounded a warning against the dangers of freedom and declared that human beings could "stand little of the cup of joy." He scanned the American metropolis for signs of

[30] Hansen, in *Studies and Records,* 9:1–28.

drinking, dancing, and amusements; and soon he was thundering among the immigrants against dancing and drinking as the principal causes of ungodliness among them.[31] He exemplified a Puritanism that was carried across the ocean from Norway and that in some ways out-Puritaned the Puritanism of the New Englanders. That this general interpretation is historically sound is suggested not only by ample evidence from the history of the Norwegian Americans but also by the similarity of Swedish-American Puritanism. The Swedish immigrants also had a deep strain of Puritanism that was firmly rooted in the pietistic movements of their mother country.[32]

Death was such a frequent visitor in the early immigrant communities, especially during cholera or other epidemics, that it was not always possible to observe the customary solemnities of the church in the matter of funerals. Rølvaag does not allow the body of Per Hansa, recovered months after his death, to be laid to rest until the minister finally arrived in the community. Ordinarily, however, funeral services would be held in the absence of the minister, and when he next visited the settlement "he would chant and cast earth upon the grave and deliver a sermon." Aaste Wilson pictures the frontier immigrant burial customs in stark detail. "For funerals," she writes, "people always had to be invited." There were always two meals, "one before they went to the graveyard, the other after they came back." Simple black homemade coffins were used, with nails driven halfway into the covers. The service opened with a hymn: "Who knows how near me is my death." Aaste's father, a layman, usually had charge of the services in the Wisconsin settlement where he lived: "He would give a talk in remembrance of the departed one and give thanks for him." Thereupon the people walked past the coffin for a

[31] See Eielsen's letters in *Lutheraneren,* 15:489, 548.

[32] Dr. Stephenson gives much attention to Puritanism among the Swedish immigrants in his *Religious Aspects.*

last look, "and immediately afterward we heard the sad sound of the hammering of the nails on the coffin lid." Then Aaste's father would say, "The day is passing and time is advancing, and the dead must go to his grave and final resting place." The coffin was carried out of the church while the people sang, "Though I must now depart, depart not Thou from me." The coffin was put in a wagon, driven to the graveyard, and the mourners walked behind it. Men took turns in digging the grave. When it was ready they placed their spades crosswise on it and sang, "Now the grave is a comfort to me, for Thy hand shall cover me." Then all said the Lord's Prayer, and that was the end. "It was simple but dignified and there was a Christian spirit and a deep sincerity in it all," writes Aaste Wilson. "They did it as well as they could."[33]

The majority of the immigrants seem to have accepted the hazards they met on the ocean crossing and in the western settlements with a degree of stoicism, but not a few were terror-ridden, haunted by the fear of disaster in the wilds of an unknown country. Most poignant were the anxiety for sick children and the anguish of their loss. Rølvaag pictures a woman who went mad when her small child died and was left behind in an unmarked grave on the prairie. Fear and sorrow, combined with the monotony of the prairie and a deep nostalgia, threw a pall of melancholy over many pioneer mothers, and unbalanced some. Per Hansa's wife fell into a trauma after the birth of her son Peder. She was tortured by many things, not least the grim power of the prairie to thwart her ambitious husband. Finally, half maddened, she concealed herself in an immigrant chest, a self-chosen coffin that seemed holy ground to her in the strange prairie land. The episode is fiction, but Rølvaag knew prairie life and hu-

[33] Wilson, in *Telesoga,* no. 33, p. 31, 32. She describes burial customs in the community of Otsego Township, Columbia County, Wisconsin, in the 1850's. When cholera ravaged the community in 1851, she says, there were reported to have been eighteen burials in two weeks.

man beings, and his portrayal of the psychological turmoil in the spirit of Beret is an authentic study of one aspect of the emotional history of immigration.

In early years many settlers had family burial plots on their own land, but usually the immigrant cemeteries were in or near the churchyards. When Ole Svendsen's wife Gro died, he wrote a description of her grave in an Iowa cemetery and sent it to his wife's parents in Norway. "I want to tell you about Gro's grave," he said. "It has been decorated with a white marble stone on which are engraved the date and place of her birth as well as of her death, how many of her family survived her, and a verse from David's Psalms. . . . I myself have planted a tree on the grave to keep weeds from spreading over it. Her friends have planted flowers and it has been enclosed with a very nice railing."[34]

In no realm do folkways express themselves more revealingly than in family life and the ways of children; and the realm is of particular significance for an understanding of immigrant transition. That it has been so largely neglected by American social historians is partly due to the inadequacy of the historical records of child life and the difficulties of exploring the activities and thoughts of youngsters in a bygone age. The setting is the home, however, and letters and diaries make it possible to get some pictures of the intimacies of the immigrants' home life. One does not read much or long without realizing that people were people in the pioneer era. Some immigrant children had a pitifully bleak life, but many knew good homes, childish joys, normal happiness. Parents had overweening pride in their offspring. They wrote eagerly to their parents across the ocean of little triumphs in the family circle. They were concerned about bringing up their children in accordance with the familiar

[34] Ole Svendsen to relatives in Norway, April 7, 1880, Nielsen Papers. The father of Rasmus B. Anderson had a private cemetery which is still in existence. Anderson, *Life Story,* 6.

precepts of the church. They transmitted to their children the folklore that they themselves had learned in childhood, and the second generation knew about trolls, woodland and mountain pixies, and traditional fairies. Immigrant parents took pride in reporting that their children could use and understand the speech of the old country, but they were no less proud to mention that they also were mastering the language of the new. Sometimes, like Beret, they feared a potential alienation of the second from the first generation and refused to have anything but their native tongue used in the home.

Contemporary pictures of frontier family life are etched in such charmingly subjective sources as Mrs. Koren's diary, the family letters of Olaus Duus, and those of Gro Nielsdatter Svendsen — the Gro whose grave was so affectionately decorated by Ole Svendsen — a buoyant and life-loving pioneer mother. Mrs. Koren was a lady of fastidious tastes, and sometimes she was dismayed by the number of children she found in small houses, especially when they were noisy and dirty. Once, however, in a "tiny log house," she found a flock of children who were "so clean and tidy it was a pleasure to look at them." She thought it unusual "to see children who were not all smeared with the everlasting molasses that they are constantly eating." Some youngsters, she observed, were carried papoose-fashion by their mothers. One day Anne Aarthun called "with no less than five children, the oldest nine, the youngest not yet a year." They brought "life enough into the house for one day and they raced up and down the attic stairs." Later they "went out and drove with my sled and horse and took care of the chickens." The "terrible uproar," Mrs. Koren said, "has certainly kept my fingers moving steadily all afternoon."

But Mrs. Koren, like all women on the frontier, found children a great comfort in the fight against loneliness. "Yes, now it is different to be home alone," she wrote after the birth of her first child. Naturally she was able to travel with her husband less than before. "No," she explained to him on one occasion, "we two shall stay at home to take care of the house and the chickens." Her husband, on his missionary journeys, had to give much attention to baptisms. In one day, on a trip in southern Minnesota, he baptized twelve. Sometimes after returning home, he was busy all day with baptisms. Usually they were solemnized in church on Sundays, and sometimes there were so many that services were very much protracted.[35]

Olaus Duus drew word pictures of family scenes in the 1850's that retain a startling vividness across the years.[36] His idol was his boy Olaf: "You should see him now as he sits on his mother's lap, eating prairie chicken and brown chicken broth with a piece of chicken in his hand. We can't give him any of our venison or any pork because he frightened us the other day by choking himself until he was quite blue in the face. . . . He is large for his age and quite a man." The minister returned from a drive on a bitter winter day: "The horse dashes along, urged both by my whip and by the comfortable assurance of oats and corn, and presently the equipage is out in the drive, while Wife and Little Boy stand at the window with beaming faces. Little Boy is all excitement. He stamps with his feet on the kitchen bench and claps with his hands on the windowpanes; he wants to get his hands on both Papa and Kitty [the horse], and Mamma has to hold him with both hands lest he make too hasty an acquaintanceship with the floor." The father sent a lock of the boy's hair to Norway. He reported that the boy liked to trot all over the house and to bring "Papa shoes, handkerchiefs, whip — whatever I ask for." Olaf was

[35] *Fra pioneertiden,* 82, 110, 113–118, 127, 139–141, 201–206. Since the particular items naturally have their setting in Mrs. Koren's story as a whole, it is of interest to read the entire diary from the point of view of homes and family relationships.

[36] This section on the home life of the Duus family is based upon the Duus Papers.

never quiet except when asleep. "You should see him when he comes stamping along in his long bodiced dress, with his little neck bare, his hair standing up in a cockscomb, red roses in his cheeks, with large and almost black eyes." Duus built a fence around his house and garden since Olaf and the pigs could never become reconciled. When the pigs were impudent Olaf liked to seize them by the snout and bite their ears.

Olaf sent his thanks for a toy wagon that he received from Norway. The boy was often in the garden. "He races around with a straw hat on and a short little frock, with bare feet and legs, his father's driving whip in his hand," rushing after the goose with shouts of "Get up! Get up!" The father thought Olaf a singularly pious boy, for the "minute he sees me take down the Book, he crawls up on the sofa and folds his hands." A letter pictures a scene of domestic felicity: two rocking chairs in front of the stove, Sophie holding Morten, the newly arrived baby, Duus holding Olaf and singing "Kitty, My Old Horse" and a ballad about Viggo, the pony. Probably most of the Norwegian immigrant children heard such rhymes as:

Ride, ride ranke
Hesten heter ikke saa,
Hesten heter Abildgraa.
Rask av sted nu skal det gaa,
Skjønt jeg dig ei fanger
Med min rappe ganger.

One moment Olaf was "romping and shouting so that we could hardly hear ourselves think"—then he was fast asleep. The boy learned to talk, and the father recorded his words, some English, some Norwegian. In time a second son and a daughter were added to the family circle. A gift box came from Norway and was unpacked amid great excitement, Olaf "blowing large blasts with his harmonica." Duus's two boys played in the ash pile and emerged looking like Espen

Askelad in the fairy tale. Another time they played "Confirmation," and Olaf solemnly asked the bishop, his young brother, "Will you please read me the fourth article?"

Amid such scenes an immigrant family arrived from Quebec. The father and mother had been crowded and pushed; all three of their children had had measles during the trip; despite "wind and weather" the parents had held them in their arms night and day. One child died and was buried by Pastor Duus. He tried to comfort the mother. She said, "Oh, if only the child could have been spared the tortures of the journey." A few days later the second of their children, a boy of ten and a half, died; and the third, a younger boy, grew steadily weaker.[37]

Gro Svendsen, pioneer mother, came to America in 1862 from her home in Aal, Hallingdal, as a bride, a merry, light-hearted, affectionate girl of twenty-one who was blessed with a lively curiosity.[38] Crossing the ocean, she made friends with the captain and crew and was given the "freedom of the ship." She relates that on "Easter evening there was dancing on the deck, and if we had only known how to waltz, we could have danced; but since we did not know how and apparently lacked the desire to learn, we shall have to live without waltzing." A bird flew onto the deck and was killed by the captain's dog — Gro was heartbroken. "Poor little creature that sought haven with us, but instead was torn to pieces!" she exclaimed. The dog whelped — Gro was delighted with its five puppies. Gro's mother-in-law had a baby — Gro took care of it and held it in her arms when the captain baptized it. She took note of the Seventeenth of May, and though it seemed to be ignored by the emigrants generally, she celebrated the day by herself, for she knew

[37] The story of this immigrant family is told in Duus's letter of August 9, 1857, Duus Papers.

[38] This section, dealing with the family life of Gro Svendsen, is based upon her letters written in the 1860's and 1870's. The particular letters here used form p. 157–302 of the Nielsen Papers.

what it meant to her native land. One night after midnight the seamen called her on deck to see an eclipse of the moon. When she reached Quebec she was pleased to have a taste of wheat bread and a drink of fresh milk. She was charmed, after the long voyage, by the sound of cocks crowing and of church bells ringing — the bells of six Quebec churches whose spires, she wrote, were "shining like silver in the morning sun."

And so Gro's party made its way to the American interior. Shortly after reaching St. Ansgar, Iowa, the baby that had been born at sea died and was buried. Gro and her husband went farther west and settled near Estherville, Iowa. They had not been long in America before Gro's first child was born; and at the first opportunity she sent a daguerreotype of her husband, baby, and herself to her people in Norway. She wanted to know as soon as possible what they thought of her child.

With a boy in her arms Gro attended an English school, "held at no great distance from here." She was determined to learn the language of her adopted country. Before long she herself was teaching school three days a week at twelve dollars a month, doing her heavier housework on the other days. Her boy grew and flourished, learned to say a few words, was smarter and prettier, his mother believed, than any other child in the community. "But one thing more," she wrote to her father, "can you tell me how I am to get my little boy vaccinated?" Later she thanked him for sending vaccine from Norway. A second son was born. And then, in 1864, Gro's husband Ole was drafted and marched away to the Civil War — she was left at home, she said, like a "lonely bird." The second son was baptized on the day Svendsen departed, and Gro insisted upon naming him Niels Olaus, using two names, an unusual thing in her family. The second was a form of her husband's name. She hinted in one letter at her reason for thus naming the boy:

she evidently had a premonition that the father would be killed in the war — she sent him away to the battlefields but, by the device of the name, she also kept him at home by her side. A third son was born while the father was away. Svendsen served in Sherman's army and returned home safely in August, 1865. He was discharged as an "honorable soldier," Gro explained to her parents in Norway, and in seven thousand miles of traveling and marching "he has seen and heard and felt much." She sent a picture of him in uniform to show her relatives in Norway what an American soldier looked like.

After the war the family grew steadily larger, and its activities were faithfully reported in letters to Norway written by Gro. Presently Svend was able to "handle the oxen very well, hitch and unhitch them to the wagon, and drive them long stretches alone, drive them down to water for his father, and do a number of things better than boys several years older than he is." Gro had a never-ceasing interest in the education of her boys. "But reading has been at a standstill this summer," she wrote in 1868. "Now, however, we have begun again, and in this district we are going to have three months of English school during the winter, and an American as schoolteacher. The school is to be held in Erik Sando's house." She also reported that the community would "have Norwegian school for several months, with Ole Johnson from the Bergen district as the teacher." Gro liked to tell about the progress of her children. There was Svend, for example. He had been at school for two months, was the youngest pupil, but won special praise for his unusual attentiveness and diligence. He had read through the first reader and was plowing through it again.

When Gro's fifth son was born, there seems to have been some difference of opinion between the father and the mother about naming him. The name, selected by Gro, was Albert Olai — the "Albert" in honor of "old Aslag," but she was unwilling to give the boy a name that would be so strange on American lips as "Aslag." In 1871 "little Steffen" arrived, and Gro wrote, "I thought I'd select a name that was a little more in conformity with American so that he wouldn't have to change it himself if ever he went out to live among Americans." This American tendency was also indicated when a pony on Gro's farm was named "Greeley." Gro had a genuine interest in names. In one letter she explained in careful detail the meaning and pronunciation of "Iowa." It signified, she said, "the beautiful land," and she told a circumstantial story of how the Indians gave it this poetical name. She also explained how the village of Estherville got its name — in fact, she said, she herself had on one occasion entertained the American lady named "Esther," for whom the village was named. Gro lived in Petterson Township, and she gave full information about the Norwegian pioneer whose memory was thus perpetuated. Her farm she called "Skrattegaard," her husband's somewhat infrequently used surname and the name of his home farm in Norway.

In 1873 a daughter was born to Gro and named Birgit. In due time another daughter, Sigri, appeared. Meanwhile Gro was not wholly satisfied with the progress of her sons. They were attending both Norwegian and English schools, but she feared they were not making rapid strides. "Had they been at home," she exclaimed impatiently, "I know well enough that they would have been much further advanced. Here Norwegian school is held so rarely, and it is so difficult to try to teach them at home." Her seven-year-old Ole, she reported in 1874, had the sharpest mind of all the children, and she was teaching him both English and Norwegian. Albert puzzled her, for he seemed remote and liked to ask "strange, disturbing little questions" on such extraordinary subjects as creation. Another son she described as the "actor" of the family.

The first house of the Svendsens was small and ugly, Gro thought, but it was replaced after the Civil War by a better one, and she explained that the new one would have come sooner had not her husband gone to war. Gro was always interested in the church and its successive ministers. Halvard Hande she regarded as exceptionally able, a man more interested in human needs than in church controversies. When he left to become a newspaper editor in Chicago and a new minister arrived, she expressed a grave doubt that the new man was of sufficient intellectual stature for the position. Of her husband she always wrote proudly, on one occasion explaining that he had held various positions of honor — constable, town trustee, and deacon in the church.

In 1876 woes struck the Svendsen family — measles, the death of Sigri, a scourge of grasshoppers that destroyed the crops, and other disappointments. Gro, usually buoyant and dauntless, wore an air of resignation to fate. In all these happenings she saw the will of God. Morbidly she took a picture of Sigri a few days before the child died. When, the next year, another girl was born — Gro had ten babies in about a decade and a half — the mother named it Sigri and thought of it as a gift from God to replace the lost Sigri. The new baby, with its dark brown eyes, seemed to her to be the image of the first Sigri. Gro continued to be depressed, however, and she felt that the "little thing" probably would be with her "only a short time." But presently her interests began to revive. All six of her boys were "going to English school every day." On Wednesdays two of them were "studying for confirmation at our pastor's." Some of them also attended the Norwegian Sunday school. "So we strive to do what we can to help them learn something useful both for life and eternity," wrote Gro. But she confessed discouragement as she thought of "our sacred duties as parents and the heavy responsibilities laid upon us." She lacked the means to do all that she wanted to do for her children, and she was frankly discontented. She talked the problem over with her husband and records his philosophical answer: "We must try to do our best by them according to our own lights and our means, and then entrust the rest to the Lord, who will help us if we pray him to."

It was in the midst of such speculations about the duties of parents and concern over the future of her children that this gallant and faithful lady died in 1878 in childbirth at the age of thirty-seven. She had described her husband as an "honorable soldier"—she herself was an honorable pioneer wife and mother who typified the best in both the immigrant and the American tradition. After reading her letters one can understand why Ole sent a lock of her hair to Norway and decorated her grave with marble and planted a tree on it, and why her friends planted flowers in her honor. The husband soon departed from the Iowa scene to pioneer in the Dakota country west of the Red River. Gro's boys wrote to their grandfather in Norway on Easter Sunday, 1880, from their new home in Dakota. Carl had been working on the farm of Tosten Nyhus. He had attended the Norwegian school and in his confirmation class had learned the Explanation and Bible history. "We are all well," he wrote, "and getting along nicely, for which we must thank the Lord." Ole, thirteen years old, had studied the Explanation up to the second article, had learned number 239 in Landstad's hymnbook, was attending school every day. Albert, seven, said, "My good grandfather, I must write to you to tell you that I am also going to school at Ole M. Bole's and have learned the second commandment in the Explanation and two little songs." He was the boy who asked strange and disturbing questions, but his letter does not tell us what questions he asked of Ole M. Bole. Nils, sixteen, said that he was planning to read for confirmation with Pastor Hagbø. "Greet grandmother from me," he added. Steffen, nine, explained that he was "the first one to learn

'Oh, grant it, God,'" and sent his best wishes to grandfather and "Gommo." Birgit and Sigri also transmitted their greetings. Barren and stiff little missives they are — after the warm and vivid letters of Gro — but they were treasured in a Norwegian home for more than a half century.[39]

Growing children found many ways of amusing themselves in frontier times. They went sledding, skiing, and tobogganing in winter, swimming, fishing, trapping, hunting, and flower-picking in summer. One of the Heg boys at Muskego was a hero to the community when he shot a swan.[40] Youngsters tried to tame wild animals — foxes, woodchucks, possums, coons, coyotes, wolves, and even skunks. A household animal was usually assigned to each child — an artful way, perhaps, of insuring a more cheerful care of the animals. On some frontiers neighbors lived very far apart, and families were obliged to be socially self-sufficient for considerable periods of time. But families were large. Birth control was unknown and ordinarily there were annual additions to the family. The number of children frequently ranged from a half dozen to a dozen or more. Professor Larson tells of a neighbor who could never remember offhand how many

[39] Gro Svendsen was a gifted writer as well as a personality of force and charm. In one of her letters she mentions the fact that she occasionally sent contributions to the Norwegian-American newspaper *Fædrelandet og emigranten.* She often served as "secretary" to her neighbors, helping them to write letters. One of Gro's brothers was the Reverend Ole Nilsen, of whom Laurence M. Larson, in his *Log Book,* 233, writes, "Even the finest clerical types of modern fiction could scarcely be an improvement on the character of this country pastor." Gro died on June 24, 1878, and was buried in the Brujeld cemetery near Wallingford. The grave, I discovered on a visit in 1940, has been marked with a new monument in recent years. The Reverend L. A. Mathre of Estherville kindly allowed me to examine the Estherville church records, which are in his possession. I am translating Gro's letters into English and expect to bring them out in book form. Some years ago Ole Nilsen published a short novel entitled *Dalrosen: Fra virkelighetens verden paa begge sider av havet* ("The Rose of the Valley: From the World of Reality on Both Sides of the Sea") in which Gro, whose name is changed for the purposes of the story to Aase Dalro, is the principal character. The story, which runs to seventy-six pages, was brought out by the Augsburg Publishing House in Minneapolis (n.d.). It is a moving tale, based upon the true experiences of Gro and her husband, and the characterization of Gro herself is done with genuine understanding of her quality.

[40] Bache Diary, April 8, 1846.

children he had, though by calling the roll he generally managed to list them all.[41] Such large families meant that each farm was a little community in itself.

After confirmation class, children often frolicked, though this was not always possible, for some had to go many miles on foot and wanted to get home before darkness came on. Rølvaag in *Peder Victorious* gives a vivid account of recess time in a Norwegian school, when hot rivalries had full swing and the teacher frequently had to intervene. There were also interracial rivalries. Hamlin Garland, recalling the district school that he attended as a boy, writes, "Here I came in contact with the Norwegian boys from the colony to the north, and a bitter feud arose (or existed) between the 'Yankees,' as they called us, and the 'Norskies,' as we called them." Garland remembers that sometimes the feud broke into open war, when "showers of sticks and stones filled the air, and our hearts burned with the heat of savage conflict." It was usually at parting that diplomatic relations were broken. The boys might walk pleasantly together for half a mile, when they "suddenly split into hostile ranks, and warred with true tribal frenzy as long as we could find a stone or a clod to serve as missile." Garland recalls no "personal animosity" in this feud; to him it was Pict fighting Angle.[42]

Such rivalries among the boys sometimes had parallels in the relations between adult Norwegian Americans and other groups. Larson, for example, has told the story of a riot in an Iowa community where the Norwegian element seemed to be getting control of a local political convention. Fence rails and neck yokes were the weapons in a fight between a gang of malcontents, largely Irish, and a crowd of Norwegians. Larson pays tribute to the fighting qualities of the Irish, but they were finally driven from the field by their

[41] *Log Book*, 43.
[42] *A Son of the Middle Border*, 77 (New York, 1917).

opponents, who outnumbered them. "Clan sentiment," Professor Larson asserts, was definitely present in the 1870's, but he points out that "racial antagonism could not long endure the wearing force of daily contact, and soon it disappeared altogether."[43]

In the summer the immigrant children often went on berrying expeditions, and in the autumn parties went nutting in the woodlands — unless they chanced to live on the treeless plains. Lulla Preus recalled excursions to pick flowers, plums, grapes, walnuts, hickory nuts, and hazelnuts; and Larson remembered the attraction of prairie flowers, especially the violet, which he called "night and day." Rosinweed was the frontier boy's chewing gum. There were also indoor amusements. Lulla Preus spoke of the invariable readiness of her mother "to entertain the young people. Either she played the piano for us, told us stories, or taught us any number of games which she could take part in, too, and thus give them added life." She remembered twilight scenes when her father would tell stories or sing. "There seemed to be no end to the hymns and little songs which my parents knew."[44] There appear to have been relatively few competitive sports. Wrestling was popular among boys, however, and both boys and girls took part in spelling matches. In some games old counting-out rhymes were used, not unlike "eeny, meeny, miney, mo":

Elle melle
Mig fortelle
Skibet gaar
Ut paa haar
Rygg i rann
To i spann
Snipp, snapp, snute,
Ute.

The immigrant frontier boy, according to Larson, was looked upon as sufficiently developed at fourteen to do the

[43] See Larson's essay on "The Convention Riot at Benson Grove, Iowa, in 1876," in the *Changing West*, 39–48.

[44] Preus, in *Symra*, 7: 7–12; Larson, *Log Book*, 29.

work of a man; and many a farmer found the road to prosperity cleared for him by the man power of his own family as his many boys reached the age when they could share in the rough work of the fields. Sometime between fourteen and sixteen, confirmation was solemnized. When this event took place, "in some respects a person was considered as having attained his majority." One reminiscent writer says that confirmation "for us settlers' children was the day when boys or girls had to begin supporting themselves."[45] If this was its practical significance, it must be remembered that it was primarily a religious landmark. Larson's minister insisted that he be confirmed as he neared his sixteenth year, and his parents acquiesced, though the son seemed not to be impressed with the necessity of the rite—and his parents were sadly aware of the state of his mind. It is apparent that he cannily realized how stereotyped the ceremony often was, and the seeming futility of hammering required answers into the heads of some of the country dolts. "Dost thou renounce the devil and all his works?" the minister asked a terrified youngster who had no idea of the meaning of the strange word "renounce." "No," he answered in swift relief, to the horror of the congregation. The clergyman rephrased the question, avoided the word "renounce," and put the matter so that it called for a negative answer; but the boy now aware that his original "No" was wrong, blurted out "Yes." The sacrament was, of course, a solemn occasion, prepared for by a period of "reading for the minister"; and the confirmands, as well as the proud parents, were dressed in their best when the fateful day of public examination and vows arrived. Sometimes guests visited the homes of the young confirmed people after services were over, and occasionally there were "confirmation gifts."[46]

A little-recognized role of pioneer immigrant children was

[45] Ylvisaker, *Eminent Pioneers,* 31.
[46] Larson, *Log Book,* 131–134.

that of mitigating the nostalgia of the pioneer mothers. So common and so deeply rooted was this immigrant nostalgia that it was a part of the folkways of the people. "Fate has indeed separated me from my native land and all that was dear to me there," wrote Henrietta Jessen from Wisconsin in 1850, "but it is not denied me to pour forth my feelings upon this paper. My dear sisters, it was a bitter cup for me to drink, to leave a dear mother and sisters and to part forever in this life, though living." This was a typical note, echoed over and over again in the America letters and the ballads of the emigrants, but usually it was accompanied by an assurance of trust in an all-wise providence. Henrietta thought that of all the emigrants from Arendal, "none went on board with a heavier heart" than she. She hoped that time would heal her wounds, though, she added, "up to the present I cannot deny that homesickness gnaws at me hard." Yet she thanked "the Lord who gave me strength to carry out this step, which I hope will be for my own and my children's best in the future." She was confident that God "protected me and mine over the ocean's waves and led us to a fruitful land, where God's blessings are daily before our eyes."[47]

Henrietta Jessen and thousands like her found companionship and comfort in their children, and they held their courage. There was a never-ending round of tasks and activities — loom and spinning wheel to be run, meals to be cooked, the sick to be cared for. There was childbearing year after year — and the incessant demands of infants and children of varying ages. Time, and not least the unrelenting work that packed its passing hours, did indeed heal their wounds. The initial ordeals of pioneering were met, and for

[47] Mrs. Jessen's letter, in *Studies and Records,* 5:22–26. Mrs. E. G. Quamme in an essay on "The Norwegian Pioneer Mother" suggests three outstanding traits that seem to find confirmation in the story of Henrietta Jessen: devotion to family ties, faith in the future of America, and firm religious convictions. Guttersen, "*Norse-American Women,*" 23–25.

many there came the "better days" that had beckoned them. Events crowded upon the homes and upon the communities of which the homes were a part. Time and interest were poured into church and social relationships. There was the eternal march of the seasons, each posing its particular problems and challenges. Children passed from infancy to their teens, girls shared in the work of the house as boys went out to share in the work of the field, and presently the second generation came of age. Some of the pioneer mothers did not survive their ordeals to win final rewards, but many had the satisfaction of seeing their children solidly established on prosperous farms or in the near-by towns, sometimes making places of trust and service for themselves in the life of community and state.[48] The hunger for schooling and education that marked the spirit of Gro Svendsen was characteristic of very many pioneers, and a significant phase of the frontier folkways. For Gro and her kind saw education as the path to the larger opportunities that America offered. The hunger was that of parents ambitious for the welfare of their children, and in many instances it communicated itself to those children. It became a common thing for the younger generation to go to school and to push on to academies, colleges, and universities — and they began to make careers in the professions. So in a thousand ways the transition to American life, working across the years and generations, made good the hope that gave confidence to the Henrietta Jessens and Gro Svendsens and their husbands of the frontier era — the hope that strengthened the souls of the immigrant fathers and mothers as, with courage and patience, they grappled with their many ordeals.

[48] For a vivid portrait of a pioneer wife and mother, Mrs. Gjertrud Hilleboe, whose "training, knowledge of the English language, American ideas of housekeeping, and other accomplishments, made her a teacher and leader among the women who came directly from their foreign homes," see Guttersen, "*Norse-American Women,*" 28–43.

VIII. THE IMMIGRANT AND THE COMMON SCHOOL

IN THE UNITED STATES, said Ole Rynning in 1838, public education "is within the reach of all." The American "realizes very well what an advantage the educated man has over the ignorant, and he spares nothing in the instruction and education of his children." Though Rynning wrote only a short time after the Norwegian immigrants had begun to arrive in the Middle West, he was able to report that two schools, "where the children learn English," already had been established among his countrymen in the Fox River settlement. He anticipated a quick transition to English, for the Norwegian language, he thought, "seems destined to die out with the parents." He noted that the children "do not learn to read Norwegian." Speaking for the benefit of "peasant and commoner" in Norway, he drew attention to the allotment of the sixteenth section in each township as school land, the proceeds from the sale of which could be used to set up a township school fund.[1]

[1] Rynning, *True Account of America,* 89.

So typical was the early note thus sounded by Rynning, and so widespread the immigrant desire to learn English and to become familiar with the institutions of the adopted country, that it seems startling to learn that a long and bitter controversy centering about the American common school was carried on among the Norwegian immigrants. This fact is the more surprising when one searches in vain for records of any similar controversy among the Swedes. And the curiosity of the historian is piqued when he learns that the majority of the Norwegians, like the Swedes, cheerfully supported the public school system.

Was the Norwegian-American school controversy a projection of the battle that the Americans themselves had fought over the merits of the common school? That school was a symbol of democratic reform in young America. It was defended and promoted as a cornerstone of American democracy by Horace Mann and others in a period of rising democracy, but it encountered sharp charges of ineffectiveness and of godlessness. "Excepting the battle for the abolition of slavery," writes E. P. Cubberley, "perhaps no question has ever been before the American people for settlement which caused so much feeling or aroused such bitter antagonisms. The friends of free schools were at first commonly regarded as fanatics, dangerous to the State, and the opponents of the free schools were considered by them as old-time conservatives or as selfish members of society." Certainly the beginnings of the American common school were humble and inauspicious. Terms were short, teachers poorly trained, funds inadequate, effective school laws lacking. There were indeed school lands, but in sparsely settled areas even the allotment of the sixteenth section of each township did not magically set up a common school. The defects of the common school were many, but it was a changing and developing, not a static, institution. As time went on, the original three-month terms were lengthened, salaries for teachers were increased, normal schools established, teachers better trained, state and local supervision inaugurated, studies better planned, tax support increased, buildings and equipment improved.[2]

Norwegian-American critics seized upon palpable defects in the common school as targets for their criticisms and they took cognizance of the fact that Americans were themselves conscious of these defects. Yet their point of view seemed to be little affected by the obvious advance and improvement of American elementary education as the country grew in wealth and population. It seems evident, therefore, that the roots of the Norwegian-American controversy on the school question go deeper than a concern about the efficiency of the common school. A review of the story discloses the fact that these roots strike into a subsoil in which Lutheran orthodoxy is the chief ingredient, with a considerable admixture of Norwegian nationalism. Of the two factors, Lutheran orthodoxy is clearly the major one, but even that, taken in its general significance, scarcely offers a conclusive explanation for the phenomenon of the school controversy. One must not forget that the Swedes did not quarrel about the public schools, and yet they were, for the most part, orthodox Lutheran in their faith, believers in the Augsburg Confession, deeply interested in transmitting their Lutheranism to their children and grandchildren. Unless one believes that the Norwegians fought a bitter battle on the question of elementary education because of contentiousness, exuberance, or sheer love of controversy, one must therefore probe further. In doing so, one brings to light a set of circumstances present in the Norwegian-American school discussions which was wholly lacking among the Swedish-American Lu-

[2] Ellwood P. Cubberley, *History of Education,* 672, 676–708 (Boston, 1920); Merle Curti, "Education and Social Reform: Horace Mann," in *Social Ideas of American Educators,* 101–138 (New York, 1935); Carl R. Fish, *Rise of the Common Man, 1830–1850,* 201–203 (New York, 1929); Luther A. Weigle, *American Idealism,* ch. 9 (New Haven, 1928).

therans. This was the extreme Lutheran orthodoxy of the clergy of the Norwegian Synod, whose theological training in the national university of Norway was reinforced in America by an absorption of the religious and educational ideas of the German Lutheran Missouri Synod. This factor, buttressed by a genuine concern about retaining the native speech and traditions of the Norwegian immigrants in conjunction with "pure doctrine," was unquestionably the pivot of the school controversy.

In the period of the 1830's and 1840's the Norwegian immigrants gratefully sent their children to such district schools as were available. When Elling Eielsen in 1846 organized his church followers, he recommended, in his church constitution, the training of the immigrant children in both English and Norwegian. He placed Norwegian first, but specified that instruction in the mother tongue should be given "in such a way that the district school is not neglected."[3] Eielsen understood the importance of reaching the children in his church through the medium of the language they were learning in the district schools, and it is significant that his English translation of Luther's Smaller Catechism, brought out in 1841, was intended for the use of immigrant children who could not read Norwegian.[4]

As congregations took form, parochial schools were established with a view to teaching the children the religion of their fathers; and in the late 1840's some of these schools had longer terms than the common schools. The Norwegian traveler, Ole Munch Ræder, who visited the Wisconsin settlements in 1847, pointed out this fact after observing conditions at Rock Prairie, where C. L. Clausen was the pastor:

[3] Article 13 in the "Old Constitution," in Rohne, *Norwegian American Lutheranism,* 109.

[4] Carlsen, "Elling Eielsen," 129. Carlsen, citing Eielsen's *Organ,* June, 1866, points out that in 1865 the Eielsen church body determined to have all its books of religious instruction made available in English translations. For an account of the *Organ* which was published at La Crosse, Wisconsin, by the Evangelical Lutheran church see Carlsen's bibliography, p. vii.

"A parochial school has been established, in which instruction is given six months of the year; the teacher, who is also the precentor, is paid ten dollars a month, I believe. He will presumably be made the teacher at the public school also because practically only Norwegians live in the vicinity; the former teacher there was likewise a Norwegian, but now the position is vacant. In the public schools instruction is given only three months a year as a rule; and, as a result, no matter how well the teacher is paid during the short term, he has to engage in some other business as well in order to support himself."[5]

When the aggressive Norwegian minister J. W. C. Dietrichson arrived at Muskego in 1844, he found that only a few Norwegian children attended the nearest district school, which was conducted in a "little, poor log house." With characteristic energy he helped to organize a district school to which all the children of the settlement had access, and he also established, in 1845, a parochial school, employing with his own private funds a teacher for three months at ten dollars a month. In the parochial school instruction was restricted to religion and choral singing, with the understanding that the common school would furnish instruction in English and other studies. Dietrichson also set up a congregational library; and he appealed to the people of Norway for financial aid in building churches and schools and supporting ministers and teachers. The moral and religious conditions among the Norwegian immigrants were, to his mind, deplorable; but he apparently accepted the common school as a desirable adjunct to the congregation in meeting the problem of immigrant primary education.[6]

The Reverend H. A. Stub, fresh from Norway, investigated immigrant conditions in 1848 and sounded a more critical note. He was appalled by the "spiritual and educa-

[5] Ræder, *America in the Forties,* 136.
[6] Dietrichson, *Reise,* 40, 41, 48, 49; *Nordlyset,* June 8, 1848.

tional darkness" that he found. It was, he said, "more dreadful than I had imagined." He was shocked to find that some of the immigrants considered the common schools quite adequate to their needs. This meant that they did not regard instruction in Norwegian as essential. Stub believed, however, that the American school was far from adequate, that in fact an intimate connection with the public school system would inevitably cause many Norwegians to be lost to the Lutheran church, their language and heritage alike despised and forgotten. Some immigrants in Chicago, he learned, had even married outside the Norwegian nationality and he regarded them as wholly lost both to the church and to the immigrant social group.[7]

The emerging Norwegian Synod, under the leadership of recently arrived clergymen, meanwhile gave increasing attention to the problem of educating the immigrant children. In 1851 the church set up rules for examining the qualifications of parochial school teachers, and the following year, meeting at old Muskego, it defined a general policy. This called for early training in the Norwegian language. The immigrant children, it was suggested, after a basic grounding in the speech of the homeland, should take up the study of English at about the age of thirteen. The church thus took a stand against any quick immigrant transition to English and at the same time revealed a critical attitude toward the American common school, whose spirit and discipline, it declared, were not conducive to the Christian development of children. The clergy felt that the common school might prove an obstacle in the way both of Norwegian-American group solidarity and of the influence of the church upon the people of the second generation. The church group urged congregations to establish parochial schools, and incidentally to build up good congregational libraries; and the next year it enjoined the pastors to visit the parochial schools regularly

[7] *Nordlyset*, November 8, 1849.

and to conduct annual public examinations of the school children. Thus, coupled with definite reservations as to the efficacy of the public schools, the idea of congregational schools was given a powerful stimulus in the pioneer years of the Norwegian church in America.[8] Such schools, oftentimes peripatetic like the Norwegian *omgangsskoler,* were held for brief terms from farmhouse to farmhouse, or in the buildings of common schools when the latter were not in session, or perhaps in church or parsonage.

As time went on, the parochial summer school became a characteristic institution in Norwegian-American Lutheran communities. Many of the parochial school instructors in the earlier years were schoolteachers trained in Norway—*seminarister*—but in due time students from Norwegian-American theological seminaries and colleges took their places.[9] Normally supplementary to the common schools, the parochial schools placed their major emphasis upon religion, the Bible, church history, and the singing of Norwegian religious hymns, but sometimes they found room for spelling, reading, arithmetic, and other subjects. At a meeting centering about the problems of parochial school teachers held in the late 1850's, the teacher at Koshkonong pointed out that as a matter of pedagogy, particularly in the matter of interesting the minds of young pupils, an unvaried diet of religion was inadvisable; and he therefore urged the inclusion not only of arithmetic and writing, but also of geography, natural history, and "world history."[10] The parochial school masters were not seldom influential figures within the circles of the church communities they served. Sometimes, among other things, they helped to build up congregational

[8] Rohne, *Norwegian American Lutheranism,* 116, 122, 124, 131.

[9] Osm. Aslakson, "De burde havt et ord," in *Symra,* 10:253–260 (1914); Norlie, *Norwegian People in America,* 215, 216; A. L. Lien, "Kirke og skole i Bluemounds settlementet," in *Samband,* no. 62, p. 362 (June, 1913).

[10] *Kirkelig maanedstidende,* 4:103, 104 (July, 1859). The school conference was held at Rock Prairie on October 1 and 2, 1858. The teacher at Koshkonong was J. Agerholm.

libraries that made genuine contributions to the cultural life of the pioneer settlers.

During the 1850's, notwithstanding the skepticism of the clergy, the Norwegian immigrants in general seem to have sent their children to the rural and town schools, accepting the opportunities thus given them to learn English and to gain a primary education. At the same time they were supplementing this training by religious instruction in parochial schools. In the same period, however, the clergy, recruiting its strength by new arrivals of ministers from Norway, was becoming increasingly powerful, and its feeling of doubt as to the virtues of the common school was deepening.[11] The contacts of the Norwegian Synod with the German Missouri Synod, originating with a careful study by two Norwegian clergymen in 1857 of the Missouri Synod's educational institutions and eventuating in the selection of Professor Laur. Larsen in 1859 as the occupant of the Norwegian chair at Concordia Seminary in St. Louis, brought within the orbit of Norwegian-American knowledge and interest the Missouri system of parochial school education as a substitute for the American common school.[12] In 1858, at a Norwegian conference on parochial schools at Coon Prairie, attended by parochial teachers and Synod preachers, the problem of religious education was discussed in detail. President A. C. Preus, acting as spokesman for the conference, rejected the idea of rapid Americanization, "idolized by the Norwegians" in the early years; conceded that if the discipline of the American common school was good, children might be sent there for part of the year; urged that religion should be taught the immigrant youth in the language of their homes — "the mother tongue is the language of the heart" — and

[11] See Larson's essay on "Skandinaven, Professor Anderson, and the Yankee School," in *The Changing West*, 116–120. Larson describes Preus, Ottesen, Koren, Larsen, and Muus as the "architects of the Norwegian Synod." This essay is the most illuminating study in print of the common-school controversy.

[12] Larsen, *Laur. Larsen*, ch. 5, 6.

touched upon the possibility of enlarging the parochial schools, expanding their studies to include English and other subjects, and ultimately supplanting, rather than supplementing, the American common schools among the Norwegian immigrants, as the Germans had done for their church groups in various cities. At a second conference, held in October, 1858, at Rock Prairie and attended by eleven ministers and seventeen parochial school teachers, President Preus's views were unanimously endorsed.[13]

Hitherto there had been no open controversy on the question of Norwegian-American support of the common school, but the stand taken at the parochial school conference was promptly challenged. It was a Danish-born schoolmaster at Scandinavia, Waupaca County, Wisconsin, who cast down the gauntlet before the clergy in 1858 on the school question. Rasmus Sörensen had been trained in a Danish academy, and before he became a leader of Danish immigration to America he had been active in his native land in the fight for popular education and social reform in the interest of the *bønder*.[14] He now submitted a lengthy article to *Emigranten* in which he defended the American public school system and denounced the Norwegian-American clergy.[15] He praised American lawmakers, who were advancing "education and enlightenment for the whole people." Public education in Wisconsin, he said, was in its childhood and needed to be watched and nurtured. All the immigrant children, in his opinion, needed to be kept "regularly and diligently in attendance at our American free schools." Instruction in English was essential to their advancement in

[13] The Coon Prairie meeting, held on June 28, 1858, is reported by J. A. Ottesen in *Kirkelig maanedstidende,* 3:134–140 (September, 1858); and the minutes of the Rock Prairie conference are in the same publication, 4:33–42, 103–112 (March–April, July, 1859).

[14] An interesting account of this remarkable Danish-American pioneer is in *Danske i Amerika,* 1:337–346. In 1859–60 Sörensen himself edited a periodical entitled *Organ for religion, landökonomie og politik.*

[15] *Emigranten,* November 1 and 8, 1858.

"their real and true fatherland, America." If the counsels of the Norwegian clergy were followed, the immigrant children would be shaped and molded as "Norwegian Indians in America" and ultimately would be treated as "outcasts and trash."

He called on the immigrants to give the Norwegian preachers "the answer they deserve" for their hostility to the American district school system. The inevitable result of such a reply, he believed, would be that the children would become "true Americans, one nation, together with all other Americans." As to the omission of religion from the American public school, he pointed out that, while the common school did not bar the reading of the Bible or the learning of Bible stories, it naturally could give no place to the creeds and customs of particular sects. The subjects it did teach were essential to one's lifework and citizenship in America. He reserved his sharpest words for the clergy's general position on parochial schools. He declared that the settlements had witnessed a process of "pastoral Norwegianization." "Can Americanism grow and thrive in the Norwegian settlements in America," he asked, "before it is planted in the children and in the young people?" He urged that "God's Word" should be read and expounded in the "American language," at any rate for the rising generation, reserving Norwegian for the benefit of the elderly and of newly arrived immigrants. If each one of the various national groups established a district school system of its own, looking upon English as a foreign language, he saw as the outcome nothing but national and religious wars in America; and he closed by excoriating what he called a "stupid imagined fear of everything American."

This was a frontal assault, indeed, and it was met by an answer from the pen of the Reverend A. C. Preus, the president of the Norwegian Synod.[16] As to the common school,

[16] *Emigranten,* November 27, 1858.

Preus said that he had no objection to it if it enjoyed the services of a "competent, zealous, and conscientious teacher," but after much observation of American district schools in the West he had been forced to the conclusion that they were "as bad as it is possible for them to be and still deserve the name of schools." Neither laws nor buildings nor money could assure good schools, he said, if they lacked good teachers; and in his opinion nine out of ten teachers in the American common schools were so young, ignorant, and lacking in experience that they were incapable of conducting a decent school. To make matters worse, most teachers stayed on for only one term — from three to six months — and hence the school derived no profit from the experience that the teacher gained during that period. "Such a thing as discipline in the school, or respect for the teacher," he declared, "is rarely seen in the West." He had himself sent his own children to the common schools, but the results had been discouraging. His daughter, six years old, reported that her teacher addressed her class as "Ladies and Gentlemen!" Preus said that he by no means opposed the learning of the English language; in fact, his own children read English and Norwegian almost equally well; nor did he have any wish that the immigrant children should not become enlightened American citizens; but he took the position that "a bad school is worse than no school at all." As to the problem of parochial schools and the use of Norwegian, until English actually supplanted Norwegian in the immigrant homes, the Norwegian language necessarily must be used in the church and the parochial schools. Religious teaching and preaching should employ the language of the heart, which he defined as the language in which one thinks and prays. English, for the Norwegian-speaking immigrants, was obviously not their mother tongue; hence it must seem a foreign language.[17]

[17] The documents of this debate appear with an excellent introduction by Professors Paulson and Bjørk, in *Studies and Records,* 10:76–106. It is of interest

This exchange of opinion had many echoes in the press, but it did not open up a controversy in full force. A satirical and humorous letter, ostensibly supporting Sörensen, was couched in the mixed Norwegian-American, and in its way threw more realistic light upon the problem of language than all the other contributions combined.[18] "Peder Paars" offered, in heavy sarcasm, mock praise of Norwegian teachers and schools. Preus returned to the attack by marshaling American criticisms of the common schools to prove that the Americans themselves were not blind to the shortcomings of their system; and Sörensen ventilated his views on the respective merits of American and Scandinavian literature.[19] But perhaps the most significant outcome of the discussion was a joint declaration, in the summer of 1859, by eleven clergymen of the Norwegian Synod setting forth their general position "On Schools and Language Conditions." This declaration, whose signers included Professor Larsen, Koren, Ottesen, H. A. Stub, A. C. and H. A. Preus, and Brandt, took the characteristic form of a series of theses.[20]

The ministers began with a forthright statement that the Norwegians in America needed a thorough knowledge of English and that it was their duty to secure it so far as they were able to do so, that they might the better fulfill their duties as citizens. Such a knowledge was necessary not only from the point of view of their material well-being, but also in order to be able to understand American writings and

to note that Preus issued a Norwegian spelling book in 1857. *Emigranten,* August 26, 1857.

[18] *Emigranten,* December 27, 1859; *Studies and Records,* 10:100–106.

[19] The "Peder Paars," Preus, and Sörensen items are in *Emigranten,* February 1, 8, April 18, 1859. See also a sharp criticism of Sörensen by Aslak Halvorsen Houchum, in *Emigranten,* December 13, 1858; a contribution on the other side by Joseph Larson of Goodyears Bar, California, April 4, 1859; and a general discussion entitled "Lidt om skolen," November 21, 1859.

[20] *Kirkelig maanedstidende,* 4:156, 157 (October, 1859). The document, reported by Ottesen as secretary, also appeared in *Emigranten,* October 31, 1859. The signers included, in addition to those named above, P. M. Brodahl, C. F. Clausen, N. E. Jensen, and C. F. Magelsen.

judge the various religious teachings in America. They went on to praise religious freedom as one of the greatest advantages of the American system and to pledge their purpose to retain, under this freedom, their Lutheran faith and old Norwegian church order, and to bring up their children in this faith. Since most of the Norwegian-American church members did not yet sufficiently understand English, it was necessary to conduct church services and to teach religion in Norwegian, "the language of home prayer and devotions." They proposed to teach the Norwegian-American children the Norwegian language and religion not only because of their natural love for the old fatherland but also because, viewing religion as the most essential of all knowledge, they looked upon the language in which it was taught as "more significant to us than anything else." They regarded it as perfectly possible both to study religion in Norwegian and to learn English, but issued a warning against the use of the common schools if they placed children in danger of being cut away from their Lutheran faith. As to the common schools, they pointed out that they had little discipline and that children should be sent to them only after careful investigation, and they urged parents meanwhile to do all in their power to improve them so that their children would not need to be denied the important knowledge that such schools offered. If the district schools were good, they concluded, children might safely be sent to them, and they recommended an energetic patronage of them. Some attention was given to the school question in the Synod meeting of the same year and it was decided, among other things, not necessarily to exclude from the church those who refused to give active support to the congregational schools of religion. The local situation was to be the deciding factor.[21]

The moderate tone of this ministerial declaration of 1859, coupled with the Civil War, seems to have been responsible

[21] *Emigranten,* October 22, 1859; Larson, *Changing West,* 121, 122.

for a postponement of a thoroughgoing discussion and controversy on the school question, but the Synod leaders were not inclined to let them rest permanently. After the Civil War, in 1865, Pastor Koren and Professor Schmidt of Luther College proposed to the Synod that a committee should undertake a study of the religious schools and particularly of the prospects of including additional subjects in their curricula so that the common schools could be made superfluous for the Norwegian immigrants or at any rate that some of the main difficulties in the way of the parochial schools might be removed. This proposal led to an elaborate report by Pastor Brandt and Professors Schmidt and Larsen, and this, in turn, placed before the Synod for action at its meeting in Manitowoc, Wisconsin, in 1866, set off the larger controversy that had been brewing ever since the clergy began to challenge the public school system.[22] The report and the Synod action that followed it definitely steered the church in the direction of the Missouri Synod system of parochial schools, not to supplement, but to supplant the American public schools; and this tendency came into conflict with the views of Norwegian-American laymen throughout the country.

The committee conceded that the common schools deserved praise and support as a state institution, and it accepted without cavil the fact that the state schools could not permit instruction in Christianity, that an attempt to introduce such instruction would have the character of an assault upon religious freedom. But it put forward the view that Christian instruction would produce good citizens and that the state had no cause for complaint if the church chose to send its children to its own schools. In a word, it said that the state should not compel children to go to the public schools. All this served as a preface to a series of twenty-seven theses

[22] *Kirkelig maanedstidende*, 11:210–223 (May, 1866); *Synodalberetning*, 1866, p. 19–40.

that were placed before the Synod for consideration and action. Of these only eight were acted upon, most of them after changes of one kind or another, but these touched the heart of the question.

The Synod began by accepting the dictum that "For Christians it must be regarded as natural to employ only Christian schools for their instruction." It then went on to declare that "In this country it must therefore as a general rule be looked upon as desirable for Christians to set up parochial schools that will permit the teaching of approximately the same things which are taught in the so-called 'Common Schools' and that the latter therefore will not need to be used." It recognized a civic responsibility, however: "As citizens it is our duty to support these common schools even if we do not utilize them for our own children." But it asserted that the "greatest service of these religionless schools" was for the non-Christian portion of the population which "does not desire Christian instruction." The fifth thesis, modified in the course of debate, finally read: "That religion is not taught in these schools is a necessary result of the religious freedom which we consider ourselves fortunate to enjoy under the present constitution of the state." The question arose, however, whether Christian parents should in all cases keep their children away from the public schools, and the Synod was not prepared to take this position. It recognized that an adequate system of parochial schools to supplant the common school could not be attained in any near future, and it therefore urged its church members to attempt to secure a large degree of influence in the management of the district schools, particularly in the matter of the appointment of teachers and the determination of the length of the school terms. But where such influence cannot be gained "and the district school is so conducted that it is a serious danger to the Christian faith or the morality of the children, then it is the definite duty of Christian parents to keep their children away and to work so much more actively for the development of the parochial school." The final thesis, upon which no formal action seems to be recorded but which represented the generally accepted view of the clergy, was a counsel to send the children — in the event that other arrangements were not practicable — to the public schools for instruction in English only after they had been confirmed, that is, at about the age of thirteen.[23]

In a series of lectures held in Norway in 1867, President H. A. Preus of the Synod explained that the central point in the opposition to the American common schools was that they were "religionless." He declared himself unwilling to turn over Norwegian Lutheran children to the guidance of teachers who were, for example, Catholics, Methodists, or atheists. He spoke of the lack of discipline in the district schools, the steady shift of teachers, and, though conceding that pupils did learn to read and write, he had little to say for the efficiency of the schools. He realized that many Norwegians would be dissatisfied not to derive advantage from an institution that they supported through taxation and that they would have difficulties of their own in building and conducting schools, but these considerations, to his mind, did not make the goal any less desirable — that of broadening the parochial schools and of making the district schools unnecessary for the Norwegian church group. He further was aware that the parochial schools themselves lacked good teachers and were not too advanced — a general point that the critics of the Synod position were soon to hammer home relentlessly — and that the people in the congregations needed to be aroused to the general need of good schools.[24]

Meanwhile, a storm of opposition to the Synod's stand on

[23] See the report of the Synod discussion and action in *Synodalberetning,* 1866, p. 32–40.

[24] Herman A. Preus, *Syv foredrag over de kirkelige forholde blandt de Norske i Amerika,* 32–36 (Christiania, 1867).

the school question was rising in the Middle West. It found one of its most pertinacious spokesmen in Knud Langeland, the doughty editor of the Chicago *Skandinaven,* launched in the very year of the Synod's meeting at Manitowoc. He took sharp issue with the theses adopted by the church body, declared that the clergy evidently intended salvation to be the reward of "ignorance and superstition," and called upon the common people to speak out on the issue. They had been largely occupied with their pioneering and, in his opinion, were being led into paths that would be genuinely injurious to their future. The choice was between being overrun by the Missouri Synod spirit and arousing the "free, patriotic Scandinavian element." The common school was the road to enlightened participation by Norwegian Americans in the life of their times, and the times demanded efficient and fruitful teaching of the young. He saw no hope in parochial schools as a substitute for public education, for they would surely be handicapped by financial difficulties, a dearth of teachers who could handle the English side in adequate fashion, and general inefficiency. As he warmed to his theme he even hinted that it might be treasonable to reject the American common school.[25]

As the controversy began to resound in the Norwegian-American press, Langeland found himself emphatically supported by the young and aggressive Rasmus B. Anderson, recently expelled from Luther College in Decorah, Iowa, for leading a student revolt, and just launching his long career as a teacher, writer, and public figure.[26] Anderson appeared as a delegate at the Synod meeting of 1868 and called for a reconsideration of the school question. He proposed that the congregations be asked to take an active interest in their American common schools and, among other things, to secure

[25] A general survey of the controversy is published as an editorial in *Skandinaven,* May 26, 1869. See also Larson, *Changing West,* 123–126.

[26] Anderson, *Life Story of Rasmus B. Anderson,* 47 ff., 71, 72, 98, 99 (Madison, Wisconsin, 1915).

the appointment of teachers who were competent in both the English and the Norwegian languages. He believed that it might prove possible to find a place, in the Norwegian communities, for the study of Norwegian in the common schools, and he suggested the advisability of petitioning the Wisconsin legislature to permit the introduction of this language in its schools. He also was prepared to point the way to reforms in teaching, and in particular he recommended that students should study at Luther College in order to perfect their Norwegian and at American institutions of higher learning to improve their English. He believed too that some effort should be made to bring about the appointment of Norwegian professors at certain American colleges and universities. But he was unable to bring about a general discussion in the Synod assembly, and his resolutions were quietly referred to the synodical pastoral conference.[27]

The school issue could not be shelved in this fashion, however, and in the spring of 1869 it was brought before the Norwegian Americans in so dramatic a fashion that it set off an explosive public discussion, and the controversy entered upon its most turbulent phase. Anderson, after conferring with such men as Langeland, C. L. Clausen, J. A. Johnson of Madison, and C. F. Solberg, the pioneer editor, took the initiative in developing plans for a Scandinavian Lutheran Education Society. A meeting was called at the county courthouse in Madison on March 4, with a degree of popular interest evidenced by the attendance of some three hundred persons from various parts of the Northwest.[28] R. B. Anderson later referred to this education society as a "stillborn child,"[29] but its importance did not hinge upon a long life

[27] *Synodalberetning,* 1868, p. 51, 52; *Skandinaven,* July 22, 1868.

[28] The Norwegian-American newspapers gave a great deal of attention to the organization of the education society. See especially *Skaninaven,* March 3, 17, April 4, 21, May 26, 1869; *Fædrelandet og emigranten,* March 4, 11, 1869; and *Nordisk folkeblad* (Minneapolis), March 17, 1869. Larson tells the story of the society in his *Changing West,* 128–131.

[29] *Life Story,* 117.

so much as upon the stimulus that its birth gave to thought and discussion upon the problem of education. With H. A. Preus and other hostile critics present, the convention immediately encountered a deadlock that led to a secession of this group, for all the members were asked to subscribe, as a preliminary, to a pledge to support "genuine public education among the Scandinavian people in this country, and especially to bring about the establishment of Scandinavian Lutheran professorships in American higher schools." Clausen accepted the presidency of the society and several pastors of somewhat liberal views joined it, but Preus and his adherents, unwilling to sign this pledge, withdrew to form an organization of their own which opposed all efforts to create Scandinavian professorships in American institutions of higher learning.

Meanwhile the main body proceeded with its deliberations and adopted a constitution setting forth its aims. These included the encouragement of the training of Scandinavian Lutheran teachers for positions in high schools, the establishment of Scandinavian professorships in universities and colleges, perhaps the creation ultimately of a Scandinavian-American university, the training of teachers versed in both Norwegian and English for positions in the common schools, and the general encouragement of higher education for the Scandinavian younger generation. The society also called for a wider interest in Norwegian history and literature and in the building up of good libraries throughout the Norwegian communities.[30] The somewhat vague plans for a Scandinavian-American university soon vanished in the smoke of controversy; and the officers of the society, believing at first that they would have to raise considerable sums of money, quickly discovered that no funds for the salaries of teachers were needed, since both American high schools and

[30] *Nordisk folkeblad,* March 17, 1869; *Skandinaven,* March 17, 1869. The seceding organization took steps looking toward the establishment of an academy at Stoughton, Wisconsin. See *Kirkelig maanedstidende,* 15:26 (January 1, 1870).

colleges, when inquiries were made, evidenced a willingness to employ Scandinavian teachers if properly qualified candidates appeared and if the young people from the Scandinavian communities should seek out these institutions as places of study.[31]

It is not without significance that when the Scandinavian Lutheran Education Society held its second meeting, at Decorah in June, 1870, it centered its discussions about the common-school question, proposing two main theses—that the American common school is right in principle and the best system proposed or known for promoting general popular education; and that parents should send their children to the common school and take an active interest in securing good teachers for it and in having good discipline maintained.[32] This swing to the old question of the common school is not difficult to understand, for it was after all the basic question, and in the months that followed the Madison meeting it was the problem accorded the most concern in the renewed give-and-take of the controversy. And yet the education society had broadened the horizons of immigrant thought on the school question by its emphasis upon high schools and colleges. It was evident to an increasing number of people that the issues had wide ramifications, that education was a wider process than the common school, and that the sons and daughters of the pioneers were facing opportunities that had not been open to their parents.

A. C. Preus spoke a faint word of praise for the common schools about the time the education society was being formed, advocated the spread of parochial schools and the establishment of middle schools, with Luther College as the goal for those seeking a higher education. His sharp

[31] See a letter by F. S. Winslow setting forth the objectives of the education society, in *Fædrelandet og emigranten,* May 12, 1870; and a detailed report of the executive committee of the society, signed by Clausen, J. A. Johnson, and Winslow, in the same paper, May 19, 1870. The latter is also in *Nordisk folkeblad,* May 25, 1870.

[32] *Fædrelandet og emigranten,* May 19, 1870; *Nordisk folkeblad,* May 25, 1870.

denunciation of American institutions of higher learning brought upon his head the vigorous rebuttal of Langeland, who asserted that there was nothing blasphemous about the devotion of the universities to scientific truth and sounded a fresh note when he insisted that religion and science were not in conflict.[33] *Skandinaven,* opening its columns wide to controversial essays and letters, offered a general review of the school question, striking sharply at what it described as the priestly domination and tyranny of Missouri.[34] H. A. Preus continued to inveigh against the "religionless common school."[35] J. A. Johnson, replying to taunts against the smallness of the knowledge gained in the common school, declared that even a little knowledge in basic fields is important, recalled with pride that he himself had enjoyed a common school training, and said that it was absurd to suppose that five or ten families could support an adequate school.[36] Knute Nelson, then a young politician in Wisconsin, called attention to a law which he had succeeded in getting passed by the Wisconsin legislature, under the authorization of which an hour a day could be devoted in the common schools of the state to the study of Norwegian.[37]

The dissenters from the Madison meeting, under the lead of H. A. Preus, issued a signed document explaining their position and inveighing against the spread of "indifferentism" with respect to "Lutheran pure doctrine." An anonymous contributor to *Skandinaven* developed the theme that the newer science harmonized with Christianity and wrote much about Hegel. A minister, S. M. Krognaes, explained

[33] *Fædrelandet og emigranten,* March 4, 1869; *Skandinaven,* April 7, 14, 1869.

[34] April 21, 1869.

[35] He also advocated the launching of Norwegian-American academies. *Skandinaven,* March 17, 1869. Replies to Preus are in the same newspaper for April 7 and 14, 1869.

[36] Johnson, "The District School," in *Skandinaven,* April 13, 1869.

[37] Nelson states that he was encouraged in this effort by A. C. Preus. *Skandinaven,* April 14, 1869; Wisconsin, *General Laws,* 1869, ch. 50. The law was general in scope. It authorized school authorities to provide for instruction "in any of the foreign languages, not to exceed one hour each day."

that he sent his own children to a common school, that members of his congregation were on the school board, and that he met the problem of religious education by means of a two-month parochial school. R. B. Anderson reported that eleven Scandinavian students were registered at the University of Wisconsin. He called upon Norwegians to accept the American public schools, but at the same time to cherish their mother tongue. There will be no good schools, he said, "if every little nationality and church party puts up its own."[38] A school society at St. Ansgar, Iowa, reported that it had worked out a plan looking toward systematic instruction in religion so handled that it would not interfere with attendance at the common school, in which incidentally it hoped to have an hour a day set aside for the study of Norwegian.[39] Thus the controversy progressed. *Skandinaven* still served as the chief spokesman for the common school and led the attack upon the Synod party, which in turn could always be assured of a welcome in the columns of *Fædrelandet og emigranten* of La Crosse. As the spring of 1870 approached much attention was given to the forthcoming meeting of the Scandinavian Lutheran Education Society, to be held at Decorah in June. Its executive committee no longer favored a Scandinavian-American university, but it ranked the common school as essential to American civil and religious freedom and presented as its principal address at Decorah a dissertation on "The School" by Halle Steensland of Madison — a stalwart defense of the common school which incidentally described the Norwegian *omgangsskoler* of Steensland's youth as institutions of negligible educational worth.[40]

This concentration of attention upon the common school

[38] The document of the dissenters is in *Skandinaven,* May 12, 1869, and the other items referred to above are respectively in the issues for May 12 and 26 and October 27, 1869.

[39] *Skandinaven,* December 28, 1870; January 11, 1871.

[40] *Fædrelandet og emigranten,* May 19, June 23, 1870.

was undoubtedly influenced by controversial winds sweeping out of Minnesota, where the Reverend Bernt J. Muus of Goodhue County, Synod circuit rider, uncompromising debater, and hostile critic of the public schools was a storm center. Muus attempted to translate his ideas into action. In 1869 on his own initiative he had established an academy in connection with his church at Holden, secured a teacher for it, and planned a general course of studies that included Bible, Christian faith and doctrine, church history, English, Norwegian, geography, history, penmanship, arithmetic, physics, geometry, drawing, and singing. Late in 1869 he announced a term of three months to begin on January 7, 1870, with a tuition charge of ten dollars. He wanted to found a school, he said, "in which the youth of the congregations could acquire a better education than could be obtained in our parochial and common schools."[41] This venture was a precursor of St. Olaf's School, which opened its doors at Northfield in 1875 largely through the initiative of Muus. While he was busying himself with such plans, the rank and file of Norwegian immigrants were undoubtedly giving increasing support to the common school in Minnesota and other states of the Middle West; and there can be no doubt that the schools themselves were making progress. The school superintendent of McLeod County, Minnesota, reported in 1869 that the Norwegians took deep pride in their common schools, exercised particular care in the selection of teachers, and made unusual efforts to retain good teachers so as to avoid the ill consequences of frequent changes. "Some of our best schools," he wrote, "are composed entirely of children whose parents were born 'beyond the sea,' and many of them had not been with us long enough to learn our language, yet they have cheerfully taxed themselves to

[41] An announcement by Muus, headed "Academy in Holden, Minnesota," appears in *Kirkelig maanedstidende,* 14:383, 384 (December 1, 1869) and is translated in I. F. Grose in his article on "The Beginnings of St. Olaf College," in *Studies and Records,* 5:113.

build comfortable school houses, and to pay for the best American teachers." [42] In Pope County, where the majority of the settlers were Norwegians, the superintendent said that there were some school districts in which the officers "are unable to speak a word of the English language"— and they "are anxious for the education of their children, and are not backward in supplying the means for that purpose." [43] More than nine hundred new school buildings were erected in Minnesota alone in the three-year period from 1867 to 1869, but many of the pioneer schools were still housed in settlers' cabins. In Mower County, for example, a school made up exclusively of Norwegian children occupied a log cabin attic, with two Norwegian families living below. The county superintendent there witnessed twenty-four children "as studiously at work as I ever saw." He noted incidentally that "myrtle vines and prairie wild flowers adorned the walls" of this improvised school room and that the teacher's desk — a flour barrel — was graced with a bouquet.[44]

In one Minnesota county, however, the superintendent of schools reported for 1869 a spirit of hostility, especially among the Scandinavian clergy, toward the common school. H. B. Wilson, surveying events in Goodhue County, pointed out that the clerical distrust found expression in the charge that the common school was "heathen." [45] The attitude of the clergy had impeded school attendance in some districts; and Wilson found that in some instances children were sent to foreign-language private schools at the same time that the public schools were in session. All this was manifestly an allusion to Pastor Muus and his academy. Wilson took account of the fact that in some districts where the popula-

[42] Minnesota, *Executive Documents,* 1869, p. 242. The McLeod County superintendent bore the name of Liberty Hall.

[43] Minnesota, *Executive Documents,* 1869, p. 250. The superintendent was E. Lathrop.

[44] Minnesota, *Executive Documents,* 1869, p. 244, 245.

[45] Wilson's report is in Minnesota, *Executive Documents,* 1869, p. 223, 224.

tion was wholly Norwegian "good commodious and comfortable school houses have been erected, and schools have been sustained for a period of six months." He pointed out that no fewer than fourteen Scandinavian teachers had taught in the county and emphatically endorsed the need for the services of such teachers, who spoke the Scandinavian languages as well as English. He defended the public schools as the best means of bringing about, through processes of union and assimilation, "one homogeneous and harmonious community." The Norwegian-American press took prompt notice of Wilson's report. *Nordisk folkebladet* of Minneapolis, for example, reprinted it in full, endorsing its point of view and expressing the hope that Wilson would have success in improving school conditions in Goodhue County.[46]

Muus promptly responded with a polemical article on "Schools and a Good School" which made him for the time being the focus of the controversy, not only in relation to the American school authorities in Minnesota but also among the Norwegian Americans.[47] He declared that the common school was an institution "which because of its essential principle must work in opposition to the kingdom of God." It was religionless, or heathen, a center of dangerous influences from which Lutheran youth should be guarded. He did not regard it as always a sin for Christian parents to send their children there, for he conceded the necessity of learning English and the fact that for many no other school was available, but he denounced the common school as ineffective, giving only a smattering of such elementary subjects as geography, reading, and arithmetic, together with "a romance with the title of 'United-States History.'"

[46] *Nordisk folkeblad,* February 2, 1870. A good account of the school controversy, with reference particularly to Minnesota and to the treatment of the subject in Norwegian-American newspapers published in Minnesota, is presented in a master's thesis in sociology prepared at the University of Minnesota in 1932 by John A. Fagereng. It is entitled "Norwegian Social and Cultural Life in Minnesota, 1868–1891: An Analysis of Typical Norwegian Newspapers."

[47] *Fædrelandet og emigranten,* March 10, 1870.

Even the Americans themselves, he believed, were skeptical about the merits of their public schools. And when he looked at the American youth educated in them, he confessed that " these young republicans " terrified him. He compared them with " wild animals " and was even prepared to claim that the children of the native Indians were better educated.

To Wilson, whose rejoinder was translated and spread before Norwegian Americans in their own newspapers, this essay by Muus revealed " a spirit of the most narrow-minded bigotry and intolerance it has ever been my fortune to read."[48] He accused Muus of bitter hostility to American institutions, but exonerated the mass of Norwegian Americans from the charge of entertaining such views; and in fact he said that he had certain knowledge that a majority of Muus's own church members did not agree with him. To his mind Muus, " a foreign priest and aristocrat," stood for perpetuating in America " a foreign language, a foreign sentiment, and foreign institutions." He poured out his indignation upon the phrase Muus had employed with reference to " United-States History," and, while asserting that the common school could not teach sectarianism, declared that it could give place to the " majesty of truth, the beauty of integrity, benevolence and the Christian graces." Asserting that Muus was in the wrong latitude for such sentiments as he had voiced, Wilson closed by predicting that the time would come when, owing to common-school instruction, " a wave of progression will roll over our prairies and will bury all bigotry, intolerance and superstition, ten thousand fathoms deep." To all this Muus replied that he had by no means implied that American history was a " romance," but merely that some of the textbooks of United States history warranted that name. Criticism, he said, does not mean hostility to American institutions. The common schools, he con-

[48] Wilson's reply is in the *Goodhue County Republican* (Red Wing, Minnesota), May 5, 1870; the Norwegian version is in *Nordisk folkeblad,* May 18, 1870.

tended, were unsatisfactory to Christians, who, if they can have better schools, ought to have them. As to the place of Christian morality in the schools, Muus said, "That Christianity, in which there is no religion, and that religion, in which there is no Christianity, I love not overmuch"—adding tartly that this probably was because he was a "foreign priest and aristocrat."[49]

While this spirited clash went echoing through the Norwegian-American settlements, Muus's own countrymen joined heartily in the discussion, and the argument ranged over the entire ground. The common school as a factor in developing good citizenship was constantly emphasized; the economic difficulty of supplanting the public system with any degree of effectiveness was set forth; and some writers charged the parochial schools with gross inefficiency. Giving up the common schools, said one Norwegian American, meant a retreat to the Middle Ages. Langeland, no less belligerent than before in his defense of the American system, urged immigrants of the first generation not to pass on to their children the difficulties and losses that inevitable circumstances had forced upon them; and he declared that he would oppose any system that promised to keep Norwegian Americans "in an alien state or condition beyond the limits of necessity."[50] When he withdrew as editor of *Skandinaven* in 1872, the banner of the common school was immediately hoisted by his successor, Svein Nilsson, who urged the church, in the interest of good citizenship, to abandon its hostility to the common school and also suggested that secular primary education was quite outside its proper sphere of activity. The same year saw the emergence of a new Norwegian-American newspaper, *Budstikken* of Minneapolis,

[49] Muus's answer, in English, is in the *Goodhue County Republican*, June 2, 1870; and he contributed to the same paper for July 7 a supplementary essay entitled "Sectarianism the True Christianity." The *Republican* took sharp issue with him.

[50] *Skandinaven*, May 17, 1871.

which was no less energetic than *Skandinaven* in defense of the common school.[51]

The acceptance of the common school by increasing numbers of Norwegian Americans, coupled with the economic cost of any serious attempt to supplant it, placed the Norwegian Synod in a difficult position. At its meeting in 1873 President H. A. Preus laid before it a formulation of the problem in nearly a hundred points, or theses, but no action was taken save to print and make available for study his views.[52] Preus considered the common school inadequate for Christians, since it is "religionless." It is suited primarily, he contended, for non-Christians or for those who "neither will nor can establish Christian schools for their children." He conceded that, if the teacher is a Lutheran Christian and church discipline permitted, Lutherans might utilize the common school, particularly if they have not established equivalent Christian schools; but when, from a variety of causes, the children are exposed to spiritual dangers, Lutherans cannot defend the sending of their children to the public school. Nevertheless, as citizens they must give the common school powerful support and seek to make it as good and useful as its destiny permits.

Turning to the parochial schools, Preus pointed out that they were in existence in most of the congregations, running usually from one to three months and conducted ordinarily

[51] Larson, *Changing West,* 131–136. For Norwegian-American replies to Muus, see *Skandinaven,* March 30, 1870 (a statement by an "old farmer in Wisconsin"), April 13 (John A. Johnson); and *Fædrelandet og emigranten,* May 12, 1870 (a layman who makes much of the fact that Muus admits the common school to be effective in teaching children English), June 23 (Halle Steensland, who spoke of the retreat into the Middle Ages), and August 3 (A. J. Berdahl, who made a sharp criticism of the parochial schools). Nilsson's views are set forth in *Skandinaven,* May 29, 1872.

[52] *Synodalberetning,* 1873, p. 25–34; *Skandinaven,* July 22, 29, 1873. One must not underestimate the sincerity and conviction that marked such leaders as Preus and Muus. Of Preus a colleague has written: "The Christian common school and education of the children lay upon his heart as a life matter, seemingly more than any other single aim. He preached, wrote, brought the topic up at congregational meetings, ministerial conferences, and synodical meetings." Adolf Bredesen, "Pastor Herman Amberg Preus," in *Symra,* 6:122 ff. (1910).

by teachers trained in Norway. The studies included reading, religion, and singing, with some writing and arithmetic. They faced many difficulties, however, and in general were in a sorry condition. The common school took up from five to seven of the best months of the year, and pupils neglected the parochial school when it conflicted with the common school. It was difficult to secure and to keep good teachers, partly because the compensation was very small. In some instances the parochial teacher had also been appointed the teacher in the common school, but this practice was usually frowned upon by Americans and was possible only where Norwegian Lutherans controlled the school board.

Preus proposed that every effort should be made to stress the importance of the school question, and his general program included the organization of Norwegian-English congregational schools wherever possible; attempts to bring about the appointment of the Lutheran parochial schoolmaster as the teacher of the common school; the development of the training of teachers at Luther College; the establishment of Lutheran academies in districts of concentrated Norwegian population; attempts to secure the appointment of able Lutheran teachers of the Norwegian language in American universities and colleges; and finally, encouragement and financial help to Norwegian-American young people who wished to train themselves for the teaching profession.

Returning to the subject in 1874, the Synod once more found it inadvisable to take action. The meeting was held in Muus's own church at Holden, Minnesota, and he himself put before the Synod a new set of theses. These amounted to a condensed restatement of his general position that the revealed Word of God should stand at the center of education. Lacking such a center, the common school, in his view, omitted the essential means of attaining the basic goal of education. Muus did not regard it as necessarily a sin to use the common school, but Christians should attempt to set up Christian schools. Only a few of Muus's many points were discussed by the Synod, and these without action, but the discussion impinged upon the broad question of the Christian's responsibilities to state and church, and here it was quickly apparent that there was a divergence of opinion among the clergy. Muus and Preus, placing parental authority above the state and arguing that a parent might be obliged to disobey and even oppose the state, could not carry with them such leaders as Professor Schmidt and Pastor Koren, who posed the dilemma of the individual if he must pick and choose the laws that he will accept. As the discussion spun to an indecisive end, it was evident that within the Synod there was an undercurrent of skepticism as to the seriousness of the alleged dangers of the common school.[53]

In Norwegian-American church circles, outside the Synod, the general attitude was one of hearty defense of the common school. The more liberal Norwegian-Danish Conference, for example, under the leadership of such men as Professors Sven Oftedal and Georg Sverdrup of Augsburg Seminary, took a decisive stand. Oftedal urged that all Norwegian children in America should be sent to the public schools; in his "Open Declaration" of 1874 he challenged the Synod's "definite hostility to any instruction, whether in the common school or in national Norwegian schools, which is not controlled by the Synod"; and a few years later he accepted election to the Minneapolis board of education.[54] It remained for Professor Sverdrup to pen the most incisive essay that the common

[53] *Synodalberetning*, 1874, p. 61–71; *Skandinaven*, July 21, December 15, 1874; *Budstikken* (Minneapolis), June 30, July 4, 1871. Muus tried to have the correspondent of *Skandinaven*, J. A. Johnson, ejected from the Holden meeting on the ground that the paper was "unchristian," but his effort was not sustained by the Synod. Professor Laurence Larson calls attention to the fact that Laur. Larsen of Luther College "could discover no hidden peril in the subjects taught in the common school." *Changing West*, 135.

[54] Bergh, *Den norsk lutherske kirkes historie*, 232; *Skandinaven*, December 22, 1874; Larson, *Changing West*, 138.

school controversy produced.[55] This Norwegian-American theologian said that the way was "clear and certain" for all Norwegians: "Let the school of religion be and continue to be the business of the congregation, and let the state continue to be without religious instruction as before." The Norwegian people in America, if they are to take their rightful place in the national life, and "if there is to be a fresh and living current in the development of America," must earnestly employ and improve the common school. "Our children," said Sverdrup, "must grow into the language and history of this country." To call the common school "heathen" was, to his mind, merely using a bad word to frighten people. It was, not a heathen, but a civic school, and there was no reason why Christians should not send their children to it. Indeed, those children could not play their part in the New World unless they went to the common school. Sverdrup even suggested, with a characteristic touch of ironic humor, that all the Norwegian Americans ought to attend the common school in order to adjust themselves to American life. Their destiny was not to be a people by themselves but to be "a little part of a great people." Furthermore, Christianity was no hothouse plant. Even if one conceded, as he did not, that the American schools "were filled with an ungodly spirit," isolation from it was no solution. A free people, he believed, needed two things: a powerful civic school and a living religious school. If the state undertook religious schools, the result would be a dead and empty church; if the church undertook civic schools, the result would be priestly rule. For Christians it is a duty and a right to participate both in the public and in the congregational schools in order that "the people shall not be without salt and the congregation without contact with the people." The Conference in

[55] Helland reprints the essay in his edition of Sverdrup's *Samlede skrifter i udvalg*, 1:358–384. It appeared originally in two parts, the first entitled "Commonskolen" and the second "Commonskolen og kristendommen" in the theological *Kvartalskrift* (Minneapolis), 2:184–190 (1876), and 3:73–95 (1877).

1877 discussed the school question in detail and heard one of its prominent ministers, M. Falk Gjertsen, put forward the thesis that "No congregation has a right to give instruction in any subject except the Word of God."[56] Its leaders looked upon the principles of American public education as basic to free citizenship. From the Norwegian Episcopal minister, E. L. Peterson, came a defense of the common school similar in spirit to that of Professor Sverdrup.[57]

Meanwhile, fuel was heaped upon the controversial fires by the launching in the middle 1870's of several ambitious parochial schools, in such centers as Decorah, Madison, and Chicago, as experiments in supplanting the public schools, each with a wider program of studies than the usual short-term parochial schools. These schools seem to have been short-lived and significant chiefly for the virulent opposition that they created. R. B. Anderson, in particular, entered the arena with all his combative energy, termed the common school the cornerstone of the constitution, interpreted the experiment at Decorah as war on the public school and treason to the country, called upon Norwegian Americans everywhere to defend American education, and to set their faces against what he considered the road to Rome. As for parochial schools he declared them "pitiful" and "miserable" in comparison with public schools. If the Norwegian language and the Lutheran church could not stand alongside the public school, he for one was ready to let both disappear. This was no casual fight to him. It was a crusade. Every letter he wrote carried this printed letterhead: "Whosoever directly or indirectly opposes the American common school is an enemy of education, of liberty, of progress. Opposition to the American common school is treason to our country."[58]

[56] Larson, *Changing West,* 139; *Budstikken,* July 4, 1877.

[57] Fagereng, "Norwegian Social and Cultural Life," 93, 94, quotes contemporary statements by Peterson in *Budstikken.*

[58] Anderson, *Life Story,* 598; Anderson, "Declaration of War against the Common School!" in *Skandinaven,* October 17, 1876. See also *Skandinaven,*

Skandinaven continued to thunder against the opponents of the public schools, and *Budstikken* of Minneapolis was scarcely less vociferous. *Norden* of Chicago was edited by a Synod minister, Halvard Hande, but like *Fædrelandet og emigranten* of La Crosse it found itself obliged by circumstance to open its columns to both sides. No controversialist appeared on the clerical side who matched the fervor and skill of R. B. Anderson. Bernt Askevold of Decorah, editor and novelist, broke into print to characterize the "Yankee school" as "pernicious"—"not even moral, much less Christian"—but he was able to make no notable contribution to the discussion. The pioneer novelist Tellef Grundysen took his stand with Anderson, dryly suggested that the Bible can be read in one language as well as another, and objected to a postponement of the learning of English until children were in their teens. "First English, then Norwegian," he said.[59] The Synod in its annual meetings took no challenging stand: it tended more and more to limit itself, in so far as it dealt with the school question, to the supplementary, short-term parochial school.[60] As the controversy trailed out, *Skandinaven* ran a series of anonymous satirical articles which reported (in dialect) an imaginary educational convention at Decorah. Solemn resolutions were adopted—that "we establish our own schools to prevent our children from learning anything in the common school"; that "education is a good thing in itself but dangerous in others"; and that R. B. Anderson was a menace because he embodied the

January 16 and August 21, 1877; Larson, *Changing West,* 141, 142. Anderson was infuriated by an essay on "Menighedsskolen," in *Evangelisk luthersk kirketidende* (Decorah, Iowa), 3:621–628 (October 6, 1876). This article tells of the decision of the Norwegian Lutheran church in Decorah to establish a congregational school to be conducted throughout the year. The school opened on September 16 for a ten-month term, with sixty-nine students. *Ibid.,* 628, 629.

[59] *Skandinaven,* November 21, 1876. Grundysen's article is in *Skandinaven,* January 16, 1877; and J. A. Johnson contributed a lengthy essay to the issues for January 9 and 16.

[60] See, for example, *Synodalberetning,* 1876, p. 43–47.

general principle of education buttressed by wit, courage, and will. Masked by the genial air of these articles was as biting and vicious an attack as the entire controversy witnessed.[61] *Budstikken,* meanwhile, carried on a persistent campaign during the late 1870's in defense of American public education, contending that the setting aside of the common school would be nothing less than a crime against posterity; that that school breathed the spirit of tolerance and breadth of interest as opposed to bigotry and narrowness; and that the Lutheran church was placing itself alongside the Catholic by its stand on parochial and public schools.[62]

The average Norwegian immigrant quietly accepted the public schools through all the years that the Synod ministers denounced them as "heathen." As the schools progressed, that acceptance deepened among Norwegian Americans. They followed the drama of controversy with alert interest, however, and it probably helped them to appreciate more fully the place of the public school and its benefits to an immigrant people in the new democracy — the advantages of at least some education *common* to all the people. Led by a vigilant press and outspoken laymen, the Norwegian immigrants rejected the doctrine of parochial schools supplanting common schools. They found such a system inexpedient on the grounds of cost and efficiency, but their chief reason for rejecting it was a belief in the soundness of the democratic idea of primary education available, at public cost, to all. Even the propagandists for the parochial plan looked upon support of the public schools as a civic duty and opposed all suggestion of public subventions for parochial schools.

When states began to enact compulsory attendance laws —

[61] This episode took place in the summer of 1877 after a period in which the Norwegian-American newspapers published scores of articles and letters on the common-school question. Larson gives an excellent account of it, with references to *Skandinaven,* in his *Changing West,* 144–146.

[62] See, for example, *Budstikken* for April 24, 1878, and June 10, 1879. An interesting article by P. P. Iverslie on "Skolen" appears in the same paper for November 28 and December 5, 1876.

Wisconsin, for example, in 1879 — Norwegians accepted them cheerfully. It is true that many of them joined with the Germans in the movement to repeal the Wisconsin Bennett Law of 1889. This law called for compulsory attendance of children from seven to fourteen years of age at a school within the district of the pupils' attendance, and it specified that no school was a school in the meaning of this law unless it taught various common subjects in the English language for a stated period of time. Even such a stalwart defender of the public schools as Rasmus B. Anderson opposed this law, as much on the basis of its rigid district provision as because of his conviction that the "English language in this country was no such invalid that it needed the nursing or protection of law." But the Norwegians had few parochial schools that could be affected by such a law and their patronage of the public schools was general. Thus their opposition to the Bennett Law did not have the emotional drive that moved the Germans. A Wisconsin historian asserts that the Scandinavians in Wisconsin were drawn into the anti-Bennett Law camp because of the district provision, which they interpreted as forbidding them "to patronize any schools but those of their own district," and that therefore many who even "favored teaching English in all schools" voted to repeal the law. There is undoubtedly some truth in these assertions, but it is also true that many Norwegians, like Anderson, viewed the Bennett Law as essentially nativistic in spirit.[63]

The summer parochial schools, conducted by local congregations as a supplement to the civic schooling of the children, became very general, though perhaps not so strong as their advocates had anticipated. A generation after the days of the school controversy, in 1909, four Norwegian Lutheran synods, reporting on activities in 3,001 congregations, dis-

[63] Louise Phelps Kellogg, "The Bennett Law in Wisconsin," in *Wisconsin Magazine of History*, 2:23 (September, 1918); Anderson, *Life Story*, 594–600.

closed that 1,715 of them had conducted such congregational schools.[64] Preus and Muus at an early date had suggested the founding of Norwegian-American academies in Norwegian population centers; and much of the drive of these men and their associates turned to this field. Before the end of 1874 Muus, for example, announced to the Norwegian-American public the launching of "St. Olaf's School, an evangelical Lutheran high school in Northfield, Minnesota." He set forth a twofold purpose: to "give the confirmed youth a higher education for practical life than home schools can do" and to "direct the moral conduct of the students."[65] This coeducational institution, which opened its doors on January 8, 1875, typified a Norwegian Lutheran academy movement that gained momentum in the last quarter of the nineteenth century. This was the period in which the public high school emerged in the Middle West, and for the majority of Norwegian Americans the high school proved to be the avenue of education beyond the grades and of preparation for college. Under church auspices, however, an attempt was made to set up denominational academies, and by the opening years of the twentieth century no fewer than thirty Norwegian-American institutions of this type had been launched.[66] Meanwhile, the college movement, inaugurated by Luther College in 1861, advanced with rapid strides, and Norwegian-American youth, the children and grandchildren of the pioneer immigrants, sought higher education in increasing numbers, not only in their own denominational colleges but also in American institutions of higher learning.

[64] Knut Takla, *Det norske folk i de Forenede Stater*, 223, 224 (Christiania, 1913).

[65] From an announcement by Muus, in *Fædrelandet og emigranten*, December 10, 1874, translated by Professor Grose, in *Studies and Records*, 5:118.

[66] See J. J. Skordalsvold's accounts of Scandinavian schools in Minnesota, Iowa, and Wisconsin, in O. N. Nelson, *History of the Scandinavians and Successful Scandinavians in the United States*, 1:317–334; 2:75–81, 129–134 (Minneapolis, 1904); and Norlie, *Norsk lutherske prester*, 25, 26, 29, 30, 34, 35, 38, 39, 43, 44.

IX. LAUNCHING AN IMMIGRANT PRESS

THE RISE of a newspaper press among the Norwegian pioneers in America took place during the 1840's and 1850's in the face of many difficulties. "Perhaps the worst obstacle for us to overcome," complained one early Norwegian newspaper in the Middle West, "is the indifference generally entertained by our people for newspapers of any description." For this apathy the editor sought an explanation in the Old World background of the settlers. "To keep a newspaper was a luxury never thought of by most of them in Norway," he explained. "They were too poor for that, and . . . they did not care, because they were in the habit of entrusting everything to others and had too little self-dependence to express any judgment as to right or wrong in questions of public interest."[1]

That this opinion was harsher than the facts justified is demonstrated by the growing power and articulateness in Norway, in the 1830's and 1840's, of the *bonde* movement. Yet the criticism probably was not without an element of

[1] *Emigranten,* January 23, 1852.

truth. The Norwegian immigrant had known a society in which there was a real cleavage between commoners and members of the official class. It is true that the commoners were challenging the Norwegian bureaucracy with increasing force during the early nineteenth century, yet the traditional cleavage undoubtedly had left marks upon the mental habits of the people.

To some writers the meager schooling of the early immigrants explains the difficulties of founding a successful press and in general the apparent slowness of pioneer social and cultural progress. That the education of the Norwegian immigrants was in most instances sharply limited does not admit of doubt. Dr. Gjerset in fact contends that they had had virtually no school instruction: "In the period following the Reformation no public school system was built up in Norway for the education of the common people. There were some Latin schools in which the sons of the officials and privileged classes were educated, and in 1811 Norway established a university, which for a long time was attended almost exclusively by the sons of the same classes. It was not until 1869 that the country passed a law providing for the establishment of public schools, and it took another decade or two before the provisions of this law could be carried into effect. By that time the great wave of Norwegian immigration to America had almost spent itself."[2] This generalization is too sweeping, however, for not only was there comparatively little illiteracy among the immigrants, but most of them had had some schooling, formal or informal.

In 1837 there were some two hundred schools in the Norwegian country districts, with an enrollment of 15,500 pupils; and 160,000 children received instruction in country homes from itinerant teachers for a short time each year. A child was expected to begin his schooling at the age of eight; and

[2] *Lutheran Herald* (Rock Island, Illinois), 16:682 (May 31, 1932).

most children were withdrawn from instruction in their twelfth year. More than eight thousand country children received no formal schooling at all, most of them because of poverty and sickness. The efficacy of the peripatetic school system was limited, for the government estimated that of the 160,000 children reached by the traveling teachers, only 35,000 were taught to write. In the towns the common schools were under the poor-relief administration. There were but eighty-nine such town schools in the kingdom in 1837, with 12,000 pupils, of whom it was estimated that 8,500 learned to write. In that year 4,200 town children of school age received private tutoring, and some 3,600, for one reason or another, did not go to school at all.[3]

With whatever the defects of the system, and they were many, it still remains true that a majority of all the Norwegian children of school age received some schooling in this period of Norway's educational history. It has been estimated, in fact, that less than five per cent failed to receive any.[4] The school system was uneven, terms were short, and there was a crying need for reform. Yet it must be borne in mind that the system was supplemented by informal instruction in many, indeed most, Norwegian homes. Religious reading was common, not least in homes that had come under the influence of Haugeanism, and children gained some additional training, by no means negligible, through their preparation, under the local minister, for confirmation. Many of the ministers were deeply interested in the school problem and helped to promote the movement for an improved system.[5] Meanwhile, the situation disclosed by the statistics of

[3] The Norwegian government reports on education were issued in 1840 by the department concerned with church and instruction. A convenient summary is presented by Wilhelm Keilhau in *Det norske folks liv og historie gjennem tidene,* 9:259 ff. (Oslo, 1931).

[4] Halfdan Raabe, *Norges folkeskolevæsen i hundrede aar,* 9 (Christiania, 1914).

[5] On early aspects of the ministerial attitude see Torstein Høverstad, *Norsk skulesoga: Det store interregnum 1739–1827,* 31–72 (Christiania, 1918) — a valuable study in which the story of the schools is viewed in its broad social setting.

1837 opened the way to reforms that led to a unified system of public education. In 1848 a law was passed requiring every town to have one common school; and in the following decades the situation continued to improve. The number of *omgangsskoler,* or ambulatory schools, was greatly reduced, and from 1860 to 1890 no fewer than 2,600 new schoolhouses were built throughout the Norwegian districts.[6]

An interesting picture of the nineteenth-century home schools of Norway is given by the late Andreas Ueland in his *Recollections.* He explains that the school which he attended was an itinerant one, like those of colonial New England. "The schoolmaster," he writes, took the school "from farm to farm with all the material in a satchel, and stayed at each place long enough to make his board and lunch for the children liquidate the school tax. The lunch was invariably a thick porridge from flour of oats, ground with the bran, and thick, sour milk — good nourishing food, but not appetizing. The children who lived within a reasonable distance had to go home to lunch." He goes on to say that the pupils had to learn Luther's Smaller Catechism by heart as well as Pontoppidan's explanation of it, and that the only school reader was the New Testament. In appraising the significance of such training one must of course bear in mind the fact that, in speech as in government and church, there was a thoroughgoing cultural dichotomy in Norway. The language of the government, the press, and the clergy was that Dano-Norwegian which to the normal man and woman in the Norwegian valleys was a book language, markedly different from the traditional vernacular which commoners used in everyday life. Yet it is surprising how large a proportion of the Norwegians were able to write something approaching the literary language. This was, in fact, essentially the language of the uncounted thousands of America letters that recorded immigrant experience. It may be added that Ue-

[6] Keilhau, *Det norske folks liv,* 9:264–267.

land, the son of a remarkable father, lived in a home that took one daily newspaper and boasted a library in which such writers as Snorre Sturlason, Saxo Grammaticus, and Holberg were represented.[7]

Probably the chief difficulty in the way of founding an immigrant press lay, not in deficiencies in schooling and cultural backgrounds, but in the economic situation of the frontier settlers. It was only natural that the immigrants who settled the Mississippi Valley during the 1830's and 1840's should have devoted their first and most vigorous energies toward meeting their economic problems. These were a primary challenge to them, but other problems and difficulties crowded upon them, too. Their language, customs, and institutions were as strange to the new surroundings as the immigrants themselves. They had little understanding of the workings of the American order. They were naturally not without a certain general interest in that order, but in their concern with the immediate problem of making a living they had comparatively little incentive to express that broader interest. And the fact that they were widely scattered in Middle Western settlements was an undoubted obstacle to unified action.

During the 1840's and 1850's, however, the Norwegian immigrants began to understand that they needed something more than the church as a steadying point. They came to realize that a newspaper in their own language would be a focus for common interests, a medium for exchange of ideas, an instrument for easing the transition they were facing, a means of defining political standpoints, perhaps of winning social and political recognition. Dispersed as they were, the immigrants felt that a press of their own, printed in their own language and projected from their own cultural backgrounds, might give them a certain sense of solidarity. They

[7] Ueland, *Recollections of an Immigrant*, 3–13 (New York, 1929). See also the picture given of the *omgangsskole* by Raabe in *Norges folkeskolevæsen*, 9–12.

believed also, and rightly, that it would supply, in enlightenment and entertainment, an ameliorating influence in the midst of the hard circumstances of the frontier.[8]

In thus groping their way to a more assured status, the immigrants were aware of the fact that they had not yet fully won the respect and understanding of the people among whom they lived. Indeed, they recognized that their own language difficulties and their lack of knowledge of American affairs accounted in part for the somewhat unflattering opinions of themselves that they occasionally heard expressed, though evidence indicates that not a little of the adverse comment centered about the primitive living conditions that obtained among the earlier pioneers. An eminent Wisconsin politician, in the heat of a debate in the first Wisconsin constitutional convention, gave it as his judgment that the "Negroes here were more intelligent, more civilized, better acquainted with our institutions than the Norwegians." He added that he had seen "the Norwegians living without what any other people would have considered the most absolute necessaries of life, burrowed so to say in holes in the ground, in huts dug in the banks of the earth." This assertion evoked an immediate retort from another member of the convention. "Go into Iowa," he said, "and you will find half of the people living in the same manner."[9]

Praise and flattery were not lacking. As early as 1847 a Wisconsin newspaper, not wholly unaware of the "foreign

[8] The history of the early Norwegian press in the United States has been the subject of several good studies by Carl G. O. Hansen. See especially his article in Wist, *Norsk-amerikanernes festskrift*, 1–40, and his two preliminary studies of the subject, which may be found in *Kvartalskrift* (Eau Claire, Wisconsin), vol. 3, no. 1, p. 14–28 (January, 1907), and *Symra*, 4:25–44 (1908). Other interesting articles are Albert O. Barton, "The Beginnings of the Norwegian Press in America," in Wisconsin Historical Society, *Proceedings*, 1916, p. 186–212; Juul Dieserud, "Den norske presse i Amerika," in *Nordmands-forbundet*, 5:153–176 (April, 1912), and an article by the same author on the newspaper *Skandinavia* in *Nordmands-forbundet*, 22:14–17 (1929); and Wist, "Pressen efter borgerkrigen," in *Norsk-amerikanernes festskrift*, 40–203.

[9] M. M. Quaife, ed., *The Movement for Statehood 1845–1846*, 98, 99 (*Wisconsin Historical Collections*, vol. 26 — Madison, 1918). The first speaker was Marshall M. Strong.

vote," spoke of the foreigners as the people "by whose energy and skill Wisconsin is being transformed magically from a wilderness to a garden," and it burst into rhapsody in its allusion to the Norwegian immigrants: "From Norway's snowy hills and icy plains rush on and on succeeding hosts, with hearts alive to Liberty's sweet inspirations, asking no other privilege than the common equal rights and privileges of men among men."[10] Such flattery, which often synchronized with the approach of elections, lacked the note of sincerity, and the sharp and realistic condemnation that was frequently heard, though it naturally did not contribute to immigrant complacency, had a ring of honesty about it that the immigrants themselves recognized as authentic. The lack of cleanliness in the frontier settlements received much comment in contemporary records, while, on the other hand, the quickness with which the immigrants picked up English was looked upon as a point in their favor. The Norwegian traveler, Munch Ræder, met an American in the Middle West who said to him, "Never have I known people to become civilized so rapidly as your countrymen; they come here in motley crowds, dressed up with all kinds of dingle-dangle just like the Indians. But just look at them a year later: they speak English perfectly, and, as far as dress, manners, and ability are concerned, they are quite above reproach." Munch Ræder, who was himself a sharp observer and probing critic of American society and institutions, did not like some of the unconscious implications of this statement, and in his narrative he adds, with a touch of reluctant humor, "Of course I tried to explain to him that their original mode of dress certainly could not make Indians out of them and that they were not entirely devoid of culture or those habits of diligence and regularity which one expects to find in a well-ordered and civilized society, even among the poorest

[10] The *Milwaukee Courier*, February 24, 1847, quoted in M. M. Quaife, ed., *The Struggle over Ratification 1846–1847*, 578 (*Wisconsin Historical Collections*, vol. 28 — Madison, 1920).

classes out in the country, but he seemed scarcely disposed to make any concessions on that point."[11]

The Norwegian immigrant press that took its rise during the 1840's and 1850's was intended to reach and to serve people in many settlements throughout the country. It was not a local press. The news items that it contained came from a wide area. Its special flavor was derived from the circumstance that it served and drew its support from a widely scattered but numerically restricted group of people whose cultural backgrounds were similar. It served, as time went on, to weld these people together in common interests, to give reality to the geographically nebulous concept of a "Norwegian America." The founders of the pioneer Norwegian newspapers, it is interesting to note, understood also that their work would have value for posterity as well as for their contemporaries. Perhaps no one saw the possibilities of the early press more clearly than did the pioneer editor and minister, C. L. Clausen.[12] He particularly emphasized the value of the Norwegian-American newspaper as a source of precise information for the future historian of the frontier settlements. He called upon the people in these settlements to contribute such information, and in his paper he listed a dozen topics that seemed to him particularly important. These included the people who founded the settlements, land and locality, the marketing of products, the growth of the settlements, education, the language problem, and temperance. The University of Wisconsin, he pointed out, had invited editors to deposit in its archives complete files of their newspapers. By accepting that invitation, he concluded with admirable prevision, "we give to our children and posterity an opportunity to know about us and our days."[13]

[11] *America in the Forties,* 37. Ræder writes of the Norwegian immigrants, "Cleanliness is, here as in Norway, for many of them an unheard-of thing. The entrance to one of the houses I visited was guarded by a formidable cesspool" (p. 38).

[12] See Andersen, *Clausen,* and Jorgensen, "Clausen."

[13] *Emigranten,* January 30, 1852.

A special purpose of the immigrant press was that of supplying news from the old country, but its founders were also aware of the role that it might play in furnishing the people of Norway with news about the immigrants and about Norway. The press was an international cultural bridge. Newspapers in Norway often reprinted articles and news items that appeared in the columns of the pioneer publications. Clausen was alert to the importance of the immigrant press in this respect. "Our friends and relatives in the old country," he wrote, "ought to be able to find in our paper reliable information concerning our land and condition, in order that they can thereby decide for themselves whether or not it would be advisable for them to emigrate." The immigrant newspapers, to his mind, were composite America letters in which many of the limitations of individual letters were absent. Of the America letters he explained: "The majority of the letter writers know very little about any other locality than the one in which they reside, but from this limited knowledge they do not hesitate to judge the entire country. Some describe America as an entirely wooded country . . . others as only a prairie. One employs great diligence in persuading his friends to come, depicting the country as a rediscovered paradise where neither thistle nor thorn grows, and in boasting of his own success he describes his log hut as a three-story building, though it has a hole under the floor as a cellar and a few pieces of board under the ceiling as an upper room. Another describes the country as consisting of merely marshes and swamps, of barren prairie, or of decayed oak forests, and containing nothing except villains, rattlesnakes, and ague." Such letters obviously were not to be depended upon. Greater reliability and more interest, Clausen believed, could be secured in a public paper, which gathered its material from many individuals and different settlements. He even went so far as to request that one member of each immigrant party send the paper a brief account of the leading motives that caused its members to leave their native land, a statement concerning the social class in Norway to which they had belonged, and a description of their journey. And he offered the use of his columns for criticism and correction of these accounts.[14]

It was in the middle 1840's that the Norwegians in the West began to interest themselves in the possibility of a newspaper of their own. The initial impulse came from laymen, not from the clergy. The clergy were to exercise in due time a considerable influence upon the immigrant press, but its launching was accomplished by lay leaders. The press took its rise in the Muskego settlement of southeastern Wisconsin, which cradled many significant Norwegian-American movements and enterprises.

James Denoon Reymert, an immigrant of 1842 who lived in the Muskego settlement, desired to edit a Norwegian newspaper. He was born in Farsund, Norway, in 1821. As a youth he had spent five years in Scotland, the native land of his mother Jessie Sinclair Denoon, and there he had learned English. He was a man of background, considerable training, and marked ability whose association with the pioneer Norwegian-American press launched him on a career of characteristic frontier versatility. He served as a member of the second Wisconsin constitutional convention, as school superintendent, justice of the peace, member of the state legislature, presidential elector, government land agent, and editor; he was a builder of sawmills and plank roads; and he ran for Congress in 1860.[15]

In the middle 1840's, however, Reymert was perhaps less influential in the Muskego settlement than Even Heg and Søren Bache. Heg was the leader of the settlement, and Bache, who had some wealth, was its unofficial banker.[16]

[14] *Emigranten,* January 30, 1852.

[15] See Barton, in Wisconsin Historical Society, *Proceedings,* 1916, p. 194.

[16] A remarkable picture of the Muskego settlement is given in the Bache Diary. On the earlier history of the settlement, see Blegen, *Norwegian Migration,* 125 ff.

SKANDINAVIA.

1. Aarg: NEW-YORK, den 15. Marts, 1847. No. 5.

O, lad os aldrig glemme,
Hvor fjernt, hvor langt vi gaae,
At *Nordens Aand* har hjemme,
Hvor *Nordens Hjerter* slaae!

CONSTITUTION

FOR

DET SKANDINAVISKE SELSKAB I NEW YORK.

1.

Den 9. Juli 1844 har dette Selskab constitueret sig under Navn af "*Skandinavia*," og skal dets Formaal være at udvide Bekjendtskabet med det gamle Fædrelands Literatur, saavelsom og til Selskabelighed, Belæring, Opmuntring og Underholdning i Almindelighed for de Skandinaver, der ere her, eller ankomme hertil. Til Selskabets ovennævnte Tendens skal endvidere et velgjörende Öiemed knyttes, bestaaende i et *Understöttelses Fond* til Hjælp for *Selskabets Medlemmer i Særdeleshed*, og, forsaavidt som Selskabets pecuniaire Kræfter tillade det, for *enhver trængende Skandinav i Almindelighed*.

2.

Som berettiget til at optages i dette Selskab betragtes *enhver Skandinav*.

3.

Selskabets Bestyrelse bestaaer af en Præsident, en Vice-Præsident, en Secretair, en Bogholder, en Casserer og en Bibliothekar.

4.

Embedsmændene udvælges af Selskabet paa følgende Maade: Ethvert Medlem foreslaaer en Candidat, og iblandt de tre, som til hvert af de respective Embeder have de fleste Stemmer, udvælges een ved Ballotering.

5.

Embedsmændenes Function vedvarer i sex Maaneder, og er det Præsidentens Pligt at paasee, at en ny Embedsmand udvælges en Maaned forinden Vacancen indtræffer.

6.

Hvert Halvaar blive Regnskaber og Böger reviderede af en af Selskabet dertil valgt Revisor.

7.

Alle Forhandlinger föres i det skandinaviske Sprog.

8.

Selskabet holder et regulairt Möde een Gang i hver Maaned, dog kan Præsidenten med 4 Medlemmers Samtykke sammenkalde et Extra-Möde.

9.

Til Bestridelse af Selskabets Udgifter betales ved hvert Medlems Optagelse, *af sammes Proponent*, \$4. Det maanedlige Contingent er 37½ cents.

10.

Forslag til Optagelse af Medlemmer skal fremlægges Selskabet en Maaned förend Indballoteringen finder Sted.

11.

Medlemmer optages med $\frac{2}{3}$ Stemmer.

12.

Ingen uden Selskabets Medlemmer tilstedes Adgang til de Möder, hvori Forhandlinger finde Sted.

13.

For at kunne foretage Forretninger ved et Möde skulle i det mindste 15 Medlemmer være tilstede.

14.

Intet Medlem kan gjöre Krav paa Understöttelse mere end 12 Uger i et Tidsrum et Aar. I anmeldt Sygdomstilfælde er Understöttelsen bestemt til \$4. pr. Uge, hvilken Sum *skal* modtages af Vedkommende.

15.

Intet Medlem kan fordre Understöttelse, forinden han har været sex Maaneder i Selskabet.

16.

Intet Medlem kan nyde Understöttelse i det Öieblik hans Bopæl er beliggende 10 Miil fra "City Hall."

17.

Understöttelse til Ikke-Medlemmer og Extra Understöttelse til Medlemmer kunne tildeles med $\frac{2}{3}$ Stemmer.

18.

Naar et Medlem er skyldig til Selskabets Casse \$1 50. eller derover, kan han ei gjöre Krav paa Understöttelse, forinden 3 Maaneder efter at hans Gjæld er betalt.

CONSTITUTION

FÖR

SCANDINAVISKA FÖRENINGEN I NEW YORK.

1.

Den 9de July 1844 constituerade sig detta sälskap under namn af "Scandinavia", och skal dess föremål blifwa att utwidga bekantskapen med det gamla fäderneslandets literatur, som ock till sällskaplighet, kunskap, upmuntran och trefnad af de Scandinaver, som äro här eller ankomma hit. Till ofwanberörda föremål skall vidare förbindas välgörenhet, bestående i en understöds fond till hjelp för sälskapets medlemmar i synnerhet och så widt pecuniera tillgångar medgifwa, för hwarje behöfwande Scandinav i allmänhet.

2.

Enhwar Skandinav anses berättigad att uptagas i detta sällskap.

3.

Sälskapets styrelse utgöres af en president, en secreterare, en bokförare, en casseur och en bibliothekarie.

4.

Embetsmannen utwälgas af sälskapet på följande wis: Hwarje medlem föreslår en candidat ock ibland de tre, som till hwarje embete har de flesta röster, utwälges en genom ballotering.

5.

Embetsmännens befattning fortfar sex månader, och är det presidentens pligt att tillse, det en ny embetsman utwälges en månad före inträffande vacance.

6.

Hwarje halfår blifwa räkenskaper och böcker reviderade af en af sälskapet dertill wald revisor.

7.

Alla förehandlingar föras i det Scandinaviska språk.

8.

Sallskapet håller en regulier sammenkomst hwarje månad; dock kan presidenten med 4 medlemmars bifall sammankalla ett extra möte.

9.

Till bestridande af sälskapets utgifter betalas vid hwarje medlems inträdande, *af densammes proponent*, fyra dollars. Månadsafgiften är 37½ cents.

10.

Förslag till intagande af medlemmar skall föreläggas sälskapet en månad förän inballotering kan företagas.

11.

Medlemmar uptagas med $\frac{2}{3}$ röster.

12.

Ingen forutan sällskapets medlemmar tillåtes tillträde till de sammankomster, der förehandlingar äga rum.

13.

För att kunna företaga förrättningar wid ett möte, skola minst 15 medlemmar wara tilstädes.

14.

Ingen medlem kan göra anspråk på mera än 12 weckors understöd under tidrymden af ett år. Wid anmäldt sjukdomstillfälle är understödet bestämdt till \$4 00 i weckan, hwilken summa *skall* möttagas af vidkommande.

15.

Ingen medlem kan begära understöd, förrän han warit 6 månader i sälskapet.

16.

Ingen medlem kan erhålla understöd från det ögonblick hans hem är 10 mil från "City-Hall."

17.

Understöd till icke medlemmar och extra understöd till medlemmar kunna tilldelas med $\frac{2}{3}$ röster.

18.

När en medlem är skyldig till sälskapets cassa \$1 50 eller derutöfwer, kan han icke göra anspråk på understöd, förrän 3 månader sedan hans skuld blifwit betald.

[From the only known original of this issue, in the Library of Congress.]

Both were interested in the founding of a Norwegian newspaper at Muskego. Doubtless their interest was sharpened during the Christmas season of 1846 by the visit of a Norwegian Whig from Illinois who was collecting subscriptions for "the establishment of a newspaper among the Norwegians in America." About the same time Knud Knudsen, a Democrat, visited the settlement in the interests of a proposed newspaper.[17] Meanwhile, a somewhat similar enterprise was likewise taking form in New York. In January, 1847, the Scandinavian colony in that city, which boasted an organized Scandinavian society, inaugurated a newspaper called *Skandinavia.* This preceded the appearance of a western Norwegian newspaper; it employed both Danish and Swedish in its columns and allotted about equal space to information about Norwegian, Danish, and Swedish affairs, emphasizing news from the Scandinavian countries.[18] Though at least eighty-three of the paper's 220 subscribers in May, 1847, were Norwegian settlers in Wisconsin, *Skandinavia* does not seem to have gained a firm foothold, perhaps because it failed to take a definite political stand, possibly because its tone was Pan-Scandinavian. "I really believe that it is on account of its Scandinavian tendencies that a newspaper which is published in New York has been declared

[17] Bache Diary, December 26, 1846. According to Munch Ræder, several Norwegians in 1846 took steps looking toward the establishment of a newspaper to be called "De norskes opmærksomhed" ("The Norwegian Observer"). It was intended to be published in Chicago. A constitution for the enterprise was drawn up, a motto — "Liberty and Equality, without regard to rank or nationality" — was adopted, and the contents of the paper were planned. It was to present information on religious and political affairs, scientific progress, and daily events in order "to instruct and edify the reader, and promote his welfare and happiness, for time and eternity." One of the promoters of this abortive project was Gudmund Haugaas, the Mormon. *America in the Forties,* 179.

[18] Mr. Malmin tells of his discovery of *Skandinavia* in his historical introduction to Ræder, *America in the Forties,* xx–xxi. Photostats of numbers 5 to 8 (March 15 to May 15, 1847), made from originals in the Library of Congress, are in the possession of the present writer. See also Dieserud, in *Nordmands-forbundet,* 22:14–17. For a contemporary account of the New York Scandinavian Society see "Axel Felix," *Langtfra Danmark,* a work published at Copenhagen in three volumes from 1850 to 1855. "Axel Felix" was Christian Hansen, the editor of *Skandinavia.* A copy of this rare work is in the library of the Minnesota Historical Society.

by the Norwegians here in the West to be just a 'little too high-toned' for them," wrote the observant Munch Ræder, adding, "certainly I cannot see anything particularly 'high-toned' in it otherwise."[19]

In the spring of 1847 the three leaders in the Muskego colony who were interested in founding a newspaper signed the following contract:

An Agreement entered into this Twenty second day of March A. D. 1847, between Soren Bache, Even H. Hæg and J. D. Reymert all of Muskegoe and Norway, Wisconsin, to vit. We all and each one of us agree to enter into a Copartnership of the following Nature; we each one of us agree to advance an igual share in the purchase of a printing press and all requisite utensils of materials for carrying on the printing business in Muskigoe and to establish a weekly Newspaper "Det Skandinaviske Ugeblad" to be edited by Mr. J. D. Reymert for which we agree to pay him the sum of three hundred Dollars annually for the term of Three years from the commencement of the first Number. — We are to bear an equal share in the expences of printing and all other requisite incidentals.

S. Bache
Even H Heg
J D Reymert

On the day this agreement was signed, Bache and Reymert set out on a fortnight's trip to the smaller Norwegian settlements at Mineral Point, Dodgeville, Hamilton's Diggings, and Monroe, Wisconsin, and found that their countrymen were interested in the proposed Norwegian paper at Muskego but lacked money with which to encourage the enterprise.[20] In June a post office, with Even Heg in charge, was established at Muskego, and Bache promptly recorded in his diary the belief that the postal business would prosper once a newspaper was started.[21] A printing press was ordered from Philadelphia, and on July 29, 1847, the first issue

[19] *America in the Forties*, 70, 71.
[20] See the entries in the Bache Diary from March 22 to April 7, 1847.
[21] Bache Diary, June 3, 1847.

of the pioneer Norwegian paper appeared in print, with Reymert as editor, and his two associates and himself as publishers. The name originally planned, "The Scandinavian Weekly," was abandoned in favor of *Nordlyset* ("The Northern Light"). The type was set by Erick Anderson, who had had experience on the *Chicago Tribune,* and the paper was printed in Heg's log cabin. Bache confided to his diary the hope that the Scandinavian people in America would support the paper "so that it would prosper and enlighten them about all those branches of affairs of which they were ignorant" and that at the same time the immigrants "might raise themselves to be a respected people in the land where they now lived and where they expected to remain the rest of their days."[22]

Bache's confidential hopes were but an anticipation of the announcement that *Nordlyset* made in its first issue. It declared that its purpose was to enlighten the Norwegian immigrants, who could not as yet readily read the American newspapers, concerning the history and government of the country, to present general news of social and religious interest, to purvey information about happenings in the old country, and to do "everything else that may be appropriate and useful toward the enlightenment and entertainment of our readers and in harmony with the strictest neutrality in political and religious matters, an ideal that we always and most rigidly will attempt to maintain."[23]

Nordlyset emphasized its American tone by including a translation of a portion of the Declaration of Independence; by publishing "a few remarks by Daniel Webster, member of Congress, and one of the most keen-minded American citizens"; and in other ways. It announced a subscription price of two dollars a year and made it known that no sub-

[22] Bache Diary, June 27, 1847; Hansen, in Wist, *Norsk-amerikanernes festskrift,* 10.

[23] *Nordlyset,* July 29, 1847.

Nordlyset.

No. 42. Thorsdagen den 8de Juni 1848. 1ste Aarg.

FRIHED og LIGHED.

Nordlyset,

trykt af Bache, Heg og Reymert;
og redigeret af J. D. Reymert

[illegible] ugentlig. Abonnementsprisen er 2 Dollars aarlig i Forskud. Ingen Subscription modtages for mindre end et halvt Aar. Enkelte Nummere erholdes for 6 cents.

Alle Breve, Indsendelser o. s. v. adresseres til „Nordlyset, Norway Post-Office, Racine County, Wisconsin" og Post Portoen derpaa maa være betalt.

Avertissementer eller Bekjendtgjørelser betales saaledes: [illegible] cts for 16 Linier (en Firkant) eller mindre for 1ste Gang 25 cts for hver Gjentagelse deraf. $5 aarlig for 16 Linier (en Firkant) eller mindre. $1. 50 for 6 Linier eller mindre aarlig.

Agenter for Nordlyset.

[Ch]icago	Iver Lawsen	Koshkonong	Ingolf Hemstad
[Mi]lwaukee	D. A. Fresho		og Lars Johannesen
[...]eta	K. Knudsen	Jefferson Pr.	E. Eielsen
[Ro]dgerville	John Lee	Slaten	Chr. Newhouse
[G]eneral Point	Ole Torsen	Lucunan Pr.	An. A. Seee
[Por]t Washington	A. Olsen	Boon Co. Ill.	T. Knudsen
[Mu]skemewec	H. B. Pauss	La Salle Co.	H. E. Furly
[W]atertown	L. J. Fribert	Newark Ill.	Ole Olsen
[M]ukbenaw	Sjur Kleiti	Lutver Valley	H. Ommeltstad
[Ne]w-York	Johan Hel.	Rock Run	Ole Olsen Sune
[...], 32 Rector Street.		Stephensen Co. Ill.	

Indsendt.

[af Svend Jensen.]

[K]om lader os see hvordan Tiden, den gaaer,
hvor ganske umærket den rinder,
At standse dens Løb ingen Jordisk formaar;
men Alt til sit Maal sig henskynder
[K]om lader os agte paa Tidernes Strøm,
og paa vore henrundne Dage.
De hare hendilet, just ret som en Drøm
og kommer ei mere tilbage.

[Hv]ad Tanke skal dette lede os til,
hvor [illegible]
[Hv]er fremgaaer om Livet er anvendt vel
og om vi kan ogsaa være glade
Naar Dødsbudet kommer og kalder os ud
fra denne vor Vandring her nede
Om Sjælen kan svinge sig op til sin Gud,
til evige salige Glæder.

[K]om lad os tilbage til Vuggen hengaae,
og betragte vor Barndoms Dage
[B]etænke vor Ungdom og mangen Aar,
men vi ei har Aarsag at klage
[M]en blide Erindringer Dæmring kom hos
i Sjælens lønlige Hjemme
[M]en heller i Minde som giør os Uro,
naar vi det kun ret vil fornemme.

[U]skyldig vi smilede i Moderens Skjød,
udkendt med vor Sorrig og Nød,
[D]e sov disse Glæder, hun [illegible] sad,
og tænkende saa vi [illegible]
[U]skyldige Glæder i skyldfrie Aar,
vort Kaldn som Foraarets Morgen
[Ei] Synd eller Sorg aabnede Hjerterne saar,
det da var os ganske forborgen.

[U]skyldige Alder, saa er du men kort,
forsnart du ilet tilsidst,
[M]en kommer vi fremad, blier Tiden meer sort,
men Synd er Aarsag maa vi vide.
[D]en Ene forfører den Anden til Synd,
utænksom vi Banen betræder
[Hv]arsomt vi vandre blandt Skarn og Dyn,
som skade kan ærbare Sæder.

[D]u Unge, som iler paa Banen saa frit,
nyd stedse uskyldige Glæder
[V]ogt Dig for det farlige og farligste Skjæmt,
som skade kan ærbare Sæder
[V]ogt Dig for det farlige, saa verder Du frie,
frie er Du i al' Dine Dage;
[O]g med blid Erindring i Alderdoms Lye,
vil Mindet Dig kalde tilbage.

[D]e forbiden: Glæder, de være kun kort,
som Skuggen de hastig bortfarer
[M]en Mindet Du haver tilbage heel fort,
men Lyden den længere varer
[D]en Krands som blier flettet ved Dydernes Haand
og vunden af ærbare Sæder
[D]en tæres ei bort udaf Tidernes Land,
men blomstrer til evige Glæder.

[S]el Lasterne have kan Herredet op
og giøre tan Dyden [illegible] Skade
[K]an rive dens Blade men ikke dens Knop,
den førrer dog at er saa Fage
[D]en blomstrer og bærer den deiligste Frugt,
dens Sødhed boer inde i Skalen
[D]en smager som Balsoms, dens sødeste Lugt,
hver som have Jesu til Delen.

[Na]ar tænker vi os til de modnere Aar,
da haver vi meget at sige
[M]en tægne hvert Feiltrin vi ikke formaar,
Endres havet visselig sine
[De]t Flæste maa vist lægge Haanden paa Mund
og have vort Bie til det Høie,
[Ti]l Jesu Forsonings og kraftfulde Fynd,
som ene kan Hjertet fornøie:

O søde Jesu i Troen og Haab
vil vi til dig Frelsere ile.
Dit guddome Løfte vi lide vil paa
og aldrig [illegible] mere tvivle
Du haver [illegible] Din Fred
den Fred som ei Verden kan give
Naar vi kun vil stræbe at følge de Fjæd,
som Du i Dit Ord os tilskriver.

O værdige Aand kom fra Himmelen ned
og skjænk os Din Kraft og Din Styrke,
Saa at vi kan vandre i Frelserens Fjæd,
saa ret vi Din Guddom kan dyrke
Og drag os paa Veien til Himmelens Land
til evige salige Glæder;
Saa vi kan istemme med jublende Sang
treenige Gud, Priis og Ære·

O Herre vor Svaghed Du kjender heel vel,
hvor ofte tilbage vi falder
Fra ædle Bestemmelser udi vor Sjæl,
hvor kjærlig og blid Du end kalder;
O reis os igjen ved Din kraftige Haand,
thi ene vi ere for svage;
Vi holder os fast ved Forjettelsens Baand
og troer Du ei os vil forlade

Ja kjærligste Fader Almægtige Gud,
mit varmeste Tak jeg Dig sender
Du haver fra Vuggen af heelt indtil nu
mig baaret just ret som paa Hænder
Har stundom en Kummer bekymret mit Sind
og Dit faderlige Ris mig har smertet.
I Glæde for Med- som for Modgangens Stund
det tjener mig Altng til Bedste·

O søde Jesu naar Samfundets Baand
skal løses og endes her [illegible],
O Herre tag Sjælene udi Din Haand
saa at vi kan samles med Glæde,
Og seirende svinge med Palmer i Haand
blandt Englenes talløse Skarer
Og glade istemme den frydefulde Sang,
Dig evig til Lov, Priis og Ære.

Saa lad os da agte paa Tiden heel vel,
og varsomt anvende de Dage
Som er os tildeelt udaf Almægten selv,
vi ved ei hvormange tilbage
Fra [illegible] Haand
og et Vaaer med Døden vil skjænke
Og Sjælen udløses fra Legemets Baand,—
see dette er Bard [illegible]tanke.

Maadeholdssagens Fremskridt. Vi glæde os ved at have Anledning til at meddele et Beviis paa denne hæderlige Sags Fremme blandt os. Den 1ste dennes organiseredes et Maadeholds-Samfund i Settlementet Yorkville i Forening med Samfundet i Norway. Hr. Mons K. Aadland blev udnævnt Ordfører, Hr. Aslag S. Aae vice Ordfører og Hr. Jens Olsen Hatlestad Sekretær. 26 Medlemmer indskreve sig og undertegnede Forpligtelserne. En god Begyndelse, som med Guds Hjelp vil forfremmes saa Whiskey og alle andre berusende Drikke blive fordømte og banlyste fra vort Settlement og Ædruelighed og Maadehold i alle Ting vil stemple vor Karrakteer, som agtbare Borgere. Uden Ædruelighed er det umuligt at det menneskelige Sind eller Legeme kan udvikles— uden denne maa alle Fremskridt standse—og eftersom Intet er stillestaaende saa følger det af sig selv at uden Ædruelighed maa Alt gaae tilbage—baade Sjel og Legeme synke i Uduelighed og Elendighed.

Heil til Foretagendet! et frimodigt Forsvar af Maadehold vil endog vinde Drukkenboltens Anerkjendelse—og Sandhed fører stedse sin egen Løn med sig. Hvor viis er ikke den som forhindrer eller forebygger en Ulykke, fremfor den som er tvungen til at afskaffe et allerede existerende Onde. Det første Glas—vogt Dig for det første Glas—Svælg aldrig det første Glas og vær forvisset at ikkun paa den Maade vil Du—Yngling være viis paa at leve hæderligt og døe savnet af Dine Venner og med et lykkeligt Haab. Men viis er ogsaa den som afstaaer fra en Vane der allerede har nedværdiget og fordærvet ham. Bedre seen, end aldrig, siger Ordsproget, og dette bør tjene som en Opmuntring til den Faldne. Sagen anbefaler sig selv til enhver menneskekjærlig Mand.

Rusland, Sverige og Danmark have sluttet et Forbund til fælleds Angreb og Forsvar.

Landboedrift.

Byg.
(fortsat.)

Bygget kan ikke modtage nogen senere Kultur, naar det er saaet tværs over Furene. Alligevel er det upaatvivlelig fordeelagtigt at bruge Valtsen, naar Planterne er to eller tre Tommer høie, især naar der ikke er faldet betydelig Regn. Valtsning giver Jorden en hensigtsmæssig Fasthed, da den om Vaaren letteligt bliver løs og porøs samt fuld af Revner som en Følge af afvexlende Frost og Tøveir, vaadt og tørt Veir; Valtsningen ødelægger en Mængde Insekter og, fremfor Alt, tjener den til for en Deel at dække Toppen af Planterne og at fremkalde en Formerelse af Kornsorter. Jeg kan anbefale denne Fremgangsmaade af egen Erfaring. Naar Græsarter saaes sammen med Byg, qvæler undertiden det frodige unge Græs Kornet, berøver det sin Næring og formindsker kjendeligen Afgrøden. For at forebygge denne Ulempe, har man anbefalet, at saa Græsarterne efterat Bygget er kommet op, dække dem med en let Harving og Valtsning, og man paastaaer, som jeg troer med Grund, at denne Fremgangsmaade ikke skader Kornet i nogen væsentlig Grad. I tørre Aaringer angribes Sæden, medens den er ung, undertiden af Orme. I dette Tilfælde bør man bruge Valtsen og lægge saa stor Vægt paa den, at den maa trækkes af to til tre Oxer.

Tiden til Indhøstningen og Fremgangsmaaden ved samme. Naar Jordbunden er fed og Aarstiden gunstig, er denne Kornsort meget udsat for at lægge sig. Dersom dette skeer, efterat den har sat Ax, lider Afgrøden ingen væsentlig Skade; indtræffer det derimod førend, da formindskes Avlingen betydeligt. Dette viser, hvor skadeligt det er at gjøre Jorden for fed og bruge frisk Gjødsel.— [illegible] paa Byggets Modenhed er, at de rødagtige Skjær paa Axet, eller hvad de engelske Landmænd kalde „Redreans" forsvinder, at Axene begynde at helde og bøie sig om mod Stilken og at Straaet bliver skjørt og gulagtigt.— Dette er den rette Tid for Skuuraanen, da Axene brækkes, dersom man lader dem staa længere, og Kornet falder af ved den mindste Berørelse. Bygget kan, efter Omstændighederne, skjæres med Meie (cradle), Sigd eller Lja. Staar Kornet ret og det ikke er for tungt, bør Meien foretrækkes, er det derimod tungt eller det har lagt sig, bør man bruge Sigd eller Lja. Men da Kornet er blødt og Straaet indeholder betydelig Vædske naar det skal skjæres, bør man lade Axene vel tørres forend de samles i Baand, bringes i Laden eller sættes i Stak. Dersom Kornet skjæres med Meie eller Sigd, lægger man det i Baand; men en sædvanligere Maade er det, at skjære det med Lja, rage Jorden og tærske Kornet paa med Byggaffelen.

Byg bliver bedre til Malt naar det ligger til Oktober forend det tærskes, hvorvel det ofte tærskes strax efterat det er indbjerget. Den største Vanskelighed ved at gjøre det færdigt til Handelen, er at skille det ved Skjægget. Dette kan gjøres med Tærskeplevlen efterat Kornet først er gaaet gjennem Rensemaskinen, og hvor man har Byg i betydelig Mængde, kan man brede det ud paa Loen i et Lag paa fire til sex Tommer og lade det udtræde af Heste.

Avlen og dens Fordeelagtighed. Middelavlen i England angives af Donaldson til 32 Bushel paa en Acre. Afgrøden i N. Y. afvexler fra 15 til 70 Bushel efter Aarstidens og Jordbundens Beskaffenhed, og jeg troer, Middelavlen er noget mindre end i Storbritanien. Sammenlignet med Hvede forholder Bygavlen sig som to eller to og en halv til een; sammenlignet med Havre er den omtrent lig denne, forudsat at Jordbunden er skikket til denne Kornart. Man maa imidlertid lægge Mærke til, at hverken Hvede eller Havre passer for Bygjord, fordi den første udfordrer et mere stivt og seigt, det sidste et mere koldt og tungtigt Jordsmon. Byg er en mindre usikker Kornart, mindre udsat for Sygdomme og er ikke saa meget udsat for Angreb af Insekter som Hvede.

En Korrespondent for Agerdyrknings-Selskabet i Bath skriver Følgende:

„Da sidste Vaar var mærkværdig tør, udbløde jeg mit Sædebyg i det sorte Vand, jeg tog af en stor Kum, som bestandig optager det Vand, der afsondrer sig fra Møgdyngen og Stalden. Da de lette Korn flød ovenpaa, skummede jeg dem af og lod Resten staa i 24 Timer. Da jeg havde taget Kornet ud af Vandet, blandede jeg det med et tilstrækkeligt Qvantum af sigtet Træaske for at faa det til at sprede sig regelmæssigt, hvorpaa jeg tilsaaede tre Agre dermed. Avlingen beløb sig til 60 Bushel Acren: Jeg tilsaaede nogle andre Agre med samme Kornsort i tør Tilstand, men Avlingen var ~~[illegible] som mine Naboer, meget knap,~~ ikke over 20 Bushel Acren og blandet med umodnet Korn og Ukrud da jeg høstede. Jeg saaede ogsaa noget af mit Byg i tør Tilstand paa een Bakke paa hver af mine Agre, men Avlingen var meget ringe i Sammenligning med de øvrige Dele af Agren."

Efterretninger fra Oregon— Til St. Louis er der nylig ankommet Efterretninger fra Oregon. Indbyggerne ere komne i en blodig Krig med Indianerne og der er forefaldet adskillige Slag.

Meek, den Mand, som bragte Efterretningen til St. Louis, var afsendt til Washington for at anholde om Hjelp.

Følgende er den Skildring, han leverer om Oregon:

„Da jeg forlod Walla Walla den 26de Januar var Folket i Territoriet Oregon i aaben Krig med fire Indianerstammer, Cayuse-, Walla Walla-, Shaster- og Day- Indianerne. Fire Slag vare forfaldne mellem dem forend jeg forlod Landet. Det første Slag fandt Sted ved Foden af „Dalles of the Columbia" den 8de Januar med en liden Troppeafdeling under Kapitain Lee's Kommando,—den næste Fægtning forefaldt nogen Tid senere med Avantgarden af Oregonregimentet under Major Lee. Han blev nødt til at trække sig tilbage efter et saare lidet Tab og forenede sig igjen med Regimentet.

Den følgende Dag rykkede Regimentet op langs Shaster-Elven under Anførsel af Oberst C. Gilliam. Omtrent Klokken 12 blev det angrebet af et betydeligt Corps Indianere, men disse bleve snart slagne af Tropperne—deres Landsbyer bleve indtagne og opbrændte En stor Mængde Lev, som var opbevaret til Føde, saavel som andre Artikler blev ødelagt.

Saasnart Oregonregimentet var blevet forstærket saaledes, at det talede 500 Mand brød det op i Retningen mod Walla Walla. Den 18de Februar viste Fienden sig i talrige Skarer paa Sletterne og Tropperne blere stillede i Slagorden Fægtningen begyndte omtrent Klokken 10 og varede indtil Natten afslutte de

scription would be accepted for less than a half year. "All letters and communications," the same notice continued, "should be addressed to *Nordlyset,* Norway Post Office, Racine County, Wisconsin, and the postage thereon must be paid."[24]

Thus was launched the first Norwegian newspaper in the United States. It attained ultimately some two hundred subscribers, but the number was not large enough to support the paper, which proved a failure financially. It probably was read, however, by many in addition to its subscribers. What kind of reading matter did it put before the eyes of the immigrants? It made available public documents—presidential messages, the constitution adopted by the Wisconsin convention (to which one entire number was devoted), the laws of Wisconsin, the message of the governor in 1849, the inaugural address of President Taylor, and the American treaty with Mexico. It printed local documents of special interest, for example, a circular entitled "From the Democratic Central Committee in Milwaukee to the Norwegians in Wisconsin," to which it appended a spirited reply.[25] It summarized for the Norwegians the stories of noted Americans, such as John Quincy Adams. It brought news from Mexico, Texas, Oregon, California, and other distant places. When a group of young Norwegians started off on the long trek to the California gold fields it arranged to publish a series of letters reporting their progress.[26] It carried much news "From Norway" and occasionally it gave a budget of general European news. It called upon its readers for accounts of Norwegian settlements in the West and published several responses. It carried items that reflected changing local conditions. In its columns one can learn of the organization of a temperance society at the home of Even Heg on

[24] *Nordlyset,* July 29, 1847.

[25] *Nordlyset,* February 10, November 16, 1848.

[26] Letters written by Hans C. Heg telling of the trek to the Far West appear in *Nordlyset,* May 17, June 7, and October 11, 1849.

January 31, 1848;[27] of a protest by a mass meeting of Milwaukee Norwegians against the activities of the minister Dietrichson in appealing for funds in Norway for the relief of immigrants in the West;[28] and of a meeting of Norwegians in Chicago to plan for the publication of antislavery tracts.[29] Notwithstanding its earlier declaration of political neutrality, it placed the names of Van Buren and Adams, the Free-Soil party candidates, at its masthead in September, 1848, and gave much information about the course of American politics, with special reference to the antislavery cause. The motto of the paper was changed from "Freedom and Equality" to "Free Land, Free Speech, Free Labor, and Free Men." Its interest in politics did not prevent the inclusion of much information on American agriculture and on religious questions. And there was room for an announcement by L. J. Fribert that he had Norwegian and German books for sale at his establishment in Watertown.[30]

Advertisements were also given space, including one of a Milwaukee store that took pains to report "Norwegian Spoken Here." Munch Ræder, a contemporary reader of *Nordlyset,* was impressed by the fact that the immigrants had already learned American advertising methods, and he gives some examples. "If you care about your health at all," ran one advertisement, "go to H. M. Hansen's Norwegian Drug-Store in Kilbourntown, Milwaukee, at the sign of the red mortar, near the upper bridge. You will find an assortment of the following medicines, prepared by the best doctors in the United States and Germany." To the list that followed, the druggist appended a personal note: "N.B. My medicines haven't that fine property of curing all sorts of diseases at once, but I can truthfully say that they will satisfy every reasonable demand. I don't intend to sell today

[27] *Nordlyset,* February 3, 1848.
[28] *Nordlyset,* March 30, 1848.
[29] *Nordlyset,* April 6, 1848.
[30] *Nordlyset,* February 24, 1848.

and run away tomorrow with the money. I want to earn my bread by conscientiously discharging all the duties of my calling. Come everyone who has faith in wholesome medicines and who prefers good health to sickness and misery." Another item that caught Munch Ræder's eye as an example of a mode of advertising unfamiliar to the old country opened thus: "Hey, Ole! Watch my oxen awhile, will you, while I go in to Morgans? They say he has the best coffee in the country and my old woman she said I had to buy a few pounds before it was all gone." [31]

Before long Reymert found a congenial relationship with the Democratic party and plunged into state politics, using the newspaper as his springboard. He went to the state legislature, apparently the first Norwegian in the country to attain such a distinction, and on February 1, 1849, *Nordlyset* published his farewell as editor. As early as the spring of 1848 he had established a second newspaper, possibly only as a temporary organ. This was *Democraten,* printed, like *Nordlyset,* at Norway in Racine County. How long it continued to appear is not known, for only one number, that for April 27, 1848, seems now to be available. This number shows that the paper was offered to subscribers for three months at twenty-five cents. In it Reymert states that "as the name indicates, the paper is devoted to the spreading of Democratic principles." He declares that it is "of importance for everyone to understand correctly the intentions as well as the principles of the party," and stresses equality at the ballot and special privileges for none.[32]

After the withdrawal of Reymert *Nordlyset* was published by "Heg and Company." In the summer of 1848 the press had been removed to the neighboring village of Rochester,[33]

[31] See Ræder's interesting chapter, "From the Pages of a Norwegian-American Newspaper," in *America in the Forties,* 177–185.

[32] A copy of *Democraten,* dated April 27, 1848, is in the library of the Luther Theological Seminary, St. Paul.

[33] *Nordlyset,* August 24, 1848.

and late in the fall of 1849 it was sold and removed to Racine, where, under the editorship of Knud Langeland, the last ten issues of *Nordlyset* appeared from March 9 to May 18, 1850. Langeland, who was aided in his newspaper enterprise by his son-in-law O. J. Hatlestad, understood, with a characteristic grasp of realities, that the Democratic party had a considerable following among the early Norwegian immigrants and that the Free-Soil proclivities of *Nordlyset* had failed to win any very wide support. He determined to change the name of the paper and to make it Democratic in policy. The paper in its new form made its appearance with the name *Democraten* on June 8, 1850, and continued under that title until October 29, 1851. Langeland did not at once take a forthright position in favor of the Democrats. He explained that the change in name was a matter of convenience. He desired a name that Americans would readily understand, and he implied that the former name had caused inconvenience because of the inability of American postal officials to cope with its spelling, pronunciation, and meaning.[34] The renamed paper, however, soon began to set forth the principles of the Democratic party.

Langeland did not make the paper primarily a political organ. His aims were general: the enlightenment and progress of the Norwegian pioneers who formed his constituency. As early as the summer of 1850 he presented his views, for example, on methods of settlement. Immigrant settlement had proceeded on an individual basis, he pointed out, and as a consequence the Norwegians had not reaped the full benefits of group undertakings. They had, for example, established no Norwegian-American cities. He proposed that an organized colonization plan be worked out, a society formed, and a commission sent out by this society to select sites for settlement.[35] There is no evidence that his ideas were car-

[34] *Democraten*, June 8, 1850.
[35] *Democraten*, August 10, 1850.

ried out, though the pioneer minister Clausen by his initiative and activity in launching immigrant settlements in northeastern Iowa and elsewhere fulfilled a function not wholly unlike that suggested by Langeland.

Langeland was an outstanding figure in Norwegian-American journalism. He was born at Samnanger, near Bergen, in 1813 and was a schoolteacher and sexton in his home district before emigrating to America in 1843. Three years later he appeared at Racine, Wisconsin. This honest, stubborn, and on the whole enlightened pioneer was an editor for forty years and gained his greatest fame as the guiding spirit of the newspaper *Skandinaven,* published in Chicago. He was widely known as a supporter of the Republican party and a defender of the American common-school system. For him, as for Reymert, journalism led to politics, for he served as a state legislator in Wisconsin in 1860.[36]

In attempting to win the Norwegian settlers to the Democratic standard, *Democraten* soon fell into a sharp controversy with *De norskes ven* ("The Friend of the Norwegians"), a rival paper established at Madison, Wisconsin, in the summer of 1850 under the editorship of one Ole Torgersen. *Democraten* charged that this short-lived paper was financed by, and was an organ of, the Whig party. This Torgersen flatly denied, declaring that in his opinion a course designed to offset extremes in the political field was the wisest policy for Norwegians to follow. "It was for this purpose," he asserted editorially, "that I hoisted a neutral flag in political matters."[37] A contemporary observer of tendencies in the Norwegian press wrote in 1853, however, that *De norskes ven* "was an entirely unsuccessful attempt to establish a Whig press among the Norwegians. It was bound to fail; for the attempt was made by a man with no talents for

[36] Knud Langeland's own story is interwoven with his account of *Nordmændene i Amerika: Nogle optegnelser om de norskes udvandring til Amerika* (Chicago, 1888).

[37] *De norskes ven,* January 28, 1851.

such work." He adds, "I am not aware that this Whig paper made a single proselyte during its political existence."[38] That existence was very brief, only about a half year. Meanwhile *Democraten* was having its difficulties. In 1850 it discussed some of the criticisms that it had encountered and made this plaintive plea: "Still, do not forget to recommend *Democraten* and to enlarge its circulation. Despite its shortcomings, the paper is worth its money. With God's help and as our typesetters gain in proficiency, the paper will gradually improve."[39]

Many years later Langeland explained that *Nordlyset* and *Democraten* were premature. The time had not yet come when a political, or secular, newspaper could be self-sustaining among the immigrants. The subscription list of *Democraten* contained at one time the names of immigrants in twenty-nine Wisconsin and twelve Illinois communities as well as in Iowa, Indiana, Missouri, New York, and Rhode Island — a far-flung constituency — but the total number of subscribers was only 280. There were sixteen exchanges, including the *Sun* and *Tribune* of New York, the *National Era* of Washington, the *Argus* and *Express* of Madison, and the *Daily Wisconsin, Volksfreund, Banner,* and *Free Democrat* of Milwaukee.[40] Such a list is evidence of the part that the obscure immigrant newspapers played in establishing contacts between the newcomer communities they served and the nation. The newspapers opened doors to immigrant understanding of American life.

The Whig party had little influence upon the mass of the Norwegian immigrants in the United States. That party, in fact, was entering upon its decline in the period when the Norwegian-American press was taking its rise. The Norwegians were strongly attracted by the name and traditions of

[38] *Emigranten,* May 20, 1853.
[39] *Democraten,* June 22, 1850.
[40] Langeland, *Nordmændene i Amerika,* 94–107.

the Democratic party, but were at the same time antislavery in their views. It is of interest to note that not a few antislavery pamphlets appeared in Norwegian and were advertised by the press in the late 1840's. The translated titles of three are "A Proof that the Liberty Party Has the Same Fundamental Principles Now as the Liberty Party of 1776," "The Fundamental Principles of the Liberty Party," and "Slavery Causes Hard Times."[41]

Nordlyset, in editorials, special articles, and extracts from speeches, put the case against Negro slavery at the same time that it declared support for free land, free speech, and Van Buren. That support, notwithstanding the early strength of the Democratic party among the Norwegians, is significant of an underlying trend of opinion among the immigrants on issues that were soon to bring about shifts in American party allegiances. Meanwhile an American newspaper, commenting in caustic tone on the defeat of the Whig party in Wisconsin, blamed that alleged disaster on the foreigners and summed up the situation thus: "Our English are generally Whigs; many of our most intelligent Irish are Whigs. Our Germans, who talk only German, are never Whigs. Our Norwegians are Democrats to a man — and so would be the Chinese if we had them among us."[42]

The Norwegian press was begun only a few years after the pioneer Norwegian colonies of Wisconsin were founded. The papers that first appeared were short-lived. They had small circulations. In their views they reflected both the flux that marked American politics at the mid-century and also the gropings of newly arrived immigrants toward a definite political alignment. Their editors were conscious of a need for an immigrant press and they tried, despite obvious limita-

[41] A copy of *Slaveriet foraarsager haarde tider* is in the library of Luther Theological Seminary, St. Paul. It is signed "En sandheds forkynder" and its origin is indicated in the words, "Written by a member of the Liberty Party in Illinois; printed and distributed through the contributions of a number of Norwegians." For a contemporary newspaper reference see *Nordlyset,* April 6, 1848.

[42] *Nordlyset,* June 8, 1848.

tions, to meet it effectively. One after another the pioneering papers fell by the wayside, but the movement for a Norwegian-American press persisted. It was only a matter of time before that press struck out on new lines, found itself politically, and attained a position of expanding power and influence. Save for an interval of less than a year, the Norwegians in America have not been without a newspaper press of their own since *Nordlyset* made its modest appearance in Even Heg's log cabin at Muskego in 1847.

X. THE PRESS AND IMMIGRANT LIFE

To THE IMMIGRANT mind America was, among other things, the "land of newspapers."[1] On more than one occasion Norwegian travelers expressed surprise at finding newspapers published in small American communities. Thus the newly arrived minister J. A. Ottesen, visiting a Pennsylvania town of four hundred inhabitants, pointed out to his Norwegian friends that this village had a weekly newspaper "four times as large as Morgenbladet," the leading newspaper in the capital of Norway.[2] It is part of the larger process of the American transition of the immigrants that they made Norwegian America a land of newspapers. In the many decades that have passed since *Nordlyset* and its immediate successors were launched, the Norwegian immigrants have founded more than four hundred newspapers, whose dates and places of publication incidentally reflect a westward movement of the press synchronizing with the larger westward movement of the immigrants themselves. It was in

[1] The pioneer editor, Knud Langeland, uses this phrase in his *Nordmændene i Amerika,* 94.

[2] *Den norske tilskuer,* November 20, 1852.

the decade of the 1850's that they first achieved a substantial newspaper press, building upon the foundations laid in the late 1840's.

The clergy, conspicuously absent as a factor in the initiation of the Norwegian-American press in 1847, played a prominent role in its expansion a few years later. The ministerial interest centered at first, however, in the problem of establishing a religious organ. As early as December, 1847, the Reverend C. L. Clausen drafted an appeal for public support of a church paper. This statement, which appeared in *Nordlyset* in January, 1848, was conceived in a broad and tolerant spirit. Clausen proposed that the paper, to be called the "Norwegian Lutheran Monthly" ("Norsk luthersk maanedskrift"), should cover a wide range of news and discussion, including the various Lutheran and Reformed groups, the church in the Scandinavian countries, and missionary enterprises, with ample opportunity for the expression of differences of opinion save in certain matters looked upon as Christian fundamentals. The appeal was definitely to the Scandinavians, not to the Norwegians alone, for support of what might be considered an intersynodical organ. Knud Langeland, the editor of *Nordlyset,* in endorsing the project, stressed the possible service of such a monthly as an offset to the partisan feeling that raged in the immigrant communities. Clausen's goal of five hundred subscribers as a condition to publication was not reached, however, and as a consequence the plan did not mature.[3]

By 1850 the time was ripe for a new move toward the establishment of a church paper. In 1847 Clausen had complained that, apart from himself, the only possible editor for a proposed church publication was the Reverend J. W. C. Dietrichson, who firmly declined to undertake the duties of

[3] Clausen's proposal is in *Nordlyset,* January 20, 1848, and is reprinted in Bergh, *Den norsk lutherske kirkes historie,* 83–86. Langeland's endorsement appears in *Nordlyset* for February 3. For discussions of the proposal, see also Rohne, *Norwegian American Lutheranism,* 138; and Jorgensen, "Clausen," ch. 7.

such a post. Three years later, however, the clergy had been reinforced by the arrival of two university-trained ministers from Norway, Hans A. Stub and A. C. Preus, the former established at Muskego, the latter at Koshkonong. These ministers joined Clausen in an announcement made late in 1850 that early in 1851 they would embark upon the publication of a paper to be called "Maanedstidende," or "Monthly Times," to serve the interests of the Norwegian Lutheran church.[4] This periodical, which its promoters intended to issue first in January, 1851, actually appeared in March, and became the organ of the Norwegian Synod. The objectives of the paper were framed along somewhat narrower lines than those proposed in 1847 by Clausen and the constituency was more restricted. The appeal to the Scandinavian Lutheran group as a whole was no longer in evidence. *Maanedstidende* did not narrowly circumscribe its areas of discussion, however, for it proposed to deal with the doctrines and practices of the American synods as well as with parties within the Norwegian Lutheran sphere. With some change of title, and with the exception of a lapse of nearly two years from 1853 to 1855, it has continued publication to the present day, gaining and sustaining a position of importance and influence in Norwegian Lutheranism.[5]

The establishment of *Maanedstidende,* printed at first in Racine on the press of *Democraten,* was the signal for the setting up, also in 1851, of a rival, independent paper, *Kirketidende* ("The Church Times"), under the editorship of O. J. Hatlestad at Racine. A schoolteacher in Norway and also, after his migration to America in 1846, at Jefferson Prairie in Wisconsin, Hatlestad had been associated with the publication of both *Nordlyset* and *Democraten.*[6] He was an

[4] *Nordlyset,* February 24, 1848.

[5] See *Maanedstidende,* March, 1851, and Laur. Larsen, "Vort kirkeblad," in Halvorsen, *Festskrift,* 215.

[6] On Hatlestad see Norlie, *Norsk lutherske prester,* 100; and also Hatlestad's own *Historiske meddelelser.*

Ellingian lay preacher, low-church in sympathy, who joined the Synod of Northern Illinois in 1854, and he employed his paper as a vehicle for the defense of lay preaching and for spirited attack upon the ministers who were supporting both *Maanedstidende* and the emerging Norwegian Synod. *Kirketidende's* existence was marked by vigorous assaults upon the state-church tradition. One appeal, addressed in particular to Haugeans, asked, "Ye have emigrated from Norway, and have set your feet on the noble soil of human freedom — America — do ye still wish with downcast eyes to permit yourselves to be led by blind and inexperienced shepherds of souls?"[7]

Thus the year 1851 witnessed the appearance of two religious periodicals among the Norwegian immigrants voicing two widely different points of view in Lutheranism — instruments for the deepening of a controversial tradition destined to absorb much of the intellectual energy and fertility of the Norwegian Americans in the next two generations. That 1851 was indeed a banner year in the advance of Scandinavian-American journalism is evidenced by the fact that it saw also the establishment of two secular newspapers and the planning of a third, which came into existence early in 1852. The two launched in 1851 were short-lived and relatively uninfluential, but the newspaper that was founded in 1852, *Emigranten* ("The Emigrant"), was a major enterprise, an institution that in itself placed the Norwegian-American press on a solid and permanent basis, for it lasted not only through the entire decade of the fifties but, with changes of name and location and consolidations with other papers, on into the twentieth century; and it came to reflect, as no other pioneer Norwegian-American newspaper did, the life and the position of the majority of the immigrants.

[7] Translated by Rohne in *Norwegian American Lutheranism*, 141. In noting the removal to Illinois in 1853 of the press on which *Kirketidende* was printed, Rohne remarks that this was the end of the paper's "bilious existence"; but the unkind adjective seems scarcely justified.

The newspapers of 1851, *Skandinaven* ("The Scandinavian") and *Friheds-banneret* ("The Banner of Freedom") represent pioneering ventures in immigrant journalism in the metropolises of America. *Skandinaven* of New York, like the earlier *Skandinavia,*[8] was an attempt to set up a distinctively Scandinavian press. It employed Swedish and Norwegian as well as English in its columns, was edited by the Swedish A. G. Öbom, and was characterized by a harsh western critic as an organ of slander, if not of "communistic—red republicanism."[9] This uncompromising charge probably was based mainly upon its animus toward royalty and its onslaughts upon Swedish officialdom and the fact that the paper was Democratic. It is of interest to note that in one surviving copy of the newspaper there is a contribution in verse by a Wisconsin Norwegian physician, Dr. J. C. Dundas, whose theme was "Democratic Independence."[10] *Skandinaven* was a weekly paper, issued somewhat irregularly from 1851 to about 1853.[11] *Friheds-banneret* of Chicago, edited by John Mauritzon and published in 1851 and 1852, was also described by the western critic as "red republican"—a radical and controversial paper whose editor was a "political Don Quixote."[12] When the paper expired, a rival editor in Wisconsin caustically remarked that it died of

[8] See *ante* p. 288.

[9] The characterization is quoted from an anonymous critic who contributed an essay entitled "Den skandinaviske presse i Amerika" to *Emigranten* for May 20, 1853. There is a brief mention of the paper by Oliver A. Linder in a chapter on "Newspapers" in Adolph B. Benson and Naboth Hedin, *Swedes in America 1638–1938* (New Haven, 1938). Linder refers to it as the "*very* first newspaper in the Swedish language" in the United States (p. 183). See also Hansen, in Wist, *Norsk-amerikanernes festskrift,* 14.

[10] Barton, in Wisconsin Historical Society, *Proceedings,* 1916, p. 198 n. Mr. Barton states that a copy dated June 19, 1852, was in the possession of the Reverend C. M. Esbjorn of New Haven, Connecticut.

[11] Linder, in Benson and Hedin, *Swedes in America,* 183. Some writers state that *Skandinaven* existed less than a year. Dr. Norlie, who erroneously identifies it with the Republican party, which was not organized until 1854, gives the dates 1851–53. *Norwegian People in America,* 226.

[12] *Emigranten,* May 20, 1853. See also Hansen, in *Norsk-amerikanernes festskrift,* 14, 15.

a "stroke, after periodic attacks of insanity,"[13] but it must be borne in mind that such judgments reflect a conservative viewpoint in an era of bitter editorial partisanship. Like the New York *Skandinaven,* the Chicago paper appears to have been radical primarily as an exponent of republican, as opposed to royal, institutions—flaunting both in title and in editorial columns the "banner of freedom."

Meanwhile, Langeland's *Democraten,* which had been removed from Racine to Janesville in June, 1851, was nearing its end.[14] Before its last number appeared, on October 29, 1851, the indefatigable Clausen initiated a plan for the organization of a Scandinavian Press Association, with the purpose of purchasing Langeland's press and employing it for the publication not only of *Maanedstidende* but also of a secular newspaper and of religious books and pamphlets for use in schools and homes. A preliminary meeting was held at Koshkonong in September, 1851, where Clausen set forth his plan, with Langeland, several ministers, and others present. It was decided to incorporate the proposed association, and to sell stock at ten dollars a share. By mid-November, when the second meeting was held, more than seventy shares had been distributed, a board of directors was chosen, and the association took under consideration the problem of employing an editor and a bookkeeper, or business manager. It has been generally assumed that the Scandinavian Press Association was an organization of Norwegian Synod pastors, but laymen held the majority of its shares. There is no

[13] Quoted from *Emigranten* by Hansen, in *Norsk-amerikanernes festskrift,* 23. According to Hansen, B. O. Dahly and Niels H. Ellichson were associated with Mauritzon as publishers of *Friheds-banneret,* and its editor, toward the end of its existence, was George P. Hanson.

[14] Langeland and Hatlestad, who had jointly published *Democraten,* divided their printing equipment, the former removing to Janesville, Wisconsin, to print *Maanedstidende,* and the latter remaining at Racine to issue *Kirketidende.* Most historians state that Langeland's removal followed the demise of *Democraten,* but as a matter of fact a half dozen numbers of *Democraten* were printed after the removal to Rock County and are dated at Janesville. See Barton, in Wisconsin Historical Society, *Proceedings,* 1916, p. 200; and Blegen, "The Early Norwegian Press in America," in *Minnesota History Bulletin,* 3:510, 511 (November, 1920).

doubt, however, that the ministers exerted great influence, especially at the outset. The association's constitution, for example, was drafted by a committee of four, three of whom were Lutheran pastors—Clausen, A. C. Preus, and G. F. Dietrichson. And when, on December 4, 1851, the association selected an editor for the proposed secular newspaper, it chose Clausen himself, offering him a salary of three hundred dollars a year plus five per cent of the income from the press.[15]

This was the general background for the emergence of the most important pioneer newspaper of the Norwegian Americans, *Emigranten,* which began publication on January 23, 1852, from a farm in the heart of a Wisconsin Norwegian rural community. Inmansville was the official place of publication, but actually the printing press, removed from Janesville, was set up in a Norwegian farmer's log cabin in the town of Newark, in the Rock Prairie region, and made use of the name "Inmansville" merely because a post office under that name was housed at a near-by farm owned by one Inman.[16] Impressive as is the name of the Scandinavian Press Association, the fact is that most of its shares had not been sold for cash, but on subscription, and in launching its newspaper and planning for the erection of a building it was obliged to proceed upon the basis of credit and borrowed money.[17] It was a humble beginning.

[15] *Emigranten,* January 23, 1852; April 1, 1853; Hansen, in *Norsk-amerikanernes festskrift,* 16; Barton, in Wisconsin Historical Society, *Proceedings,* 1916, p. 200, 201; Langeland, *Nordmændene i Amerika,* 109.

[16] Inmansville was in Plymouth Township and when, on August 1, 1852, the Scandinavian Press Association filed its articles of incorporation, with a capital stock of two thousand dollars based upon two hundred equal shares, its location was given as Plymouth, Rock County. G. F. Dietrichson, A. C. Preus, H. A. Preus, Iver Ingebretson, and James D. Reymert were the incorporators. It may be noted that at a meeting held in Luther Valley on March 10, 1852, Reymert, former publisher of *Nordlyset,* was elected president of the association. Its secretary, or bookkeeper, was John Holfeldt. Barton, in Wisconsin Historical Society, *Proceedings,* 1916, p. 201; Hansen, in *Norsk-amerikanernes festskrift,* 16.

[17] See Adolf Bredeson, "Pastor Nils Brandts erindringer fra aarene 1851 til 1855," in *Symra,* 3:107 (1907).

Adopting the motto of "Unity, Courage, and Perseverance,"[18] Clausen set forth his purposes and platform in the initial number of *Emigranten.* He evidently thought of the paper in terms of a general Scandinavian-American constituency, for he wrote, "I realize that it will be very important for the Scandinavians in America to have a newspaper in their mother tongue, whereby they may be informed of institutions and conditions in the country of their adoption; through it they will learn of their American privileges and responsibilities."[19] To his American friends he addressed a special message in English. "Through our paper," he assured them, "we hope to hurry the process of Americanization of our immigrated countrymen. We want to be one people with the Americans. In this way alone can they [*Clausen here meant the immigrants*] fulfill their destination [*sic*] and contribute their part to the final development and character of this Great Nation."[20] As an earnest of his sincerity he shortly embarked upon the publication of a translation of a general history of the United States from colonial times to Jackson, running this serial of more than eighty chapters regularly in a prominent position on the first page of *Emigranten.* In the summer of 1852 he also began publication of a history of Wisconsin. Thus he sought to make his readers familiar with the story of both nation and state and typified an aspect of immigrant transition in which not only Scandinavian but also German and other foreign-language newspapers have played an important role.

There could be no dissent from these large purposes, but the problem of a definite political stand offered difficulties. There was evidently both Democratic and Whig opinion in the ranks of the press association, and the result was a com-

[18] "Enighed, Mod, Udholdenhed."

[19] *Emigranten,* January 23, 1852, translated in Harold M. Tolo, "The Political Position of *Emigranten* in the Election of 1852," in *Studies and Records,* 8:94, 95.

[20] *Emigranten,* January 23, 1852.

promise.[21] *Emigranten,* Clausen announced, would be an "independent Democratic" organ. He explained that "although we in general join and make common cause with the Democratic party, we by no means pledge ourselves to follow it through 'thick and thin.'" It has sometimes, he said, been led by demagogues and office hunters. That other parties had been similarly culpable did not excuse the Democrats, whose "better political principles," he believed, "ought also to be accompanied by a better practice." The "majority of our people coincide with us in our strong predilection for those principles." He called for the service of "Truth and Right and the interests of the people" and promised that if the Democratic party betrayed such principles "we stop short and care not a straw for any of the too common party denunciations that may be hurled against us."[22]

Clausen felt called upon to explain that he did not intend to "carry on a quasi religious, political controversy with the dissenters in our church." The newspaper would not "become merely an addendum to *Maanedstidende,* wherein the pastors may discuss more freely the current political problems." He took the view that, since each "church faction already has its own publication," a "third paper of that sort is quite unnecessary."[23] It should be added, however, that the church pastors some years later declared in *Maanedstidende* that they promoted the establishment of *Emigranten* in order "to insure our countrymen a political organ which would not become a source of corruption, immorality, and infidelity."[24] The files of *Emigranten,* examined in the light of a later time, reveal the fact that neither Clausen nor his successors were able to prevent the paper from giving much space to religious controversy. *Kirketidende* lost no time in assailing *Emigranten* as the "pastors' paper" and in

[21] Hansen, in *Norsk-amerikanernes festskrift,* 16.
[22] *Emigranten,* January 23, 1852.
[23] Tolo, in *Studies and Records,* 8:95.
[24] *Kirkelig maanedstidende,* 1:1 (March, 1855).

offering sharp criticism in the name of civil and religious freedom. *Emigranten,* it declared, depended upon a group "whose interest in many things is so different from the people that it would be folly to expect impartial justice from them."[25] *Emigranten* naturally could not ignore such criticisms, pastors did not hesitate to wield the pen in defense of their positions, and Clausen soon was in an unhappy situation, drawn into controversies which as a matter of newspaper policy he desired to avoid and finding himself, furthermore, at odds with a majority of the board of directors of the press association. Fearing serious disruption, he withdrew after seven months, gently suggesting that his dual interests as editor and pastor inevitably conflicted, for as editor of a Norwegian paper in America he could not avoid offending many people.[26]

Meanwhile *Emigranten* was viewing the larger scene of American politics with an observant eye. In its third issue it took up the public land question and delivered a blast against land speculators that undoubtedly reflected the convictions of the frontier immigrants. It did not yet call for free land, but demanded that no public land should be sold to speculators. "Land speculation," it declared, "is a curse and a national evil, the destroying influence of which is not half realized." It pointed out that "most settlers wish to locate in more settled communities where they may have schools for their children and where they may gather for religious service." Speculation interferes with this natural wish, however, for, "At the first sign of settlement, the speculators have been buying up land warrants and if settlers wish to stay there they must give the speculators a four or five hundred per cent profit. In this way the land-speculating

[25] Quoted by Jorgensen in "Clausen," 62.

[26] *Emigranten,* August 27, 1852; Jorgensen, "Clausen," 65. Clausen was succeeded as editor by a layman, and another layman was now the president of the press association, whose stock was mainly in the hands of laymen. It is clear that *Emigranten* was less a "pastors' organ" than has usually been assumed.

evil tends to divide up — to retard and to barbarize — our Norwegian settlements."[27]

Emigranten was initiated in the year of a presidential election and its columns throw light upon the early political trends among the Norwegian immigrants. Most of them were antislavery in view, favored a liberal public land policy, and shared the hostile frontier attitude toward the land speculator. There was little concern at first, however, about national politics, and during the campaign of 1852 one contributor complained to *Emigranten* that "whenever you meet a Norwegian, the conversation veers toward farming problems or toward religious controversies; politics is, for him, a closed book." The Norwegian immigrant farmer, he went on, must remember that he is no longer in Norway but in a country where each citizen assists in the machinery of government. One of the roles of the immigrant press was that of stimulating general interest in national politics, and *Emigranten* as early as March, 1852, reviewed the prospects for the coming election, declaring with reference to the Democrats that Lewis Cass of Michigan, W. L. Marcy of New York, and Stephen A. Douglas of Illinois were "all able men and the one selected will be firmly supported by the entire Democratic party."[28] The campaign had not advanced far before a Scandinavian Democratic Association was formed in Wisconsin, limited in membership to "those of Norwegian, Swedish, or Danish descent who are citizens of Wisconsin." This organization had the warm support of *Emigranten*, which, however, expressed disgust over the nomination of Franklin Pierce as the Democratic candidate. When the Whigs nominated General Scott, *Emigranten* described him

[27] *Emigranten*, February 13, 1852, translated by Tolo, in *Studies and Records*, 8:98, and here quoted with one minor change in the translation. The discussion of the land question, Clausen states, was based upon an editorial in the *New York Tribune*.

[28] Tolo, in *Studies and Records*, 8:92–111, reviews the story of *Emigranten's* relation to the campaign of 1852 and translates many items that appeared in that paper.

as a soldier but no statesman, and solemnly congratulated the Democrats upon their selection of Pierce. In due time it issued an extended serial account of "The Large American Political Parties." An editorial on "The Christians in Politics," reprinted from the *Lutheran Standard,* expressed the hope that pastors would "have enough sense not to defame the pulpit by speaking of politics in their sermons; politics have no place in the church and its services"; but it also defended the right of the pastors to political views and to their expression at the proper time and place.[29]

It was in the midst of the campaign that Clausen, on August 27, 1852, withdrew as editor of *Emigranten.* His place was taken by Carl M. Riise, whose name was later metamorphosed into Charles M. Reese, like Clausen a Dane by birth but identified largely with Norwegian immigrant life. He continued to devote the first page of the paper to American history, for he considered it vital to the immigrants to know the story of their adopted land. He was definitely more controversial than Clausen and promptly invited the expression of dissent and opposition. This, he explained, by stimulating other readers to write to the editor, would have a wholesome effect. Reese accepted the independent Democratic position of *Emigranten,* though he said, "I consider myself more in accord with the so-called Free-Soil or Antislavery party — a view which I believe is held by the majority of Norwegians in America." Replying to a declaration that the Democratic party was a slave party and that Norwegians as good Christians could not conscientiously give such a party their support, he hastened to explain that he was not a proslavery Democrat. He feared, however, that a fight for abolition would imperil the Union.[30] As the campaign progressed a biography of General Scott was issued in Norwegian by the Whigs, who also distributed a Norwegian

[29] Tolo, in *Studies and Records,* 8:104.

[30] Hansen, in *Norsk-amerikanernes festskrift,* 16, 17; *Emigranten,* September 3, 24, 1852.

version of Horace Greeley's *Why I Am a Whig.* Reese meanwhile ran a Norwegian biography of Franklin Pierce and gave support to a mass meeting in Beloit at which a Democratic address was made in the Norwegian language. "Let us show the Whigs," he wrote, "that Pierce and King have no warmer friends than the Norwegian farmers." *Emigranten* rejoiced when the Democrats won the election, noting that Pierce carried Wisconsin and even the county in which *Emigranten* was printed. "Rock County," it said, "has up to this time been a strong Whig center, but this time we have carried through the Democratic ticket, 'a nice clean sweep.'"[31]

Some measure of political education there undoubtedly was in the election of 1852 for the Norwegian immigrants as a whole. The door to active interest and participation was opened wider than it had been, but an air of unreality hovered over the scene. There was little fundamental discussion of issues, even of the Compromise of 1850 and the Democratic determination to "resist all attempts at renewing, in Congress or out of it, the agitation of the slavery question," on which in a sense the election was "a kind of popular referendum."[32] A more clearly defined issue than the "organized incompatibility" known as the Whigs was able to present and a more realistic grappling with national problems by national parties were needed before the immigrants could place politics above immediate farming problems and the drama of religious controversy. New immigrants were surging into Wisconsin and other Middle Western states in the early 1850's, and to them, as to the old, the problem of wresting a living from the soil came first. The church, just then taking on the compact form of organized bodies, was closer to the realities of their everyday life than such institutions as national political parties.

[31] Tolo, in *Studies and Records,* 8:106–111.
[32] John D. Hicks, *The Federal Union,* 546, 547 (Boston, 1937).

The immigrant newspapers continued, however, to probe into political matters, both state and national; and as party divisions were more closely drawn and important issues defined in the middle 1850's, the subject began to claim more attention. A lengthy essay on political parties in the United States appeared in *Emigranten* in the spring of 1853.[33] The following summer the newspaper announced that, *Frihedsbanneret* having ceased publication, *Emigranten* remained as the only political newspaper in the United States printed in the Norwegian language. Its subscribers, it was reported not long thereafter, numbered between five and six hundred.[34] In the state elections held in the fall it endorsed, as usual, the Democratic ticket.[35] Meanwhile, it was having serious difficulties in its management, for Reese, balked in an attempt to gain ownership of the newspaper from the press association, ceased to be its editor, and a committee was given editorial control. Reese's connection, said *Emigranten* on January 27, 1854, has "entirely ceased with the present number." The acting editor during the period from 1854 to 1857 was Knud J. Fleischer, a newly arrived immigrant from Norway who possessed considerable competence and a marked literary talent.[36] For some time, under his management, *Emigranten* betrayed comparatively little interest in the political scene, but a new note of concern appeared after the passage of the Kansas-Nebraska Act, and in the fall of 1854 the paper gave its support to anti-Nebraska candidates. It described the Wisconsin Republican convention as composed of "men united in the cause of freedom" and declared that the immigrants "have not left their native country beyond the waters to give support, either directly or indirectly, to the spread of slavery here."[37]

[33] *Emigranten,* March 18, 1853.
[34] *Emigranten,* June 10, 1853; Hansen, in *Norsk-amerikanernes festskrift,* 24.
[35] *Emigranten,* October 21, 1853.
[36] Hansen, in *Norsk-amerikanernes festskrift,* 24.
[37] *Emigranten,* September 22, 1854.

Avertissementer.

Please attend!

BOARD OF DIRECTORS OF THE SCANDINAVIAN PRESS-ASSOCIATION do hereby notify: that we are induced to inform our subscribers and others, by whom we are connected in any branch of business, concerning this establishment, that K. J. FLEISCHER, AND HE ALONE, is entitled to receive and give receipts for money, due to the Office: whether it be for subscription, advertising, job-printing, or sale of books etc.—and, that, a receipt made out by any body else, will not be authentic or sufficient.

Dated Inmansville, Rock Co. Wis., January 21st 1854.

J. D. REYMERT, President.

G. F. DIETRICHSON. A. C. PREUS.
J. INGEBRETHSON. H. A. PREUS.
Directors.

K. J. FLEISCHER, Cashier.

☞ EDITORS of Madison, Milwaukee, Janesville, Beloit and Chicago, would do us a favor by inserting this notice in their papers

Märk!

Direktionen for den Skandinaviske Presseforening bekjendtgjör herved, at vi ere foranledigede til at underrette vore Subskribenter og alle andre, med hvem vi staae i venskabelig Forbindelse, i Henseende til Bogtrykkeriets Affairer, at K. J. Fleischer, og Ingen uden ham alene, er berettiget til at modtage og qvittere for Penge for Bogtrykkeriets Vedkommende: det være sig enten for Subskription, Avertissementer, Job-Trykning eller Salg af Böger rc., — og at enhver Andens Qvittering vil af os blive anseet ugyldig.

Inmansville, Rock Co. Wis. d. 21de Jan. 1854.

J. D. Reymert, Foreningens Formand.

G. F. Dietrichson. A. C. Preus.
J. Ingebretfsen. H. A. Preus.
Direktører.

K. J. Fleischer, Kasserer.

Den aarlige Generalforsamling

i den skandinaviske Presse-Forening afholdes Onsdagen den 22de Februar 1854 Klokken 12 Fm. i New England House i Janesville.

Da Gjenstande af särlig Interesse og Vigtighed ville blive Actieihaverne forelagte, önskes Forsamlingen saa talrig som muligt.

Enhver, som ikke kan möde personlig, bedes at sende Fuldmagt. De Beslutninger, som ved Mödet maatte fattes ville blive forbindende for de Fraværende. Actiehavere, der have anmeldt at ville have deres Actier udlöste med Linderots Huuspostiller have ingen Stemmeret.

Inmansville, Rock Co. Januar 11te 1854.
(43,3w) Directionen.

Efterlysning.

Torger Hansen, Gartner, ankommen til Milwaukee i afvigte Aar, ville behage at underrette Undertegnede om hans Opholdssted og Adresse.

Belvedere, Jll. Sigur Halvorsen Berg,
(42,3w) boende paa Banegaarden.

Hörfrö! ☜ ☞ Hörfrö!

25000 Bushels Hörfrø kjøbes i

Beloit - Drug - Store.

Den høieste gangbare Priis vil for samme blive betalt contant ved

Carey & Gordon.
Beloit, Wis. 33,3m

Bestandig i Spidsen.

En ny stor Samling af Sommervarer.

Et betydeligt Oplag af de skjønneste og modernete Sager. Varerierne i Persien, China, Italien, Frankrig og England have sendt os nogle af deres bedste Producter, hvilke vi nu have den Ære at fremlægge for Publikum.

Iblandt vort uhyre Oplag vil findes:

1000 Yards smukt dobbelt broderet Atlask i alle Farver fra 8 Shilling til høiere Priser. Ligesaa deiligt sort og hvidt dito til Sorg;

1000 Yards glat, stribet, tærnet og changant Silketøi til forbausende billig Priis;

1000 Yards ægte Italiensk sort Silketøi, som vi sælge for 6 Shilling pr. Yard;

500 Yards Tyrkisk Atlask af alle Farver; samt mange andre Sorter til umaadelig billige Priser.

Linon, Linon,

en uendelig Mængde af alle Slags, Farver og Mønstre. Franske Broderier og Borter i nyeste Mønstre, Kraver, Underærmer, Lommetørklæder, kort sagt Alt, hvad man i denne Retning kan ønske sig.

Shawler Shawler!

I denne Retning kunne vi tilfredsstille Enhvers Smag, da vi have fra de simpleste til de kostbareste. Ligeledes have vi 10,000 Hatte af alle Slags, deriblandt 1000 Stykker til 6¼ Cent.

Vi have nu arrangeret os saaledes med vore Indkjøb, at vi kunne undersælge ethvert andet Etablissement i Vesten. Vi have

1000 Frakker, Veste og Beenklæder, gode syede;

500 linnede Frakker til $ 1,00;

10,000 Par Sko og Støvler af første Qualitet;

forskjellige Slags Thee fra 3 Shill. til høiere Priser.

Pedlere, Landhandlere og Modehandlere kunne kjøbe hos os til New-York Priser for Contant. Bomuldstøi og Lärred til Lagener og Pudevaar, samt grovere Sorter findes hos os i Masse.

Vi have engageret en Norsk Clerk, Oluf Petersen, som vil glæde sig ved at see sine Landsmänd i Boutiken, og vi opfordre derfor de Norske til at komme og undersöge vort Oplag, og sikkert ville de blive tilfredsstillede.

M'Key og Broder, Main Str. Janesville.
M'Key & Br. 76 Main Str. Racine.
M'Key & Br. Mineral Point.
M'Key & Br., Madison.
M'Key & Co. Waukegan, Jll.
M'Key & Co. Woodstock, Jll

VEXLER PAA EUROPA, DE FORENEDE STATER OG CANADA.

VEXLER OG CREDITBREVE i store og smaae Summer, efter Behag, paa fölgende Herrer og Banker:

PAA NORGE:
Jacob Dybvad, Forenede Staters Consul, Christiania.

PAA DANMARK:
Suhr & Søn Kjøbenhavn.

PAA SVERRIGE:
C. D. Arfwedson, Forenede Staters Consul, Stockholm.

PAA ENGLAND:
Dhrr Aubertin Brødre. London.
Guion & Co. Liverpool.

PAA IRLAND.
Hibernia Bank og Branches, Dublin.

PAA SCOTLAND:
National-Bank of Scotland og Branches.

PAA FRANKRIG:
Allies & Grand. Paris.

PAA TYDSKLAND:
I. Langs, Sønner, Widon & Co. Bremen.
I. Goll & Sønner. Frankfurt am Main.
Mendelsohn Bartholdy. Hamburg.
I. H. Stametz & Co. Wien.

PAA HOLLAND:
Goll & Co. Amsterdam.

PAA DE FORENEDE STATER:
C. E. Habicht. Norsk og Svensk Consul, New York.
Geo. S. Robbins & Sønner. N. York.
Bank of Attica. Buffalo N. Y.
M. Judson & Co. New Orleans.
L. P. Swift. Milwaukee, Wisconsin.
David Decker. Dubuque, Iowa.
Page & Bacon. St. Louis, Missouri.
Blake Ward & Co. Boston Mass.
W. H. Newbold. Philadelphia Pa.
E. Swift. San Francisco California.

PAA CANADA:
Bank of British North America } Quebec, Montreal & Toronto.

Undertegnede indkasserer ligeledes Penge Norge og Sverrig og andre Europæiske Lande, ligeledes i alle de Forenede Stater og Canada.

Personer, som i Norge, Sverrige og Danmark, eller i andre Egne af Europa, agte at udvandre til de Forenede Stater, og som maatte ønske nœrmere Oplysning, kunne henvende sig til Undertegnede (i portofrie Breve), hvorpaa al ønskelig Oplysning med Beredvillighed vil blive meddeelt. Penge indbringe her fra 10 til 12 pCt. lovlig Rente.

Personer i Norge, Sverrig og Danmark, som ønske at sende Penge til deres Venner i America ville i Almindelighed finde det for deelagtigt at anskaffe og tilsende Vexler paa London eller paa suffisante Banker paa Fastlandet i Europa; slige Vexler bringe al mindeligviis en Premium i de forenede Stater. Undertegnede vil til alle Tider betale den høieste gangbare Priis for Vexler udstædte af gode Bankerer i Norge, Sverrige og Danmark, for Guld og Sölv.

R. K. SWIFT,
Office Nr. 45 Clark Street
Chicago Illinois
(5) U. S of North America.

A. Poole,

I Närheden af Broen og lige overfor Rock-River Hotel i

Beloit

er bestandig forsynet med et godt Assortemen af alle Slags Varer saasom Manufacturvarer, Groceri-Varer, Jernkram, Søm, Bindusgrammer, Steentøi, Glas og Porcellain, Skotøi og et stort Oplag af

færdigsyede Klæder,

bestaaende af Frakker, Beenklæder og Veste af enhver Bonitet. Alt sælges til de laveste Priser for Contant.

(42) A. Poole.

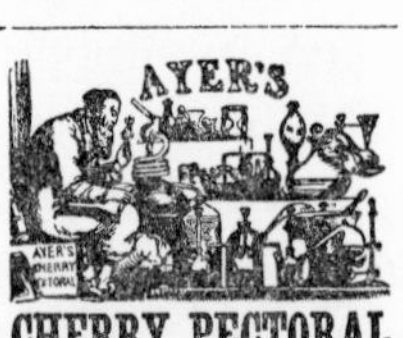

CHERRY PECTORAL

For the rapid Cure of

COUGHS, COLDS, HOARSENESS, BRONCHITIS, WHOOPING-COUGH, CROUP, ASTHMA, AND CONSUMPTION.

Ayer's Cherry Pectoral,

Lägemiddel mod

Hoste, Forkjölelse, Rygsmerter, Halsbetändelse, Häsbed, Kighoste, Asthma (Trangbrystighed) og Täring.

Dette Lägemiddel har ved dets helbredende Virkning i alle mulige Lungesygdomme vundet en saa almindelig Anerkjendelse, at det er aldeles unödvendigt at opregne alle de Vidnesbyrd om dets gode Egens ber, som ere afgivne paa alle de Steder, hvor det värel benyttet. Da det allerede i lang Tid har v i Brug her i Landet, behöve vi kun at forsikkre P likum om, at dets Qvalitet for Närvärende er saa som den nogensinde har været, og at den ägte u falskede Artikel sälges hos

Carey & Gordon i Beloit.

AYER'S PILLS.

Ayer's Piller

ere et nyt og särdeles heldigt Lägemiddel til Hel delse af alle Slags Galde-Sygdomme — Fors pelse, Mangel paa Fordöielse, Guulsot, Vatter Värk i Lemmerne, Feber, Podagra, Sindsli Nervesvaghed, Pirrelighed, Inflamation, Hoved Smerte i Bryst, Side, Ryg og Lemmer, qvind Upasseligheder, etc. etc. Der er sandelig faa S domme, til hvilke der ikke mere eller mindre udfor et rensende Lägemiddel, og der vilde forebygges m ge Lidelser, naar man mere hyppigt benyttede et u digt, men virksomt Afföringsmiddel. Ingen ka finde sig vel, naar Forstoppelse tager Overhaa saameget mere som denne gjerne afstedkommer al lige og ofte slemme Sygdomme, som kunde v undgaaede ved en betimelig og skjönsom Brug a godt Renselsesmiddel. Dette gjälder ligesaam om Forkjölelse, Kjendetegn paa Feber, og Uorden Galden. Thi disse Onder udvikle i Almindeli en dybt rodfästet Sygelighed, som jevnlig bel Liigvognen hele Landet over. Derfor er et paal ligt Familie-Medicament af störste Vigtighed for almindelige Sundhed, og disse Piller ere tilber med den merst paalidelige Duelighed i denne Rein Den grundige Undersögelse, som Läger, Profes og Patienter have anstillet, har givet et Resultat, overgaaer Alt, hvad man tidligere kjendte. Man de neppe troe de Cure, de have udfört, hvis ikk dygtigste Mänds Udsagn vidnede for dem.

Blandt de Mänd, vi ere bemyndigede til at h vise til, ere:

Prof. Valentin Mott, den berömte L i New York.

Doct. A. A. Hayes, practisk Chemiker i B ston, og Geolog for Massachusetts.

Ira L. Moore, M. D. en udmärket Chir og Läge i Lowell, som länge har anvendt dem sine Cure.

H. C. Southwick, en af de förste Kjöbm i New York.

C. A. Davis, M. D. Overläge ved de St. Marine-Hospital i Chelsea, Mass.

Disse Piller, Resultatet af en lang Undersö og Studium, tilbydes Publikum som det bedste fuldständigste Middel, den nuvärende Lägeviden kan give. De ere sammensatte, ikke af tilbere Lägemidler, men ene af vegetabilske Midlers be Essentser, som ere fuldkommen rene og blandede s ledes, at de sikkre det bedste Udfald.

Denne Maade at blande Mediciner paa har b de i Brystsaften og Pillerne viist sig at danne et v sommere Middel, end man hidtil har kunnet erh og Grunden dertil er fuldkommen tydelig. Med ved den gamle Blanding enhver Medicin er besä med mere eller mindre skarpe og skadelige Egensk findes ved denne kun alle de säregne Egenskaber, önskes for at det skal väre helbredende. Derfor er diensynligt, at Virkningen maa vise sig, som den o har viist sig, mere reent lägende, og at Pillerne m väre en sikkrere og kraftigere Modgift mod Syg end nogensomhelst anden Medicin.

Da det ofte er rettest, at mine Mediciner ta under en Læges Veiledning, og da denne ikke vel dömme om et Lägemiddel uden at kjende dets S mensätning, har jeg forsynet alle Läger i de Fore Stater og de Britiske Provindser med en nöiagtig F klaring over, hvorledes baade min Brystsaft og n Piller ere fabrikerede. Hvor faa af alle tilbudte P tent-Mediciner vilde blive tagne, hvis deres B ding var bekjendt! Deres Liv bestaaer i deres H melighed.

Jeg har ingen Hemmeligheder: mine Medicin Blanding ligger aaben for Enhver, og Alle, kunne bedömme Sagen, erkläre frit deres Ove viisning om deres store Fortjeneste. Brystsa blev af videnskabelige Mänd erkläret for en udmä Medicin, förend dens Virkninger vare bekjend mange Läger bevidne det Samme om mine Pil og endog mere sikkert, og de ere rede til at bevidne deres Forventninger bleve overtrufne ved Forsöget

De virke ved deres stärke Kraft paa de l Dele, saa at de rense Blodet og bringe det i f Circulation, de häve Sygdomme i Maven, Ind dene og Levren, idet de ordne deres uordentlige V og modarbeide Smaating, som ere den förste Op delse til Sygdomme.

Da de ere overstrøgne med Sukker, ere de b gelige at tage, og da de ere reent vegetabilske, k de uden Skade tages i saa stor Mängde man öns

Närmere Underretning findes paa Äskens O slag.

Tilberedte af James C. Ayer, practisk analytisk Chemist, Lowell, Mass.

Carey & Gordon, Beloit,

Chikago Store.

Østre Side, Main Street, Janesville W

Vi ville herved underrette vore Landsmänd at vi have oprettet en Norsk Boutik her Stedet.

En vel assorteret Beholdning af Manu tur- og Colonialvarer, samt färdiggjorte & Støvler, vil altid väre at erholde til de vest mulige Priser.

Enhver, som vil beäre os med et Besøg, altid finde en opmärksom og retskaffen handling.

(23) Eckstorm & Brow

ADVERTISEMENTS IN A PIONEER NORWEGIAN NEWSPAPER
[From *Emigranten*, February 17, 1854.]

In December, 1854, *Emigranten* found itself obliged to face a new rival in the newspaper world when *Den norske Amerikaner: Et blad for folket* ("The Norwegian American: A Newspaper for the People") was established at Madison, Wisconsin, by Elias Stangeland. This paper appeared weekly and was issued up to May 27, 1857. Stangeland, whose activities as an emigration agent had recently been under sharp fire both in Norway and in America and who had published an important emigrant guide in Christiania in 1853,[38] seems to have launched the newspaper as an organ for his own defense, which took the form principally of counterattacks against those who had denounced him. One historian, noting that he opened his columns generously to the Reverend P. A. Rasmussen, then engaged in a controversy with certain prominent Synod ministers, suggests that *Den norske Amerikaner* "was started in 1854 by all the forces opposed to *Emigranten* and the Synod 'pastors' in general."[39] The truth is that both motives coalesced and were in turn reinforced by a distinctly political motive, for the paper was belligerently Democratic in its policy. Stangeland withdrew after two years, and the editorial management was taken over by Reese, former editor of *Emigranten,* now hostile to the paper he once had served.[40]

Den norske Amerikaner promptly threw down the gauntlet to its rival and the air was filled with the sounds of controversy. It ranged over a wide field — Stangeland's work as emigration agent, Rasmussen and the Synod pastors, and the respective merits of the Democratic and Republican parties. *Den norske Amerikaner* was quick to raise the Know-Nothing issue, charging that the new party was tainted with hostility to foreigners. It was keenly aware of the fact that

[38] See Blegen, *Norwegian Migration,* 339–342.

[39] Rohne, *Norwegian American Lutheranism,* 152. Rohne points out that Reese, Hans Borchsenius, and Reymert were on the staff of *Den norske Amerikaner.* "All cordially hated the Synod pastors for one reason or another," he adds.

[40] Hansen, in *Norsk-amerikanernes festskrift,* 26.

the Norwegian immigrants were antislavery, however, and was on the defensive when it said, "We have always been against slavery and we intend to oppose its extension as well as we can. But to work for freedom and the ballot for the Negroes, while at the same time we obstruct and sacrifice our own, is indeed expecting too much of us."[41] *Emigranten* in the spring of 1855 still described itself as "independent Democratic," but it was in fact Republican. It declared that it saw in the Wisconsin legislature of 1854 what vultures and "political speculators" paraded under the name of "Democrats," with Irish, Germans, and some Norwegians in their footsteps. For itself, it preferred to separate from these groups and to oppose the "old hunkers," joining the Republicans, "whose platform agreed with our principles" and whose reforms, it believed, would "set the ship of state on an even keel."[42] Thus the issue was joined, and in the fall of 1855 *Emigranten* ran the Republican state ticket at the head of its editorial column. In presenting the party platform it said, "We, for our part, and undoubtedly the majority of the Scandinavian voters, are to be found standing upon the Republican platform."[43]

The national election of 1856 was discussed among the immigrants in terms far more realistic than those employed four years earlier. *Emigranten* gave its cordial support to Frémont and the Republicans, *Den norske Amerikaner* was fiercely Democratic. There was no halfway position. To *Emigranten* the battle was "between liberty, equality, and enlightenment on the one side, and slavery, despotism, and ignorance on the other."[44] *Den norske Amerikaner* saw the fate of the Republic hanging in the balance and the "basic principle" of the Union endangered—"that every man is capable of governing himself and his own affairs." It con-

[41] February 28, 1855.
[42] May 4, 1855.
[43] August 24, 1855.
[44] November 21, 1856.

temptuously described the Republican party as "Republican Know-Nothing"—"a party of all sorts of tinker-politicians, abolitionists, spiritualists, Whigs, desperate turncoats, and dissatisfied, sulking Democrats,"[45] while *Emigranten* published the story of Thorgnyr Landmand at Upsalathing, pointing out that the struggle of the Swedish *lagmand* against Oluf Skotkonnung should "serve us as a model in our present situation, when our inalienable rights as free and liberty-loving citizens of the republic are seriously threatened by the petty slavocratic kings of the South."[46] At the end of the campaign, *Emigranten* sounded a grim warning that, although the Republicans were defeated, defeat did not mean annihilation, the "reading, thinking, and conscientious public" were on their side, and another election was coming.[47] Although the immigrant press indulged in a vast amount of invective, issues were joined sharply, and much space was given over to documents, speeches, and detailed information on the campaign. National problems were clarified to the immigrants and party lines took on definite meaning for them.

In 1857 the perennial problem of the editorial management of *Emigranten* was solved by the selection as editor of Carl Fredrik Solberg, a native of Christiania who had had an academy education in Denmark. He immigrated to the United States in 1853 with his father, who was engaged by Ole Bull to be the director of his colonization project in Pennsylvania. After the collapse of Oleana, the younger Solberg went west, worked for a time on the printing press at Inmansville, and was made editor of the paper upon its removal, in 1857, to Madison. He was a man of unusual competence, fertility of ideas, and broad human interests,

[45] November 1, 1856.

[46] August 22, 1856. With its July 11, 1856, issue, *Emigranten* distributed a broadside, in Norwegian, from the Republican state central committee urging the Scandinavians to vote for Frémont — to keep slavery out of the free states and new territories. "Everyone who in his heart hates slavery will vote for Fremont."

[47] November 21, 1856.

and he ranks as the greatest editor of *Emigranten.* He expanded the paper in size, varied its contents, increased its interest and value as a literary magazine, reached out to all parts of the Northwest for news of Scandinavian Americans, and built up its circulation until, in Civil War times, it had nearly four thousand subscribers. Three years after he took charge, he bought *Emigranten* from the press association.[48]

Solberg accepted gladly the position of *Emigranten* on the slavery and public land issues and made it even more influential than it had been as a spokesman of the Republican party. Bitter personal squabbles were given less space than formerly, and the "editorials dealt for the most part with the great political questions—the preservation of the Union and the slavery controversy."[49] The clash on public questions, however, was sharpened in 1857, when *Den norske Amerikaner* was sold to the Scandinavian Democratic Press Association, which had been formed on April 1 of that year.[50] Its name was changed to *Nordstjernen: Et national demokratisk blad* ("The North Star: A National Democratic Newspaper"), with Reese continuing as editor. Solberg had taken office as editor of *Emigranten* in April, 1857, and the new rival issued its first number, in Madison, on June 10. *Nordstjernen* announced that it would "follow in the footsteps of Thomas Jefferson and Andrew Jackson." It explained, furthermore, that it would "present to the Scandinavian public in this country the views of the various political parties, their position and attitude toward the American Union,

[48] See Carl Fredrik Solberg, "Reminiscences of a Pioneer Editor," with an introduction by Albert O. Barton, in *Studies and Records,* 1:134–144. The number of readers of *Emigranten* probably was many times the number of subscribers. Dr. O. Fritiof Ander, in writing of the Swedish paper *Hemlandet,* calls attention to an instance of seven families reading one copy of that paper and suggests that when *Hemlandet* had less than a thousand subscribers, it probably had from seven to ten thousand readers. *T. N. Hasselquist: The Career and Influence of a Swedish-American Clergyman, Journalist and Educator,* 159, 160 (Rock Island, Illinois, 1931).

[49] Hansen, in *Norsk-amerikanernes festskrift,* 29.

[50] Hansen, in *Norsk-amerikanernes festskrift,* 26.

in a detailed, clear, and nonpartisan way."[51] Notwithstanding this claim, its avowed policy was to "tear the mask from Black Republicanism." It continued the attacks of *Den norske Amerikaner* upon *Emigranten,* which now boldly proclaimed as its motto: "No Slavery for Black or White." *Nordstjernen* supported the Fugitive Slave Law and criticized severely the hostile attitude of *Emigranten* toward the enforcement of that act. So warm did the controversy become that in the autumn of 1857 an effort was made to arrange a public debate between the editors of the two papers. It is evident, however, that *Nordstjernen* enjoyed little support from the Norwegian element, which was rapidly going over to the Republican side, and after a half year it began to appear irregularly. Hans Borchsenius leased the paper from the Scandinavian Democratic Press Association in 1858 and two years later Solberg himself purchased *Nordstjernen* and consolidated it with *Emigranten.*[52]

The attempt to defeat the swing of the Norwegian immigrants toward the Republican party resulted in 1857 in the advance of the Norwegian press into Minnesota, then on the eve of statehood. The first Norwegian newspaper in Minnesota, *Folkets röst* ("The Voice of the People"), appeared on October 1, 1857, about two weeks before the election in which the people of Minnesota Territory were to vote on the question of statehood and choose their first slate of officers for the future state. Democratic and Republican strength was about evenly divided in Minnesota and there was a spirited campaign going on in the attempt to win the election. The editor of *Folkets röst,* O. Nelson, described himself as a "true Minnesotan and a thorough Democrat." His paper was frankly a Democratic campaign sheet, probably subsidized with a view to winning the "Scandinavian vote" for

[51] *Nordstjernen,* August 12, 1857.

[52] Solberg, in *Studies and Records,* 1:139, 140; and Blegen, in *Minnesota History Bulletin,* 3:514.

the Democrats. He appealed to the Norwegians to vote in the coming election "as it behooves foreigners and adopted citizens," and he explained that "it is as natural for you to be Democrats and to vote for the Democratic candidates as it is for a farmer to sow wheat and plant corn." [53] A Minnesota correspondent of *Emigranten* definitely asserted that Nelson was employed by the Democrats and quoted him as saying, "If it were not for that damned 'Emigranten,' I could get every Norwegian vote." [54] The second issue of *Folkets röst* did not appear until July 24, 1858, when, still Democratic, it said that its central purpose was to "contribute something toward holding our free political position as Scandinavians with dignity and honor." In a strain familiar among the pioneer Norwegian editors, Nelson called upon his readers to shake off their political lethargy, "inherited from our forefathers in our native country." There, he declared, the "doctrine of political economy consisted chiefly in a blind obedience to the instituted authorities." Perhaps this was intended as a thrust at *Emigranten,* for Nelson was keenly aware of the influence of the Wisconsin journal in the Norwegian settlements of Minnesota and he took occasion to make the scurrilous statement that *Folkets röst,* unlike its "illustrious co-temporary," was not edited by "Priests, deacons, and fugitives from justice, under the guise of a committee." For some years *Emigranten* had had agents in Minnesota, and in 1856 no less than eight were attempting to recruit subscribers in that territory for the Wisconsin Republican newspaper.[55]

The predominance of *Emigranten* was not merely a matter of management, organization, and activity in hunting for new subscribers. It was fundamentally a matter of policy

[53] *Folkets röst* (St. Paul), October 1, 1857.

[54] See an interesting letter from James Crowley of Kenyon, Minnesota, in *Emigranten,* November 18, 1857.

[55] H. Paulson Rosendahl of Spring Grove was the *Emigranten* agent listed in the paper for September 7, 1855. *Emigranten* had subscription agents in Wisconsin, Illinois, Iowa, Missouri, and Texas, as well as in Minnesota.

on the issues of the day. One of those issues was a homestead law, not achieved until the Civil War period, but vigorously demanded by Westerners in the 1850's. Knud Langeland, employing the columns of *Emigranten,* put the case in 1859, pointing to the Republican party as the exponent of the doctrine of free land to settlers. "We have not forgotten," he wrote, "how the Democrats last year treated the proposed bill of the Republicans with reference to a piece of free land for every family." He glanced back at the election of 1856 and said, "Had we laboring immigrants understood earlier our situation, we should now under Frémont have had the pleasure of seeing every poor family in possession of a 160-acre farm free." And he looked forward: "But there is yet hope; only let us not continue to oppose stubbornly the best interests of ourselves and of our adopted country—for such an attitude does not befit a Christian, free, and intelligent people such as the Scandinavians."[56]

In 1859 the realities of American politics were driven home to the consciousness of the Norwegian immigrants by the emergence of Norwegian candidates for state office. In Iowa and Minnesota, as well as in Wisconsin, Norwegian immigrants appeared as candidates for membership in state legislatures, but the most dramatic contest involving the immigrants was for a Wisconsin state office—that of prison commissioner. The Democratic party took the initiative by nominating Henry C. Fleck, a Norwegian farmer of Dodge County, for this post; and the Republicans responded by presenting the name of Hans Christian Heg of Racine County, a son of the noted pioneer Even Heg. Both nominations undoubtedly reflected a desire on the part of the respective political groups to fend off charges of nativism. Although the Republicans and Democrats had adopted antinativist planks as early as 1857, there was still much talk

[56] *Emigranten,* October 22, 1859.

about Know-Nothingism.[57] The nominations equally reflected a desire to capture the foreign vote. *Emigranten* gave valiant support to Heg, who won the election over Fleck by a majority of 2,673. It was evident that the Norwegian voters by this time were definitely on the Republican side. When Heg was nominated, the Republican convention was reminded of the fact that he was the son of one of the founders of the first Norwegian newspaper in the United States and that that newspaper was Free-Soil and advocated "the principles that now form the Republican platform." Heg, who came into the state field by the route of service in many local political positions, declared in an address, "I went aboard the Republican ship when she was launched. I was aboard when she made trips up Salt River. I am still aboard, but I believe she is now heading toward a different port. But whether she be destined for one port or another, so long as she sails under true Republican colors, you can rely upon finding me among the working members of her crew." The Norwegian immigrants, he said, were for the most part working people with deep antislavery convictions, who had been drawn to America because it was a free country.[58]

The Northwest, according to an American historian, was the critical contested area of the 1860 national election and was won by the Republicans "only on the narrow margin by the votes of the foreigners whom the railroads poured in great numbers into the contested region."[59] This statement may or may not be true, but it is clear that, so far as the Norwegian immigrant voters were concerned, the "fight for

[57] An excellent study of "Know-Nothingism in Wisconsin" by Dr. Joseph Schafer is in the *Wisconsin Magazine of History*, 8:3–21 (September, 1924).

[58] On this election see Blegen, *The Civil War Letters of Colonel Hans Christian Heg*, 16–19 (Northfield, 1936); and Hansen, in *Norsk-amerikanernes festskrift*, 30, 31. Heg had been an unsuccessful candidate for the Wisconsin assembly in 1852 as a Free-Soiler.

[59] William E. Dodd, "The Fight for the Northwest, 1860," in *American Historical Review*, 16:788 (July, 1911).

the Northwest" had been won long before the election of Lincoln in 1860. It was won in the second half of the 1850's, and the leadership of the immigrant press was an important factor in the victory. The Swedish Americans had similarly swung over to the Republican cause in the 1850's. Their great pioneer newspaper, *Det gamla och det nya hemlandet* ("The Old and the New Homeland"), launched at Galesburg, Illinois, in 1855 under the able leadership of T. N. Hasselquist, like Clausen a clergyman-journalist, had been stoutly antislavery in policy from the outset; in 1856 it suggested that the Scandinavian would dishonor himself and his ancient liberty "by giving his vote for Slavery"; and in 1858 it called upon its readers in Illinois to support Lincoln in his memorable contest with Douglas. It has been said that *Hemlandet* and Hasselquist "did more than any other agency in forming the political opinion of the Swedes in America." *Hemlandet* was read by many Norwegians, just as *Emigranten* was read by many Swedes. Both had, to a certain extent, a general Scandinavian constituency. And that constituency was becoming political-minded. Of the Swedes, as well as of the Norwegians, it is true that by 1860 "politics was an absorbing interest, second only to the affairs of their church." [60]

Emigranten had followed the rise of Lincoln with sharp interest, and on July 2, 1860, it announced that it would be in the "thickest of the fight" for "Lincoln and Hamlin, for free territories, for Homestead, for throwing out the Cuba bill, for a moderated tariff." Before the campaign began, the Scandinavian Press Association, in which the ministerial influence had notably declined, passed out of existence, and Solberg took over his faltering Democratic rival *Nord-*

[60] Larsen, *Laur. Larsen,* 127. On Hasselquist and *Hemlandet,* see Ander, *Hasselquist,* ch. 9. A paper entitled *Ugeblad for Skandinaver i Amerika* ("Weekly Paper for Scandinavians in America"), edited by T. M. Holst, a Dane, was appearing in Chicago in 1859. See an advertisement in *Emigranten,* March 7, 1859.

stjernen.[61] How far the trend to the Republican cause had gone is evidenced by the fact that Reese, Solberg's erstwhile Democratic opponent, blossomed out as a Republican, editing a short-lived (and possibly subsidized) Chicago Norwegian newspaper called *Folkebladet* ("The People's Gazette"), the first number of which appeared on September 22, 1860. Reese asked for the election of Lincoln "not because he has split rails or run a flatboat, but because we consider him an honest man" and the people "ought to try an honest administration of the federal government." Solberg, meanwhile, printed a biography of Lincoln,[62] a vast amount of campaign material, and, after the election, jubilant reports of victory.

The pioneer Norwegian immigrant newspapers were not merely organs for political and church controversy and for the dissemination of news. They served also as magazines, and it is of interest to note that in the period when the slavery controversy was reaching its climax, much of the first page of *Emigranten* was being devoted to the writings of Bjørnstjerne Bjørnson, who just then was winning wide fame as a result of his stories of Norwegian country people. *Synnøve Solbakken,* an "epoch-making work in Norwegian literature,"[63] was published by Bjørnson in Norway in 1857. It began to appear serially in *Emigranten* in January, 1859; and Solberg on the eve of the Civil War launched the similar publication of *En glad gut.*[64] Even after the Civil War had begun and his newspaper space was largely claimed by the great conflict, he went serenely on with his attempt to make available to the immigrants the literature of Norway. Bjørnson's *Arne,* for example, began to appear serially in *Emigranten* on January 6, 1862. Earlier, in 1858, he had drawn

[61] Hansen, in *Norsk-amerikanernes festskrift,* 31. H. A. Preus remained to the last as a member of the board of directors of the press association. *Emigranten* announced on January 23, 1860, that Solberg had taken over the paper.

[62] *Emigranten,* September 24, 1860.

[63] Theodore Jorgenson, *History of Norwegian Literature,* 278 (New York, 1933).

[64] January 21, 1861.

Emigranten.

8de Aargang. No. 2.

Et uafhængig demokratisk Blad.

Løbende No. 344.

Udgivet af den Skandinaviske Presse-Forening.

Fremad til Sandhed og Oplysning!

Redigeret af C. Fr. Solberg

Madison, Dane Co., Wisconsin, Onsdagen den 12te Januar 1859.

Emigranten,
a weekly paper,
Published at Madison, Dane Co. Wis.
Edited by **C. Fr. Solberg.**
Adress: Box 82.

TERMS.
8th vol. ending 31th Dec. 1859,
in advance $1,50; not in advance $2.

RATES OF ADVERTISING.

	1 w.	3 w.	3 m.	6 m	1 y.
Sq	$1,50	$2,00	$4,00	$6 00	$12 00
Cl.			8,00	12,00	18,00
Cl.			10,00	15 00	21,50
Cl.			12,00	18,00	25,00
Cl.			18,00	25,00	35,00

The space of 13 lines, close matter, make a square.
BUSINESS-CARDS $1 pr. year each line.

Synnøve Solbakken
af
Bjørnstjerne Bjørnsen.

1ste Capitel.

I en stor Dal kan der være et til alle Sider fritliggende hoit Sted, som Solen bærer Straaler paa, fra det den gaaer op, til den falder, og de, som boe lættere under Fjeldene og sjeldnere faae Sol, kalde da hiint Sted en Solbakke. Den, hvorom her skal fortælles, boede paa en saadan, hvoraf Gaarden havde sit Navn. Der lagde Sneen sig sidst om Hosten, der braanede den ogsaa forst om Vaaren.

Gaardens Eiere vare Haugianere og kaldtes Læsere, fordi de havde det travlere med at læse i Bibelen end andre Folk. Manden hedte Guttorm og Konen Ingrid; de fik en Gut, som døde for dem, og i tre Aar kom de ikke paa den østre Side af Kirken. Efter dette Tidsforløb fik de en Jente, som de kaldte op efter Gutten; han havde hedt Syvert, og hun blev døbt Synnöv, da de ikke fandt noget Nærmere. Men Moderen kaldte hende Synnøve, fordi hun, saalænge Barnet var lidet, havde for Viis at lægge "min" til, og det da syntes hende at falde lettere. Hvordan det var og ikke var: den Tid Jenten blev større, kaldte Alle hende Synnøve efter Moderen, og de fleste sagde, at i Mandeminde var ikke saa fager en Jente voxet der i Bygden, som Synnøve Solbakken. Hun var ikke gammel, for de hver Prækensøndag tog hende med i Kirke, skjønt Synnøve i Forstningen ikke vidste bedre, end at Præsten stod og skjendte paa Slave-Bent, som hun saae sidde lige nedenfor Prækestolen. Dog vilde Faderen hun skulde være med — forat faae Vanen, sagde han; og Moderen vilde det Samme, "da Ingen vidste, hvorledes hun imidlertid blev passet hjemme." Var der paa Gaarden noget Lam, Kid, eller liden Gris, som vantrivdes, eller en Ko, som noget Ondt kom over, blev det altid givet Synnøve til Eiendom, og Moderen syntes vide, at fra den Stund kom det sig; Faderen troede ikke rigtig, det kom deraf, men det var i alle Fald det Samme, hvem af dem eiede Fæet, naar det blot trivtes.

Paa den anden Side i Dalen og tæt under det høie Fjeld laae en Gaard, som hedte Granliden, saa kaldet, fordi den laae midt i en stor Granskog, den eneste i en vid Omkreds. Eierens Oldefader havde været blandt dem, som laae i Holsteen og ventede Russen, og fra denne Færd bar han mange fremmede og forunderlige Frøsorter med hjem i Turnistret. Dem plantede han rundt sine Huse; men i Tidens Længde var en efter en gaaet ud; kun nogle Grankongler, som fæst nok var kommen iblandt, havde sat stærk Skov og skyggede nu Husene til alle Sider. Holsteensfareren havde hedt Thorbjørn efter sin Bedstefader; hans ældste Søn Sæmund efter Faderen, og saaledes havde paa den Gaard Eierne skiftevis hedt Thorbjørn og Sæmund — op i umindelige Tider. Men det Ord gik, at i Granliden havde blot anden hver Mand Lykken med sig, og det var ikke ham, som hedte Thorbjørn. Da den nuværende Eier, Sæmund, fik sin förste Søn, tænkte han mangehaande derved, men turde dog vanskeligt bryde Slægtens Skik, og kaldte ham derfor Thorbjørn. Grundede han da over, om ikke Gutten kunde opdrages slig, at han kom forbi den Skjæbnesteen, Snakket havde lagt i hans Vei. Han var ikke rigtig vis paa det, men han syntes formærke stridigt Sind hos Gutten; "det skal plukkes ud", sagde han til Moderen, og saasnart Thorbjørn var bleven tre Aar, satte Faderen sig stundom hen med et Riis i Haanden, tvang ham saa til at bære alle Vedtræer tilbage paa sin Plads, tage op igjen den Kop, han havde kastet, klappe Katten, som han havde knebet. Men Moderen gik gjerne ud, naar det Sind kom over Faderen.

Sæmund undredes ved, at alt som Gutten blev større, var der mere at rette hos ham, og det uagtet han stedse blev strengere medfaren. Han voldt ham tidlig til Bogen og lod ham gaae med paa Marken forat kunne have et Øie med ham. Moderen havde stort Huus og Smaabörn; hun kunde ikke mere end klappe og formane Sønnen hver Morgen hun klædte ham paa, og tale sagte med Faderen, naar Helligdagene samlede dem. Men Thorbjørn tænkte, naar han fik Hug, fordi a b sagde ab og ikke ba, og fordi han ikke havde Lov til at give liden Ingrid Riis, som Faderen gav ham: — det er dog underligt, at jeg skal have det saa slemt og alle Smaasöskende mine skal have det saa godt.

Da han var meest omkring Faderen og han ikke turde tale synderligt til ham, blev han ordknap, skjøndt ikke saatænkt. Engang undslap det ham dog, medens de drog paa det vaade Ho: "Hvorfor er alt Hoet tørt og inde derovre paa Solbakken, og her er det vaadt?" "Fordi de have oftere Sol end vi." — Det var første Gang han lagde Märke til, at den Solglands der borte, han tidt havde siddet og glædet sig ved, stod han selv udenfor. Siden den Dag faldt hans Öine oftere paa Solbakken end før. "Sid ikke der og gab," sagde Faderen og gav ham et Puf; "herovre maa vi slide det vi kunne, baade Liden og Stor, skulle vi faae Noget i Huus."

Sæmund skiftede Tjenestegut, da Thorbjørn kunde være omkring de Syv, Otte. Aslak hedte den nye, og han var nok allerede vidtreist, skjøndt han blot var Unggutten endda. Den Kveld, han kom, var Thorbjørn gaaet tilsengs, men den næste Dag, han sad og læste, slog En op Døren med et saadant Spark, som han aldrig havde hørt før, og det var Aslak, der kom drivende med et stort Fange Ved, — slængte det med Fart ned paa Gulvet, saa Skirne føg til alle Sider. Selv hoppede han høit i Veiret forat trampe Sneen af sig, og for hvert Hop raabte han: "Det er koldt ja' Troldbruden, hun sad i Jis til Beltet!" Faderen var ikke inde, — men Moderen sopte Sneen sammen og bar den stiltiende ud. "Hvad glaner Du efter?" sagde Aslak til Thorbjørn. "Ikke efter Noget," svarede denne; thi han var ræd. "Har Du seet den Hanen, som Du har bag i Bogen der?" "Ja". "Han har fuldt af Høns omkring sig, naar Bogen er lukket i, — har Du seet det?" "Nei". — "Saa see efter!" — Gutten gjorde saa. — "Du er en Tosk!" sagde Aslak til ham. — Men fra den Stund havde Ingen den Magt over ham som Aslak.

"Du kan Ingenting", sagde Aslak en Dag til Thorbjørn, — denne piltede som sædvanlig efter ham for at give Agt. "Jo, jeg kan til den fjerde Part." "Pyt! Nei, Du har ikke engang hørt om Troldet, der dandsede saalænge med Jenten, til Solen randt, og det revnede som en Kalv, der har spiist Suurmelk!" I sine Levedage havde Thorbjørn ikke hørt saa megen Kundskab paa eengang. "Hvor var det?" spurgte han. "Hvor? — Ja det, — jo, det var borte paa Solbakken der!" Thorbjørn stirrede. "Har Du hørt om ham, som solgte sig til Fanden for et Par gamle Støvler?" Thorbjørn glemte at svare, saa forundret var han. "Du tænker vel paa, hvor det var — he? — — Det var ogsaa borte paa Solbakken der, rigtig lige nede i den Bæk, Du seer! — — — Vorherre bevar' os! Det staaer daarligt til med din Christendomskundskab," sagde han videre. "Du har vel ikke engang hørt gjetti hende Kari Træstak?" Nei, han havde Ingenting hørt. Og medens Aslak nu arbeidede fort, fortalte han endnu fortere, — og det var om Kari Træstak, om Kvarnen, der malte Salt paa Havsensbund, om Fanden med Træsko paa, Troldet, som fik Skjægget fast i en Træstamme, de syv grønne Jomfruer, som nappede Haarene af Skyttepeers Lægge, medens han sov og umulig kunde vaagne, — og Altsammen foregik borte paa Solbakken. "Hvad i Guds Navn gaaer der af Gutten?" sagde Moderen den næste Dag. "Han har nu staaet paa Knæ der borte paa Bænken og seet ud over til Solbakken, fra det blev lyst. "Ja, idag har han det travelt," sagde Faderen, som laae og hvilte sig den lange Søndag. "Aa, Folk siger, at han har fæstet Synnøve Solbakken," sagde Aslak; "men Folk siger ogsaa saa meget," lagde han til. Thorbjørn forstod det ikke rigtig, men blev dog ildrød over det hele Ansigt. Da Aslak gjorde opmærksom herpaa, krøb han ned af Bænken, tog sin Catechismus og begyndte at læse. "Ja, trøst Dig med Guds Ord, Du," sagde Aslak; "Du faaer hende saa ikke alligevel."

Da det led saa langt frem i Ugen, at han tænkte de havde glemt det, spurgte han Moderen ganske sagte (thi han var undseelig ved det): "Du, — hvem er Synnøve Solbakken?" "Det er en liden Jente, som engang skal eie Solbakken" — "Har hun ingen Træstak da?" Moderen saae forundret paa ham: "Hvad er det Du siger?" sagde hun. Han følte det maatte være noget Dumt og taug. "En har aldrig seet vakkrere Barn, end hun er," lagde Moderen til, "og det har hun faaet i Løn af Vorherre, fordi hun bestandig er snild og brav og flittig til at læse." Nu vidste han det med.

En Dag Sæmund havde været i Marken med Aslak, sagde han om Kvelden til Thorbjørn: "Du skal ikke oftere være sammen med Tjenestegutten." Men Thorbjørn agtede ikke videre paa det. Saa lød det en Stund efter: "Dersom Du findes oftere sammen med ham, gaaer det Dig ikke godt!" Da sneg Thorbjørn sig efter ham, naar Faderen ikke saae det. Denne kom over dem, der de sad og talte sammen; da fik Thorbjørn Prygl og blev jaget ind. Men siden pasiede Thorbjørn Aslak op, naar Faderen ikke var hjemme.

En Søndag, Faderen var i Kirke, gjorde nok Thorbjørn Ugang hjemme. Aslak og han kastede Snebolte paa hinanden. "Nei, nei, Du kvæler mig," bad Thorbjørn; "lad os kaste tilsammen paa noget Andet." Aslak var strax færdig, og saa kastede de først efter den spinkle Gran borte ved Buret, saa efter Burdøren, og endelig efter Burvinduet, — ikke dette selv, sagde Aslak, men Listen omkring det. Thorbjørn traf imidlertid Ruden og blev bleg. "Pyt, hvem saaer vide det? Kast bedre!" Han saa gjorde, men traf nok en. "Nu vil jeg ikke mere." I det Samme kom hans ældste Søster, liden Ingrid ud. "Kast efter hende, Du!" Thorbjørn var strax færdig, Jenten græd og Moderen kom ud. Hun bad ham holde inde. "Kast, kast!" hviskede Aslak. Thorbjörn var hed og ophidset; han gjorde saa. "Jeg mener Du gaaer fra Viddet, jeg," sagde Moderen og rendte mod ham. Han foran, hun efter — Gaarden rundt; Aslak lo og Moderen truede. Men der fik hun ham fat oppe i en Snedrive, og gav sig ifærd med rigtigt at dænge ham. "Jeg staaer igjen, jeg, det bruge de her" — Moderen holdt forundret inde og saae paa ham. "Det har en Anden lært Dig," sagde hun saa, tog ham stiltiende ved Haanden og førte ham ind. Hun sagde ikke et Ord mere til ham, men stellede godt for hans Smaasøskende og talte med dem om, at nu kommer Fader hjem fra Kirken. Da begyndte det at blive dygtig hedt i Stuen. Aslak bad om Lov til at besøge en Slægtning; det fik han strax; men Thorbjørn blev meget mindre, da Aslak var gaaet. Han havde frygtelig ondt i Maven og var saa klam i Hænderne, at han svedede Bogen, naar han tog i den. Bare Moder ikke vilde sige Noget til Fader, naar han kom hjem; men at bede derom, fik han ikke over sig. Alt, han saae paa, skiftede Udseende, og Stueuhret sagde: Bank, Bank — Bank, Bank! Han maatte op i Vinduet og see paa Solbakken. Den alene laae tilsneet, stille og perlede i Solen, som bestandig; Huset stod og loe ud af alle Ruder, og der var visselig ikke en eneste itu; Røgen foer forfærdelig glad op af Piben, saa han kunde forstaae, at de ogsaa der kogte for Kirkefolket. Der gik bestemt Synnøve og saae ud efter sin Fader, og skulde slet ikke have Hug, naar han kom hjem. Han vidste ikke, hvad han skulde tage sig for, og blev paa eengang saa kjærlig mod sine Søstre, at det var ingen Ende paa det. Ingrid var han saa god mód, at han gav hende en blank Knap, som han havde faaet af Aslak. Hun tog ham om Halsen, og han tog hende om Halsen: "kjære, vesle Ingrid min, er Du sindt paa mig?" "Nei, vesle Thorbjørn! Du kan gjerne kaste saa meget Snee paa mig, som Du vil." Men der trampede En Sneen af sig i Svalen! Det var ganske rigtig Faderen; han syntes mild og god og det var endnu værre. "Nu?" sagde han og saae sig omkring, — og det var forunderligt, at ikke Stueuhret ramlede ned. Moderen satte Maden frem. "Hvordan staaer det til her?" spurgte Faderen, idet han satte sig og tog Skeen op; Thorbjørn saae paa Moderen, saa Taarerne kom ham i Øinene. "Aa — jo," sagde hun reent uroelig langsomt, og hun vilde sige endnu Mere, det saae han nok. "Jeg gav Aslak Lov til at gaae ud," sagde hun. — Det var nu dengang, tænkte Thorbjørn, — han tog paa at lege med Ingrid, som om han ikke tænkte paa nogen Verdens Ting. Saalænge havde Faderen aldrig spist, og Thorbjørn gav sig tilsidst ifærd med at tælle hver Bid; men da han kom til den fjerde, vilde han see, hvormeget han kunde tælle op mellem den fjerde og femte, og saaledes gik det istykker for ham. Endelig reiste Faderen sig og gik ud. Ruderne, Ruderne, klirrede det for Ørerne paa ham, og han saae efter, om de vare hele, de, som vare i Stuen. Jo, de vare hele allesammen. Men nu gik ogsaa Moderen ud. Thorbjørn tog liden Ingrid i Fang og sagde saa blidt, at hun maatte forundret stirre paa ham: "Vi To skulle lege Gulddronning i Enge, vi!" Det vilde hun da gjerne. Og saa sang han, medens Benene skjalv under ham:

> Vesle Blomme,
> Enge-Blomme
> hör nu lidt paa mig!
> Og vil Du väre Kjärestell min,
> saa skal Du faae en Kaabe fin
> af Fioiel og Guld,
> af Perler fuld.
> Ditteli, Dutteli, deja, —
> og Solen skinner paa Heja.

Saa svarte hun:

> Gulddronning,
> Perledronning
> hör nu lidt paa mig.
> Jeg vil ei väre Kjäresten din,
> Jeg vil ei have Kaaben fin
> af Fioiel og Guld,
> af Perler fuld —
> Ditteli, dutteli, deja —
> Og Solen skinner paa Heja!

Men som nu denne Leg var bedst igang, kom Faderen ind og satte Øiet vist paa ham. Han trykkede Ingrid tættere i Fang og faldt slet ikke af Stolen. Faderen vendte sig bort, sagde Ingenting; en halv Time gik, han havde endnu Intet sagt, — og Thorbjørn vilde næsten begynde at være glad, men turde ikke. Han vidste ikke, hvad han skulde troe, da Faderen selv hjalp til at klæde ham af; han begyndte saa smaat at skjælve igjen. Da klappede Faderen ham paa Hovedet og strøg hans Kind; det havde han ikke gjort, saalangt tilbage Gutten kunde huske, og derfor blev han saa varm om Hjertet og over den hele Krop, at Frygten randt af ham som Iis for Solstik. Han vidste ikke, hvorledes han kom i Seng, og da han hverken kunde give sig til at synge eller raabe, lagde han Hænderne stille overkors, bad Fadervor fer Gange fremlængs og baglængs, ganske sagte — og følte, idet han sovnede ind, at der var dog Ingen paa Guds grønne Jord, han holdt slig af som Fader sin.

Den næste Dag vaagnede han i en forfærdelig Angst, fordi han ikke kunde skrige; thi han skulde nu alligevel have Prygl. Da han slog Øinene op, mærkede han til stor Lettelse, at han havde bare drømt det, men mærkede ogsaa snart, at en Anden skulde netop have Prygl, og det var Aslak. Sæmund gik op og ned ad Gulvet, og Thorbjørn kjendte nok den Gang. Den noget lille, men undersætsige Mand saae en og anden Gang under de buskede Bryn saaledes hen til Aslak, at denne nok følte, hvad der laae i Luften; Aslak selv sad oppe paa Bunden af en stor Tønde, nedad hvilken hans Been dinglede eller krogede opover. Han havde som sædvanlig Hænderne i Lommen og Huen paa Hovedet trykket let ned, saa at det tykke morke Haar stak i Dusker frem under Skyggen. Den lidt skjæve Mund var endnu skjævere, det hele Hoved holdt han lidt paa Skakke og saae til Sæmund fra Siden af under halvt tillukkede Øienlaag. "Ja, Gutten din er gal nok," sagde han; "men værre er det, at Hesten din er troldskræmt." Sæmund standsede: "Du er en Gap!" sagde han, saa det dronede i Stuen, og Aslak lukkede Øienlaagene endnu tættere til. Sæmund gik paany; Aslak sad en Stund stille. "Jo, gu er den troldskræmt, jo," og skottede efter ham forat see hvad Virkning det havde. "Nei, men den er skogræd, er den," sagde Sæmund, fremdeles gaaende; "Du har fældet Træ over den i Marken, din uvorne Slusk, og derfor kan Ingen længer faae den til at gaae rolig der." Aslak hørte en Stund paa dette. "Jaja! troe Du det! Troen skjæmmer Ingen. . . . . Men jeg tvivler paa den gjør Hesten din god igjen," lagde han til og skubbede sig i det samme længer ind paa Tønden og dækkede for Ansigtet med den ene Haand. Sæmund kom ganske rigtig hen til ham og sagde sagte, men uhyggeligt nok: "Du er en ond . . . ." "Sæmund!" lød det borte fra Aaren; det var Ingebjörg, Konen, som tyssede paa ham, ligesom hun sad og tyssede paa den Mindste, der var bange og vilde skrige. Barnet havde tiet før, og nu taug ogsaa Sæmund; men han stak dog sin for en saa undersætsig Mand meget lille Næve opunder Næsen paa Aslak og holdt den der en Stund, idet han ludede sig frem og brændte ham med Øinene ind i Ansigtet. Derpaa gik han som før og saae hen til ham en og anden Gang i Hast.

(Fortsættes).

upon the Norwegian historian P. A. Munch for the story of Olaf Tryggvesson.[65] From the same historian he produced, in four installments, the history of the Norse discovery of America. Henrik Wergeland, Peter Christen Asbjørnsen, Hans Christian Andersen,[66] and many other familiar Scandinavian names appear among the authors represented. *Emigranten* in the period of Solberg's editorship was definitely richer in its Scandinavian literary content than the same paper in its earlier period or than other pioneer Norwegian newspapers. Not a little of the documentary publication in the earlier years consisted of distinctively American materials, such as the history of the United States, and of political and social essays, sermons, and the like. As the press more and more fulfilled its purpose of acquainting its readers with American history and conditions, however, the editors took greater cognizance of the cultural ties with the Scandinavian North and increasingly supplemented their budget of news "From Norway" with the writings of Norwegian and other Scandinavian authors.

The immigrant press was "a clearing house for immigrant thought as well as a round-robin letter."[67] In it were discussed, in addition to religious and political questions, many problems of immigrant transition, such as that of immigrant children and the common schools, the possible submergence in America of the Norwegian language, and the desirability of temperance among the settlers.[68] Perhaps its most char-

[65] *Emigranten,* May 26 to July 7, 1858.

[66] "Flaskehalsen," in *Nordstjernen,* November 22, 1859; January 2, 1860.

[67] Richard B. Eide, comp., *Norse Immigrant Letters: Glimpses of Norse Immigrant Life in the Northwest in the Fifties,* 6 (Minneapolis, 1925).

[68] There actually was a temperance publication called *Avholdenhedsvennen* published at Racine, Wisconsin, in 1852, edited by P. L. Massin, or Mossin, of Milwaukee. This Norwegian paper appeared monthly and was aimed against the liquor traffic "which has ruined and poisoned the whole social life." The present writer knows of no existing copies of this paper. A clue to the paper is in *Emigranten,* June 11, 1852: "We have received a paper called *Afholdsvennen,* edited by L. P. Mossin. It is published monthly, and costs twenty-five cents a year." O. J. Hatlestad, in *Friheds-banneret,* March 12, 1853, quoted by Gjerset and Hektoen, in *Studies and Records,* 1:13.

acteristic feature, however, was its service as a round robin, giving news from the Scandinavian countries for the immigrants and reports from the immigrant settlements and settlers. It served not only for their own enlightenment in a period of much migration to new frontiers but also as a kind of composite America letter, such as Clausen had envisaged, for the common people of Norway. The immigrant newspapers were thus a regional press carrying reports from Minnesota, Iowa, Missouri, Dakota, Kansas, California, Washington, Texas, New York, Pennsylvania, and many other parts of America in which Norwegian immigrants were establishing themselves. Settlers debated the relative advantages of various areas, Cleng Peerson and J. M. C. Wærenskjold, for example, adjuring immigrants not to go to the bleak North but instead to join the Norwegians who had pioneered in Texas,[69] other settlers arguing that the climate and land of Wisconsin were infinitely preferable to those of Minnesota.[70] The difficulties of travel, the ordeal of pioneering on remote frontiers, and social and economic conditions attending the daily life of the immigrants are among the subjects that are illuminated in the immigrant press. A scholar, selecting items from *Emigranten* in the period 1857–59 for "Glimpses of Norse Immigrant Life in the Northwest in the Fifties," writes, "Many of these news-letters, though they may not add a great deal to the knowledge of important events at the time, contain a variety of interesting detail: there is a striking account of a May 17th celebration on board the immigrant ship 'Norge'; an account is given of the Norwegian settlement at Bonnet Prairie, Columbia county, Wisconsin; accounts are given of Norwegians in Dakota and Blue Earth counties in Minnesota; an interesting letter from Mankato is included; an unusual scene at a land sale in Iowa is described; there is a complete account of a

[69] *Democraten,* August 20, 1850; *Nordstjernen,* October 14, 1857.
[70] *Nordstjernen,* June 24, 1857.

journey through the middle and western parts of Minnesota; there are a few notes from Council Bluffs areas; as well as accounts of Indian cruelty and cunning and an account of how the cholera drove the devil out of one community."[71]

That the immigrants themselves fully understood the value of newspapers as America letters is evidenced by the establishment in 1857 at Leland, Illinois, of a small Norwegian newspaper called *Wossingen,* the central purpose of which was to afford a convenient "means of communication between the expatriated Vossings and their countrymen in the Old World." In the 1840's emigrants from the Norwegian district of Voss had banded together in a correspondence society "with the special object in view of giving systematic enlightenment to the Norwegian people concerning the status of their emigrated countrymen and of refuting false assertions and correcting wrong impressions regarding America and the Norwegian immigrants." This organization, beginning in the autumn of 1848, dispatched eight monthly manuscript letters to the old country. A similar society was started in 1856 by two Chicago Norwegians who had returned from a visit to Norway. Though the principal purpose of this "Vossing Emigration Society" was that of collecting funds to aid "needy and worthy families to America," its activities led to the founding of the newspaper *Wossingen,* with Nils T. Bakkethun as editor.

This unique newspaper was sending about a hundred copies of its issues to Norway in 1858. One number in that year "contains over a dozen letters, about an equal number being contributed from each side of the water." In addition to letters it contains announcements of marriages and deaths, advertisements for missing Vossings, appeals for money to help needy immigrants, occasional verse, now and then an article, and several interesting news items. The paper ap-

[71] Eide, *Norse Immigrant Letters,* 6, 7.

peared irregularly for a little more than two years, when, having been removed to Milwaukee, it suspended publication in March, 1860, to be resumed in Voss, Norway, under the same title in 1871. Apart from its interest as an America-letter newspaper, *Wossingen* is an early illustration of the immigrant tendency to emphasize solidarity along the lines of the special *bygd,* or district, in Norway from which given groups had emigrated — acquaintanceship, dialect, and local traditions serving as bonds of mutual interest. Much later this tendency was to give rise to a half-hundred *bygdelags,* each primarily interested in a particular *bygd* and the story of the migration of its sons and daughters to the New World.[72]

On the eve of the Civil War the Norwegian immigrant press had the momentum of a decade and a half of experience. Some fifteen newspapers and periodicals had been established during that period. They voiced many different points of view — Free-Soil, Whig, Democratic, Republican, nonpartisan. Their careers, for the most part, had been stormy, as a result not only of furious controversy but also of financial difficulties; and most of them had gone the way of the world. Yet they served their constituencies effectively. They were textbooks for the political education of the immigrants, whose outlook was clarified and defined as, year after year, they read news reports, speeches, documents, editorials, and controversial essays. In their columns the papers employed of necessity the literary language of Norway, not the salty and vigorous, but dialectally varied, vernacular that was on the lips of the majority of the immigrants, hail-

[72] The finding of a file of *Wossingen* and the piecing together of the history of the early organizations among the Vossings constitute a contribution of extraordinary interest in the Norwegian-American field. The man responsible for both is Mr. Albert O. Barton of Madison, Wisconsin. See especially his "Norwegian-American Emigration Societies in the Forties and Fifties," in *Studies and Records,* 3:23–42; and his essay in Wisconsin Historical Society, *Proceedings,* 1916, p. 202–205, with a reproduction of the first page of *Wossingen* for June, 1858. The quotations above are drawn from these two articles. Contemporary accounts of *Wossingen* are in *Emigranten,* November 15, 1858; March 7, 1859.

ing as they did from the scattered Norwegian districts where this type of speech had behind it the wear of centuries.

This fact also explains the circumstance that Danish-born editors like Clausen and Reese were able to enter the field of Norwegian-American journalism with entire ease. The leaders of the pioneer press were, in general, men of considerable competence, who naturally represented a somewhat higher level of training, experience, and cultural outlook than that of the ordinary immigrant. The newspapers were therefore leaders along many lines, especially in the transition of the Norwegian settlers, new and old, who were adjusting themselves to American ways. As reporters, purveyors of literature, debaters on problems of church and state, and fathers of a regional Norwegian-American family, the newspapers gave direction and solidarity to immigrant life. They helped to shape and to make articulate a Norwegian America that has lasted, notwithstanding time and new circumstance, to the present day. They added to that life an imponderable element of interest. Viewed in the full range of their services, therefore, the pioneer Norwegian newspapers constituted a basic social and cultural immigrant institution.

XI. NEW WORLD SAILORS

A LARGE PROPORTION of the nineteenth-century immigrants from Norway were country people, tillers of the soil with generations of farming behind them, but many who came to America knew the way of life of seamen and fishermen. Innumerable fingers of the sea reach into Norway, and on its storm-battered western coast the country faces the north Atlantic. The "flung spray and blown spume" are part of the history of its people across the centuries from Viking raiders to modern commerce and fishing. There is a tang of the sea in their sagas and tales, in their songs and sayings. To many a Middle Western Norwegian-American farmer the prairie was an ocean, the covered wagon a vessel, the entire scene reminiscent of sailors and ships and sky-rimmed sea. Rølvaag's caravan of pioneers crossing a western plain left behind it a track "like the wake of a boat—except that instead of widening out astern it closed again." To the fisherman-novelist it was natural to think of Per Hansa, the land-taker, as a Viking of the prairie; and the pioneers themselves never forgot—there were times when the remembering meant consolation — that they were descendants of men who had voyaged to American waters a millenium before the era of emigrants and caravans. "And so, as in saga days Norse ships were tossed about on the sea," sang an immigrant poet in mid-Atlantic in 1837, "even now the Norwegian fronts without fear the might of storm and wave, and hails once more the distant strand of Vinland the Good."[1]

In colonial days Norwegians had found their way to that strand, too. A native of Norway, Jens Munk, commanded an ill-fated expedition of two vessels dispatched in 1619 by King Christian IV of Denmark and Norway in search of the Northwest Passage. After a disastrous winter of sickness and death on the shores of Hudson Bay at the mouth of the Churchill River, Munk and two of his crew, the sole survivors, managed to sail one of the vessels to Norway, where they arrived in the autumn of 1620.[2] In the seventeenth and eighteenth centuries sailors occasionally made their way to America, coming by way of Holland, England, and Germany. In that stirring age when England and Holland were competing for the European carrying trade, Norwegian sailors enlisted for service on the trading vessels of both countries. "The best seamen of the King of Denmark are the Norwegians," wrote an English diplomat, "but most of them are in the service of the Dutch, and have their families established in Holland."[3] In the eighteenth century as many as eight or nine thousand Norwegian, Danish, and Holstein seamen assembled at Amsterdam when the Dutch merchant fleets were congregated there; and the lumber trade between Norway and England brought Norwegian sailors into close contact with the English merchant fleets. Since both the

[1] Blegen and Ruud, *Norwegian Emigrant Songs and Ballads*, 28, 29.

[2] Munk's narrative of the expedition, originally issued at Copenhagen in 1624, has been edited by C. C. A. Gosch in an English translation and issued as book 2 of *Danish Arctic Expeditions 1605 to 1620* (Hakluyt Society, *Works*, no. 97 — London, 1897).

[3] Robert Molesworth in his account of Denmark in 1692, quoted in John O. Evjen, *Scandinavian Immigrants in New York 1630–1674*, 13 (Minneapolis, 1916).

Dutch and the English had colonies in the New World, it is not surprising to learn that Norwegians now and then appeared in colonial ports. A noted historian has been able to present biographies of some fifty-seven Norwegians who settled in New Netherland from 1630 to 1674.[4]

When Norwegian seamen flocked to the United States in the nineteenth century, therefore, they followed a tradition in maritime circles. The havoc played with Norwegian shipping during the Napoleonic wars made the plight of sailors even more dire than that of their predecessors in earlier centuries. The rebirth of Norwegian shipping and the expansion of commerce with the United States, Brazil, and other countries would absorb and hold thousands of Norwegian sailors, but American shipping offered inducements that many could not resist—increase in wages, steady employment, and the prospect of independence in the form of captainships and even ownership of vessels. The sailors were by no means immune to the contagion of "America fever." Here, as in the entire migration from Norway, economic motives played a basic role.

Large numbers of Norwegian sailors were naturally attracted to American waters as a result of the expansion of both emigration and commerce, and in the course of time Norwegians began to figure in the American merchant marine, not only in ocean shipping but also in the commerce of the Great Lakes. If the export of iron from Norway to America was a result of emigration, so also was the export of sailors. The precedent was set as early as 1825 by the captain of the "Restoration," the "Mayflower" of the Norwegian immigrants. "It is the captain's intention," reads a report in a contemporary newspaper, "to remain in this country, to sell his vessel and prepare himself to navigate our

[4] Evjen, *Scandinavian Immigrants*, 19–147. See also Knut Gjerset, *History of the Norwegian People*, 2:239–247 (New York, 1915); and Ludvig Daae, *Nordmænds udvandringer til Holland og England i nyere tid* (Christiania, 1880).

waters, by entering the American merchant service, and learning the language."[5] Many Norwegians entered the American service in a wholly regular manner, coming into the country as immigrants with valid passports. A Great Lakes captain recalled that as a Norwegian seaman he had to sign a contract pledging him to remain with a vessel for a period of two years. "We might sail with lumber to Liverpool," he said, "then load with coal for the West Indies, where we might take a cargo of sugar for England, or go in ballast to Mexico, where we would load with mahogany for Havre, Liverpool, or Hamburg." A seaman might get an opportunity to return home during the two-year period, but a succession of voyages often meant a full two years before such a return. "As I desired to find a place where I could enjoy home life," said the captain, "I decided to go to America. I came to Manitowoc, where I built me a home and began to sail on the lakes."[6]

This captain was an example of the normal immigration of Norwegian seamen to America, and there were many who came in a similar frame of mind. On the other hand, it is certain that thousands joined the American sailing service without benefit of legality. Not only was there widespread desertion from Norwegian vessels in American harbors, but the practice was common in various ports of the Old World. In the middle 1850's, for example, a consular official at Havre lamented the prevalent desertion from Norwegian ships and said that the chief sinners were North American skippers, who combined cunning with brutality in their efforts to entice Norwegian sailors.[7]

[5] The captain of the "Restoration" was Lars O. Helland. The passage is from the *New York Statesman*, October 12, 1825, reprinted from the New York *Daily Advertiser*.

[6] The narrative of Captain Harry Gresholdt, quoted in Knut Gjerset, *Norwegian Sailors on the Great Lakes: A Study in the History of American Inland Transportation*, 10 (Northfield, 1928).

[7] Worm-Müller, in *Den norske sjøfarts historie*, vol. 2, pt. 1, p. 579, uses the report of Consul Broström of Havre for 1854.

The principal reason for the desertions was the sharp difference between the Norwegian and American rates of wages for seamen. A Norwegian sailor in New York, accustomed to a wage running from six to nine specie dollars a month, found it difficult not to be drawn by an American offer of fifteen dollars a month, particularly when he knew that sometimes after a desertion, he might be re-engaged on a Norwegian vessel at the American rate and normally would escape Norwegian penalties for his desertion. The Norwegian seamen were looked upon as very skillful, men who knew the sea and the business of sailing, and there seems to have been a special effort to draw them away from the vessels of their native country. Often the agents seeking Norwegian seamen were themselves Norwegians who met the sailors casually in lodginghouses and persuaded them to desert at the last moment before their vessel was scheduled to depart. Sometimes to the argument of higher wages was added the promise of a discipline less rigid than that on the Norwegian ships; and now and then violent methods, lubricated by liquor, undoubtedly were tried.

By reciprocal treaty agreements nations were pledged to help apprehend and punish sailor deserters, but relatively few deserters were actually caught. The Norwegian-Swedish chargé d'affaires, Sibbern, reporting on the general problem in 1851, indicated that the complexities of American jurisdiction added to the difficulty.[8] Three ordinary Norwegian seamen were arrested in New York City for desertion in 1849; they were held for forty-three days and then, under habeas corpus proceedings, released by a New York state court for lack of jurisdiction. An act of Congress in 1829 to give effect to treaty agreements in the matter of sailor deser-

[8] Sibbern's report appears in full in *Christiania-posten*, September 13, 1852, under the title "Om den hyppige rømning af norske søfolk i Amerika." I have had a photostat made. Worm-Müller indicates that the report, prepared upon special instructions from the government, was made in 1851.

tions had made enforcement mandatory on federal courts, whereas for state courts it was merely discretionary or optional.

Sibbern reported that 256 Swedish and 212 Norwegian merchant vessels had entered New York harbor from 1846 to 1850. There had been 910 Swedish deserters with only 36 apprehensions, and 502 Norwegian desertions, with 25 apprehensions. The Norwegians got higher wages than the Swedes, but both were unfavorably paid as compared with American seamen, though Sibbern contended, probably with some justification, that the higher American wages were to a certain extent illusory and that not a few of the deserters ultimately drifted back to their own flag. The disparity of wages continued to be a powerful factor, however, and as the Norwegian merchant marine expanded and its commerce grew — and the 1850's were foundational for the modern Norwegian merchant service — desertions steadily increased in volume, creating a constant problem for ship captains and for consular officers. The situation in Canada was no better than that in New York, for desertions were common from the beginning of the Norwegian trade with Canada. In 1866 there were 145 Norwegian deserters at Quebec, and in 1872 there were 340 from a total of 382 ships. In 1872, also, 812 seamen deserted from 320 Norwegian ships in New York, and of these only 13 were apprehended. That is, in a single year there were 1,152 Norwegian desertions in Quebec and New York alone. In 1880, a total of 1,389 seamen deserted from 935 Norwegian ships in New York. Obviously, neither treaties nor laws had any appreciable effect upon the practice. In both the United States and Canada it had become an everyday affair; and meanwhile the disparity in Norwegian and American wages for seamen tended to become greater rather than less. In that general period American wages for seamen ran close to twenty-five dollars a month, whereas the Norwegian ships paid only slightly over nine dollars.[9]

How stubborn and long-continued the problem of desertion was is indicated by an official Norwegian report made in 1915, which stated that from 1856 to 1865 about 4,050 Norwegian sailors deserted; from 1871 to 1880 the estimated number was 11,200; and from 1876 to 1890 — unfortunately there is some overlapping of figures — the number was 19,487.[10] The committee report corroborated Sibbern's early impression that many deserters ultimately returned to their native decks, for of the 11,200 deserting from 1871 to 1880, no fewer than 5,200 returned to Norwegian service; and 9,262 of the 19,487 from 1876 to 1890 returned. That is, nearly half of the deserters returned. However comforting such figures may have been to Norwegian authorities, the fact remains that large numbers of sailors did not return to the Norwegian vessels. For the period from 1876 to 1890 the number unaccounted for among those who returned is precisely 10,225. And 10,225 trained seamen, by any standard, must be considered a very large number.

The pioneer Norwegian sailors, whether regular immigrants or irregular transfers from the Norwegian merchant fleet, appeared in American waters at an opportune time. The sailing vessel as the great instrument of maritime traffic was nearing its last phase. The steamboat had already put in an appearance, and a few enterprising shipowners realized that this rival meant quick doom to white sails unless energetic steps were taken to meet its threat. More efficient service, greater speed, better accommodations, cheaper rates — these were among the reforms demanded. The fast packet was devised and came into use on the more important lines.

[9] An illuminating discussion of the Norwegian desertions, with detail for both New York and Quebec, is in Worm-Müller, vol. 2, pt. 1, p. 579–583.

[10] Emigration Committee, *Lov om utvandring,* 161 — the second part of the report of the Norwegian committee on emigration, 1912–13.

Fixed routes and definite schedules struck at waste and uncertainty. Presently the sleek clipper ship superseded the fast packet, offering greater speed on maritime routes that were becoming longer as the Pacific trade blossomed. Ship designs and mechanical improvements were important, but the American shipping companies were insistent also on securing good seamen. The coming of Norwegian sailors seemed to some shipowners and captains a happy circumstance indeed, for by and large they brought with them manifest skill in handling sailing vessels; they were amenable to discipline; and they had the sailor's distaste for steam. So they played a part in the fight to maintain the dominance of sails; by their work they helped to give the sailing vessels something of that deceptive prosperity which they enjoyed for a half century. Ultimately the Norwegian sailors, like their fellows of other nationalities, had to make the transition from sail to steam, and they soon learned that steam removed neither the need of skill nor the hazards of navigation.[11]

The earliest Norwegian seamen in American ports made a reputation for themselves which assured both them and their successors of a hearty welcome in American waters — and perhaps contributed to the popularizing of the game of desertion. In small harbors as well as large, Norwegians soon were familiar figures. They were present, for example, in numerous New England ports where Yankee captains seemed to like the ruggedness of these Scandinavian men and took them on to fill places left vacant by reluctant New England

[11] The two basic monographs for the story of the Norwegian sailors in America are Dr. Gjerset's *Norwegian Sailors on the Great Lakes* (1928) and his *Norwegian Sailors in American Waters: A Study in the History of Maritime Activity on the Eastern Seaboard* (1933). Both were brought out by the Norwegian-American Historical Association. Dr. Gjerset tells the story with an almost bewildering amount of biographical data. In trying to present a broad survey of the field — something hitherto lacking — I have been obliged for the most part to omit such detail. The reader who wishes to secure information about specific persons is referred to the indexes in the two volumes cited. Unfortunately Dr. Gjerset did not include the subject of desertions. Nor does he deal with the area of the Pacific coast. In my citations I have abbreviated his titles to *Great Lakes* and *American Waters*.

youths. The Norwegians accepted whatever work was to be found. Active service at sea they preferred, of course, but they were not unwilling to go into maritime industry on shore; and they were seen hard at work in shipyards as carpenters or sail riggers, behind the counters of ship chandling establishments, and in the offices of marine surveyors. They also appeared as members of wrecking and salvaging crews, as fishermen, and as keepers of lighthouses or lightships. Of the three departments on board ship — deck, engine room, and the steward's domain — they naturally preferred the deck, but they were willing to tackle any job. Until the Italian immigrants took over the work of longshoremen, they were active in that field. In the winter when some of the northern harbors closed down, they often went south for the trade in lumber, cotton, cattle, and sugar — and, in course of time, oil and fruit.

So the Norwegians gradually fitted into a great American industry, made themselves a part of it, and were to be seen all along the Atlantic seaboard, from Portland to Pensacola, and on the gulf, from Mobile to New Orleans and Galveston. They appeared on the Great Lakes, too, borne forward by the westward trek. Many, in fact, preferred the Great Lakes to the Atlantic, for its relatively short runs made possible some semblance of a natural home life. And the smaller capacity of the lake vessels meant that they were less expensive — perhaps within the potential reach of ambitious sailors who dreamed of command or ownership. Furthermore, the sails held on somewhat more stubbornly on the lakes than on the Atlantic. The work on the lakes, it is true, was seasonal, but there was always the chance of employment in the hinterland during the winters; and not a few Norwegians formed the habit of spending their summers on the Great Lakes and their winters on the eastern seaboard. "Deckhands, mates and boatswains are often Norwegians, who form the real backbone of the sailing crews on the lakes till this day," said an old Great Lakes captain. "Many of them are salt water men who in the spring come to sail on the lakes and return to salt water for the winter. These men are ninety-five per cent single men."[12]

The actual number of Norwegian seamen who have engaged in American service is difficult to estimate, for statistics are incomplete, omit some of the port towns, do not distinguish too carefully between native-born and naturalized citizens, and often reflect the Yankee's airy unconcern about the boundaries of nationality that mark off Norwegians, Swedes, and Danes. Some clues there are, however. The commissioner of navigation reported in 1894, for example, that "In the coasting trade four-fifths of the sailors are Scandinavians, and most of the sailors on our yachts are of the same nationality."[13] In 1903, there were reported in the merchant service 36,761 native Americans and 22,737 naturalized Americans, with 7,615 Norwegians, 6,268 Swedes, and 1,571 Danes—a total of 15,454 Scandinavians. By 1919 the number of native Americans was 97,160 and of naturalized Americans, 24,676, with the Norwegians numbering 10,237, the Swedes 10,054, and the Danes 5,843—a total of 26,134 Scandinavians. Such figures may mean much or little, but they are obviously inadequate.[14] Even less satisfactory are those for the Great Lakes service. In the 1870 census the number of sailors listed for the port of Chicago was 1,959, and of this total the Scandinavians comprised 516. This is enlightening, but one looks in vain for figures on the smaller ports, where many of the Scandinavians actually lived—Duluth and Superior, for example. Dr. Knut Gjerset, after a careful study of all the evidence, concluded that the Scandinavian element on the sailing vessels and steamboats plying Lake Michigan in 1869–70 comprised sixty-three per cent of the

[12] Louis W. Norteman, quoted in *Great Lakes,* 121.

[13] Quoted in *American Waters,* 75, 76.

[14] See the tables in *American Waters,* 74, 75, and supplementary material on p. 249.

total and that the Norwegians alone made up not less than fifty per cent.[15]

Other testimony is perhaps more revealing than statistics in appraising the place of the Scandinavian sailors. Arthur H. Clark, who served as an officer on clippers, recalled their services. "During the first half of the nineteenth century," he said, "American ships trading upon voyages to China and India carried crews composed chiefly of Scandinavians—splendid sailormen who could do any kind of rigging work or sail-making required on board of a ship at sea and took pride in doing it well, and who also had sufficient sense to know that discipline is necessary on shipboard. These Scandinavians, who were as a rule fine seamen, clean, willing, and obedient, were the first and best class among the men of whom the clipper ship crews were composed. A vessel with a whole crew of these strong, honest sailors was a little heaven afloat."[16] Another captain, harking back to experiences in the middle of the nineteenth century, wrote, "The 'Rocket' was lying at Central Wharf, Boston, loading a cargo for the East Indies. Wishing to choose for myself who should sail with me for so many months, the shipping master was told to send on board any good men who appealed to him, giving preference to Norwegians and Swedes, these being in my opinion, both in seamanship and docility, the best class of sailors that man our vessels."[17] A writer in 1893 said that Scandinavian seamen "have been in great demand, and American captains as well as English employ them in preference to other seamen. Young Americans, on the other hand, do not care to go to sea, as they can find more agree-

[15] *Great Lakes*, 75–77. Through a long period citizenship was not regarded as an essential requirement of seamen in service on American vessels; and until relatively recent times many of the Norwegian-American seamen, mainly because of difficulties in establishing continued residence, appear to have been aliens. In general, however, like their countrymen who sailed the prairie schooners of the West, the Norwegian seamen sought naturalization.

[16] Quoted in *American Waters*, 67, from Clark's *Clipper Ship Era*.

[17] Quoted in *American Waters*, 63, from Robert C. Adams, *On Board the "Rocket."*

able and lucrative employment on land. The result is that the number of Scandinavians, and especially of Norwegians, in this harbor is greater than that of any other nationality."[18] Similarly the commissioner of navigation in 1894 spoke of the preponderance of Scandinavians in the coasting trade and quoted reports from leading American seaports indicating a strong preference for Norwegian and Swedish sailors, as much for their strength and endurance as for their submission to discipline and freedom from insubordination.[19]

All this would seem to indicate that the Norwegians were in a sense a preferred class. Unemployment in their field was for a long time virtually nonexistent. Railroad competition, it is true, struck a blow at Great Lakes navigation, but iron, copper ore, and wheat nevertheless continued to furnish a substantial basis for a merchant fleet. That the Norwegian sailors inhabited a Utopia does not follow as a corollary of the favorable opinions that their services won for them. There was evidently a constant shifting in the profession. Men returned to Norway and to the Norwegian merchant fleet, and others found escape from the roving life of the sailor in the Homestead Act and the agricultural "western front," where so many of their countrymen were in the furrows. Nevertheless, evidence is convincing that the Norwegians have been a constant factor in the American merchant marine, both on salt water and on the inland lakes, since before the middle of the nineteenth century.

The economic base of this constancy was the wages paid to seamen in American service. These wages fluctuated, sometimes were difficult to collect, and in accord with maritime tradition had a way of vanishing into thin air — or across the bar — once the sailors were on dry land, with its

[18] *Annonce tidende (Nordisk tidende),* February 7, 1893, quoted in *American Waters,* 71, 72.

[19] *American Waters,* 75, 76, 83, 84.

varied avenues to a handsome dispersion of ready money. But the wages earned in the Norwegian merchant service seemed almost ludicrously low as compared with the American. A Norwegian sailor, born in 1848, who came to the United States at the age of twenty-four, received $3.00 a month when he began his services before the mast in Norway; when he married, after some years as a sailor, he earned $8.50 a month. Another seaman who began at $3.00 a month advanced to the position of first mate on a full-rigged ship — and in that capacity earned $19.00 a month. A Great Lakes captain who began his career in the Norwegian service in 1866 hired out at the initial rate of $4.00 a month; and it will be recalled that Sibbern in the 1850's spoke of the Norwegian seaman's wages as ranging from $6.00 to $9.00 a month.[20] In the American merchant marine, wages varied according to the general state of shipping; and there was some disparity between rates on ocean-going vessels and on the Great Lakes, where short runs, long watches, and the seasonal character of the employment were special factors. Sibbern indicated that about 1850 wages of $15.00 a month were common among American seamen,[21] and a quarter of a century later they evidently had been advanced to $20.00 or $25.00. On the Great Lakes before the Civil War seamen received from $1.25 to $2.50 a day, or even more, for wages were higher late in the season when grain crops were moving east and there was a rush of business before the lakes froze over. During the abnormal war years, wages went to $3.50 and $4.50 a day, but with peace they resumed former levels. In 1870, according to Dr. Gjerset, they were from $1.25 to $2.25 a day for ordinary seamen, while captains earned from $80.00 to $100.00 a month. The Chicago fire boomed the business of Great Lakes shippers, and wages for seamen increased, but they soon fell back to earlier levels. And sailors,

[20] *Great Lakes,* 4, 5.
[21] *Christiania-posten,* September 13, 1852.

like farmers and businessmen, felt the pinch of the depression that came on the heels of the panic of 1873. Wages in 1877 ran from \$1.00 to \$1.12½ a day. Not a few of the older sailors turned their backs upon the lakes — but the gates of immigration were wide open and there were always young Norwegian recruits available to fill their places.[22]

The reshaping of navigation with the advent of steam and the organization of the Lake Carriers' Association in 1885 served as a general tonic. The association took pride in high labor standards and emphasized fair treatment to employees. A high wage level has been maintained, and in modern days positions on Great Lakes steamers and barges have been as eagerly sought as they were in the days of sails. On ocean-going vessels the American merchant marine continued the policy of paying sailors higher wages than were current in other countries; but in 1894 a New York official reported that the wages of ordinary seamen — rarely over twenty dollars a month — were still out of all proportion to the demands made on them by captains and shore agents. In the same year the commissioner of navigation, aware of the preference for Scandinavian sailors, inquired in leading ports whether or not they enjoyed wage differentials, but learned that as a rule they accepted current wage schedules.

The advance of the status of American seamen in more recent times was due in considerable measure to their unionization and to the efforts of a fearless and singularly able leader, the Norwegian-American Andrew Furuseth. He carried on a bitter and long struggle to forward the interests of the American sailor, with a living wage as one of his demands. When American shipowners alleged that they were already paying more than their European competitors, Furuseth called for an international equalization of seamen's wages. He would repeal all the laws and abrogate all the treaties penalizing desertion in American ports, help finance

[22] *Great Lakes*, 87–96.

the deserter in his hunt for a new job, and force foreign competitors to raise wages or lose their crews. He would have American wage standards dominate the maritime commercial world. The Furuseth Seamen's Act of 1915 translated his ideas into action; and in 1919 a magazine pointed out that the American wages for seamen had risen 164 per cent since 1914.[23] The chief competitors of the United States—England and Norway—were in turn forced to take action. Thus Norway in the cases of eight vessels clearing from New York in December, 1918, found itself obliged to pay both its seamen and firemen according to the American rate in dollars. It appears, therefore, that the efforts of a Norwegian-American maritime reformer, striking at an age-old problem, had achieved substantial results not only in the American merchant marine but also in that of the Old World.

Many Norwegian-American sailors rose to leadership in maritime circles. Both on the Atlantic and on the Great Lakes, Norwegian names soon began to appear in the lists of captains and mates. On the lakes, where small craft were numerous and opportunities great, the process was quicker than along the Atlantic seaboard, but there, too, the number of advances into positions of responsibility increased. Among the seamen whose names appeared in the Chicago directory for 1839 is Captain George Peterson of the schooner "St. Joseph," the first known Norwegian lake captain, according to Dr. Gjerset. In the Atlantic trade there were Norwegians in command of ships as early as 1842, and many more appeared in the ensuing years, especially after the Civil War. With the coming of steam, there was no apparent decline in the number of Norwegian officers, though in proportion perhaps fewer were captains and more held other positions. Some of the captains of Great Lakes schooners could not adjust themselves to the transition from sails to steam and so they retired, but a large number qualified. Dr.

[23] *New Republic,* 19:9 (May 3, 1919).

Gjerset gives the names of about 425 Norwegian captains who had been in command of sailing vessels or steamers in the Great Lakes service and of 110 who were in service in 1928, when he was writing. In the Atlantic service Captains Hans D. K. Doxrud, L. Morton Jensen, John Ibsen Stousland (a nephew of the great Norwegian dramatist), N. Kvande, Fredrik W. Hvoslef (a son of a distinguished Norwegian bishop), Tom Olsen, and Martin Thompson made notable careers for themselves. The integration of Norwegian and Norwegian-American shipping lines and the fact that American shipping brokers often chartered Norwegian vessels made it easier than it had been for Norwegian Americans to rise to command. And the vast increase in the American merchant marine occasioned by the World War was a boon for both ordinary seamen and officers. In September, 1918, the United States Shipping Board appointed 27 Norwegian captains on new vessels built in Washington and Oregon shipyards. A society of Norwegian sea captains organized in New York in 1918 had 100 members before it was two months old, nearly all in active service.[24]

In early days a ship captain was often responsible for the advantageous sale of his cargo, and the trading instinct in many instances led him on to buy and own a vessel of his own and to conduct his own shipping and trading. On the Great Lakes, where relatively little initial capital was needed, some Norwegian captains came into possession of fleets of schooners. During the Civil War, S. T. Gunderson, whose two brothers Gabriel and Martin were lake captains, owned six lake vessels, most of them employed in the grain business; and Gunderson was one of a half dozen Norwegians in the trade. John Oleson, owner and captain of the schooner "Dawn," is said to have transported the first lumber used in building the Chicago stockyards.[25]

[24] See *Great Lakes*, 16–50, 123–199; and *American Waters*, *passim*.
[25] *Great Lakes*, 54, 55, 57, 58.

As business languished for sailing vessels, many owners and captains turned to the towing trade. Along the Atlantic coast several Norwegian firms are still engaged in running lighters, tenders, barges, and steam tugs; and in similar service not owned by Norwegian companies, many of the captains are of Norwegian origin. Of fifty lighters belonging to the Clyde Line in 1928, for example, twenty-nine had Norwegian captains. The Great Lakes trade tells a similar story — in many instances gallant old schooners were stripped of their rigging and ingloriously turned into steam barges.[26]

In pioneer days Norwegian shipbuilders flourished on the Great Lakes — in Chicago and Milwaukee, as well as in numerous small Wisconsin and Michigan port towns, including Manitowoc, Green Bay, Sheboygan, Racine, Sturgeon Bay, and Holland. Some stately schooners and sloops were built by them, many of the schooners as large as three or four hundred tons. The Norwegians were less conspicuous after the introduction of steam, though their shipyards turned out workaday craft such as steam tugs and launches; and in the great shipyards of the Pacific coast large numbers of Norwegians found employment. Dr. Gjerset believes that the Norwegian element contributed little or nothing to the designing of new types of craft, but that it evidenced excellency of craftsmanship in building standard models. After the World War as many as twelve Norwegian shipbuilding firms sprang up in New York alone; and at present Norwegians throng American shipyards, forming staunch Norwegian communities in shipyard districts along the water fronts of Brooklyn, Long Island, Staten Island, and New Jersey. Of thirty riggers and spar makers in a Massachusetts shipyard in 1928, twenty-three were Scandinavian. Many of the Norwegian-American builders were chiefly engaged in filling

[26] *American Waters*, 89, 90; *Great Lakes*, 98, 174–197.

orders for Norwegian companies. The World War boom was followed by collapse, and many companies which had been ambitiously launched were docked in the laps of receivers.[27]

Norwegian-American firms have engaged with profit in the time-honored occupation of ship broking. They have acted as liaison agents in procuring ships for shippers, and cargo — passenger and freight — for otherwise idle vessels. One of the first Norwegian-American firms in this field was that of Benham and Boyesen of New York. For many years Bennett, Hvoslef, and Company was the outstanding Norwegian-American ship broking firm of that city; and there have been various others. Similar Norwegian-American firms were established in Philadelphia in 1875 and Savannah in 1894. Norwegians have also engaged in the picturesque business of ship chandlery, with shops along the water fronts of leading Atlantic ports and also on the Great Lakes. One of the pioneers of this business was Aanon Anson of Christiansand, who emigrated with his family and settled in Brooklyn in 1849. These are but illustrations of the spread of Norwegians into many of the collateral occupations and services associated with seafaring. They have played their part in piloting, wrecking and salvaging, diving and lifesaving, the care of lighthouses and lightships. They have entered the Coast Guard service, as well as the American navy and marine corps.[28]

Many Norwegian Americans were born into the fishing trade. More at home on a fishing smack than on solid ground, they were quick to enter the American fisheries. As time went on, Norwegian fisherfolk settled along the Atlantic seaboard, on the Great Lakes, the Gulf of Mexico, and the Pacific coast. Dr. Gjerset has found that they played on

[27] *Great Lakes*, 61–71; *American Waters*, 149–154.

[28] *American Waters*, 142–148, 154–157, 196–216; *Great Lakes*, 133, 163, 178, 183, 190.

the whole a minor role in the eastern whaling industry, but a more important one in mackerel and bluefish expeditions. The oyster beds of the Chesapeake and the seafood industry along the Gulf of Mexico commanded their interest. In the interior they vied with Indian fishermen in early years along the shores of Lake Superior, and since 1890 they have been conspicuous in that industry. An official of a Norwegian-American fishing firm estimated some years ago that between eighty and ninety per cent of the fishermen along the North Shore of Lake Superior, between Duluth and the Canadian border, were Norwegians.[29]

The Pacific coast, with its salmon, halibut, cod, herring, tuna, and other varieties of fish, was a paradise for fishermen; and the Norwegians have played an active role in the development of the industry at many points. There were only sixty-five Norwegians in Washington Territory in 1870, but that decade witnessed Norwegian-American beginnings in fisheries. John Brygger, for example, established a pioneer salmon fishery at Salmon Bay, not far from Seattle, in 1876. Peter Thams Buschmann, who reached Tacoma from Trondhjem in 1891, viewed the fishery possibilities of the Pacific coast with genuine business imagination, installed the first salmon trap on Lummi Island in Puget Sound, and saw that establishment become enormously valuable. Fishing was only one of several basic economic interests of the Norwegians on the Pacific coast — shipping, lumbering, and farming were among the others. The fisheries, however, help to explain the charm of the Puget Sound region for Norwegians.[30]

In 1894 Buschmann struck northward to Alaska, where his canneries were the nucleus of an important fishing center named Petersburg in his honor, a village whose approximately

[29] Dr. Gjerset has material on fishing in his *Great Lakes,* 178; and *American Waters,* 118–141.

[30] Qualey, *Norwegian Settlement,* 188–191.

fifteen hundred inhabitants were reported to be ninety per cent Norwegian. A few years later Buschmann installed a salmon trap in Icy Strait. Meanwhile, all along the Pacific coast Norwegian Americans took a keen interest in the fishing industry in its various branches and phases. Thus the "mildcure" salmon industry was initiated in 1893 by representatives of Einar Beyer of Bergen, who ultimately commanded large interests on the coast. In the halibut fisheries it is said that approximately eighty per cent of the fishermen are Norwegians; and the fleets of halibuters, which are very largely owned by Norwegians, include craft with such names as "Ibsen," "Eidsvold," and "Tordenskjold." Norwegian Americans have been active, too, in applying modern techniques to the sardine and tuna industry in California.

The Alaska herring business has developed since the late 1890's, when Buschmann introduced salting and reached out to the Scandinavian-American market of the Middle West. How large the industry ultimately became is indicated by the fact that in one year (1918) more than a hundred thousand barrels were produced. The Norwegians entered the west coast codfishing industry late, for it was one of the pioneer American enterprises of the Far West, but they have established themselves as a factor there, too. A writer in the early 1920's said that the codfishing "boats are chiefly manned by Norwegian crews and Norwegian masters." According to the same authority, the contributions of the Norwegians to the whaling industry of the Pacific coast consisted primarily in the introduction of modern ships and methods.[31]

In most parts of America fishing at first, and indeed for a long time, was essentially an individual enterprise, in which the fisherman owned and manned his own schooner or smack,

[31] On the Norwegian factor in the fishing industry of the Pacific coast, see Thomas H. Kolderup, "Contributions to American Fisheries," in Harry Sundby-Hansen, ed., *Norwegian Immigrant Contributions to America's Making,* 69–75 (New York, 1921); and the same author's interesting essay, "Det praktiske livs norsk-amerikanere paa vestkysten," in *Nordmands-forbundet,* 19:1–7 (1926).

made his own catch, and marketed his products. Like other industries, however, it was transformed by the industrial revolution, and big business tended to take over most of the fisheries, consolidating them in a relatively small number of powerful companies. At the end of the process the great majority of the Norwegian-American fishermen found themselves occupying subordinate positions. For the most part they were actual fishermen, not the managers and magnates of the industry. To many, fishing meant a frugal existence, but it was a way of life that the Norwegians thoroughly understood, and they accepted it—its modest rewards as well as its accompanying hazards of storm, exposure, and peril.

Yachting and racing opened new opportunities to Norwegian-American sailors as steam tended to relegate white sails to the realm of sport. These hobbies of the rich were not taken up by the Norwegians as owners of craft or as members of yacht clubs, but nevertheless they were familiar figures in yachting circles. Captain Niels Olsen as early as 1871 became the superintendent of the New York Yacht Club and later served as the yacht reporter for the *New York Herald* and for some time as editor of the *American Yacht List*. In the valiant days of yachting as an international sport, Norwegians served both in command and as crew members of many a well-known yacht. In fact, not infrequently as large a proportion as three-fourths of the crew were Norwegian, serving under a Norwegian captain and mate; and often the races pitted Norwegians against Norwegians. Sir Thomas Lipton engaged the services of Norwegian sailors on his various "Shamrocks" which competed with yachts also manned to a large extent by Norwegians.[32]

Few Norwegian sailors built up great wealth. According to Dr. Gjerset, the Norwegians lacked the imagination to

[32] "Norwegian-American Yachting Sailors," in *American Waters*, 101–117.

grasp many of the great advantages open to them. They applied small-gauge standards to an American system whose gigantic pattern could be grasped only by big standards and a wide-ranging outlook. They were too often extremely conservative and individualistic, and most of them tended to play a lone hand. Small partnerships and companies, preferably within the limits of their own families, they readily accepted, but they shrank away from the huge corporate organization of the world into which immigration, the march of the industrial revolution, and the growth of America had taken them. Venturing beyond a certain conservative point seemed profligacy; and in a critical period of transition from one form of navigation to another, their conservatism did not keep them abreast of business progress. As a consequence these sailors did not emerge as the magnates of a new maritime order. Their skill and traditions, after all, were those of the sea rather than those of business management.

All this did not mean that they were without the cooperative spirit. Shipowners of the Great Lakes welcomed the Lake Carriers' Association, organized in 1885 to further common interests, and Halvor Michelson, a Chicago shipbuilder and owner, was for some years its president. Norwegian seamen took part in developing the Great Lakes harbor towns, accepted public office, and bore themselves as public-spirited citizens who left marks on such cities as Chicago, Milwaukee, Sheboygan, Racine, Green Bay, and Manitowoc.[33]

The ordinary seamen raised up a conspicuous leader whose efforts to improve their conditions transcended racial and national considerations. Andrew Furuseth, born in Romsdal, Norway, in 1854, arrived in the United States as an ordinary seaman in 1880 after voyages that had carried him all over the world. For a half dozen years he engaged in sailing and salmon fishing and then became secretary of the

[33] *Great Lakes,* 16–50, 59, 84–86.

Coast Seaman's Union. This modern Viking had gained a wide outlook into the conditions surrounding the seamen, and he possessed both the ability and the force to carry on a stubborn fight for reform. The treatment of ordinary seamen since time immemorial had been disgraceful to all nations. Cruel disciplinary methods, violence in securing enlistments, the vicious practice of shanghaiing, sordid living conditions aboard ship, inadequate wages, and the monstrous business of flogging were among maritime traditions that smacked of medievalism but were continued, in greater or less degree, down to the present century. Crimps traded upon the necessities of both sailors and shipmasters: deals were made with ill-smelling characters among boarding-housekeepers in port cities; extortionate fees were charged; a complex of conditions made the manning of vessels a hideous matter for sailors and captains alike.

The Norwegians, like other sailors, were victimized by this vicious racket, and it was the Norwegian-American Andrew Furuseth who led the fight to abolish it. The chief instruments of this fight were the seamen's protective associations which first appeared on the Great Lakes and the Pacific coast and ultimately coalesced in the International Seamen's Union of America. In 1908, thirteen years after its formal organization, Furuseth, who for many years had served in a secretarial capacity or as a Washington agent for one of the regional organizations, was chosen president of the union. This was a position of strategic national eminence, and he used it to full advantage, ably seconded by Victor Olander of Chicago, the son of a Swedish father and a Norwegian mother. The union kept up an unceasing fight against sharp opposition, made periodic gains in the form of ameliorating acts of Congress, and finally, with the aggressive aid of Senator Robert M. La Follette of Wisconsin, prevailed upon Congress to pass in 1915 that Seamen's Act which has been termed the seamen's Great Charter of Liberty. The "most unforgettable man I ever knew," said Peter B. Kyne of Andrew Furuseth. "He had an ideal and never lost sight of it, never quit fighting for it and never fought unfairly." When he died in 1938, his "ashes were scattered at sea, as he had asked"—in mid-Atlantic.[34]

Other Norwegian Americans had not been unaware of the plight of the sailors. The missionary work done by ministers of the Norwegian Lutheran faith in New York, Brooklyn, and other American seaports was designed to protect the social and economic, as well as the spiritual, welfare of the seamen. The Norwegian Seamen's Mission Society of Bergen, Norway, had begun its work in New York City as early as 1867, co-operating with the Norwegian Synod, which organized a church for seamen in 1866. This church, backed by both Norwegians and Norwegian Americans, was removed in the 1920's to Brooklyn, the strategic central location for an institution seeking to serve the sailors. There it helped hundreds of thousands of sailors—provided reading rooms, writing facilities, a banking institution, helped sailors to transmit money to their families, and gave aid to families hunting for missing sailors. The Scandinavian Sailors' Temperance Home, established in Brooklyn in 1886, tried to protect sailors from the machinations of crimps and boardinghousekeepers, including among its services an employment bureau. Institutions similar to the Norwegian Seamen's Church of Brooklyn have been established in many other cities, including Philadelphia, East Boston, Baltimore, Norfolk, Newport News, Pensacola, Mobile, and New Orleans, as well as Quebec and Montreal.[35]

While Norwegians thus entered and made themselves a

[34] Peter B. Kyne's article on "Saint Andrew the Sailor" is in the *Reader's Digest,* vol. 35, no. 212, p. 9–14 (December, 1939). See also an excellent article by A. N. Rygg, "Andrew Furuseth," in *American Scandinavian Review,* 26:123–133 (June, 1938); and Dr. Gjerset's discussion of "Life and Labor at Sea: Andrew Furuseth and the Seamen's Act of 1915," in *American Waters,* 158–184.

[35] A Norwegian observer who visited New York in 1874 was shocked by the morals of the sailors and the prevalence of "temptation" in the American metropo-

part of the merchant marine of America, the merchant service of Norway expanded in extraordinary fashion until it was ranked as one of America's greatest competitors, with a half dozen great Norwegian shipping firms plying a flourishing trade in American waters, on both the west and the east coasts, and elsewhere. As American shipping needs widened, many Norwegian ships, sailed by Norwegian captains and manned by Norwegian crews, were chartered by American firms, particularly for the fruit trade of Central and South America. Norwegian-American and American effort and funds, mobilized by such broad-visioned businessmen as Birger Osland and E. H. Hobe, played a notable part in the launching, shortly before the World War, of the Norwegian-America Line for direct service between Norway and the United States.[36] Dr. Gjerset presents figures showing that by 1916 no fewer than 2,532 Norwegian steamers with a tonnage of 3,522,263 and 273 sailing vessels with a tonnage of 388,184 traded in American ports. A dozen years later approximately seventy Norwegian vessels commanded by Norwegian captains were reported in charter for the West India trade. In recent years a vast Norwegian tonnage has passed through the Panama Canal. The Norwegian flag, as Dr. Gjerset says, "has become one of the best known in American waters."[37]

So the story of Norwegian immigrant transition includes the men who went down to the sea in ships — sailors who

lis. He was comforted by a visit to a Norwegian seaman's boardinghouse on the East Side, an institution that he found to be both religious and "temperance" in atmosphere. The cost to the sailor of living at this house was a dollar a day, including meals. Jørgen Gjerdrum, "Fra Amerika," a letter dated New York, November 19, 1874, in *Dagbladet* (Christiania), December 10, 1874. Dr. Gjerset tells of "Religious and Social Work among Norwegian Seamen in America," in chapter 10 of *American Waters*.

[36] On the general background of the Norwegian-America Line, see Carl J. Hambro, *Amerikaferd: Av emigrasjonens historie* (Oslo, 1935). The first vessel of the line, the "Kristianiafjord," reached New York on June 17, 1913.

[37] *American Waters*, 77, 97–100, 183. For a broad survey see Brækhus, *Fra "Restaurationen."*

mastered sail and steam, fishermen skilled in gathering up flapping treasures from the waters. Migration means transfer, not alone of human bodies that can be counted and tabulated in statistical tables, but also of culture and lore, skills and trades, traditions and ideas. Such things elude the statistical tables, but they are drawn into the life and institutions of the people in the new environment to which they are brought. The men who homesteaded on ocean and inland waters transferred from Norway to America a share in the maritime traditions and skills of a people who had navigated the seas of the world for more than a thousand years. As compared with such a range of time, the century or more that has passed since the "Restoration" brought its load of pioneer emigrants to America seems short enough. Yet the modern saga of Norwegian sailors in the New World has a sweep of its own — a sweep across a century that has been profoundly important in the making of a new nation, a geographical sweep that embraces the seven seas and America's Great Lakes, and a sweep of occupation and talent.

In the American midlands, in the valleys and plains of the good earth, Norwegian pioneers left place names as footprints. The place names on the Great Lakes were borne by vessels that sailed those waters, names like "Arendal," "Ole Bull," "Anna O. Hanson," "Helvig Holst," "Walhalla," "Ole Olsen," "Norway," "North Cape," "Anna Thorine," and "Col. H. C. Heg." These names and vessels have alike vanished, but it seems probable that the Norwegian imprint upon American maritime history will not soon be erased.

XII. CANADIAN INTERLUDE

TO THE SCANDINAVIAN immigrants who landed at the port of Quebec in the 1850's and 1860's, Canada was a corridor, not a place for permanent settlement. Many of them had friends or relatives, already established in the United States, who had written home of their experiences; and information thus transmitted determined the destinations of immigrants before they left Norway. A migrating people directs itself to regions where opportunities for land and labor seem best — and the Scandinavians, accepting the testimony of the America letters, were flocking to the area west of Lake Michigan.[1]

The Canadian immigration authorities gave the Scandinavians every aid. Sick passengers were cared for at the immigrant quarantine station; those who were impoverished were furnished with passage money to help them to reach their destinations; and for the benefit of all the most convenient routes to Illinois and Wisconsin were mapped out.[2]

[1] Edith Abbott, *Historical Aspects of the Immigration Problem,* 536 (Chicago, 1926).

[2] Report of A. C. Buchanan, chief emigration agent, for 1855, in Canada, *Sessional Papers,* 5 Parl., 2 Sess., vol. 14, no. 5, appendix no. 44 (1856).

The tide began flowing through the northern ports in 1850, when 250 Norwegian immigrants came to America by way of Quebec; in 1854 the Scandinavians, chiefly Norwegians, numbered over 5,000; and the total for the period from 1850 to 1865 was more than 51,000.[3] Nearly all these immigrants went on to the United States. As early as 1856, however, the Canadian authorities began to question the wisdom of allowing the northern immigrants to continue south and west without offering them some inducement to remain. Late that summer a party of sixty indigent Norwegians were offered free passage from Quebec to Ottawa City and promised employment for the winter. Fellow passengers came to their aid, however, and they went on to Chicago.[4] A. C. Buchanan, the general emigrant agent for Canada, in his report for 1856, proposed that an immigration agent be sent to the Scandinavian North. A Norwegian settlement in the Ottawa country, he believed, would be highly desirable, but it could not be brought about unless a "judicious Agent" were sent abroad under governmental authority to advertise the province among Norwegians before their emigration. Buchanan thought that "if a few families could be once introduced into the Ottawa section of the country they would soon draw others around them."[5]

In 1856 an announcement from the Canadian minister of agriculture placed before Norwegians the prospect of securing lands in three specified areas. To take advantage of this offer the settler was required to be at least eighteen years of age, to occupy the land within a month after claiming it, to bring a stated part of it under cultivation within four years, and to build on it a house measuring at least twenty by

[3] Blegen, *Norwegian Migration*, 350–352; Christopher A. Closter to A. C. Buchanan, December 27, 1858, in *Sessional Papers*, 6 Parl., 2 Sess., vol. 17, no. 3, appendix no. 19 (1859).

[4] *Sessional Papers*, 5 Parl., 3 Sess., vol. 15, no. 8, appendix no. 47, return no. 8 (1857).

[5] *Ibid.*, return no. 4.

eighteen feet, with the proviso that if groups of families so desired, they might build one large central dwelling. The statement that these vacant lands could accommodate eight million people — more than five times the population of all Norway — suggested something of Canada's boundless possibilities.[6] The next year at Quebec the Canadian department of agriculture published, primarily for distribution in Norway, five thousand copies of a Norwegian translation of a handbook for immigrants. Useful details were combined with broad generalization: "Canada is in truth a 'land of hope, which will not be disappointed,' where work of every kind wins well-deserved rewards." Labor and bread await every worker in this "market for all the world's products."[7]

In 1853, before any such efforts had been made, two Norwegians had settled near Sherbrooke in the Eastern Townships.[8] These townships comprise eleven counties in the province of Quebec, in a district a hundred miles east of Montreal and about the same distance southwest of the city of Quebec. The territory, netted with lakes and traversed by part of the Appalachian range, is some four and a half million acres in area.[9] In June, 1854, fourteen Norwegian families, comprising sixty persons, arrived at Quebec on the "Flora" from Christiania. Their goal was Sherbrooke, where their two countrymen were making good progress and were held "in high estimation by the Inhabitants." Four of these families purchased farms; the rest found employment on the railroad; and in December of that year Buchanan commented hopefully on the prospects of the colony. "This is the first party of Norwegians, of any consequence," he wrote, "who have established themselves in Canada, and

[6] *Morgenbladet,* November 2, 1856.

[7] *Canada: En kortfatted skildring af dets geographiske beliggenhed* (Quebec, 1857). The translation was made by A. Jorgensen. A copy of this rare pamphlet is in the library of the University of Oslo.

[8] *Sessional Papers,* 5 Parl., 1 Sess., vol. 13, no. 13, appendix D. D. D. (1854–55).

[9] Beckles Willson, *Quebec, the Laurentian Province,* 185 ff. (Toronto, 1912).

their attraction thereto is attributed to the favorable reports which they had received from two of their countrymen, who settled in that district in 1853. Should they prove successful, and of which I have little doubt, we may look for a further addition to their numbers, during the ensuing season."[10]

Johan Schrøder, who traveled in the United States and Canada in 1863, reported that a group of Norwegian immigrants, led by an agent, settled in Bury in the Eastern Townships in 1856. A land company had four thousand acres of land for sale at that place; the settlers paid from two and a half to five dollars an acre for their farms, did some clearing of the wooded lands, and built houses, but a number of them abandoned their property after a year or two.[11]

In 1857 Christopher Closter, a Norwegian, was appointed emigration agent by the Canadian department of agriculture; he was to spend the immigration season, beginning about June 1, at Quebec and was to be paid fifty pounds for his services.[12] Closter was a brother of Asbjørn Kloster, the noted temperance reformer and Quaker leader at Stavanger. He had emigrated to the United States before 1850, was a commission merchant at Hamilton, Canada West, in 1855, and soon thereafter, with another Norwegian, formed a company in Quebec to promote the Norwegian lumber-carrying business.[13] In 1857 he petitioned the Canadian government for a tract of unappropriated land in Canada West for the establishment of a Norwegian colony. He said that he considered the Norwegians well suited for the task of clearing the soil; that he had previously tried to persuade them to

[10] *Sessional Papers*, 5 Parl., 1 Sess., vol. 13, no. 13, appendix D. D. D. (1854–55).

[11] Schrøder, *Skandinaverne i de Forenede Stater og Canada*, 53.

[12] Public Archives of Canada, Department of Agriculture, Report of Committee of Executive Council, May 21, 1857.

[13] Several letters from Closter to his brother from 1850 to 1859, in the Kloster Papers, give information about his early activities in the United States and Canada. A circular in 1859 announces that Closter and A. Jorgensen are in the lumber-forwarding business at Quebec.

settle in Canada rather than in the United States; but that their destinations were determined before they left Norway and they would not remain in Canada until some reliable offer was made them. The commissioner of crown lands, to whom this petition was referred, suggested the Gaspé district, Ottawa County, or St. Maurice as most suitable for Norwegians. Closter next proposed the establishment of a colony on the eastern shores of Lake Superior. He said that he had made arrangements with a number of English-speaking Norwegians in Wisconsin to settle in Canada at once; he believed he could establish three thousand families in five years if the land grant were made.

The minister of agriculture received this plan favorably. He was willing to provide land and to arrange for the construction of roads, but he would assume no responsibility for the immigrants if they became destitute. The price of the land was not to exceed four shillings per acre.[14] By September, 1857, Closter was reported to be in Norway, working to attract large numbers of his countrymen to Canada.[15]

Some time in 1857 ninety Norwegians were persuaded by C. H. Tambs, agent for the British-American Land Company, to settle in the Eastern Townships;[16] and in June of the same year some young men, members of a Norwegian party on its way to the West, were sent to that area for work because they were without funds.[17] All the settlers had been destitute when they arrived; but through the influence of Tambs they obtained work that enabled them to survive the first winter. They cleared some ground and by the autumn of

[14] Public Archives of Canada, Department of Agriculture, Report of Committee of Executive Council, June 17, 1857.

[15] William Hutton to Henry Chesshyre, September 25, 1857, in Public Archives of Canada, Agriculture and Statistics, Letters Sent, 1857 to 18—.

[16] Closter to Buchanan, December 27, 1858, in *Sessional Papers,* 6 Parl., 2 Sess., vol. 17, no. 3, appendix no. 19 (1859).

[17] Buchanan's report for 1857, in *Sessional Papers,* 6 Parl., 1 Sess., vol. 16, no. 7, appendix no. 41 (1858).

O. E. Rølvaag

CANADA:

A BRIEF OUTLINE OF HER

Geographical Position,

PRODUCTIONS, CLIMATE, CAPABILITIES,

EDUCATIONAL AND MUNICIPAL INSTITUTIONS,

&c., &c., &c.

Published by Authority.

TORONTO, CANADA WEST
1857.

Cover Page of O. E. Rølvaag's Copy of a Canadian Pamphlet

1858 they had supplies stored up for the second winter. Some settlers had even been able to make payments on their land.[18]

Closter was appointed Norwegian interpreter at Quebec for the season of 1858 at a salary of a hundred pounds,[19] and on December 27 he submitted to Buchanan a lengthy report. Before beginning his activities at the port he had investigated the situation in the Eastern Townships. The satisfactory progress of the settlers convinced him that there was the place to which to direct Norwegian immigrants; he was sure, however, that certain "kinds of underhanded work were practised, to prevent any of them from settling in Canada, by parties interested to forward them westward." Thirty of the settlers, "influenced by parties from the West," had left the Eastern Townships that spring; some returned, however, "evidently convinced that their industry would be equally as profitable in this country as in the States"; and they were pleased with the climate of the province. They settled down, purchased land, and got along well considering their belated start. Closter believed that they had a prosperous future in store for them.[20]

He thought it a good plan to secure a few families that year from each district in Norway. When they were settled and contented in the Eastern Townships, this instance of successful colonization would refute any statement that Canada was an unfavorable country for immigrants. Apparently this plan operated successfully; the number of Norwegian families in the Eastern Townships increased to twenty-five, with 126 persons. "All are of the working classes," Buchanan wrote, "possessing but small resources, but if industrious as they generally are hardy and economical,

[18] Closter to Buchanan, December 27, 1858, in *Sessional Papers,* 6 Parl., 2 Sess., vol. 17, no. 3, appendix no. 19 (1859).

[19] William Hutton to Closter, May 18, 1859, in Public Archives of Canada, Agriculture and Statistics, Letters Sent, 1857 to 18—.

[20] *Sessional Papers,* 6 Parl., 2 Sess., vol. 17, no. 3, appendix no. 19 (1859).

they cannot fail shortly to be independent. . . . [They] appear well satisfied with their future prospects."[21]

The settlers had purchased more than three thousand acres from the British-American Land Company, at three dollars per acre. Closter considered that in view of the convenient location of the farms this price was not exorbitant; nevertheless it would be considered so by immigrants who were not well acquainted with the general price of farm land, and who knew at what low prices land was being offered in the United States. A large tract of Canadian land should be set aside for the immigrants, he suggested, and "additional inducements" offered them.[22]

When the immigration season ended, Closter visited the Norwegians in the Eastern Townships for eight or ten days, in order to make his own estimate of the country itself and of the new colony's progress. During his stay he called a meeting of the settlers and questioned about forty of them individually as to their intentions. They were contented and eager to have more of their countrymen join them, he reported; they were pleased with their new home and with the climate, which so much resembled that of Norway; and they looked prosperous. Nevertheless they would give Closter no guarantee that their residence was permanent. He evidently feared that they would ultimately be drawn to the American West.[23]

Of more than twenty-six thousand Norwegians who had entered Canada, said Closter, all save some three hundred had gone to the United States. He stressed Canada's need for agriculturists of the type of these immigrants, and pleaded for more definite efforts to persuade them to remain. He was confident that if inducements had been offered the Norwegians, at least a fourth of them would be living in Canada.

[21] *Ibid.*

[22] Closter's report to Buchanan, December 27, 1858, in *Sessional Papers,* 6 Parl., 2 Sess., vol. 17, no. 3, appendix no. 19 (1859).

[23] *Ibid.*

He urged a land grant and "the appointment of some respectable person thoroughly informed of this Province, and the Norwegian language, one who has the interest of the country at heart, and possesses the confidence of the Government so that they would feel secured from dangers, errors, or deception." [24] It seems evident that he had Christopher Closter in mind as a suitable appointee.

In March, 1859, William Hutton, secretary of the bureau of agriculture, wrote Buchanan that he questioned Closter's reliability, considered him a "slippery person," and doubted the wisdom of giving him another appointment. Closter had as much as admitted that he would direct the Norwegian immigration elsewhere if by so doing he could line his own pocket.[25] Buchanan, however, felt that he would get nowhere with the Norwegian immigration if he had to dispense with Closter's services.[26]

In July, 1859, fifteen families, consisting of forty-nine persons, arrived from Norway on the "Brødrene," went to join their countrymen at Bury in the Eastern Townships, and purchased more than a thousand acres of land from the British-American Land Company. "They appeared so well pleased with their situation," said Buchanan, "that two of them have proposed returning to their native land this winter, in order to make known the advantage Canada offers, and to induce others of their countrymen to join them." [27]

Closter, reporting on his activities for 1859, mentioned that three of these colonists had been sent by relatives and friends in Norway to select localities for settlement. He accompanied them when they examined the land; it far exceeded their expectations, as they had been informed both

[24] *Ibid.*

[25] William Hutton to Buchanan, March 22, 1859, in Public Archives of Canada, Agriculture and Statistics, Letters Sent, 1857 to 18—.

[26] A memorandum of Hutton, March 31, 1859, quoting Buchanan, in *ibid.*, Letters Sent, 1857 to 18—.

[27] Buchanan's report for 1859, in *Sessional Papers,* 6 Parl., 3 Sess., vol. 18, no. 3, appendix no. 18 (1860).

in Norway and when they arrived in Canada that Canadian lands were the least desirable in North America for agriculture. Later in the year Closter received a letter from the Eastern Townships indicating that the three investigators, and the settlers as a whole, were pleased with their selections and confident that when this news reached Norway it would do much to counteract misrepresentations of Canadian conditions.[28]

Closter had now worked out a plan of five lines of action which he urged the government to take. Three townships should be set apart for the exclusive use of Norwegians, one on Chaleur Bay in the Gaspé Peninsula, another in the Eastern Townships, and the third on the north shore of Lake Huron. Roads should be laid through each of these townships and the settlers should be employed in building them or given small contracts for the construction work in order to "assist the new comers during the first year." A government representative speaking both English and Norwegian should be posted in each of the settlements as an adviser to the settlers. Ten years should be allowed for the exclusive settlement of these townships by Norwegians. Finally, a free grant of a hundred acres should be given each head of a family, with certain stipulations as to its cultivation.

Closter believed that if three different townships were available, each settler would be able to choose a place suitable to his own occupation — farming, lumbering, mining, or fishing. "Many large families with small capital would avail themselves of such an offer," he said, "when assured that their friends and relations would be offered the same privileges on joining them in future in the same Townships."[29]

A general emigration pamphlet on Canada issued by the department of agriculture in 1860 recommended the Eastern

[28] Closter, "Report of Norwegian Assistant," in Buchanan's report for 1859, in *Sessional Papers*, 6 Parl., 3 Sess., vol. 18, no. 3, appendix no. 18 (1860).
[29] *Ibid.*

Townships for settlement. Two million acres of land were available, with special opportunities for grazing and dairying; and it was proposed to build "Colonization Roads" for the benefit of the settlers. The population consisted of English, Scotch, and Irish, and "a large and thriving settlement of Norwegians has recently been formed." The district had railroad and steamboat connections not only with Quebec and Montreal but also with Portland, Boston, and New York.[30]

Closter's request for a definite area for Norwegian colonization was approved by the Canadian government in 1859, and a site was selected in the vicinity of Gaspé, a village situated on a deep bay in the Gaspé Peninsula, an arm of the province of Quebec which projects into the Gulf of St. Lawrence. Land within a stated area was to be restricted to Norwegians, who would have the privilege of selecting a hundred acres each for a total of twenty dollars, payable in five years. It was a heavily wooded, remote fishermen's settlement in a region of long and severe winters. Isolated it may have been, but it was nearer Norway than was the American West. Many immigrants arrived in Canada without funds with which to pay fares to Wisconsin or Minnesota. Why not promote a settlement that would be within easy reach of these enterprising but impecunious people? As for the climate, Norwegians were accustomed to long and cold winters; and both fishing and farming opened up possibilities on the Gaspé shores.[31] Buchanan, late in 1859, encouraged the establishment of such a settlement: "In the development of the inexhaustible wealth which this country possesses in her fisheries along the seacoast and the Bay of Chaleur, the hardy fishermen of Norway might find a large encouragement; and fishing establishments, in connection

[30] *Canada: A Brief Outline of Her Geographic Position,* 24 (Quebec, 1860).

[31] For an interesting reminiscent account of the Norwegian settlement at Gaspé, see N. C. Brun, "Første aars oplevelser," in *Symra,* 7:110–119 (1911). Brun was a fifteen-year-old boy when he went to Gaspé.

with settlement, would greatly conduce to the general prosperity of the country."[32] The department of agriculture's pamphlet of 1860 pictured the resources of Gaspé as abundant and varied.[33]

It was not intended, however, to restrict Norwegian settlement to the Gaspé area. In March, 1860, an agent named Helge Haugen was sent to Norway as Canada's official representative. A letter addressed to him at Bury, Eastern Townships, just before his departure, by P. M. Vankoughnet, commissioner of crown lands, instructed him to distribute maps and pamphlets, to give information about "such places as the Sault Ste Marie, Lake Nippissing and the Ottawa Country in Upper Canada," and to tell also of "the Ste Maurice Territory, the Eastern Townships and Gaspe in Lower Canada." The commissioner warned Haugen against making dishonest claims: "You will take care not to state anything which you do not know to be true."[34]

On August 6, 1860, Closter, accompanied by seven families of Norwegians (thirty-four persons in all), left by steamer from Quebec for the Gaspé Basin, where his group was joined by another party which had gone ahead three weeks earlier and was awaiting the arrival of its leader before its members selected land. Closter secured employment and lodging for most of them and with four others went into the interior to inspect the country. They found that there was plenty of good land but no passable road; and no property having a seacoast frontage was available from the crown — a disappointment to those interested in combining fishing with farming. After spending twelve or fourteen days investigating possibilities, Closter and his associates filed applications for all available land in Malbay Township. The seventeen men in the party went at once to Malbay to begin building log

[32] *Sessional Papers,* 6 Parl., 3 Sess., vol. 18, no. 3, appendix no. 18 (1860).

[33] *Canada: A Brief Outline,* 12.

[34] P. M. Vankoughnet to Haugen, March 1, 1860, in Public Archives of Canada, Agriculture and Statistics, Letters Sent, 1857 to 18—.

houses. "I am happy to be able to state," wrote Closter in September, "that I left them perfectly reconciled to their new home." There were fifty Norwegians then at Gaspé, twenty-eight adults and twenty-two children.

Closter was not confident, however, that the colony could survive without assistance. Its members had been delayed in Quebec and their funds had been nearly exhausted. Meanwhile, prices were high at Gaspé.[35] He suggested that Gaspé could be colonized only by a "class of emigrants who by their former habits are so peculiarly adapted to the character of that part of Canada, which has hitherto been almost rejected by all other European emigrants." The Norwegians, he believed, could succeed either as farmers or fishermen. Roads needed to be built, and in particular the Norwegian settlement must be made accessible from the main road. Closter also requested assistance in the construction of a schoolhouse, which would serve incidentally as a meeting-house. If the settlers were given aid, "they would then feel perfectly at home in their choice of locality, and by their influence during the winter, will, in all probability, induce a large number of their countrymen to come and join them next season."[36] Nine of the colonists, in a letter written in November, 1860, sang the praises of Gaspé, wrote that they were building houses and would have a schoolhouse of their own, and expressed satisfaction with the land.[37] Buchanan's report of February, 1861, indicated satisfactory beginnings at Gaspé. John Eden, the crown land agent at Gaspé, in November had reported "great progress" among the Norwegian settlers, who were "perfectly satisfied" with their lands.

[35] Closter to A. C. Buchanan, September 10, 1860, in Buchanan's report for 1860, in *Sessional Papers*, 6 Parl., 4 Sess., vol. 19, no. 3, appendix no. 14 (1861). Closter's report is printed as paper no. 6 in the Buchanan report.

[36] *Ibid.*

[37] A letter of December 18, 1860, signed by Halvor Jordal and Elling H. Vigen, and one written in November, signed by Petter A. Berg and eight others, were published in Stavanger and Christiania newspapers and reprinted in *Emigranten* for April 29, 1861.

They had "six habitable houses of a good size," and considerable road-building had been done. "I shall watch with much interest the future progress of this settlement," wrote Buchanan, "as on its results will in a great measure depend the success of our Norwegian settlements within Canada." [38]

In 1861 Closter, who had gone to his native land in his official capacity, brought out a revision of the earlier Norwegian edition of the handbook for immigrants, with its store of condensed information about Canada, its lands, minerals, fisheries, government, laws, and people. The book contains many practical details for the prospective settler on such subjects as the pioneer's equipment and the prices of supplies and tools. Gaspé is mentioned briefly but generously: "The lands in the Gaspé district have a light but rich soil, which produces all kinds of grains and vegetation. In these districts are millions of acres still in their natural state and covered with beautiful woods." And again: "The population in the Gaspé district and the northern coast of St. Lawrence River and Bay comprises 32,000 souls. In this district alone 500,000 people could make their living." [39] In March of the same year, William Hutton, secretary of the bureau of agriculture, wrote to Closter in Christiania, cautioning him against encouraging a general immigration to Gaspé. Hutton referred to reports of a crop failure in Norway and of the prospective emigration of large numbers of very poor people. "I think you ought to take care," he said, "that these poor people have no false hopes that the Can[n] Gov[t] will aid them." [40]

Closter's brother, the Norwegian Quaker leader, had no official connection with the Gaspé plan, but he was interested

[38] *Sessional Papers,* 6 Parl., 4 Sess., vol. 19, no. 3, appendix no. 14 (1861).

[39] C. O. Closter, *Canada: En kortfattet skildring af dets geographiske beliggenhed,* 16, 47, 48, and *passim* (Stavanger, 1861). The writer found a copy of this rare book in the Deichmanske Library at Oslo.

[40] Hutton to Closter, March 15, 1861, in Public Archives of Canada, Agriculture and Statistics, Letters Sent, 1860.

in it and privately encouraged it. He was in communication with a Swedish Quaker, Carl Schöllström of Upsala, who was contemplating emigration in order to escape religious intolerance in Sweden. Schöllström reported the existence of a Swedish Quaker society of some fifty members, for whom the outlook was dark because they were at odds with the established church.[41] Early in 1861 he suggested that Quakers in the North might unite in a colony somewhere in North America, for he was convinced that emigration was their only hope. A little later he came to the conclusion that it was God's will that he should emigrate. The book on Canada, sent him by Asbjørn Kloster, had caused him to consider seriously the choice of Gaspé as his destination. And in 1862—his name by that time metamorphosed to Charles Shieldstream—he wrote to Kloster from Gaspé Basin.[42]

Meanwhile, however, Christopher Closter's plans for a Norwegian colony in Canada East had been sharply attacked by the Reverend G. F. Dietrichson of Stavanger, recently returned from a pioneer pastorate in Wisconsin. On January 8, 1861, he publicly invited Closter to debate with him on the emigration question or, if he preferred, to publish fully his reasons for recommending Canada to prospective emigrants. This invitation occurred before the Canadian handbook had appeared, and Asbjørn Kloster replied on behalf of his brother that the latter's book about Canadian conditions would shortly appear in print.[43] In the early spring, newspapers announced that two barks soon would leave for Canada with Gaspé colonists. This announcement aroused the ire of the pugnacious Dietrichson, who forthwith declared that he would give a public lecture on emigration and emigration agents; meanwhile he cautioned people under no circum-

[41] Schöllström to A. Kloster, May 29, 1859, in Kloster Papers.

[42] Schöllström to A. Kloster, March 1, 18, May 22, 1861; March 15, 1862, in Kloster Papers.

[43] *Stavanger amtstidende og adresseavis,* January 10, 15, 1861.

stances to make arrangements with Closter to emigrate to Gaspé. On April 2 he delivered his address before an audience of several thousand people in Stavanger and some days later, with Dietrichson present, Closter made a public answer, after which the irrepressible minister delivered a spirited rebuttal. Much interest was aroused by this clash and it was widely reported in the Norwegian press.[44]

Dietrichson began his lecture by sketching the history of emigration, which he declared was now setting strongly toward Minnesota and eventually would sweep westward to the Pacific coast. He asserted that civil war was imminent in the United States and that a Southern invasion of the upper Mississippi Valley would inevitably follow. Because of this general situation, he advised against all emigration. Nevertheless, if people must emigrate, he said, the American West was the proper region in which to select sites for settlement. Gaspé he disposed of as a bleak, isolated, heavily forested region that could be recommended only by one having a commercial interest in its promotion. Closter with his reply exhibited wheat and timothy which he asserted had been grown at Gaspé; sketched the perils of the journey to the American interior, which could be avoided by those who chose Canadian settlement; defended Canada as a suitable land for immigrants; and denounced Dietrichson as a land speculator. When Closter suggested that people who were dissatisfied with Gaspé would have the privilege of migrating elsewhere, Dietrichson pounced upon the statement, explaining that the poor ordinarily would find it difficult to avail themselves of so expensive a privilege; hence the necessity of good judgment in primary land selection. The personal attack he brushed off by stating that he did not own a foot of land in the West and by reminding Closter that he was on record as opposed to all emigration. After the debate, news-

[44] *Stavanger amtstidende og adresseavis,* March 11, 20, 27, April 2, 4, 8, 15, 1861. Dietrichson's lecture also appears in *Almuevennen,* April 13, 20, 1861.

papers announced that many prospective colonists had withdrawn their names. Oscar Malmborg, at that time active in Norway and Sweden as the agent of the Illinois Central Railroad, also struck out against the influence of Closter and urged the officials of the railroad to be on guard at Quebec against Canadian "runners," who "spare no pains or expense in inducing the arriving to settle in the Canadas."[45]

Nevertheless not a few set out for Gaspé. Meanwhile Haugen, the second Canadian agent, had made Trondhjem his northern headquarters and had carried on an extensive advertising campaign from that northern center, distributing books and maps, encouraging migration both to the Ottawa region and to Gaspé, reaching the Lofoten fishermen with his propaganda, and making plans to charter two emigrant vessels. "We have had very satisfactory letters from Mr. Haugen," wrote Hutton to Closter on March 15. "If you both work together you may materially aid one another."[46] Haugen succeeded in recruiting about a hundred prospective emigrants to Canada, and some of these eventually arrived at Gaspé. A large part of Closter's emigrant group sailed on the "Iris" from Stavanger on May 4. They reached the quarantine station at Grosse Isle on July 10 and finally landed at Gaspé on July 25, 1861. Disease and death usually marked the emigrant passage in that period, and this voyage was no exception. Yet the toll of dead was light compared with the usual crossing. Only three persons died on the "Iris," whereas on the "Norge," sailing from Bergen about the same time, there were thirty-one deaths, and on the "Northern Light," which left Christiania on April 27,

[45] *Stavanger amtstidende og adresseavis,* April 15, 1861. Dietrichson's general criticisms of conditions in the United States were sharply refuted in *Emigranten,* May 27, 1861. On Malmborg, see Paul W. Gates, "The Campaign of the Illinois Central Railroad for Norwegian and Swedish Immigrants," in *Studies and Records,* 6: 72, 73.

[46] *Stavanger amtstidende og adresseavis,* May 3, 1861; Hutton to Closter, March 15, 1861, in Public Archives of Canada, Agriculture and Statistics, Letters Sent, 1860. Haugen's report is summarized by Hutton in *Sessional Papers,* 6 Parl., 4 Sess., vol. 4, no. 23 (1861).

twenty-one passengers had succumbed before the vessel arrived on July 7 at Grosse Isle.[47]

Closter evidenced his own good faith in Gaspé by bringing to it his wife and family, his aged father and mother, a brother, and various other relatives. Eden wrote that about four hundred Norwegians and Swedes had settled to the north and south of Gaspé Bay, "more especially in the Basin of Malbaie," during the year 1861.[48] The story of the little colony has been characterized as the saddest chapter in Norwegian-American history.[49] In the light of the initial difficulties and hardships that some groups of early Norwegian settlers in the upper Mississippi Valley were compelled to meet, this characterization is an exaggeration. There is no doubt, however, that the Gaspé colonists had an unhappy experience. The colony failed. Its members dispersed after the winter of 1861–62. In addition to difficulties of climate, land (especially the fact that the settlers were not able to secure tracts along the shore), and employment, there were financial troubles for which Closter himself seems to have been responsible. He had purchased a tract of fifteen hundred acres some fourteen miles from the village and also a smaller tract, with a sawmill and a flour mill, near Gaspé. Evidently there was a plan for organized effort, for one emigrant was made manager of the workers. There were also rumors of lead deposits and future mining operations on Closter's lands.[50] Some of the colonists were optimistic. "For my part," wrote Bertha E. Kloster to a relative in Nor-

[47] See *Stavanger amtstidende og adresseavis,* December 9, 1861, and April 7, 1862, for some information on Haugen and the Trondhjem group. Haugen evidently tried to persuade some of the immigrants to take up land in the Ottawa country. See also "Report of the Quarantine Hospital at Grosse Isle," in *Sessional Papers,* 7 Parl., 1 Sess., vol. 20, no. 4, appendix no. 19 (1862).

[48] "Report on Colonization Roads in Lower Canada, for the Year 1861," in *Report of the Commissioner of Crown Lands,* in *Sessional Papers,* 7 Parl., 1 Sess., vol. 20, no. 3, appendix no. 11 (1862).

[49] Hjalmar R. Holand, "Gaspé: Et trist blad i vor nybyggersaga," in *Symra,* 5:2–8 (1909).

[50] Nils O. Closter to A. Kloster from "Gaspe Basin," October 25, 1861, in Kloster Papers.

way in October, "I like Gaspé much better than any place I have been before and I don't doubt you would do as well here as there." [51]

The shadow of disappointment soon lay over the colony, however. Closter gathered up from the colonists about twelve hundred dollars and set off for Quebec to buy supplies; but his return, for some reason, was long delayed. The settlers for the most part failed to get work for wages and were soon in such want that a public subscription was taken up for them at Gaspé.[52] A letter of December 27, 1861, in the files of the department of agriculture, states that the Norwegians at Gaspé were suffering great distress and were unable to obtain supplies for winter consumption; the government was studying the case and would take measures for their relief. At the end of December aid was sent to Gaspé.[53] The privations of that winter damned the Gaspé colony for most of the settlers. According to a Canadian official, three hundred Norwegian families had been living in Gaspé; by the fall of 1862 all except ten had gone to the United States or to Upper Canada.[54] In March the Quaker Shieldstream wrote Asbjørn Kloster that Dietrichson had been right, that no emigrants should be advised to go to Gaspé; and he branded Closter as untruthful and unchristian. He himself, he said in a later letter, was the only colonist who was satisfied—and his peace of mind came from the fact that he had escaped from worse conditions in his native land than those that confronted him at Gaspé.[55] A colonist's letter published in Norway in the fall of 1862 charges Closter with having used part of the money to pay off private debts, but states

[51] To her sister, Ellen Maria, October 25, 1861, in Kloster Papers.

[52] Shieldstream to A. Kloster, March 15, 1862, in Kloster Papers. A letter of Andrew Closter, March 8, 1862, mentions the death of a son of Christopher at Gaspé the preceding November.

[53] E. Campbell to H. S. Scott, December 27 and 30, 1861, in Public Archives of Canada, Agriculture and Statistics, Letters Sent, 1860.

[54] *Sessional Papers*, 7 Parl., 2 Sess., vol. 21, no. 3, appendix no. 4 (1863).

[55] Shieldstream to A. Kloster, March 15, 1862; March 18, 1863, in Kloster Papers.

that finally he did send supplies, though some of the colonists received nothing in return for their money. Closter's wife, who was "sick with sorrow," was said to have mortgaged her own property in order to aid the needy settlers.[56]

Canadian officials do not agree as to whether the responsibility for the failure of the colony lay with the settlers themselves, the government, or conditions beyond the control of either. These officials do not confirm the report that Closter had appropriated the colonists' funds. In fact, they make no mention of any defection by him. The minister of agriculture, F. Evanturel, felt that the wrong class of immigrants had been established there. "The Norwegian colony which the late Government tried to plant on the banks of the St. Lawrence, has not succeeded so well," he wrote. "Being composed of a class of immigrants who were poor, burthened with families, and unused to agriculture, they became of course, notwithstanding the aid which they received from the Government, discouraged in a strang[e] land, and betook themselves elsewhere to settle. . . . It was, therefore, impossible for the present Government to keep them in Lower Canada, and the charge of neglect, which has been brought against the Government in this behalf, is accordingly unfounded." The minister went on to criticize severely the policy of bringing over immigrants incapable of supporting themselves on the property selected for them, "and who, like these Norwegians, end by moving off, breathing curses on the persons by whose persuasion they were led to settle in Lower Canada." Eden wrote to Buchanan in a strain similar to that of Evanturel. The "last Norwegian emigrants," he said, were "but little better than paupers and not over fond of work." In general, he concluded that the Norwegians were "of a rambling disposition, very similar to English Gipsies." Among numerous causes of immigrant discontent he mentioned the absence of a "church or minister of their own

[56] *Stavanger amtstidende og adresseavis,* October 6, 1862.

principles." He also was inclined to believe that some "secret agency" made them discontented with Gaspé and turned "their attention to the United States."[57]

The emigrant agent at Hamilton questioned some of the Norwegians from Gaspé — and some who had been living on the Ottawa — when they passed through his station on their way to the United States. They informed him that the localities chosen for them in Canada were neither what they liked nor what they needed. Many of them, he said, conversed quite readily in English; they told him that they would have preferred to remain in Canada had they been able to support themselves there, but that they had found it impossible to do so. The agent added, as his own opinion, that their desire to live among their own countrymen was an additional incentive to their abandoning Canada.[58]

Meanwhile the Illinois Central Railroad, acting upon the advice of its agent in Sweden and Norway, sent agents to Quebec in the summer of 1861 to meet arriving immigrants and to take every possible step looking toward their going on to the Middle West. The following summer the railroad engaged the Reverend Abraham Jacobson, a Norwegian-American minister, to continue this work and among other things to distribute circulars among the immigrants. Jacobson spent four months in Quebec, but gave most of his energy to humanitarian and missionary work among the sick and needy — a service for which he was rewarded by a grant from the Canadian government. This kind-hearted Midwestern pastor took occasion to visit Gaspé and there learned at first hand the story of the hardships and disappointments met by

[57] *Sessional Papers,* 7 Parl., 2 Sess., vol. 21, no. 3, appendix no. 4 (1863).

[58] *Ibid.* The agent at Hamilton, W. Gillespie, recorded that three thousand Norwegians passed through that place during the season. He suggested the desirability of a permanent Norwegian colony and named the north shore of Lake Huron as a suitable area. "The Norwegian," he said, "does not care to be isolated from his countrymen; he prefers being surrounded by them, and has no desire of mixing with other people." See also an interesting report on the failure of the Gaspé colony in a discussion of roads in Gaspé County, included in the report of the minister of agriculture and statistics for 1862.

the colonists and gave to them the ministrations of the church.[59]

So the ill-fated colonization enterprise gradually came to an end. Most of the members of the Gaspé settlement set their faces toward the West, choosing to identify themselves with the main stream of Norwegian migration. Closter helped some of them to meet the expenses of their journey. He himself, with his family, was in Chicago in 1864, though he appeared in Montreal again late in 1865. Shieldstream removed to Norwich, Canada West, and in 1867, writing to ascertain the whereabouts of Closter, said, "I have nothing against him, and I am very glad to say that he has done right to me, and I don't write for the sake of hurting him." He was then inclined to believe that the colonists made a mistake when they abandoned Gaspé in favor of the West.[60]

Canadian officials continued to watch the Norwegian migration with interest and to deal with the ever-present problems of sickness and relief that accompanied it. The Ottawa agent in 1863 observed that, although the German settlements in the Ottawa district were progressing, "It is different . . . with the Norwegians, who are abandoning this

[59] Gates, in *Studies and Records,* 6: 77; Clara Jacobson, "A Pioneer Pastor Who Knew Lincoln," in *Scandinavia,* vol. 1, no. 3, p. 38, 39 (March, 1924); and Holand, *Den sidste folkevandring,* 331. The Bishop of Quebec made All Saints' Chapel in Quebec available for Jacobson's use in holding church services for his countrymen and also put him in touch with Episcopal clergymen at Gaspé. See a letter from the Bishop to Jacobson, September 2, 1862, in St. Olaf College archives. Miss Clara Jacobson of Decorah has kindly furnished the author with information about her father's visit to Quebec. Unfortunately a letter by Jacobson, September 16, 1862, on conditions at Gaspé, though listed in "Agriculture Letters," Public Archives of Canada, cannot be found. Jacobson carried with him to Quebec a letter signed by C. J. P. Peterson and Erl. Carlssen, Chicago, May 26, stating that he went "as a missionary in order to assist Norwegian and Swedish emigrants in their spiritual and temporal affairs." He was a member of the Scandinavian Augustana Synod. A copy of this letter is in the St. Olaf College archives.

[60] Endre and Niels Kloster to A. Kloster, October 27, 1864, and Shieldstream to A. Kloster, January 8, 1867, in Kloster Papers. The sale of a tract of land at Gaspé by Henry Price to Closter for four thousand dollars was completed on November 16, 1865, and a letter patent was issued to him on February 24, 1866. See transcripts of two letters by Closter, dated at Montreal on December 13, 1865, and January 25, 1866; also L. A. Richard of Quebec to Agnes Larson, October 4, 1928, in St. Olaf College archives.

THE EMIGRATION FROM EUROPE DURING THE PRESENT CENTURY.

ITS CAUSES AND EFFECTS.

TRANSLATED FROM NORWEGIAN STATISTICS AND REPORTS, AND FROM EXTRACTS OF "HISTOIRE DE L'ÉMIGRATION EUROPÉENNE, ASIATIQUE ET AFRICAINE, AU XIX SIÈCLE,"

By A. JORGENSEN.

QUEBEC,
PRINTED BY C. DARVEAU, No. 8 MOUNTAIN HILL.
1865.

part of the Province altogether."[61] One Canadian official shrewdly suggested that a successful Norwegian colony demanded a leader, perhaps a clergyman or a schoolteacher, in whom all the emigrants had confidence, and declared that this had been essential in the western settlements in the United States. He favored action by the Canadians to retain a part of the Norwegian immigration and characterized the people as "a fine, hardy race . . . considered by the Western States to be the best class of emigrants they get."[62] The foreign interpreter for the government immigration office was A. Jorgensen, who reported that 5,525 Norwegians and Swedes landed at Quebec in 1864 and expressed regret that there was no settlement of their nationality in Canada to which they could go — an indication that Norwegian settlement in the Eastern Townships had fallen away. Many of the emigrants expressed a wish to settle in Canada, but said they felt that the prospects of employment were too uncertain.[63] Buchanan brought the question of organizing a settlement before the Canadian Land and Emigration Company, and indicated that some preliminary steps had been taken. Jorgensen, incidentally, reported that some sixty-five young emigrants, on a vessel bound for Portland, were under contract with the Foreign Emigration Association of Maine and presumably intended for the Northern armies, but were prevailed upon, instead, to land at Quebec. They were all artisans and mechanics and were given work in Montreal, Ottawa, and Kingston.[64] In 1865 Jorgensen published an enlightening pamphlet on *Emigration from Europe during the Present Century: Its Causes and Effects*, a large part of which was translated from Norwegian official reports and

[61] Buchanan's report, in *Sessional Papers,* 8 Parl., 2 Sess., vol. 23, no. 3, appendix no. 32 (1864).

[62] *Ibid.*

[63] Jorgensen's report on "Foreign Immigration," December 14, 1864, is addressed to Buchanan, the chief agent. *Sessional Papers,* 8 Parl., 3 Sess., vol. 24, no. 2, appendix no. 6 (1865).

[64] *Ibid.*

dealt with the migration from Norway.[65] That year the Scandinavian arrivals at Quebec dropped to 4,382. Jorgensen again suggested that the reasons why the immigrants did not remain in Canada were "principally the want of immediate employment, and there being no settlement of their countrymen in the Province." [66]

The failure of the Gaspé project was not soon forgotten in Norway. In 1867 the British-American Land Company, backed by the shipping firm of A. Sharpe and Company, offered to set aside twenty thousand acres of land in Canada for a Norwegian colony, selling it in fifty-acre lots at $2.50 an acre, requiring immigrants only to pay interest for the first three years and thereafter the capital in six installments. The company even promised to contribute two hundred dollars a year for three years to the salary of a minister and to give land for a church and a parsonage if as many as one hundred families joined the colony. But the proposal was quickly attacked in the Norwegian newspapers, which reminded readers that Canadian colonization by Norwegian groups had had no success, and incidentally warned emigrants against doing business with private land companies instead of with the Canadian government.[67]

The time was to come when large numbers of immigrants from the Scandinavian peninsula would join in the westward movement into the Canadian prairie provinces — but that time was still far in the future. Meanwhile the official Canadian efforts to attract immigrants in the early period seem generally to have been unsuccessful. Early Norwegian settlement in Canada was an interlude. The reasons for the

[65] The pamphlet (23 p.) was printed at Quebec. The writer has a photostat.

[66] Jorgensen's report, February 17, 1866, is in *Sessional Papers*, 8 Parl., 5 Sess., vol. 26, no. 2, appendix no. 5 (1866).

[67] *Morgenbladet*, February 4, 15, 1867. See a Canadian land advertisement in the same paper for October 2, 1865. Among Norwegian settlers in the West, Canadian colonization, after the Gaspé affair, was sometimes held up to ridicule. See "Ogsaa en amerikafarer," in *Drammens blad*, November 18, 1862, reprinted from *Emigranten*.

failure of the plans for Norwegian colonization in Canada were more fundamental than mismanagement or an unfortunate choice of land for a particular colony. An American scholar concludes that the "two chief difficulties against which Canada was struggling were the Canadian land system, which was less liberal than the American land system, and the attraction which the United States with its greater economic opportunities for labourers and capitalists had over the industrially backward country to the north." [68]

[68] See an admirable study by Paul W. Gates, "Official Encouragement to Immigration by the Province of Canada," in *Canadian Historical Review,* 15:37 (March, 1934). I am indebted to Professor Gates for calling my attention to various manuscript items in the Public Archives of Canada relating to Gaspé and Norwegian settlement in Canada. The more important of these materials I have had photostated.

XIII. THE ERA OF THE CIVIL WAR

NORWEGIAN IMMIGRANTS were aware of the friendly attitude of the West toward the colonization of its open lands by Europeans, for that attitude had been expressed in many ways during the 1850's. Nativism had been rampant in the East, especially during the early part of the decade, and there were traces of it in the western states, but in general these states opened their arms to foreigners and natives alike. In fact, Wisconsin and Minnesota, in the very period of nativistic squalls and storms in the East, embarked upon aggressive advertising schemes designed to attract to their respective areas as large a proportion as possible of the westward-moving crowds of immigrant and native land seekers. The frontier wanted and needed men to break sod, conquer prairie and forest, build roads, lay railroads, and raise up towns and cities; and it found ways of making its need known to the immigrants.

Early in 1852—the year after the Minnesota Indian land treaties served notice that a new stage was at hand in the history of white settlement in the Northwest—Wisconsin established the office of commissioner of emigration. Gysbert Van Steenwyck, the appointed commissioner, took up his duties in May and set about advertising Wisconsin among the incoming immigrants at New York. A Wisconsin pamphlet was brought out in various foreign-language editions, including the Norwegian; a Norwegian was employed in the agent's office to help in answering Scandinavian inquiries; advertisements were inserted in various American newspapers; and other avenues of exploitation were followed. The office was continued in 1853 under Herman Haertel, a German land agent of Milwaukee, who like his predecessor was shocked to learn of the numerous kinds of impositions that were practiced upon immigrants in New York by unscrupulous agents and runners. In 1854 a subagency was established at Quebec, the chief port of entry for Norwegians. The appointment as subagent of Elias Stangeland, who appears to have continued to act as an agent for the forwarding house of Maxwell and Patten, was looked upon with disfavor by many Norwegians in the West, however. Late in 1854 a writer in *Emigranten* declared that Wisconsin had lost hundreds of immigrant families to Minnesota and Iowa because Stangeland had thus continued his private agency.[1]

In 1855 Wisconsin gave up its official promotion of immigration; but Minnesota Territory, which was trumpeting in newspapers and other unofficial forms of printed matter its advantages for prospective settlers, took up the work in that year.[2] It sent a commissioner of emigration to New York, where for two years he represented the territory officially, advertised its resources, and gave practical aid to newly arrived immigrants. In the competition of these western areas for immigrants much attention was devoted to the question

[1] *Emigranten*, December 8, 1854.

[2] Blegen, "The Competition of the Northwestern States for Immigrants," in *Wisconsin Magazine of History*, 3:3–29 (September, 1919); Blegen and Livia Appel, "Official Encouragement of Immigration to Minnesota during the Territorial Period," in *Minnesota History Bulletin*, 5:167–203 (August, 1923).

of climate. The first agent sent by Minnesota to New York, for example, wrote, "Our high northern latitude particularly, has, in many instances, been made a bug bear to the emigrant and frightened him from risking his life among the alleged *mountains of ice* in this Territory." He even declared that "interested and officious parties" were guilty of misrepresenting the situation in Minnesota.[3] Iowa followed the example of its neighbors by establishing a similar office in 1860, which was retained for two years.[4] These efforts of the commonwealths of the Northwest are perhaps more important as revelations of point of view than as factors that played a notable influence upon the trend of settlement. They served as a public declaration by Wisconsin, Minnesota, and Iowa that these commonwealths were looking for immigrants to settle upon their lands, and the immigrants swarmed to the Northwest, glad of the welcoming hand extended to them and no doubt eager to apprise their friends and relatives in the old country of the cordial attitude that they encountered in the "Land of Canaan."

Norway, meanwhile, was increasingly conscious of the attractions of that Canaan. The highest point in the earlier Norwegian emigration was reached in 1861, the spring and summer when the American Civil War was in its opening phases. Disastrous crop failures in Norway in 1860, coupled with reports of improving economic conditions in the West and especially of the glories of the upper Northwest, help to explain a phenomenal rise in emigration from 1,900 in 1860 to 8,900 in 1861 — a figure higher by 2,500 than the previous peak in 1857. This large migration of 1861, curiously enough, does not figure in the United States immigration statistics for that year. According to the American official records, the total of both Norwegian and Swedish immigrants

[3] See the annual report of Eugene Burnand, in *Minnesota History Bulletin,* 5:194.

[4] Marcus L. Hansen, "Official Encouragement of Immigration to Iowa," in *Iowa Journal of History and Politics,* 19:159–195 (April, 1921).

in 1861 was 616, but the government statistics are perversely blind to the patent fact that nearly all of the 8,668 Scandinavians who landed from emigrant vessels in Quebec in 1861 passed on to the United States. It may safely be assumed that the official Norwegian emigration figure for 1861—8,900—is substantially correct.

That it was so high, notwithstanding the outbreak of civil war in America, is not difficult to understand. Early frosts in 1860 killed both the crops and the hopes of many Norwegians. The chief official of one county, commenting later on the effect of the failure of 1860, said that the farmers were caught in the grip of economic pressure, their powers stunned. In the great county of Kristian, crop failures were general in 1860, save in Faaberg and northern Gudbrandsdal. A general economic report on Norway for the period from 1861 to 1865 declares that agriculture, beginning with a disastrous year, had made less progress than in earlier periods, had in fact gone backward.[5] Commenting on the rise of emigration in 1861, a newspaper pointed out that the serious effects of the crop failures were now being felt and that people were emigrating despite the imminence of war in the United States. It admitted that the soil was poorly cultivated in Norway, but declared that in other countries where agriculture was no more scientific, the people were better off. "The primary fact," it concluded bitterly, "is that Norway lies north of the 58th degree and consists of large masses of rock." And so, though it clung to the belief that emigrating to the United States was like jumping from the frying pan into the fire, it did not blame the emigrants.[6]

The emigrants themselves did not seem to be afraid to make this dire "jump." In the history of American immigration it is customary to speak of the Civil War reaction,

[5] Sections on Akershus and Kristians *amt,* in *Beretning om rigets oeconomiske tilstand i aarene 1861–65,* vol. 1. See also vol. 2, p. i, ii, lx.

[6] *Morgenbladet,* March 6, 1861.

but the term is hardly applicable to the Scandinavian immigration. For the five years from 1860 to 1865, Norwegian immigration was higher by more than three thousand than in the gala period from 1851 to 1856; and Swedish emigration showed a gain each year from 1859 to 1865. Only one year, 1863, witnessed a marked decline in Norwegian emigration. As Kendric C. Babcock says, "The Civil War disturbed comparatively little the conditions favoring Scandinavian immigration, for the Northwest was never in danger of invasion, and nominal prices for farm products ranged higher and higher. Furthermore, the Homestead Act of 1862 gave new and cumulative impetus to the immigration which sought farming lands."[7] On the other hand, it is conjecturable that the great swelling of numbers that actually began in 1866 would have come sooner had there been no Civil War, especially with the new and potent magnet of free land and after the removal of the Indian menace on the frontier of the Northwest.

While Norwegian farmers were lamenting the poor harvest of 1860, the older forms of stimulation of the emigrant trade persisted, the propaganda for Gaspé and Canadian colonization as managed by Closter and Haugen was in full swing, and a new type of emigration advertising promotion was making itself felt in Norway. The Illinois Central, first of the land-grant railroads, had experimented tentatively in 1854 with the advertising of its lands in Norway and Sweden through a Scandinavian agent, Oscar Malmborg, a Swede by birth. His work had then been cut short by his recall to America, but in 1860 he was sent back to the Scandinavian countries, and this time, though he went for only a four-month stay, his campaign was prolonged and he continued on through the winter of 1860–61. Making the shipping firm of A. Sharpe and Company his headquarters in Christi-

[7] *Scandinavian Element,* 68.

ania, he traveled about the country to Bergen, Stavanger, and other places, distributed maps and circulars, offered credit for as long a period as six years on land purchases, held meetings, won some newspaper endorsement, and in the spring appeared at such ports as Bergen, Drammen, and Christiania to talk with prospective emigrants.[8] It was hoped that, as a result of his activities, large tracts of railroad land in eastern Illinois would be settled compactly by Scandinavians, but the president of the Illinois Central came to the conclusion that Malmborg's mission had been a failure, for few Swedes and Norwegians were drawn to the railroad's lands. The Norwegians, following the main immigrant routes, went to northern Illinois, Wisconsin, Iowa, and Minnesota. The Illinois Central later had some success in colonizing Swedish immigrants on its lands, but it seems to have attracted relatively few Norwegians. The significance of Malmborg's work lay principally in its foreshadowing of a kind of propaganda that became highly important in the period after the Civil War when, as Paul W. Gates points out, "Norway and Sweden as well as other northern European countries became literally honeycombed with a hierarchy of emigration agents maintained by Canadian provinces and American states, railroads, and steamship companies."[9]

Meanwhile the immigrants in America were confronting ordeal by battle. The Civil War marked a new step in the identification of the Norwegian immigrants with the fortunes and ideals of their adopted country. It solidified trends of opinion and politics that had emerged and become articulate

[8] An advertisement by Malmborg is in *Adressebladet* (Christiania) for September 29, 1860, and succeeding issues, and his circular is reprinted in that paper for February 9, 1861. *Almuevennen* endorsed Malmborg's work in its issue for September 29, 1860, making much of the fact that the agent had the approval of the Norwegian-Swedish consul in New York. Advertisements of the Illinois Central Railroad appeared frequently in *Emigranten;* see, for example, the issue for June 27, 1859.

[9] Gates, in *Studies and Records,* 6:88; the principal documents of the Malmborg mission are printed in the *Swedish-American Historical Bulletin,* 3:9–52 (June, 1930).

in the 1850's; and it bound the Norwegians, and indeed the Scandinavian-American group as a whole, to the Republican party with bonds that were not to be loosened until the economic discontents of western farmers of a later day took form in independent agrarian political protest. In a word, the Civil War, to the accompaniment of death and suffering and stern trial, made a contribution to the larger immigrant transition to American life. New and old, the Norwegian immigrants responded cheerfully and with enthusiasm to President Lincoln's call for volunteers when the war broke out. "At last the North has wakened from its slumber," wrote Hans Christian Heg, then state prison commissioner of Wisconsin, "cast all political differences to the winds, and all are as one in crying: 'To arms for the defense of the old Union, established by Washington.' Of the outcome there can be no doubt."[10] A newly arrived immigrant in 1861 wrote, "Many of the young men who came on the 'Flora' have already enlisted in the war."[11] These notes are typical of the immigrant feeling about the war.

It has been estimated that at least eight hundred Norwegians in Minnesota, over four hundred in Iowa, approximately three thousand in Wisconsin, and proportionate numbers from the old Norwegian settlements in Illinois joined the colors.[12] It is difficult to gauge the totals with exactness. One Scandinavian-American historian believes that one in every six Norwegians in the northwestern states served in the Civil War; another has placed the total between six and seven thousand, including four thousand from Wisconsin.[13] These

[10] Heg's letter, sent to Norway, is quoted in *Stavanger amtstidende og adresseavis*, July 15, 1861.

[11] *Stavanger amtstidende og adresseavis*, April 7, 1862.

[12] Babcock, *Scandinavian Element*, 77; Nelson, *Scandinavians in the United States*, 1:303, 304; 2:66–68, 119–121. The figures for Minnesota and Iowa are from reports of the adjutant generals of those states; that for Wisconsin is Nelson's estimate, based upon the "original and unpublished records of the adjutant-general" of that state.

[13] Nelson, *Scandinavians in the United States*, 1:304; Waldemar Ager, in Nordahl Rolfsen, ed., *Norge i Amerika*, 399 ff. (Christiania, 1915).

figures appear to be based primarily upon studies of names rather than upon dependable statistics of national origin; and it is not impossible that some of the estimates have been colored by filiopietism. There can be no doubt, however, that, as the American historian Babcock says, many hundreds of Scandinavians "gave their strength and their lives for the unity and safety of their adopted country no less bravely and no less cheerfully than did the native-born American."[14] For the most part they served in the ranks, but some rose to regimental commands, notably Colonel Porter C. Olson, the son of one of the sloopers of 1825, who raised a company made up chiefly of Norwegians from the Fox River colony in Illinois, led it to the war as a captain, rose to the command of the Thirty-sixth Illinois Volunteer Infantry, and was killed in action at the battle of Franklin;[15] and Colonel Hans Christian Heg, who commanded Wisconsin's "Norwegian regiment" and led a brigade at Chickamauga.

This regiment, the Fifteenth Wisconsin, has been regarded by the Norwegian immigrants and their descendants as a symbol of the patriotism of the Norwegian Americans; and its achievements have been celebrated and remembered in Norway as well as among Norwegian Americans. It originated soon after the war began. This was an era when the loyalty of various immigrant groups was not infrequently expressed through the organization of entire regiments made up of immigrants of given nationalities. The Ninth Wisconsin, for example, was mainly German and the Eleventh, Irish. And so the Scandinavians launched a movement for a regiment of their own, asked the governor of Wisconsin to commission Heg as its colonel, and in the fall of 1861 set about recruiting soldiers, with the Norwegian paper *Emigranten* taking the lead in forwarding the cause. Heg and nine other Scandinavians called upon their countrymen late in Septem-

[14] *Scandinavian Element,* 75.
[15] Anderson, *First Chapter,* 113–127.

ber to come to the support of the proposed regiment, emphasizing the unique opportunity that it presented to the Scandinavians of the West to serve in the army under officers and with comrades who used their own speech; and appealing to their national pride by declaring that the Scandinavians could not allow themselves to be outmatched in patriotism by the Irish and Germans.[16] Heg himself was the chief recruiting officer. He visited settlements in Wisconsin, Iowa, Minnesota, and Illinois, calling for the enlistment of a thousand Scandinavians. Never had there been a better opportunity for young men, he declared, "to fight for a noble cause, to win an honored name and proud memories for the future, and an experience that could not be had elsewhere." He invoked their ancient traditions: "Come, then, young Norsemen, and take part in defending our country's cause, and thus fulfill a pressing duty which everyone who is able to do so owes to the land in which he lives. Let us band together and deliver untarnished to posterity the old honorable name of Norsemen."[17]

The appeals were successful. The regiment was brought together at Camp Randall in Madison, built up to a total membership of approximately nine hundred, and on March 2, 1862, left for the South. The pioneer minister, C. L. Clausen, served as its chaplain; Dr. S. O. Himoe, a Kansas Norwegian, was its surgeon. The men, drawn generally from the Scandinavian settlements of the Northwest, included some Swedes, Danes, and native Americans, but they were preponderantly Norwegians, who tagged their companies with such salty names as the Wergeland Guards, Odin's Rifles, the Norway Bear Hunters, the St. Olaf Rifles, the Scandinavian Mountaineers, and Clausen's Guards. Olsens, Johnsons, Petersons, and Hansens were numerous, and in

[16] *Emigranten,* September 30, 1861.
[17] *Emigranten,* November 18, 1861. See also the issues for October 7 and 14.

the regiment as a whole there were 128 men who bore the first name of "Ole."

So the Fifteenth Wisconsin went to the war. It participated in the Union movements in Missouri, Kentucky, Mississippi, Tennessee, Alabama, and Georgia. It fought at Island No. 10, Perryville, Murfreesboro, Chickamauga, Chattanooga, Resaca, New Hope Church, Kenesaw Mountain, and other places. It lost eighty-five in dead and wounded at Murfreesboro; was nearly torn to pieces at Chickamauga, where Colonel Heg himself was killed; but it managed to retain its identity and was later commanded by Lieutenant Colonel Ole C. Johnson, who had been taken prisoner at Chickamauga but escaped from Libby Prison and rejoined the regiment. Finally, after the march to Atlanta, the Fifteenth was mustered out early in 1865 at Chattanooga, a thin remnant of the regiment that had left Madison in 1862. An even one-third of its men had been killed in battle or died in hospitals from wounds and sickness.

Colonel Heg, whose career was cut short at Chickamauga, became the war hero of the Norwegians, the personal symbol of their contribution to the preservation of the Union, and heroic bronze statues of him stand at the state capitol of Wisconsin, in the Muskego community where his people had settled in 1840 as charter members "of the new Scandinavian-American civilization which was growing up in Wisconsin prior to the Civil War," and in Norway at Lier, from which the Hegs had originally come.[18] An American historian has suggested that Colonel Heg was a potential Norwegian Carl

[18] On the Fifteenth Wisconsin and Colonel Heg, see Blegen, *Colonel Heg;* Waldemar Ager, *Oberst Heg og hans gutter* (Eau Claire, Wisconsin, 1916); and the numerous bibliographical references listed in the first of these works. The quoted phrase is from Joseph Schafer, "Hans Christian Heg," in *Wisconsin Blue Book,* 1933, p. 37, 38. Norway followed with great interest the Civil War achievements of the Norwegian Americans, and its press had many stories about the Fifteenth Wisconsin. Norwegian soldiers also reported such phases of the war as the battle of the "Monitor" and the "Merrimac" and the fluctuations of the Peninsular campaign. See, for example, *Morgenbladet,* May 27, July 24, 25, 1862; January 3, 1863.

FÆDRELANDET

Et uafhängigt Unionsblad for "Ret og Sandhed."

No. 29. | La Crosse, Wisconsin, Thorsdag den 25de August 1864. | 1ste Aargang.

"Fädrelandet" udgaar hver Thorsdag. Bladet koster 2 Dollars Aargangen. 1 Dollar for 6 Maaneder og en halv Dollar for 3 Maaneder.

Betales en hel Aargang forskudsvis koster den 1½ Dollar.

Kirkelige Avertissementer, Ægteviel- ser og Dödsfald optages uden Betaling.

Adresse: "Fädrelandets" Office.
La Crosse, Wisconsin.

Oberst
Hans C. Heg.

Bland er Nordens stolte Sön,
Blaa hans Öies Flamme;
Blade skyder evig grön
Odins gamle Stamme.
Hil dig, Nord med Kraftens Börn!
Med dit Ord det Rige!
Gid din Aand som frie Örn
Stolt mod Lyset stige!

Klar og klangfuld Stemmen er
Paa de norske Fjelde,
Som Naturens Farve der
Skjön med al dens Välde.
Sölvermalm i dyben Grund
Gjemmer stendägt Ager;
Men dets Klang i Nordmands Mund
Herlig sig gjentager!

Hans Heg var Nordmand. Hans Livslöb fra den förste Udflugt fra Fädrenehjemmet til Amerika, hans Anerkjendelse som brav Borger i dette Land i Fredens Dage — alt dette er allerede saa ofte bleven behandlet i Lidsskrifter og Aviser, at vi ikke gjorde vore Läsere nogen synderlig Tjeneste ved her at fremstille disse Dele af Hegs Liv.

Det var Hegs Opträden som som sit adopterede Fädrelands Forsvarer, der udödeliggjorde hans Navn for Alle. Men vi Nordmänd nävner ogsaa hans Navn med Kjärlighed og Taknemmelighed; thi Heg arbeider derhen, at den Glorie, som

Det Femtende Wisconsin Regiment har paataget sig en ansvarsfuld Opgave; men til Dato har det löst den hederligt. Vor Del af Krigshistorien hänger ved det Femtende Wisconsin, og idet vi har dets förste Kommandör Hans Hegs Henfald i Tankerne, vil vi benytte Leiligheden til baade paa Nutidens og Fremtidens Vegne at takke det Femtende Wisconsins brave Officerer og Soldater, fordi de har givet Nordmändene i Amerika en Krigshistorie, og det en häderlig Krigshistorie.

Heg faldt i det blodige Slag ved Chickamauga i Tennessee den 19de og 20de September 1863. Han kommanderede da som Brigadegeneral, og han faldt i Spidsen for sin Brigade, fordi han og hans Nordmänd ikke vilde vige, naar de var befalet at staa; og det er ikke den eneste Gang, at Femtende Wisconsin har lidt frygtelige Tab fordi det löd Pligtens og Ærens Stemme istedetfor Klogskabens.

En stor Del af Brigaden faldt. Ja vi kan gjerne sige, at der fulgte Störsteparten af Nordmändene deres Brigadegeneral Heg i Döden.

Mangen en Moder og Söster har grädt og gräder over Slägts og Venners Blod, som der flöd; men lad det väre en Tröst, at Nordmänd i Amerika og Norge aldrig vil glemme, hvad de skylder Heg og hans faldne Brigades Minde.

Naar Femtende Wisconsins Soldater engang vender tilbage til sine Hjemsteder, saa vil mangen en Kjär savnes. Men han har nydt den störste Ære. Han kunde ikke komme tilbage til Slägt og Venner:

"Thi han er gaaet til Hegs Brigade."

uden at regne, at vore Interesser vare saare forskjellige, bidroge ogsaa andre Omständigheder til at fjerne os fra hinanden. Vi vare begge forsynede med Anbefalingsbreve til Familier, der bevägede sig i forskjellige Kredse, men B.s Bekjendte hörte til Ludvig Philips Parti, medens min Moders gamle Veninde, Marquisen af O., indförte mig hos lutter Tilhängere af det fordrevne bourbonske Dynasti. Nu var det mig vistnok temmelig ligegyldigt enten den äldre eller den yngre Gren af Bourbonnerne herskede i Tuillerierne, og udstedte Indbydelseskort til Hoffesterne der, og jeg havde ringe Haab om, at Carl den Tiende vilde blive tilbagekaldt, men jeg kom til at holde af den gamle Marquise, og stiftede i hendes Hus Bekjendtskab med Folk, hvis politiske Meninger vare saare forskjellige fra min Medreisendes Venners. Vi havde opholdt os i Paris i tre Uger, og skjönt vi boede i samme Hotel, havde jeg ikke seet B. paa nogle Tage, da vi tilfältigvis möttes paa Trappen.

"Vi blive aldeles fremmede for hinanden. Hvor gaar Du hen?"

"Til Madame O."

"Hvad? Du vanker fremdeles hos den legitimistiske Marquise? Skulle vi ikke spise Middag sammen?"

"Hjertelig gjerne. Möd mig her Kl. 6."

B. lovede det, og saaledes skiltes vi. Klokken var omtrent 3.

Det var meget varmt i Paris den Dag. Stenbygningerne vare gjennemhedede af Solen, og de brändende Straaler syntes at fortörre alt muligt. Brostenene föltes varme under Skosaalerne. Jeg gik ind i Tuilleriernes Have for uu-

Nordmanden Hans Heg,

OBERST I FEMTENDE WIS. REGIMENT.

vanskeligt for mig at beskrive min Tilstand. Jeg fölte mig, som om Livet lidt efter lidt gled fraväk mig, og Livskraften svandt hen indtil der tilsidst blot var en liden Gnist tilbage. Jeg var dog fremdeles i Live, thi jeg havde min fulde Be-

Lad mig vide, om Du staar paa en fortrolig Fod med din Livjäger, og om I have agtet at väre i Fölge den hele Tid." Alle disse Tanker for mig gjennem Hovet i nogle faa Sekunder. Jeg vidste, at jeg maatte väre geraadet i etslags

lagde Haanden paa mit Bryst og holdt den der en Stund.

"Hans Hjerte slaar ikke länger."

"Föl hans Puls—"

"Jeg kan ikke märke den svageste Banken. Han ser ud til at väre stendöd."

Personer i näste Värelse samtalte om min Tilstand; jeg kunde ikke skjelne Ordene, men snart blev Stemmerne tydeligere og de Talende kom aabenbart närmere. Det Kläde, som bedäkkede mit Ansigt blev trukket tilside og jeg fik Öie paa de Konstabler, som havde baaret mig ud af Haven tilligemed nogle Andre. Der saa jeg ogsaa den brune Mand fra Haven; det var utvivlsomt den selvsamme Person; jeg fölte mig overbevist om, at han var Doktor og glädede mig til at han vilde oplyse disse taabelige Mennesker om, at jeg ingenlunde var död.

"Han er allerede ganske stiv. Det hender ikke sjelden, at Folk, som lide af visse Hjertesygdomme faa en saa pludselig Död. Jeg er tilböielig til at tro, at at han har väret död over en Time, altsaa längere end I sige. Jeg spadserede selv der i Eftermiddag. Og hverken Navn eller Adresse? Det er da besynderligt. Hvad, er Klokken allerede sex! Og jeg som skal i Middagsselskab om et Kvarter! Stakkels unge Menneske! Luk hans Öine, Ludvig; de se aldeles levende ud. De tillader mig vel, mine Herrer at ende Skjönsforretningen strax og indföre min Erklaring i Protokollen? Kom lader os gaa."

Af Lägehjälp havde jeg nu ikke mere at haabe. Derpaa sagde en af de Tilstedeväerende i en bydende Tone: "Lad ham strax bringe derhen, Ludvig." Döeren lukkedes, og Alt var tyst.

Jeg begyndte nu at faa Öinene op for det rädselsfulde i min Stilling. Höitideligen erkläret for död, gjennemgik jeg den voldsomme indre Kamp, som vel er uundgaaelig, naar et sundt og friskt Menneske med et lösrives fra Livet og ser sig

bleven erkläret död af Doktor og Övrigheden; Hvad kunde det väre? Jeg fölte plumpe Greb i mine Arme og Been. Man trak Kläderne af mig; vilde man lägge mig i Ligkisten? Jeg antog nu at alt Haab om at vende tilbage til Livet var forbi, og fölte mig trät og ör. Mine Sandser begyndte at slöves, og dette gjorte, at jeg led meget mindre, end Tilfäldet ellers vilde väret. Jeg laa fremdeles i stille Forventning, opfattede Alt, som foregik omkring mig, forsaavidt min Mangel paa Synsevne tillod mig det og undrede paa, hvad der videre vilde ske. Man afförte mig alle mine Kläder og bar mig ind i et andet Rum, hvorfra en eiendommelig og kvälende Stank strömmede mig imöde. Jeg blev lagt paa Ryggen paa et haart Leie, saaledes at Hovedet laa lidt höiere end Födderne. En ubeskrivelig Rädsel greb mig. Blev jeg lagt i Graven? Jeg var i nogen Tid uvis, men Intet blev lagt over mig undtagen et Kläde, som bedäkkede mine Länder. Maaske man havde lagt mig i en Kiste, for imorgen at begrave mig paa de Fattiges Kirkegaard. Barmhjertige Forsyn, hvor vilde jeg väre, naar jeg vaagnede til Livet igjen!

Nei, jeg kunde alligevel ikke ligge i en Ligkiste. Pludselig begreb jeg, hvor jeg befandt mig. Jeg var paa La Morgue. La Morgue er en Bygning, hvori findes et stort Värelse, som paa Midten er afdelt af en hel Glasväg. Paa den ene Side af Glasväggen ligger lange Stenheller i en heldende Stilling ud fra Väggen. Paa Hellerne lägges Lig af Forulykkede, som paa en unaturlig Maade er kommen afdage, og hvis Navn eller Opholdssted man ikke kan komme efter i

den Dag. Min Blindhed og Hjälpeløshed var paa en hvis Maade til Held for mig; jeg antog, at det nästen vilde träde mig at tilbringe en hel Nat indespärret paa et saadant Sted i sund, frisk Tilstand. Bedre, langt bedre var det at väre slöv og afmägtig. Hvis jeg blot kunde falde isövn og tabe den Smule Bevisthed, som jeg havde tilbage!

Martret af Angst og pinlige Betragtninger laa jeg efter min Beregning mange Timer paa mit haarde kolde Leie. Snart maatte vel Dagen bryde frem. Hvad vilde den bringe?

Pludselig for en sälsom Gysen gjennem mit hele Legeme. Blodet strömmede mig voldsomt til Hovedet, og mine Lemmer zittrede som i Krampe. Var Anfaldet nu när ved at gaa over, og vilde jeg paany blive istand til at röre mig og tale? Jeg önskede neppe at dette skulde ske endnu. Jeg fölte en voldsom Smerte i Hovedet; instinktmässigt vilde jeg löfte Haanden for at knuge den mod min Pande; Armen hävedes; jeg havde nu gjenvundet mine Lemmers Brug.

Skjönt jeg fölede mig beroliget ved at märke at jeg ikke längere var tryllebunden, dvälede jeg ved at forsöge paa at röre mig. Jeg holdt fremdeles mine Öine lukkede, og tog ikke Haanden väk fra Panden. Derpaa besluttede jeg at anspende alle mine Kräfter for at komme väk. Jeg prövede, om jeg havde gjenvundet Brugen af min Stemme, udstödte först en uartikuleret Lyd og udtalte derpaa nogle Ord, löftede den anden Arm, og derpaa et af mine Ben iveiret. Smerten i Hovedet var aftaget, og den krampagtige Skjälven aldeles ophört, men jeg fölte en underlig Trätthed og Ulyst til at

A CIVIL WAR NEWSPAPER, WITH AN ARTICLE ABOUT COLONEL HEG

[From *Fædrelandet* (La Crosse), August 25, 1864.]

Schurz,[19] but it seems somewhat doubtful that he warrants such an appraisal. He was a young, zestful, confident, ambitious, forceful leader who grew in powers as experience taught him the realities of war. He won the devotion of his soldiers, and one of his captains said after his death, "We miss him in our regiment, for he was more than a friend to us all. The influence he exerted among us will long be felt. Our hearts are crowded with sorrow." He had particularly impressed his soldiers by his personal bravery and by his "power to dispel gloom and sorrow." He was the leader of a brigade at the time of his death, and his commanding general said that, had he lived, he would have received the formal rank of brigadier general. A man of distinct promise he was, and withal very human, as his recently published private correspondence shows, deeply interested in every detail of the situation at home while in the thick of his campaigns, never losing his contact with Muskego and Wisconsin and the Norwegian Americans. "The 'Gen.' will call and see you the first thing you know—probably surprise you," he wrote in his last letter to Mrs. Heg the day before he rode to his death at Chickamauga. He was a symbol of the patriotism and the ambitions of his countrymen in the West, even if he did not, in the brief span of his life, disclose promise of the intellectual powers and broad-ranging interests of a Carl Schurz.

What the Civil War meant to Colonel Heg's soldiers may be suggested by drawing upon some of their letters, diaries, and recollections. Bersven Nelson, an immigrant who arrived in Wisconsin in the summer of 1861, explains how he happened to go to war. After helping to put up a "handsome log house constructed in Norwegian fashion," he worked in a sawmill for a few weeks and then met a sergeant who was recruiting soldiers for the Fifteenth. This officer told him about Colonel Heg's regiment and discussed the war be-

[19] Charles R. Wilson, in *Journal of Southern History*, 2:540 (November, 1936).

tween the North and the South, which he believed would not last long. "Yes," says Nelson, "and then there was a bounty of a hundred dollars, and thirteen dollars a month, free clothes and free food. This seemed very good to me, and furthermore I would have an opportunity to travel and to see a great deal." So he enlisted. He tells of the training at Camp Randall in Madison, where on Sundays there was an interlude: "On Sundays we marched up into town to the church. The minister there, Pastor Preus, preached to us." On March 2, with his regiment, he marched to the Madison station, where "a tremendous number of Norwegians had met to say good-by to husbands, sons, brothers, and sweethearts. When the train started, there was a waving of hats and handkerchiefs." Nelson did not come back to Wisconsin until 1865, a seasoned veteran who had had ample opportunity to travel—and to fight.[20]

Nils J. Gilbert, in a letter to his mother, describes a special event on Island No. 10: "I will also report to you that we held a 'fest' here on the 17th of May in honor of Norway's freedom, which we celebrated very joyously, for we sent to Cairo, Illinois, for beer and our company got a barrel and a half and the other companies also got some. At first, in the morning, we discharged thirteen cannon shots as a salute to the day just as the sun came up. Later we had a parade. When we got back from that we drank freely and happily."[21] War was not just a parade, however, and not many months later Gilbert was writing from a hospital to report that he had been wounded: "I have survived the great battle of Murfreesboro and was wounded, but I thank God that it is no worse than it is and that I have hopes of regaining my health." He had found himself lying on the battlefield, bleeding badly. "After a while I recovered strength sufficiently to lift myself up, and, between the two lines, I hopped on one

[20] Ager, *Oberst Heg,* 15–61.
[21] Ager, *Oberst Heg,* 78.

leg toward ours." He soon was able to return to duty and was promoted to the rank of sergeant. Less fortunate than himself, he explained, was Svend Borgarsen, also wounded at Murfreesboro, "who had his leg amputated above the knee."[22]

Lars O. Dokken, writing to his relatives from Camp Lyon, Bird's Point, in the spring of 1862, told of the capture of New Madrid and Island No. 10, but confessed that he knew little about the progress of the war. "I believe," he said, "that you learn much more about the war than we do, except for events in our neighborhood, for you get *Emigranten* before we do." There was much sickness among the troops, and on one occasion Dokken exclaimed, "May God strengthen all the sick and suffering both at home and here in the land of the enemy." He took note of problems of discipline. One of the Norwegian boys went to sleep at his post, and Dokken was afraid that this would mean the death penalty for him. Another soldier failed to clean his tent: "He was hung up by the hands for a short time — as long as they thought he could stand it. We have to do what our officers command us to do or else we are punished." After long marches he wrote, "Sometimes we get a little coffee and sometimes not, and it is pretty hard to stand it with such food and such marching." The common soldier had an unending interest in prices, and Dokken noted sorrowfully, in camp near Nashville, that "A pound of butter now costs seventy-five cents and a pound of tobacco $1.50." At Murfreesboro he was badly wounded. "I remained lying on the ground and the rebels came about me from all sides, and one swore and said, 'Here is a damn Yankee.' I lay still; but they had to have something from me and so they took my coat and my water bottle and a red hide-covered notebook in which I kept all the letters I had received from you. They took also a little packet in which I had needle and thread and other small

[22] Gilbert's interesting letters are printed in Ager, *Oberst Heg*, 74–101.

things; and then they took my double Explanation from me, and that I miss most." But, he wrote later, "That time I was wounded and lay out during the night, I suffered no harm, for the rebels made up a fire for me so that I was warm both at night and in the day." He bore his sufferings bravely: "It is hard to be kept in bed for so long a time, but I must be patient, and God will help me, for He will not lay heavier burdens upon me than I can carry with patience."[23] Not many days after that he died.

"Everybody in the company gets letters except myself," complained John Thoe from Island No. 10. From Humboldt, Tennessee, he wrote, "In this town most of the people have been rebels; but now they are Union people, for they don't dare to oppose the Union troops." Writing after the battle of Perryville, he said that he had "had an opportunity to see the rebels since he last wrote." At the end of his letter: "I see by your letter that the Indians are restless in northwestern Minnesota and Iowa, which is sad to hear." A little later: "It was extremely pleasant to receive the letter from Norway. It is so long since I have heard from them." After Chickamauga, Thoe remarked, "I have now been in three great battles, but this was the hardest one. God be praised and thanked! He held His hand over me, as He always has done, so that I came unharmed out of this." He participated in the Georgia march and fell at New Hope Church.[24]

"All the Negroes are running away from their masters and coming to our camp, where they can be safe and beyond the range of the cat-o'-nine-tails," wrote one soldier.[25] Another sent a solemn letter from Murfreesboro to a young brother: "You are now at an age in which, for better or worse, one

[23] Dokken's letters, running from March 8, 1862, to March 16, 1863, are in Ager, 101–120.

[24] John Thoe's letters, from April 21, 1862, to May 22, 1864, are in Ager, 127–136.

[25] Thomas Emerson, from Island No. 10, May 25, 1862, in Ager, 140.

establishes habits that last for life. Therefore I recommend that you use all your time to broaden your understanding. You must remember that you now have three brothers in the army and you alone remain behind with our dear sister, which is a big responsibility. You must remember that war is a very risky business."[26] How risky it was Knud Knudsen Stjernes could testify, for after Murfreesboro he wrote, "The battle began on the 31st of December, New Year's Eve, and lasted six days, but I was wounded on the first day of the fight, and I got a bullet in my right arm and one through the calf of my left leg, and I have one in my back just under the shoulder blade, which has grown in, and one in my hip which has grown in, and another through my hip which came out again, and one I got in my right side and the bullet came out through my stomach on the upper side of the navel." He spent five months in a hospital, then wrote a letter in which he said that he was well and ready for work, though he had three bullets left in him. His letter, printed in Norway, occasioned an editorial comment that the outlook for the Confederates was not good if they had to spend so many bullets on one Union soldier and even then failed to do away with him.[27]

Morten J. Nordre, advancing with Sherman, records in his diary a succession of fights, and occasionally comments on the weather. "It is frightfully hot today," he wrote on June 28, 1864. "We are keeping ourselves in some holes which we have dug in the ground to protect ourselves from the rebel sharpshooters. But it is so hot in these holes that it almost kills us." On July 1 he sounds a philosophic note: "Though we have entered upon a new month, our business with reference to the war is the same as before." On July 4: "This day is a great day in all the United States. But we

[26] Sergeant Albert Emerson, May 18, 1863, in Ager, 144. His phrase, in the original, reads as follows: "Du maa huske, at Krig er en meget risikabel Forretning."

[27] *Stavanger amtstidende og adresseavis,* December 14, 1863.

had to get up and eat breakfast at four and prepare for an attack on the rebels." A joyful entry occurs on July 25: "Colonel Ole C. Johnson, who has escaped from Dixie, came to us today." Nordre on one occasion paid a tribute: "I must admit that the ladies of the South are fine and brave women. Whole flocks of them go among the rebel soldiers even in the worst hail of bullets, where they are in danger of losing their lives every minute." [28]

To Captain Hans Hanson the outlook seemed dark and discouraging early in 1863: "For my part I am tired of the whole business and I look with longing eyes to the day when peace shall be declared — not the kind of peace which the so-called Peace Democrats want, but peace won by our armies, which I believe will be the only lasting peace." "War is like a thunderstorm which will clear the air of dangerous mists," wrote another officer on May 30, 1863, to relatives in Norway. He was aware of the sympathy for the South in England and France and believed that it was based upon cotton and a monarchic suspicion of American free institutions. But to him the freeing of the slaves and the preservation of "the best form of government on earth," both for the present and for future generations, were the great things. The North would win the war, he prophesied, but at a vast cost in human blood and treasure.[29]

Not a few of the soldiers were taken prisoners and knew the terrors of Andersonville and other southern prisons. Ole Steensland fought in the battle of Chickamauga, saw Ole Milesten die on his right and Chris Thompson on his left. "I got a bullet through my hat," he said later, "and that did no harm; but I was taken prisoner, and that was something that did hurt." Forty-three men of his regiment died at Andersonville, but he survived. "Scurvy and diarrhea," he

[28] Selections from Nordre's diary are in Ager, 154–159.

[29] Captain Hanson's letter, written from Murfreesboro on February 28, 1863, is in Ager, 164. See also a letter of Lieutenant Ole Rasmussen, in Olaf Yderstad, "Et amerikabrev fra 1863," in Nordmør historielag, *Årskrift*, 1931, p. 30–32.

said, "took the lives of most of the boys. I had scurvy very badly and nearly lost my life. My teeth were so loose and my gums so sore that I could see blood on the hard bread for each bite I took. My feet were so swollen that I could hardly walk. If I had given up and quit trying, as so many others did, I should have yielded up the ghost like them; but I hobbled around and vowed that they would not get my life if I could prevent it."[30]

In the immigrant home communities, while Heg and his comrades were at the war, women took up men's duties, ran farms, attended to the business and financial affairs entrusted to their care, pored over the reports in *Emigranten* from its editor, C. F. Solberg, who accompanied the regiment to the South as a war correspondent, and treasured the letters that came in an increasing stream from homesick soldiers at the front. They found time, also, to organize soldiers' aid societies, which forwarded bandages and supplies for wounded and sick soldiers as well as gifts of clothing and food for those on active duty — gifts that gave intense gratification to the recipients. One of these organizations that devoted its particular attention to the Fifteenth Wisconsin was the Soldiers' Aid Society in Norway and Raymond townships, in Colonel Heg's own community. Acknowledging gifts from this organization, Heg on one occasion wrote that the kindness of the givers "speaks to the heart of every soldier in the Army." He predicted victory. "Our army is bound to crush this terrible rebellion," he said, "if the people of the North will only stand by the army, and by all their power encourage the soldiers."[31]

That the immigrants who remained at home did in fact stand by the army is amply evidenced by the reports and editorials in the Norwegian-American press of the time.

[30] Steensland lived to tell the story of his imprisonment at a regimental reunion in 1900. Ager, *Oberst Heg*, 166–181.

[31] Blegen, *Colonel Heg*, 32, 219.

When the war election of 1864 occurred, *Emigranten* advocated the re-election of Lincoln, but did so without undue partisanship. "We have attempted to keep out all bitterness and bickering," it announced after the election, "maintaining instead a proper decorum and adhering to the truth as far as we are able to discern it through the haze of misrepresentation and falsehood with which party interests have enveloped it. We have endeavored to be temperate in our attitude — a course which we considered best suited for our time, when party controversies may so easily and so dangerously inflame the temper of the people." As to its central stand, it said, "We have supported the re-election of Lincoln because, in our opinion, the policies he advocated were the most beneficial to the future welfare of the Union."[32] Less temperate was Knud Langeland, who in a communication to *Emigranten* said, "The old folks, I believe, have an adage to the effect that 'Those whom the gods wish to destroy, they first make mad.' If God has determined to destroy us, the only thing He now needs to do is to make us mad enough to elect General McClellan for our next president." Urging Lincoln's re-election, he added, "I prefer to die with the conviction that I have not been unfaithful in time of distress to the oath of allegiance I made my adopted country."[33]

Throughout the Civil War years *Emigranten* maintained its position as the leading Norwegian-American newspaper, but it was not without a rival. The *Skandinavisk post,* established in New York late in 1863 and edited by the Swedish-American Gustav Öbom, was another attempt to conduct a general Scandinavian newspaper. It devoted itself mainly to matters of local interest to the growing Scandinavian element in New York and Brooklyn, and it had no noticeable influence in the West.[34] More important was

[32] *Emigranten,* November 16, 1864.
[33] *Emigranten,* October 22, 1864.
[34] Hansen, in *Norsk-amerikanernes festskrift,* 31, 32.

Fædrelandet ("The Fatherland") of La Crosse, established early in 1864 by Frederick Fleischer and Johan Schrøder. This paper was destined ultimately to absorb *Emigranten* and it marked a natural step northwestward in the development of the Norwegian-American press. Fleischer was the son of a Norwegian clergyman. He had enjoyed a good education in Norway, studied law, dug gold in California, been a sailor on the Great Lakes, and taught school in southern Wisconsin. "This is an independent Union paper, for truth and justice," he said in his first issue, and "at the present time for the policies of Abraham Lincoln and nothing else."[35] In the campaign of 1864 *Fædrelandet* declared that the "main current" favored Lincoln and that if his policies were not carried out, American life and greatness would become a thing of the past. "Therefore, countrymen, keep abreast of the times, and do not be deceived, either through ignorance or by turn-coats and pettifoggers who are interested in your votes not for the sake of McClellan but in order that they themselves may secure political plums."[36] Perhaps the asperity of this appeal was induced by the activities of a Norwegian Democrat, B. A. Frøiseth of St. Paul, who on behalf of the Democratic party issued a broadside (in an edition of forty thousand copies) to the Scandinavian voters of Minnesota, Iowa, Wisconsin, and Illinois, calling upon them to vote for McClellan as a "champion of freedom and justice." In impressing upon the Scandinavian voters the importance of their vote, Frøiseth made the interesting statement that they held the balance of power in the Northwest between the two great parties. There is no evidence, however, that this Democratic appeal had any appreciable influence among the Scandinavian-American voters.[37]

[35] *Fædrelandet,* January 14, 1864; Wist, in *Norsk-amerikanernes festskrift,* 42, 43. Fleischer was a cousin of the former editor of *Emigranten,* Knud J. Fleischer.

[36] *Fædrelandet,* October 27, 1864.

[37] Hansen, in *Norsk-amerikanernes festskrift,* 35.

The reading matter that the Norwegian-American newspapers carried to homes throughout the Northwest was by no means limited to the war and national politics. For one thing, *Emigranten* devoted column after column to a diverting, if little understood, controversy on the momentous question whether slavery was a sin or not, with a phalanx of Synod ministers stoutly upholding the negative.[38] There was a stir of interest when in 1862 and again in 1863 and 1864 the Norwegian bark "Sleipnir" docked at Chicago, direct from Bergen, with large parties of emigrants and with Norwegian goods consigned to a Norwegian-American firm in Chicago, taking for the return voyage cargoes of flour, wheat, corn, and other articles. This exploit seemed to open new possibilities in trade relations between Norway and the Midwestern metropolis. The captain of the "Sleipnir" in 1863 undertook to guide his party of emigrants to the Mississippi and thence northward to Iowa, Wisconsin, and Minnesota.[39]

Emigranten kept a sharp eye on the scattered Norwegian settlements in Minnesota, Iowa, and other areas. It found room for a lengthy communication from a Norwegian at Virginia City, telling of the Idaho gold mines; and for an account of Norwegian farmers in Meeker County, Minnesota.[40] It glanced at the newly organized Dakota Territory, where, it was pleased to note, three Norwegians were serving as members of the territorial legislature. It was always interested in evidence that the immigrants were acquiring

[38] For a full discussion of this controversy see chapter 14.

[39] There was also keen interest in Norway in this trade contact between Bergen and Chicago. *Morgenbladet* for November 8, 1862, has a lengthy article on the exploit of the "Sleipnir," quoting at length from the Montreal *Daily Witness* for October 7. The 1863 trip is recorded in *Stavanger amtstidende og adresseavis,* August 17, 27, 1863. The "Sleipnir" was sixty-three feet in length, forty-five tons, and had a six-man crew. The voyage from Bergen to Chicago in 1863 took ninety-six days.

[40] See a letter written at Virginia City by Chr. Northfos, in *Emigranten,* January 16, 1865. The Meeker County settlement is described in the issue for April 18, 1864.

training in the fundamentals of American local government. It took note in 1864, for example, of a northern Wisconsin county which boasted a Johnson as sheriff, a Larson as county attorney, a Jensen as surveyor, an Anderson as county clerk, another Anderson as register of deeds, and an Ole Aslakson as county superintendent of schools, leaving only one county office, that of coroner, to be occupied by a non-Scandinavian.[41] There were long articles on agriculture — crops, stock, and current problems. Now and then the puritan note was sounded in articles on the evils of tobacco or liquor and the advance of the temperance cause in Norway and America. The advertisements, ranging from such items as Manny's reaper and mower to patent medicines that promised cures for nearly all earthly ailments, were not without interest. *Emigranten* found place for a list of nearly a hundred different books available at Ole Monsen's "Norske Boghandel" in Madison and for a notice of a similar establishment in Decorah.[42] Amid the excitement and swift pace of American events there was always the note of interest in the old country, revealed perhaps in a novel of Norwegian rural life by Bjørnson, or in special news letters from Christiania, or in stories in 1864 about Seventeenth of May celebrations in such widely separated places as Quebec, Madison, Wisconsin, and Lawrence, Kansas.[43] But always in the foreground were the great events that were taking place on the national stage of American affairs.[44]

The reverberations of a great civil war and of the internal problems and crises of President Lincoln's administration

[41] See Hansen, in *Norsk-amerikanernes festskrift,* 34, 37.

[42] *Emigranten,* October 31, December 5, 1864.

[43] The Quebec celebration was attended mainly by the captains of Scandinavian vessels then at Quebec. *Emigranten,* July 18, 1864. See Hansen, in *Norsk-amerikanernes festskrift,* 34, 35.

[44] Following the close of the war and the assassination of the president, *Emigranten* carried a somewhat extended biography of Lincoln. It is of interest to note that it gave attention now and then to masterpieces of American literature. Beginning on October 2, 1865, it ran, in installments, a Norwegian translation of *Rip Van Winkle.*

did not dry up the immigrant stream from Norway. But that stream became very thin when the Old World caught the echo of Indian war whoops on the frontiers to which its sons and daughters had gone. The smallness of the emigration in 1863 — the year after the Homestead Act had swung wide the gates to the immigrant land seeker — may indeed have been due, in part, to the intensification and increasing grimness of the Civil War, but it was probably mainly a result of the panic among settlers caused by the Sioux War of 1862 in Minnesota. It is well known that the Indian outbreak spread a wave of fear into the neighboring states of Iowa and Wisconsin, but that the terror crossed the ocean and influenced the decisions of people in the valleys of the Scandinavian North is an aspect of the uprising that has been somewhat neglected by historians.

In commenting on the Civil War, immigrants writing to friends in Norway frequently reminded them that the theater of action was the South, where few of their countrymen had settled. An Iowa settler in 1861 expressed the opinion that immigration would stream into the West, unhindered as usual, and an immigrant in Wisconsin the next year reported that no economic harm had resulted from the deflection to Chicago and the East of the former down-river trade, for both wages and prices were high.[45] It was a different matter, however, when the fierce Sioux went on the warpath in the heart of Minnesota, the new Mecca for Norwegian immigrants, for now there were sent to Norway general reports, followed by settlers' narratives, of countrymen scalped and killed, of destruction of property, of abandoned farms, of panic, and of a marked feeling of insecurity. The massacre at Norway Lake, where Swedish and Norwegian settlers felt the fury of the Indian vengeance for white men's wrongs, was reported in detail in the press of the old country; and the

[45] *Stavanger amtstidende og adresseavis,* August 26, 1861; *Drammens blad,* December 30, 1862.

earlier accounts were soon supplemented with lists of casualties. An immigrant letter written from St. Peter on September 9, 1862, a few weeks after the initial uprising, was used as the text for newspaper arguments against emigration. This letter perfectly reflected the horror inspired by the outbreak. The author believed that he was penning his last message. With his family he had taken refuge in St. Peter. The near-by village of New Ulm, he reported erroneously, had already fallen. "Axes and scalping knives," he wrote, "have already claimed many victims; helpless children are as a rule burned alive or hanged from trees; destruction goes from house to house; the Indians burn everything in their path — houses, hay, grain, and the like — and I feel that my pen can't paint the horror in such terrible colors as it deserves."[46] As late as November 22, 1862, a farmer in Dodge County, Minnesota, reported that the Indians were ten thousand strong. "We never go to bed without fear," he said, "and my rifle is always loaded." In the midst of the excitement, he reported, the preliminary enrollment for the draft took place and he faced the prospect of leaving his wife and family without his protection.[47] These are but a few of many items that appeared in Norwegian newspapers, but they afford clues to the nature of numerous unprinted America letters of the period. The next spring a marauding party of Sioux murdered several Norwegians in southern Minnesota, on the South Branch of the Watonwan River, and this affair also was given prominent notice in Norway.[48]

[46] The letter is reprinted in *Stavanger amtstidende og adresseavis,* October 27, 1862, from *Buskeruds amtstidende,* which had published it with an accompanying warning against emigration. The Norway Lake massacre is reported in *Drammens blad,* October 8, December 18, 19, 1862. An early general report, from *Morgenbladet,* is in *Stavanger amtstidende og adresseavis,* October 13, 1862, and a list of casualties at Norway and Eagle lakes is in the same paper for January 15, 1863. Many items on the Sioux War were reprinted from the Norwegian-American paper *Emigranten.*

[47] *Morgenbladet,* November 22, 1862.

[48] A letter by Lars Lee, from South Bend, Minnesota, April 21, 1863, is in *Morgenbladet,* June 7, 1863. See also the issue for June 13, 1863.

The Sioux War, for the Norwegian immigrants as for Yankees, Germans, and others who lived in the Minnesota frontier area, was a severe pioneer ordeal, indeed. The immigrants learned by grim experience that they could not accept the promise and the rewards of the West without accepting at the same time its hazards and dangers. By meeting both they undoubtedly wove themselves the more firmly into the fabric of American life. And sometimes, in the face of crisis, they made modest contributions to the heroic legends of the West. Thus one of the epics of the Sioux War is the story of a humble Norwegian immigrant woman, Guri Endreson, who with her husband and a family of five children lived in 1862 in a small log cabin not far from the frontier village of Willmar, Minnesota. A Sioux War party burst suddenly upon this peaceful farm scene, shot down her husband and one of her sons, severely wounded another son, and carried away her two daughters. Guri herself, with a third daughter, managed somehow to elude the fury of the red men, and when they had galloped off, she succeeded in getting her wounded son and her daughter to the cabin of a neighbor, where she found two men, both badly wounded. She promptly took charge, bandaged the wounds of the men, put them in a wagon, and set out for the village of Forest City, thirty miles away. The journey took two days and nights, with Guri Endreson driving the wagon by day and keeping sleepless watch by night, until the haven was reached. Her two daughters escaped from their captors and rejoined her, but the wounded son died within a year. Guri waited four years before she could bring herself to write the story of this ordeal to her relatives in Norway. "God permitted it to happen thus," she said, and went on to tell about her resumption of farming. After four years, she had gone back to her farm and taken up again the homely tasks of daily life. She reports that during the first summer following her return she churned 230 pounds of butter. Many years later the state of Minnesota put a monument over the grave of Guri Endreson "in memory of her heroic deeds."[49] The monument recalls her courage in the face of the tragedy that she met in 1862, but her less dramatic heroism in going back to her farm is typical, too, of the fortitude with which most of the pioneers, immigrants and native Americans alike, met the frontier ordeal.

In general, the Sioux War tended temporarily to retard Norwegian settlement. Pioneers got out of the zone of immediate danger, but eventually most of them returned, and soon their numbers were augmented by new arrivals from the older settlements to the south and from abroad. In the north central region of Minnesota, for example, there were a few more than a hundred Norwegians in 1860. Many of these people evacuated the region after the uprising, but from 1864 on, they began to reoccupy the area, and many Norwegians newly arrived from Norway or migrating northward from the older settlements in Wisconsin and Iowa joined them. By 1870 there were more than six thousand Norwegians in the region, and five years later the number had increased to nearly sixteen thousand — a quarter of all the population of that portion of Minnesota. If Norwegian immigrants were victims of the uprising, it should be noted that they also participated in the government's campaigns that drove the Sioux westward across the Dakota plains. Thus Ole Paulson, a young theological student who enlisted in the army just before the Sioux Outbreak, served as a second lieutenant in Sibley's western campaign of 1863; Paul Rosendahl of Spring Grove also marched with Sibley's troops; many privates of Norwegian origin were in the ranks; and there were Nor-

[49] Blegen, *Building Minnesota*, 212–214 (Boston, 1938); *Studies and Records*, 5:14–29; Agnes C. Laut, "Daughters of the Vikings — Guri Endreson," in *Outing*, 52:413–423 (July, 1908). The writer found in Norway the letter that Guri Endreson wrote to her relatives on December 2, 1866. The Norwegian-American Historical Association has a copy.

wegian immigrant soldiers in the Dakota expeditions led by Sully.[50]

The alarm occasioned in Norway by the Sioux Outbreak began to subside in 1863. O. E. Dreutzer, the American consul at Bergen, issued a stream of circulars from his office with a view to allaying fears and answering inquiries about conditions in the United States. Dreutzer was a Swedish-born American who lived in the South, served in the Seminole War, pioneered as a farmer in Wisconsin in the vicinity of the Unonius colony, studied law, and became a county judge two years before his appointment, in 1862, to the Bergen post. He was aggressively Northern in spirit and equally zealous in his espousal of the cause of emigration. In one of his consular publications, dated November 12, 1862, he complained bitterly about the early European reaction to the Civil War.[51] He declared that the enemies of the Republic, both in America and in Europe, had "spread the view that the great North American Republic, which had advanced so rapidly upon the highways of civilization, art, and science, was near its destruction, that it had proved that a democratic government cannot endure, and that there remained only scenes of anarchy and of social and industrial confusion, coupled with ruined finances, which undoubtedly meant failure and ruin for all persons who emigrated to America." The educated classes, he believed, had not been misled by such reports, but the workers and in general those who were not well informed had accepted them as true. He

[50] Ole Paulson, *Erindringer,* ch. 13–16 (Minneapolis, 1907); Rosendahl's diary, in the possession of the Minnesota Historical Society; a letter from a Norwegian soldier in Sully's expedition, in *Emigranten,* October 24, 1864. Qualey, *Norwegian Settlement,* 125 and *passim,* gives an excellent picture of the effect of the Sioux War upon settlement in Minnesota, with special reference to the Norwegians.

[51] *Fra de forenede nordamerikanske staters konsulat i Bergen.* Two copies of this two-page, double-column circular were sent by Dreutzer to Secretary Seward as enclosures with his letter of December 9, 1862. They are filed with the Dreutzer-Seward correspondence here mentioned in the National Archives at Washington in a volume of manuscript documents entitled "Bergen — Dept. of State — 1862–68." For further information about Dreutzer, see Stephenson, *Letters Relating to Gustaf Unonius,* 102 n.

proceeded to refute this unsympathetic view, told about the Homestead Act, the wages of labor, the flourishing condition of manufactures, and various other matters. The leaflet was a reprint of an article which he had published in *Bergensposten,* a newspaper which promptly replied to the consul, tartly suggesting, among other things, that the prospect of being scalped was "not so inviting that it should entice emigrants to the distant West."[52] Transmitting a copy of this circular to Secretary of State Seward, Dreutzer said that the Indian troubles in the West had been "the hardest blow to emigration."[53]

In a second circular, issued early in 1863,[54] Dreutzer devoted a section to the Sioux Outbreak, explained that only eight Norwegians and fifteen Swedes had been murdered, stated that the removal of the Sioux from Minnesota was assured and that settlers were freed from the danger of further attacks, and told of the punishment that had been meted out to the Indians. He repeated much of the material that had appeared in the leaflet of 1862, describing American conditions and institutions in attractive colors. Owing to the war, he said, labor was scarce and wages were high. In fact, no period in American history had been so favorable in the matter of wages. Much of the pamphlet was devoted to an exposition of the Homestead Act, which Dreutzer printed in full. Here, announced by an American governmental official in Norway and in the prospective emigrant's own language, was perhaps the most important news ever

[52] Dreutzer's article appeared in *Bergensposten* for November 14, 1862, and that newspaper's reply was printed in the issue for November 17. Dreutzer had first sent his article to *Morgenbladet* in Christiania, which rejected it. "I think this is a fair indication of the feeling of the press towards our government," he wrote to John H. Andresen on October 17, 1862. Consular Archives, Oslo: Letters Received, 1858–63.

[53] Dreutzer to Seward, December 9, 1862. Dreutzer printed five hundred copies of the circular.

[54] *Cirkulære fra de nordamerikanske staters consulat i Bergen* (Bergen, Chr. Dahl, 1863). A copy of this sixteen-page circular is with Dreutzer's letter to Seward of February 9, 1863. Only one other copy of the circular, preserved in Norway, is known to be in existence.

put before the emigrants: "The Congress has passed a law by the terms of which every adult male, who has reached the age of twenty-one, is entitled to receive 160 acres of governmental land in consideration of a total payment of only ten dollars together with about three dollars to the treasurer and register of the land office. A patent will be issued to him after he has cultivated the land for five years." Citing the authority of Seward, he made it clear that no one, not a native-born or naturalized citizen, could be pressed into military service. He took account, however, of the possibility that many emigrants might wish to enter the Union armies and incidentally explained the financial benefits that they thus could obtain; but he declared that the primary need was for laborers rather than soldiers. He had no desire to entice anyone to America, he said, but he reminded the Norwegians that people had a right to seek the best livelihood they could find. "It is a very peculiar patriotism," he said, "that insists upon remaining in a land under oppressive circumstances merely because one has been born there, when one is fully convinced that he can meet the future elsewhere with the happiest anticipations both for himself and his dependents."

Dreutzer returned to the attack in yet another circular dated November 10, 1863, published in conformity with instructions from Seward and devoted principally to assuring emigrants that they would not be pressed into war service when they reached America.[55] The circular also offered a broad comparison of North and South and expressed confidence in the ultimate triumph of the Union government. "The newspapers in this country," Dreutzer wrote to Seward, "are generally opposed to admitting anything in their columns which in any way might have a tendency to encour-

[55] *Cirkulære fra de nordamerikanske forenede staters konsulat* (Bergen, Dahls Bogtrykkeri, 1863). A copy of this eight-page document is filed with Dreutzer's letter to Seward of December 7, 1863.

age emigration, but eagerly take up anything discouraging."[56] The circular was soon brought out in a new edition, with some added matter on the Homestead Act and the advantages of emigration.[57] "The idea that the emigrant will be upon his arrival in the United States compelled to perform millitary [*sic*] duty," Dreutzer informed Seward, "is generally prevailing throughout this country."[58] He was interested in all aspects of the emigration problem. In 1862, reporting in much detail upon the prevalence of leprosy in western Norway, he advocated the establishment of immigrant controls, and particularly a consular bill of health as a condition of admission to the United States.[59] In 1864 he actually urged upon Seward the advisability of having the United States appropriate money to cover the cost of transportation for the poorer classes of emigrants from Quebec to the West.[60] In the autumn of 1864 he brought out a new and expanded edition of his circular for emigrants; and he never ceased to believe that the emigrants were the "nerve and sinew of the Norwegian peasantry."[61]

On the whole, opinion among the common people in Norway, as in Sweden, was favorable to the North. Traditions of free labor, deep-rooted hostility to slavery in any form,

[56] Letter of December 7, 1863.

[57] *Cirkulære fra de nordamerikanske forenede staters konsulat* (Bergen, H. J. Geelmuydens Enkes Officin ved J. C. Hagen, 1863). Two copies of this eight-page document accompany Dreutzer's letter to Seward of January 6, 1864.

[58] Letter of January 6, 1864.

[59] Dreutzer to Seward, June 17, 1862. With this letter is an enclosure consisting of an elaborate essay on leprosy in Norway.

[60] Letter of May 9, 1864.

[61] *Cirkulære fra de nordamerikanske consulat, Bergen* (Bergen, 1864). Two copies of this sixteen-page circular are filed with Dreutzer's letter to Seward of October 3, 1864. This was the seventh in the series of circulars issued by Dreutzer at Bergen. Only five have been mentioned in the foregoing notes. One, entitled *De forenede staters konsulat Bergen 14 Sept 1863,* was a broadside on the subject of tariffs. A copy of it accompanies Dreutzer's letter to Seward of September 29, 1863. Another was a newspaper translation of a dispatch from Seward on homestead and military matters, a copy of which is filed with the letter cited above. With a single exception (mentioned in note 54), the only known copies of these consular circulars are those preserved in the National Archives. Dreutzer's letter to Seward dated March 23, 1866, comments on the quality of the Norwegian emigrants.

and the influence of emigrant letters reflecting the Northern point of view were among the forces that account for this position. But among the official classes in both Sweden and Norway, as Dreutzer's circulars imply, there was considerable skepticism over the cause represented by Lincoln. This was not expressed in any breach of neutrality. The Confederate side got neither vessels nor armament from Norwegian or Swedish sources. But the feeling crops out unmistakably in connection with certain American events. Writing of Lincoln's re-election in 1864, for example, James H. Campbell, the American minister to Sweden and Norway, said, "It was not what the 'governing classes' expected or desired. They preserve 'friendly relations,' but would prefer the dismemberment of a power jealously regarded as too great, and the success of the aristocratic rebellion." Professor Hovde may be correct when he comments that this was "more true of Sweden than of Norway," but it applied in a measure to Norway also.[62] "For the general welfare of the world in the immediate future," commented *Morgenbladet* after Lincoln's success in 1864, "this re-election is a misfortune." Even by his own party, this paper asserted, President Lincoln was not looked upon as a "man of outstanding ability."[63] Such an attitude was not shared, however, by the brilliant Norwegian leader of liberal democratic reform, Johan Sverdrup, who believed in Lincoln and consistently spoke of America as the land of the future, destined to achieve leadership in politics, science, and art.[64]

[62] Brynjolf J. Hovde, *Diplomatic Relations of the United States with Sweden and Norway, 1814–1905*, 49–58 (University of Iowa, *Studies in the Social Sciences*, vol. 7, no. 4 — 1921). Hovde quotes Campbell from *Diplomatic Correspondence of the United States*, 1865, part 3, p. 188. Dreutzer, in a letter of February 2, 1863, to Carl Kraby, the United States consul at Porsgrund, declares that pro-Southern opinion was widespread in Norway and attributes it to ignorance of American conditions. "It is astonishing to me," he writes, "that a people as enterprising as the Norwegians know so little about America notwithstanding the great tide of emigration to that country." Consular Archives, Oslo: Letters Received, Porsgrund, 1863.

[63] *Morgenbladet*, November 24, 1864.

[64] Blegen, *Abraham Lincoln and European Opinion*, 9, 10 (Minneapolis, 1934).

Despite the Civil War, the prospects for emigrants seemed to be brightening; and Norwegian emigration rose in 1864 to 4,300 and stood on about the same level in 1865. In the West farming was booming; wheat from western grainfields was dethroning King Cotton, playing a prominent part in the economic life of the North, and aiding in the diplomatic struggle to keep England neutral. From immigrant farmers in Minnesota came brighter reports. "Of the Indians," wrote Torsten C. Levig late in 1863 from Blue Earth County in a letter that was published in the Christiania *Aftenbladet*, "we now hear nothing and we hope that for the future we shall suffer no more from this pack of thieves." He reported that troops were guarding the frontier and that only six miles from his farm there was a frontier fort. The farmers were doing well, he said, and in some places wheat yielded as much as thirty-five bushels an acre. It was low in price, but barley brought seventy-five cents a bushel. The Norwegians in his community now had a minister who held services every fifth or sixth Sunday. Good land was still available, and Levig's advice was summed up in the one word "Come!"[65]

The Homestead Act was beckoning; the war was nearing its final stages; and in 1864 Congress passed a law legalizing labor contracts made by American employers with immigrants in Europe. The American Emigrant Company, with a labor office in New York, "chartered for the promotion of Foreign Immigration," set about to organize on a large scale the importation of contract labor in accordance with the terms of this act. It advertised for mechanics, miners, farm and railroad laborers, and offered to advance money for the cost of passage, which the contract laborer would repay in installments. In the autumn of 1864 this company had an agent in Sweden and one of the American consuls in Norway seems to have been co-operating with him.[66]

[65] *Aftenbladet*, January 23, 1864.

[66] See a circular letter of August 6, 1864, from the American Emigrant Company, signed by its general agent, John Williams, in the Consular Archives, Oslo:

Meanwhile at Bergen in 1864 Dreutzer appears to have given some encouragement to the emigration of laborers to America for employment by mining companies in the Upper Peninsula of Michigan. For this activity he was sharply attacked in the press. *Morgenbladet,* for example, suggested that his real purpose was to secure "cannon fodder" for the Union armies. In defending himself, he explained that hundreds of prospective emigrants had applied to his office for advice and had indicated their eagerness to pay for the cost of passage with labor. The mining companies, which had lost many laborers as a result of the war, had sent an agent to Europe to recruit laborers who would not be liable to the draft. Dreutzer declared that his only connection with the transaction was as a notary public in legalizing the contracts, but he took the view that so long as he did nothing to fan discontent in Norway, it was entirely proper for him to take an active interest in emigration.[67] Early in 1865 he explained to the state department that the emigrant contracts had been made with Henry F. Tefft as the agent of officials of the Quincy and Pewabie mining companies. More than a hundred Norwegian families—"good, healthy and moral people"—had gone to Bergen as a result of the advertising of the mining companies and many had been obliged to return to their homes. The general effect, Dreutzer said, was "unfortunate." A copy of the contract, forwarded to Washington by Dreutzer, discloses the conditions that the mining companies established. They agreed to pay the expenses of the ocean voyage and of the journey to the interior and to provide house and food for the miner after his arrival. He in turn pledged himself to remain in the employ of the companies for two calendar years at wages of two hundred and sixty dollars a year, with half of his monthly

Letters Received, Porsgrund, 1864; also a letter from Williams to Consul Kraby at Porsgrund, November 11, 1864.

[67] *Bergensposten,* August 28, 1864.

payments withheld to satisfy his debt. At the end of the two-year period he was to receive a bounty of fifteen dollars. An experienced miner was offered forty dollars additional wages per year. The companies also offered to pay a third of the cost of transporting a wife and children to America, upon condition that the expense should later be defrayed from the miner's wages.[68]

The employment of prospective copper miners was promoted vigorously in the far northern districts about Tromsø, from which 589 emigrants are recorded as having left in 1864. There the active agent was one Christian Taftezon, a Norwegian emigrant who was reported to have lived in America for thirty-five years. The laborers enrolled by him were transported via Newcastle and Liverpool; a Trondhjem newspaper item in August refers to some two hundred Norwegian copper miners herded for a night on the Newcastle station platform. The newspaper asserted that Taftezon, who was paid so much "a head" for the emigrants he forwarded, was fooling the people and that his activities ought to be checked by the public authorities. Later reports from emigrants, however, indicated that the wages and conditions of work in the copper mines were satisfactory.[69]

In 1865 Taftezon was again active as an emigrant agent. He published a lengthy article "On Conditions in America," in which he criticized the farming West as a goal for emigrants and urged people to go to the copper mines, particularly the Quincy mine at Portage Lake; and he arranged for a ship to leave Trondhjem in July and promised to meet the emigrants in Quebec. The cost of transportation was announced as from thirty to thirty-five specie dollars, the emigrant to furnish his own food. Taftezon agreed to forward a portion of the cost of the journey, to be made up later

[68] Dreutzer to William Hunter, acting secretary of state, January 27, 1865. "Bergen — Dept. of State — 1862–68," in National Archives.

[69] *Tabeller vedkommende folkemængdens bevægelse 1856–1865,* 180; *Adressebladet,* August 2, 9, 23, October 25, 1864; *Tromsø stiftstidende,* May 8, 15, 1864.

by labor on contract, but each emigrant was required to have a minimum of twenty dollars.[70]

Michigan had been somewhat outside the main path of Norwegian emigrant settlement, though both the lumbering and the sailing industries had attracted substantial groups, who for the most part settled in the eastern counties along the Lake Michigan shore. Now, in part as a result of the activities of Tefft and Taftezon, Norwegians appeared in the Upper Peninsula, notably in the area of the copper mines in Houghton County and the iron mines in Marquette County, and in both areas there has been a large contingent of people from the far north in Norway. A traveler in the middle 1870's, for example, found from six to eight hundred Scandinavians in the city of Ishpeming, most of them Norwegians from the northern parts of Norway. In 1880 there were some six hundred Norwegians in Houghton County, concentrated for the most part in Calumet.[71]

[70] Taftezon's article "Om forholdene i Amerika" appeared in *Tromsø stiftstidende,* May 25, 28, 1865, and was also issued separately. Further details about the activities in 1865 are in the same newspaper for June 29, September 10, October 5, 1865. In 1865 Taftezon appears to have secured, in all, about 180 emigrants, including some Lapps.

[71] See Qualey, *Norwegian Settlement,* ch. 8.

XIV. THE SLAVERY CONTROVERSY AND THE CHURCH

THAT THE SLAVERY controversy should have invaded Norwegian Lutheran church circles, leaving in its wake bitterness and dissension, seems, at first thought, an anomaly. For the great majority of the Norwegian immigrants from the beginning had cherished, alongside a deep faith in American liberty, an equally deep aversion for slavery. The America letters that flowed in a steady stream to the old country almost universally praised the spirit of American freedom, and immigrant voices were quickly raised in condemnation of Negro slavery — an "ugly contrast," as Ole Rynning wrote in the late 1830's, "to this freedom and equality which justly constitute the pride of the Americans." Twenty-three years before the fall of Fort Sumter, Rynning predicted that the "infamous slave traffic" would inevitably lead either to a political partition of the United States or to a bloody civil war.[1]

When, a few years after Rynning's time, the oldest Nor-

[1] Rynning, *True Account of America*, 87, 88.

wegian Lutheran church organization in America condemned slavery in scathing terms, hardly a word of dissent was heard either within or outside that church body. The antislavery resolution of Eielsen's Synod, adopted in 1846 and reaffirmed four years later, bears the accent of earnest conviction: "We, standing united, wholly repudiate the fearful sin of giving our approval to the slave traffic; rather shall we employ all possible diligence to promoting and supporting opposition to it, with a view to the freeing of the Negroes, for Jesus has said: 'Therefore all things whatsoever ye would that men should do to you, do ye even so to them; for this is the law and the prophets' (Matt. 7: 12). They also are redeemed and intended to inherit the same glory as other people. We counsel everyone to take this matter under a more careful consideration."[2]

The stand of Rynning and Eielsen was prophetic of Norwegian immigrant opinion. The Norwegian press, launched under the Free-Soil banner, voiced an antislavery point of view that became increasingly emphatic with the march of events in the 1850's; the Norwegian people in America, accepting "antislavery" as the dominant spirit of the Republican party, gave an overwhelming majority to Lincoln at the end of the decade; and when the Civil War came the immigrants went to the battlefields of the South with fervor and loyalty. Though a few Norwegians had settled in the South, they did not cause any division or controversy among their countrymen along sectional lines.[3] The apparent

[2] The Norwegian text is in Bergh, *Den norsk lutherske kirkes historie,* 30. P. A. Rasmussen, who accepted the Eielsen Constitution in 1850, later broke with that group and in 1857 he publicly objected to the antislavery resolution on the ground that it was a political rather than a church, or religious, question. *Kirkelig tidende* (Lisbon, Illinois), 2:102–106 (May, 1857).

[3] In the early 1850's Mrs. Wærenskjold, one of the leading Norwegian Americans in Texas, expressed horror of slavery and asserted that there could be no compensation for the loss of freedom, but she said that the slaves received kindly treatment and often were in better circumstances than laborers in Norway. Some of the Texas Norwegians, it is interesting to note, did own slaves before the Civil War. One of them explained, some years later, that such ownership was "in keeping with the society in which they then lived." But such slaveholding had

anomaly becomes the more striking when it is recalled that the Swedish immigrants, antislavery and Republican like the Norwegians, witnessed not a ripple of controversy within their church organizations on the slavery question.

Yet, like all other historical developments and unlike a real anomaly, the intrusion of the slavery controversy into the Norwegian-American church submits to a rational explanation. Its immediate background was the connection of the Norwegian Synod with Concordia Seminary of the Missouri Synod at St. Louis, which the Norwegian Synod as early as 1857 had recommended as a place of training for potential ministers in their own church and where, beginning in 1859, Professor Laur. Larsen had occupied a chair in order to serve primarily as a teacher and guide for the small group of Norwegian students who had gone there for training. The arrangement was clearly intended as a temporary one, pending the establishment of an institution of higher learning by the Norwegian Synod, but meanwhile it served as a bridge between the German and Norwegian church bodies. Professor Larsen, brought under the pervading influence of Dr. C. F. W. Walther and other great churchmen, became himself an "ardent Missourian," and there is no doubt that the Missouri influence, tending generally in the direction of strict "purity of doctrine," permeated the wider circle of Norwegian Synod clergymen, in many instances no doubt confirming views to which their training in Lutheran orthodoxy had already committed them. It was inevitable that, among the many questions discussed, that of slavery should have come under consideration.[4]

More than a year before the slavery controversy arose in the Norwegian Synod, its president, A. C. Preus, turned to

no reverberations among the Norwegians in the North and had nothing to do with their controversy on slavery. It seems doubtful that the northern Norwegians had any knowledge of slave ownership among southern Norwegians. See Ella Lonn, *Foreigners in the Confederacy,* 37, 38 (Chapel Hill, 1940); Qualey, *Norwegian Settlement,* 207; and Blegen, *Norwegian Migration,* 186.

[4] Larsen, *Laur. Larsen,* ch. 6.

Dr. Walther himself for counsel on this important question. It is interesting to learn that the head of the Synod then took the view that slavery was sinful, arguing that since it existed under human laws that were unchristian and contained sinful stipulations, the institution itself was sinful. This, Walther contended, was a great misunderstanding of the case, and he proceeded to lay down a doctrine which, in essentials, was later voiced by the Norwegian Synod clergy amid the clamor of controversy. Slavery, according to Dr. Walther, is an intermediate thing, and what is intermediate remains intermediate. In a word, its use does not make the institution itself sinful. The sinful element is in the nature of an accident. "What God permits even to the Christian in the New Testament and does not command him to abolish, but even regulates, can in itself be no sin." Preus, in Walther's opinion, had put himself in the position of arguing that "not only Roman slavery, which the apostles sanctioned as an institution, but also Jewish slavery, which God regulated, becomes a sinful institution." And so the Missouri theologian suggested that the pioneer minister was fighting against Moses, the apostles, and even against God himself; and that, furthermore, his stand was as revolutionary as if he had declared the state itself to be sinful. Walther took pains to point out, however, in declaring slavery in itself to be no sin, that one is not thereby justified in excusing, extenuating, or vindicating the sin allied with it. "Fight against the abuse, not the use," he urged. The abuses should be heartily condemned. "They — but not slavery itself — have cried aloud to Heaven, and the misery of the South is unquestionably a deserved punishment from God for the abuses that have so fully accompanied slavery." He even suggested that American slavery might be sinful, but firmly insisted that it is not a sinful institution. But Walther was well aware of the explosive character of the question, and he offered a word of caution, asking Preus to take into account the "quiet, the peace, and the unity of the church" and not to be a needless troublemaker. It is significant that he took occasion to send a copy of his letter also to the Reverend Jakob A. Ottesen, another pillar of the Norwegian Synod. A modern writer scouts the view that the Synod clergymen acquired their views on the slavery question from St. Louis, but Dr. Walther's letter is proof that the Missouri Synod leader emphatically impressed his doctrine upon them.[5]

Not Preus, but the march of events precipitated the controversy and disturbed the "quiet, the peace, and the unity" of the Norwegian Synod. Only eleven days after President Lincoln called for volunteers and the Civil War began, Professor Larsen wrote an announcement for publication in *Emigranten* that Concordia College had closed its doors and sent its students home owing to disturbed political conditions; and in the same issue in which this announcement appeared the editor of *Emigranten,* C. F. Solberg, seized the occasion to inquire about the point of view of the Concordia College teachers, suggesting that it was important to his countrymen to know whether or not the faculty stood for the Union. Though he conceded that they might hold to the strict Lutheran view that revolution is ungodly, he nevertheless felt that the confidence of the Norwegian people in the institution would be increased if they could be assured that the teachers were Union men, whereas if they were not, the situation would be very questionable. Since some returned students had indicated that the teachers sympathized with the South, Solberg made his inquiry, he said, to clear up this point. Most of the church leaders in the South, he pointed out, were on the other side, and in his opinion it was an issue on which one could not be passive.[6]

[5] Walther to A. C. Preus, January 8, 1860, and to Ottesen, January 9, in L. Fürbringer, ed., *Briefe von C. F. W. Walther,* 1:124–130 (St. Louis, 1915). The modern writer alluded to is Adolf Bredesen, *Slaveristriden i ny belysning,* 21, 22 (Decorah, Iowa, 1905).

[6] *Emigranten,* May 8, 1861. Professor Larsen's announcement was dated April 26.

This inquiry, moderate in tone, undoubtedly reflected a sincere concern on the part of an immigrant group just then rallying to the cause of the Union. For Larsen, however, it offered difficulties. For one thing, his sympathies were Democratic and he accepted the principle of state rights; for another, he felt no obligation upon himself as a clergyman to ventilate his political views, and he scarcely needed the fervent counsels of discretion offered him by Ottesen and President Preus to realize the danger of launching both himself and the Synod upon a controversy potentially explosive in a period of crisis and tense feeling.[7]

It has been said the spirit of Lutheran individualism is that of retiring "behind the line of battle of all external events" into "a purely personal spirituality, into the citadel of a freedom which no events of the external order can touch." In this instance A. C. Preus urged Larsen to issue a statement that nobody could compel him to air his political faith.[8] Larsen chose, instead, to make no reply whatever, but his silence was not met by silence. After about a month an anonymous contributor was given space in *Emigranten* for an exposition of his views on "Concordia College and the Rebellion."[9] He flatly asked whether or not the Concordia teachers were secessionists. Were they sympathetic with the rebels? Accepting Professor Larsen's silence as an acknowledgment of the truth of the rumors that had occasioned the original inquiry, he advocated the immediate severance of the Norwegian Synod from Concordia College and the establishment of a school of its own. The launching of such a school, he was glad to notice, was to be discussed at a Synod meeting to be held during the summer. The contributor said that the rebels declared that neither slavery nor opposition to the execution of the laws of the United States

[7] Larsen, *Laur. Larsen,* 127–129.

[8] Ernst Troeltsch, *Social Teaching of the Christian Churches,* 2:542 (New York, 1931); Larsen, *Laur. Larsen,* 128.

[9] June 3, 1861. The contribution was signed "H."

was a sin. On both points he presented a rebuttal, remarking, among other things, that not one person in a hundred in the North would question the accuracy of the view that slavery is a sin.

In the next issue of *Emigranten* another contributor urged Larsen not to make any accounting of his political views and advocated sending students to Concordia as long as Professor Larsen was able and willing to teach them "pure Lutheran doctrine."[10] Larsen, however, now concluded that he must answer, consulted with President Preus and Ottesen, who aided him in drafting a statement, and on June 17 his reply appeared in print.[11] It marshaled scriptural authority from both the Old and the New Testament in support of the view that slavery is not sin, took the position that rebellion invariably is sin, but expressed some doubt that secession constituted rebellion. In fact, Larsen said, he had heard some good reasons why a state has a right to secede, but he did not consider himself sufficiently familiar with the constitution, laws, and history of the United States to pass judgment on that question. He would go to war himself, he declared, if the governor of Wisconsin called upon him to do so.

Solberg, in his rejoinder, pushed aside as irrelevant the point "that slavery as an abstract conception is sin," but characterized it as America's "greatest civic evil." The important thing to him was the preservation of the Union and loyalty to the national government, and here he found the position of the Concordia faculty, in the light of Larsen's statement, unsatisfactory. The assurance that Larsen would go to war upon call of the governor implied, in Solberg's opinion, that he would do the same thing if he were a resident of a Southern state. What the editor wanted was a forthright position on the question of the hour. "Our countrymen," he said, "have followed the rebellion step by step

[10] Jacob Nielsen of Janesville, in *Emigranten,* June 10, 1861.
[11] In *Emigranten.* Compare Larsen, *Laur. Larsen,* 129.

and long since formed their opinion of it."[12] The anonymous contributor, a week later, invited Larsen to reveal the "good reasons" which he had heard put forward for the right of a state to secede, insisted that the Southern states were in actual rebellion, and attempted, like Solberg, to shunt to one side the question of slavery as sin.[13]

It was at this stage of the discussion that the Norwegian Synod convened on June 26, 1861, at Rock Prairie, in the Luther Valley church, for its annual deliberations, with pastors and lay delegates from the various congregations present. The peace and solemnity with which the sessions began did not reflect the excited state of feeling beneath the surface of things. The nation was at war. The incipient slavery discussion, in which Professor Larsen was a central figure, was in the minds of all; and he himself was present at the meeting. A majority of the laymen wanted to cut off the St. Louis connection and to set up at once a school of their own. And in the hearts of most of the people there was a feeling of hostility to slavery in the South. These were among the factors that broke the outward calm and precipitated a debate on slavery that was to have repercussions throughout the decade.[14]

The school question led inevitably to the slavery question; for while there was agreement on taking steps toward establishing a Synod school and on a permanent site for the proposed institution, there was sharp disagreement on the question of launching the school at once in a temporary location. A committee reporting on this problem was divided between clergymen and laymen — the clergymen advocating maintenance of the Concordia connection if the St. Louis

[12] *Emigranten,* June 17, 1861.

[13] *Emigranten,* June 24, 1861.

[14] *Emigranten,* July 15, 1861; *Kirkelig maanedstidende,* 6:225 ff., especially 258–262 (September, 1861); *Synodalberetning,* 1861; Larsen, *Laur. Larsen,* 130–136; Rohne, *Norwegian American Lutheranism,* 204–207. Dr. Rohne devotes a chapter to a survey of the slavery controversy.

institution should again open its doors, the laymen urging the immediate establishment of a school of their own. On this particular issue the laymen were a majority and they carried the Synod with them, but the discussion naturally widened into a debate on slavery, for this matter was the heart of much of the lay opposition to Concordia.

It was a curious debate. The laymen, led by Erik Ellefsen, an Iowa farmer, had a sharp eye on the living reality of slavery in the South, and wanted to discuss slavery as an institution existing in contemporary life; but the clergy, led by Professor Larsen, rejected such a discussion as essentially a political and historical question that had no place in the deliberations of the church. Larsen therefore discussed "slavery in itself," going to Biblical authority to prove that it is not, "in and by itself," a sin, although, precisely as Walther had pointed out, he recognized that it was closely allied with many sins. It proved difficult for the laymen to come to grips with an "objective and ideal slavery" that apparently had no contact with living people and institutions. Nor was there unanimity among the clergy themselves, for John N. Fjeld urged that slavery was against the entire spirit of the New Testament and therefore a sin; and Bernt J. Muus suggested that, since Christianity would lead to the end of such a "terrible institution," it was sinful to countenance its retention. C. L. Clausen, soon to emerge as the leader in the fight against the position that slavery was not a sin, declared it to be one of the greatest temporal evils, an institution that every Christian should attempt to abolish, but at the time conceded that it was not a sin "in itself." It remained for Ellefsen to declare stoutly that it was against "God's Word" for one person to hold property rights over another. He argued that personal freedom was both a good and a right, that none could rob another of it, and that slavery clashed with the precept that one should love one's neighbor; but the ministers promptly pointed out to him that freedom, though a good, was temporal, given by God and not a natural right, that in fact human beings have no natural rights.[15]

In the evening following this indecisive debate the ministers foregathered to consider some possible way of easing the situation. Under the leadership of Ottesen and H. A. Preus it was concluded to draft a ministerial declaration that all the ministers could sign and to place it before the laymen for approval. It is evident that the pastors were alarmed by the potentiality of discord in the Synod and were earnestly seeking some means of disposing of the issue. The "basic texts" were threshed over and those ministers who had not been in accord with Larsen's central thesis were prevailed upon to endorse a statement that slavery "in and by itself" is not a sin, coupled with a characterization of it as an evil and a punishment from God, condemnation of abuses and sins allied with it, and even a conditional pledge to work for its abolition. The name of President A. C. Preus headed the list of those who signed the resolution: "Although, according to the Word of God, it is not in and by itself a sin to keep slaves, nevertheless it is in itself an evil and a punishment from God. We condemn all abuses and sins connected therewith, and furthermore, when our official duties require it and when Christian love and wisdom demand it, we will work for its abolition."[16]

If the pastors had high hopes of allaying the feelings of the delegates with this resolution, they were quickly quashed, for when it was put before the laymen for their vote, only twenty-eight out of sixty-six indicated approval. Ten voted an outright "No" and twenty-eight declined to vote. Ellefsen, who later declared that the pastors were trying "to pull the wool over the eyes" of the laymen, and eight other delegates

[15] *Kirkelig maanedstidende,* 6:258–261.

[16] *Kirkelig maanedstidende,* 6:261, 262. The translation is Miss Larsen's; a slightly different one is in Rohne, *Norwegian American Lutheranism,* 206. On the ministers' resolution see also the Synod church council's *Historisk fremstilling,* 5, 6 (Madison, 1868), and Claus L. Clausen's *Gjenmæle,* 13–18 (Chicago, 1869).

meanwhile drafted a counterresolution which was placed in the minutes but not put to a vote: "Slavery, viewed as an institution, can exist only under definite law, and since the laws upon which it is based stand in manifest conflict with the Word of God and Christian love, it is sin; and since slavery in the United States has been one of this country's greatest evils both for church and state, we look upon it as our absolute duty as Christians and good citizens to do everything in our power, by legal means, to alleviate, lessen, and if possible abolish slavery when our country's welfare and Christian love demand this of us."[17]

A full report of the Rock Prairie meeting went before the readers of both *Emigranten* and *Maanedstidende* and it was soon evident that the controversy had by no means been stilled. Larsen went into print soon after the church meeting to deny a report that the line of division had been between clergy and laity, but drew a quick rejoinder from Halvor Steensland, who asserted that there was precisely such a division and that it arose from the fact that the clergy refused to discuss slavery as it is, but chose instead to consider a concept of it without regard to the slavery on which the church members as citizens wanted information; and he insisted that the vote on the pastors' resolution therefore had no significance.[18] This was but a minor incident, however, in comparison with the sensation of Pastor C. L. Clausen's formal retraction of his approval of the resolution.

Soon after the Rock Prairie Synod meeting, Clausen had entertained serious doubts about the resolution he had been prevailed upon to sign. These were not diminished when at a summer ministerial conference attended by Dr. Walther he

[17] Translated from the original in *Kirkelig maanedstidende,* 6:262; a different translation is in Rohne, *Norwegian American Lutheranism,* 207. Ellefsen's remarkable phrase, "blæse os Blaar i Øinene," occurs in an article which this pugnacious layman wrote on "Slavery and the Bible," in *Emigranten,* December 23, 1861.

[18] *Emigranten,* July 22, 29, 1861.

Gjenmæle

— mod —

Kirkeraadet for den Norske Synode

i Anledning af dets Skrift,

kaldet:

"Historisk Fremstilling af den Strid som i Aarene 1861 til 1868 inden for den Norske Synode i Amerika har været ført i Anledning af Skriftens Lære om Slaveri."

Af

C. L. Clausen,

Præst for St. Ansgar og annekterede Menigheder.

Chicago. 1869

I Kommission hos Fritz Franizen, 43 West Kinzie St.

Trykt i "Skandinavens" Bog- og Accidents-Trykkeri.

THE TITLE PAGE OF C. L. CLAUSEN'S PAMPHLET ON THE SLAVERY CONTROVERSY

heard the noted Missouri leader characterize the federal government as a "fanatical abolitionist government" which was employing arms to enforce anti-Christian teachings about the sinfulness of slavery as well as about freedom, equality, and natural rights.[19] Late in July Clausen informed Larsen and Ottesen that he no longer accepted the pastors' declaration and that he considered his signature to that document to have been given under pressure.[20] A. C. Preus, meanwhile, was urging Larsen not to issue public statements on political matters unless they had previously been approved by his associates.[21] In November Clausen attended another ministerial conference, at Decorah, Iowa, where a warm discussion took place, starting with slavery and the applicability of the fourth commandment to the point at issue, but eventuating in a wide-ranging debate on liberty and governmental authority. The Synod church authorities later said that Clausen took the position that "liberty was not one of the things over which the government and parents have the power of dispensation" and that "whatever rights these have, they are given them for the good of the subjects, and if those in authority used these rights to the detriment of the governed, they could not expect to be obeyed as rulers; they had then violated their trust and exceeded the rights given them." This doctrine, which has a Jeffersonian ring, naturally implied a justification of revolution. This, however, the ministers pointed out, was sin. They declared, some years later, that Clausen withdrew this "heresy" in 1864, but Clausen himself not only denied that he made any such withdrawal but said that the ministers did not accurately report the position that he took at the Decorah conference. He had not

[19] Clausen, *Gjenmæle,* 19. The ministerial conference was held at Spring Prairie from July 4 to 11.

[20] *Historisk fremstilling,* 7. Clausen felt that the resolution was put through with undue haste and that its sponsors exaggerated the gravity of the crisis so far as the need of quieting the laymen was concerned. *Gjenmæle,* 15, 16.

[21] Larsen, *Laur. Laursen,* 146.

denied in 1861 that government and parents had the power of dispensation of liberty, but had asserted that there were limitations, centering in the security and welfare of individual, family, and society, upon the use of that power. To the pastors, revolution was revolution — and Clausen records that they briefly disposed of the American Revolution as an "ungodly rebellion."[22]

And so, having first announced his position to his own church at Luther Valley, Clausen published early in December a formal retraction of his agreement to the pastors' declaration on slavery.[23] On reviewing the entire matter in his mind he had come to the conclusion that slavery was in direct opposition to the spirit of Christianity, particularly the injunction to "love thy neighbor as thyself"; and in his retraction he described the pastors' declaration as a "web of sophistry." Rearguing the case, he pointed out that all were in agreement that slavery was an evil, like poverty or disease. Was it not, then, a sin to keep other people in such a condition by force? To do so, he asserted, violated both nature's laws and all true Christianity. He reduced his argument to syllogistic form: slavery is an evil; it is a sin forcibly to keep people in a state of evil; keeping slaves, therefore, is a sin.

Clausen's retraction opened the floodgates of controversy. Ministers and laymen alike took to the pen. *Emigranten* published one article after another — attack and defense, dissertations packed with Biblical citations, essays exploring the views of the church fathers, refutations, charges, and countercharges. The church periodical similarly devoted much space to the controversy, but without the give and play of debate open to both sides, and it even declined to print Clausen's retraction. Pamphlets furnished a medium for biting irony and a parody of the ministerial polemics. Alongside diatribes in *Emigranten* on the sinfulness or non-

[22] *Gjenmæle*, 21–30; *Historisk fremstilling*, 21.
[23] *Emigranten*, December 2, 1861.

sinfulness of slavery ran reports of the progress of the war and stories about the organization, training, and departure of the Fifteenth Wisconsin — the Norwegian regiment — with Pastor Clausen himself as its chaplain. In the thick of the controversy he issued a call for contributions of money and books for a soldiers' library; and H. A. Preus and Ottesen, two of his principal opponents, planned a book of devotions for the soldiers.[24] Solberg left for the South as a war correspondent to keep the Norwegians in touch with the exploits of the Fifteenth. A lengthy account by him "From the Norwegian Regiment," telling of the Mississippi expedition, appears in the same issue of *Emigranten* that carries a polemical article by A. C. Preus on slavery.[25]

To students of American history this controversy has a familiar ring. What was unusual was the fact that it did not develop until after the Civil War began and that it was carried on within a church and among a group of people who had virtually no actual contact with slavery and who at heart almost unanimously were against it, whether they stood on one side or the other of the controversy. The historic schism in the Methodist church in 1844, between North and South, was precipitated by the ownership of a Negro slave by a Methodist bishop in Georgia. The secondary schism between the northern and central Methodists, in 1860, also was a break between sections. And the schisms among the Baptists, Presbyterians, and other church groups were based upon the clash of belief and practice among members of church bodies whose areas and constituencies were intersectional.[26] One group after another had formulated declarations setting forth its point of view. In the middle 1850's, for example, conservative northern opinion among the Methodists was embodied in these points: "(1) There is not a passage

[24] *Emigranten,* January 6, February 3, 1862.
[25] April 21, 1862.
[26] William W. Sweet, *The Story of Religions in America,* ch. 13 (New York, 1930). This chapter is on the "Slavery Controversy and Slavery Schisms."

in the New Testament expressive of approbation of slavery. (2) The early Church indicated her disapproval of slavery indirectly. (3) The early Church laid down general principles which, when carried out, would necessarily work its abolition. (4) Finding slavery in existence, the early Church laid down certain rules for master and slave." [27] The immediate occasion for the Methodist schism of 1860 was a declaration that "the buying, selling, or holding of human beings as chattels is contrary to the laws of God and nature; inconsistent with the Golden Rule." [28]

The Norwegian Synod ministers were in a difficult position. As the controversy wore on, they defined the issue more and more clearly in terms, not of slavery, but of the authority of the Bible, with "free thinking" and the belief in freedom as a natural right among the enemies around the corner. The Synod position can be understood more clearly when one recalls Professor Larsen's statement that the "words in the Bible are to be taken in their primary, natural sense in accordance with common linguistic usage, unless it has been proven by unequivocal and unshakable arguments that they cannot possibly have their usual meaning." This rule, he said, "has determined our Lutheran faith and confession" in most of its disagreements with other churches.[29]

But since the issue began with slavery and involved the question of Biblical authority on that particular issue, they could not divorce the controversy from the emotion and aroused opinion about contemporary slavery in an age that saw North and South locked in a desperate war — an age, too, of increasing humanitarianism. Save for its statement that slavery "in and by itself" is not a sin, the Synod pas-

[27] Sweet, *The Methodist Episcopal Church and the Civil War,* 36 (Cincinnati, 1912). See also a scholarly study by Charles B. Swaney, *Episcopal Methodism and Slavery* (Boston, 1926). On the Lutheran side see Charles W. Heathcote, *The Lutheran Church and the Civil War* (Chicago, 1919).

[28] Sweet, *Methodist Episcopal Church,* 39, 40.

[29] Larsen, *Laur. Larsen,* 179, 180.

tors' declaration of 1861, by even a strict interpretation of its language, was distinctly antislavery in tone. In defending its premise, however, the Synod debaters put forward, in full panoply, the Biblical argument of the Southern defenders of slavery, doing so, not to sprinkle "holy water on the slave-pen and lash,"[30] but to maintain a theological position. That argument had echoed south and north for more than a quarter of a century. It had sounded in the halls of Congress, where a Southern spokesman in 1858 said, "We learn from the Holy Scriptures that Abraham and many wise and good men of that day not only held slaves but exercised acts of ownership over them; and that God Himself, after He had rescued the children of Israel from the house of bondage, sanctioned and recognized slavery both in principle and in practice."[31]

The Biblical argument ranged over the Old Testament, massing evidences of divine sanction of slavery from the patriarchs onward, with Abraham heading the list of Biblical slaveholders.[32] Even positive sanction was cited in Lev. 25:44, a passage that Larsen included in his first review of the problem and which served the South as the "Rock of Gibraltar in the Old Testament case."[33] The argument also included the fourth and tenth commandments, the former enjoining a master's authority over his servant. These and other items in the Old Testament were reinforced by many citations from the New, including, among others, the fact that the Apostles taught slaves to submit to their masters; that Paul returned Onesimus to his master Philemon, a point

[30] Samuel E. Morison and Henry S. Commager, *Growth of the American Republic,* 421 (New York, 1930).

[31] Quoted in Charles A. and Mary R. Beard, *Rise of American Civilization,* 1:705 (New York, 1927).

[32] William S. Jenkins, *Pro-slavery Thought in the Old South,* ch. 5 (Chapel Hill, 1935); *The Pro-slavery Argument* (Charleston, 1852), especially the argument of the Virginian Thomas R. Drew; and James Ford Rhodes, *History of the United States from the Compromise of 1850,* 1:370, 371 (New York, 1902).

[33] Jenkins, *Pro-slavery Thought,* 202. Larsen's argument at Rock Prairie is summarized in *Kirkelig maanedstidende,* 6:259.

popularized throughout the country in the 1850's because of its use by the defenders of the Fugitive Slave Law;[34] and especially the prescription (in I Tim. 6 : 1, 2) of the duties of both master and slave.[35] Affirmative sanctions were in turn given greater force by the absence of any Biblical condemnation of slavery. Why, if slavery was sin, Larsen argued at Rock Prairie, did not the Bible call for its abolition?[36] The Synod ministers, of course, had many other angles of approach. A. C. Preus, asserting that he stood against slavery just as he did against barbarism and ignorance, claimed that in seventeen hundred years of Christendom no Christian teacher had taught that slavery was sin; and he said that if slavery was a sin every citizen supporting the constitution had taken an oath to support sin, for slavery was protected by the constitution.[37] Koren, reviewing the entire problem, emphasized, among other things, the difference between temporal and spiritual freedom, suggested that Clausen was on the wrong track in the matter of natural rights, and incidentally declared that the abolitionists were not motivated by any love for the "poor Negroes."[38]

Clausen was a humanitarian who hated slavery; he was democratic, close to the laity, sympathetic to popular feeling, and had identified himself with the common life as an editor, as a settlement promoter, even as a member for a time of the Iowa legislature; and it need hardly be added that he was

[34] Rhodes, *History of the United States from the Compromise of 1850,* 1:370.

[35] On Larsen's use of this passage at Rock Prairie, see *Kirkelig maanedstidende,* 6:259; and Rohne, *Norwegian American Lutheranism,* 204.

[36] Rohne, *Norwegian American Lutheranism,* 204.

[37] *Emigranten,* December 16, 1861.

[38] See a lengthy essay by V. Koren in *Emigranten,* March 31, 1862, reprinted in his *Samlede skrifter,* edited by Paul Koren, 3:5–44 (Decorah, Iowa, 1911); H. A. Preus and J. A. Ottesen in *Emigranten,* February 17, 1862, and their "Reply to Pastor Clausen's Attack upon the Biblical Teaching about Slavery," in *Kirkelig maanedstidende,* 7:108–134 (April and May, 1862). See also Larsen's own summary of the entire controversy in *Historisk fremstilling.* A clash of Larsen with the editor of *Emigranten,* in its issues for January 20 and February 17, 1862, is of collateral interest. In general, Larsen did not take much part in the newspaper controversy.

Historisk Fremstilling

af den Strid, som

i Aarene 1861 til 1868

indenfor den norske Synode i Amerika

har været ført

i Anledning af Skriftens Läre om Slaveri.

Udgiven af

nävnte Synodes Kirkeraad.

Madison, Wis.

Trykt i B. W. Suckows Bogtrykkeri.

1868.

The Title Page of Laur. Larsen's Historical Review of the Slavery Controversy

unlearned in Hebrew and Greek. His antagonists were men of learning, university-trained for the most part, skilled in dialectics, clear and firm in their views, and considerably less responsive than he to popular currents. Clausen, opening with a retraction, was guilty in many details of inconsistency, and this his opponents pounced upon, trying both in private conferences and in public discussions to make him confess that he had sinned against the Word of God. He himself admits that he was tortured with doubt and struggle and discouragement, but he clung to his main position. Attempting to meet the clergy on their own ground he tried to prove that the Biblical "servant" was not a "slave" and that the slavery of the Bible was vastly different from American slavery; and on many other points he sought to weaken the force of his opponents' reasoning.[39] But in the main his defense was similar to that of Northern reasoners generally in the argument with the South. Rhodes, summing it up, says, "The spirit of Christianity was certainly opposed to slavery; under the Roman empire it had ameliorated the condition of the slaves, and during the middle ages it had been the chief influence in the abolition of slavery in Europe"; and on this general ground Rhodes contends that the Northerners had the better of the argument.[40] Clausen, though he tried to meet the ministerial arguments in the field of Biblical citation and interpretation, continued to view them as a distortion and sophistry since, as he believed, they shifted "a question of great practical interest to an absolutely abstract question."[41] He did not go so far as did the lay pamphleteer, Dr. S. J. Hansen, who, in a biting attack upon "orthodoxy," declared that the Synod clergy were indulging in a "soulless

[39] See his first discussion in *Emigranten,* December 2, 1861, and a controversial essay in the issue for February 17, 1862; also his later *Gjenmæle.* Miss Jorgensen devotes a chapter to the slavery controversy in her "Clausen."

[40] *History of the United States from the Compromise of 1850,* 1:372, 373.

[41] *Emigranten,* February 17, 1862.

game of sham with the letter of the Scriptures, not a genuine interpretation of their true spirit of Godliness."[42]

In the summer of 1862 Clausen, returning on leave from his duties as chaplain of the Fifteenth Wisconsin, put before the Synod meeting at Holden, Minnesota, a new resolution which in its first form omitted the pronouncement that slavery is a sin: "Since the owning of slaves is nowhere in the New Testament explicity sanctioned, much less recommended, and since it is in opposition to the spirit and nature of Christianity as well as to natural right and justice to hold other people as slaves (save as a consequence of criminal offenses), and since furthermore experience teaches that slavery customarily promotes and is related to all kinds of open and gross sins, it is the duty of Christian citizens wherever slavery exists to work for its amelioration, restriction, and abolition by the use of Christian means." With this statement his ministerial opponents seemed to be in agreement. They were unwilling to pass it, however, since it failed to define the issue between them and Clausen, and they therefore prevailed upon him to add the words that slavery "consequently is sin." Thus amended, it was spread upon the minutes, with some ten signatures appended to it.[43] The ministers had no wish to encourage a discussion of slavery in the midst of the Civil War; and the following year when the matter was again brought up a discussion was postponed. Nothing conclusive occurred in 1864 or in 1865.

From time to time pastoral and private conferences were held at which Clausen was insistently urged to recant, and indeed on one occasion, after long and fatiguing discussions, he appears to have been on the verge of confessing publicly, in his congregation, both false doctrine and evasion, Ottesen undertaking to formulate the confession for him. But Clau-

[42] *Menneskelighed og orthodoxi casuelt afhandlede i aabne breve til norske præster i Nord-Amerika,* 9 (Madison, 1861).

[43] *Kirkelig maanedstidende,* 7:238–240 (August, 1862); Rohne, *Norwegian American Lutheranism,* 210, 211.

sen, once he was removed from the immediate and strangely compelling influence of men like Ottesen and H. A. Preus, found himself unconvinced. Recalling later his confused thoughts and emotions at the time, he said that, notwithstanding the extraordinary force of the personalities and exhortations of the pastors, his conscience would not permit him to surrender. "No! No!" he exclaimed. "Slavery is a sin—for it does not harmonize with the love that God requires of us to our neighbor."[44] To the great chagrin of his opponents, he would not make the desired recantation. In 1865, however, he appeared before the Synod in the role of a peacemaker calling for mutual tolerance. The war was over, emancipation was a fact, and Clausen now proposed that bitter remarks should be withdrawn and that he and his opponents should agree that they might have different opinions on slavery and still work together peacefully in the church as Christian brothers. Some of the pastors appeared to be willing, but Clausen asserts that H. A. Preus, who had succeeded the milder and more sympathetic A. C. Preus as president in 1862, was unwilling to accept this overture and hence no action was taken.[45] Disturbed feeling had invaded many congregations and one of them, with its annexes, had withdrawn from the Synod in 1865 and had been persuaded to continue in it only upon the condition that the pastor called to serve it would not give public countenance to the doctrine that slavery is not a sin.[46]

Meanwhile an extraordinary chapter in the development of the slavery controversy had been kept hidden from the knowledge of Clausen and the public. On March 17, 1862, A. C. Preus, at that time president of the Norwegian Synod, had addressed a formal request to the theological faculty of Norway's national university at Christiania, where most of

[44] Clausen, *Gjenmæle*, 56–64; *Historisk fremstilling*, 21–28.
[45] *Gjenmæle*, 66–70.
[46] *Gjenmæle*, 64–66; *Historisk fremstilling*, 28–30.

the Synod clergy had been trained, for an opinion on the pastors' resolution about slavery. More than a year and a half went by without an answer, but on September 30, 1863, this faculty, headed by the distinguished professors and theologians C. P. Caspari and Gisle Johnson, delivered its opinion, which was brought to America by Pastor Ottesen, who had visited Norway that summer.

The reply of the Christiania scholars was by no means what the Synod leaders had anticipated. To them it seemed to be both "Yes" and "No." It apparently accepted, for the most part, their textual exposition, but by its definition of slavery and its conception of Biblical "slavery," it shifted the base for meeting the central question from textual exegesis to history and a broad interpretation of the Christian spirit; and its tone from first to last was profoundly antislavery. Postulating slavery as an institution in which a human being is treated as property — as a thing — it declared this to be contrary to God's original will to man, for God placed men in a relationship of essential equality as persons. Slavery, it went on, was no divine institution, but a fruit of sin intruding upon the world against God's will. Slavery pertains to the heathen world and Christianity must seek its abolition. In fact, the conquest and abolition of slavery are fruits of the cleansing and transforming influence of Christianity upon human society, working not through externals but by means of the rebirth of human hearts. After first pointing out that the slavery of the Old Testament was so modified as compared with heathen slavery that it could scarcely be called a slave relationship in the real meaning of the word, and that there was even further modification in Christian times, the faculty presented doctrines more acceptable to the Synod clergy, for it said that nowhere in the New Testament is slavery condemned or forbidden and nowhere is there a demand for its abolition. It conceded that the Scriptures not only do not make it an unqualified sin to hold slaves, but in fact place the slave relationship under the fourth commandment, and even admonish slaves to be submissive to their masters. It cited the familiar case of Paul and the runaway Onesimus. It then went on to emphasize the spirit of inner equality and suggested that with time this inner spirit of brotherhood brought about changes in external form. Slavery, it concluded, if considered in general, apart from the form in which it appears in specific cases, conflicts with God's original will to man and cannot be harmonized with Christianity, and is therefore sin " in and by itself " ; but it rejected the view that being or holding a slave is in every individual instance a sin, and it elaborated the opinion that it is not unqualifiedly sinful and unchristian to be a slaveholder. It then closed with an emphatic condemnation of slavery. Its re-establishment in the Christian world, it declared, is unquestionably a return to the ancient heathen system long since overcome by Christianity. Slavery is a " blot of shame upon the Christian name which every Christian in his heart must wish to see done away with again." The Norwegian theologians made it plain that they understood the nature of American slavery, in which the slave was definitely a chattel.

This document was not made public until a year after the close of the Civil War.[47] The Synod church council later explained to the Christiania faculty that contemporary publication was withheld because it would have caused confusion. Opponents of the clergy, it was suggested, could have pointed triumphantly to one part of the opinion, the clergy to another.[48] The excited feeling of Civil War times and the conviction of the clergy that part of the faculty opinion was not only not based upon the word of God, but actually in conflict with it, were alleged to be factors in the delay. But Clausen,

[47] The faculty opinion and other documents pertaining to it are printed in the *Synodalberetning*, 1866, p. 40–66. The opinion is conveniently reprinted in Bergh, *Den norsk lutherske kirkes historie*, 152–158.

[48] Bergh, *Den norsk lutherske kirkes historie*, 166.

who himself did not know about the opinion until it appeared in 1866, was not satisfied with any of these explanations. He said that it both provoked and saddened him that his opponents should have been so little candid that they concealed the opinion for three years " while they maintained that all the ablest theologians of the Lutheran church were on their side." [49] They had ample opportunity to show him the document during their many pastoral and private conferences with him, in the period when as friendly colleagues they were calling upon him to confess himself guilty of " evasions." But they did not choose to share their secret with him.

Meanwhile President H. A. Preus on March 31, 1864, had replied to the theological faculty in Christiania, requesting a reconsideration of the matter and enclosing a refutation which had been prepared by the Luther College professors, Laur. Larsen and F. A. Schmidt, probably mainly the former.[50] This refutation was a closely reasoned analysis which took sharp issue with much of the theological faculty's argument. It insisted that there were fundamental contradictions in the faculty position, particularly in the assertion that slavery, in general, is a sin in itself but that it is not, in every particular circumstance, a sin to keep slaves. Larsen and his colleague could not reconcile the two parts of this generalization. To their minds, if slavery itself was a sin, it was sinful both to own and to be a slave; and they challenged the faculty contention that the Bible, when it speaks of "slavery," implies something other than an actual slavery. As to

[49] *Gjenmæle,* 68. Clausen was particularly grieved that his colleagues had not evinced a " brotherly spirit " by showing him the opinion at the Perry conference in 1864, where they " pressed him hard." But he had no word of the opinion until the Synod meeting of 1866. See his article in *Emigranten,* November 19, 1866. In an essay in the issue for July 30, 1866, he suggests that the great majority of the people in the congregations would undoubtedly have agreed with the Christiania opinion and that the Synod leaders, aware of this, therefore held it back.

[50] This refutation, which is in *Synodalberetning,* 1866, p. 45–57, is unfortunately not reprinted by Bergh with the other major documents relating to the faculty opinion. It was dated March 14, 1864.

the general position that Christianity, altering external forms by its spirit, tends to make men equal, they argued that the logical consequence of such reasoning, applied not only to slave and master but also to rich and poor and other unequal classes, was communism.

Perhaps the most interesting part of the refutation, however, was its rejection of the faculty postulate of slavery as an institution under which one human being is treated by another as a "thing." This definition, they reasoned, confused physical with spiritual slavery. A slave is not a "thing," but a moral person whose spiritual self cannot be owned by another, and who, since a master's jurisdiction extends only to the temporal man, does not lack human rights. In a word, they rejected the faculty's primary definition of slavery, and in doing so they took precisely the ground that the Southern slaveholding moralists took when they insisted that the soul could not be sold, that property rights did not destroy "the rights of the slave as a man," and that it was "ridiculous to say that human legislation could convert mind into matter or matter into mind."[51]

The Norwegian theologians replied on June 6, 1864, that the communication from President Preus, with its enclosure, had occasioned a reconsideration of the matter, but that they did not find themselves moved to withdraw their opinion or to undertake any essential change in it. This communication in turn led to a heated rejoinder from the Synod church council on February 16, 1865, which reviewed the points at issue, indicated that the documents would be laid before the Synod, and attempted to define the broad issues underlying

[51] In the refutation Larsen and Schmidt suggest that slavery was introduced into America by a "monk" and that the institution, in God's hand, had forwarded a far more effective civilizing and Christianizing of the Negroes than had been possible through missionary enterprise in Africa. The "monk" was doubtless Bishop Las Casas, who, according to Jefferson Davis, "with philosophical humanity inaugurated the importation of the race of Ham." Jenkins, *Pro-slavery Thought*, 205. Clausen vigorously assailed this defense of slavery in *Emigranten*, July 30, 1866.

the dispute. The council said that the question was not merely one of slavery, but was rather a phase of the anti-Christian program of the times, involving temporal freedom as one of the "natural and inalienable rights of men: freedom, property, security, and opposition to oppression." It had learned "how violently party sickness can blind the eyes and embitter the heart," and how difficult it was "in a time of political upheaval to prevail upon men to analyze questions quietly in the light of God's Word." [52] To this rejoinder the Christiania theologians vouchsafed no reply.

Naturally this correspondence must have been fresh in the mind of President Preus at the Synod meeting of 1865 when Clausen, still completely uninformed about the opinion from Norway, proposed tolerance, within the church, of differing views on the slavery question. Preus and the council realized that the subject could not yet be closed, for they had indicated to the Christiania faculty that in all probability the documents would be laid before the Synod and the subject rediscussed in that body.[53] It was not until 1866, however, that Preus presented the correspondence to the Synod. The emergence of this new material did not at the time occasion a discussion and decision on the central problem by the Synod, but it set off a violent resumption of the controversy in the press, which had given the entire matter little attention since 1862, and it soon was evident that the Synod itself could not long postpone a thoroughgoing consideration and, if possible, a settlement of the question.

The subject was again debated in pastoral conferences, and Clausen, who was delighted with the general tone of the theological faculty's opinion, once more appeared as the central spokesman for the thesis that slavery is a sin. Dissen-

[52] The faculty reply and the council's rejoinder are in Bergh, *Den norsk lutherske kirkes historie,* 164–171.

[53] In their communication of February 16, 1865. Bergh, *Den norsk lutherske kirkes historie,* 171.

sion and trouble in the Synod congregations, common since the beginnings of the controversy in 1861, added to the fire. The chief secular organ for the controversy soon became *Skandinaven,* the Chicago newspaper established in the spring of 1866 by Knud Langeland and John Anderson, but other Norwegian-American newspapers were also keenly alive to the public interest in the discussion. Langeland gladly gave space to controversial articles on the subject. He had been a Free-Soiler in the 1840's and was a man of intense antislavery feeling. With this was coupled a hostility to all signs of what he considered the fastening of a clerical aristocracy upon the Norwegians in America reminiscent of the state-church clergy as he remembered it from his youth in Norway.[54] Clausen took up the discussion in *Emigranten* again, in July, 1866, and Schmidt and Larsen and others joined in it. And so it echoed throughout the Norwegian settlements with *Skandinaven* particularly active as the controversy developed. "How *Skandinaven* rages nowadays you can well imagine," wrote Larsen on one occasion in a private letter. "It not only keeps on rehashing the slavery question continually, but attacks us for intolerance." The "indifferentism and religious promiscuousness" of the editors and of Clausen himself, Larsen thought, made it possible to get "a good hold on them," but he suggested that "the realization that the pure doctrine is important is entirely too weak in many of our people, so that our opponents will not lack support on this score also."[55]

[54] Wist, in *Norsk-amerikanernes festskrift,* 50.

[55] *Historisk fremstilling,* 30, 31; Larsen's letter to his wife, in Larsen, *Laur. Larsen,* 175–177. The entire Christiania correspondence was printed in *Emigranten,* July 9, 23, and 30, 1866; and Clausen opened in the issue for July 30 with an article entitled "The Professors in Christiania and the Professors in Decorah on Slavery." Larsen and Schmidt jointly appeared with controversial articles on September 10 and October 22 and 29; and there was an elaborate reply by Clausen, October 1, 15, 29, November 5, 1866. A clash of Muus and Clausen is recorded in *Emigranten,* December 10, 1866; January 14, and February 18, 1867; and there were many other contributions to the discussion, including a somewhat moderate statement by A. C. Preus, September 17, 1866.

The controversy did not become intersynodical, though the Augustana Synod took notice of the subject in its ministerial proceedings, declared that slavery is a sin, and indicated its agreement with the Christiania faculty.[56] Hasselquist long since had declared that slavery is "ungodly in its very foundation and cannot stand the test of Christianity."[57] Eielsen had never wavered in his opposition to slavery, and after seeing actual slavery on a visit to the South in 1859 was more than ever convinced that it was not consonant with Christianity. Though he criticized the stand of the Synod ministers, they engaged in no open controversies with him on this issue.[58] H. A. Preus and Clausen, who were both in Norway in the early winter of 1867 (the former lecturing there on Norwegian-American church conditions), had a joint conference with Professor Johnson, one of the signers of the theological faculty's opinion, and each came away feeling that his cause was strengthened.[59] The Synod leaders also consulted a German theologian, Dr. Von Harless of Munich, who suggested that the famous declaration of 1861 should substitute for the words "Although, according to the Word of God, it is not in and by itself a sin to keep slaves" the following phrase: "Although the writings of the New Testament do not make it a sin for Christian masters to keep slaves."[60]

And so, finally, in 1868, at a meeting held in Chicago, the Synod reached a decision on the problem. There were extended conferences with Clausen, and ultimately a series of ten theses on the slavery question was laid before the church

[56] Preus, *Syv foredrag,* 131. In one of these lectures Preus gave an exposition of the position of the Synod leaders on the slavery controversy.

[57] Ander, *Hasselquist,* 153.

[58] See Mørstad, *Elling Eielsen,* 211. Eielsen's Synod in 1865 adopted resolutions of regret at the murder of President Lincoln and of rejoicing over the triumph of the Northern cause. Carlsen, "Elling Eielsen," 127.

[59] *Historisk fremstilling,* 47; *Gjenmæle,* 76–80; *Synodalberetning,* 1867, p. 86. Compare A. Weenaas, reporting on Gisle Johnson's lectures of 1867–68, in *Skandinaven,* January 31, February 7, 1872.

[60] *Synodalberetning,* 1867, p. 86–103; *Historisk fremstilling,* 47, 48.

body. Eight of these Clausen found himself willing to accept, but the theses that to his mind were fundamental and which amounted to acceptance of "the doctrine of slavery as a divine institution protected by God's Law, and giving the owner the right of inheritance and sale of slaves," he rejected The tenth, in particular, he regarded as crucial: "The condition of bondage spoken of in the New Testament is an actual servitude, or an actual slavery." He had been willing to agree that the "forced servitude" of the New Testament is "not in and by itself sinful," for he did not regard this as actual slavery; but when nailed to the final thesis, it meant nothing less than the doctrine which he had been fighting since 1861, that slavery is not a sin. Accused by his enemies throughout the entire controversy of inconsistencies and changing viewpoints, Clausen, ever since his retraction of 1861, had clung to his main position. And now, at the end, he held his ground. He himself proposed an alternative set of resolutions, but it was accepted only after a committee had gone over it and purged it of what they considered "false doctrines." The Synod was willing to concede that it is sin in itself for a human being to treat another as a "thing"—a chattel—but it rejected the view that this was a correct description of the property relationship existing between a master and a slave. By a large majority, it accepted the ten theses which made official doctrine for the Synod the basic doctrine that the clergy had underwritten in 1861—that slavery, according to the Word of God, is not a "sin in and by itself." Clausen had no alternative save to resign from the Synod. This he did, on June 28, 1868, and a dozen or more congregations of the Synod similarly broke away or were split in two.[61]

So long and bitter a controversy could not be ended at a

[61] *Historisk fremstilling,* 48–54; *Gjenmæle,* 80–86; *Synodalberetning,* 1868, p. 22–37, with Clausen's letter of resignation on p. 34; Larsen, *Laur. Larsen,* 173–176; Rohne, *Norwegian American Lutheranism,* 218–220.

stroke, however, and the Synod action of 1868 was not the final curtain of the drama. The newspapers continued to carry controversial articles. Professor Larsen, on behalf of the church council, combed Clausen's utterances for contradictions and prepared for publication by the council in 1868 an analytical and controversial essay entitled "Historical Presentation of the Conflict Which Was Carried On within the Norwegian Synod in America on the Biblical Doctrine concerning Slavery."[62] The next year Clausen brought out his side of the story in a booklet called "Refutation of the Church Council of the Norwegian Synod"—a chronological survey of the controversy, subjective, somewhat rambling, and lacking the precision of Larsen's analysis, but by no means an ineffective statement.[63] He was on the defensive, for Larsen had devoted a major share of his attention to alleged inconsistencies on Clausen's part. Though Clausen insisted that many of them were "merely imaginary or at most derived from a lack of clarity"[64] in his many discussions through the years since 1861, he conceded that he had known doubt and struggle and had made mistakes, but he said that these did not affect the essential correctness of his cause. That he himself may not have been the best man to defend that cause did not make the cause itself any the less worthy. Both Larsen and Clausen were partisan and controversial in their approach and each is a necessary corrective to the other.[65] An interesting statement endorsed by

[62] The full title is *Historisk fremstilling af den strid, som i aarene 1861 til 1868 indenfor den norske synode i Amerika har været ført i anledning af skriftens läre om slaveri.* It was issued in a booklet of fifty-five pages by the Synod's church council at Madison in 1868. The authorship is proved in Larsen, *Laur. Larsen,* 177. Professor Larsen was asked by the Synod president to prepare a "concise presentation of Pastor Clausen's different positions during the slavery controversy, his remarkable assertions, concessions, and contradictions."

[63] *Gjenmæle mod kirkeraadet for den norske synode i anledning af dets skrift kaldet: "Historisk fremstilling af den strid som i aarene 1861 til 1868 inden for den norske synode i Amerika har været ført i anledning af skriftens lære om slaveri"* (86 p.).

[64] *Gjenmæle,* 55.

[65] A twentieth-century repercussion of the controversy occurred in 1905 when Adolf Bredesen published his *Slaveristriden i ny belysning,* in which he pictured

the Synod church council was that "No Christian can be a proslavery man."[66] In the spring of 1869 A. C. Preus offered a "word of conciliation." Though he considered Clausen's Biblical exposition wrong, he had been discontented with the unwillingness of his colleagues to discuss American slavery, which would have met the original problem and satisfied the layman. He himself frankly believed that slavery as carried on in America was a sin, that the Word of God and Christian love forbade Christians to deal with human beings as they were dealt with under the institution of American slavery. He also considered the Christiania opinion sound, and he deplored the efforts of the Synod leaders to refute it.[67]

The adoption of the ten theses by the Synod in 1868, establishing "purity of doctrine" and limiting the church's action to Biblical passages and authority, evidently left a contemporary feeling that something yet remained to be said. In 1869 the Synod returned to the subject, this time to deal with American slavery, which in 1861 had been put aside as a political-historical matter that had no place in the Synod's deliberations. The resolution of 1869 condemned the "sins and ungodliness" that accompanied slavery in the United States. It declared that "American slavery," if by that term "in the less precise speech of daily life" one implied the use of laws and regulations as a cover for such

the Synod leaders of the slavery controversy as spokesmen of the Republican cause and declared that the blessing of Lincoln rests over them. A Clausen adherent, the church historian J. A. Bergh, challenged Bredesen's reasoning as specious, pointing out that among his many quotations from Lincoln he had failed to include the famous assertion "If slavery is not wrong, nothing is wrong" and that he had made no allusion to the "House Divided against Itself" address. *Slaveristriden: Nogle rettelser til Pastor Bredesens nye indlæg i den gamle strid* (Madison, 1905).

[66] *Historisk fremstilling,* 4. A criticism of the council's document by Wilhelm Winslow is in *Skandinaven,* March 3, 10, 1869; and a criticism of *Gjenmæle* is in *Kirkelig maanedstidende,* 15:33–37 (February 1, 1870).

[67] A. C. Preus, "Et mæglende ord i slaveristriden," in *Skandinaven,* March 3, 10, 1869. Clausen, though pleased that Preus accepted the Christiania opinion, did not wholly agree with various phases of Preus's general view of the problem. See "Et par bemärkninger," in *Skandinaven,* April 7, 1869.

accompanying sins and ungodliness, was in this sense "a sin and an abomination." But it reiterated the central position of the Synod on slavery, and it said that masters who treated their slaves "in love according to God's Word" did not sin by keeping slaves. And it closed with a fervent hope that "this strife about an institution which has never existed in our congregations and which now, God be praised, has been abolished in our country, may be ended among all who really love the Word of God, and that their hearts may again be united in peace and love on the rock of truth." [68]

The central reality in the minds of the Synod leaders in the slavery controversy was the authority of the "Word of God." They fought for Lutheran orthodoxy as they conceived it, for a strict Biblical interpretation, for theological dogma. The central reality in the mind of Clausen was slavery in the United States and an unwillingness to have the church countenance it. He fought against contemporary slavery and for human freedom — a part of the same crusade that drew him to the Southern battlefields as an army chaplain.

Neither of these realities found a direct opposite, a forthright enemy, to come to grips with. Clausen's antislavery passion did not collide with a proslavery passion; and the ministerial orthodoxy did not confront a challenging religious liberalism. It is true that the Synod clergy betrayed no great enthusiasm for the Civil War and that they utilized in their polemics the Biblical arguments which the Southern

[68] *Synodalberetning*, 1869, p. 86. An echo of the slavery controversy was heard in 1874 when Sven Oftedal and August Weenaas of the Norwegian-Danish Conference issued a very sharp "Open Declaration" challenging the Synod on many grounds, including the "doctrine, adopted by the Synod, of the divine justification of slavery, mocking all individuality and personality, all human freedom and right." The text is in Bergh, *Den norsk lutherske kirkes historie*, 231–234. Weenaas later withdrew his assent to this "Open Declaration," but in his *Wisconsinismen belyst ved historiske kjendsgjerninger*, 127–132 (Chicago, 1876), he delivered a blast against the Synod doctrine on slavery. He incidentally characterized the controversy as the "longest, sharpest, and most bitter" in the history of the Norwegian Lutheran church in America (p. 127).

slaveholder employed as the basic element in his moral defense of slavery, but they regarded slavery as an evil and a punishment from God, and they declared themselves willing to work for its abolition. It is true, also, that Clausen turned more to the broad spirit of Christianity than to the letter for basic support of his position and that he represented a more liberal outlook than that of his opponents, but he was scarcely a spokesman for an elastic Biblical interpretation, and his fight was not directed against the fundamental concepts of Synodical orthodoxy.

Since there was no head-on clash between these two central realities, the controversy has about it a certain air of unreality. The two combatants do not seem to be fighting in opposite trenches. The only document of the controversy that seemed to grasp this curious aspect of the affair was the opinion of the Christiania theological professors. That subtle opinion voiced the Christian spirit in its denunciation of slavery in the modern world; it understood clearly that the American slave, unlike the slave in Mosaic law, was a chattel; it was unwilling to anchor the kite of chattel slavery to the Christian church; and at the same time it took cognizance of the Synod pastors' Scriptural exposition. Its spirit was that of mediating the two central realities, and when it encountered a Brand-like attitude of "all or nothing" on the part of the Synod leaders, the Norwegian theologians as a group had nothing more to say.

The story of the controversy has, of course, its human side. Larsen and other leaders of the Synod cause were men of considerable theological scholarship, of earnest religious belief, and of courage. They were human enough to be conscious of the dignity and authority of a trained clergy, but they were driven primarily by a zeal for the "Word of God"—for an uncompromising orthodoxy—and in this spirit they were formidable antagonists. Their orthodoxy had been stiffened by the Missouri connection, which also swung ajar the door to controversy and may have colored to some extent their political views. They were not closely in touch with the realities of contemporary American feeling, not easily moved by popular clamor. Clausen, as has been noted, was sensitive to the common life, democratic, emotional, stirred by the war and the problem of American slavery, and possessed of a stubborn courage which fully matched that of his opponents. Notwithstanding his ministerial rank, he was essentially a lay leader. Some historians reject the idea that the struggle was in any sense one between the common people and a clerical aristocracy — a transfer to American soil of the antipathy of Norwegian commoners for an entrenched officialdom; but in a wide-ranging controversy, many elements crowd about the central issues, and there undoubtedly was some contemporary interpretation of the controversy in terms of such a class division, especially during its later stages.

Larsen and the Synod clergy won the fight in the sense that the church body officially sanctioned the clergy's doctrine. The Synod attained doctrinal unity and harmony and came out of the struggle with a heightened orthodoxy, but in winning this victory it lost not only Clausen but to a certain degree that flavor of a realistic touch with the common life of the age which he represented. He in turn lost the theological battle within the Synod and felt compelled to secede, but his basic cause — antislavery — triumphed; the Synod, though accepting the clergy's doctrine on slavery *per se,* gave praise to God Himself that American slavery, which was the only slavery that had any actual significance to Clausen and the laymen, had been abolished; and its church council accepted the dictum that "No Christian can be a proslavery man." Both Larsen and Clausen, as leaders in the controversy, left marks on Norwegian-American life, the one through his scholarship and theological austerity, the other through his democratic sympathy and humanity, both through their sincerity and controversial stubbornness. Each side, for better or for worse, both won and lost — as is sometimes the case in theological and other wars. Meanwhile, for Americans north and south, perspective gradually lengthened, and there was a growing tendency to consider slavery, not in theological terms, but as an economic and social institution to be viewed, in its setting of time and circumstance, as wise or unwise, just or unjust, humane or inhuman.

XV. PEOPLE IN DISPERSION

THE TENACITY of the Norwegian impulse to emigrate during the Civil War years was an augur of the coming flood, but few appear to have anticipated the extraordinary outpouring of the postwar years from 1866 to 1873. In all the years from 1820 to 1865 the total of Norwegian migration had amounted to only 77,874. Now in the space of eight years, no fewer than 110,896 Norwegians left their native country for the promise of fortune overseas. And even this was not high tide. A period of a half dozen years followed in which the total emigration was only 28,597—in fact, in five of those years the annual total was less than 5,000. A rise in 1879 to 7,607 signalized the approach of a new period. The figures leaped to more than 19,000 in 1880, to 25,000 in 1881, and to 28,000 in 1882—the highest figure for a single year in the entire history of Norwegian migration to America—and, with various shifts but never dropping below 10,000 a year, the numbers totaled 254,666 for the entire period from 1880 to 1893. Thereafter for another six years the figures were low, but in 1900 there was another upward surge, and the first decade of the twentieth century witnessed the third great outflowing of population, the volume reaching a total of almost precisely 25,000 in the one year of 1903.[1]

Thus Norwegian emigration became a major exodus, a colossal movement in proportion to the total population of Norway. The "America fever"—that contagion of excitement about the New World—spread over the entire country, touching every district, every hamlet, almost every family. This was no casual episode, no passing phenomenon, but a great social and economic force generated by a combination of the magnetic attraction of America with fundamental changes in the national economy of Norway. It was a folk movement that had far-reaching effects upon the life of the Norwegian people. It was a stream of hundreds of thousands of living beings that flowed to the valleys and prairies of the West, contributing to the vigor of American growth.

As the migration swelled after 1865 the Norwegian sailing vessels, which hitherto had carried most of the emigrants, faced sharp competition from voracious English steamship lines. The Norwegian vessels did, indeed, manage to convey all but some fifteen per cent of the emigrants in 1866, but three years later the English carriers, utilizing the magic of steam and propeller, had captured more than half the trade. And as that trade mounted year after year beyond the ten-thousand mark, many of the rising British companies, including the White Star, Allan, Cunard, Anchor, Inman, and Guion lines, established central offices in Norway.[2] Agents

[1] A convenient table giving the figures for Norwegian emigration is in *Utvandringsstatistikk,* 104ff. (Departementet for Sociale Saker, *Norges officielle statistikk,* series 7, no. 25—Christiania, 1921); Qualey, in his *Norwegian Settlement,* 251, gives both the Norwegian and American tabulations for the period from 1820 to 1910. Arne Skaug points out that the general level of emigration was raised after the Civil War "so that a migration that we now characterize as 'lower' is high compared to the emigration during the earliest years." See his *Fluctuations in Migration from Norway since 1900,* 15, a work issued by the International Institute of Intellectual Co-operation in Paris in 1937. It is a scholarly study of much broader chronological range than its title indicates.

[2] Ingrid Gaustad, "Utvandringen til Amerika 1866–73," in *Historisk tidsskrift* (Oslo), 31:272, 273 (1938).

were sent to the interior districts during the winter to fan emigration interest and to enroll passengers for the coming season. The toils of people in dispersion promised money profits, dividends. Late in 1866 *Morgenbladet* published an article "On Emigration Agents," calling attention to the lengths to which the emissaries of the shipping companies were going. Thirty years earlier Norwegian skippers had occasionally visited the rural districts to enroll passengers and perhaps had indulged in some exaggeration of the glories of America. Now, with foreign competition rapidly developing, numerous agents were regularly engaged in recruiting emigrants. They were on a winter hunt, with commissions dependent upon the size of their bags. They carried with them impressive documents praising their vessels and captains, extolling America, and describing Norway in dark colors. *Morgenbladet* called upon the Norwegians to offset this propaganda, and it particularly urged ministers and teachers to use their influence to check the prevalent mania, to save their countrymen from exposure to what was politely referred to as the "rawness, impudence, and sectarianism" of America.[3]

The popular hurly-burly was accentuated in 1866 by an alleged scandal centering about the new passenger steamer "Ottawa," backed by the American Emigrant Aid and Homestead Company, a corporation organized shortly after the passage of the American law of 1864 which legalized contract labor. This company, looking for laborers from the Scandinavian countries, engaged the firm of Blichfeldt and Knoph to recruit emigrants for the "Ottawa." A large number of Norwegians enrolled as a result of this arrangement were tradesmen and artisans who were unable to pay more than a small part of the costs of their passage and therefore signed labor contracts. This pledging of future labor shocked many freedom-loving Norwegians, and the "Ottawa" had scarcely

[3] "Om udvandringsagenter," in *Morgenbladet,* December 21, 1866.

Columbia.

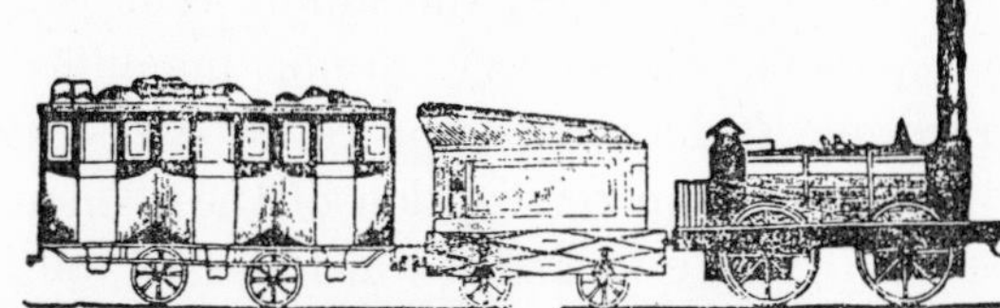

Udvandrer-Befordring

til alle de væsentligste Havne i Amerika og Australien,
hver 8de Dag regelmæssig,
ved Morris & Comp. i Christiania.

Udvandringen var tiltaget saa betydeligt i den senere Tid i Norge, at vi have fundet os foranledigede til under Dags Dato foruden vort Hoved-Bureau i **Liverpool** og **Hamburg**, ogsaa i **Christiania** at grunde et Bureau til den **hurtigste, prompteste** og **billigste** Befordring for Udvandrere — herfra over England. Det er et ubestredet Faktum, at Skibene fra Liverpool tilbagelægge deres Reise i den korteste Tid, da af alle de europæiske Hovedhavne Liverpool er de amerikanske Landingspladse nærmest beliggende. Ved Reisen over Liverpool undgaaes desforuden aldeles den for Passagererne i Almindelighed saa ubehagelige Fart gjennem Kanalen og langs med Kysten samt Sandbankernes Farlighed. Den direkte Befordring af Udvandrere fra Christiania bliver udført med Dampskib og Jernbane til Liverpool hver 8de Dag regelmæssig, i et Tidsrum af omtrent 4 Dage; og da den sædvanlige Overreise til de nævnte nordamerikanske Søstæder bliver tilbagelagt i 20 a 22 Dage fra Liverpool, saa vilde hele Reisen fra **Christiania** til et af Nordamerikas Hovedstæder kunne tilbagelægges i 25 a 26 Dage,

et vigtigt Forsprang for de fra Christiania direkte afgaaende Skibe.

Reisen fra Liverpool til Australien tilbagelægges i Almindelighed i cirka 70 Dage.

Alle vore Skibe, med hvilke vi befordre Udvandrere fra Liverpool, ere første Klasses, kobberbudede Tremastere, byggede ifølge de engelsk-amerikanske Love og særegent indrettede til dette Maal; de tør ei optage flere end det lovligt foreskrevne Antal Passagerer.

Uden videre Ordprunk for at anbefale vort nye Etablissement i Norge, henvise vi kun til vort længe med Agtelse bestaaende Firma, og bemærke, at vi ved de i Hamburger Commerce (øverste Finantsforvaltning) kontant deponerede **12.000 Mark Hamburger Banco**, og de ifølge Loven i Liverpool deponerede **1000 £ Sterling**, byde fuldkommen Garanti at de Udvandrere som benytte vort Firma, blive ifølge Forpligtelse reelt betjente.

Prospecti, hvoraf det Nærmere er at se, blive **gratis** udleverede i vort **Bureau, Hjørnet af Prindsens- og Skippergaden No. 22**

Christiania, 1ste August 1853. **Morris & Comp.**

NB Solide og redelige Personer, som skulde kunne ønske at overtage Agenturen for os udenbyes, ville i frankerede Breve derom henvende sig til os, hvorimod vi tilstille dem alle Oplysninger og Prospekterne.

AN ADVERTISEMENT OF AN EMIGRANT AGENCY IN NORWAY
[From *Christiania-posten*, August 3, 1853.]

left Christiania when wild rumors spread that the emigrants had been branded like cattle and were in the hands of malevolent slave traders. The bankruptcy of the forwarding company added fuel to the fire. Evidently it was the intention of the American concern to send the immigrants west to work on the Pacific railroad. The "Ottawa" had an uneventful voyage, apart from the solemn christening of a newborn babe with the beguiling name of Ottawa Atalanta; the passengers were duly landed in New York; and a few of them went on to the steppes of Missouri. Some of the immigrants were acutely discontented, it is true, but the records do not seem to prove that they were defrauded or victimized. In Norway, however, the affair went echoing through the newspapers, with every rumor magnified, occasionally in grotesque fashion; and the result was a deepening concern about the commercialization of the economic distress of the people. Many looked toward the establishment of governmental control of the promotion of emigration by commercial agents.[4]

The competition of runners and agents for the emigrant business in Norway, as indeed in New York, Quebec, and Chicago, was a sordid scramble for profits. An old ballad is more revealing than government documents in its portrayal of the tactics of emigration agents. Probably it is a truthful record in its reflection of the greedy psychology of these officials. The ballad celebrates the adventures of an emigrant who made his way to Christiania, where he was to embark for America:

> Last night I arrived in Christiania, and was about to find a lodging; but as I stepped out of the station I was besieged by "runners" from Henderson's, Heitmann's, and Sharpe's. "We've got to land him," they yelled. "You're going to America, aren't you?"
>
> I said yes, and then there was a riot. Hats and caps flew in the air; Henderson Brothers' tugged at my coat, and the men from Sharpe's cried, "Hei, what a picking." And not one of them gave an inch.
>
> Soon there was a free-for-all fight; mud spattered everywhere, and rags of clothing flew about. The Hendersons howled and the Sharpes they pulled, and the minions of Heitmann put them both to flight. Good God, how I laughed. I never had such sport in my life.[5]

[4] An advertisement of Blichfeldt and Knoph is in *Aftenbladet,* July 28, 1866. The "Ottawa" affair was discussed in *Morgenbladet* for August 20, September 1, 11, 12, 13, 26, 27, October 1, 11, 17, 18, 24, 28, November 1, 29, 1866, and in various other issues of that paper. The subject was threshed over by Wilhelm Sommer in *Den saakaldte "Ottawahistorie" upartisk belyst* (Copenhagen, 1866). An article in *Folketidende* (Mandal), interpreted the outcry about the "Ottawa" as a phase of the opposition to emigration. See "Et par ord om udvandringen," in *Folketidende,* November 28, 1866.

[5] Blegen and Ruud, *Norwegian Emigrant Songs and Ballads,* 333–336.

To many emigrants, however, the business was not sport but tragedy. That there was brazen skullduggery in the art of collaring prospective emigrants was proved in the case of an unctuous scoundrel named Myles W. Gunderson, who in 1867 promoted emigration, issued a guide for those seeking to learn English, published briefly a monthly paper entitled "The Norwegian Emigrant,"[6] and devoted himself particularly to the unholy business of searching out as victims those prospective emigrants who were converted Christians. With a wealth of advance payments in his pocket, this pious thief incontinently disappeared from the scene.[7] Obviously, a ministerial opinion was needed. The Reverend H. A. Preus, then in Norway, was called upon to give his judgment on the entire problem of America.[8] He knew nothing about Gunderson, advised people not to have too high hopes of America and to be fully prepared for hard work there, but he took occasion to urge everyone to take with him his church papers, and he called attention to the abundance of public land still available in the West, especially in Iowa and Minnesota. "It is not too much to say," he added, "that if the entire population of Norway emigrated and took up land, there still would be room for more."[9] This was scarcely comforting to those who hoped to dam the flood, and Preus was answered sharply in the newspapers. One writer even questioned publicly the truth of the assertion that in America public land was free to settlers. The correctness of what Preus said, however, was driven home when *Morgenbladet* printed the text of the American Homestead Law on its front page and a returned emigrant who had been in America for

[6] J. B. Halvorsen, *Norsk forfatter lexikon,* 2:457.

[7] Gunderson organized the "Norwegian American Emigration Society," urged emigrants to plan to go beyond Chicago and to take the shortest possible route. He seems to have given special praise to Colorado and Idaho. See *Morgenbladet,* January 23, 25, February 7, 9, 13, 23, March 6, 13, 18, 1867. *Morgenbladet* declared on March 6 that cheating emigrants had become an occupation in Norway.

[8] *Morgenbladet,* March 6, 1867.

[9] *Morgenbladet,* March 16, 1867.

several years pointed out that the minister had stated only the simple truth about American land.[10]

Meanwhile, there could be no question, in the light of the conditions themselves and the popular agitation in Norway, of the need for governmental control of some kind. It came in a series of provisional regulations in 1867 and a law of 1869 which made these regulations permanent.[11] Without analyzing the new controls in precise detail, it may be said that they accomplished the needed reform of placing all emigration agents in Norway under governmental supervision and regulation. The measures were designed to prevent fraud and to protect the interests of the emigrant. The agent was required to put up as security a sum ranging from two thousand to seven thousand specie dollars, to secure written permission to act as an agent from the chief of police in the city where he established his headquarters, and, most important of all, to submit every emigration contract to the police for endorsement. Among other things the government ruled invalid all stipulations with reference to the compensation through labor in America for all or part of the passage money of the emigrant. Thus Norway struck at the contract labor provision of the American immigration law of 1864 which Lincoln, confronted by the crisis of the Civil War and the dearth of laborers in industry and agriculture, had urged Congress to enact. The emergency had passed with the war, however, and the United States in 1868, only a year after the Norwegian regulations were first put into effect, repealed the law of 1864. This repeal removed a troublemaking factor in the emigration situation, though it did not signify any

[10] *Morgenbladet,* March 17, April 3, 4, 1867.

[11] A mass of material relating to the Norwegian action of 1867 and 1869 is in Socialdept., Oslo: Lovkontor, Utvandringen, Forarbeide til lov av 1869 ogsv., folder 1. This material includes letters from the Norwegian consuls in New York and Quebec, and information on the British passenger act of 1855, the Hamburg decree of the same year, and the French law of 1860, all of which were aimed at a control similar to that desired by the Norwegians. See *Morgenbladet,* April 12, 14, 1867; May 11, 1869.

abandonment of the general American attitude of encouragement to the immigration of Europeans. The Republican party in 1868 adopted a resounding declaration favoring such encouragement, and Congress took under advisement, though it did not pass, a bill imposing upon the American consuls in Norway and other countries of Europe the responsibility for spreading information about the attractions of America.[12]

Even without such legal authorization the American consuls in Norway during the Civil War period had played an active part in advertising the United States among the common people. But their efforts were only one item in an overwhelming grand total of influences that reached across the ocean from the western world. America letters continued to reach Norway in a ceaseless and steadily widening stream, and though details might differ, the major emphasis was usually the same: free land, fresh opportunity, release from old burdens, a new life. The Norwegian settlements in the West had passed the preliminary experimental stage. The immigrants could, and did, speak with assurance. "Yes," wrote one in 1868, "we can truthfully call to the burdened cotter, the many hungry and impoverished families of servants, and the poor laborers and craftsmen in the old dear Norway: 'Come over to us. Here is land for the landless and bread for the breadless, so that you and your children can have a happy future.'" The promise of economic betterment was implicit in the thousands of letters that told of individual progress in America, however difficult the road. And often it was accompanied by a vibrant social note: the workingman in America is not obliged to stand with his hat in his hand when the big fellows come along; all eat at the same table; here "there is equality before the law."[13] The complacent *Morgenbladet* might talk about the "rawness, impudence, and sectarianism" of America, but that organ had

[12] Stephenson, *American Immigration,* 139, 140.
[13] *Hamars stiftstidende,* April 14, 1868; Gaustad, in *Historisk tidsskrift,* 31:273.

slight influence upon the masses who read with breathless interest the personal reports out of America which revealed, scene by scene, the drama of life in a new nation bursting with resources and energy.

While steamships were cutting down the costs of transportation so that in the late 1860's it became possible to make the entire journey from Norway to the Midwestern metropolis of Chicago for less than fifty dollars, the America letters never ceased to focus attention upon free land under the Homestead Act, good wages for labor, and the opportunities for the common man in the American democracy. The America letters did more. They often carried enclosures that told a more convincing story than any airy generalizations about the opportunities of the West—prepaid tickets, money to cover the costs of the long journey by vessel and train. This language needed no interpreter. "A man from Birid who left home ten years ago and now lives in Wisconsin sent his aged parents three hundred dollars," ran a newspaper item in 1866, "and thus they and eleven other members of the family were enabled to follow after him." From 1872 to 1875, of 18,372 emigrants who left Norway by way of Christiania 7,247, or thirty-nine per cent, had prepaid tickets.[14] The percentage might vary in different periods, and ordinarily women were more likely to have such tickets than men, but evidence indicates that through all the ups and downs of emigration to the twentieth century, prepaid tickets continued to play an important role. From 1905 to 1916, for example, there was no single year in which the percentage of the Norwegian women emigrants having prepaid tickets fell below thirty-three, and in five separate years it ran well above forty per cent. For both men and women in the same period the percentage ranged from 28.4 to 42.3.[15] Thus the America letters, endorsing their stories of immigrant expe-

[14] *Morgenbladet,* May 3, 1866; Gaustad, in *Historisk tidsskrift,* 31:274.
[15] *Utvandringsstatistikk,* 86, 87.

rience with precious tickets, bought and paid for by American dollars, implemented the tumultuous propaganda that steamship lines, railroads, land companies, American states, and other agencies concentrated upon the transfer of thousands of people to the New World. The magnetic potency of America is a central force in emigration. The sensitiveness of the movement to the economic swings in America is too well known to need emphasis. Invariably after an American panic—1857, 1873, 1893, 1907—the volume of the stream was greatly reduced, only to swell again as times in America improved.

Søren Jaabæk in 1866 attributed the potency of America as a magnet to two major forces: its great civic liberty and its wonderfully fertile soil. These forces, acting upon a country in which there obviously was much discontent, would produce, he believed, a mass emigration. Emigration, it was argued in Jaabæk's paper, "The People's News," is the only available relief; the doors at home are closed for poverty-stricken people; they face dark night. This paper saw the America letters as part of an endless chain of circumstance that forwarded migration. The more people that go, it said, the more letters; the more letters, the more reliable information; the more reliable information, the more emigration. A similar point of view was expressed by *Aftenbladet* in Christiania, which pointed out the absurdity of defining emigration in terms of enticement on the one side and folly on the other. The Norwegians in America had already developed an organized society of old neighbors. A mass of questions had been raised and answered, back and forth across the Atlantic, between that society and the people of Norway.[16]

[16] *Folketidende,* August 8, November 28, 1866; February 20, 1867; *Aftenbladet,* May 4, 1867. Jaabæk, it may be added, was a believer in the republican form of government. "It is my firm belief," he said in a preface to his volume of poems, "Song and Rest," "that the future belongs only to the republicans, and I therefore open with a song to the future in the hope that the cultural development of the twentieth century will bring to republicans, by legal and proper means, a general victory throughout the civilized world."

That hundreds of thousands of Norwegians traveled the road of emigration, a path cut broad and clear by the pioneers of the earlier period, means not only a powerful pull from America but also a powerful ejective force in Norway. On the Norwegian side the searcher for explanations is confronted, not by a simple category of emigration causes, but by the entire economic and social web of the common life as it was spun on the loom of the nineteenth century.[17] For Norwegian emigration to America was one aspect of a turbulence and jostling within the Norwegian economy which accompanied a national transformation; and as American contacts deepened, New World influences tended more and more to play into the emerging Norwegian patterns. The scene is that broad field of Atlantic history — the merging of European and North American history — which the English scholar, H. Hale Bellot, has defined; but it is a Norwegian scholar, Ingrid Gaustad Semmingsen, who has most clearly envisioned the larger interrelations of emigration with the economic and social evolution of Norway.[18]

Her interpretation centers about the unprecedented and constant increase in the population of Norway which shot the total, notwithstanding a tremendous emigration drain, from 883,440 in 1801 to 1,792,833 in 1875, to 2,217,971 in 1900, and 2,810,592 in 1928. Norwegian population expanded to twice its size in the half century from the end of the Napoleonic wars to 1865.[19] Had this extraordinary increase, with

[17] See ch. 8, on "Emigration Causes and Controversy," in Blegen, *Norwegian Migration*.

[18] See Mrs. Semmingsen's "Norwegian Emigration to America during the Nineteenth Century," in *Studies and Records*, 11:66–81; her article, published by her as Ingrid Gaustad, in *Historisk tidsskrift*, 31:237–279; and "Grunnlaget for utvandringen," in *Nordmanns-forbundet*, 29:207–209 (July, 1936). Dr. Skaug, in his analysis of the Norwegian emigration statistics, reaches conclusions somewhat similar to those of Mrs. Semmingsen and his tabulations offer a substantial body of supporting material.

[19] An excellent discussion of births, deaths, and the growth of the Norwegian population in relation to emigration is in Skaug, *Migration from Norway*, 20 ff. He writes, "In spite of heavy emigration and the beginning of the decline of the

a variety of factors accounting for a decline in infant mortality, been accompanied by a quick and energetic swing from an agricultural to an industrial economy, it is conjecturable that much of the population surplus would have been absorbed within the boundaries of Norway. But for various reasons the great development that has marked recent Norway in the fields of industry and urbanization was relatively late in getting under way; and agriculture, shifting from a very limited self-contained economy to one of money profits and international competition, developed slowly and encountered severe crises, especially in the 1860's and 1880's, the very periods of mass migration to America.

This was the background for the emergence of a great population surplus which, in a continuing agrarian society, tended to be projected to a considerable extent into a landless class of laborers, servants, and unemployed people. It was no local, no isolated, but rather a general Norwegian problem, the profile of which is revealed by the fact that in the first gigantic wave of emigration, that from 1866 to 1873, 63.42 per cent of the birth surplus found its way out of the country.[20] But the swarming of the population surplus was by no means confined to the lanes of emigration. Norway witnessed also an extensive internal migration as the folk comprising the economically frustrated surplus sought outlets for their energies and potentialities — and bread for their mouths. This migration and the emigration to America were different aspects of the same large movement; and one of the most interesting of the Norwegian scholar's conclusions is that the later urban migration from Norway to America was very largely the old rural migration delayed by briefer or longer pauses in the Norwegian cities. In a word, it may be compared with the immigration which sought temporary

birth-rate from the 1870's, thanks to the improvement in the mortality-rate, we have a growth of population the like of which we have never had before" (p. 32.).

[20] Skaug, *Migration from Norway*, 24.

haven in Chicago or Minneapolis before pushing on to the valleys and plains of the West.[21]

The picture must not be oversimplified. The stresses were not equal in all parts of Norway; and the ways of relief differed. As Mrs. Semmingsen points out, in some areas nearly the entire population surplus went off to America; highlanders, at a far remove from urban life and conditions, were likely to emigrate, whereas lowlanders tended to be drawn toward Christiania; in some districts special industrial trends were developed which provided sanctuary for youthful energy and so the emigration was relatively small.[22] For the early migration the available data make it exceedingly difficult to analyze the migrants from the point of view of occupations and status, but the materials for the period after the Civil War are somewhat more informing. They indicate a solid representation of the substantial class of independent landowners, the traditional rural aristocracy of Norway, but much of the migration is drawn from the landless class of cotters, laborers, servants, and others who might naturally be expected to emerge as the surplus in a rapidly growing population. Mrs. Semmingsen offers an analysis of the migration in the period from 1868 to 1875 which is not without interest in this connection. Her tabulations show that of 27,669 men over fifteen years of age who emigrated from the country districts, 2,882 were *gaard* men and 2,628 the sons of *gaard* men — that is, 5,510 represented the class of independent landowners with their proud traditions. Cotters numbered 1,905 and cotters' sons 920 — a total of 2,825. There were 2,449 men drawn from mining and other industries, and 995 from trade and shipping. Those who did not report any occupation numbered 6,613 — a class that probably included a considerable number of wage earners, cotters, and servants. Those classified in personal

[21] Semmingsen, in *Studies and Records,* 11:78–80.
[22] Semmingsen, in *Studies and Records,* 11:73–75.

Fra D. D. sælge Undertegnede sine Varer pr. Contant til saa lavt nedsatte Priser, at de trodse enhver Concurrence. Credit staar fremdeles aaben.

Hamar den 14de December 1869.

G. Falk. Chr. Platou. A. Steen. P. Traaseth. P. Ilsaas. S. Steen. O. Østbye. M. Soelberg. N. Petersen. E. Skappel. P. Jolstad & Co. Finstad & Schjerden. I. T. Hansen. M. H. Imislund.

God, hurtig og billig Befordring

til alle bekjendte Steder i

Amerika med Guion & Co.s

nye, store, hurtigseilende og bekvemt indrettede

1ste Klasses Kongl. Post-Dampskibe:

„Colorado"	3000 Ts.	„Dacotah"	3100 Ts.
„Manhattan"	2900 „	„Wyoming"	3100 „
„Minnesota"	2900 „	„Wisconsin"	3100 „
„Nebraska"	3500 „	„Somerset"	2000 „
„Nevada"	3100 „	„Worcester"	2000 „
„Idaho"	3100 „	„Carroll"	2000 „

Post-Dampskibe over Hamburg til **New-Orleans** og **Galveston i Texas:** „Hammonia", „Cimbiria", „Allemania", „Borussia", „Holsatia", „Saxonia", „Bavaria", „Teutonia", „Westphalia", „Silesia".

Seilskibe til Quebec:

DHrr. Johannes Rods Sønners velanbefalede Emigrantskib
Columbia, Capt. O. Rød, afgaar 24de April,
Edda, „ Andersen, do. 13de do.

Emigranter behage at henvende sig til Undertegnede, hvor fornødne Oplysninger meddeles og Indskrivning naarsomhelst sker til billigste Overfragtpriser.

C. F. Omang, Hamar,
autoriseret Emigrations-Agent for **Blichfeldt & Co.**

Emigrant-Indskrivning.

sker paa **Grundset Marked** ved vor autoriserede Agent

Hr. C. F. Omang,

der er at træffe i „**Nor**", hvor Udvandringslystne behage at henvende sig.

Blichfeldt & Co.,
autoriserede Emigrations-Agenter i **Christiania.**

Til Amerika

fra Christiania over England og Kjøbenhavn.

Ved Dampskibsfartens Aabning befordres **Emigranter** gjennem **Amerikanske Emigrant-Compagny** med store, nye og velindrettede **første Klasses Jern-Skrue-Dampskibe hver Uge** til **New-York.** Det fra Kjøbenhavn først afgaaende Dampskib „**Danmark**", der expederes den **15de April.** Gjennemgangsbilletter til alle Dele i de Forenede Stater i **Amerika** og **Canada** erholdes til **billigste Pris.**

Alle nødvendige Oplysninger erholdes og Indskrivning foregaar
i Ringsaker hos Herr L. Ingeberg og
„ C. Simenstad,
i **Hamar** „ „ **O. H. Enger**
samt hos **O. Svenson.**
Autoriseret General-Agent,
Contor: Store Strandgade,
Christiania.

Dame-Søm.

Jeg tillader at bekjendtgjøre for det ærede Publikum, at jeg fremdeles modtager Skrædderføm, baade hvad angaar simpelt og bedre Arbeide. Prisen for Kjoler i simpelt Udstyr, beregnes til 48 ß pr. Stkr. og om finere Udstyr skulde ønskes, da vil selvfølgelig Prisen blive forhøiet. Damer fra Landet, der ønsker sin Bestilling færdig, Dagen de kommer, vil blive expederet snarest muligt.

Mathea Johansen,
boende i B. Larsens Gaard
ved Torvet.

Sædekorn.

Paa Svennæs i Birid er tilsalgs et større Parti Byg 2 radet og 6-radet, Rug, Blandkorn, Havre hvid og sort, alt af meget god Kvalitet.

Norsk Landmandsbog

for 1870 udg. af Asbjørnsen, Pris 36 ß, erholdes hos **H. A. Samuelsen.**

Ny Brev- og Formularbog

Pris indb. 48 ß er udkommet i ny Forsyning hos **H. A. Samuelsen.**

Til Salgs.

En Ko, tjenlig til Slagt, er tilsalgs ved Sæhlie Brænderi; man henvender sig til Madm. Gjestvang, Vangs Klettergaard.

Rug, Byg, Blandkornhalm, Erterris samt Hø og Avner, en Del Haa sælges af Madm. Gjestvang.

Vangs Klettergaard, 22de Febr. 1870.

Det norske Udvandringsselskab

befordrer **Emigranter** direkte til **Amerika**

til **billigste** Priser:

1. med 1ste Klasses norske Klipperskibe fra **Christiania** til **Quebec,**
2. med „the Northamerican Loyds"

1ste Klasses store, hurtigseilende og for Passagerer bekvemt indrettede **Dampskibe**, hvormed følger dansk Læge, skandinaviske Opvartere og serveres Kost, tillavet saaledes som her er brugeligt.

Da Passagererne paa denne Linie gaar direkte fra Christiansand til Newyork, saa er det ventelig at Mange vil foretrække samme, da de her undgaar at gaa iland i England og at komme isammen med fremmede Nationaliteter, hvorfor alle de, der ville benytte sig af denne Fordel, bør tegne sig i betimelig Tid.

Enhver nærmere Oplysning meddeles af Selskabets befuldmægtigede Agent hersteds,

N. Petersen.

Den billigste og korteste Vei til Amerika.

Indskrivning af Emigranter til alle Steder i de Forenede Stater i Amerika og Canada med **Ankerliniens** velanbefalede, store, bekvemme og hurtigseilende Dampskibe, som afgaar hver Uge fra Christiania ved første aabent Vand via Leith og Glasgow til New-York. Tolk følger hele Veien til Chikago. Emigranter behage at henvende sig til Undertegnede, hvor nærmere Oplysning erholdes og Indskrivning naarsomhelst foregaar til billigste Fragtpriser.

L. A. Lindberg, Hamar,
autoriseret Agent.

Billigt Brødmel—Eftersigtmel

af Hvede, Rug og Byg — saakaldet Dernæstmel, Kringlemel og Bygpillemel samt bedste Sort Rugsjærmel sælges i Partier og sækkevis hos

J. C. Helgesen.

Bekjendtgjørelse.

Det bekjendtgjøres herved i Henhold til Konkurslovens § 13:

At Gaardbruger i Furnæs Sogn, **Mikkel Magnusen Grinager** idag har overleveret sit Bo til Skifterettens Behandling som Konkursbo og at Overretssagfører Petersen foreløbigt er beskikket til midlertidig Bestyrer,

At en Skiftesamling er berammet til Afholdelse i det almindelige Retslokale **Tirsdagen den 8de Marts førstkommende Kl. 10 Formiddag.**

De Gjenstande, som der ville blive forhandlede, ere:

1) Spørgsmaal om nogen midlertidig Bestyrer bør beskikkes og i bekræftende Fald Valg af en saadan samt 2 raadgivende Mænd efter Konkurslovens § 22.
2) Spørgsmaal om Underholdningsbidrag til Skyldneren og Familie af Boets Midler samt om disses Realisation.
3) Valg i Tilfælde af Inkassator.

I Forbindelse hermed opfordres Alle og Enhver, der maatte have Fordringer at gjøre gjældende i Boet, til **skriftlig** at anmelde disse senest **inden 20de April** førstkommende samt til at fremsende i Original eller Afskrift de Dokumenter, hvortil Fordringerne støtte sig.

Endelig indkaldes Fordringshaverne til at afgive Møde her paa Kontoret **Onsdagen den 11te Mai førstkommende Kl. 11 Formiddag** for at overvære og deltage i de anmeldte Fordringers Prøvelse.

Hamars Sorenskriveries Skifteret, den 23de Februar 1870. Harald Gram.

Frøkorn

velbjerget, fuldvægtig, godt Byg, Blandkorn, Havre og Rug, sælges paa Gaarden Regstad i Stange.

Auktionsplakat.

Mandagen den 7de Marts førstkommende, og om fornødiges den og de paafølgende Dage, Kl. 2 Eftermiddag bliver offentlig Auktion afholdt paa Gaarden Mælum i Furnæs over endel Føderaadskone Anne Eriksdatter Mælums Dødsbo tilhørende Gjenstande, saasom Korn, Poteter, Kjøreredskaber, Indbo, Sølvtøi, gode Sengklæder og flere andre Løsøreeffekter.

Som Appendix bortsælges Frøkorn af forskjelligt Slags.

Hamar Sorenskriverkontor den 21de Februar 1870. Harald Gram.

Sæter i Østerdalen tilleie.

Sæteren Storbækdalen under Gaarden øvre Sjølie i Rendalen, hvorpaa haves Havneret til 35 Stykker Storfæ og 7 a 8 Heste, er ledig. Den er beliggende omtrent en og en halv Mil fra Sjørbunden og kan faaes paa et eller flere Aar.

Om Leien akkorderes med Ole Øvergaard i Stange.

Handelsbetjent.

En rutineret Handelsbetjent søger Plads enten hersteds eller ved et Landhandleri. Gode Anbefalinger kan præsteres. Avis-Expeditionen anviser.

En Karl og en Pige kunne faa Tjeneste om nogle Uger ved Meieriet paa Gaarden Folkhoel i Stange ved at henvende sig til E. Holmboe, der bor paa Gaarden.

En sort Fruentimmerkrave er for en 3 Uger siden funden mellem Hamar og Tommelstad som Eieren kan faa tilbage paa Vienrie i Vang mod Omkostningerne.

Den, der ved Branden paa Løken fik forbyttet en Pensylvanstindshue, kan faa ombyttet sammesteds.

Redigeret af Kand. O. Arvesen.

Udgivet, trykt og forlagt af Th. A. Hansen.

NEWSPAPER ANNOUNCEMENTS OF EMIGRANT SAILINGS
[From *Hamar stiftstidende,* February 25, 1870.]

service were 9,011. It would appear, therefore, that nearly 22,000 of the total of 27,669 represented classes that might be described as essentially underprivileged. In the same period, the emigrant men over fifteen years of age who came out of the Norwegian towns and cities numbered 6,388, of whom 2,104 represented mining and industry, 2,236 personal service, and 1,336 unspecified vocations.[23]

One of the notable things about nineteenth-century Norway was a novel and contagious readiness to turn aside from well-worn traditions of occupation and place. "A transformation of values had taken place among the country youth," writes Mrs. Semmingsen. "Many of them refused to remain in the home community any longer."[24] It was this intransigent spirit that the Norwegian national poet Bjørnson caught when he sang of breaking the bonds of circumstance, of hastening beyond the lofty mountains that encompassed him. Certainly many a young emigrant joined him in his passionate "Forth will I! Forth!"—and echoed his impatient "I will be crushed and consumed if I stay." The individual setting out for the city or for the distant glories of America departed from his home community, but his going left widening waves of influence. The American West was a Norwegian frontier. "One of our chief ways of subsistence," said a Norwegian newspaper in 1869, "is the way to America."[25] In going that way and in breaking away from his old environment the emigrant, dissenting from the tradition of acceptance of things as they were, helped to implant in the minds of his fellow Norwegians the idea of new frontiers and of a dissent that might take other forms than that of emigration. As Mrs. Semmingsen suggests, there was a "more conscious self-assertion" instead of a "dull hopeless

[23] See a statistical table in *Historisk tidsskrift,* 31:246; and Skaug's careful analysis of the "Character of the Norwegian Emigration," in *Migration from Norway,* ch. 4.

[24] In *Studies and Records,* 11:76.

[25] *Verdens gang* (Christiania), April 14, 1869.

spirit," and this tended to spread throughout the large class of landholders as well as among the landless.[26] As it spread, the America letters, with their story of American opportunity and equality, continued to be a leaven in Norwegian society, especially among the classes at its bottom, and there unquestionably developed a community of spirit between the people who remained behind and those who made their way to the frontier democracy of the West.

The America letters were reinforced by the testimony of Norwegian Americans who visited the mother country. "I will not report the impression that I got of the economic and social condition of the Norwegian *bonde* as compared with that of a farmer in America," said an immigrant after visiting Norway in 1868. "If I did, people would either not understand me or else accuse me of madness. Even the person who has grown up in one of the poor districts of Norway and then has lived many years in the midst of the American abundance tends to forget how the poverty in Norway actually tasted. The dear fatherland is always in his memory — perhaps more correctly in his imagination — with a vague charm over it which he cannot explain. Distance lends enchantment to the view. Only when he makes a trip home and sees the reality close at hand does he cast aside the pictures which have enchanted him as if by magic."[27]

What was taking place in Norway was the transformation of an ancient agricultural society, with centuries of tradition, into a new order, varied in its economic interests and closely allied with the modern industrial world. This transition marked the emergence of modern Norway and expressed itself in manifold ways, not only along economic and industrial lines, but also in the realms of politics, literature, and the social and cultural life of the people. Every great movement functions both as effect and as cause. Emigration

[26] In *Studies and Records,* 11: 76.
[27] *Folketidende,* April 14, 1869.

from Norway is projected out of basic conditions in both Norway and America. It is an outpouring of people that accompanied fundamental changes in Norwegian economic life; and it is an inpouring of people that accompanied the rise and continental expansion of the American Republic. Both as outpouring and inpouring, it is an effect; but so mighty a movement inevitably sets up trains of consequence.

Emigration as cause, so far as the history of Norway is concerned, needs more searching analysis than scholars have yet accorded it, but Professor Hovde has drawn attention to the large role that it has played in the economic and social changes of that country.[28] The people of Norway could not witness an annual exodus of their young and energetic people without being obliged to consider its reasons. It was only a step from studying the economic problems that largely occasioned emigration to asking for a planned development of the economic life. Let the government take action, it was urged. In parliament and in his newspaper articles, O. G. Ueland, the *bonde* leader, pointed to the United States as the standard for reform. A Swedish commentator blandly suggested that America should be moved to Sweden. The pull of America is the thing, said a Norwegian newspaper in the late 1850's. It argued that there was little in Norwegian society to keep the people. The need was for liberal and popular reforms. A modern historian asserts that America was the ideal state for a larger proportion of the Norwegian people and that it was against this background that they demanded higher standards of living, freedom of occupation, and democratic laws.[29] Norwegian critics suggested that if the immigrant must alter his methods and techniques in America in order to achieve success, why should he not do so in Nor-

[28] Brynjolf J. Hovde, "Notes on the Effects of Emigration upon Scandinavia," in *Journal of Modern History* (Chicago), 6: 253–279 (September, 1934).

[29] Ernest Beckman, in 1883, cited by Hovde, in *Journal of Modern History,* 6:258; *Aftenbladet,* May 14, 1857; Arne Odd Johnsen, *Utvandringen og bygdehistorien,* 12–14 (Oslo, 1937), a reprint from *Heimen.*

way — and thus obviate the necessity of emigrating. "It is a pity," according to a statement in a newspaper of 1871, "that Norway's better and best sons and daughters of the working class cannot realize just as great expectations as to future success and well-being here as in the states."[30] Since so many of the emigrants were agricultural in their interests, the discussion tended to give much emphasis to the problems of the farmer. Professor Hovde believes that the spectacle of emigration not only created a demand for reforms in Norway but played some part in producing needed legislation and funds, while the exodus itself relieved the pressure upon the soil and tended to set limits to the advance of parcelization. He also finds that the more modern tendencies toward mechanizing the processes of agriculture, establishing tariff protection, and intensifying farming itself are not unrelated to emigration.

Closely related to the problem of agriculture was that of land distribution. As early as the 1840's emigrant leaders called upon the Norwegian state to lend its aid to the settlement of uncultivated, waste, and state lands in Norway, even to the point of advancing loans without interest to prospective farmers of such lands.[31] This approach to the emigration question — a move toward inner land colonization — was never wholly lost sight of, but it was not until the twentieth century that it took form in organization and aggressive action. In 1909, after preliminary steps over a period of two years, the Society for the Restriction of Emigration was formed in Norway. It received wide support, both in its initiation and after its formal establishment. It emphasized such matters as controlling the agencies that sought to promote emigration; and it made every effort to ease the return of emigrants to Norway, but gradually it

[30] J. A. Budde, *Af et brev om Amerika* (Stavanger, 1850); Blegen, *Norwegian Migration,* 261; *Verdens gang,* June 21, 1871.

[31] See the discussion of Reiersen in Blegen, *Norwegian Migration,* 157 ff.

turned its major attention to a constructive attack upon the internal land problem. In 1916 it changed its name to "New Soil: A Society for the Inner Colonization of the Country and for the Restriction of Emigration."[32]

"It is remarkable," said one of the leaders of this movement, "how little people know about their own country. Those in Gudbrandsdalen and Valders as a rule know extremely little about conditions in Smaalenene and Jarlsberg. No, they are much better acquainted with conditions in Dakota and Minnesota."[33] The same leader believed that one of the central objects of the organization should be that of facilitating the return of emigrants. In particular, he believed that it would be an advantage to Norway if many emigrants returned to that country, purchased Norwegian *gaards,* and there applied the ability and experience that had been built up by their work in America. "It is not the United States but Norway that is the land of the future for the Norwegian people," said one of the society's speakers in 1917.[34] New Soil received generous subventions from the central government and widespread support from organizations and localities. With the decrease of emigration in the World War years, it found that anti-emigration activity was less needed than formerly but that the flow of the rural-urban movement needed to be checked. The "importance of cultivating and colonizing our own land so as to make ourselves as independent as possible," it said, "has become greater, and we note that sympathy and interest for this part of the society's work is steadily growing as it becomes better

[32] Selskapet til emigrationens indskrænkning, *Beretning om virksomheten fra dannelsen til og med aaret 1909* (Christiania, 1910); *Beretning om emigrationsselskapets virksomhet i aarene 1910 og 1911;* Johan E. Mellbye, "Ny jord," in *Ny jord* (Oslo), May, 1916, p. 68–81. On the change of name, see *Ny jord,* March, 1916, p. 27.

[33] Mellbye, "Utvandringen," in *Mot emigration,* I–IV, p. 10, 11 (Christiania, 1909).

[34] The phrase was used in a lecture by Knut Takla, "Forholdene i de Forenede Stater," in *Ny jord,* March, 1917, p. 58–83.

known throughout the country."[35] The men who led the work were well aware of the attraction of America. Johan E. Mellbye, for example, in advocating the beautification of farm homes and gardens and the adoption of a national style of architecture, said, "We ought to have more charm over our country life." The "gray of everydayness," he explained, "lies over life and work here at home in houses and *gaards,* and then come reports in letters or from relatives about all the unknown, great, fabulous, and inviting things in the fairyland on the other side of the Atlantic."[36]

Among other effects of emigration upon Norway, Professor Hovde suggests the economic gain derived through gifts, bequests, and other forms of contributions from Norwegian Americans to people in the old country. In the period after 1910 such contributions were running as high as approximately ten million dollars a year and were regarded as an offset to the economic losses occasioned by the emigration. "Churches, hospitals, and old people's homes have been built, and legacies established, by means of gold from the West," writes Johnsen.[37] Of special interest is the remigration of Norwegians from America to their native land. The Norwegian census of 1910 indicated that more than nineteen thousand Norwegian Americans — that is, returned emigrants and their children — were then living in Norway; and more than eighty per cent of them were located in the rural districts. The total number of Norwegian Americans in Norway was placed at nearly fifty thousand in 1920 by a Norwegian scholar.[38] It was precisely such returns of people that the Society for the Restriction of Emigration wished to

[35] *Beretning om ny jords virksomhet 1916–17,* 2 (Christiania, 1917).

[36] "Utvandringen," in *Mot emigration,* I–IV, p. 6, 7.

[37] Johnsen, *Utvandringen og bygdehistorien,* 12–14; Hovde, in *Journal of Modern History,* 6:259, 260; *Lov om utvandring,* 217.

[38] *Utvandringsstatistikk,* 77; a table shows the distribution in Norway of the Norwegian Americans in 1910. See also Andr. M. Hansen, "Indflytterfolk i Norge," in *Nordmands-forbundet,* 18:3 (1925); Hovde's essay; and Qualey, *Norwegian Settlement,* 252.

promote; and it is clear that the Norwegians interpreted such remigration in somewhat broader terms than those of mere numbers. The national commission which investigated the emigration problem in 1912–13 definitely saw in this tendency a transfer from America to Norway of new methods and a new spirit. "All those who come from America," said the commission, "begin to till the soil better than it was tilled before. . . . Crop rotation is introduced, machinery is acquired, the buildings of the farm, dwellings as well as others, are improved, more rational dairy methods are practiced, and gardens are laid out. In all these respects there have been great advances in *Sørlandet* during the past 10–15 years; the returned Americans have had their very considerable part in it, in some places even the largest part. They bring home with them much practical experience and understanding, which redounds to the advantage of the whole region. Furthermore, they have a will to take hold, and have in America learned a rate of work, which is different from what people are accustomed to here at home." [39]

Within the general domain of industry it is difficult to set bounds to the influence of emigration upon Norway, for as Dr. Skaug says, "emigration has contributed towards a continuous heightening and increase of the claims as to wages and conditions of labour on the part of the labourers. This has in its turn promoted the organisation and development of the employers and capitalists, and of rational methods in industrial life." [40] Professor Hovde also emphasizes this side of the picture, among other things touching upon the emigration influence in mechanizing industrial production. He points out, too, that the Norwegians were well aware of the American labor tempo. This awareness is implicit in the emigration commission's comment on agricultural influences, but it is of wider consequence than the field of agriculture.

[39] Quoted by Hovde, in *Journal of Modern History,* 6:278.
[40] *Migration from Norway,* 71.

Virtually all Norwegians are impressed by the intensity of American effort; and they realize that among the many things that have marked the transition of the Norwegian immigrant has been his ready acceptance of that intensity, or tempo.

The lines of influence run, on the one side, to the sharp impulse that emigration gave to the development of the Norwegian merchant marine, both in the expansion of business and in the improvement of vessels and the organization of the shipping trade; and on the other, to the labor movement in Norway. Emigration, as Professor Hovde well says, "helped to create the necessary conditions for a vigorous labor movement."[41] This is not the less true because such a class as the cotters found in emigration an avenue of escape and almost disappeared from the Norwegian economic and social scene; or because leaders like Marcus Thrane, prominent in the arbortive labor movement of the mid-century, turned away, disillusioned, and sought refuge in America. The very threat of emigration, however, coupled with the constant play of the status of American labor as reported in letters and by returned emigrants, aided in establishing those "necessary conditions." If the effects of emigration upon the home country seem comprehensive, it should be borne in mind that the social consequences of the movement were not less important than the economic. In a word, emigration turned men's minds in the direction of social ills and shadows, just as it had compelled a closer scrutiny of economic problems. The "conscious self-assertion" that Mrs. Semmingsen stresses was bound to find expression in movements for reform, and the field of reform was extensive enough to include social defects of many kinds, even in the realms of education and religion. This is not equivalent to saying that emigration was the basic cause of social and economic reform movements in Norway, but it does imply that emigration

[41] In *Journal of Modern History*, 6:270–273.

was part of the broad picture, and that it had wide-reaching influences.[42]

Since emigration touched so many vital Norwegian interests, and since America bulked so large in the consciousness of the Norwegian people, one expects to find that these twin themes play a part in the literature of Norway. That they do indeed has been convincingly demonstrated by the Norwegian scholar, Arne Odd Johnsen, in a study of "Bjørnson's Reaction to Emigration."[43] Wergeland's last play, *The Mountain Hut,* was centered upon the subject of emigration and in particular was a sharp attack upon emigration agents who "enticed" the people. Its spirit was that of romantic nationalism. As the poet considered the throngs of people leaving for the western world he sang songs begging them to remain at home:

> For go you east or go you west,
> The Norwegian home remains the best.[44]

Ivar Aasen in his play *The Heir* makes a returned emigrant the hero and causes him to sing in a romantic strain of the beautiful land that has drawn him back from America:

> Here I know the parishes and homes
> And the mountains in their far-flung ranges.
> Fjords and cliffs and skies and sun
> Seem lovelier here than anywhere else.

Bjørnson's first play, "Valborg," written in 1851, was an anti-emigration document, probably similar in spirit to Wergeland's *The Mountain Hut,* but the play was never produced and the poet destroyed the manuscript. One of his most noted stories, *Arne,* from the late 1850's, was an elaboration of the view that "talented persons who find themselves cramped in their native country can do better by remaining at home and enriching life there than they can by

[42] *Journal of Modern History,* 6: 268–270.
[43] In *Studies and Records,* 6: 133–145.
[44] Blegen and Ruud, *Norwegian Emigrant Songs and Ballads,* 75–98.

emigrating." Mr. Johnsen, taking note of such writings of the national romantic school, suggests that possibly emigration was one factor in the tendency of authors to picture the native country in idyllic colors.[45] Certain it is that the focus of the idealization of the fatherland was upon the people of the old rural stock; it was these people who served as heroes to all the disciples of the national romantic school, not only to poets and writers of stories and plays but also to folklorists and historians. Yet, as Professor Oscar J. Falnes points out, the "peasant had been influenced by the spirit of modern progress and had begun to regard his traditions as outworn and backward, as something to be discarded."[46] One mark of this spirit was precisely that refusal to stay on in the home community, which Mrs. Semmingsen interprets as a sign of the transformation of the country youth.

It is interesting to learn that even the America letters made their way into the high literature of Norway. In Bjørnson's play *The King*, the king asks about such letters. He is told that they are letters from relatives in America, that there "is now scarcely a family in the country that does not have relatives in America." The king makes an inquiry: "And these write home — about self-government, about republican customs?" The answer is: "And institutions. So it is!" The king then asks, "Have you read any such letters?" and receives the reply, "Many of them!"

Bjørnson himself ultimately visited America and took a position different from that advanced in his early romantic writings. "Our fatherland," he wrote, "cannot demand that we shall curb our own abilities. If it cannot provide opportunities for the development of our talents, we must go where such conditions are to be found."[47] He and many other writers, from the mid-nineteenth century down to the

[45] In *Studies and Records,* 6:136, 137.
[46] Oscar J. Falnes, *National Romanticism in Norway,* 58 (New York, 1933).
[47] Johnsen, in *Studies and Records,* 6:140, 144.

present, including Bojer and Hamsun, could write again and again about emigration and America, knowing that these were familiar themes to a people bound by ties of blood to a vast emigrant population in the New World — a people who, as the spokesman of the New Soil movement said, "are much better acquainted with conditions in Dakota and Minnesota" than with those in some other valley of their own country.

A newspaper reporter wandered down to the docks in Christiania in 1868 to visit an emigrant vessel just before it left for America. Wergeland, many years earlier, had written a jeering song in which he said,

> So many a fool went over the sea
> Went over to North America.

But the reporter was constrained to reject the idea that these emigrants were either "fools or adventurers." Most of them, he concluded, "know both what they are leaving and what difficulties they face in seeking a new home, but it is need that drives them, and that breaks all laws." He went down into the steerage, where a "confusion of speech, song, laughter, weeping, and music" greeted him. He saw farmers and young folk from the towns — probably the young folk dominated the scene, for in the later as well as in the earlier periods of emigration the typical emigrant was, usually, from twenty to twenty-four years of age. The movement was a young people's movement.[48] The reporter saw a boy and his mother saying good-by to one another; an old man with a meerschaum pipe; a band of Mormons off for the New Jerusalem; a countryman playing a Hardanger violin.[49] He saw "women, old and young, weeping their bitter tears" and "strong, broad-shouldered men, silently gazing at the hills." He left the vessel and watched it sail, "A breeze springs up from the North and the ship vanishes behind the

[48] *Lov om utvandring*, 192.
[49] *Verdens gang*, April 29, 1868.

hills of the island. Soon the coast disappears, and the emigrant whispers softly, 'My native land, farewell.'"[50] So the "people in dispersion" sail westward for America, where they are to merge with an emigration movement which is firmly woven into the national history since 1825, particularly into the social and economic development of those localities and regions where immigrants in preponderant numbers have settled and lived their way into American life.

[50] "An Emigrant Ship Leaving Christiania," in Blegen and Ruud, *Norwegian Emigrant Songs and Ballads,* 296–300.

XVI. CHANGING FRONTIERS

THE SCENE in America, after the emigrants have broken old ties and crossed the seas, is one of continuing dispersion. Immigration becomes migration and merges with the American westward movement. There is a panorama of settlements and frontiers, of the coalition of old and new immigrants, of human beings by the thousands pushing their way toward goals of economic security and of happiness. It is dispersion in the mass, but individuals are striking root. They may indeed move and move again, but their search is for the ordered life of established settlements—even if they do the establishing themselves. So, in the midst of what seems a restless human jostling, people are settling down, making places for themselves in community life, building farms and villages and states. There are covered wagons and long treks, but the caravan, as in *Giants in the Earth,* is the symbol of the search for a goal.

The Fox River settlement in Illinois, representing the initial pioneering of the Norwegians in the West, is important less for its priority than because it generated a social ferment in the immigrant's world, served as a center for the play of religious ideas and forces, harbored such leaders as Elling Eielsen, symbolized to Norway the destiny of its emigrated sons and daughters, and became a fertile mother colony. Cleng Peerson himself, the restless founder of the settlement, set the fashion of making it a base for new adventures in settlement. Not a few Norwegian-American communities are the termini of lines of migration and influence starting from Fox River. It was for many years one of the objectives of immigrants fresh from the seaboard, though colonies farther north soon challenged its primacy. Many immigrants stopped at Fox River to consult with older immigrants and to study prospects before setting out for Wisconsin, Iowa, or Minnesota. The Fox River colony itself expanded with time until it occupied parts of La Salle and several near-by north-central Illinois counties. In the northern tier of the counties of that state, near the thriving Norwegian settlements of southern Wisconsin, there was also a substantial Norwegian farming area.[1]

The strategic position of Illinois in Norwegian-American history after the pioneer era, however, was derived mainly from the increasing importance of Chicago. For this Midwestern metropolis became one of the most significant urban centers of the Norwegian immigrants in America. They were attracted to Chicago as early as the foundation period in the city's history—the decade of the 1830's. Sailors looking for employment or kept in port by ice-locked lakes lounged about the pioneer town. By 1850 there were 562 Norwegians there, and from that time on, the number increased rapidly, reaching 1,573 by 1860 and 6,825 ten years later. By 1890 the Norwegian-born in Chicago numbered

[1] See Carlton C. Qualey, "The Fox River Norwegian Settlement," in Illinois State Historical Society, *Journal*, 27:133–177 (July, 1934), and his *Norwegian Settlement*, ch. 2. For the earlier history of the Fox River colony see Blegen, *Norwegian Migration, passim;* also consult, on the Illinois settlements generally, A. E. Strand, ed., *History of the Norwegians of Illinois* (Chicago, 1905).

about 22,000; forty years later the Norwegian-born and children of Norwegian-born totaled 52,708.[2] The Norwegian interest in Chicago well justifies, therefore, an emphasis upon the urban aspect of Norwegian immigrant settlement. Dr. Qualey correctly points out that "large numbers took advantage of the demands for labor in such large cities as Chicago and Minneapolis, and in the iron and copper mines and the lumber camps of Michigan, and that many who had been professional men or tradesmen in Norwegian villages and cities sought to pursue their old occupations in the New World. The wages offered in such metropolitan centers as Chicago provided immediate support for thousands of impecunious immigrants, many of whom, after having obtained a competence, went farther west and purchased or claimed the farm of which they had dreamed." The same writer also takes note of the social significance of the creation of a Chicago Norwegian colony: "As the Norwegian element in the city grew, newspapers and periodicals, both secular and religious, appeared. The city became not only a dispersion point for settlement and itself a home for immigrants, but also a center for news, education, and the preservation of Norwegian culture in America."[3]

Thus the Norwegians had a share in the epic growth of Chicago; and it is interesting to observe that from the beginning the city attracted Norwegian-American youths from the rural settlements. It is true enough that some of the artisans and laborers in the city saved their money in the hope of acquiring farms, but Norwegian youth in the country felt the pull of the big city. Consider, for example, the case of Iver Larson Bø, or Iver Lawson, as he was called in America. He was an immigrant from Norway in 1837 who went with his parents to Fox River, but two years later he decided to try

[2] Otto Clausen, "Det norske Chicago," and Leif B. Buch, "Innvandringen til Chicago," in *Nordmanns-forbundet,* 26:142–146 (May, 1933); 27:75–78 (March, 1934).

[3] *Norwegian Settlement,* 38, 39; Strand, *Norwegians of Illinois,* 180 ff.

his fortune in the infant Chicago. He ran a clothing store, interested himself in real estate, and gradually established himself in the business life of the city. He was active in Norwegian-American affairs, helped Paul Andersen to set in motion a Norwegian Lutheran church in 1848, and joined with John Anderson in founding the important Norwegian newspaper *Skandinaven* shortly after the Civil War. Public interests found a place in his career, too, for he was made the Chicago city marshal in 1860, served in the municipal council for several years, and became a member of the state legislature. In the state lawmaking body he presented, among other things, a measure to create Chicago's Lincoln Park. Iver Lawson built up a fortune of perhaps a million dollars, but suffered disaster in the great fire of 1871, which left destruction and ruin in its ashes; and the next year he died. This immigrant story, in its Chicago setting, now passes to the second generation as the figure of Iver's son, Victor Fremont Lawson, emerges. He was born in Chicago in 1850 and was sent to Phillips Academy for his schooling. By 1876, still a young man, he was the owner and publisher of the *Chicago Daily News* and from that point of vantage he went on to a notable career in American journalism and in the life of Chicago and the Middle West.[4]

The story of the Lawsons illustrates the business opportunities that made Chicago an enticing city for ambitious men, whether immigrants or native-born Americans. Another illustration is afforded by the career of Christian Jevne, who had worked in a store in Norway before coming to Chicago in 1864. In an America letter written not long after his arrival, he conceded that there were disappointments in America, but he believed that the chances for a young man were definitely better than in Norway. Those who came expecting an easy road to "wealth and ideal conditions" would

[4] Charles H. Dennis, *Victor Lawson: His Time and His Work* (Chicago, 1935). The account of Iver Lawson is on p. 20–23.

be disillusioned, for everybody was challenged to work. In America, he said, "nothing may be had for nothing." Jevne clerked in a grocery store in the daytime and went to school in the evenings to learn "English, bookkeeping, banking, and brokerage." Probably he made use of those horsecars which he described with such care in his America letter: "In most of the streets there have been laid rails, on which very handsome cars are operated, quite similar to railway coaches, which are drawn by two horses, it costs five cents to travel upon them either for a short or a long distance."[5] Jevne established his own business in 1865 and ultimately developed it into "the largest wholesale and retail grocery business in Chicago," importing "coffee direct from Sumatra and Arabia; tea from Japan, China and Ceylon; wine from Europe; cheese, fish, canned goods and aquavit from Norway, Sweden and Denmark."[6]

While Norwegians were entering the business, industrial, and professional life of Chicago, with a considerable residential concentration in the Wicker Park area, they gave a compact support to a Norwegian-American cultural life that expressed itself in a variety of ways. To Chicago, for example, came in the 1860's the brilliant Marcus Thrane, the Norwegian labor leader and social reformer. He became a newspaper editor and the leader of a Norwegian theater which from 1866 to 1868 produced more than thirty plays, some of them written by himself. The support of the Norwegians for such an enterprise took form in a Norwegian Dramatic Society which presented plays in the period from 1868 to 1872.[7] The Norwegian interest in music was displayed through many clubs, notably Nordmændenes Sang-

[5] Brynjolf J. Hovde, ed., "Chicago as Viewed by a Norwegian Immigrant in 1864," in *Studies and Records,* 3:65–72. The document translated by Dr. Hovde is a letter written by Jevne on December 10, 1864.

[6] A brief account of the firm of "C. Jevne and Company" is in Strand, *Norwegians of Illinois,* 244, 245.

[7] Napier Wilt and Henriette C. Koren Naeseth, "Two Early Norwegian Dramatic Societies in Chicago," in *Studies and Records,* 10:44–75.

forening, organized in 1870.[8] Churches, fraternal societies, and other kinds of social and cultural groups tended to knit the Norwegians of Chicago into a unit. And *Skandinaven* served as an organ not only for this unit but also for the Norwegians far and wide throughout the country.

In Norwegian immigrant expansion the pioneer settlements of Wisconsin were developed by two human streams, one flowing north from Illinois, the other moving through the Great Lakes and discharging upon the west shore of Lake Michigan, with Milwaukee as a central point.[9] By the 1860's the earlier Wisconsin settlements, which were founded in the 1830's and 1840's, were already old by frontier standards. Lore and tradition had gathered about Muskego, Jefferson and Rock prairies, and Koshkonong. There fateful Norwegian-American enterprises had been cradled — in church and education, in the press and social life, in politics and war. These communities had struggled through the trying preliminary years of hardship, sickness, and distress. Now they bore the marks of prosperity and triumph, and from them emanated impulses and forces that were spreading over the entire domain of Norwegian-American life.

Young men born in America or reared from early boyhood in the frontier communities were stepping onto the stage of leadership alongside the leaders, clerical and lay, who had come to Wisconsin from Norway in their adult years. Hans Christian Heg, whose boyhood was spent in old Muskego, had marched to the Civil War at the head of his regiment of immigrant soldiers and had fallen at Chickamauga. He was one of the 29,557 Norwegians of Wisconsin whose names were written down in the federal census of 1860.[10] These thousands had been drawn to the old settlements, occupied and

[8] "The Nordmændenes Sangforening," in Strand, *Norwegians of Illinois*, 203–206.

[9] See Blegen, *Norwegian Migration*, ch. 5.

[10] Qualey, *Norwegian Settlement*, 40. The number by 1870 was 59,619. Dr. Qualey in his chapter 5, "Pioneering Wisconsin," describes in detail the spread of settlement in that state.

expanded their lands, wrestled with the problems of American agriculture, and sought out new areas for settlement, with an increasing tendency to work toward the western side of Wisconsin and northward in the valley of the Mississippi. The magic allure about Wisconsin and the West was still land, but as the farming communities grew, more and more of the Norwegians found their way to the cities and villages that functioned as markets and trading centers — such towns as Stoughton, Cambridge, Deerfield, and Madison.

The Norwegians did not ignore the attractions of the lands in eastern Wisconsin, however. With the Swedes and Danes they helped to develop the Pine Lake settlement northwest of Milwaukee, the region in which Unonius led the settlers into the Episcopalian church. And a notable migration of people from Valders was directed toward the lake-shore counties to the north, particularly Sheboygan and Manitowoc, under the leadership of one Stephen Olsen.[11] One of the men who came out of the Norwegian valley of Valders has been described as "slow, deliberate, and without fear, a man of might, poise, and balance, like an 'unchiselled grey rock.'"[12] He was a friend of Stephen Olsen who in 1847 came to America, where he got temporary work in Olsen's fanning mill while his wife served as a maid in an American family. By trade he was a carpenter, but he had the Norwegian love of land. He occupied a claim but was forced off it, took a farm, then moved to another location, this time in Cato Township, Manitowoc County, where he remained until 1865, when he pushed on to Minnesota. The census report for 1860 indicates that he had made considerable progress, for he then owned 160 acres, occupied a house that he had built with his own hands, and his farm in 1859 had produced seven hundred pounds of butter, one hundred bushels of oats, sixty bushels of potatoes, and various other products. So

[11] Holand, *Den sidste folkevandring*, 78–84.
[12] Joseph Dorfman, *Thorstein Veblen and His America*, 4 (New York, 1934).

this farmer's story seems typical in many respects. It becomes unusual, however, because of an extraordinarily gifted son. For this farmer's name was Thomas Anderson Veblen, and among his many children was a boy named Thorstein Bunde Veblen, born on the Wisconsin farm in the summer of 1857 and eight years old when the family moved on to Minnesota. Out of the Valders migration and the life of a frontier farm came one of America's original economic thinkers—the author of the *Theory of the Leisure Class* and the *Theory of Business Enterprise*.[13]

Still farther north along the Michigan shore were the Norwegian Moravian settlements promoted by Nils Otto Tank, regarded by Holand as the "most remarkable emigrant" from Norway to America,[14] and A. M. Iverson, in the Green Bay vicinity and on the Door Peninsula, with Ephraim as its central point.[15] Lumbering and fishing played an important part in the economic support of these communities, and across Green Bay, in Oconto County, lumbering and mining supplemented the agrarian interests of the Norwegian settlers. Inland, in Winnebago, Waupaca, and Portage counties, there were large and compact Norwegian settlements; but many forces were directing the immigrants to western Wisconsin, along its Mississippi boundary, which swings in an arc toward the west. The lands of the older settlements in the south and southeast were filled and in some instances overflowing. Railroads in the 1850's were binding the Mississippi Valley to the market towns of the East, touching Rock Island in 1854, Prairie du Chien three years later, and La Crosse in 1858. Advancing settlers were sending back in their America letters enthusiastic reports of the wonders of western Wisconsin. As in the American westward move-

[13] Dorfman, *Veblen*, ch. 1. Thorstein Veblen's mother, Kari Veblen, has been described as high-spirited, religious, and a "counsellor, adviser, and often physician and surgeon in the community" (p. 11).

[14] *Den sidste folkevandring*, 85.

[15] Blegen, *Norwegian Migration*, 335, 336; Holand, *Old Peninsula Days*, ch. 6, 7.

ment generally, a union of time and a series of interacting circumstances explain a large trend of settlement.[16]

So the Norwegians swarmed to the Wisconsin area alongside the great river. There were 135 there in 1850—in one county, Crawford. Ten years later—in fifteen counties—there were 5,658. And by 1870—now spread into seventeen counties—there were 22,571. There were pioneer thrusts in the 1850's, usually shaped by overland migration and ox-drawn wagons, but the principal expansion came after 1860, when railroads and steamboats supplemented the older forms of transportation. In the rich hills, valleys, and prairies above Prairie du Chien are the Coon Prairie and Coon Valley colonies—in Vernon County—founded in the late 1840's and compactly settled by Norwegians in the decades that followed. Holand describes this region as the first and largest *bygd* of the Gudbrandsdal folk in America—"the most densely populated Norwegian area" in the country, a highly prosperous region in which the farmers diversified their agriculture and exploited dairying and tobacco raising. Farther north is the La Crosse region, where Norwegians pioneered as early as 1850 and numbered more than three thousand by 1870. The city of La Crosse developed as a center in which Norwegian newspapers and books were printed and both business and cultural interests came to a focus. The immigrants sought also the Trempealeau region, pioneering it in the 1850's; struck farther away from the Mississippi when they went into the Eau Claire country, the Chippewa Valley, and found work in the Wisconsin lumber camps. Many years later Waldemar Ager was to write a Norwegian-American novel describing the life of the Wisconsin lumber camps and mills. Still farther northward were Norwegian settlements in Pierce and St. Croix counties, centering at Rush River, where Laur. Larsen arrived in 1857 to serve frontier congregations. Thus there was a sweep of Norwe-

[16] Qualey, *Norwegian Settlement,* 59–69.

gian settlement from the south central colonies in Rock and Dane counties toward the northwest, running alongside the Mississippi from Crawford County on, reaching up into the valleys of such tributaries as the Chippewa and the St. Croix — a great area of combined lumbering and farming interests, with a sufficiently compact Norwegian population to encourage a concentrated interest in social and religious cooperation and organization.[17]

The Norwegian settlements in Iowa bear out Dr. Qualey's contention that much of the colonization of the early West represented domestic migration rather than direct immigration. The impulse for the founding and development of the Norwegian colonies in Iowa came from the older Norwegian-American communities. It expressed itself in a search for new frontiers, a removal from old. In the very early period Cleng Peerson, the original Norwegian trail blazer in America, helped to found a new settlement in the southeastern corner of Iowa as well as one in northeastern Missouri.[18] A typical picture is that of a party of settlers in 1850 starting from Muskego, stopping at Koshkonong to recruit other migrants, pushing on as a company of more than a hundred people in every manner of vehicle, including wagons with wheels "made of solid sections of oak logs." At Prairie du Chien the caravan divided, some heading north for the Coon prairie and valley country, the others crossing the great river into Iowa and making their way to Winneshiek County in the northeastern part of the corn state.[19]

[17] Holand, *Den sidste folkevandring*, ch. 10, and *Coon Valley* (Minneapolis, 1928); Qualey, *Norwegian Settlement*, 63–75; Larsen, *Laur. Larsen*, ch. 3, 4.

[18] H. F. Swansen, "The Sugar Creek Settlement in Iowa," in *Studies and Records*, 9:38–44.

[19] See the reminiscences of Abraham Jacobson in Edwin C. Bailey, *Past and Present of Winneshiek County, Iowa*, 1:217 ff. (Chicago, 1913); George T. Flom, "The Coming of the Norwegians to Iowa," in *Iowa Journal of History and Politics*, 3:375–383 (July, 1905); and Qualey, *Norwegian Settlement*, ch. 4 — "On into Iowa." Dr. Qualey suggests (p. 14) that Norwegian settlement should not be thought of "as a part of the process of emigration from Norway" but rather as "a separate process — an integral part of the westward movement of the American population." A summary of a thesis on "The Norse in Iowa to 1870," by

Another picture of domestic migration is that of the Reverend C. L. Clausen's expedition of 1853 from the Rock Prairie settlement in southern Wisconsin. The colonizing minister had carefully scouted the north country and he led a caravan of some forty covered wagons to Mitchell County, Iowa, the valley of the Big Cedar River — a journey of three weeks in which, as one of the migrants said, "most of us walked the whole way, driving the cattle."[20] When, the next year, a hundred additional families joined this colony, which Clausen named St. Ansgar, the movement seemed like an exodus.[21] "I believe the entire population of Wisconsin is on the way to the west now," wrote Mrs. Koren when a visitor told her that he had passed more than three hundred wagons on their way to northeastern Iowa and southern Minnesota.[22] A third picture from the Iowa saga is that of the Story City colony, which was an organized project planned in the parent colony of Fox River in the middle of the 1850's. Advance scouts were sent out a year before the migration. Then in 1855 the main group, numbering more than a hundred, started on its trek, first organizing as a congregation, with a minister and a schoolteacher. These pioneers carried with them to the new frontier of their choice the institutions of an established society.[23]

Thus the Norwegians moved to the beckoning Iowa frontier. By 1860 there were more than eight thousand of them in that state, and the number vaulted to more than twenty-five thousand in the following decade. The pioneering of the 1850's marked out the main lines of the Norwegian advance

H. F. Swansen, is in the University of Iowa, *Studies in the Social Sciences,* vol. 10, no. 4, p. 81–93 (1938).

[20] Mrs. Assur H. Groth, quoted by Gjerset and Hektoen, in *Studies and Records,* 1:11.

[21] Qualey, ed., "Claus L. Clausen: Pioneer Pastor and Settlement Promoter," in *Studies and Records,* 6:12–29.

[22] Koren, *Fra pioneertiden,* 168.

[23] Holand, *De norske settlementers historie,* ch. 54; Qualey, *Norwegian Settlement,* 93, 94; Oley Nelson, *En kort historie af det første norske settlement i Story og Polk counties, Iowa* (Chicago, 1905).

into Iowa, for the areas of intensive settlement continued to be the northeastern counties, with an extension toward the west in the upper tier of counties; and central Iowa, with Story City as a nucleus. There were tentative moves toward the prairies, though the Norwegian settlers usually chose the traditional lands of woods and waters before venturing onto the treeless plains. People of all classes they were, of every kind of background, including a cattle herder in the vicinity of Estherville, who was the proud owner of forty acres of land and bore the name Nicolai Alexander Ibsen — a brother of Norway's greatest dramatist.[24]

The rapidity of the growth of population after 1860 meant that streams of new immigrants were joining the old, that the various agencies of promotion were making themselves felt — letters, the reports of scouts, the surge of railroad building which shot the Iowa mileage from 655 in 1860 to 2,683 in 1870, and the momentum of settlement which was created by the development of communities where people of like language and customs were grouped together. So the immigrants came, looking with curious eyes at the lands that they found. "As we approached Forest City," writes Laurence M. Larson, telling of a "little cavalcade" of Norwegians in 1871, "those in the company who still had an eye for beauty looked ahead with wondering eyes. It was the season of the year when nature is at its loveliest; and the outlook, with heavy forests to the right and boundless prairies to the left, must have been highly attractive and even impressive." The choice of land was of first importance. The younger people were evidently more daring than the older. "Grandfather," writes Larson, "loved the timber and lived for several years in the woods near Forest City. The others turned their faces toward the open prairie." Norwegians had penetrated this area in the middle 1850's, but it

[24] Cyrus F. Savereide, "Henrik Ibsen's Brother," in *Norden* (Chicago), 5:4, 5 (May, 1933).

was in the period after the Civil War that the numbers of settlers became large. "The newcomers came from the older Norwegian settlements in southern Wisconsin and northern Iowa; but a considerable number came direct from the old northern shores. By the close of the century four-fifths of the population of Winnebago County was of Norwegian origin." Larson, recalling the pioneer period, remembered the animal life, the birds, the prairie flowers — pasque flowers, violets, which the Norwegians called "night-and-day," sunflowers, goldenrod. "Everywhere," he said, "there was life and loveliness. But the pioneer had come with traps and plows and shotguns," he added regretfully, "and in a few years much of this delightful variety of living things had disappeared."[25]

As the Norwegian settlements expanded, there were inevitable thrusts northward into Minnesota and westward toward the Dakota country, but the main Iowa Norwegian areas remained those of the 1850's and 1860's. And it was in the heart of the northeastern corner of the state — the region of most intensive settlement — that the urban-church-cultural center of Decorah grew up. Here was the home of Luther College, the educational nucleus of the Norwegian Synod, where such leaders as Laur. Larsen, Friedrich A. Schmidt, Ulrik Koren, Christian K. Preus, and Knut Gjerset were familiar figures.[26] Decorah was a center for church and lay publication in the Norwegian-American field — magazines such as *For hjemmet* in early days and *Symra* in a later time, newspapers such as *Decorah-posten,* still appearing and influential in 1940. And in Decorah a great Norwegian-American Historical Museum has been created, its collections centering about the Norwegians in America — "their life and culture and the general conditions surrounding them from the time

[25] Larson, *Log Book,* 23–29.

[26] See Luther College Faculty, *Luther College through Sixty Years 1861–1921* (Minneapolis, 1922).

when their fathers and mothers first set foot on American soil."[27]

The Norwegians, breaking away from the old settlements in Illinois and Wisconsin, and reinforced by waves of immigration from the Old World, were moving north and west. Striking root in the Wisconsin country adjacent to the Mississippi, reaching into Iowa, spreading out on both sides of the river, they faced Minnesota at the north. They accepted the prophecy voiced by Fredrika Bremer in 1850, just after the northern region, emerging from its fur-trading era, had been organized as a territory: "What a glorious new Scandinavia might not Minnesota become!" For here were wide-stretching fertile lands waiting for the touch of plow. Here was a veritable Land of Canaan, with lakes and rivers, woods and prairies, and seemingly boundless resources.[28]

By 1860 the Norwegian element in Minnesota — it had become a state of the Union in 1858 — numbered nearly twelve thousand.[29] These people had pioneered in the southeastern area, especially in the lower tier of counties, from Houston and Fillmore toward the west, and, somewhat farther north, in the Goodhue County area. Spring Grove was the village center of the Houston settlements, which were compactly Norwegian, with many lines of connection reaching to Muskego, Rock Prairie, Koshkonong, and the Iowa colonies. In Spring Grove as late as the 1930's Norwegian was "spoken commonly on the streets."[30] The Goodhue area won wide fame as a prosperous farming country. "By

[27] Knut Gjerset, "The Norwegian-American Historical Museum," in *Studies and Records*, 6:153–161.

[28] Fredrika Bremer, *Homes of the New World*, 1:56 (New York, 1853); John T. Flanagan, "Fredrika Bremer: Traveler and Prophet," in *Minnesota History*, 20:129–139 (June, 1939).

[29] Two scholarly studies by Dr. Qualey are "Pioneer Norwegian Settlement in Minnesota," in *Minnesota History*, 12:247–280 (September, 1931), and his chapter on "A Glorious New Scandinavia," in *Norwegian Settlement*, 97–129.

[30] A collection of pioneer stories relating to this region is O. S. Johnson, *Nybyggerhistorie fra Spring Grove og omegn* (Minneapolis, 1920). See also Qualey, "A Typical Norwegian Settlement: Spring Grove, Minnesota," in *Studies and Records*, 9:54–66.

1855," writes Theodore Nydahl of this region, "practically all the desirable land was taken. Land seekers came from Iowa, from Wisconsin, from Illinois, and directly from Europe. Of the pioneer group the largest element by far was Scandinavian, the Swedes settling in the northern part of the county and the Norwegians in the southern and southwestern sections."[31] They had learned the first principles of frontier adaptation. "Naturally there were no houses awaiting them," wrote a pioneer, "but they had houses along with them which they had become thoroughly accustomed to in the last few weeks—their covered wagons." These were of course merely temporary: "Log houses were built, generally about ten by twelve feet, and sometimes twice as large. These huts were always open to welcome those who came later, and often housed two or three families."[32] In 1857 a minister praised the Goodhue settlers and their choice of a site. "They are almost all old farmers," he said, "who have sold their property in the older settlements, partly in Wisconsin and partly in Illinois, and have come to this blossoming territory with not inconsiderable amounts of money."[33]

The Minnesota pioneers, like those on other frontiers, had their ordeals—the pinch of hard times after the panics of 1857 and 1873, the terror of the Sioux Outbreak, the invasions of devouring hordes of grasshoppers in the 1870's; but good times succeeded bad, the Indians were dispersed, and there was an end to the insect armies. Meanwhile, railroads, beginning in 1862, threw paths of steel across the state, machinery and milling and other forces made much of Minnesota into a vast field of hard spring wheat, homestead lands were available as the Sioux were pushed out, and numerous agencies, including the state itself, the railroads, and land companies, held

[31] Theodore L. Nydahl, "Social and Economic Aspects of Pioneering as Illustrated in Goodhue County, Minnesota," in *Studies and Records*, 5:50.

[32] P. M. Langemo, in *Festskrift, Holden menigheds jubelfest 1906*, 48 (Minneapolis, 1908), quoted by Nydahl, in *Studies and Records*, 5:51.

[33] H. A. Stub, in *Morgenbladet*, June 4, 1857.

out hands of welcome to the immigrants in the spirit of the old ballad:

> We have room for all creation and our banner is unfurled,
> Here's a general invitation to the people of the world.[34]

The Norwegians accepted the invitation gratefully, and ran their Minnesota totals up to 49,569 in 1870 and 83,856 by 1875, when they constituted a seventh of all the people in the state. In the older areas of the south and southeast, where they had begun their pioneering in the 1850's, there was expansion in the later period and a jostling of people as these areas overflowed. A great settlement launched in the 1850's inside the bend of the Minnesota River, in Nicollet and Sibley counties, flourished in the next two decades. The Norwegians pushed into the upper reaches of the Minnesota River, beginning in the late 1850's, but developing the movement in the next two decades so that by 1875 there were no fewer than 1,254 Norwegian families on lands lying on the north and south banks of the river in that area. Among these families was that of Ole S. Gjerset, who came to Chippewa County from Romsdal in 1871. A kindly Swedish family near Litchfield gave the Gjersets the hospitality of their log cabin, and there, pausing on the journey west, the immigrant family waited for the birth of Karen Marie Gjerset's fifth child. Not long thereafter a wagon was loaded with chests and baggage and the family set out for its destination. Gjerset was a land taker in the saga sense, a *landnamsman,* who, according to his son, looked beyond the commercial value of land to the stability and dignity inherent in land ownership. He soon owned 640 acres, including a quarter section that he acquired under the Timber Culture Act by planting and caring for forty acres of trees. This western Minnesota farmer had wide interests. His farmhouse boasted a library containing " volumes of his-

[34] See Blegen, *Building Minnesota,* ch. 15–27, for the general Minnesota background; and " Minnesota's Campaign for Immigrants," with accompanying documents, in Swedish Historical Society of America, *Yearbook,* 1926, p. 3–83.

tory, geography, sagas, travels, psychology, law, medicine, religion, language, music, and mathematics"; he himself had been a schoolteacher in Norway before becoming an emigrant. One of the five children later won distinction as a scholar and historian, Dr. Knut Gjerset, author of the *History of the Norwegian People*.[35] By 1875 the Norwegians had been drawn also into the rich lands of central Minnesota, looking northwestward from Kandiyohi to Pope, Douglas, and Otter Tail counties.[36] It was in the summer of 1871 that Knute Nelson, a young Civil War veteran and lawyer, a native of Voss, Norway, moved from the Koshkonong settlement in Wisconsin to Alexandria in Douglas County, Minnesota, to combine the practice of law with farming on the frontier. Law and politics became his central interest as he entered local politics, then moved into the state field, became a Congressman, and ultimately, governor and United States Senator.[37]

These western regions were close to the fertile lands bordering the Red River. They had been scouted for the Norwegians in 1869 by Paul Hjelm Hansen, a newspaper writer who gloried in his wagon journey from Alexandria to the western river. He knew the tread of oxen, kept warm at night under a buffalo robe, used a sack of flour for a pillow, and, like the Vikings, "had the blue heavens for a covering." There was no doubt in his mind about the coming agricultural greatness of the Red River Valley. "It is my opinion and the opinion of every man who has seen this country," he wrote, "that it offers so many advantages for Scandinavian farmers that immigrants will stream into this region in the near future. Doubtless within ten years the whole country will be settled and under cultivation, and it will then be one of the most beautiful and fruitful sections of America."[38] By 1875 the Min-

[35] Knut Gjerset, "A Norwegian-American Landnamsman: Ole S. Gjerset," in *Studies and Records*, 3: 82–100.

[36] Qualey, *Norwegian Settlement*, ch. 5.

[37] Martin W. Odland, *Life of Knute Nelson*, ch. 5, 6 (Minneapolis, 1926).

[38] *Nordisk folkeblad*, August 11, 1869; and Blegen, in Swedish Historical Society of America, *Yearbook*, 1926, p. 18–20. In a report to the Minnesota board of

nesota side of the Red River had attracted 1,234 Norwegians, who constituted forty-two per cent of the total population of that region.[39] So the people from Norway endorsed the judgment of Paul Hjelm Hansen, and the endorsement was written into the soil in the following decades by thousands of their countrymen who struck westward from southern Minnesota and other areas where the lands had been taken and in some instances almost exhausted by the one-crop system of agriculture that was practiced. Throngs arriving from the old country also joined the trek to the Red River Valley.

The North Star State was the new Mecca of the Norwegian immigrants. They were jubilant as they swarmed onto its lands, sweeping northwestward through the varied farming areas from the southeastern corner to the valley of the river that ran north. It was essentially the trans-Mississippi country — the Sioux lands and the northwestern Chippewa tracts — that they selected, though in time they also penetrated the areas lying east and north of the river, including the north Superior shore, where fishermen were active, and the range country, where men got work in the mines. Norwegians in large numbers went into the pine woods as lumberjacks in the gala days of lumbering, and in the later days of the industry the typical lumberjack was Scandinavian. Artisans and tradesmen found opportunities in the villages and towns for the skills that they brought with them from the old country. The census, it is said, turns living people into figures, but the figures stir the imagination of the reader who can see them in terms of living people. They catch in the large the outlines of the Scandinavian influx into Minnesota. In that state in 1860 there were 8,425 Norwegian-born people; thirty years later there were 101,169 — more than twelve times as many. For the Swedes, too, Minnesota was

immigration Hansen contended that native Americans commonly sold their farms and moved into the cities. The Scandinavians, he said, " buy these farms and stay " to " settle the lands under all kinds of troubles and sufferings." *Yearbook*, 1926, p. 49.

[39] Qualey, *Norwegian Settlement*, 127.

a potent magnet, and the number of Swedish-born people in the state increased in the same period from 3,178 to 99,913. In that tumultuous generation Fredrika Bremer's "new Scandinavia" grew with a prodigious speed that put even the prophecies of its pioneer boosters to shame. Its population stood at 172,023 in 1860. In 1890 it had 1,301,826 inhabitants. The number of foreign-born people in Minnesota in 1890 was 467,300, and of these the Scandinavians made up nearly half.[40]

While the farm lands were filling up, Norwegians were also filtering into the towns and cities, sometimes with educational institutions setting up cultural centers, as in the case of St. Olaf College in Northfield. It was Minneapolis, however, that tended to become the cultural capital of Norwegian America, in sharp competition with Chicago and other nuclei of settlement. The Norwegians preferred the milling and manufacturing city about the Falls of St. Anthony to the old commercial center and political capital at the head of Mississippi navigation, and as early as 1875 there were nearly five times as many Norwegians in Minneapolis as in St. Paul.[41] Minneapolis offered openings for men trained in the skilled trades, and there was work, too, for unskilled day laborers. To that city came professional men — doctors, lawyers, and engineers, including the noted bridge and tunnel builder, Olaf Hoff. The removal of Augsburg Seminary from Marshall, Wisconsin, to Minneapolis in 1872 symbolized the emergence of the Minnesota metropolis as a Norwegian-American church and educational center, with dominant figures like Georg Sverdrup and Sven Oftedal in the foreground. There was a northwestward movement of the Norwegian-American press,

[40] Blegen, *Building Minnesota,* ch. 25 ("Immigrants and Settlement") and ch. 39 ("A Changing Population"). Qualey, in the appendix of his *Norwegian Settlement,* analyzes the Norwegian element in Minnesota for 1857, 1860, 1870, and 1875. By 1930 there were 267,912 Norwegians of the first and second generations in Minnesota. See R. W. Murchie and M. E. Jarchow, *Population Trends in Minnesota* (Minneapolis, 1936).

[41] The figures in 1875 were Minneapolis, 2,318; St. Paul, 481. Qualey, *Norwegian Settlement,* 129 n.

also, and Minneapolis witnessed important ventures in the field of immigrant journalism — especially such newspapers as *Budstikken* and the *Minneapolis tidende*. In Minneapolis, also, many of the musical, artistic, and social forces among the Norwegians found expression in one form or another, sometimes in organization, sometimes in the achievements of an individual, such as Jacob Fjelde, the sculptor. The growing city on the banks of the upper Mississippi was an urban, cultural, and professional center for the scattered agricultural empire that the immigrants were developing in the Middle West.

The people of Koshkonong, looking west, spied the prairie lands between the Big Sioux and Missouri rivers in 1858, the very year the land cession of the Yanktonai cleared the way for white settlement in that area; and in 1859 six wagons of Norwegian pioneers set out from Stoughton, Wisconsin, for Dakota, to take advantage of the land opening.[42] This was two years before the Territory of Dakota came into official being. Here was hunger for land and a readiness to face the hazards of a far frontier, but for the Norwegians it meant something more. It meant challenging the Great Plains. Even in the prairie land the Norwegians instinctively went near rivers, or hunted out lakes if there were lakes to be found, but the day of limiting their land choice to forested areas was over. In one of the old emigrant ballads a Norwegian singer confesses that as settlers he and his friends had something to learn from the Yankee:

> We had come from a national quarry
> And of land claims we didn't know beans,
> So the Yankee would settle the prairie,
> While we clung to the woods and the streams.[43]

[42] G. Bie Ravndal, "The Scandinavian Pioneers of South Dakota," in *South Dakota Historical Collections,* 12:299 ff. (1924); and Qualey, *Norwegian Settlement,* 132. Dr. Qualey presents the story of the spreading Norwegian settlements in South Dakota in a chapter entitled "The Giants' Country."

[43] The text of this ballad, "Korleids dæ gjek," with a prose translation, appears in Blegen and Ruud, *Norwegian Emigrant Songs and Ballads,* 344–350.

The Norwegians who pioneered in the area that was to become South Dakota served notice that the immigrants were ready to grapple with the prairie frontiers, though for many of them, especially the women, it was an ordeal to do so. The forlornness of Beret in *Giants in the Earth* found its most poignant expression in her anguish over the lack of trees. In Norway friendly and beautiful woods clothed the hillsides everywhere; here, on the devouring plains, there was not even a tree to hide behind.

That the early pioneering did not quickly lead to a large wave of Norwegian settlement in the Dakota country was not due to the treeless landscape, however. Some Norwegians did go to that area in 1860 and 1861, and a newspaper of that period reported that about 150 Norwegian and Danish families were settled near Vermillion and along the Missouri River.[44] But the prairies were swept by the scourge of Indian wars in the 1860's, and it was not until after the menace of the Sioux had been removed that immigration and settlement on an intensive scale began to develop. Soon the familiar pull of free land, the attraction of good crops in wet years, the agitation of public and private agencies seeking to advance settlement, and the pressure of restless farmers in the older colonies, coupled with the surge of incoming thousands of immigrants, began to forward the movement to the South Dakota country. By 1870 there were 1,264 Norwegians in the Missouri–Big Sioux region, with the southeastern counties — notably Union, Clay, and Yankton — as the heart of the farming development in the Missouri Bottom area. The

[44] *Emigranten,* February 18, 1861; Blegen, *Norwegian Migration,* 363. A pioneer minister, Abraham Jacobson, visited the Dakota settlements in the fall of 1861, going by wagon from Decorah with a party of eight Norwegians. He found the Norwegians in three colonies: " Elk Point, Vermillion, and the tract between the present location of Gayville and the James River at Yankton." He also found many Norwegians on the Nebraska side, waiting for the opening of Dakota land. Near Vermillion he saw the Norwegians fight a prairie fire — " an ocean of flame, which seemed about to swallow everything in its way." Abraham Jacobson, "A Pioneer Pastor's Journey to Dakota in 1861," translated by J. N. Jacobson, in *Studies and Records,* 6: 53–65.

Norwegian element there rose to 2,776 by 1880 and 5,850 by 1900.[45] Relatively small numbers of Norwegians went to Nebraska and Kansas.

Farming was the great interest of the pioneers who entered the country of Rølvaag's *Giants in the Earth,* but the frontier offered other interests, too. These may be illustrated by the story of a number of young Norwegians of the Opdal group who arrived in the Dakota country in 1869 and 1870. These Opdal folk, representing the best stock in their native Norwegian valley, had selected Dakota as their objective even before leaving Norway. Their migration to the region that became South Dakota drew others, and even today a considerable proportion of the Opdal element in America is located in South Dakota. Some of the young men were attracted to the employment of the United States at such places as Fort Sully, Fort Thompson, and Fort Randall, and on the steamboats of the Missouri, and many of them made their way west in a special caravan of 1870 from Yankton. Men like Iver Furuness and Halvor Aune thus tasted the adventure of the military frontier and, with their fellows, made a contribution to the early history of the plains. "By their work as hewers of wood and drawers of water," writes Einar Haugen, "they helped to supply the basic needs of these frontier communities. Their strong arms aided in keeping the means of communication moving on the Missouri River. Their mechanical skill as carpenters and blacksmiths helped to create and preserve, even in the wilderness, the implements of civilization. They acted as assistants and managers for the government agents, and as their intermediaries with the Indians; their wives kept boarding houses and gave to the wilderness a touch of home."[46]

The great stretch of Norwegian settlement in the Giants

[45] Qualey, *Norwegian Settlement,* 133 ff.

[46] Einar Haugen, "Norwegians at the Indian Forts on the Missouri River during the Seventies," in *Studies and Records,* 6:89–121; "Opdalinger ved fortene langs Missourielven i 70-aarene," in *Opdalslagets aarbok,* 1933, p. 11–21.

country lay in the Big Sioux Valley in the counties north of the union of the Big Sioux and the Missouri rivers. Here are several famous centers of Norwegian-American life. Canton, in Lincoln County, became the home of an important Norwegian-American newspaper, and it had in time a Lutheran school called Augustana College. To this school in 1899 went a young South Dakota farm hand with a "fierce desire for knowledge,"[47] who many years later was to write the saga of the prairie. His name was O. E. Rølvaag. Farther north are intensive settlements clustering about Sioux Falls and Brookings. Norwegians had sought out some of these areas before 1860, but their major impetus came in the 1860's and 1870's. In Brookings County, for example, a significant pioneering enterprise took place in 1873.

The story of the immigrants' trek to Lake Hendricks in Brookings County centers about eleven "canvas hooded wagons, commonly called 'prairie schooners,'" in which a party of more than thirty persons, all hailing originally from the Trondhjem region in Norway, made their way from Houston County in Minnesota and Allamakee and Winneshiek counties in Iowa. Their saga, preserved by Gustav Sandro, is a parallel in real life to the trek across southern Minnesota that is described vividly in the opening pages of *Giants in the Earth*. The covered-wagon journey lasted from May 15 to July 14, 1873. It was jointly planned by the Iowa and Minnesota groups, who met by prearrangement in Minnesota. Some of the members of the party were newly married couples, for whom the trek was a honeymoon, while others came in families that included small children. The objective was not a fixed spot, but the free prairie land of Dakota Territory, where particular sites would be selected after the party arrived in that country. So the caravan made its way across the plains. Canvas coverings gave protection from sun, rain, and wind; and at night the emigrants slept in the schooners.

[47] The phrase is from Mr. Lincoln Colcord's introduction to *Giants in the Earth*.

Behind the wagons moved a herd of thirty cattle. On Sunday mornings the trekkers would camp. "Seated together there on the ground, or on wagon poles," writes Sandro, "they had a short religious service. They would sing some hymns, one would lead in prayer and read the text, according to Lutheran custom, and then they would close the service by singing another hymn." On one occasion a team of young oxen took fright and ran away with one of the wagons. Guri Troøien, with her baby Kirsti in her lap, was seated on an emigrant chest at the front of the wagon, and seemed to be in serious peril; but the oxen, after pounding through a slough and "splashing mud and water high into the air," were slowed down by a hill and came to a stop. When the party reached the Blue Earth River, it was ferried across the stream, the ferryman charging fifty cents for each wagon. At Jackson the travelers entered a scene of desolation, for this was the first year of the grasshopper invasions and they had already "devastated the region." As the caravan approached the Dakota country, scouts were sent out to make reconnaissances. Ultimately two men explored the vicinity of Lake Hendricks and their reports led the party to go there for land. This area proved to be journey's end for the travelers. The wagon boxes were lifted off the trucks and served temporarily as houses, but soon cabins were built for the settlers and sod stables for the oxen. "Two babies were born that summer while the colonists still lived in the wagons," and three more arrived in the autumn. Some of the bachelors set out when cold weather came to find work in the lumber camps of the north country, while the main party settled down to the ordeal of prairie frontiering. Thus was founded a Norwegian-American community which in the course of time was to wax prosperous.[48]

[48] Gustav O. Sandro, *The Immigrants' Trek*. This is one of the most vivid accounts available of western pioneering. See also Sandro and C. N. Troøien, "Pionererne ved Lake Hendricks," in *Trønderlagets aarbok*, 1932, p. 31–37. A narrative by Anders J. Berdahl, "Et par reiser til Dakota Territory i 1872," in

The upper end of the Big Sioux Valley settlements extended north of Brookings into Deuel County; and there was some advance also into the areas immediately to the westward. With such village centers as Toronto and Brandt, the settlers in the Deuel area gradually developed a thriving farming community. It was there that the pioneer pastor R. O. Brandt and his wife "followed and sustained the Per Hansas, gave spiritual aid to the settlers, set up a focus for pioneer social activities, brought books to the prairie, sometimes played the roles of doctor and nurse, and in many other ways made their influence felt."[49] Farther toward the north were fairly compact Norwegian settlements, centering especially in Day and Roberts counties, launched in the 1870's but developed largely in the 1880's and 1890's, with Aberdeen as a center; and by 1900 there were no fewer than 10,745 Norwegians in this general area. There were scattered settlements still farther west, beyond the Big Sioux and James River regions, but on no such intensive scale as in eastern South Dakota. Some few Norwegians joined the Black Hills gold rush, but the element was never large in the mining area.[50] For the most part the Norwegian pioneers were takers of farming lands, men and women of the mold of Per Hansa and Beret. Their saga in real life runs parallel with that of Rølvaag's Giants, who, like the people of the Lake Hendricks caravan of 1873, steered their course through the whispering grasses of southern Minnesota for "Sunset Land."

If Norwegian settlement in the southern part of Dakota antedates that in the northern area by a decade, this does not mean that there was any less enthusiasm for the prairies stretching westward from the Red River than for the region farther south. The Norwegian exploitation of what became

Samband, no. 71, p. 265–272 (March, 1914), tells of migration from Fillmore County, Minnesota.

[49] The phrase is from my preface to vol. 7 of *Studies and Records*, which contains Mrs. R. O. Brandt's charming and informative article on "Social Aspects of Prairie Pioneering."

[50] Qualey, *Norwegian Settlement*, 147–150.

North Dakota opened with a paean of praise and was carried forward on a wave of high hopes. The paean was sounded by the trail-blazing journalist, Hjelm Hansen, who wrote in lyric phrases about the rich black soil of the prairie, its invigorating air, its ample room, and the ease of cultivating land "where there is not so much as a stone or stump in the path of the plow."[51] The settlers themselves supplied the high hopes as the Norwegian element in North Dakota increased from 10 in 1870 to 8,814 in 1880 and to 73,744—nearly a fourth of the entire population of the state—in 1900.[52] "The Master of Life has placed us here and gave the land to us for an inheritance," protested a Chippewa chief in 1863, but his protests were unavailing, and the Chippewa were obliged to cede the wonderful valley of the Red River to the whites.[53] The inheritance to a large extent was taken over by immigrants from the Scandinavian North.

North Dakota—it did not become a state until 1889—was frontier land when the pioneer Norwegian caravans arrived. Wet years in the late 1870's and early 1880's reinforced the booming of the area by railroads, which were building to the prairie's edge and then across the plains, opening markets, sponsoring towns, and transporting people from the older settlements and immigrants only recently arrived from overseas. Yet many went, not by railroad, but in the covered wagons of the traditional pioneer trek. A boy living near the rim of the Dakota country in 1882 long remembered the pageant of pioneer caravans that passed on their way westward. "We watched the schooners come up from the south," he wrote many years later, "zigzagging up the tortuous trail like ships beating up against the wind. Slowly

[51] *Nordisk folkeblad,* August 11, 1869.

[52] Dr. Qualey has traced the processes of North Dakota settlement in an article on "Pioneer Norwegian Settlement in North Dakota," in *North Dakota Historical Quarterly,* 5:14–37 (October, 1930); and his chapter on "North Dakota and Beyond," in *Norwegian Settlement,* 151–171, is a mine of useful and well-organized information.

[53] Ella Hawkinson, "The Old Crossing Chippewa Treaty and Its Sequel," in *Minnesota History,* 15:282 (September, 1934).

they drew nearer — sometimes one, sometimes five or six in a fleet. Out to the road we went to watch them pass, and it was the only event of interest from one day to another. Usually the woman was sitting at the front driving the team, and beside her or peeking out of the front opening were a flock of dirty, tousled, tow-headed children. Often she held a small baby in her arms. Behind followed a small herd of cattle or horses driven by the man and the boys on foot, for the rate of travel was a walk." Sometimes the travelers would stop. "They told us where they came from, Fillmore or Goodhue County in Minnesota, or Wisconsin, or Iowa. Most of them were on their way to Larimore, Devil's Lake, Church's Ferry, or some other point far distant from a railroad in Dakota." Day after day the caravans moved by, from ten to fifty schooners each day, symbols of the prairie hegira. "Slowly the wagons passed on, the children now peeking from the opening in the rear, the schooner receding into the distance, very much like a real ship plowing its way over a trackless sea and then disappearing below the horizon." [54]

That was the period of the "Dakota fever," of folk migration to the wheatlands; but before these caravans of the 1880's, the pioneers of the preceding decade had pushed out onto the Dakota side of the Red River. The old fear of the prairie was breaking down, but the Norwegian farmers liked the river valleys, especially the Red and its various tributaries. The prairie was alluring, but the flowing water of streams still had a place in their conception of the good earth. Before the end of the 1870's they had swarmed into Dakota in its eastern counties, from Richland, in the southeastern corner, up through all the rich counties lying beyond the Red River; and it was this fertile eastern Dakota land that remained a center of Norwegian concentration from pioneer days to the twentieth century. The Norwegians also liked

[54] William A. Marin, "Sod Houses and Prairie Schooners," in *Minnesota History*, 12:153–156 (June, 1931).

the Sheyenne country and pioneered there, too, in the 1870's, building up their settlements in the 1880's and finding a trading and cultural nucleus in the Dakota town of Valley City.

When the great boom came, from 1879 to 1886, the lines of immigrants from Norway and of older settlers from Wisconsin, Minnesota, and Iowa converged upon upper Dakota. There was a land rush, with settlers scrambling for claims along the water courses or near them. They established themselves along the Wild Rice at many points, including its headwaters in Sargent County—in the lowest tier of North Dakota counties—in the early 1880's. A pioneer said that the Sheyenne Valley became "solidly Norwegian." About 1883 settlers poured into the valley of the James; and in approximately the same period they headed for the Devils Lake region, pushed into the rich Mouse River country beyond Devils Lake, and built compact settlements in north central Dakota, with Minot as a center. By 1900 the Norwegians had exploited in the main a North Dakota triangle of some twenty counties bounded on the north and east by state lines, and on the west by a slanting boundary running from Richland and Sargent in the southeast corner to Bottineau at the northwest. This was the heart of Norwegian North Dakota, but in later days Norwegian settlers struck farther into the central, southwestern, and northwestern areas of the state. The Norwegian novelist, Johan Bojer, in his story of *The Emigrants,* wrote of Erik Foss, who was searching for Dakota farm lands, "He had to go a long way before finding the best land, but what matter? Provided you began in the right place, the railway was bound to come and hunt you out before very long, and then flourishing settlements and towns would spring up; that always happened here now. Only, you had to be first in the field to secure the best land." [55]

[55] Bojer, *The Emigrants,* 74. See Qualey, ch. 7, and a good map showing the distribution of the Norwegians in North Dakota in 1900. A general treatment of interest is Harold E. Briggs, "The Great Dakota Boom, 1879 to 1886," in *North Dakota Historical Quarterly,* 4:78–108 (January, 1930).

Beginnings were often humble. John H. Blegen, a professor in Augsburg Seminary who traveled across Dakota in 1886 on a missionary journey, found a Norwegian family living in a sod hut at a dismal spot far from trees and water. A traveling chest with a flat lid served as a dining table and was the only piece of furniture in the house. The settler had a young ox team but no plow. It was almost impossible for him to get either wood or water. The prospects seemed so hopeless to him that he broke down and wept, expressing bitter regret that he had left his "humble but happy home" in his native land. But the visitor comforted him and encouraged him to persist in his struggle. After all, he did have a cow and some chickens — he was not likely to starve. Reflecting philosophically on the plight of the settlers, the visitor wrote, "Naturally, it will be a little hard for them to come through the first two years, the period before they can get any crops of importance. But after that time has passed by they will probably no longer regret the fact that they journeyed to America. At least that is the way it goes with most people." Professor Blegen incidentally got a glimpse of the prairie boom. At a spot called Church's Ferry, just reached by a railroad, he observed men laying the foundations of the first houses and was told that a station and a town would soon emerge, but he was skeptical and said to himself, "It will take some time before any town appears here." A few weeks later he passed the same spot and recorded that his eyes "met a surprising sight" — for the town had in fact taken form. It was not large, but it already had saloons, shops, hotels, houses. "So rapidly," he exclaimed, "can development go in the Northwest! Towns spring up faster than mushrooms." [56]

Pioneer farmers began to raise great crops of spring wheat. Railroads pushed westward, bringing markets within reach of frontier settlements and delivering increasing numbers of pioneers to the flat lands. Norwegians endured blizzards

[56] John H. Blegen, in *North Dakota Historical Quarterly*, vol. 1, no. 3, p. 16–29.

and some of them, like Per Hansa in *Giants in the Earth,* lost their way amid the relentless fury of such storms and were frozen to death. The Norwegians knew the flaming rage of prairie fires. The very summer in which the Augsburg professor made his journey across the plains, a Dakota prairie fire swept across five hundred square miles of land northwest of Bottineau.[57] The pioneers lived through summers when the pitiless sun of the Great Plains baked the unprotected expanse of land and settlers accustomed to cool Norwegian slopes and valleys gasped for breath. But there were occasional compensations. In the 1880's a Norwegian farm laborer in Dakota observed the cloudless sky, the wide-stretching sea of wheat, the appalling bigness of bonanza farms. "Fie, what a country, this Dakota!" he exclaimed. But he was moved by the spectacle of the Dakota sunset, "blood-red in hue and of an intensity almost defying description." This was no ordinary laborer, this observer of the prairie sun, but a genius who would one day write the *Growth of the Soil* and win the Nobel Prize—Knut Hamsun.[58]

Moments of beauty there were, blood-red sunsets, rain that left the prairie fresh with the promise of growth, winds that turned fields of broad-bladed wheat into billowing seas, the sight of prairie flowers—harebell, wild rose, goldenrod, aster, blazing star. The dominant note, however, was not beauty, but work—toil and drudgery—and the settlers lived lives without glamor as they patiently tried to realize their hopes. Yet across the years the drudgery of hours and days shaped a drama of change and achievement. The one-room

[57] Federal Writers' Project, *North Dakota: A Guide to the Northern Prairie State,* 239 (Fargo, 1938).

[58] John T. Flanagan, "Knut Hamsun's Early Years in the Northwest," in *Minnesota History,* 20: 404, 405 (December, 1939); Kristofer Janson, *Hvad jeg har oplevet,* 222–224 (Christiania, 1913). "The doors of the hut stood open, gasping for air," wrote Bojer of the Dakota heat, "and who could hope to rest at night when the room felt like an oven and the air was thick with mosquitos? The men cursed and struck out in their sleep." *The Emigrants,* 121.

sod huts gave way to frame houses, improvised furniture was replaced by table and chairs and beds from the prairie stores, churches and schoolhouses were built, Norwegian-American newspapers were established, a Norwegian-American community life was set in motion, and in prairie homes one heard talk of American politics, church controversies, and other interests in the world beyond the rim of the grainfield. The things out of Norway had a stubborn vitality. Even today a Dakota handbook speaks of the prevalence of the Norwegian dialects on the plains, of the Dakota love of coffee and Norwegian pastries, of the cultivation of Norwegian music and dance and sport.[59] Fargo, where half the people are of Norwegian descent, has a Dovre ski slide and cherishes monuments to Gange Rolf and Henrik Wergeland. The sod-hut pioneer of the 1880's was disconsolate as he faced his initial problems, but the wise teacher who consoled him read the future of the prairie. For the pioneers brought its flat expanse under cultivation and won the rewards of the soil. The time came when their granaries were bursting with hard wheat to be sent to the mills to make white flour. Their children and grandchildren attended the prairie university or went to college in Northfield, Decorah, or Minneapolis. And ultimately Dakota governors bore such names as Olson, Nestos, and Sorlie, and the experiences of the men and women — and children — of the sod huts were woven into the state saga. There came a day, too, when the very success of the pioneer farmers, based as it was upon a prodigal and unscientific exploitation of the soil, precipitated grave economic problems upon the modern state.

If the block of a half dozen states of the Northwest — Illinois, Wisconsin, Iowa, Minnesota, South and North Dakota — represents the main domain in which the Norwegian immigrants met the frontier challenge, it must be borne in mind

[59] See the chapter on "Racial Groups and Folkways," in Federal Writers' Project, *North Dakota,* 78 ff.

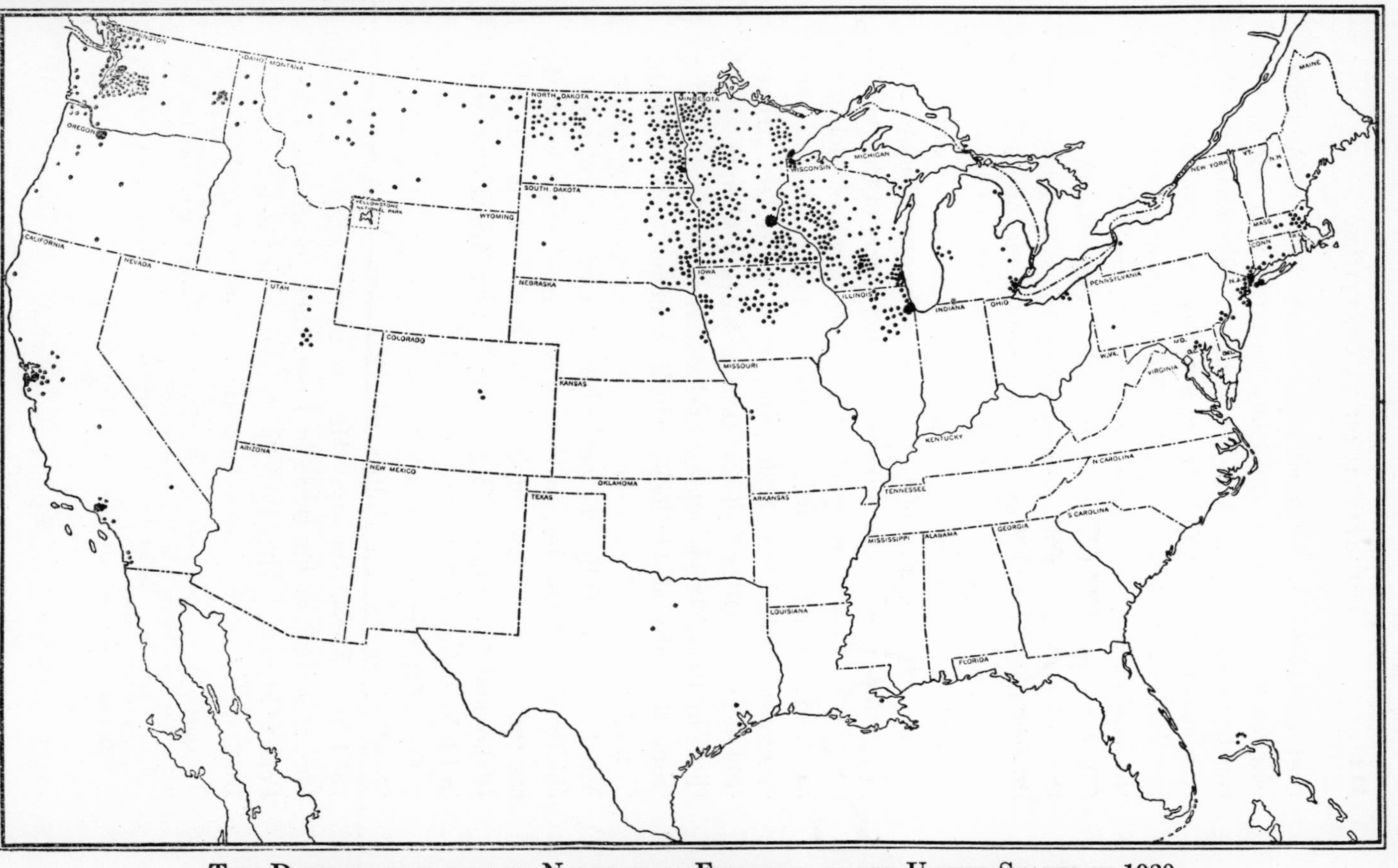

THE DISTRIBUTION OF THE NORWEGIAN ELEMENT IN THE UNITED STATES IN 1930

[Each dot represents a thousand persons. From a map in Qualey, *Norwegian Settlement,* 202.]

that the migration touched many other parts of America. Michigan, for example, especially on its eastern side and in the Upper Peninsula, attracted many Norwegians, with the emphasis more upon industry and wages than upon land and farming. They went to the logging camps and sawmills, to the copper and iron mines of the northern region, to the Great Lakes ports where seamen found opportunities to use their special skills, and in more recent times to the great industrial centers, where mechanics and engineers secured profitable employment.[60] Beyond North Dakota to the north, the Norwegians joined in the trek to the prairie provinces of Canada, an extension of the American frontier, though the pioneers who made this advance became a part of the British Empire. Many Norwegians followed the trail of such men as P. M. Henriks, a fisherman from northern Norway who emigrated in the late 1860's, pioneered in western Minnesota — first in Otter Tail and then in Kittson County — and then, in 1902, struck out for Saskatchewan, settling not far from the site of Outlook, which became a Norwegian-Canadian center.[61] To the west the Norwegians moved into Montana, especially its agricultural northeastern corner, chiefly since 1900; but in the earlier period some were attracted to the mineral empire in western Montana — and in Idaho and Colorado. Thirty-one Norwegian miners were in Idaho before 1870.[62]

One of the immigrants who made their way to the mineral kingdom was A. M. Holter, who had come to America in 1854 from Moss, Norway. He was a carpenter and worked for some time at his trade in Iowa, then joined the Pike's Peak gold rush. After three years he returned to Iowa, and in 1863, with a team of oxen, he again went west, this time pass-

[60] Qualey, *Norwegian Settlement*, ch. 8, including a map showing the distribution of the Scandinavians in Michigan in 1880.

[61] O. B. Grimley, "En høvding blandt nybyggerne," in *Nordmanns-forbundet*, 28:159–161 (May, 1935).

[62] Qualey, *Norwegian Settlement*, 170, 171, 193–196.

ing on from Colorado to Montana. He hauled a "second-hand sawmill outfit" more than a thousand miles to Bevin's Gulch, near Virginia City; was robbed and nearly murdered by the notorious bandit George Ives; set up his mill; built a cabin and a blacksmith shop; soon opened lumberyards in Nevada City and Virginia City; moved on to Helena when gold was discovered at Last Chance Gulch, and started a mill there; installed the first planer used in the territory; expanded his business in the face of formidable difficulties; and by 1868 was running the first sash and door factory in Montana. Holter, with this background of pioneering, went on to become a magnate of the industry of his choice, and in later years he was hailed as the "father of lumbering in Montana."[63]

Norwegians in the 1840's and 1850's had responded to the lure of California gold, going direct from Norway or overland from the Middle Western settlements, and by 1860 there were more than seven hundred Norwegians in that state.[64] Others had joined the Mormons in their trek from Nauvoo to Utah or had been converted in Norway to the doctrines of the Latter-day Saints and made their way to the Mormon paradise. In the main, however, Norwegian settlement in the Far West has been a trend of more recent years. As Dr. Qualey suggests, it has been a jump from the edge of the Great Plains to the area about Puget Sound and the rich valleys of Oregon and Washington. The bridging of the continent by railroads was a large factor in the migration, but it was also coupled with discontents in the older regions and the widely heralded advantages of the Pacific slope. The Puget Sound region attracted the majority of the settlers,

[63] An undated pamphlet of twenty-three pages entitled *Pioneer Lumbering in Montana,* issued by the *Timberman* of Portland, Oregon, contains Holter's own reminiscences of his career in Montana. A copy of this little-known item is in the library of the Minnesota Historical Society. See also Rolfsen, *Norge i Amerika,* 521–529.

[64] See the chapter on "Emigrant Gold Seekers," in Blegen, *Norwegian Migration,* 267–286.

and in 1930 more than four-fifths of all the Norwegians in the Pacific Northwest were to be found there. The immigrants who went into the Far West took jobs in lumber camps, worked in sawmills, entered the fishing industry, sailed on vessels out of Pacific ports, and in many instances made farms for themselves, notably in eastern Washington. Seattle, Tacoma, and Portland became important urban centers for Norwegian Americans, where newspapers were published, churches built, and an active social and cultural life developed.[65]

An illustration of the mechanics of organized migration from the Middle West to the Pacific Northwest is afforded by the story of the Bella Coola colony of British Columbia. Discontented farmers in the Red River Valley, meeting in 1894 at Vineland in Polk County, Minnesota, selected two men to act as scouts on a trip to Washington and British Columbia. One of the two chosen was the Reverend C. Saugstad, a versatile Lutheran pastor who had been a farmer and lumberjack, wrote hymns and composed music, and left among his papers the manuscript of an unpublished novel. The two agents returned from their scouting trip and reported with enthusiasm on the prospects offered by British Columbia. And so a company was formally organized "to induce moral, industrious and loyal Norwegian farmers, mechanics, and business men to come to Bella Coola and make their homes there under the laws of British Columbia." Canadian officials promised to reserve lands for the colony, to build a needed wagon road, and to allot 160 acres of land free to each settler. Officers were chosen, including Saugstad as president, and in the autumn of 1894 more than eighty people set out for the West. They reached their intended destination, founded their colony, received not a few recruits the next year, and in general won measurable suc-

[65] Qualey, *Norwegian Settlement*, 188–193.

cess, notwithstanding caustic criticism of the entire project in the Norwegian-American press of the Middle West.[66]

The story of the Norwegians in dispersion runs over a long period and has a wide range both in geographical area and historical interest. It begins with the arrival of fifty-three immigrants in the sloop "Restoration" in 1825. More than a century later the census reported that there were in the United States 1,100,098 people born in Norway or of Norwegian parentage in whole or in part; and some scholars estimate that perhaps a million more persons in America represent a Norwegian ancestry at a farther remove which is not reflected in these census figures. The sloop folk made an advance from the eastern seaboard to the New York frontier. The Norwegian immigrants pushed on to Illinois and the Middle West in the 1830's and ranged upward in the Mississippi Valley during the following decades. They moved into the trans-Mississippi West and out onto the Great Plains, thrust northward into the Canadian prairie provinces, reached out to the mineral kingdom and the Mormon state, and found their way to the Pacific slopes, from California to British Columbia — and Alaska, too. The pre-Civil War settlements in Texas had a surprising vitality, retained their identity though relatively few Norwegians followed Cleng Peerson's trail into the Southwest, and by 1930 the Texas Norwegian element was placed at 5,543. The circle is complete when one ranges northward along the Atlantic coast, pauses to note that there is a village called Norge in the old dominion of Virginia, and observes that in 1930 there were 118,135 Norwegians in ten states of the East. It is not surprising to learn that three-fifths of all these people live in

[66] Iver Fougner, "The Founding of Bella Coola," in *Canadian Magazine* (Toronto), 23:529–536 (October, 1904); and Clifford R. Kopas, "Norse Canadians," in *Maclean's Magazine* (Toronto), 48:26, 54 (April, 1935). Thanks to the kindness of Mr. Fougner, I have been enabled to make photostats of many documents relating to this colony, including the constitution, the minutes of the annual meeting of 1901, and various newspaper clippings, some of them containing contemporary reports by Saugstad.

Greater New York, for one of the principal Norwegian-American economic, professional, and cultural centers is to be found in Brooklyn. The eastern city, as part of America's metropolis, is a lively center of Norwegian institutional and social activity; it is the home of *Nordisk tidende,* one of the most influential of all Norwegian-American newspapers; and it represents fresher contacts with modern Norway than do the settlements of the Middle West.[67]

[67] Qualey, *Norwegian Settlement,* 198–214; H. M. Gundersen, "Norge i Virginia," in *Nordmanns-forbundet,* 28:8–10 (January, 1935); E. N. Figved, *En historisk skisse om de Norske i Boston og omegn* (Brooklyn, 1925); and Th. Tallaksen and Paul H. Wiig, *Norske paa Staten Island* (Brooklyn, 1927).

XVII. THE PROBLEM OF HIGHER EDUCATION

The widening of the social and cultural frontiers of Norwegian-American life is a subject so far-reaching in scope and challenging in precise detail that it invites a separate volume. The larger historical significance of the present story of immigrant transition can scarcely be understood, however, if some of the outlines of its broader cultural consequences are not sketched in the final chapters of this study. The extension of the frontiers of culture was not unrelated to that of the frontiers of settlement. Norwegian-American cultural pioneering, in fact, often synchronized with agricultural pioneering and usually had its roots in the struggle of the immigrants to gain a firm foothold in the New World.

The challenge of higher education came to an early focus in the need of educating ministers for the Norwegian-American Lutheran church, but it broadened at once into a movement for colleges and academies where the younger generation, whether aspiring to the ministry or not, could acquire a liberal education. Dietrichson and Clausen, as has been noted, took under advisement as early as 1847 the problem of launching a Norwegian Lutheran seminary, but their efforts were fruitless, notwithstanding the willingness of Clausen to guarantee a salary for a teacher.[1] The Synod ministers in 1852 considered an invitation to utilize Capital University in Columbus, Ohio, in conjunction with the Joint Synod of Ohio, but doubts of the wisdom of such an affiliation blocked action. In the middle 1850's the Norwegian Synod began to give thought to the possibility of establishing an independent educational institution, but confronted a lack both of funds and of available teachers. The feasibility of utilizing the University of Wisconsin for the classical training of prospective ministers also was studied.[2]

Nothing was accomplished, however, until 1855, when the Synod sent two delegates on a journey of investigation of Lutheran institutions of learning in St. Louis, Fort Wayne, Springfield, Columbus, and Buffalo. The upshot of this tour was an emphatic recommendation that a Norwegian professorship should be established at Concordia Seminary in St. Louis. The Norwegian Synod in 1857 endorsed this recommendation, which brought the rising church body into close contact with the German Missouri Synod. This action by the Norwegians is not difficult to understand. The Synod, growing rapidly, already had many parishes without pastors; it found it impossible to induce many young ministers trained in Norway to come to America; it felt assurance as to the complete orthodoxy of the Missouri group; and it concluded that the time was not yet ripe for an independent college or seminary. Meanwhile, the utilization of the gymnasium and seminary at St. Louis promised an early easing of the problem of supplying vacant parishes with pastors. The step was tentative, however, for the Synod acted favorably upon

[1] *Nordlyset* (Trondhjem), November 19, 1847; and *ante*, p. 159.

[2] Gisle Bothne, *Det norske Luther College 1861–1897*, ch. 2 (Decorah, 1897); Laur. Larsen, in *Katalog for det norske Luther-college i Decorah*, 4, 5 (Decorah, 1872).

a proposal to collect funds for the establishment of a "Norwegian Lutheran University." [3]

Norwegian students matriculated at Concordia Seminary as early as 1858, but there was some delay in finding a Norwegian professor for the proposed chair. This problem was solved by the appointment of Laur. Larsen, who took up his duties in 1859 as the director of the group of Norwegian students in the Missouri Synod institution. He served in that capacity for two years. Meanwhile, in 1859, the Synod pledged itself to make an effort to establish its own "Norwegian University" within three years; and in 1860 it authorized student patronage of the Missouri Synod's practical seminary at Fort Wayne, in addition to the school at St. Louis, as a means of meeting the insistent demand for ministers. The outbreak of the Civil War and the explosion of the slavery controversy within the Norwegian Synod precipitated the decision of that body, however, to establish without any further delay its own institution of learning. The clergy preferred a continuance of the arrangements with Concordia Seminary, but the laymen in the synodical meeting of 1861, as we have seen, insisted upon launching an independent school at once. The idea of Luther College, as Professor Karen Larsen correctly maintains, had its inception among the clergy, whereas it was the laity, agitated about the slavery issue, who turned the idea into action in 1861. As Laur. Larsen said later, the decision to set Luther College in motion perhaps would not have been taken for a considerable time if general conditions had been normal and peaceful. [4]

[3] See President Larsen's account of the early history of Luther College in the 1872 *Katalog*, 4–16; Luther College Faculty, *Luther College*, 16, 24–26; and Bothne, *Det norske Luther College*, 27 ff. Brandt and Ottesen were commissioned as delegates to examine Lutheran institutions of higher learning as early as 1853, but they did not report until 1857.

[4] *Luther College*, 24–26; Larsen, in the 1872 *Katalog*, 8; Larsen, *Laur. Larsen*, 136. Miss Larsen devotes ch. 6 of this work to her father's experiences as "Professor at Concordia College."

Thus it came about that the first of the Norwegian-American colleges was established in 1861 and passed through its initial struggles during the fateful years when North and South were locked in Civil War. Larsen, who became the first president of the college, and his associates in the Synod accepted the educational principle of working from the bottom up rather than from the top down. Although launched with the avowed purpose of training ministers, Luther College never became a theological school. Larsen, in a public announcement, called it the "Norwegian Lutheran School for the Education of Ministers,"[5] and so it was, but it conceived its task in terms of the basic education of men who would later add, in some other institution, the necessary specialized training in theology. Luther College opened its doors to boys as young as fourteen, functioned as a preparatory school, gradually expanded its program until by 1865 it was offering a six-year Latin course,—running from the lowest form Sexta to Prima at the top,—and ultimately built a four-year college course superimposed upon a three-year preparatory department. President Larsen believed in the ideal of a thorough classical education for prospective ministers, and this ideal Luther College exemplified. Dealing with the problem of training boys from the Norwegian-American farms of the Middle West, however, it could take almost nothing for granted in the way of preliminary preparation. Larsen's thought was centered upon the needs of the church; he was acutely aware of the importance of filling empty pulpits without undue delay; but he clung steadfastly to his concept of a broad fundamental education, with "thoroughness" as its watchword, as an essential for an enlightened clergy, and the passing years bore witness to the solidity of the contribution that he thereby made to Norwegian-American cultural history. So it came about that the de-

[5] Larsen, *Laur. Larsen,* 137.

pendence upon the Missouri Synod for formal theological training continued for many years after the Civil War. Indeed, it was not until 1876 that the Norwegian Synod established its own theological seminary.[6]

The beginnings of Luther College were humble. It was housed for the year 1861–62 in a parsonage at Halfway Creek, near La Crosse, Wisconsin. This building, erected for the use of one family, accommodated President Larsen and Professor F. A. Schmidt and their respective families as well as the student body — a squad of some ten or eleven boys. The house was dormitory, classroom, dining hall, and library, and the conditions were those of tutors living with their charges after the manner of a large family. Conveniences were absent, books few, teachers overloaded with duties, students deficient in preliminary training, funds limited; the first year ended in a deficit; but the institution had two teachers of uncommon ability and force, and it was supported by staunch purpose in the Synod congregations. Larsen himself was filled with the "youthful, hopeful energy of the pioneer and with impassioned zeal for a great cause."[7]

So these builders of a pioneer college went serenely on with their task, reduced the tuition from $32.00 to nothing the second year, and removed the institution from the country parsonage to Decorah, Iowa, where it was temporarily housed in a hotel building. The student body grew in numbers as the curriculum was expanded year by year into a six-year course and as clergy and laymen alike accepted the idea of foundational training not only for future ministers but also for the sons of the immigrants, whatever their professional

[6] A statement by Larsen setting forth his ideals for Luther College is translated in *Laur. Larsen,* 184. His views were pungently expressed in the phrase "no pretense without content, no shell without kernel."

[7] The Halfway Creek phase is dealt with in Miss Larsen's chapter, "Luther College Born in Storm and Stress," in *Laur. Larsen,* 126–155; and in Bothne, *Det norske Luther College,* 38–43. The study plan for the form Quarta at Halfway Creek included the following subjects: Latin, Greek, religion, German, English, Norwegian, algebra, history, singing, and penmanship.

aims. One of the most remarkable facts in Norwegian-American pioneer history is that Luther College, so humbly initiated in the frontier era, so beset with difficulties in the trying years of the Civil War, was able to dedicate in 1864 a magnificent college building that cost no less than $75,000. In its cornerstone reposed this record: "Emigrated Norwegians, Lutheran Christians, living in Wisconsin, Iowa, Minnesota, and Illinois, united in erecting this building to educate teachers of the Church"; and its tower framed the motto: "Soli Deo Gloria."[8] A measure of the significance attached to the event by the pioneers themselves is afforded by the fact that six thousand people crowded into the little Iowa town to see the new college building and to attend the ceremonies of its dedication.[9]

President Larsen knew that a building did not make a college. He tried to get a faculty of competent teachers devoted to the idea of a classical education and at the same time faithful to the religious views embodied in the Synod. He secured some men whose training had been gained in the old country, but he also was aware of the transition that the Norwegians in America were undergoing and he tried to keep step with it by finding teachers trained in American institutions. "We need fresh forces," he said in the early 1870's, "while everything imported from Norway invariably has to be more or less recast."[10] As early as 1866 he took time to visit such American colleges and universities as Wisconsin, Beloit, Oberlin, and Michigan, an enterprise unusual, if not unique, among the pioneer Norwegian-American educators. Critical and observant of minute details, he found relatively little in these institutions upon which to model changes at Luther College. The University of Michigan did, indeed, impress

[8] The text of the cornerstone statement is given in full in *Luther College*, 27. See also Larsen, *Laur. Larsen*, 170 ff.

[9] Bothne, *Det norske Luther College*, 82–110; W. Sihler, in *Luther College*, 21.

[10] Quoted in Larsen, *Laur. Larsen*, 239.

him favorably, but at Wisconsin he found little to praise. The desks and benches were admirable, but "there was little questioning about analysis" in Virgil, the students in Xenophon were often not prepared, the class in Schiller "went miserably," a lecture on school discipline was "quite dry," and one class was devoted to "mental philosophy — terrible humbug." At Beloit College, where he found a Norwegian from the Muskego settlement, he attended a Greek class and observed "the most wretched teaching I have heard," though this was somewhat offset by a recitation under Professor Joseph Emerson — "the best I heard." Oberlin he viewed as the "pinnacle of Yankee humbug and conceit."[11]

Larsen looked at college education in the Middle West in its primitive stages, but whatever his disillusionment about American institutions of learning, he was aware of the fact that Luther College was facing changes. These changes, worked out over a period of many years, constituted, in the words of President Larsen's daughter, a transition "from a Latin school, built on a European model, into an American college which nevertheless was to remain true to its original character and purpose." The transition was signalized in the early 1880's by the separation of the college proper from the preparatory course as well as by curricular changes and the gradual displacement of Norwegian by English in class instruction and campus speech. Men like Larsen himself, Schmidt, and the pioneer minister Brandt were the core of the faculty, which at one time or another also included such teachers as O. J. Breda, Thrond and Gisle Bothne, L. S. Reque, Adolf Bredesen, Christian A. Naeseth, A. A. Veblen, and J. D. Jacobsen. In the later history of Luther College the faculty included such men as Christian K. Preus,

[11] Professor Karen Larsen has made available in English the remarkable diary kept by her father on his visit to American colleges in 1866. See "A Newcomer Looks at American Colleges," in *Studies and Records,* 10:107–126. The characterization of Oberlin College is quoted from a private letter, in Larsen, *Laur. Larsen,* 187.

who succeeded the venerable Larsen in 1902; Dr. O. M. Norlie, the historian and statistician; and Knut Gjerset, the noted historian and builder of a unique pioneer museum on the Luther College campus which fittingly includes the pioneer parsonage of Ulrik V. Koren. The Synod clergy were always in close touch with the college, and men like Koren were influential figures in its life. So, decade after decade, through all the years since 1861, Luther College sent graduates into the professions and built a tradition of service to the Norwegian immigrants and their descendants.[12]

Professor A. A. Veblen, who taught at Luther College from 1877 to 1881, saw it in a period of transition.[13] He was surprised to be invited to teach at the Norwegian college, for he was a graduate, as was his brother Thorstein, of Carleton College, an American Congregational school in Minnesota. He was even more surprised to be assigned the class in beginning Latin, for the Luther College leaders, he felt sure, were sharply critical of American methods in teaching the classical languages. Probably Veblen did not quite fathom Larsen's quiet interest in introducing "new forces" into the life of the college. Veblen was deeply interested in his six colleagues and has left vivid characterizations of some of them. The rugged and plain-spoken Thrond Bothne, Norwegian-trained, could find nothing more severe to say in condemnation of a

[12] The most informing and valuable sources of information on Luther College are Karen Larsen's admirable biography of her father; Bothne's *Det norske Luther College;* and *Luther College through Sixty Years.* The latter is a co-operative work dealing topically with various aspects of the development of Luther College. It includes a useful bibliography by O. M. Norlie (p. 485–487) and a chronological summary by O. A. Tingelstad (p. 488–490). A brief essay of considerable interest on "Luther College," by Ola A. Solheim, is in *Symra,* 6:217–238 (1910). The catalogues and student publications of the college, as well as the synodical reports and church periodicals, naturally contain a vast amount of information about the institution. Luther College has also appeared in fiction, for Peer Strømme's novel, *Hvorledes Halvor blev prest,* gives a faithful account of student life at Luther in the 1870's. This novel appeared in Norwegian at Decorah in 1893; an English translation by Inga B. Norstog, *How Halvor Became a Minister,* was issued in Minneapolis in 1936.

[13] Professor Veblen's unpublished recollections, entitled "At Luther College (1877–1881)," are preserved in the Veblen Papers, in the possession of the Minnesota Historical Society.

person than that he was "Americanized."[14] Nevertheless, the Americanization of the college itself went steadily forward. For one thing, the "English party"—that is, the group favoring increasing use of English in class instruction—was gaining ground, and when Veblen left Decorah in 1881 he believed that English had "practically displaced Norwegian as the language of the campus." Most of his energy and time was devoted to teaching English grammar, composition, and rhetoric—no simple task, for he found Sexta an "untrained and miscellaneous flock of country boys." And, like all the other teachers on the faculty, he had a heavy program. The average teaching "load" of the professors ran from twenty-four to twenty-seven hours a week.

Veblen was active in a student military company which bore the name "Luther College Phalanx." Baseball was the chief sport of the students, who also played a "sort of very simple Rugby." The discipline of the college had some self-governing features: each dormitory, for example, had a student superintendent, and there were also student supervisors of woodcutters. Students over eighteen might smoke, but only in one specified building, a structure politely referred to as the "chicken coop." This became, Veblen says, a social center, and a club with bylaws and officers was organized—"Niffelheim," the home of smoke. Soon a competing club of nonsmokers—"Muspelheim"—was started. Veblen found that the general ministerial conferences, held in the college chapel, were memorable events. When such conferences occurred, students were allotted a week in which to prepare for examinations. At the conferences Veblen learned how the "solidarity of the clergy was promoted and the well-known uniformity of pastoral management was built up and maintained." Incidentally, he watched the rise of the church controversy on predestination, which was leading toward

[14] A fuller characterization of Bothne is offered in "Thrond Bothne som lærer," by P. J. Eikeland in *Symra,* 4:10–24 (1908).

schism before he left. He himself resigned after four years. Among other matters, he found himself criticized by his colleagues for "puritan and illiberal objection" to the use of wine at a college celebration — an evidence that the deeper Puritanism of the Norwegian Americans, however severe the discipline of Luther College, did not have its main roots in the Synod group.

Widespread as was the support of Luther College, it represented only one wing of Norwegian-American Lutheranism, and one is not surprised to learn that rival, low-church forces in the immigrant religious scene also responded to the challenge of higher education. Augsburg Seminary, established at Marshall, Wisconsin, in 1869, and removed to Minneapolis in 1872, had its roots in the Scandinavian Evangelical Lutheran Augustana Synod, which in turn grew out of the movement centered in the Scandinavian affiliation with the Synod of Northern Illinois and its "university" at Springfield. In 1860 the dissatisfaction of the Scandinavians with that "polyglot Lutheran synod" came to a head, as has been noted, in secession. For about a decade thereafter Swedes and Norwegians co-operated in the Augustana Synod, supporting an independent school — Augustana College and Theological Seminary — located first in Chicago and after a few years at Paxton, Illinois. There men like Esbjörn, Hasselquist, and S. L. Harkey gave instruction to Swedish and Norwegian students, and occasionally a Norwegian was engaged to give special attention to the needs of the Norwegian contingent. In 1868 August Weenaas, who had studied at the national university in Christiania from 1853 to 1860 and had served as a minister and teacher in Norway, arrived at Paxton to occupy a special Norwegian chair in theology.[15]

[15] The standard history of Augsburg Seminary, and the best historical review yet published of any Norwegian-American college, is Helland's *Augsburg Seminar gjennem femti aar 1869–1919*. Professor Weenaas has recorded his experiences in *Mindeblade eller otte aar i Amerika* (Volden, 1890) and *Livserindringer fra Norge og Amerika* (Bergen, 1935). An account by a man who studied in the old

The coming of Weenaas, far from cementing the Swedish and Norwegian union, proved a prelude to schism, with language and nationality as the chief divisive factors. Even before Weenaas arrived, the co-operative experiment was beginning to falter. Its principal weakness lay in the fact that it did not extend into the congregations. The Norwegians were organizing, as were the Swedes, congregations of their own throughout the Middle West. In 1866 they established an organ of their own, *Den norske Lutheraner,* which emphasized their solidarity; they set about raising a special fund with which to support a Norwegian professor; and as their numbers increased, the impulse toward separation gained force.[16] It should be noted, however, that their particularism did not bar wholehearted co-operation with the Danes. The explanation of this fact lies in several circumstances: there were relatively few Danes; traditionally the Danes and Norwegians had stood very close to one another in the New World; and the language problem between them was nonexistent so far as the printed page was concerned. At first there was some thought of breaking the Augustana Synod into two church bodies, Norwegian-Danish and Swedish, while continuing to co-operate in support of one institution of higher learning. Weenaas had not been long in America, however, before he was convinced that the establishment of a separate school for the Norwegians and Danes was a matter of vital importance. The outcome was that

Augsburg at Marshall is C. Saugstad, *Augsburgs historie* (Minneapolis, 1893). A brief survey of "Augsburg Seminarium" is contributed by H. C. Caspersen to *Symra,* 6:163–184 (1910). Documentary material of high value has been assembled by Professor Lars Lillehei in his *Augsburg Seminary and the Lutheran Free Church* (Minneapolis, 1928). An unpublished essay of interest is Bernhardt J. Kleven's "History of the Norwegian-Danish Evangelical Lutheran Church in America," a University of Minnesota master's thesis submitted in 1930. It contains a comprehensive bibliography. Mr. Kleven has also written a pamphlet, *The Story of Augsburg,* issued recently by the college.

[16] *Den norske Lutheraner,* edited by O. J. Hatlestad, J. P. Gjertsen, and S. M. Krognæs, began publication at Chicago in 1866. Mention of the "professor fund" occurs in the issues for February 10 and March 10, 1868. I have used a file of this rare paper in the Augsburg Archives.

the Scandinavian schism came first on the question of a separate school rather than on that of a separate synod. In 1869 Weenaas and his band of students, under authorization from the Augustana Synod, broke away from the institution at Paxton to establish Augsburg Seminary at Marshall, a village in Dane County, Wisconsin, where an American academy building had been secured to house the seminary. The division of the Augustana Synod itself did not occur until the following year.[17]

Meanwhile, at Marshall the first theological seminary of the Norwegian Lutherans in America took form. The Norwegians had agreed to launch an academy alongside the theological school; both were set in motion in September, 1869. A Norwegian magazine in Madison hailed the new enterprise as one befitting a "free and enlightened people that has the responsibility of governing itself" and also as one "worthy of the children of the evangelical Lutheran church." It welcomed a higher school at some central point among the Norwegians east of the Mississippi, and urged the Scandinavians not to lag behind the Americans and the Germans in supporting such an institution, which raised the question of "duties to ourselves, our children, and our posterity." It viewed the new Wisconsin school as presenting "a rare and favorable opportunity to forward sound popular education."[18]

The beginnings of Augsburg Seminary, like those of Luther College, were humble. The seminary enrolled eleven students during the first year; the academy, or preparatory department, ten.[19] President Weenaas presided over the seminary; an assistant, Caesar Boeck, taught Latin, Greek,

[17] Weenaas, *Mindeblade,* 22–27; Helland, *Augsburg Seminar,* ch. 2, 3. See an article by Weenaas, "Hvad vi ville," in *Den norske Lutheraner,* 3:17–26 (February 10, 1869).

[18] The article in *Billed-magazin* was entitled "Marshall College." It is reprinted in Helland, *Augsburg Seminar,* 40 ff.

[19] The original record book for the first year of the school is preserved in the Augsburg Archives. Weenaas tells of Augsburg's first year, in *Mindeblade,* 27–38.

and German; J. J. Anderson was the principal of the academy. Funds were slim and there was a constant struggle to meet running expenses. In October, 1869, Weenaas gratefully acknowledged gifts which included eight bushels of wheat, one and a half of potatoes, a hundred pounds of butter, a large tablecloth, five stoves, a bedcover, and sundry gifts of money, including twenty dollars from the Milwaukee Ladies' Aid.[20] On November 10, 1869—the anniversary of Luther's birth—the school was dedicated in ceremonies that included addresses on such subjects as "The Need of a Junction between Moral and Intellectual Education," "Intellectual Culture and the Individual and Society," and "The Lutheran Reformation." It was the president, Weenaas, who spoke on the Reformation, and he emphasized two points which, according to Professor Andreas Helland, are major chords in the history of Augsburg Seminary. One was the sovereignty of the congregation; the other, the need of "an ever deeper sense of the truth." In emphasizing the first, Weenaas put the congregation over any churchly authority which might try to enslave it; in explaining the second, he struck at sterile orthodoxy, the formulation of theses, scholasticism, and traditionalism.[21]

The second year of Augsburg Seminary proved a critical one. In the summer of 1870 the Norwegian-Danish group separated peacefully from the Scandinavian Augustana Synod and formed a synod of its own—the Norwegian-Danish Augustana Synod. Its strength lay chiefly in the newer elements within the group, men more recently out of Norway

[20] *Den norske Lutheraner,* 3:76 (November 10, 1869). A sketch of the Augsburg plan of studies appears in the same paper for January, 1870. Subjects included in the theological school were New Testament, church history, dogmatics, Old Testament, symbolics, New Testament Greek, and singing. The proseminary offered, among other subjects, Greek, Latin, German, English, Norwegian, history, geography, mathematics, and religion.

[21] Helland, *Augsburg Seminar,* 45–47. One of the Norwegians who studied at Paxton and Marshall was N. E. Bøe. His daughter A. Sophie Bøe devotes an interesting chapter (p. 26–34) in her *Story of Father's Life* to his student experiences.

than Paul Andersen and his associate Andrewson; while the older elements, those most active in the earlier Synod of Northern Illinois, opposed the move. An effort was made to secure the affiliation of C. L. Clausen with the new body, and in the course of events it was metamorphosed into the Conference of the Norwegian-Danish Evangelical Lutheran Church in America. Clausen, recently estranged from the Norwegian Synod, became the president of this Conference, the very title of which emphasized a decentralized church body. It was supposed that the Norwegian-Danish Augustana Synod had been dissolved when the Conference emerged to take its place, but the dissident elements did not accept this view. Instead, they continued that synod, with O. J. Hatlestad as president, and proceeded to claim the academy building at Marshall. The result was that Weenaas, shortly after Augsburg's second year opened, found himself obliged to vacate the school building and to carry on the theological seminary in his own home, while the Augustana group took over the academy. Behind this secondary schism there was evidently a feeling on the part of the older leaders that Weenaas and his followers were bent on introducing the liturgy of the Norwegian state church, whereas men like Andersen and Andrewson had consistently resisted the transfer of the Old World church forms to the immigrant churches. Weenaas in turn insisted that a common liturgy in nowise conflicted either with a genuine Lutheranism or with congregational freedom.[22]

These events led to the removal of Augsburg Seminary from Marshall to Minneapolis in 1872. A continuation at Marshall was clearly impossible. Apart from its forlorn situation, the theological seminary was not enough: there must be a foundation built for the specialized training of

[22] Kleven, "Norwegian-Danish Evangelical Lutheran Church," ch. 5–7; Helland, *Augsburg Seminar,* ch. 4; Weenaas, *Mindeblade,* 38–59, and *Livserindringer,* ch. 9.

ministers. A university city offered possibilities of bridges between the struggling Norwegian institution and an American university; and the University of Minnesota in fact offered free instruction in English to the Augsburg students. This offer harmonized with the ideas of Weenaas, who foresaw the disintegration of the Lutheran church among the Norwegian Americans unless its pastors learned to speak and preach in English and made an effort to reach the English-speaking second generation. Moreover, Minnesota in the 1870's was close to the major stream of Norwegian-American settlement, and Minneapolis, stirring with metropolitan ambitions, joined the local Lutheran pastor, Ole Paulson, in extending a cordial welcome to a Scandinavian institution of higher learning. Civic interest took the form, in fact, of offers of land and of financial aid.[23]

Thus it came about that Augsburg was located in the Minnesota metropolis. A period of rapid development followed. A building had already been erected when Weenaas and his students arrived in the autumn of 1872. This was soon enlarged and other equipment was added. The program of the school was widened to include preparatory and college departments. A successful effort was made to secure the services of a number of university-trained theologians from Norway. Sven Oftedal arrived in 1873, and a year later Georg Sverdrup and S. R. Gunnersen appeared. When Weenaas returned to Norway in 1876, his place as president was taken by Sverdrup. As the student body quickly increased in numbers and the curriculum was broadened, other teachers were added to the faculty. The supporting Conference, meanwhile, grew by leaps and bounds and by 1883 numbered no fewer than 360 congregations.[24]

It is no chance circumstance that many of the early records

[23] Paulson, *Erindringer,* ch. 21; Helland, *Augsburg Seminar,* 73–87.

[24] Professor Helland's *Augsburg Seminar* is a guide to these events. See especially ch. 5 and 7. Weenaas deals with Augsburg at Minneapolis in *Livserindringer,* ch. 10, 11, and in *Mindeblade,* 60–97.

of Augsburg Seminary center about the ideas and the leadership of Sverdrup and Oftedal, for they were men of unusual qualities and far-reaching influence. Sverdrup, of a distinguished Norwegian family, was an original and incisive thinker who combined scholarship with singular power as a writer and teacher. He stood for a trained, democratic ministry functioning in a low-church atmosphere; turned aside from the traditions embodied in the European Latin school and gave Greek a large place in the Augsburg curriculum; emphasized the central importance of the free congregation, rejecting hierarchy on the one side and unorganized religion on the other; and, like Weenaas, raised his voice against a sterile orthodoxy. Dr. John O. Evjen, his most acute interpreter, describes Sverdrup as a "conservative eclectic Lutheran, with wholesome liberal leanings."[25] Oftedal was a dynamic, breezy personality, practical in approach, skilled in the art of winning friends and funds for a cause, a versatile linguist, and a dramatic fighter. He had hardly arrived on the American scene before he threw down the gauntlet to his theological opponents, particularly the Norwegian Synod, in an "Open Declaration" which Dr. Evjen characterizes as a "spirited, personal declaration of independence." Only a few years earlier H. A. Preus in his controversial lectures published in Norway had blasted the opponents of the Norwegian Synod with unusual virulence. The "Open Declaration" of Oftedal accepted the gage of battle in terms quite as searing as those Preus had employed; and Norwegian Lutheran controversy entered upon a phase in which theological learning, dialectical skill, and firmly held convictions on the one side were matched, for better or

[25] The quotation is from Evjen's brief account of Sverdrup in the *Dictionary of American Biography,* 18:229. A longer essay, also by Evjen, is *Georg Sverdrup* (Leipzig, 1913) — a reprint from vol. 24 of Albert Hauck's *Real-enzyklopädie für Protestantische Theologie und Kirche.* Volume 3 of Helland's edition of Sverdrup's *Samlede skrifter i udvalg,* a six-volume work, is devoted to "Augsburg og frikirken."

for worse, against similar qualities on the other.[26] Both sides were well equipped for the fray.

John H. Blegen, who studied at Augsburg in the 1870's, has left a vivid description of the conditions that prevailed in the pioneer institution at that time.[27] He arrived in Minneapolis in 1875, walked to the edge of the town, and then trudged out on the prairie, where the Augsburg building loomed up. He found a student body of more than a hundred, an enrollment that was a tribute to the recent strengthening of the faculty. The teachers at the time included Weenaas, Sverdrup, Oftedal, Gunnersen, and two instructors, one of them a graduate of an American college who was teaching English to the Augsburg students.

The organization of the college was just then being worked out. It was being modeled in the direction of four classes, from first to fourth Greek, but only two of these were then functioning. Blegen entered a preparatory class during his first year, then took the Greek, or college, classes in their four-year sequence, was graduated in 1880, and went on to study theology for three years. In preparing for the ministry, he spent eight years of study at Augsburg Seminary. He recalled later that the bewhiskered students of the time were industrious, notwithstanding the rarity of tests. He himself was called upon to pass no formal examinations until the end of his senior year in college, when he took lengthy written examinations in such fields as Greek, Latin, English, and Norwegian. Those in English and Norwegian consisted of philosophical essays, and one of the subjects on which he wrote was "The Relationship between the History and the Literature of a People."

[26] See Evjen's sketch of Oftedal in the *Dictionary of American Biography*, 13: 635; Lillehei's account in *Augsburg Seminary*, 16–21; Helland, *Augsburg Seminar*, ch. 6; Kleven, "Norwegian-Danish Evangelical Lutheran Church," 25–28. The "Open Declaration" appeared in *Skandinaven*, January 30, 1874. See also Weenaas, *Mindeblade*, 81 ff. and his *Wisconsinismen*.

[27] The narrative of conditions at Augsburg is part of John H. Blegen's unpublished "Biografiske optegnelser," in the possession of the writer.

Many of the student interests in the college were religious, but a prominent place was accorded the debating societies, which dealt in their programs with a wide range of subjects. In one of these clubs, the Demosthenian, only English was used; its suggestive Latin motto was "Si vis pacem, para bellum." The social life of the college centered in a boarding club, with a student "boss" at its head. After his initial year as an Augsburg student, Blegen attended the annual meeting of the Conference, where he witnessed a controversial preliminary to the conflict between the "old and the new tendencies"—the latter upheld by Sverdrup and Oftedal. There were sessions day and night, heated debates, sharp questions and answers, with voices rising from every part of the church in eager cries of "Mr. President! Mr. President!" After thus being introduced to the excitement of church controversy, Blegen went on to grubbing trees, wielding an American cradle, and tackling various harvest jobs, though in later summers he usually taught parochial school—several times in the Red River Valley or on the Dakota prairie. Upon his college graduation he delivered an oration in English on "The Duties of an American Citizen." Ultimately he returned as a professor of Greek and German, and for more than thirty years played a part in the development of this college, which like its sister institution at Decorah fashioned a tradition of service to the Norwegian-American people. On the faculty, at one time or another, were such men as Hans A. Urseth, a skilled teacher and writer; Wilhelm Pettersen, a poet who lectured on history; John O. Evjen, a church historian of wide learning; Andreas Helland, a theologian and the editor of the elder Sverdrup's writings; and George Sverdrup, who served as president for a generation after the pioneer era of his father.

St. Olaf, advancing from the status of school to that of college in 1886, was rooted in the efforts of B. J. Muus to establish an academy for the education of boys and girls under Lutheran auspices. As we have already seen, Muus turned his ideas into practice as early as 1869 with the founding of an academy in his own parsonage at Holden, convinced, as he said, that he was offering his countrymen "a valuable help for the education of their youth."[28] By 1874, amid the din of the controversy on the merits of the common school, he called on the Synod to back a plan for a more ambitious academy, and when that body contented itself with pious hopes minus action, Muus struck out independently. With the co-operation of Harald Thorson, a public-spirited Norwegian business pioneer, he proceeded to arouse sentiment in his own churches, secure support from the people of Northfield, Minnesota, and raise money in the form of subscriptions. "We extend to our Norwegian brethren a cordial invitation to locate their college at Northfield, and we pledge them our hearty sympathy and support," said the Northfield citizens, with an accompanying subscription of more than five thousand dollars. St. Olaf's School was incorporated in the fall of 1874, with Muus as president of its board and Thorson as secretary. Thorbjørn N. Mohn, a graduate of Luther College who had studied theology in St. Louis, was chosen president of the institution, an old public school property in Northfield was purchased, and on January 8, 1875, the school began to function with a half hundred students. In its initial class it offered such courses as history, English, religion, geography, penmanship, Norwegian, and singing. Muus was indefatigable in his efforts to promote the enterprise and took the lion's share in the task of raising more than twenty thousand dollars for the school during its early years.[29]

It was these funds that made it possible for the school to move to a new site, the beautiful Manitou Heights of the

[28] See *ante*, p. 263; Grose, in *Studies and Records*, 5:113.

[29] C. A. Mellby, *St. Olaf College through Fifty Years 1874–1924*, 23–27 (Northfield, 1925); Grose, in *Studies and Records*, 5:116–121.

present St. Olaf College, and to erect for use by 1878 an impressive main building. Professor C. A. Mellby speaks justly of the "faith, courage and persistency of the founder" and of the readiness of immigrants to give funds out of their "slender savings," though they were barely emerging from their pioneering and for the most part had not themselves enjoyed the kind of education they were now asked to support.[30] But another aspect of the emergence of St. Olaf should also be emphasized. Both Luther and Augsburg were the fruits of a desire to forward the education of a Norwegian-American clergy. These institutions did indeed serve the broader purpose of opening the road to a higher education for men whether they went into the ministry or not, but their central aim was to produce clerical leadership, and this occasioned their founding. St. Olaf, on the other hand, was simply aimed at giving Norwegian boys and girls an opportunity for a higher education than their community schools afforded them. It was co-educational from the start, whereas Luther and Augsburg were not open to women; and, although it drew its main support from people in Norwegian Lutheran congregations, it was not, to begin with, officially a synodical institution. This by no means implies that its spirit was not that of a strictly Lutheran institution. One of its principles was that in its classes nothing was to be taught "in contravention of the Apostolic, Nicene, and Athanasian creeds, of the Unaltered Augsburg Confession, and of Luther's Small Catechism."[31] But it means that the central drive behind it was not at first synodical. It was an independent enterprise in the general setting of the immigrant frontier. It is interesting to note that one of the historians of St. Olaf comments on the influence "of the frontier and the spirit of the early Northwest" as still traceable "in the life of the college

[30] Mellby, *St. Olaf College*, 26.

[31] Grose, in *Studies and Records*, 5:118. The phrase occurs in the articles of incorporation.

today"; and that he interprets St. Olaf against the general background of Norwegian-American society and culture, a milieu in which "the forces of young life" were at work, with "intellectual and social ferment" reshaping older ideas.[32]

Curiously enough, it was an explosive church controversy which transformed this pioneer school into a college. The early 1880's witnessed taut lines within the Norwegian Synod as the issue of predestination divided the body, setting Missourian against anti-Missourian; and when the break came in 1886 with the secession of the anti-Missourians, a body of more than fifty clergymen, from the old Synod, these dissenters were left without an educational institution of their own. It was not difficult for them, however, to come to an agreement with the managers of St. Olaf's School, for the support of that school had centered largely in the anti-Missourian group. And so, in return for active support from the Anti-Missourian Brotherhood, St. Olaf agreed to set up a college department and to make accommodations for housing (but not incorporating with St. Olaf) the theological school of the brotherhood. Thus it came about that the frontier academy blossomed into a college. Its base broadened in 1890 when the Conference, the Norwegian-Danish Augustana Synod, and the anti-Missourians, after an intensive drive toward peace and union, formed among themselves the United Norwegian Lutheran Church. The backing of St. Olaf by this body was interrupted, owing to controversies and complications, from 1893 to 1899, but at the turn of the century it was resumed, and it continued until the great merging of church forces in 1917, when the college came under the Norwegian Lutheran Church of America.[33]

These are the backgrounds of an institution which, taking its start in a modest and struggling pioneer academy, has be-

[32] Mellby, *St. Olaf College*, 10, 16. An interesting account of early St. Olaf is given by Kildahl in *Symra*, 10:232–238.
[33] Mellby, *St. Olaf College*, 28–32.

come the largest of the Norwegian-American colleges. Like Luther and Augsburg, it had outstanding personalities in its history. It relied mainly upon American-trained leadership. All four of its presidents, for example, were trained in institutions of the American Middle West. Mohn, who served as president until 1899, came to America as a small boy, and studied at Luther College and Concordia Seminary. In building St. Olaf College, he exhibited what Professor Mellby terms an "outspoken Americanism." He was of a "practical and progressive bent" and did much to liberalize the curriculum of the college. The larger modernization of the institution came, however, in the twentieth century under J. N. Kildahl, who, like his predecessor, was a graduate of Luther College. Under his leadership the college built up a strong faculty, modernized its curriculum, adopted the elective system, expanded its equipment, increased its resources, and grew to an enrollment of more than five hundred students. The progress has been continued intensively under more recent leadership, notably that of Dr. Lars W. Boe. This is the St. Olaf College of O. E. Rølvaag, dynamic teacher and creative writer; of Dr. F. Melius Christiansen, master musician and leader of a student choir that has become one of America's distinctive institutions; of Andrew Fossum, Nils Flaten, P. J. Eikeland, and other able scholars and teachers; of a student body of more than a thousand; and of an army of alumni in various fields of professional work whose basic training was secured on Manitou Heights.[34]

Luther, Augsburg, and St. Olaf illustrate characteristic forces in the Norwegian-American response to the challenge of higher education, but they form only a part of a much

[34] J. Magnus Rohne, "Johan N. Kildahl," in *Dictionary of American Biography,* 10:373; Rasmus Malmin, ed., *Dr. John Nathan Kildahl: En mindebok* (Minneapolis, 1921). Rølvaag contributes to this book a section on "Kildahl ved St. Olaf." See also I. F. Grose, *Fifty Memorable Years at St. Olaf* (Northfield, 1925); J. A. Aasgaard, ed., *Quarter Centennial 1874–1899: Souvenir of St. Olaf College* (Northfield, 1900); and K. Orlano Sattre, ed., *St. Olaf Memories: Fortieth Anniversary Souvenir* (Northfield, 1914). The latter is a collection of pictures.

larger canvas. Though the picture cannot be drawn in detail in these pages, it may be noted that there were many other colleges, seminaries, and academies, both within and outside the Lutheran fold. The Eielsen group experimented briefly with a seminary in Lisbon, Illinois, in the middle 1850's; made some effort in the next decade; and in 1879—under the auspices of Hauge's Synod—launched the Red Wing Seminary, with college and theological divisions. This institution was carried on for a generation, until after the great church merger of 1917. Another educational enterprise with roots that strike deep in Norwegian-American history is Augustana College in Sioux Falls. It will be remembered that the Norwegian-Danish Augustana Synod was continued in 1870 after a majority of its members had created the Conference. The synod conducted the academy at Marshall, Wisconsin, removed it in the early 1880's to Beloit, Iowa, and presently, in 1884, to Canton, South Dakota. Five years later a normal school was founded in Sioux Falls and was carried forward under the auspices of the United Lutheran Church. After the church merger in 1917 these two institutions were brought together at Sioux Falls, and in more recent years Augustana College has gained considerable impetus and prestige. Concordia College, at Moorhead, Minnesota, representing a thrust of the immigrant college frontier into the Red River Valley, dates from 1891; Pacific Lutheran College, at Parkland, Washington, was established in 1894.

Each main division of the Norwegian Lutheran Church, meanwhile, supported its own theological school. The Norwegian Synod established such a seminary at Madison, Wisconsin, in 1876, expanded its scope three years later, removed it to Robbinsdale, Minnesota, in 1888, and finally placed it in St. Paul in the late 1890's, where it was continued until the church merger. The United Church utilized Augsburg from 1890 to 1893, but at the end of that period broke away, and after some temporary expedients located its seminary in St. Anthony Park, St. Paul, in 1902. Thus through most of the first two decades there were four Norwegian Lutheran theological seminaries in Minnesota — that of Hauge's Synod at Red Wing, that of the Lutheran Free Church at Augsburg in Minneapolis, and those of the Norwegian Synod and the United Church in St. Paul. After the church merger of 1917 Luther Theological Seminary at St. Anthony Park concentrated in itself the ministerial training for the Norwegian Lutheran Church of America, putting one institution in place of three. The Lutheran Free Church, organized in 1897, remained outside the union of 1917, and consequently continued to sponsor Augsburg Theological Seminary and College.[35]

Numerous academies, often bearing the misleading designation of "colleges," normal schools, seminaries for ladies, and Bible institutes in the widely scattered Norwegian-American domain fill out the general picture of a persistent educational endeavor. However admirable in purpose, this endeavor has suffered by a failure, perhaps inherent in the circumstances, to concentrate support, funds, and patronage upon a very few institutions. The diversity of opinion and dispersion of strength have made it extraordinarily difficult to build colleges of the highest quality. Many of the institutions have struggled on from year to year without endowments in a hand-to-mouth existence, with inadequate equipment, small libraries, pitifully meager funds for professorial salaries, and not infrequently with thin and inadequate curricula. Sometimes their faculties have been broken by the issues of theological warfare into warring camps far removed in spirit from the tolerance and open-mindedness of

[35] See M. K. Bleken, "De norsk-amerikanske skoler," in Wist, *Norsk-amerikanernes festskrift*, 245–265. Bleken tells of thirty Norwegian-American schools active in 1914 and lists nine that had been discontinued. A useful reference book is O. M. Norlie, ed., *School Calendar 1824–1924: A Who's Who among Teachers in the Norwegian Lutheran Synods of America* (Minneapolis, 1924).

scholarship. Of the Norwegian-American domain one may say, as Professor Stephenson remarks of the American West, that "it was dotted with religious experiment stations."[36] The multiplication of colleges seems remarkable when one recalls that Norway, the homeland of the immigrants, had but one university, the Royal Fredrik University of Oslo. It is understandable, however, in the setting of Norwegian-American transition and of time and special circumstance.

The Norwegian immigrants found themselves emancipated from the authority of a state church. They lived amid fluid social conditions. They breathed the air of religious liberty, and undoubtedly noted the exuberant combat on doctrine and polity among their American neighbors on the frontier. So they gradually institutionalized their religious and educational faiths as they were stratified by processes of discussion and controversy. While rejoicing in the freedom that enveloped their battles, they were not unaware of the weakness inherent in disunion; and they wanted to improve the quality of the educational institutions they were so facile in establishing. Consequently there were sober reactions from time to time to their institutional proliferation. In a word, there were movements for harmony and union. One of these, in the 1880's, led to the emergence of the United Norwegian Lutheran Church of 1890. Gerhard Hoyme in 1887 delivered one of the most powerful orations in Norwegian-American church history on the theme of union. Many people, he suggested, defended the theological strife on the ground that the "honor of God's name" had to be defended, that the strife was necessary, and that it had led to much research in the fundamentals of religion; but he ventured the opinion that many had fought less for the honor of God's name than to defend their own assertions, that their research had been directed primarily to finding weapons to use against

[36] George M. Stephenson, *American History to 1865,* 244 (New York, 1940).

their enemies.[37] Whether this charge was true or not, three considerable groups buried the hatchet and united their efforts in 1890. Twenty-seven years later the Norwegian Lutheran Church of America emerged as the result of another powerful drive toward union. This church by 1940 had under its aegis not far from three thousand congregations. Such a union naturally made possible a progressive concentration of educational enterprise. One by one the weaker schools were discontinued, and inevitably there was a drive to strengthen the better institutions.

[37] Hoyme's address is published in Bergh, *Den norsk lutherske kirkes historie*, 327 ff.

XVIII. FRONTIERS OF CULTURE

THE NORWEGIAN-AMERICAN colleges and other educational institutions unquestionably extended the cultural frontiers of the people they served. Whatever their shortcomings, they made possible a degree of education that, under conditions prevailing in the country from which the Norwegians emigrated, would have been beyond the reach of most of them there. Meanwhile, the institutions founded by the Norwegian Americans were only a part of the broad educational scene in which they moved. American universities and colleges were legion, and immigrants and their children began to be aware of the many avenues of training that they made available. The result was an increasing patronage of such institutions, beginning in the early period of pioneering and swelling in the period after the Civil War.

Many of the sons and daughters of the immigrants went directly from their communities to such universities as Wisconsin, Illinois, Minnesota, and Iowa, to such denominational colleges as Beloit, Carleton, and Grinnell, and to normal schools and other institutions that flourished in the regions where they lived. Others, after basic training at Luther, Augsburg, St. Olaf, and other Norwegian-American schools, went to universities in the West and East to round out their training, and in some instances they sought the universities of the Old World.

Yale University conferred doctor's degrees on two Norwegians in the early 1870's, and it was to Yale that Thorstein Veblen went for his doctorate. He was a graduate of an American college of the Middle West, and before going to Yale he had studied under Richard T. Ely, George S. Morris, and Herbert Baxter Adams at Johns Hopkins. Peter Hendrickson went from the Muskego settlement to Beloit College, and after his graduation in 1867 he studied at Christiania and Erlangen, returning to become a member of the Beloit faculty and later a Norwegian-American newspaper editor. George T. Flom, who became the dean of Norwegian-American linguists, was born in a Wisconsin farming community, gained his basic education at the University of Wisconsin, and then went on to advanced study at Columbia, Copenhagen, and Leipzig, taking his degree of doctor of philosophy at Columbia. John O. Evjen, the church historian, went from Augsburg College in the Middle West to a doctor's degree at Leipzig. Dr. Ludvig Hektoen, the distinguished pathologist, went from Luther College to the University of Wisconsin, then to a medical college in Chicago, and thereafter to Upsala, Prague, and Berlin. Oswald Veblen, born in Decorah, Iowa, in the period when his father Andrew A. Veblen was on the faculty of Luther College, attended the University of Iowa and Harvard University, took his doctorate at Chicago, and went on to become a noted mathematician. Arthur Andersen, who became one of America's authorities on accounting, came up through Illinois and Northwestern universities. Julius E. Olson, born in the Koshkonong settlement and for a generation professor of Scandinavian languages and literature in the University of

Wisconsin, was himself a graduate of that institution. Knut Gjerset, the son of a Minnesota pioneer, went from a state university to Leipzig, where he rounded out his historical studies. Not a few of the earlier Norwegian-American scholars sought the graduate seminars of Johns Hopkins University for advanced training.[1]

Laurence M. Larson, who came out of an Iowa pioneer community, studied at Drake and Wisconsin, and ultimately won high distinction as a historian, has appraised the achievements of "The Norwegian Element in the Field of American Scholarship." He lists many distinguished names and calls attention to the wide range of scholarly interest that they represent. It is beyond the scope of the present inquiry to detail the specific contributions of Norwegian-American scholars, but certain generalizations suggested by Larson's appraisal call for mention. One is that the pioneering of the immigrants opened the way for another kind of pioneering, that of the frontiers of scholarship, and that the urge toward education, coupled with the signal opportunities of the New World, led in time to achievements which have touched widely different fields, from mathematics, medicine, and natural science to history, the classical languages, literature, and theology. These achievements, from the pioneering days of Rasmus B. Anderson and Hjalmar Hjorth Boyesen to the present, have taken the form of an extensive scholarly production.

That the production in the earlier era was not of greater significance is probably due to two circumstances. One was the pouring of the energy and learning of the Norwegian-American church and school fathers into religious controversy. This is not to imply that the vast amount of pamphlet and periodical literature inspired by such controversy did not re-

[1] Larson, "The Norwegian Element in the Field of American Scholarship," in *Changing West,* 16–38. See also John A. Hofstead, *American Educators of Norwegian Origin* (Minneapolis, 1931), and Norlie, *School Calendar.*

veal skilled reasoning and, in some instances, impressive learning. But, as Larson suggests, the "atmosphere of wrath," in which much of the production flourished, was scarcely conducive to the highest type of intellectual effort.[2] It must be confessed, too, with due regard to the convictions of the combatants, that many of the controversial issues offered little opportunity for original contributions to knowledge or significant advances in human understanding. Hairline theological argumentation, often dramatic as an exercise in dialectics, was frequently spun to an end in a vacuum. The second circumstance hampering a quick entrance into the domain of productive scholarship was the economic and social milieu of immigrants who, like all American pioneers, had to struggle first with the basic problem of making a living. Unlike the native American, however, the immigrant had on his hands the problem of learning the language and customs of the country and of adjusting himself to the cultural climate of the New World. It was inevitable, therefore, that the major advances beyond recognized frontiers of scholarship should have come after the first period of immigrant transition. Most of them were made when Rølvaag's "hidden America" was beginning to emerge, when creative intellectual effort was freed from the earlier theological predilections, when both the first and second generations were in direct and stimulating contact with American scholarship. They were the selective fruit of the growth of an active interest in education at the college level, when thousands of young men and women swarmed to the institutions of higher learning.

Immigrant journalism, meanwhile, offered a challenge that attracted some of the most gifted minds among the Norwegian Americans. The press was close to actual life and opinion, responsive to changes, and wide in its interests. The pioneer era from the late 1840's to the end of the Civil

[2] *Changing West*, 20.

War saw the Norwegian-American press securely established as an institution, but its period of great growth came after the Civil War. It trailed the immigrant frontiers from the Middle West to the Canadian Northwest and the Pacific coast, and it back-trailed them to the eastern seaboard. Newspapers sprang up in prodigal fashion in the shifting centers of Norwegian population, but many of them were short-lived. Between four and five hundred Norwegian papers were established in America from first to last. The immigrant press, like the American press in general, witnessed rapid changes, sharp competition, and many consolidations. A few papers took rank as leading organs of news and opinion, and these flourished during the period when Norwegian speech in America was at its high point. The stronger journals have, in fact, continued to the present. In recent years, however, their path has become difficult and uncertain, and one of the commanding Norwegian-American newspapers, located in a strategic center, was obliged to discontinue publication in the 1930's.[3]

The vitality of this immigrant press was nonetheless remarkable. *Skandinaven* of Chicago, founded in 1866 by John Anderson and Knud Langeland, still flourished seventy-four years later, in 1940. This newspaper, Republican throughout its career, was a spokesman for the common schools in its early days, low-church in tendency, and generally sympathetic with laymen. It expanded and changed emphasis with the times, so that, as Wist says, its "history in its larger aspects is that of the successful Norwegian pioneer in this country." It drew the services of several men of marked talent, including Langeland, Svein Nilsson, Peter Hendrickson, Victor F. Lawson, who stepped from immigrant

[3] The most comprehensive account of the Norwegian-American press after the Civil War is Wist's, in *Norsk-amerikanernes festskrift*, 41–203. See also Dieserud, in *Nordmands-forbundet*, 5: 155–182. A series of interesting sketches of Norwegian-American newspapers may be found in O. E. Rølvaag and P. J. Eikeland, *Norsk læsebok*, 2: 307–328 (Minneapolis, 1920).

journalism into the arena of the American press, and Nicolai Grevstad. After analyzing this paper's editorial policy in the period from 1900 to 1903, Professor Agnes Larson writes: "In assisting the immigrant to make the transition to American ways of thinking and doing, *Skandinaven* undoubtedly played a significant part. That the immigrant might not completely lose the inheritance that was his, *Skandinaven* stressed the literature and culture of the mother country. To aid him, on the other hand, to become a genuine son of the new country, its parties and politics and issues were placed before him. Perhaps government received the major emphasis, but other institutions and interests of America were given recognition as well. That the immigrant might make the best use of his opportunities, the paper kept steadily before him the possibilities for self-improvement and economic advancement in the United States. On most matters *Skandinaven* was fairly conservative, though it was critically so — it was more open-minded and independent than most of the English newspapers of the United States. Its enthusiasm for the people and its optimistic faith in the possibilities of the common man and of democracy give the key to an understanding of its faith in America and its institutions, especially the government and the school."[4]

It will be recalled that *Fædrelandet* ("The Fatherland") of La Crosse absorbed the pioneer *Emigranten* in 1868. As *Fædrelandet og emigranten* it played an influential role in Norwegian-American life. It was Republican in politics, like *Skandinaven*, but unlike the Chicago paper it inclined on the religious side toward the Norwegian Synod. Its removal to Minneapolis in 1886 brought it within the scope of one of those consolidations that marked the history of the Norwegian-American press. The chief Minnesota Norwegian paper of the 1870's and 1880's was *Budstikken*, established in 1873,

[4] Agnes M. Larson, "The Editorial Policy of *Skandinaven*, 1900–1903," in *Studies and Records*, 8: 112–135.

a sturdily independent newspaper, with such gifted men as Luth Jaeger, Paul Hjelm Hansen, and Erik L. Petersen associated with it, forthright in criticism both in literary and religious fields, and Democratic in politics. Meanwhile, a Dakota paper, launched at Grand Forks by the novelist Tellef Grundysen and bought by Thorvald Guldbrandsen, was removed to Minneapolis in 1887, where it became the *Minneapolis tidende* and by the early 1890's absorbed both *Budstikken* and *Fædrelandet og emigranten*.[5] The *Tidende* became the leading Norwegian newspaper of Minnesota for a generation, with men like Sigvart Sorensen and Carl G. O. Hansen on its editorial staff. It gave particular attention to the cultural life of the Norwegian Americans and was noted for its articles and reviews in the fields of literature and music and for its admirable weekly " summary of the political, social, literary, artistic, and intellectual life of Norway." When this well-edited and widely read journal ceased to appear in Minneapolis in 1935, the event was interpreted by many as a sign of the approaching end of the Norwegian language press in this country.[6] Jaeger, after his service on the earlier *Budstikken,* joined Colonel Hans Mattson in publishing the *North* of Minneapolis, a short-lived paper in the English language intended particularly for Scandinavian-American readers.

Meanwhile, a newspaper of notable quality and wide fame had developed at Decorah. *Decorah-posten* began in 1874 as the result of preliminary newspaper enterprises in both La Crosse and Decorah under the leadership of B. Anundsen, and in time it enlisted the services of Johannes B. Wist and Kristian Prestgard, gained a vast circulation through publishing Norwegian-American fiction, notably the novels of H. A. Foss, made all Norwegian America its field, and built

[5] Wist, in *Norsk-amerikanernes festskrift,* 57–69.

[6] See an interesting comment by Martin B. Ruud, " The Second Generation," in *Signal Fires: New World Groups* (Minneapolis), no. 6 (May, 1935).

its strength and prestige on solid foundations. If in special degree this paper has had a literary influence, it doubtless was a reflection of a central interest of Wist and Prestgard, both of them skilled writers and able editors, who lost no opportunity to promote the cause of Norwegian-American letters. In 1935 *Decorah-posten* absorbed the *Minneapolis tidende* and in 1940, sixty-six years after the paper was founded, it was still in existence, widely read and influential.[7]

It is indicative of the spread of the Norwegian element that two other newspapers which survived effectively to 1940 were located on the Atlantic and Pacific coasts — *Washington posten* of Seattle, with Gunnar Lund as its dominant figure, and *Nordisk tidende* of Brooklyn, in which A. N. Rygg and Sigurd Arnesen have played large roles. The western paper was founded in the 1880's, the eastern in the early 1890's. Many personalities of distinction in Norwegian-American life have had newspaper organs of their own. Rasmus B. Anderson reached the public, in his later days, through the columns of *Amerika* of Madison. Waldemar Ager spoke the cause of temperance and promoted an intelligent interest in literature through *Reform* of Eau Claire. Peer Strømme, roaming reporter, Mark Twain of the Norwegian Americans, poet, teacher, lecturer, novelist, and translator, found avenues for his wit and wide-ranging observation in *Normanden* of Grand Forks, *Amerika,* the *Minneapolis Times,* and various other papers, Norwegian and American, which he edited.[8] Marcus Thrane in the 1860's and 1870's employed such organs as *Den norske Amerikaner* and *Dagslyset* ("Daylight"), both of Chicago. *Dagslyset,* a "philosophical-religious" publication, served in 1875 as the instrument of the Chicago Scandinavian Society of Freethinkers.[9]

If an extensive, persistent, and various press may be taken

[7] Wist, in *Norsk-amerikanernes festskrift,* 71–80.

[8] John O. Evjen, "Peer O. Strømme," in *Dictionary of American Biography,* 18:141; and Strømme's own *Erindringer* (Minneapolis, 1923).

[9] Wist, in *Norsk-amerikanernes festskrift,* 91 ff.

Billed-Magazin.

No. 3.] Madison, Wisconsin den 21de November. [1868.

De skandinaviske Setlementer i Amerika.

Det ældste norske Setlement i Wisconsin.

(Fortsættelse fra No. 2.)

Det er allerede bleven fortalt, at Elling Eielsen ledsagede Søren Bade og Johannesen til Amerika og videre op igjennem Landet til Illinois. Det er ei Hensigten her at skrive denne Mands Biografi, hvortil der maaske vil blive Anledning i en anden Afhandling under Overskriften "De norsk-amerikanske Setlementers Kirkehistorie". Kun en almindelig Oversigt over Eielsens Levnetsløb vil her blive meddelt. Han blev født Aar 1804 paa Gaarden Sønve paa Voss. Allerede som ung Mand sluttede han sig til Hans Nielsen Hauges Venner og begyndte at udlægge Skriften for sine Medmennesker. Efter vidtløftige Reiser i Norge, Sverige og Danmark udvandrede han Aar 1839 og opholdt sig først nogen Tid i det norske Setlement ved Fox River. Herfra foretog han hyppige Reiser til forskjellige Nybyggerkolonier saavel i Wisconsin som Illinois. Efter sine Landsmænds Begjæring udførte han under disse Vandringer Sjelesørgerens Forretninger. Farmerens Stue, Skolehusene og andre Boliger benyttedes, eftersom Anledning gaves, for Gudstjenesten. Omsider begyndte Skandinaverne at sprede sig over Vestens umaadelige Vidder; men Eielsen fulgte efter, opsøgte Udvandreren i hans nye Hjemsted for at prædike Frelsens Evangelium. Her findes neppe

Hotellet Watercure ved Madison.

en Skandinav, som har saa vel gjennemvandret Amerika i alle Retninger som denne Mand. Der gives knapt et norsk Setlement af nogen Betydning, hvor han ei har været. Nu bor han paa en god, velbygget Farm i Townet Yorkville, Racine County; men Troesiveren drager ham ofte bort fra den huslige Arne, og uagtet sine 64 Aar opsøger han sine Landsmænd endog i det fjerneste Vesten. For 5 Aar siden besøgte Elling Eielsen Norge, hvor han med Glæde blev modtaget af sine mange Venner. Han er nu den egentlige Leder for det Kirkesamfund, hvis Medlemmer ofte benævnes Ellingianerne, men som selv, saavidt jeg ved, kalder sig Hauges Venner.

Heller ikke i Townet Norway var vore Landsmænd heldige med Hensyn til Valget af Opholdssted. Man maa have seet en amerikansk Urskov for at faa Begreb om det med Oprydningen forbundne Arbeide. Jordbunden bestaar hovedsagelig af maver Lere, der under indtrædende Tørke sprækker i alle Retninger og bliver haard

as valid evidence, it would appear that Norwegian-American society was distinctly articulate. The lay press represented only one side of immigrant journalism. There was a profusion of church papers emanating from the different synods, ranging from scholarly journals to children's papers. Several interesting attempts were made to establish literary periodicals. The pioneer magazine was Svein Nilsson's *Billedmagazin,* established at Madison in 1868. It had the unique distinction of publishing the remarkable series of articles that Nilsson himself, after visiting the settlements and interviewing pioneers, wrote on the early immigration. *For hjemmet,* of Decorah, founded in 1870, published what seems to have been the first novel of Norwegian-American life. There were several other experiments in literary periodicals in the 1870's and 1880's, but it was not until the twentieth century that definitely high standards were reached. *Symra* of Decorah, launched in 1905 and superbly edited by Prestgard and Wist, was beyond question the best literary magazine that the Norwegians in America ever published. It was conceived as an international organ that would be of interest on both sides of the Atlantic, promote cultural understanding between the immigrants and their motherland, and attract contributions from both Norwegian and Norwegian-American authors; and it measured up to these purposes. Its short-lived rival, *Vor tid* ("Our Time") of Minneapolis, which also began in 1905 but was forced to suspend three years later, was a well-conceived publication that took color from the versatile Peer Strømme, one of its editors. N. N. Rønning, essayist, humorist, and novelist, published over a long period of years a series of family magazines that attained a high degree of popular interest.

The political implications of the Norwegian-American press were recognized from the beginning not only by the immigrants themselves but also by American politicians who were concerned about winning their support in elections.

That press was a powerful influence in clarifying political issues, stirring political interest, and formulating a political stand for the majority of the immigrant voters before the Civil War. After the Civil War the expanding press tended for the most part to voice majority opinion, though not without discordant notes. Historical circumstance and geography both contributed to the marked Republican complexion of the Norwegian-American political viewpoint. "For a generation or more after the Civil War," according to the noted journalist N. A. Grevstad, "the Norwegians remained all but solidly republican in national and local politics."[10] It would perhaps be more precise to say that for two decades after the war, the Norwegians were held securely in the ranks of the Republican party. The masses of incoming immigrants were normally brought into the fold of the party with which the older settlers had affiliated. Its traditions were associated with Lincoln and the cause of human freedom, and with a dramatic, even heroic, chapter in the history of the Scandinavian element itself. But as the issues of the Civil War were subordinated to new questions, mainly economic, the older party ties were loosened. In the Northwest the agrarian crusade enlisted large numbers of Norwegian immigrant farmers under its banner and contributed to a new tradition of political independence.

In explaining the active and vital interest that Norwegian Americans have taken in politics, Mr. Grevstad calls attention to several contributing factors. Large numbers of the settlers became landowners; the Norwegian immigrants were quick to become American citizens; they had a background of democratic tradition; and their very compactness and strength seemed to place in their hands in crucial political situations a potential balance of power. More fundamental than these factors was the circumstance that in large farming

[10] N. A. Grevstad, "Participation in Politics," in Sundby-Hansen, *Norwegian Immigrant Contributions,* 111.

areas the Norwegian pioneer settlers had to fashion their own local governmental affairs, manipulating American institutions, often conducting district and town meetings before they could speak the language of the country. They brought with them from Norway a knowledge of local self-government. Professor Larson believes that the Norsemen were politicians by nature whose early traditions were those of a "full share in the management of local concerns." In any event, the immigrants had to grapple with the business of organizing and carrying on local government in not a few regions of the West. "The ballot was as much of a necessary tool in their life," says Mr. Grevstad, "as the ax, the spade, the hoe, the plow and the harrow." Men might talk in abstract terms about the glories of the American government; in many immigrant communities the American government that was understood in concrete terms and came closest to the life of the people was "largely of their own making."[11]

It was normally against such backgrounds of practice in local self-government that the Norwegian-American participation in state and national government was framed. Hans Christian Heg, Knute Nelson, and many other Norwegian-American leaders whose names bulk large in the immigrant hall of political fame acquired their familiarity with American politics through experiment in the laboratory of American local government.[12] Thus it may fairly be said that Norwegian-American political leadership developed from the ground up, in conformity with American democratic tradition. The domain of politics did not attract so distinguished a type of Norwegian-American ability as did scholarship and

[11] Grevstad, in *Norwegian Immigrant Contributions*, 107, 108; Larson, *Changing West*, 77. As early as 1881 a Minnesota newspaper reported that Scandinavians filled 111 county offices in that state. Of that number, 81 were Norwegians, 28 Swedes, and 2 Danes. The offices tabulated were auditor, treasurer, sheriff, register of deeds, probate judge, surveyor, coroner, clerk of court, court commissioner, and school superintendent. The report did not take into account offices in the localities within the counties. See *Freeborn County Standard* (Albert Lea), February 17, 1881.

[12] The political education of Nelson is described in Odland, *Knute Nelson*.

the professions, but its practitioners carried with them into state and national capitals the savor of local reality; and they were held responsible by constituencies that cherished the vote as one of the high privileges of American citizenship. The exercise of the privilege, for the Norwegians as for all other elements in the population, was a constant factor in their gradual Americanization. The significance of Norwegian-American participation in politics lay not so much in the fact that leaders of Norwegian origin took places on the stage of public affairs as in the more fundamental circumstance that many of the immigrants played an active part in the functioning of the democracy with which they had merged.

The persistent urge of the Norwegians to settle on the frontiers of the Northwest had definite political consequences. More than fifty per cent of all the Norwegians in Minnesota were living in the western counties of that state by 1890. In this frontier area significant defections from the Republican tradition took place about that time. Agrarian in origin, economic and sectional in fundamental character, these revolts centered in the programs of the Farmers' Alliance and the Populist party. Large numbers of hitherto staunch western Republican farmers, including a substantial quota of Norwegian Americans, broke away from their accustomed affiliations. The agrarian group had strength enough to win the balance of power in the Minnesota legislature. The broader significance of the crusade seems to lie, however, not so much in the winning of specific reforms as in the stimulation of independent political thinking and voting. The day of unbroken party loyalty was at an end. Political independence, rooted in economic and social discontents and emerging from the soil of contemporary issues, became a recurrent thing as time went on, and was always focused upon specific reforms.[13]

[13] Blegen, "The Scandinavian Element and Agrarian Discontent," in American Historical Association, *Annual Reports*, 1921, p. 219. This is an abstract of a

Norwegian-American interest in politics had indeed been active and persistent long before this period; Knute Nelson, for example, was elected to Congress from Minnesota as early as 1882 in a stirring campaign. After the era of the Populist revolt, however, there developed a marked tendency toward the political "recognition" of the Scandinavians in an attempt to hold erstwhile truants to traditional political affections. This tendency, it must be remembered, synchronized with an enlarging general interest and activity on the part of Scandinavians in the political field; and many immigrant leaders were willing to meet the American politicians more than halfway in the sordid business of bargaining for votes. Some resorted to intrigue in their efforts to secure political "recognition," but the rank and file of voters often spurned the implications of such political trading. The more vital the economic and political issues, the more marked the tendency to crowd out racial factors in voting. Many deep-lying reasons explain why in Minnesota after 1890 it became almost a custom to elect, or at any rate to nominate in one party or another, a Scandinavian for the governorship of the state. From 1893 to 1940, some ten or eleven out of fourteen governors of Minnesota were of Scandinavian origin.[14] It should be noted, incidentally, that the Northwest was the stage of a persistent crusade for the cause of temperance which drew much of its leadership and strength from the Norwegians and Swedes and took political form in the Prohibition party.[15]

Politics was only one of many interests that engaged the mind of the Norwegian immigrant. It is true that he found

paper read before a session of the association. Babcock, in *Scandinavian Element,* ch. 11, 12, discusses "The Scandinavian in Local and State Politics" and "Party Preferences and Political Leadership."

[14] Blegen, *Building Minnesota,* ch. 32, 39, 44–46.

[15] A useful survey of "Nordmænd i det offentlige og politiske liv," with information about many individuals who attained high political station, is contributed by Juul Dieserud to Wist, *Norsk-amerikanernes festskrift,* 307–329. An enlightening personal narrative by an American politician of Norwegian backgrounds is Nils P. Haugen, *Pioneer and Political Reminiscences* (Madison, [1930?]).

himself more and more deeply concerned about American institutions and political problems as he grappled with the economic difficulties that confronted him when the frontier era faded into the past. Meanwhile, the church continued to be close to his life, and the rumble of its controversies had echoes in most Norwegian-American homes. The immigrant's interest in the professional and commercial opportunities of America quickened as his children broke away from the occupational limitations that had marked the earlier period and as more and more professionally trained people joined in the Norwegian migration to America. Medicine, engineering, and law seemed in particular to interest the Norwegians who sought professional careers. In engineering, for example, men who had enjoyed the best advantages of technical training in Norway came in increasing numbers to America to find employment for their abilities. There is little doubt that this field commanded the services of some of the ablest of all the Norwegian Americans — men of the stamp of Olaf Hoff, builder of tunnels and bridges; Tinius Olsen of Philadelphia and Edwin Ruud of Pittsburgh, inventors and manufacturers; Magnus Swenson, who had a versatile career in " engineering, invention, manufacturing, business administration, and public affairs "; Thomas G. Pihlfeldt, the Chicago bridgebuilder; Ole Singstad, builder of the Holland Tunnel; and a host of others. It is of interest to know that in recent years the engineers and architects of Norwegian origin in the United States have formed a Norwegian-American Technical Society, which publishes a journal and includes among its objectives that of gathering and preserving information on the contributions of the Norwegian-American technicians.[16]

Wherever the immigrants went, they carried with them

[16] See John Hjellum, ed., *Skandinavens almanak-kalender,* 1934, p. 94–101 (Chicago, 1933). A monograph on Norwegian-American engineers and architects, to be published by the Norwegian-American Historical Association, is in course of preparation by Dr. Kenneth Bjørk of St. Olaf College.

an interest in the language, literature, and culture of Norway, and this interest expressed itself in many ways. In close alliance with the religious motive, it was at the base of widespread efforts to foster parochial schools; and it was voiced in the curricula of the Norwegian-American colleges. In many immigrant homes there were libraries, small or large, that represented the best works produced in the old country; and in many communities Norwegian literary societies were formed. Newspapers and literary magazines throughout the entire course of Norwegian-American history have given space both to the reprinting of Norwegian classics and to criticism of the drama and fiction of Norway. Norwegian publishing houses in America have on occasion brought out the works of Norwegian authors; and the bridge to American readers and to those children of immigrants who read English more readily than they did Norwegian was crossed when Rasmus B. Anderson from 1881 to 1883 translated into English seven volumes of Bjørnson's stories and pioneered in presenting modern Norwegian authors to American readers.[17]

Anderson was also a pioneer in introducing courses in the language and literature of Norway in American universities. He began to teach in the University of Wisconsin in 1869, and in 1875 he became professor of Scandinavian languages in that institution. Upon his withdrawal in 1884, he was followed by Julius E. Olson, who for a generation stirred students with his infectious enthusiasm for Scandinavian studies. In more recent times the work at Wisconsin has been headed by Einar Haugen, a scholar and teacher of high competence. At the University of Minnesota a legislative enactment resulted in the establishment of a Scandinavian department in 1883. In the years since that time teachers who have given special attention to things Norwegian have included O. J. Breda and Gisle Bothne, both of whom formerly taught

[17] Anderson brought out these volumes through Houghton, Mifflin and Company.

at Luther College. George T. Flom conducted a department of Scandinavian languages and literature at the University of Iowa, beginning in 1900, and nine years later transferred to the University of Illinois, where his learning and skill as a teacher have left deep marks. Professor Henning Larsen, meanwhile, carried on the work at Iowa in the spirit of high scholarship.

Yale University has had courses in Norwegian and in other fields of Scandinavian studies since 1889, when Olaus Dahl began to give instruction there, and in many other colleges and universities efforts have been made to develop this field. Hjalmar H. Boyesen taught Norwegian at Columbia as early as 1880; David Starr Jordan taught Norwegian grammar at Indiana in 1885; North Dakota organized a Scandinavian department under George T. Rygh in the early 1890's; and South Dakota established a similar department in the early 1900's, with O. E. Hagen and Tollef B. Thompson. In these and various other institutions Norwegian usually had a place alongside studies in Swedish and Danish, with a range from Old Norse to the modern languages and the works of outstanding writers like Ibsen and Bjørnson. In many instances such Scandinavian departments, even in centers of Scandinavian-American population, do not appear to have flourished greatly. The effort has been carried forward with persistence, however, and has been built upon a foundation of sound educational aims. The high value of the work is perhaps best illustrated in the University of Wisconsin, where for more than seventy years the combination of good standards of scholarship and high enthusiasm represented by Professors Anderson, Olson, and Haugen has borne rich fruits. In 1911 scholars in this general field organized the Society for the Advancement of Scandinavian Study.[18]

[18] George T. Flom, "Norwegian Language and Literature in American Universities," in *Studies and Records,* 2:78–103. See also Gisle Bothne, "Nordiske studier ved amerikanske universiteter," in Wist, *Norsk-amerikanernes festskrift,* 330–338.

Professional enterprise in effecting a transit of Norwegian literary culture to the world of the immigrants and their descendants was accompanied by lay efforts of genuine interest. They may be illustrated by the concerted attempt made in Chicago from 1866 to 1872 to create a Norwegian-American stage. A group of amateur players was active in that western metropolis from 1866 to 1868 under the leadership of the Norwegian exile, Marcus Thrane. It produced no fewer than thirty-two plays, drawing upon the best dramatic literature of Norway, Denmark, and the European continent, and giving place to at least five productions by Thrane himself. The repertory included Holberg, Oelenschlaeger, Hans Christian Andersen, Ivar Aasen's *Ervingen* ("The Heir"), C. P. Riis's *Til sæters* ("To the Saeter"), and Møller's *Gjæst Baardsen.* Unhappily the texts of Thrane's own plays seem not to have survived. One of them, "Syttende Mai," was definitely an immigrant play, a satirical production with its first act set in Norway, its second in America, and offering much ironical commentary upon the Americanization of the immigrants. A Norwegian-American newspaper, taking note in 1866 of the efforts to establish a theater in Chicago for Scandinavian acting, spoke of the "progress of enlightenment and cultivated society among our countrymen here" and called for "patronizing and encouraging the little step forward on the path of culture."

In 1868 the Norwegian Dramatic Society of Chicago emerged as an outgrowth of the pioneer work of Thrane, and for some four years it continued to present plays, adding such performances as Wergeland's *Fjeldstuen* ("The Mountain Hut"), two of Bjørnson's dramas, and works by Andreas Munch and C. M. Monson. As Professors Wilt and Naeseth point out, this Chicago venture bore a close relationship to the famous Norwegian theater in Bergen. It was marked by a distinct Norwegian national spirit, and ten of its plays were Norwegian. The society built up a special library of a

Den norske

Dramatiske Forening.

Præsident:—E. S. Howland...Regisseur:—E. Moyel.
Secretair:—J. Wærness.......Kasserer:—R. Andersen.

Förste Forestilling

gives i

GERMAN HALL

Lørdagen den 28de Marts, 1868.

Til Opførelse kommer:

En Hallingdøl, som Prolog,

udføres af.............. .... Hr. E. Moyel.

Derefter:

Den graae Paletot,

Vaudeville i 1 Akt af Erik Bøgh.

Personerne:

Jægermester v. Seydel............... Mr. Sporeland.
Holger hans Brodersøn........ ... .. " Wærness.
Vilhelm Valberg...................... " Moyel.
Clara Holmgaard...... ....Miss Giertsen.
Assessor Sievert ....Mr. Moller.
Peter, Holgers Opvasser. . ... " Howland.
Melchior, en Jøde.................. .... " Berg.
Skræddermester Jespersen............. " Ross.
Anette, Claras Pige............... ....Mrs. Wærness.

Til Slutning:

Soldaterløier,

Sangspil i 1 Akt af Hostrup.

Personerne:

Lange, Godseier...........................Mr. Howland.
Emilie hans Datter.....................Mrs. Sporeland.
Prokurator Barding ....Mr. Berg.
Magister Glob, h. Brodersøn........, ... " Ross.
Anker, Landskabsmaler .... " Moyel.
Loitnant Vilmer.......................... " Wærness
Mads, Gaardskar........ .... " Moller.

Handlingen foregaar paa Langes Gods.

PROGRAM OF THE FIRST PERFORMANCE OF THE NORWEGIAN DRAMATIC SOCIETY

[From the secretary's book of the society, in the possession of the Norwegian-American Historical Association, Northfield, Minnesota.]

hundred and fifty works, sponsored folk dancing, and on one occasion in 1869 made a tour to Madison, Wisconsin. Although it seems to have discontinued its activities in 1872 (one of its performances was interrupted by the Chicago fire), it pioneered a kind of Scandinavian enterprise which has "flourished up to the present day." Professors Wilt and Naeseth, who have made a scholarly and illuminating analysis of the work of the early Norwegian dramatic societies in Chicago, suggest that the need felt by these groups for "identifying themselves with their native culture while adapting themselves to a new life" illustrates "a typical immigrant phenomenon." The peculiar interest of these organizations "lies in the type of culture, the literary and artistic inheritance which they brought to the United States and to American theatrical tradition."[19] That the enterprise had any marked influence upon "American theatrical tradition" may be doubted, but it is worth noting that the Chicago societies were by no means unique. The Scandinavian Society and the Scandinavian Dramatic Society, formed in Minneapolis in 1869 and 1870, also staged Scandinavian plays, as did similar organizations in smaller towns, for example, Calmar, Iowa, and Austin, Minnesota, in the early 1870's.[20]

Although Ibsen was not represented in the dramatic efforts of the pioneer Chicago players, the Norwegian Americans were deeply interested in his plays, as they were in the writings of the national poet Bjørnson; and when Ibsen's social dramas appeared they were moved by deep emotions, as were the dramatist's countrymen in Norway and people in every country that felt the impact of his ideas and power. Professor Haugen's researches show that the first English performance of *A Doll's House* in America occurred in Milwaukee

[19] Wilt and Naeseth, in *Studies and Records,* 10:44–75.

[20] Carl G. O. Hansen, "Det norske foreningsliv i Amerika," in Wist, *Norskamerikanernes festskrift,* 272.

in 1882,[21] but two years before that event the Norwegian press witnessed an interesting controversy on this provocative drama. The organ for the discussion was the Chicago *Norden,* which Professors Paulson and Bjørk characterize as "the most literary of Norwegian immigrant papers" in 1880.[22] This paper regularly included a literary serial, so printed that it could be clipped and bound in book form, and its printing office was combined with a bookstore that carried a stock of more than two thousand volumes.

In this newspaper P. P. Iverslie, a farmer-scholar who had had some education at Luther College and who published several vigorous books, attacked what he called the "moral degeneration" in Ibsen and Bjørnson and declared that the great Norwegian poets were entering their second childhood. Ibsen's *Doll's House* he did, indeed, concede to be a masterpiece, but that consideration, he asserted, did not matter in view of the "Godless life" that the drama portrayed. The moral of the play, he believed, would lead to the "dissolution of every bond of relationship." Iverslie was taken sharply to task by O. S. Hervin, a trained newspaperman who employed the pen name of "Herm. Wang," and whose basic view was summed up in this declaration: "I look upon the play as a description of the life of the 'cultivated classes,' and not as a lesson in morality." When Iverslie intimated that the great Norwegian writers were fools and seemed to condemn Hervin as anti-Christian because of his defense of Ibsen, he was met with a sturdy declaration: "That which creates the greatest number of freethinkers is, and always has been, the intolerance and the censure which stamp one's fellow men as fools and unbelievers the moment they depart from the narrow pathways of authoritative opinion." The contro-

[21] Einar Haugen, "Ibsen in America: A Forgotten Performance and an Unpublished Letter," in *Journal of English and Germanic Philology,* 33:396–420 (July, 1934).

[22] Arthur C. Paulson and Kenneth Bjørk, "*A Doll's House* on the Prairie: The First Ibsen Controversy in America," in *Studies and Records,* 11:1–16.

versy, according to Professors Paulson and Bjørk, may be interpreted as an expression of "a vigorous intellectual life rarely associated with the frontier."[23] It exhibited the clash between a "moral and ethical" interpretation of the play and a nontheological approach. The remarkable thing about it was not Iverslie's attack, but Hervin's interpretation, which, to use an Ibsenian phrase, was in league with the future.

The controversy over Ibsen's *Doll's House* was as nothing, however, compared with the furor occasioned by the visit of Bjørnstjerne Bjørnson to America and the West in 1880–81. He came to the New World, not to tour the settlements of his immigrated countrymen, but to sense the currents of thought in Boston, which he rightly regarded as the "literary and cultural center of America" in that era. He met many prominent American writers, saw typical scenes in the East, and wrote vigorous letters to his countrymen in Norway commenting upon his experiences. Meanwhile, a storm was brewing in the West, and Bjørnson, an aggressive controversialist, felt himself drawn toward its center. Professor Paulson has analyzed the backgrounds of the storm. On the one hand, Bjørnson was a "popular idol," prized for his simple stories of Norwegian country life, admired for his republicanism no less than for his ardent nationalism. The author of *Synnøve Solbakken* and of the national anthem of Norway aroused mixed feelings among many people, however, for, on the other hand, his many crusades had included one that was anathema to the Norwegian-American church people, without regard to their particular synodical affiliations. As Professor Paulson puts it, Bjørnson "declared that Christians must interpret the Bible in accordance with the growing power of the human mind." Unless the church heeded "the dictates of culture and intellect," it would "find itself submerged"—"frightened, impotent." He rejected the doctrine of eternal punishment, threw overboard the

[23] *Studies and Records,* 11:1.

sacrament of baptism, and late in the 1870's challenged the divinity of Christ. And so he was regarded as "an apostate and heretic"—and many forces considered a visit by this orator and powerful personality a menace to the institutional assumptions of the time.[24]

Bjørnson, glorying in combat, invaded the immigrant West on a great speaking tour, with Rasmus B. Anderson as his impressario. He traveled widely, throwing down the gauntlet to the clergy in an exuberant lecture on "The Prophets," and the lay and church press quivered from the shock of his coming. Men like Sven Oftedal of the Conference and H. A. Stub of the Synod led the clerical opposition. Oftedal with manifest injustice compared the Norwegian poet to a circus clown; Stub abjectly called upon church people to stay away from his lectures, or, if they felt that they must be informed about them, to select small committees to hear and report upon them. *Skandinaven* of Chicago, forthright as usual, welcomed Bjørnson as "the champion of popular liberty, as the fearless spokesman of truth, and as the true interpreter of the modern spirit of progress," while Luth Jaeger of *Budstikken* turned upon Bjørnson's enemies with fierce diatribes, accusing one ministerial editor of "bowing to papal authority." Some observers took a middle ground. Halvard Hande of *Norden* withdrew from a welcoming committee and branded Bjørnson as "Norway's Ingersoll," but urged people, nevertheless, to attend his political lectures. And so the tour proceeded to the accompaniment of storm and turbulence. It has been said that Bjørnson lost ground because of his violence. In a final address in Chicago he spoke in angry temper, referred to the uncouthness of some of his audiences in the West, and after

[24] Arthur C. Paulson, "Bjørnson and the Norwegian-Americans, 1880–81," in *Studies and Records*, 5:84–87. See also Dr. Paulson's *The Norwegian-American Reaction to Ibsen and Bjørnson 1850–1900* (Northfield, 1937). As early as 1873–74 Bjørnson had contributed regular letters to *Skandinaven* on events in Norway and thus had become very well known to immigrant readers.

mentioning the Norwegian-American schools, exclaimed, "What do I care for schools which do not dare to give instruction in the natural sciences and in which sturdy farmer boys are driven as if in harness!" He was inevitably accused of being ungracious and insulting, but such accusations, whether true or not, had no pertinence in relation to the central issues in which the poet was interested. Had he wished, he could have alluded to a Minnesota audience that was reported to have attended one of his lectures well-armed with cabbages and ill-smelling eggs. Bjørnson was a fighter who neither gave nor asked quarter; he would not invite popular support by conciliation. Charged with being "ungovernable," near the outset of his trip he had asked, "And the Norwegians and other Scandinavians in this great American republic — were they always satisfied with conditions in Norway? Did they find everything there so splendid, so free, so noble, that they cannot meet a countryman who because of his struggle against those same conditions has become an ungovernable person?"[25]

So Bjørnson came and went. The storm subsided; clerical antagonists, after sharing a common front, resumed their battles among themselves; and the church maintained its position. The visit is significant historically chiefly for the

[25] See Paulson, in *Studies and Records,* 5:93. There was a spirited protest against a charge made by Bjørnson that there was a large amount of drunkenness in one of his audiences in a western city, but no one seems to have made an impartial investigation of the facts. In his oratorical fervor, the poet unquestionably used the language of exaggeration, but other evidence indicates that he was not the only visiting lecturer who took cognizance of the phenomenon of excessive drinking. Knut Hamsun, after lecturing in a Norwegian community of Wisconsin, declared that it was not possible to get its people " to listen to a lecture; they know only how to drink." See Hamsun to R. B. Anderson, April 21, 1883, in the Anderson Papers in the possession of the State Historical Society of Wisconsin, Madison. Bjørnson rubbed salt into the wound by urging the clergy to work against the evil of excessive drinking. When interviewed in the East, after his trip, Bjørnson said he would recommend emigration to the poorer country people when he returned to Norway. The immigrants had done well in the West, many had become " almost wealthy," none were in want, and of all the Scandinavians he thought the Norwegian pioneers the most enterprising; but he regarded them as " priest-ridden," held to a " rigid Calvinistic creed," victims of a " narrow-minded, unmodern spirit." The interview is quoted in the *Freeborn County Standard,* May 5, 1881.

relief in which it throws the Norwegian-American culture, and particularly the religious culture, of the time, but it undoubtedly left marks that were not soon erased. Bjørnson's sincerity and dynamic force touched many lives, not only those of the thousands of people who thronged to hear him despite clerical injunctions to stay away, but also those of multitudes who heard the sharp echoes of the tour in their newspapers and community conversation. The Lutheran clergy fought the man and his ideas with a fierceness equal to his own. The tradition of virulent controversy among the Norwegian Americans, deep already, was deepened further. The lusty spirit in which blows were exchanged bespoke the freedom of the American arena. The visiting poet, after spreading his ideas with all the potency at his command, carried back to Norway an admiration for the institutions and ideas of the western republic.[26]

One realm of Norwegian-American activity was little affected by controversy, though not wholly untouched by it. This was the realm of music, which, it has been said, has been "fostered as an art of the people" among the Norwegians. Their music took its inspiration, in the main, from three sources. One was the heritage of hymns out of Norway, kept alive through vigorous congregational singing, for the Norwegian Lutheran church to the present day prides itself upon being a "singing church." A second was the folk music of Norway—the multitude of ancient songs and dances, marked by regional differences of spirit and rhythm, which the immigrants carried with them to the New World. And the third was the wealth of composition poured forth by modern Norwegian composers—Grieg, Sinding, Svendsen,

[26] On Bjørnson and the Norwegian Americans, see, in addition to the essay by Professor Paulson, H. Eitrem, "Bjørnstjerne Bjørnsons Amerikaferd i 1880–81," in *Edda* (Oslo), 29:165–206 (1929); Anderson, *Life Story*, 337–344; Einar Haugen, "Bjørnson og hans norsk-amerikanske impresario," in *Nordmanns-forbundet*, 29:20–23 (December, 1936), and also his "Nyt lys over Bjørnsons Amerikatur," in *Decorah-posten*, December 2, 6, 9, 1932.

Kjerulf, and others. Most of these composers shaped their art in consonance with the musical lore treasured through centuries by mountain and valley folk in Norway; and of them all Grieg was the best loved, both in Norway and among his kinsmen in America, because of the authenticity with which his genius transmuted these treasures into lasting art.

The most characteristic musical contributions of the Norwegian Americans have taken the form of male choruses, particularly in *a cappella* singing, a form that reached its highest artistry in the performances of the St. Olaf College Choir under the direction of Dr. F. Melius Christiansen. Mr. Carl G. O. Hansen, the director of the Norwegian Glee Club of Minneapolis, asserts that "Hundreds of Norwegian male choruses, in course of the years have been active in this country and, in their local spheres as well as at district and national festivals, been instrumental in popularizing this form of amateur art." Such choruses are normally to be found in typical Norwegian-American communities and some of the "larger cities have as many as half a dozen organizations."[27]

Musical activity among the Norwegian Americans began to take organized form in the pioneer period. The Normanna Singing Society of La Crosse, for example, was formed in 1869, and the Norwegian Singing Society of Chicago a year later. In 1886 a federation of the United Scandinavian Singers of America was created. This central organization, which emphasized the unity of Norwegian, Swedish, and Danish choral singing, held great biennial musical festivals, beginning at Philadelphia in 1887; and when the festival was held in Minneapolis in 1891, there were approximately fifty constituent societies, which represented some eleven hundred singers. In music, as in religion and

[27] See a pamphlet by Carl G. O. Hansen, *Why Sons of Norway?* (Minneapolis, 1939); and also his essay "Northern Music in America: II. Norwegian," in *American-Scandinavian Review,* 4:38–43 (January–February, 1916).

education, however, Scandinavian co-operation foundered upon the rock of nationalism. After some united efforts to maintain a Scandinavian federation in the Northwest, the Swedes drew away from the Norwegians and Danes, and ultimately the Norwegians stood alone in a federation of their own. The Northwestern Norwegian-Danish Singers' Society was formed in 1906, and four years later the name was changed to the Norwegian Singers' Society of America. By the late 1930's the latter numbered more than forty societies in seven states and Canada. It arranged a tour to Norway in 1914 under the leadership of Emil Biørn of Chicago; it continued the biennial musical festivals, which had been held regularly since the early 1890's; it published a magazine devoted to the common interests of the societies; and it did much to promote a wide popular interest not only in choral singing but also in the general musical lore and the culture of Norway.[28]

The Norwegian singing societies on the Pacific coast, meanwhile, established a regional federation of their own at Seattle in 1902. By the late 1930's it numbered thirteen clubs in California, Oregon, Washington, British Columbia, and Alaska. Throughout the country there were not a few societies that were not affiliated either with the national or the Pacific coast federation. The custom of musical festivals, local, regional, and national, was contagious and soon spread to the church, which on occasion brought together many choirs for massed singing under directors of the caliber of Dr. Christiansen. A Choral Union within the Norwegian Lutheran Church of America has existed for many years and has sponsored great festivals, in some of which thousands of singers

[28] The story of the musical organizations is told by Mr. Hansen in his paper in Wist, *Norsk-amerikanernes festskrift,* 266 ff. See also Finn Rein Simonsen, "Omkring det norske sangerforbund i Amerika," in Hjellum, *Skandinavens almanak,* 1934, p. 78–82; Martin Bergh, "Det norske sangerforbund i Amerika," in *Nordmands-forbundet,* 18: 205–208 (1925); an account of "Sang- og musikliv paa østkysten" in the same magazine, p. 209–211; and J. R. Nannestad, "Lidt om norsk mandssang i Amerika," also in that magazine, 3: 296–319 (June, 1910).

have participated, in such centers as Chicago, Minneapolis, Fargo, Seattle, and Hollywood. Some of the directors of male choruses were also composers of note. Alfred Paulsen of Chicago, for example, wrote the extremely popular "Naar fjordene blaaner" ("When the Blue of the Fjords Deepens") and other songs which male choruses from coast to coast and also in the Scandinavian countries delighted to sing; and Ole Windingstad of New York proved a force in Norwegian choral and symphonic music in the East both through his conducting and as a composer.[29]

The Norwegian-American musical scene has exhibited some celebrated artists, but for the most part they have been Norwegians attracted to America by the opportunities for concert tours and operatic appearances. Olive Fremstad, a Metropolitan Opera star of Norwegian and Swedish backgrounds, came out of the Middle West, but such figures of a later day as Kirsten Flagstad and Kaja Norena were musical importations direct from Norway. Ole Bull in the 1840's and 1850's became known everywhere in the United States for his wizardry with the violin, and by virtue of his long residence in Boston, Madison, and other parts of America he was hailed by many as a Norwegian American. The truth, however, is that he was always essentially a Norwegian on tour.

In 1903 St. Olaf College at Northfield appointed Dr. F. Melius Christiansen as its director of music. This musical genius had acquired much of his training in an American conservatory and at Leipzig. During his first year at the Lutheran college in Minnesota he appeared as a concert violinist, conducted the college band, led the choir of a local Lutheran church, presented the St. Olaf Choral Union in a cantata, and held a May musical festival, with a performance

[29] Norwegian contributions in the field of music are briefly reviewed in Sundby-Hansen, *Norwegian Immigrant Contributions*, 145–149. See Hjellum, *Skandinavens almanak-kalender*, 1939, p. 55, 78–81.

of Haydn's "Creation" as its central event. During his early years at St. Olaf, the college band, which he led on a tour of Norway in 1906, won wide fame, but this was eclipsed by that of the St. Olaf Choir, which similarly toured Norway in 1913. During more than a quarter century, this choir, functioning in the St. John's Church at Northfield, drawing its talent from the St. Olaf student body, and undertaking concert tours in America and Europe, has become internationally known for the "artistic perfection" of its singing. According to Mr. Hansen, it "became the original source of the a cappella movement in this country." Dr. Christiansen, both through his directing and through his numerous compositions of chorales, religious lyrics, and other works, rounded out a musical contribution of pervasive influence. Much of it centered about his purpose to have the "rich treasure of music within the Norwegian Lutheran Church . . . taken over and adopted by all the American people."[30]

The widespread Norwegian-American interest in choral singing has not crowded out the interest in instrumental music. Perhaps the most typically Norwegian form that the latter has taken has been the attempt to preserve in America the traditional hallings, spring dances, and other examples of old Norwegian folk music. Much of this interest has centered in the Hardanger violin, and in 1914 there was formed Spelemans Laget af Amerika—a society of more than a hundred members, nearly all of them performers, whose central aim was the cultivation of that particular species of violin and its use in keeping alive the heritage of folk music. Annual conventions were held, with prizes for outstanding performances.[31]

The doors of music were hospitably open to amateur prac-

[30] Hansen, *Why Sons of Norway?*, 14; Eugene E. Simpson, *History of St. Olaf Choir*, 179 (Minneapolis, 1921). The phrase quoted is said to represent an "oft-stated wish" of Dr. Christiansen.

[31] Brief reports on this unique society are to be found in the annual issues of *Skandinavens almanak-kalender*.

titioners of the art, whereas sculpture and painting generally were more selective. There was a fairly broad base for creative work in these arts, but distinguished achievement was rare. In not a few Norwegian homes in America, the art of wood carving, handed down from father to son, was cherished; and many Norwegian women busied themselves with Hardanger and other forms of skilled handwork. It is interesting to note that Jacob Fjelde, who won fame as a Norwegian-American sculptor, was the son of a wood carver. The sculptor was active in Minneapolis from 1887 until his death in 1896 and was widely known in the Northwest. His works include the Ole Bull statue in Loring Park, Minneapolis; and the graceful monument to Hiawatha and Minnehaha which stands just above Minnehaha Falls. The tradition of creative art represented by Fjelde was carried on by his son Paul Fjelde, who was trained under Lorado Taft and has many notable works to his credit, including the Colonel Heg monument in Madison, the bust of Lincoln in Frogner Park, Oslo, and the recent bronze of the elder Charles A. Lindbergh, completed in 1940 for the Minnesota Historical Society. The extraordinary artistic talent of the Fjelde family is also illustrated in Jacob's sister, Pauline, noted for her tapestries, and his brother Dr. Herman Fjelde, a physician who found time to build monuments to such Norwegian chieftains as Wergeland, Hauge, Aasen, Ibsen, Bjørnson, and even Ganger Rolf, which are to be seen in various cities of the Red River Valley. Sigvald Asbjørnsen of Chicago was the sculptor of the Grieg statue in Brooklyn and also of the Leif Erikson monument in Chicago.[32]

In the realm of painting there have been many Norwegian-American artists of considerable local and regional fame, but

[32] Luth Jaeger, "Two American Sculptors: Fjelde — Father and Son," in *American-Scandinavian Review,* 10:467–472 (August, 1922); Sundby-Hansen, "Painting and Sculpture," in *Norwegian Immigrant Contributions,* 141–145; and Norlie, *Norwegian People in America,* 465. Other Norwegian-American sculptors of note include Gilbert P. Riswold, Alexander Grinager, and Sigurd Neandross.

few of national distinction. The best-known Norwegian-American painter probably was Jonas Lie, a nephew of the great Norwegian author of the same name. His works are to be found in many of the leading art galleries of the world. Though he seems to have had a special fondness for New York scenes, his range of interest was wide. It has been said that his subjects included the storm, the thunder cloud, snow-decked hills, rocky masses, and dark and hidden, mist-covered streams.[33]

The world of music afforded the Norwegian Americans at once the consolations of art and the pleasures of sport, for to many, the song festivals — joyous occasions when thousands of people assembled in holiday mood — were sport. In the realm of sport proper, however, the most notable contributions of the Norwegians to America have centered about skiing. Skiing itself, in fact, is a contribution of the Norwegian immigrants, for they brought this ancient sport of Norway to America and they took the lead in developing it as an American pastime. Their original purpose in carrying skis with them across the sea or in fashioning them in the western settlements, however, was utilitarian, not recreational. "In the older settlements of Illinois, Wisconsin, Minnesota, Iowa, and the Dakotas," writes Mr. Hansen, "the Norwegian pioneers more easily than others made their way through forest and over prairie on their winter journeys to town because they had their skis." One of the pioneer settlers at Rock Prairie, Wisconsin, recalled skiing in the autumn of 1841 — the earliest known instance of skiing in America. "When the first snow had fallen in the autumn," he said, "I and another Norwegian went across the prairie on skis to Beloit to buy flour. The Americans later saw the

[33] Rølvaag and Eikeland, *Norsk læsebok,* 2:358. See also *Norwegian Immigrant Contributions,* 142. Sigurd Skou, Trygve Hammer, Brynjulf Strandenaes, Herbjørn Gausta, August Klagstad, Sigvart Sievers, and Lars Haukanes are among the painters well known in Norwegian-American circles. See "American Artists of Norwegian Descent," in *American-Scandinavian Review,* 13:365–367 (June, 1925).

ski tracks in the snow, and nobody could tell what kind of animal it was that had left such a trail behind it." He went on to say that there was much speculation about the matter. Some people believed that the tracks had been made by an unknown monster of the western woods, but no one could understand how the animal could possibly get about in summer.[34]

Sometimes the Norwegian talent for skiing was employed in tasks of spectacular usefulness to the pioneers. An early illustration is afforded by the story of John Thompson, an immigrant son of old Telemark, the Norwegian region most famous for its masters of skiing. Thompson came to America in 1837, hunted for gold in California in the early 1850's, and a few years later contracted to carry the United States mail between Placerville, California, and Carson Valley, Idaho. This was a bleak stretch of ninety miles that was virtually impassable during winter, with some snowdrifts more than thirty feet deep. For nearly two decades, using skis of his own manufacture, "Snowshoe" Thompson got the mail across this barrier despite snow and storm; a pair of his pioneer skis is now preserved in the museum of Sutter's Fort at Sacramento.[35]

Skiing as a popular sport did not begin to develop until the 1880's, however, though the children of the Norwegian pioneers probably made a game of it in earlier years. The 1880's were a period of mounting interest in winter sports, an interest symbolized by the ice carnivals held by St. Paul during that decade. This was the general era in which ski clubs began to be organized, both in the West and in the

[34] Carl G. O. Hansen, "Contributions to Sports," in Sundby-Hansen, *Norwegian Immigrant Contributions,* 163–170. The Rock County pioneer was Gullik Knudsen Laugen (Springen), who settled in that area in 1841. His account of early skiing in Wisconsin is quoted by Svein Nilsson in *Billed-magazin,* 1:172 (May 1, 1869). Professor Haugen kindly called my attention to this interesting item.

[35] Holand, *De norske settlementers historie,* ch. 37; Charles M. Dudley, *60 Centuries of Skiing,* 46 ff. (Brattleboro, Vermont, 1935); William M. Thayer, *Marvels of the New West,* 261 (Norwich, Connecticut, 1888); Ylvisaker, *Eminent Pioneers,* 67–78.

East. In the West pioneer clubs were founded in such towns as Red Wing, St. Paul, Minneapolis, Stillwater, La Crosse, Eau Claire, Stoughton, and Ishpeming; and in the East, also under Scandinavian leadership, there were early ski organizations in such places as Berlin, New Hampshire, and Altoona, Pennsylvania. A factor of considerable importance in the West was the arrival at Red Wing in 1883 of a quartet of noted skiers from Norway, two of whom had won wide fame as ski jumpers. These two were Torgus and Mikkel Hemmestvedt, the former of whom set a Norwegian jumping record in 1879 that was not broken until early in the twentieth century. The Hemmestvedts were the pioneers in America of the ski jump.[36]

Both in Red Wing and in St. Paul, the manufacture of skis, modeled upon those of Norwegian make, was undertaken on a large scale; the tools of the sport became less uncommon than they had been; tournaments were held by the various clubs; and by degrees the sport gained popularity. It was not until after the National Ski Association was founded in 1904, however, that skiing made notable strides forward. The national body was created by a small group of Norwegian-American skiers, with Carl Tellefsen as president and Aksel Holter as secretary. The Norwegians, preeminent particularly in ski jumping and cross-country tests, counted among their stars such men as Oscar Gunderson, Anders and Lars Haugen, Ragnar Omtvedt, Caspar Oimen, and Alf Engen. Mechanical ingenuity solved the problem of creating ski runs where there were no high hills or mountains available; and in time huge steel scaffolds — towering artificial hills — became conspicuous landmarks in the vicinity of most northern American cities.

Two hundred thousand pairs of skis, manufactured by

[36] Aksel H. Holter, "Norwegian National Sports and Their Influence in the United States and Canada," a manuscript prepared for the Norse-American Centennial of 1925; and the same author's "Nordmænds indflydelse i Amerikas sportsliv," in *Nordmands-forbundet,* 18:198–204 (1925).

Norwegian-American industry, were sold in 1924, but it was during the 1930's that skiing became a widely popular and fashionable sport. Austrian influences and the power of the radio implemented earlier factors in promoting the sport. Enthusiasm for the winter game swept the country; millions of people experimented with its hazards; carnivals attracted great crowds — nearly sixty thousand people crowded into Soldiers' Field in Chicago for a ski exhibition; expensive resorts were developed for devotees of the sport; and special trains were made available to people who sought holiday escape from the cities to rugged snow-clad hills. Jumping was but one phase, though perhaps the most thrilling, of a sport which included among its seductive attractions the flying kilometer, the *slalom*, the cross country, the art of skijoring, and the cool delight of tumbling in the snow.[37]

If skiing was a major interest of the Norwegians, skating stood second to it. In this sport Norwegian traditions and tools were carried to America; and a considerable impetus to the sport was given by visits to the United States of masters of ice skating in Norway. In many of the larger American cities the Norwegians organized athletic clubs of their own, such as the Norwegian American Athletic Association of Chicago, which served as nuclei for wide-ranging activities. It has been said that the Norwegian Americans had a relatively small participational interest in baseball and boxing; they were deeply interested, however, in all forms of sailing; and like Americans generally they took to tennis, golf, and many other sports that have played roles in relieving the tension of American life.[38]

The impulse toward organization in music and sports

[37] Dudley, *60 Centuries of Skiing, passim;* and G. C. Torguson, "Skiing Then and Now," in *Pope County Tribune* (Glenwood, Minnesota), February 9, March 30, 1939. A vast amount of information may be found in the *American Ski Annual,* the yearbook of the National Ski Association; and there is also a *Canadian Ski Year Book,* issued by the Canadian Amateur Ski Association. See also Frank G. Menke, *Encyclopedia of Sports,* 277–281 (Chicago, 1939).

[38] Hansen, in Sundby-Hansen, *Norwegian Contributions,* 166–170.

reflects a general aspect of Norwegian-American life. The American habit of "joining," deeply rooted in the past, was adopted by the Norwegian Americans, who exhibited a marked tendency toward the formal organization of activity in every field into clubs, societies, lodges, leagues, and *lags*. They represented a wide variety of purpose, but had a certain unity in their emphasis upon common cultural backgrounds. There can be no doubt that they played an important role in the social and intellectual life of the Norwegian Americans. In the pioneer period of the 1850's and 1860's organization usually had a broad Scandinavian base, representing efforts at Norwegian, Swedish, and Danish co-operation. In New York, Boston, Chicago, Minneapolis, San Francisco, and other cities there were Scandinavian societies which centered their efforts upon music, drama, immigrant aid, and the like. This Scandinavianism was largely swept away in the 1870's, however, and numerous societies specifically Norwegian in character appeared, while the Swedes and Danes emerged with organizations of their own. In Minneapolis, the Scandinavian Dramatic Society, renamed Norden, was for some years genuinely Scandinavian in its atmosphere, but in the 1870's first the Danes and then the Norwegians seceded, and Norden continued as a Swedish society.[39]

Usually the impulse to organize societies was local and individual; and the necessary steps were simple — the framing of a constitution, the election of officers, and individual "joining." Some of the most distinguished of all the Norwegian-American societies, such as the literary societies of Symra and Ygdrasil, respectively in Decorah and in Madison, stood sturdily on their own feet.[40] The general tendency,

[39] Mr. Hansen has made a contribution of singular value in his study of "Det norske foreningsliv i Amerika," in *Norsk-amerikanernes festskrift*, 266–291. See also Simon Johnson, "Glimt av norsk foreningsliv i Amerika," in *Nordmands-forbundet*, 18: 189–197 (1925).

[40] Anderson tells of the beginnings of the Ygdrasil society in his *Life Story*, 370–373.

however, was toward regional and national associations in every field, with district and local units, and some important Norwegian-American developments came in efforts to give wide organizational scope to ideas first experimented with on a local scale. The Sons of Norway, for example, was initiated in 1895 by a group of young Norwegians in Minneapolis who leagued themselves together for mutual aid. The idea was contagious, other groups took similar action, a supreme lodge was formed, and by 1940 there were some three hundred local lodges in seventeen American states, Canada, and Alaska, integrated in a compact organization. On the material side, this organization had more than ten million dollars of insurance in force among its members, and, on the cultural side, it had interested itself actively in things Norwegian, issued a monthly organ that contained much information on affairs in Norway and in the domain of Norwegian America, and kept a watchful eye on the activities of its major districts and local lodges. The intense, and even aggressive, Norwegian interests of the latter are suggested by such typical lodge names as Terje Viken, Rølvaag, Dovre, Leif Erikson, Fedreminne, Grieg, Wergeland, Henrik Ibsen, Garborg, Ueland, and Telemark. The collateral Daughters of Norway, with approximately fifty lodges in 1940, liked such names as Camilla Collet, Solveig, Freya, and Hjørdis. Another aspect of Norwegian-American organization has taken the form of the sponsorship of more than twenty-five hospitals from coast to coast, most of them inspired by an interest in immigrant charity and welfare work and having their inception in church circles. Thus the magnificent Norwegian-American Hospital of Chicago, representing large resources, the best standards of medical leadership, and generous support by Chicago Norwegians, was the outgrowth of a Lutheran Tabitha society launched by women in that city in 1885. Closely related to hospitals and churches were large numbers of old people's and orphans' homes, hospices, and other institutions which made a useful place for themselves in the Norwegian-American domain.[41]

The general attempts made to promote Norwegian cultural interests through organization sprang in part from a belief that the rapid transition to English was accompanied by cultural losses, that bridges of understanding between parents and children were being swept away. In churches and homes the second generation more and more seemed to be drifting away from things Norwegian; and so, among those who deplored this tendency, there was a conservative effort to foster the Norwegian speech — not the Norwegian-American of everyday parlance or the dialects brought from the Norwegian valleys, but the literary language of the old country — and an appreciation among the younger folk of the culture of the Norwegian people. The Norwegian Society of America, founded in 1903, aimed at the preservation of the language, history, and traditions of the Norwegians, attempted to forward the study of the Norwegian language in American schools, gave medals to the winners of declamation contests, and paid honor to creative achievement in the domain of Norwegian-American literature. "Culturally," wrote Wist in the first number of this society's quarterly, "we are a people in migration — nomads in transition from one nation to another"; and he emphasized the need of drawing upon the cultural riches of Norway. Waldemar Ager, the editor of the quarterly, did not wholly agree with this point of view, however. He was primarily interested in the development of a Norwegian-American cultural life which,

[41] A "History of Sons of Norway: An American Fraternal Organization of Men and Women of Norwegian Birth or Extraction," by Carl G. O. Hansen, its educational director, was begun in *Sønner af Norge,* vol. 37, no. 1 (January, 1940). It is appearing with separate pagination and will ultimately be bound as a book. The pamphlet *Why Sons of Norway?* contains useful information. Mr. Hansen also issues for the Sons of Norway a series of mimeographed bulletins which have a wide interest. The names of the lodges appear in Hjellum, *Skandinavens almanak,* 1939, p. 64–70. See also the same yearbook for 1929, p. 109–116, and Nicolay A. Grevstad, *The Norwegian-American Hospital* (Chicago, 1930).

king root in the soil of the New World and drawing its urishment from its own backgrounds and interests, might yield creative fruit in literature and art. Poets, painters, musicians, and sculptors would come in time, he believed, but meanwhile the Norwegian Americans had to make it clear that they had a genuine need for artists. What Ager apparently wanted was an articulate, indigenous impulse toward beauty, springing from the normal life of the people in their own setting of time and region and cultural circumstance — something native, not borrowed.[42]

For Fædrearven ("For the Ancestral Heritage"), a society formed at La Crosse in 1919, tried to promote understanding of the value in the cultural backgrounds of the immigrants. Rølvaag was one of its founders and served as its secretary. He saw grave dangers in a quick loss of the "cultural identity" of the Norwegian Americans and believed that unless they cultivated their "ancestral heritage" they would not succeed in making their potentially largest contribution to American culture. As Professor Haugen interprets the novelist's views, Rølvaag insisted that his people "must not come empty-handed to the banquet, nor must they vanish without trace in the great maelstrom." The truest Americanization, according to Rølvaag, was to be found only in connection with the maintenance of a "cultural solidarity with the past"; and it was out of this conception that he created *Giants in the Earth.* Rølvaag did not go so far as James Truslow Adams, who maintained that the Scandinavian empire of the Northwest "is slowly absorbing, instead of being absorbed by, the older Southern and Northern American stocks, while developing as sound an Americanism

[42] A thoughtful interpretation of the work of the various Norwegian organizations is offered by Ager in "Norskhetsbevægelsen i Amerika," in *Nordmandsforbundet,* 18: 211–219 (1925). See also Johannes B. Wist, "Vor kulturelle stilling," in *Kvartalskrift* (Minneapolis), vol. 1, no. 1, p. 1–10 (January, 1905), and Ager's essay on "Vore kulturelle muligheder," in the April, 1905, issue of the same magazine, vol. 1, no. 2, p. 2–10.

as exists anywhere on the continent." What Rølvaag saw clearly was that two traditions were gradually and subtly influencing each other. What he wanted was to make as rich an immigrant contribution as possible to American life. He took a long and essentially realistic view of things, and it is possible that he would have questioned the interpretation of Mr. Adams as sharply as he did the theory of a swift melting-pot process.[43]

Yet another organization that appeared on the immigrant horizon was the Norwegian National Society in America, which represented an effort, organized on a regional basis, to federate numerous Norwegian societies of different character and purpose. It had its genesis in 1899 in the city of Chicago, where broad-minded leaders of the stamp of Birger Osland took the lead in bringing a large number of societies — ultimately some fifty — into a coherent relationship with a view to occasional joint action in important matters of common interest. In Norway, meanwhile, interest in international bridges of understanding and friendship resulted in a League of Norsemen which had a large membership among the Norwegian Americans and which utilized a well-edited monthly magazine to keep this membership informed upon events and currents of thought in Norway. In the United States, the American-Scandinavian Foundation achieved notable success in forwarding a general American interest in the culture of the Scandinavian countries, not least through the publication in English of many of the classics of Norwegian, Swedish, and Danish literature; and it set up a system of fellowships which effected an exchange of scholars between the Scandinavian countries and the United States.[44]

[43] Rølvaag's volume of essays, *Omkring fædrearven,* was published in Northfield in 1922. See also Haugen, "O. E. Rölvaag: Norwegian-American," in *Studies and Records,* 7:56; Jorgenson and Solum, *Rölvaag,* 295; and Adams, *The Epic of America,* 311 (Boston, 1931).

[44] There was spirited organizational activity in Chicago among the Norwegian Americans from early days. Mr. Birger Osland recalls particularly the Norrøna Literary Society and its successor, the Arne Garborg Club, which flourished in the

A deep consciousness of Norwegian regional origins had been present among the immigrants from early pioneer days, but it was not until much later that the *bygdelag* movement was launched. Andrew A. Veblen, who was himself American born, was one of the leaders in the organization in 1902 of the Valdris Society, and by 1909 there were a dozen organizations of this kind — each cherishing memories of a different district in Norway. The membership was made up of emigrants from given districts and their descendants; the bonds of union were dialect, common customs, songs and music, acquaintanceship, and shared traditions. In a word, organization was rooted in Norwegian locality and tribe, and was another phase of the wider Norwegian movement.[45] Encouraged by Rasmus B. Anderson, who in 1901 called upon Norwegians to tell of achievement in America in terms of the sons and daughters of particular *bygds,* the idea of *bygdelags,* or district societies, spread rapidly.[46] Each society held a summer meeting at which speeches in dialect were in special favor and the music and dancing as practiced in the ancient *bygd* were revived. Each *lag* normally published a magazine or a yearbook; ultimately a central council was formed to give cohesion to the movement; occasionally special histories were issued by the *lags* on the saga of their own dalesmen in the New World; and the central council at-

1890's and were noted for the excellent quality of their discussions and debates. When the National League was formed in 1899, no fewer than twenty-three Chicago societies joined it. By way of illustrating the variety of the organizational interests of the Norwegians, it may be noted that these included various lodges, the Norwegian Quartet Club, the Norwegian Glee Club, the Norwegian Singers' Society, the Norwegian Turners' Society, the Athletic Club Sleipner, the Normania Band, the Norwegian Old Settlers' Society, the Scandinavian Shoemakers' Society, the Tabitha Hospital Society, the Leif Erikson Monument Society, the Norwegian Women's Industrial Society, and two women's clubs, Thora and Minde. The magazines, *Nordmands-forbundet* and the *American-Scandinavian Review* are convenient guides to the work of the League of Norsemen and the American-Scandinavian Foundation.

[45] See Andrew A. Veblen, *The Valdris Book* (Minneapolis, 1920).

[46] Rasmus B. Anderson, ed., *Bygdejævning: Artikler af repræsentanter fra de forskjellige bygder i Norge om, hvad deres sambygdinger har udrettet i vesterheimen* (Madison, 1903).

tempted to promote undertakings of general cultural interest to the Norwegian element in America, such as the celebration in 1925 of the centennial of the arrival in New York of the sloop folk.[47]

The *bygdelag* movement was carried forward on the crest of high enthusiasm and ambitious plans. Some of the *lags* published valuable reminiscent and historical material, notably the Valdris, Telemark, Numedal, and Voss groups; and their periodicals and yearbooks, although chiefly antiquarian in character, have considerable interest as documents of the social history of the Norwegians in America. The movement as a whole contributed to recognition of the value of *bygd* lore, especially the dialects and the wealth of music and dance and costume that each group represented; and it encouraged among its members a popular interest in Norwegian backgrounds which may have had a wide influence. The organizations also played a significant role in forwarding Norwegian-American celebrations; and they have made many splendid gifts to institutions and causes in the Norwegian home valleys. When it is remembered, however, that nearly a half hundred *lags* were active and that they commanded widespread support and interest, it is difficult to understand why the movement did not bear more impressive fruits. The truth seems to be that the *lags* were primarily social institutions, centering about annual reunions. They were old settlers' societies, and, from the point of view of the rank and file of the membership, activities other than social probably were incidental. The editing of the magazines and yearbooks, with certain notable exceptions, was entrusted to men without training for the task. Veblen's plan to pool

[47] Mr. John A. Fagereng has written a valuable unpublished essay on "The Bygdelags" which I have had the privilege of reading. One of the best brief accounts of the movement, with emphasis upon its aims and achievements, is Dr. L. M. Gimmestad's "Bygdelagsbevægelsen," in Hjellum, *Skandinavens almanakkalender*, 1929, p. 97–103. See also his "Bygdelagene i 30 år," in *Nordmannsforbundet*, 25:260–262 (August, 1932).

resources and effort in a central publication of high quality failed to win any genuine support, though his magazine, probably the best of its kind, did tend in some measure to function as an organ for the entire movement. An ambitious scheme to gather up Norwegian-American documents and to preserve them in a central hall of records on the campus of a Middle Western university failed to mature.[48]

The urge to record in one form or another the experiences of the Norwegian immigrants in America was no new thing. The early editor Clausen called upon settlers to send records of their migration to the press in its initial period; and in the late 1860's Svein Nilsson, the editor of *Billed-magazin*, collected from the pioneers themselves their own stories and published their narratives in a series of articles entitled "The Scandinavian Settlements in America." To this pioneer of culture the emigration "from Europe to the New World discovered by Columbus" seemed one of the "most remarkable phenomena" of the nineteenth century. He viewed the movement broadly in its relation to the economy of the old country and to the wide-reaching effects in America of the "stream of immigrants" that "flowed over the immensely great western plains"; and he understood the lasting value of original accounts by those who themselves had been a part of the movement. He was not so much a historian as a collector of the materials of history; and all historians of the Norwegian migration have found his materials a treasure house of information.[49]

The 1870's and 1880's witnessed the emergence of Rasmus B. Anderson as a quickening influence in the domain of Norwegian-American letters. In rapid succession he brought out his *Norse Mythology*, *America Not Discovered by Co-*

[48] The Minnesota Historical Society has files of the publications of nearly all the *bygdelags* and it also has in its possession a large collection of manuscripts, clippings, and other records left by the late Andrew A. Veblen, who was one of the leading spirits in the *lag* movement.

[49] See D. G. Ristad, "Svein Nilsson, Pioneer Norwegian-American Historian," in *Studies and Records*, 9:29–37.

lumbus, a collection of *Viking Tales of the North,* the *Younger Edda, Julegave* (a book of fairy tales in Norwegian), and a flood of translations and other works. In most of this early and prodigal production, it was the things of old Norway, not the story of the modern immigrants, that engaged his interest and his facile pen. He wrote with a glow of enthusiasm and his interpretations were romantic, not critical. His central purpose was that of "transmitting the cultural treasures of his ancestral land into the English language," and in achieving this purpose he generated a literary contagion among his countrymen. He was a popularizer of boundless energy whose gifts as a writer were matched by his skill as a speaker and by a singularly provocative personality. He stirred the creative ambitions and widened the vistas of those who were beginning to think of a Norwegian-American literature.[50]

The tendency to interpret the Norwegian-American saga found its earlier outlets not so much in the writing of history as in fiction; and it was in the period after the Civil War that the pioneer efforts in this field were made. They marked the beginnings of a Norwegian-American literature which embraces more than a hundred novels, only a few of which have been introduced, through translation into English, to the American world. There has also been a vast distillation of poetry; and long shelves have been filled with religious works and with Norwegian-American biography and reminiscence.[51] With the exception of a few novels —

[50] Einar I. Haugen, "A Critique and a Bibliography of the Writings of Rasmus B. Anderson," in *Wisconsin Magazine of History,* 20:253–269 (March, 1937); and Anderson's own *Life Story.*

[51] Dr. Norlie, in his *Norwegian People in America,* tells of taking from the shelves of his library a hundred volumes — all in the Norwegian language — produced by eighty-four Norwegian-American writers of fiction. He also speaks of "at least a thousand" books in the field of religious literature written by Norwegian Americans in the period from 1890 to 1925 (p. 407); and of fifty Norwegian-American writers of verse who turned out one or more volumes each in the same period. Such statistics afford a quantitative, but not a qualitative, gauge of the productive urge. For some measure of the quality of Norwegian-American poetry, see Ludvig Lima, *Norsk-amerikanske digte i udvalg* (Minneapolis, 1903).

notably *Giants in the Earth* and other works of O. E. Rølvaag — Norwegian-American fiction is primarily of historical, rather than artistic, interest — a social documentation of the immigrant world. Its rise synchronized with the close of the earlier ordeals of pioneering and with the expansion of the migration into a mass movement. It was related to a growing self-consciousness that sprang from a sense of triumph over achievement not alone in subduing frontiers but also in building an institutionalized and coherent society out of scattered fragments. The expansion of the press, which mirrored this Norwegian-American society, had some share in making it more articulate than it had been. In a word, the Norwegians from the late 1860's and early 1870's onward were in a mood to look at their own story and to offer fictional interpretations of it, however fumbling and uncertain in technique.

Though the first novel by a Norwegian in the United States appears to have been Hjalmar Hjorth Boyesen's *Gunnar,* which appeared as a serial in the *Atlantic Monthly* in 1873 and as a book in 1874, this quiet romantic tale in the earlier Bjørnson tradition was set wholly against a Norwegian background, and it did not touch the immigrant world.[52] Bernt Askevold's *Hun Ragnhild, eller billeder fra Søndfjord* ("Ragnhild, or Pictures from Søndfjord"), published in 1876, was written in Norwegian and came out of the Middle West, but like *Gunnar,* it dealt with life in Norway and was remote from immigrant actualities. The beginnings of the Rølvaag tradition are to be found rather in the pioneer novels of Nicolai Severin Hassel and Tellef Grundysen. Hassel published in 1874, in the periodical *For hjemmet,* a lengthy novel entitled "Alf Brage eller skolelåreren i Minnesota: En original norsk-amerikansk fortälling" ("Alf Brage,

[52] See Larson's essay on Boyesen in *The Changing West,* 82–115. A Norwegian translation of *Gunnar* was brought out in Chicago in several editions. The third is dated 1884.

For Hjemmet.

Et Tidsskrift for nyttig og underholdende Läsning.

5te Aarg. Den 15de Januar 1874. No. 1.

Alf Brage
—eller—
Skolelæreren i Minnesota.

En original norsk-amerikansk Fortälling

af

N. S. Hassel.

Motto: Den, som overvinder sig selv, er større end den, som indtager en Stad.
(Gammelt Ord.)
Men den, som lader sig overvinde af Guds Ord, beholder Seier til evig Tid.

Förste Afsnit.

Alf Brages Forældre, hans Barndom og Ungdom.

Alf Brages Fader var en velhavende Gaardbruger i en af Norges bedste Egne, og det var et af hans høieste Ønsker, at Alf skulde blive Kjøbmand i Kristiania. Denne vilde ogsaa føie Faderen heri, skjønt han havde større Lyst til Bogen end til Alenmaalet og Pengene. Men hans Fader lovede at hjælpe ham ivei, saasnart han blev myndig, og saa trøstede han sig med, at han da blev fri og sin egen Herre, kunde kjøbe mange Bøger, faa Tid nok til at læse i dem og desuden leve saa behageligt som muligt.

Gamle Brage og hans Hustru lignede de fleste skikkelige og brave Folk i Norge. Han var en forstandig, driftig og nøieseende Mand. Nogle sagde, at han var ganske smaalig i mange Stykker, men Alle var enige i, at han var en brav og gjennemærlig Mand—man kan jo hellerikke være efter Alles Hoved; thi da skulde man vel blive underlig rar.—Baade han og hun var godgjørende; men en saare vigtig Ting forsømte de, nemlig at gjøre sine Børn tilgode med Guds Ord og Formaninger hentede derfra. Naar de paa Helligdagene ikke var i Kirke, læste han gjerne en Prædiken af Linderots Huspostil for Alle som var i hans Hus og vilde høre derpaa; men det var ogsaa alt det Guds Ord som lød der. Det var, som om de tænkte, at de kunde have Samfund med Gud hver Søndags Formiddag, men i de øvrige sex og en halv af Ugens Dage kunde være Ham foruden. Guds Ord vilde de have til Søndagsbrug, men ikke til Hverdagsbrug; om Søndags Formiddagen skulde Gud faa Lov til at komme frem og tale til dem, men Resten af Ugen skulde Han nok helst være taus og fraværende. Djævelen og Kjødet udlægger og forklarer det tredie Bud paa den Maade, og næsten hele den skikkelige Verden vil have det saaledes forstaaet. Som saa mange Andre skammede de sig for at tale om Gud og Hans Ord imellem sig og kunde hellerikke komme sig til at tale med sine Børn derom. Denne hellige Pligt blev forsømt i Brages Hus, og maaske var det netop Følelsen heraf, som drev ham til at sørge for deres Skoleundervisning saa godt, han efter sin Mening kunde. Det vil sige, han sparede ikke paa Penge, naar det gjaldt dette Øiemed, og var ikke bange for ganske alene at holde en dyr, men god Huslærer for et Aarstid ad Gangen, naar han ikke paa anden Maade kunde skaffe sine Børn en god Undervisning. En god Opdragelse er den bedste Arv, vi kan give dem, sagde han ofte, men forsømte selv det vigtigste Stykke af en kristelig Børneopdragelse. Alfs Moder havde i sin Barndom kun nydt en sparsom Undervisning og havde saa ringe Tanker om sin Kundskab og om sig selv, at dette maaske var Bevæggrunden hos hende til ikke at blande Guds Ord ind i sin Tugt og Formaning, om hun end undertiden kunde føle Trang dertil.

Alf var en meget flink Gut i Skolen, og hans sidste Huslærer, som selv var Student, vilde endelig, at Faderen skulde lade ham studere. Men Brage mente, at Alfs Skoleflid og Kundskaber vilde blive ham til ligesaa stor Nytte, naar han blev Kjøbmand; og Alf vilde jo ogsaa selv blive Kjøbmand, sagde han, skjønt han vidste, at hans Interesser vegede i en anden Retning, og at han vilde blive Kjøbmand, fordi hans Forældre ønskede det. Han havde to Brødre, men ingen af dem vilde blive Kjøbmand. Sigurd, som var den ældste, havde hverken Lyst til Bogen eller Bylivet, han vilde blive Gaardbruger. Og Halfdan, som var yngst af Brødrene, vilde blive Sømand; thi det var det Morsomste, som var til, sagde han, at kunne komme saaledes omkring i Verden og faa se Saameget.

Alf blev konfirmeret, og hans Fader tog ham med sig til Kristiania og fik ham anbragt hos en Kjøbmand, som han kjendte. Da Brage allerede havde sagt Farvel til sin Søn for at efterlade ham i Byen, tilraabte han ham endnu disse Ord: "Falskhed slaar sin egen Herre paa Halsen, men Ærlighed varer længst. I hvad du gjør, Alf, handl ærligt overfor din Principal og overfor hans Kunder, for Guds og Menneskers Øine". Dette trøstede og glædede ham; thi han havde undertiden følt Frygt for, at man i Hovedstaden vilde befale ham at gjøre, hvad der ikke var ganske ærligt; men nu kunde han staa paa sin

or the Schoolteacher in Minnesota: An Original Norwegian-American Story ") and followed it with a sequel called " Rædselsdagene: Et norsk billede fra Indianerkrigen i Minnesota " (" Days of Terror: A Norwegian Picture from the Indian War in Minnesota "). The author, a graduate of the university in Christiania, was a schoolteacher and editor, and he dealt in his stories with experiences with which he was thoroughly familiar — those of a parochial school teacher in the Middle West. The tales are freighted with heavy religious moralizing, but are authentic in their Norwegian-American flavor and, so far as is known, mark the initial attempt to deal specifically with the immigrant scene in a Norwegian novel.[53] They did not appear in book form.

Grundysen was a clerk in a Decorah drugstore who had come from a Minnesota farm. Three years after Hassel's stories had been printed, he brought out a novel entitled *Fra begge sider af havet* (" From Both Sides of the Sea ") — with the scene laid " partly in Norway and partly in America," a story influenced by the national romanticism of Bjørnson, but marked in its treatment of immigrant life in Minnesota by an atmosphere of " stark reality." As Professor Larson says, " It made no pretense to literary art and a modern critic would find little in the novel to commend," but it was an honest, if unschooled, attempt to delineate " the life and activities of the Norwegian group in its new environment." [54]

It was against this background of literary pioneering that an amazing production of Norwegian-American novels en-

[53] Hassel's "Alf Brage " appears in twelve chapters in volume 5 of *For hjemmet: Et tidskrift for nyttig og underholdende Läsning,* from January 15 to June 15, 1874; and " Rædselsdagene " runs from June 30 to October 15 of the same year. Some biographical information about Hassel may be found in *Luthersk kirketidende,* January 5, 1916. These novels, so far as I am aware, have not previously been considered in discussions of the history of Norwegian-American fiction; and Tellef Grundysen has usually been mentioned as the first novelist to deal with Norwegian-American life.

[54] There is an admirable account of " Tellef Grundysen and the Beginnings of Norwegian-American Fiction," in Larson's *Changing West,* 49–66.

sued. As early as 1876 a writer published an essay on "Norwegian-American Literature: The Obstacles to and Basic Conditions of Its Future Existence and Sound Development." The essayist was Bernt Askevold, who brought out his novel *Hun Ragnhild* in the same year. He saw only literary blight in a too rapid Americanization. A Norwegian-American literature meant both reading and writing in the Norwegian language, for obviously unless there were readers, there could be no stimulus to authors. He found no literary hope in Scandinavianism, assailed the spirit of partisanship, called for solid and unbiased literary criticism, and suggested that the Norwegians, with their numerous organizations, might well support a good literary periodical. It is not primarily his analysis, however, that is significant historically; it is rather the fact that by the middle 1870's the concept of a Norwegian-American literature was defined in a public discussion and that there was a definite consciousness of its potential fruition. It was probably no coincidence that from 1875 to 1885, as Professor Haugen points out, seven Norwegian-American novelists made their debut. Once established, the tradition of creative writing was carried forward steadily in the decades that followed.[55]

Although a detailed review of Norwegian-American fiction cannot be attempted in these pages, attention must be called to a few writers who contributed to the development of the genre.[56] O. A. Buslett, a poet, storyteller, dramatist, orator, and reformer, had a lyre in one hand and a dissecting knife in the other, according to Waldemar Ager. He published a novel entitled "Fram" in *Skandinaven* in 1882—employing

[55] Bernt Askevold, "Norsk-amerikansk literatur: Hindringer og betingelser for dens fremtidige tilvärelse og gavnlige udvikling," in *Budstikken,* November 14, 21, 1876; Haugen, *Norsk i Amerika,* 101. Mr. Haugen's chapter "Diktende trang" (p. 98–116) is a discriminating survey of Norwegian-American literature.

[56] One of the ablest critical appraisals of achievements in the field of Norwegian-American literature is Waldemar Ager's essay "Norsk-amerikansk skjønliteratur," in Wist, *Norsk-amerikanernes festskrift,* 292–306. A more recent survey is that of Simon Johnson, "Skjønlitteræere sysler blandt Norsk-Amerikanere," in *Decorah-posten,* February 24, March 3, 10, 1939.

the Bjørnson formula — and later wrote many stories of Norwegian-American life, some of them, like "The Way to the Golden Gate," searching studies in immigrant psychology.[57] A much abler writer and thinker than Hassel or Tellefsen, he exerted a significant influence upon Norwegian-American letters. The romantic theme of the humble cotter boy who wins success in America was widely popularized in 1889 by H. A. Foss in his *Husmands-gutten: En fortælling fra Sigdal* ("The Cotter Boy: A Story from Sigdal"), which, serialized in *Decorah-posten,* increased the subscriptions to that newspaper by six thousand. One of a half dozen novels by the same author, this work is of relatively small literary interest, but nevertheless came from the hand of a genuine teller of stories. In a much later work, *Valborg,* dealing with a pioneer trek from Wisconsin to the Red River Valley, Foss gives "glimpses of choral societies, seventeenth of May festivals and other social activities; of newspapers and works of Norwegian authors; as well as the toil of clearing the land and the building of homes."[58] Like many other Norwegian-American writers, he was a crusader for temperance reform and used fiction as an instrument in that crusade. Ager believes that his best novel was *Den amerikanske saloon* ("The American Saloon"), published in 1889 — a painfully didactic work which nevertheless embodies much close observation. Peer Strømme in 1893 wrote *Hvorledes Halvor blev prest* ("Halvor: The Making of a Minister"), the story of a boy from a Norwegian-American settlement who went to Luther College for an education — probably a faithful reflection of Strømme's own experience and observation. Though this

[57] Another interesting work by Buslett is his *Fra min ungdoms nabolag,* published at Eau Claire in 1916. In a long letter of December 20, 1915, to the Reverend O. Nilsen, Buslett discusses his literary career and gives an interpretation of "The Way to the Golden Gate." He mentions that he has two major works and a mass of lesser writings that have never been published. The letter is in the Ole Nilsen Papers in the possession of the Minnesota Historical Society.

[58] Aagot D. Hoidahl, "Norwegian-American Fiction since 1880," in *Studies and Records,* 5:61–83.

story and a sequel to it were highly prized by Norwegian-American readers, Strømme's best work was not fiction, but his sprightly travel accounts and his genial and vivid *Erindringer* ("Reminiscences"), published in 1923.

As Norwegian-American fiction emerged into the twentieth century, it attained higher literary levels than in the earlier period. Waldemar Ager, Simon Johnson, and Johannes B. Wist in particular made notable contributions, though none of them reached the heights attained by Rølvaag. Ager combined professional skill in writing with sharp observation and a gift for ironical humor. His *Kristus for Pilatus* ("Christ before Pilate"—1911), *Gamlelandets sønner* ("The Sons of the Old Country"—1926), and *Hundeøine* ("Dog Eyes"—1929; translated into English as *I Sit Alone*) were probing social and psychological studies that won for him a high place among Norwegian-American writers. He also produced several volumes of spirited short stories, not a few of them devised as tracts against the liquor traffic. Simon Johnson wrote *Et geni* ("A Genius"—1907) on a North Dakota farm, and his novels, which include *I et nyt rige* ("In a New Kingdom"—1914), *Fallitten paa Braastad* (The Braastad Bankruptcy"—1922), and *Frihetens hjem* ("The Home of Freedom"—1925), describe Dakota pioneering and modern life on the prairie with sensitive understanding. From the historical point of view Johannes B. Wist's *Nykommerbilleder* ("Immigrant Scenes"—1920), *Hjemmet paa prærien* ("The Home on the Prairie"—1921), and *Jonasville* (1922) are among the most interesting of all Norwegian-American novels, for this unpretentious trilogy reflects precision of observation, realistic understanding of immigrant life, and a generous interest in the minutiae of immigrant transition. That the books were written with humor and without didacticism adds to their charm and value. Wist, both as novelist and as editor, occupies a high place in Norwegian-American cultural history.

Alongside such writers as Wist, Ager, and Johnson stood poets like Julius Baumann, O. S. Sneve, Knud A. Teigen, Wilhelm Pettersen, Ditlef G. Ristad, and Jon Norstog. The latter was a prairie phenomenon, a writer of rare gifts, whose production, for the most part, took the form of colossal Biblical dramas. There were also humorists like N. N. Rønning, whose writings include the novel *Gutten fra Norge* ("The Boy from Norway"—1924) and a volume of exuberant sketches called *Bare for moro* ("Just for Fun"—1913); a popular regional novelist like Martha Ostenso, who wrote such books as *Wild Geese* and the *Stone Field* in English for the larger American public; and numerous other authors who interested themselves in immigrant backgrounds and problems.[59]

The pioneer efforts of Svein Nilsson to preserve the history of the Norwegian pioneers had no quick sequel in systematic efforts by historians, but they were not forgotten. The theme of the great folk movement was one of irresistible attraction within the Norwegian-American domain, though American historians—Frederick Jackson Turner and Kendric C. Babcock were notable exceptions—as yet had little understanding of its significance for social and cultural history. Knud Langeland, the pioneer editor, took up the theme in his *Nordmændene i Amerika* in 1889, with the Aeneas touch of a writer who had himself played a part in the events that he chronicled. In 1895 the indefatigable Rasmus B. Anderson produced his *First Chapter of Norwegian Immigration*, drawing heavily upon Svein Nilsson, and incidentally for the first time making that collector's narratives available in English. Anderson also mobilized much

[59] Some excellent criticisms of Norwegian-American literature appeared from time to time in *Symra*, a literary periodical that did much to forward general Norwegian-American interest in letters. Wist wrote about Strømme in 1:144–158 (1905); Strømme on Ager, in 3:137–147 (1907); Ager on O. S. Sneve, 7:214–224 (1911), and on Wilhelm M. Pettersen, 4:67–78 (1908); and Michael A. Mikkelsen on Boyesen, 2:60–76 (1906). A revealing autobiography is Rønning's *Fifty Years in America* (Minneapolis, 1938).

fresh material by means of his own curiosity and a wide appeal to pioneers who remembered early events.

The widening popular interest in the field was reflected in a compendious two-volume work on the Scandinavians in the United States brought out in English by O. N. Nelson in 1901; and in Hjalmar R. Holand's *De norske settlementers historie,* published in 1908. Holand made available an entertaining survey written after extensive travels in the settlements and presenting a wider geographical and chronological sweep than that of earlier works. A year later Professor George T. Flom issued a documented monograph on Norwegian immigration to 1848, prefacing it with an assertion that American historians ultimately would give greater attention than they had done in the past "to the immigrant pioneer as a factor in the development of the nation." Flom's colleague, Kendric C. Babcock, took a step toward fulfilling this prophecy when in 1914 he issued a book on the *Scandinavian Element in the United States.* Wist gave particular attention to the history of the Norwegian-American press in a co-operative volume that he edited in 1914; and Dr. Evjen two years later produced a scholarly work on *Scandinavian Immigrants in New York 1630–1674.* Many other writers, compilers, and editors, lay and professional, gradually added to the sum total of historical — and antiquarian — information in the field, and their writings were always cordially welcomed by Norwegian-American newspapers and periodicals. In 1925, at the time of the Norse-American centennial, Dr. O. M. Norlie issued an encyclopedic compilation entitled *History of the Norwegian People in America.*

It was now evident that the time had come for an integrated program of collecting, editing, and scholarly writing, spreading a wide net for materials both in Norway and in America, inviting the co-operation of many trained scholars, and employing the professional techniques and standards of modern historical research. Such a program was achieved through the Norwegian-American Historical Association, founded in the year that marked the centennial of the arrival of the sloop folk. The association was a broad co-operative enterprise which interpreted its problems in the general setting of American history, collected extensive materials in Norway, and called upon the aid of trained scholars on the one hand and business and professional leaders on the other. Men like Gjerset, Laurence M. Larson, and Rølvaag stood beside Birger Osland, Magnus Swenson, Arthur Andersen, D. G. Ristad, and Kristian Prestgard in the leadership of the enterprise. Its spirit was interpreted by Mr. Andersen, who assumed the presidency of the association in 1936. "We must strike while the iron is hot," he said. He called for a broad and aggressive program of work and pointed out that "If the task is postponed, its difficulty will greatly increase and it will inevitably suffer in accuracy and completeness." In the first decade and a half of its activity the association has published more than twenty volumes of essays, monographs, edited documents and narratives, recollections, and other historical materials centering about the story of the Norwegians in the New World.[60]

It is not without interest to recall that Rølvaag was one of the founders of the Norwegian-American Historical Association and that the year in which it was launched also witnessed the appearance, in Norway and in Norwegian dress, of the second part of his novel *Giants in the Earth*.[61] Rølvaag marked the climax of a creative experimentation in Norwegian-American letters which had been in process for more than a half century before the appearance of *Giants in the Earth*. The many writers who preceded him wrote their

[60] See the publication entitled *A Review and a Challenge* issued in 1938 by the Norwegian-American Historical Association at the instance of its president, Mr. Arthur Andersen of Chicago. An essay by Wist, "Vor historiske literatur," in *Symra,* 5:127–143 (1909), is of more than passing interest.

[61] Kenneth Bjørk, "The Unknown Rølvaag: Secretary in the Norwegian-American Historical Association," in *Studies and Records,* 11:114–149.

novels, for the most part, in Norwegian and brought them out either privately or through local publishers who had difficulty in finding an audience. Consequently these authors won almost no financial rewards and necessarily had to earn a livelihood by some other means than writing—the versatile Buslett, for example, as a dealer in groceries and meats. Rølvaag himself had almost no market for his earlier production, and it was only near the end of his career that he emancipated himself from Norwegian-American bonds and succeeded in reaching the general public of America and the world. From first to last, however, he was a Norwegian American, as his novels testify—*Amerika-breve* ("The America Letters"), *Paa glemte veie* ("On Forgotten Paths"), *The Boat of Longing, Pure Gold, Giants in the Earth, Peder Victorious,* and *Their Fathers' God.* "Everything of consequence that he wrote," according to Professor Haugen, "was either a loving delineation or a bitter scourging of his Norwegian people in America."[62]

Rølvaag's masterpiece was characterized by the *Nation* as the "fullest, finest, and most powerful novel that has been written about pioneer life in America." Its truth was not merely that of a realistic portrayal of scenes and events, but also that of a wise understanding of the psychological realities underlying the immigrant frontier experience. It is this work which, of all the Rølvaag books, is best remembered by American readers. The bigness of the theme of *Giants in the Earth,* the earthy quality of its drama, and the fecund power with which Rølvaag conceived the story and breathed

[62] See Haugen, in *Studies and Records,* 7:53; and his sketch of Rølvaag in the *Dictionary of American Biography,* 16:124. Rølvaag surveyed broadly the cultural achievements of his countrymen in America in a series of brief essays that he wrote under the general title "Skogen som klædde fjeldet," in Rølvaag and Eikeland, *Norsk læsebok,* 2:329–367. This volume, one of a series of three compiled by the two St. Olaf College professors, was wholly edited by Rølvaag himself. It is a collection of readings for academies, high schools, and homes, and many of the selections included are by Rølvaag. The work as a whole is broad in scope and remarkably interesting.

life into its characters explain the tendency to emphasize this one book. Historically considered, however, it is Rølvaag's entire production — from the immigrant letters which reflected his own experiences as a newcomer in America to his final novel, which concerned itself with the intricate problems of the second generation — that assumes increasing significance with the passing years; and the reason is plain. For Rølvaag in the sweep of his entire work, with deeper insight and greater effectiveness than any other writer, recorded and interpreted the American transition of the legions of Norwegian immigrants who made their way to the western world. That, rather than pioneer life itself, was the grand theme of his writing; and it is a clue to the dynamic quality of his whole production. His thinking was centered upon the living relationship between past and present. Understanding of the past, coupled with insight into its impingement upon the present, seemed all-important to him. "It is vital in all cultural life," he wrote in 1926, "to maintain a link between the present and the past. If there is anything history makes clear it is this, that when a people becomes interested in its past life, seeks to acquire knowledge in order better to understand itself, it always experiences an awakening of new life."[63]

[63] Quoted by Bjørk, in *Studies and Records,* 11:121. A little-known work of Rølvaag is his *Fortællinger og skildringer* ("Stories and Sketches"), a compilation issued in Minneapolis in 1932, with a biographical introduction by Waldemar Ager. D. G. Ristad, in an essay on *Den norske innsats i amerikansk kulturliv* (1927), discusses, among other things, the literature of the Norwegian Americans and suggests that it has served the double purpose of illuminating the saga of the pioneers and of forwarding an understanding of the spiritual values that the "land takers" who came into the "new kingdom" cherished.

APPENDIX

JOHN QUINCY ADAMS AND THE SLOOP "RESTORATION"

No chapter in the history of Norwegian migration to America has proved at once so fascinating and so baffling as that which centers about the sloop folk of 1825 and their diminutive vessel, the "Restauration," or "Restoration"—the "Mayflower" of the Norwegians in the New World. The story has the inevitable interest that hovers over the beginnings of an important movement. The Quaker influence and the complexity of the motives of the immigrants add appreciably to its flavor. In the background looms the somewhat enigmatic figure of Cleng Peerson, the trail blazer of the Norwegian immigrants. Elements of adventure and courage are not lacking; and there is a tang of saga about the fourteen-week voyage from Stavanger to New York by way of Funchal in Madeira.[1]

[1] The route taken by the "Restoration" has been the subject of considerable discussion, and some writers have suggested that the ship was driven off its intended course and went to Madeira by accident. There is excellent reason for believing, however, that it intended to go precisely where it did go. The same route was followed in 1818 by the Norwegian vessel "Prima" of Larvik, which carried a party of German emigrants from Bergen, where they had been stranded,

For more than two generations historians have told and retold the story of the "Restoration." In 1925 the centennial of its arrival was celebrated with pomp and ceremony; Calvin Coolidge, essaying the role of historian, spun the tale to the nation; and the United States government accorded the event due philatelic recognition. Meanwhile, scholars have hunted high and low, both in Norway and in America, for every scrap of evidence that might shed contemporary light upon the migration of 1825. A generation ago a historian of the Scandinavians in America, discussing the "Restoration" and the immigrants of 1825, declared that the "lack of documentary evidence in the case is so obvious that no writer on the topic has been able to reproduce, or even to mention, a single original document in support of his assertions or theories."[2] This was not strictly true, but it was evidence of a painful paucity of material. Since then many small bits, and a few larger items, of contemporary source material have rewarded the probing patience and industry of scholars. These fragments, pieced together and interpreted, have proved of genuine importance, and have given the story as a whole a firm foundation.[3] There have been few major "finds," however. No "Restoration" diary has turned up — perhaps none was kept. Save for a few newspaper reports of unusual interest, no contemporary narratives of the

to Baltimore. This vessel steered a course through the English Channel, south along the European mainland, and to the Madeira Islands, in order, as one of the crew said, "to avail ourselves of the eastern trade winds, which in these tropical waters at this time of year blow directly to the West Indies." The voyage took three months. See records in the Bergen tariff books, Riksarkiv, Oslo, and in the Secretary's Files, Treasury Annex, Washington, D. C. The story is told briefly by Fredrik Scheel in Scheel and Worm-Müller, *Den norske sjøfarts historie,* vol. 2, pt. 1, p. 138. When to all this is added the fact that Yankee merchant vessels bound for the Baltic region in this period customarily sailed by way of the West Indies, Fayal in the Azores, and sometimes Madeira, it seems safe to conclude that the skipper of the "Restoration" took the general course that he planned to take. "Massachusetts approached Russia," according to Samuel E. Morison, "by a long détour in Southern waters." *Maritime History of Massachusetts, 1783–1860,* 293 (Boston and New York, 1921).

[2] Nelson, *Scandinavians in the United States,* 1:126.

[3] The footnotes accompanying the discussion of the "Restoration" in the writer's *Norwegian Migration to America, 1825–1860,* 24–56, 381–396, may serve as a guide to the materials available on the subject up to 1931.

enterprise have appeared. Even the list of the passengers on the famous sloop — and there is now a society of the descendants of the sloop folk — has had to be reconstructed from stray items of contemporary evidence plus reminiscence and tradition, with the unhappy result that no two scholars agree precisely on the personnel of the party. Taking into account both the interest of the story and the scarcity of documentary evidence, therefore, it is pleasant to be able to report the discovery of some hitherto unknown, and not unimportant, contemporary material about this chapter in American history.

When the "Restoration" arrived in New York on October 9, 1825, with the first shipload of modern Norwegian immigrants to the United States, it carried forty-six passengers (including an infant born at sea) and a crew of seven. The vessel, which had been purchased by the emigrants in Norway before their departure from Stavanger on July 4 or 5,[4] measured about thirty-nine tons. Thus, as Professor Cadbury has pointed out, the Norwegian "Mayflower" was less than a fourth of the size of the original "Mayflower."[5] The United States customs officials in New York generously credited the "Restoration" with a trifle more than sixty tons, but this concession did not prevent its owners — evidently a half dozen or more of the principal persons in the party as a

[4] The interesting problem of the date of the sailing of the "Restoration" from Stavanger is discussed in *Norwegian Migration,* 393–395. The traditional date of sailing is July 4, 1825, but a Norwegian newspaper item dated July 7, 1825, refers to the sailing as having occurred "Iforgaars" — that is, the day before yesterday, or July 5. Notwithstanding this bit of evidence, it now appears that the traditional date cannot be summarily set aside, for three New York newspapers list ninety-eight days as the length of the "Restoration" voyage These are the October 10, 1825, issues of the *New York Evening Post,* the *New York Statesman,* and the *New York Mercantile Advertiser.* In order to get a total of ninety-eight days, one must include both July 4, the traditional sailing date, and October 9, the known date of arrival. In a word, if the sloop started on July 5, the total number of sailing days could not possibly have been reported as more than ninety-seven. In one of the documents printed below the sloop leaders refer explicitly to the length of the voyage as fourteen weeks.

[5] The sloop measured 18.5 commercial lasts, or 38.48 tons. See *Norwegian Migration,* 41; Scheel, in *Nordmands-forbundet,* 16:324 (1923); and Henry J. Cadbury, "The Norwegian Quakers of 1825," in *Studies and Records,* 1:60–94.

whole — from running afoul of the American federal law of 1819 which allowed only two passengers to each five tons of a vessel landing at an American port.[6] Even conceding sixty tons and a fraction, American officials found that the sloop carried twenty-one passengers too many. Under the act of 1819, therefore, its owners incurred the penalty of confiscation of the vessel and a fine of $3,150 — that is, $150 for each passenger in excess of the number legally permissible. The seizure of the sloop was an untoward and discouraging circumstance, but to the immigrants, who were almost penniless and who gratefully accepted the charity of kindhearted Quakers in New York, the fine, unless it should be remitted, meant disaster.[7]

It was this episode that Ole Rynning described in his *True Account of America,* published at Christiania in 1838: "It created universal surprise in New York that the Norwegians had ventured over the wide sea in so small a vessel, a feat hitherto unheard of. Either through ignorance or through misunderstanding the ship had carried more passengers than the American laws permitted, and therefore the skipper and the ship with its cargo were seized by the authorities. Now I cannot say with certainty whether the government voluntarily dropped the matter in consideration of the ignorance and childlike conduct of our good countrymen, or whether the Quakers had already at this time interceded on their behalf; at all events the skipper was released, and the ship and its cargo were returned to their owners. They lost considerably by the sale of the same, however, which did not bring them more than four hundred dollars."[8]

[6] "An Act regulating passenger ships and vessels." *Statutes at Large,* 3:488.

[7] Even so small a charge as $3.60 for tonnage duties must have seemed burdensome to the sloop folk. This charge was on the basis of sixty cents per ton. See "Abstract of Tonnage Duties and Light Money — Arrivals 1825–1827," a manuscript in the Custom House, New York. This tonnage measurement is dated October 14, 1825. On the aid of the Quakers, see Anderson, *First Chapter,* 64; and Rynning, *True Account of America,* 73. John Cox, Jr., in *Quakerism in the City of New York, 1657–1930,* 49 (New York, 1930), mentions the Quaker aid, but adduces no evidence on the subject from Quaker sources.

[8] *True Account of America,* 72.

In the light of newly discovered documents, it is now possible to reconstruct the events centering about the seizure of the "Restoration" with a degree of precision lacking in Rynning's account, though his version, in its main outlines, is not far from the truth. What happened was that the "Restoration" was seized and libeled in federal court in consequence of its violation of the law of 1819. The nature of the libel is set forth in a formal legal document addressed to the United States district court for the southern district of New York by the United States district attorney, Robert Tillotson, on October 13, 1825, four days after the "Restoration" arrived in New York. This document brings out the fact that the vessel was "seized as forfeited" on October 12 by the surveyor of the customs, Joseph G. Swift. The attorney called upon the district court to make the forfeiture definitive after citing the sloop people to "answer the premises." The document follows:

The Libel of the "Restoration," October 13, 1825

[Miscellaneous Admiralty Cases, Archives of the Federal District Court, Southern District, New York — D. S.]

District Court U States

At a Special District Court of the United States of America for the Southern District of New York, held at the City of New York in the said District on the thirteenth day of October in the year of our Lord one thousand eight hundred and twenty five, comes Robert Tillotson Attorney of the said United States for the said Southern District of New York, who prosecutes for the said United States in this behalf, and being present in this Honorable Court in his proper person in the name and on behalf of the said United States, alleges propounds and declares as follows, that is to say:

First — That Joseph G Swift surveyor of the Customs for the District of the City of New York, on the twelfth day of October in the year of our Lord one thousand eight hundred and twenty five, at the City of New York in the Southern District of New York aforesaid, seized as forfeited to the use of the United States, the Sloop or Vessel called the Restoration, her tackle apparel and furniture, being the property of some person or persons to the said Attorney as yet unknown.

Secondly — That the said Sloop or Vessel being of the burthen of sixty tons and no more, and being owned in whole or in part by a subject or subjects, citizen or citizens of some foreign country to the said Attorney as yet unknown, the Master or other person on board of the said Sloop or Vessel, did, after the first day of January in the year of our Lord one thousand eight hundred and twenty, take on board the said Vessel at some foreign port or place, and did bring and convey into the United States on board of the said Vessel a number of passengers exceeding the proportion of two persons to every five tons of such Sloop or Vessel, by the number of twenty one passengers and upwards; whereby the aforesaid Sloop or Vessel became and is forfeited to the use of the said United States, pursuant to the act of Congress in such case made and provided.

Lastly — That all and singular the premises are and were true public and notorious, of which due proof being made, the said Attorney prays the usual process and monition of this Honorable Court in this behalf to be made, and that all persons interested in the said Sloop or Vessel may be cited in general and Special to answer the premises and all due proceedings being had that the said Sloop or Vessel together with her tackles apparel and furniture — may for the causes aforesaid and others appearing be condemned by the definitive sentence and decree of this Honorable Court as forfeited to the use of the United States according to the form and effect of such act in such case made and provided.

R. Tillotson, Atty U. S. &c

[*Endorsed*] District Court U. S. The United States vs The Sloop Restoration. Libel Rob[t] Tillotson Atty U. S. Filed Octr 13th 1825.

On the same day that this libel was filed in the district court, the sloop was bonded in the amount of six hundred dollars, with Francis Thompson as surety. The appearance of this name, new in the annals of the sloop folk, adds another item to their Quaker connections, for Francis Thompson was a prominent New York Quaker, one of the founders of the famous Black Ball Line, which ran packet ships between New York and Liverpool.[9] Here he appears in the role of a friend to the Norwegian immigrants of 1825, whose leader was the Quaker Lars Larsen. The document relating to the bonding bears an interesting authorization by the judge of the district court, William P. Van Ness.

The Bonding of the "Restoration," October 13, 1825

[Miscellaneous Admiralty Cases, Archives of the Federal District Court, Southern District, New York — D. S.]

District Court U. S. The United States &c vs The Sloop Restoration her tackle &c — Johanes Stene[10] and other claimants.

It is agreed that the Vessel — above named may be bonded at the agreed Value of Six hundred — Dollars, and that Francis Thompson be the surety on the Bond. Dated 13. Octr 1825.

Jonathan Thompson Collector

I concur in the above.
R W. Tillotson U S A.

The Clerk is authorized to swear the petitioners to their petition in the above cause, then to transmit exemplified Copies of the proceedings thereon to the Secretary of the Treasury. Oct 13. 1825.

W. P Van Ness

[*Endorsed*] District Court U S. The United States vs The Sloop Restoration &c. Consent to Bond &c Filed Octr 13. 1825

On the next day, Friday, October 14, 1825, a hearing on the case of the "Restoration" was held in the same court, with Judge Van Ness presiding. Three petitioners appeared before him — Lars Larsen, Johannes Steen, and Lars O. Helland. They jointly petitioned the court to "enquire in a summary manner into the circumstances" of their case and to forward the facts to the secretary of the treasury with a

[9] Cox, *Quakerism in the City of New York,* 134. Francis Thompson made the "immigrant trade" his distinctive field, according to Professor Albion, and he and his nephew Samuel were "among the first and for a while the most active immigrant agents in this country." Robert G. Albion, *Square-riggers on Schedule,* 113 (Princeton, New Jersey, 1938).

[10] The name "Johanes Stene" is written above that of "Lars Larson," which has been crossed out.

District Court U. S.

The United States vs
The Sloop Restoration
her tackle &c
Johannes Stone and
others claimants —

It is agreed that the Vessel above named may be bonded at the agreed Value of Six hundred Dollars, and that Francis Thompson be the surety on the Bond. Dated 13. Octr 1825.

Jonathan Thompson
Collector

I Concur in the above —
R. H. Gibbs(?) M. D.(?)

The Clerk is authorized to swear the petitioners to their petition in the above cause, & then to transmit exemplified Copies of the proceedings thereon to the Secretary of the Treasury — Oct 13. 1825.

[illegible] Judge(?)

THE BONDING OF THE "RESTORATION"
[From the original document in the archives of the federal district court, New York City.]

view to the remission of the forfeiture and penalties they had incurred. They were required to make "solemn oath that the contents of the said petition are just and true," and after certain other formalities Judge Van Ness duly ordered the clerk of court, one James Dill, to forward the petition of the sloop leaders to the secretary of the treasury. This was done on the day of the hearing, October 14.

The petition is a document of extraordinary interest. It is nothing less than a firsthand narrative of the story of the sloop folk, signed by the three principal persons of that famous party, and dated only five days after the "Restoration" arrived in America. It is the first contemporary narrative by participants in the sloop migration that has come to light. Its interest is not lessened by the fact that Larsen, Steen, and Helland testify in their joint statement to the significant role of Cleng Peerson in the initiation of modern Norwegian migration to America. In fact, they make that role even more important than historians have considered it. They add, at several points, interesting bits of new information; and the freshness of the document is not the less genuine because it is brief and bears the marks of legal phraseology and of an interpreter. The documents do not reveal the identity of the interpreter, but one suspects that he was none other than Cleng Peerson himself.

The original of the petition, bearing the authentic signatures of Larsen, Steen, and Helland, has been found by the writer in the archives of the federal district court in New York. It is herewith printed in full:

The Petition of Lars Larsen, Johannes Steen, and Lars O. Helland, October 14, 1825

[Petitions for Remission, Archives of the Federal District Court, Southern District, New York — D. S.]

To the Honorable William P Van Ness, Judge of the District Court of the United States of America for the Southern District of New York.

The Petition of Lars Larson and Johanes Stene on behalf of themselves and others owners of the Norwegian Sloop or Vessel called the Restoration, and Lars O Helland, Master of the said Sloop

Respectfully represents — that one Clang Peerson,[11] a native of Norway, left his home upwards of four years ago, as your Petitioners are informed and believe, and came to the United States, where he purchased land for himself in the Pultney Estate or tract,[12] in the County of Orleans in the State of New York. That in the year 1824 the said Clang Peerson returned home to Norway, where he gave an account of his travels in America, and represented to his friends the favorable condition of the Country, and urged upon them the advantages they would gain by emigrating to it.[13] That the Petitioners and others, amounting in all to forty five persons, principally relatives and friends of the said Clang Peerson, purchased the said Sloop in Norway aforesaid, took on board a few tons of iron for ballast, and provisions for the voyage, and thereupon, after having been regularly cleared at the Port of Stavanger in Norway aforesaid,[14] took their departure for the Port of New York, where they arrived in the said Sloop, after a passage of fourteen weeks, on the ninth of October instant. That the said Sloop being of the burthen of about sixty tons Custom House measurement, and having on board upwards of twenty passengers above the number allowed by law to a Vessel of the tonnage of the said Sloop, in consequence whereof the Collector of this Port of New York caused the said Vessel to be seized and Libelled in this Honorable Court, as forfeited to the said United States under the second section of the act of Congress entitled "an act regulating passenger

[11] The usual spelling of the name is "Cleng Peerson." See my article on Peerson in the *Dictionary of American Biography,* 14:390. It may be added, apropos of the spelling of names, that Lars Larsen is more commonly known as "Lars Larson" and seems to have accepted that spelling later in his life. There seems to be no doubt, however, that he used the form "Larsen" in 1825. Johannes Steen appears sometimes as "Stene" or as "Steene," and in some documents his first name is spelled "Johanes."

[12] This is a confirmation of the suggestion made in *Norwegian Migration,* 39, 53, 391, of a connection of the sloop folk with the Pultney lands.

[13] On Peerson's return to Norway in 1824, see *Norwegian Migration,* 38 ff.

[14] The "Restoration's" ship papers, bearing the record of clearance at Stavanger on June 27, 1825, were turned over by Captain Helland to Consul Henry Gahn in New York. Gahn in turn entrusted them to C. H. Valeur, who sent them to the Norwegian Finance Department with a letter dated November 29, 1826. These precious papers are now preserved in the Riksarkiv, Oslo: F. D. Journalsaker 456/1826 F. I have had a transcript made of these documents, which include a list of the crew, a description of the cargo, and sundry other items.

To the Honorable William P. Van Neſs Judge of the District Court of the United States of America for the Southern District of New York.

The Petition of Lars Larson, and Johanes Stene on behalf of themselves and others owners of the Norwegian Sloop or Veſsel called the Restoration, and Lars O Helland, Master of the said Sloop

Respectfully represents— That one Clang Peerson, a native of Norway, left his home upwards of four years ago, as your Petitioners are informed and believe, and came to the United States, where he purchased land for himself in the Pultney estate or tract, in the County of Orleans in the State of New York — That in the year 1824 the said Clang Peerson returned home to Norway, where he gave an account of his travels in America, and represented to his friends the favorable condition of the country, and urged upon them the advantages they would gain by emigrating to it. That the Petitioners and others, amounting in all to forty five persons, principally relatives and friends of the said Clang Peerson, purchased the said Sloop in Norway aforesaid, took on board a few tons of iron for ballast, and provisions for the voyage, and thereupon, after having been regularly cleared at the port of Stavanger in Norway aforesaid, took their departure for the Port of New York, where they arrived in the said Sloop, after a paſsage of fourteen weeks, on the ninth of October instant. That the said Sloop being of the burthen of about sixty tons Custom House measurement, and having on board upwards of twenty paſsengers above the number allowed by law to a Veſsel of the tonnage of the said Sloop, in consequence whereof the Collector of this Port of New York caused the said Veſsel to be seized and libelled in this Honorable Court, as forfeited to the said United States under the second section of the act of Congreſs

The Petition of the Sloop Folk
[From the original document in the archives of the federal district court, New York City.]

entitled "an act regulating Passenger Ships and Vessels", passed 2 March 1819 — And your Petitioner the said Lars O Helland is informed that he has also incurred the penalty of one hundred and fifty dollars for each passenger over the number allowed by the said act to the said Vessel, which being twenty one persons amounts to three thousand one hundred & fifty dollars, under the first Section of the aforesaid act. And your Petitioners further represent that they and the said passengers are all entirely ignorant of the language and laws of this ~~United States~~ Country — That they came hither for the purpose of forming a settlement on some of the uncultivated lands in this State, and are anxious to set out for the place of their destination before the ice or snow obstruct their passage by water — And the Petitioners declare that the penalties aforesaid have been incurred in consequence of their utter ignorance of the laws of this Country and without any intent or expectation whatever to violate any law of the United States.

Under these circumstances your Petitioners humbly pray that your Honor would be pleased to enquire in a summary manner into the circumstances of your Petitioners case, pursuant to the provisions of "An Act to provide for the mitigating and remitting the forfeitures, penalties and disabilities therein mentioned," approved March 3d. 1797 — and cause the facts which shall appear upon such enquiry to be stated, and that your Honor would cause the same to be transmitted to the Honorable the Secretary of the Treasury of the United States to the end that the forfeiture of the said Vessel and the aforesaid penalty so as aforesaid incurred may be remitted to your Petitioners —

THE PETITION OF THE SLOOP FOLK — PAGE 2

And your Petitioners will ever pray &c

A Woodward
Proctor.

Lars Larsen
fuldmægtig for
Lars O. Helland

Sworn in open Court
this 14 day of October
1825 and explained
to the Petitioners by a sworn interpreter
James Dill Clerk

THE PETITION OF THE SLOOP FOLK — PAGE 3

Ships and Vessels," passed 2d March 1819. And your Petitioner the said Lars O. Helland is informed that he has also incurred the penalty of one hundred and fifty dollars for each passenger over the number allowed by the said act to the said Vessel, which being twenty one persons amounts to three thousand one hundred & fifty dollars, under the first section of the aforesaid act. And your Petitioners further represent that they and the said Passengers are all entirely ignorant of the language and laws of this Country. That they came hither for the purpose of forming a settlement on some of the uncultivated lands in this State, and are anxious to set out for the place of their destination before the ice shall obstruct their passage by water. And the Petitioners declare that the penalties aforesaid have been incurred in consequence of their utter ignorance of the laws of this Country and without any intent or expectation whatever to violate any law of the United States.

Under these Circumstances your Petitioners humbly pray that your Honor would be pleased to enquire in a summary manner into the circumstances of your Petitioners case, pursuant to the provisions of "An Act to provide for the mitigating and remitting the forfeitures, penalties and disabilities therein mentioned," approved March 3d 1797, and cause the facts which shall appear upon such enquiry to be stated, and that your Honor would cause the same to be transmitted to the Honorable the Secretary of the Treasury of the United States to the end that the forfeiture of the said Vessel and the aforesaid penalty so as aforesaid incurred may be remitted to your Petitioners.

District Court U. S.

The United States
vs
The Sloop Restoration
Johanes Stene and
others, claimants —

Petition for remission &c
A. Woodward
Proctor

Service of Copies of the Petition in this case is hereby admitted, and it is consented that the same may be presented to the Court and heard without further notice. Dated 14 Oct 1825

Jonathan Thompson
Collector
Robt. Tillotson
atty U. S.

THE PETITION OF THE SLOOP FOLK — ENDORSEMENTS

And your petitioners will ever pray &c

LARS LARSEN
JOHANES STEEN
LARS O. HELLAND

A WOODWARD Proctor.

Sworn in open Court this 14 day of October 1825, and explained to the Petitioners by a sworn interpreter.

JAMES DILL Clerk

[*Endorsed*] District Court U. S. The United States vs The Sloop Restoration Johanes Stene and others, claimants — Petition for remission &c

A WOODWARD *Proctor*

Service of copies of the Petition in this case is hereby admitted, and it is consented that the same may be presented to the Court and heard without further notice. Date 14. Oct 1825.

JONATHAN THOMPSON Collector
ROB[t] TILLOTSON Atty U. S.

Filed Octr 14. 1825

Dill, the clerk of court, transmitted a copy of this petition to Washington, sending at the same time two formal documents — printed forms with various blanks filled out. One was a report of the hearing of October 14 "In the matter of the Petition of Johanes Stene and others, claimants of the Sloop Restoration," with the judge's order that the matter be placed before the secretary of the treasury. The other was a form statement by Dill certifying "that the Writings annexed to this Certificate are true copies of their respective Originals, on file, and remaining of record in my office." All these documents have been found in the National Archives at Washington.

A copy of the petition of the three leaders of the sloop passed through the hands of the president of the United States, John Quincy Adams. Acting upon the information that it contained, he freed the sloop folk from the penalties of the law of 1819; and the document bears an endorsement

At a Special District Court of the United States of America, held for the Southern District of New-York, at the City of New-York, on Friday the fourteenth day of October 1825.

PRESENT,

The Honourable WILLIAM P. VAN NESS, *Esq.* Judge of said Court.

In the matter of the Petition of Johannes Stene and others, claimants of the Sloop Restoration —

THE Petitioners came this day into Court and presented to the Court a petition (a copy of which is hereto annexed) praying, for the reasons therein mentioned, that the Court would make summary inquiry into the circumstances of the case, and certify to the Secretary of the Treasury of the United States such facts as to the said Court should thereupon satisfactorily appear, and it appearing to the Court that reasonable notice had been given by the Petitioners as well to the Attorney of the United States as to the Collector of the District of the City of New York of their intention to present to the Court the said Petition, and the said Attorney being present in Court and the said Collector not attending, the Court proceeded to the said inquiry: **Whereupon** the petitioners made solemn oath that the contents of the said petition are just and true. And no other evidence was offered to the Court by the said Petitioners or by the Attorney of the United States or the said Collector, and the Petitioners were not cross examined on behalf of the United States: **Thereupon,**

It is ordered by the Court, that the Clerk annex a statement of the facts which so appeared upon the said inquiry to the Petition aforesaid, and transmit the same with a Copy of the said Petition under the seal of the Court, to the Secretary of the Treasury of the United States: All of which is done by these presents.

Witness, *The Honourable* WILLIAM P. VAN NESS, *Esquire,* Judge of said Court, at the City of New-York, in the Southern District of New-York, this fourteenth day of October — in the year of our Lord one thousand eight hundred and twenty five — and of our Independence the fiftieth.

James Dill

Clerk of the Southern District of New-York.

A REPORT ON THE HEARING OF THE SLOOP FOLK IN NEW YORK, OCTOBER 14, 1825

[From the original document in the National Archives.]

signed by him personally. That President Adams had any knowledge of the coming to America of the sloop folk, much less that he took official cognizance of the event in any way, has not hitherto been known. The documents link, in friendly fashion, the name of one of America's great statesmen with the saga of the "Restoration."

Endorsements Made at Washington on Copy of Petition of Lars Larsen, Johannes Steen, and Lars O. Helland

[The National Archives, Washington, D. C.: Records of the Department of State, Pardons, vol. iv (March 18, 1822, to February 19, 1836)]

Case of the Norwegian Sloop Restoration.

Petition of Johanes Stene and others,—New York, Oct. 14. 1825, Under act of congress of March 3. 1825[15] relative to passenger ships.

Let the penalty and forfeitures be remitted on payment of costs so far as the United States are concerned.

J. Q. Adams.[16]

November 5. 1825

Remission made out under date of Nov. 15. 1825, and transmitted to T. Morris, Marshal Southern D^{t} of N York Nov. 16. 1825.

W. S[lade]

A presidential pardon of the sloop folk was issued by special proclamation on November 15, 1825, and was signed by President Adams and by his secretary of state.[17] Thus is added to the story, in addition to the name of President Adams, that of another distinguished figure in American history, Henry Clay.

[15] This is an error. The correct date is March 2, 1819. *Statutes at Large,* 3: 488.

[16] This signature is in the hand of President Adams himself. It may be noted that he had once briefly visited Norway. In 1809, while on his way to St. Petersburg, Adams was detained for a few days near Christiansand, Norway. A letter written by him from that Norwegian city on September 23, 1809, is in W. C. Ford, ed., *Writings of John Quincy Adams,* 3: 343–345 (New York, 1914); and he also tells of his experiences at the time in his *Memoirs,* 2: 19–25 (Philadelphia, 1874).

[17] The documents preserved at Washington include, in addition to the finished draft of this proclamation, a rough draft containing various changes and corrections.

Case of the Norwegian Sloop
Restoration.

Petition of Johannes Stene
and others, — New York,
Oct 14. 1825,

Under act of congress
of March 3. 1825 relative
to passenger ships.

Let the penalty and
forfeitures be remitted
on payment of costs
so far as the United
States are concerned.
J. Q. Adams.

November 5. 1825

Remission made out under date
of Nov. 15. 1825, and transmitted to
T. Morris. Marshal Southern Dt. of N York
Nov. 16. 1825. W. S—

ENDORSEMENTS ON THE WASHINGTON COPY OF THE SLOOP FOLK'S PETITION

[From a manuscript copy in the National Archives.]

John Quincy Adams, President of the United States of America

To all who shall see these presents, Greeting

Whereas the Norwegian Sloop, Restoration, whereof Lars Larson and Johannes Steene and others are owners, and Lars O Helland is Master, has become forfeited by a violation of a Law of the United States, entitled "An Act regulating Passenger Ships and vessels," and the said Owners and Master have, severally, incurred the penalty imposed by the first section of said Act;—and whereas it has been made to appear, satisfactorily, that the violation of said Law as aforesaid was committed through ignorance, the said Master and owners being Foreigners, and entirely unacquainted with the language and Laws of the United States:—

Now, therefore, I, John Quincy Adams, President of the United States, in consideration of the premises, divers other good causes me thereunto moving, have pardoned, and do hereby pardon, the offence aforesaid, and have remitted, and do hereby remit, unto the said owners and master, all and singular the pains, penalties and forfeitures thereby incurred so far forth as the United States have any claim, interest or concern therein; On condition, nevertheless, that all costs which may have accrued in any prosecution for said breach of Law, be first paid and satisfied by the parties implicated therein.

L. S. In testimony whereof, I have hereunto subscribed my name, and caused the Seal of the United States to be affixed to these presents. Given at the city of Washington, this 15th day of November, A.D. 1825, and of the Independence of the United States, the fiftieth.

(Signed) J Q. Adams

By the President (Signed) H. Clay, Secretary of State.

PRESIDENT ADAMS PARDONS THE SLOOP FOLK
[From a manuscript copy in the National Archives.]

PRESIDENT JOHN QUINCY ADAMS' PROCLAMATION OF PARDON, November 15, 1825

[The National Archives, Washington, D. C.: Records of the Department of State, Pardons, vol. iv (March 18, 1822, to February 19, 1836) — State Department Copy]

JOHN QUINCY ADAMS, President of the United States of America.
To all who shall see these presents, Greeting

Whereas the Norwegian Sloop, Restoration, whereof Lars Larson and Johannes Steene and others are owners, and Lars O Helland is Master, has become forfeited by a violation of a Law of the United States, entitled "An Act regulating Passenger Ships and vessels," and the said Owners and Master have, severally, incurred the penalty imposed by the first section of said Act;—and whereas it has been made to appear, satisfactorily, that the violation of said Law as aforesaid was committed through ignorance, the said Master and owners being Foreigners, and entirely unacquainted with the language and Laws of the United States: —

Now, therefore, I, John Quincy Adams, President of the United States, in consideration of the premises, divers other good causes me thereunto moving, have pardoned, and do hereby pardon, the offence aforesaid, and have remitted, and do hereby remit, unto the said owners and master, all and singular the pains, penalties and forfeitures thereby incurred so far forth as the United States have any claim, interest or concern therein; on condition, nevertheless, that all costs which may have accrued in any prosecution for said breach of Law, be first paid and satisfied by the parties implicated therein.

In testimony whereof I have hereunto subscribed my name, and caused the Seal of the United States to be affixed to these presents. Given at the City of Washington, this 15th day of November, A. D. 1825, and of the Independence of the United States, the fiftieth.

L. S. (Signed) J. Q. Adams
(Signed) H. Clay, Secretary of State.
By the President

It was this pardon that was transmitted to the United States marshal in New York with the following letter from the department of state on November 16, 1825: [18]

W. Slade, Jr., to Thomas Morris, November 16, 1825

[The National Archives, Washington, D. C.: Records of the Department of State, Domestic Papers, vol. xxi (March 7, 1825, to July 13, 1827) — Letter Book Copy]

Department of State Washington
16th Nov. 1825

Thomas Morris Esq.
Marshal U States, for the
Southern District of New York
Sir,

I have the honour to transmit you the accompanying Act of the President of the United States in the case of the Norwegian

[18] This letter, which I discovered in Washington on December 4, 1939, opened the way to the discovery of the various other documents relating to the "Restoration" case. Unfortunately the original of the pardon has not been found in the New York archives. It seems not unlikely that it was turned over to Captain Helland.

Sloop Restoration, Lars O. Helland, Master, lately libelled in the District Court for your District. You will please give it effect and acknowledge its receipt to this Department.

Very Respectfully, Sir, etc —
(Signed) W. SLADE, Jun.

It should be noted that in the meantime the district court in New York had duly "commanded" the United States marshal to attach the sloop "Restoration" and "to detain the same in your custody until the further order of the Court respecting the same." This order also called for a hearing on November 1 at which the marshal was to report "what you shall have done in the premises" and at which all the persons claiming the vessel should appear. This document, preserved in the district court archives, bears an endorsement by the marshal, Thomas Morris, stating that he had attached the vessel and given due notice to claimants of a hearing on November 1 at which "this Court will . . . proceed to the trial and condemnation thereof, unless a claim should be interposed for the same." One may assume that this was a legal formality and that when the presidential pardon arrived in New York soon after November 16, the entire matter was settled. The document just mentioned bears the following endorsement of date: "Filed 12 May 1826."

Henry Gahn, the Swedish-Norwegian consul stationed in New York at the time the "Restoration" arrived, took a deep interest in the event and recorded it in several communications written in Swedish and addressed to the Norwegian government. Since these documents bear directly upon the seizure and release of the "Restoration," they are here made available, accompanied by translations prepared with the help of Professor George M. Stephenson of the University of Minnesota. The texts were transcribed by the present writer from the original documents in the Riksarkiv in Oslo and were collated under the direction of Mr. H. Blom Svendsen, *førstearkivar* in that institution.[19]

Henry Gahn to the Finance, Trade, and Customs Department of the Norwegian Government, October 15, 1825

[Riksarkiv, Oslo: Finans og Tolddepartementet, Kontor F, Journalsager, 1825/487 — A.L.S.]

Vördsam Berättelse:

Den Nionde innevarande October månad ankom till denna hamn, ifrån Stavanger, den Norrska Slupen Restauration, förd af Skepparen Lars Olsen Helland, med fyratio fem Passagerare, utom Besättningen, och omkring Tjugu Skeppund Stångjärn. Enligt fartygets här företedde Documenter, hvaribland så väl Fri Bref som Latinskt och Algerienskt Pass saknas, så synes det tillhöra Herr Johannes Steen i Stavanger, hvarest utklarerings Tull Passet är påskrifvit: *Passerar fritt,* och dateradt den 27de Junii 1825. Till följe af en Dessa Förenade Staters Lag (Act of Congress), hvilken jag i behörig tid inberättade till Kongl: Maj:ts och Rikets Högloflige Commerce Collegium i Stockholm, är detta fartyg nu här underkastadt Beslag, såsom förande ett långt större antal Passagerare, jämförelsevis till dess drägtighet, än åberopade Lag tillåter, hvilken inskränker detta antal till tvänne Passagerare för hvarje fem Americanska "Tons" efter hitkomna fartygs här förättade mätning. Oagtadt bästa villja till skonsamhet, har man icke kunnat uptaga fartygets nu sålunda uträknade drägt till mer än Femtio fem Tons, ehuru, för fyratio fem Passagerare, skulle åtminstone behöfvas Ett Hundrade Tolf och en half Ton; ett Barn lär hafva tillkommit under Resan, hvarföre, i Lagens strängaste mening, fartygets storlek bordt kunna beräknas till Ett Hundrade Femton Tons. Tull-Directionen härstädes är i sanning brydd öfver denna obehagliga nödvändighet att förfara efter Lag, då fartygets hela värde knapt

[19] Film copies of the Gahn documents have been made for the collections of the Norwegian-American Historical Association and for the Library of Congress. These documents have not hitherto appeared in the original Swedish or in English translations, but parts of two of them, supplied by Mrs. Gudrun Natrud of Oslo, were printed in 1925 in a Norwegian version as part of an article entitled "De kom over havet i et nøddeskal," in *Familiens magasin* (Minneapolis), vol. 36, no. 12, p. 11 (September–October, 1925). Mrs. Natrud originally found the documents and reported them in her calendar of American materials in Norwegian archives compiled for the Norwegian-American Historical Association.

4. prg. 1825 — Jour. 487 1825

Vördsam Berättelse:

Den Nionde innevarande October månad ankom till denna hamn, ifrån Stavanger, den Norrska Slupen Restauration, förd af Skepparen Lars Olsen Helland, med fyratio fem Passagerare, utom Besättningen, och omkring Tjugu Skeppund Stång Järn. Enligt fartygets här företedda documenter hvaribland så väl Förbref som [illegible] [illegible] förnas så synes det tillhöra Herr Johannes Steen i Stavanger, hvarest [illegible] klarerad [illegible] Tull Pagat om påskrift: Passerar [illegible] och daterad den 27de Junii 1825.... Till följe af en dessa Förenade Staters Lag (Act of Congress), hvilken jag i behörig tid inberättade till Kongl: Majestäts och Rikets Högloflige Commerce Collegium i Stockholm, är detta fartyg nu här underkastadt beslag, såsom förande ett långt större antal Passagerare, jämförelsevis till dess dräktighet, än åberopade Lag tillåter, hvilken inskränker detta antal till tvenne Passagerare för hvarje

Läst

First Page of Henry Gahn's Letter to the Norwegian Government, October 15, 1825

[From the original manuscript in the Riksarkiv, Oslo.]

departement af den Kongl. Norrska Regeringen. Detta var den förrsta upplagan af desse Förenade Staters Tull-Taxa, jämte åtskilliga nu gällande Handels och navigations Lagar.

New York den 15 October 1825.

ödmjukast

Henry Gahn

Vördsam Tillaggning. Sedan föregående var skrifvit har jag anmärkt en uppsats, rörande denna händelse, i Evenings Dagblad, hvaraf jag tar mig före tillägga [illegible] utdrag: Man [illegible] i [illegible] till beskaffenheten af Norrska Lasten, men [illegible] för öfrigt framställa saken i sitt verkliga förhållande [illegible] den [illegible] [illegible] [illegible] [illegible] [illegible] Amerikanska [illegible].

[illegible]

Kongl. Norrska Regeringens Finance- Handels och Tull-Departement i Christiania.

Last Page of Henry Gahn's Letter to the Norwegian Government, October 15, 1825

anses svarande emot procedurens omkostningar och besvär; och jag fruktar att denna omständighet ochså torde förhindra sjelfve Skepparen eller hvilken annan Representant som häldst af Rederiets rätt, att här fullfölje de ytterligare mått och steg som eljes ännu kunde leda till restitution af den förverkade Slupen, nemligen, igenom Ansöknings Inlaga till Finance Departementets Secreterare (Secretary of the Treasury) i Washington, hvilken Ansökning Directeuren af härvarande Tullkammare (the Collector) sjelf ädelmodigt erbjuder sig att på allt sätt och vis befordra; men det står icke eller i dess förmåga att eftergifva andras rätt till de umgälder some åtfölja de härvid oundvikeliga formaliteterna. Jag lär ej behöfva erinra att Embetsmanna-Directionen här i landet ifrån den Högsta till den Lägsta, icke kan verka emot eller utöfver gällande Lagars bestämda föreskrifter. Imedlertid skall ingen möjlig åtgärd å min sida uragtlåtas till befordrande af Intressenternes angelägenheter, for hvilka jämväl ett allmänt deltagande här väckts af sjelfva Företagets djerfhet och besynnerliga beskaffenhet. För öfrigt lär jag väl i alla fall böra tillse att icke något vidare misbruk sker med fartygets tilläfventyrs otillräckliga Documenter till fullko[mmen—*ms. torn*] rättighet att föra Norrsk Flagg i aflägsna fa[rva—*ms. torn*]tten.

Vid detta tillfälle torde det tillåtas mig att vördsammast åberopa några Handlingar, som jag, i sidstledne April månad, hade lägenhet att här anförtro en då härifrån afresande Handlande från Bergen, Herr Kentel, för att, vid dess lyckliga återkomst till Norrige, inlämna till vederbörande Departement af den Kongl. Norrska Regeringen. Deribland var den sednaste uplagan af Dessa Förenade Staters Tull Taxa, jämte åtskilliga nu gällande Handels och navigations-Lagar.

New York den 15 October 1825.

ödmjukast

Henry Gahn.

Vördsamm Tilläggning: Sedan föreståande var skrifvit har jag anmärkt en upsats, rörande denne händelse, i ortens Dagblad, hvaraf jag tror mig böra tillägga vidhäftade utdrag. Mann irrar sig väl i anseende till beskaffenheten af *Norrska Läster,* men torde, för öfrigt, framställa saken i sitt verkliga förhållande. Enligt den här förrattade utmätningen har också Slupens drägt blifvit beräknad till Femtio fem Americanska Tons.

[*Addressed*] Till Kongll. Norrska Regeringens Finance-Handels och Tull-Departement i Christiania.

[*Translation*]

RESPECTFULLY SUBMITTED:

On the ninth day of the present month of October there arrived in this port from Stavanger the Norwegian sloop "Restoration," commanded by Skipper Lars Olsen Helland, with forty-five passengers in addition to the crew, and a cargo of about twenty ship pounds of bar iron. According to the ship's documents presented here, which do not include a license and Latin and Algerian papers, the vessel appears to be the property of Mr. Johannes Steen of Stavanger; the outward clearance customs certificate bears the notation "*Duty free,*" and is dated June 27, 1825.[20] In compliance with an act of Congress, which was duly reported by myself to His Majesty's and the Kingdom's most worthy *Commerce Collegium* in Stockholm, this vessel is now sequestered at this place for carrying a much larger number of passengers in proportion to its tonnage than permitted by the said law, which limits the number to two passengers for each five American tons, according to the measurements made here of arriving ships. Despite a disposition toward leniency, it has been impossible to declare the tonnage of the vessel above fifty-five tons, whereas for forty-five passengers at least 112.5 tons are required. One child is said to have been born on the voyage; therefore, under the strictest interpretation of the law, the ship's tonnage ought to be 115 tons. The customs service here is genuinely concerned over the disagreeable necessity of taking legal steps, in view of the fact that the total value of the vessel will scarcely liquidate the costs of such action; and I fear that just this circumstance may prevent the master or any other representative of the interests of the company from carrying through the necessary measures that might assure the restitution of the forfeited sloop, that is, final appeal to the secretary of the treasury in Washington, a procedure which the local collector of customs generously offers to facilitate by every means at his command; but it is not within his power to remit the dues entailed by such an inescapable procedure. It is not necessary for me to remind you that the government officials in this country, from the highest to the lowest, may not violate or ignore existing

[20] The endorsement here referred to is as follows: "Passerer frit. Stavanger Toldkammer d: 27 Junij 1825." It is signed by three officials — Blom, Løvdahl, and S. Munch. See the ship papers, in Riksarkiv, Oslo: F. D. Journalsaker 456/1826 F. The "Restoration," it may be added, was supplied with a signal for use in communicating with Swedish ships off the African coast.

legal regulations. In the meantime, no possible measure on my part will be overlooked in behalf of the interested parties, whose daring undertaking and extraordinary situation have awakened general sympathy. Beyond this, it is necessary to see to it that no further misuse is made of the vessel's papers, which are inadequate for carrying the Norwegian flag to remote waters.

May I take this opportunity respectfully to refer to certain documents which I entrusted last April to the care of a merchant from Bergen, Mr. Kentel, with instructions to deliver them on his arrival in Norway to the proper department of the Royal Government of Norway. Among them was the latest edition of the United States tariff schedules, together with the existing trade and navigation laws.

New York, October 15, 1825.

Respectfully,
Henry Gahn

Respectfully appended: Since the above was written, I have seen an account of this affair in a local daily newspaper, an excerpt from which is herewith enclosed. The article errs with reference to the nature of Norwegian lasts, but otherwise is an accurate version.[21] According to the measurement made here, the tonnage of the sloop has been fixed at fifty-five American tons. [*Addressed*] To the Royal Norwegian Finance, Trade, and Customs Department in Christiania.

Henry Gahn to the Finance, Trade, and Customs Department of the Norwegian Government, November 24, 1825

[Riksarkiv, Oslo: Finans og Tolddepartementet, Kontor F, Journalsager, 1826/4 — A.L.S.]

Vördsam Berättelse:

Med det till Liverpool härifrån afseglade paket-skeppet William Thompson hade jag, den 15de sidstledne October månad, äran inberätta hitkomsten af den Norrska Slupen Restauration med fyratio fem Passagerare ifrån Stavanger. Detta fartyg hvars namngifne Redare, Johannes Steen, lär sjelf vara en af desse hitkomne, och till den innre deln af denna Staten New

[21] The New York *Daily Advertiser* for October 12, 1825, reporting the arrival of the sloop, spoke of it as measuring " only about 360 Norwegian lasts or forty-five American tons." Actually the sloop measured 18.5 lasts. This news story, entitled "A Novel Sight," appeared also in the *New York Statesman* for October 12 and in the *New York Advertiser* for October 15.

York afreste Passagerare, har nu blifvit af Dessa Förenta Staters Regering aldeles frigifvet ifrån det Beslag som jag haft äran anmäla, med eftergift af all plikt och betydliga omkostningar; så att egaren kan derom disponera efter eget godtycko. I anseende till den enda här legitimerade Flaggan, så lär denna Slup likväl, i hvad händelse som häldst icke kunna berättigas att, under den Kongl. Svänska och Norrska Unions-Styrelsens beskydd, idka sjöfart i dessa aflägsna farvatten; i hvilket hänseende jag fruktar att densamma befinner sig i den categorie som omtalas i Kongll. Kundgörelsen af den 17 Julii 1821, Kongl: Brefvet af den 23 Januarii 1822, och Kongll Svänska Commerce Collegii Circulaire af den 4de Februarii samma år, hvaraf innehållet i sammandrag förklaras uti 6te Artikeln, 16de Capitlet, 2^{dra} Paragraphen, pagina 431, af Herr Assessor G. M. Danckwardts år 1823 i Stockholm tryckta uplaga af gällande Forfattningar, hvilket Verk troligen finnes i Den Kong. Norrska Regeringens Samling af erhållna Handlingar ifrån Sverige. Härom har jag, till varning, underrättat en här qvarblefven Intressent i denna Slup, tillställande honom en Dansk öfversättning af åberopade paragraph. Jag känner ej bestämdt huru långt Consulernes embetsmanna-myndighet, under Konungariket Norriges Lagar, sträcker sig in anseende till anhållande af otillräckliga Norrska Skepps Documenter som endå hvarken äro *falska* eller synas annorlunda *origtiga.* Desse hitkomne Emigranters medförda Förpassningar och Bevis om god frägd lära väl i alla fall berättiga *dem* till min enskildta välvillighet och biträde; äfvensom allmänhetens deltagande för dem har här yttrat sig i betydliga gåfvor af penningar och klädespersedlar till deras utrustning vid aftågandet härifrån staden inåt landet.

Vid ytterligare efterfrågan på Tullkammaren, har jag erfarit, att man utsträckt Slupen Restaurations utmätning ända till Sextio och 2/95 Tons, men det kunde endå ej befria ifrån beslag; denna drägtighet berättigade honom endast att hitföra Tjugufyra Passagerare, enligt Congress-Acten af den 2^{dra} Mars 1819, kallad "An Act for regulating Passenger Ships and Vessels", hvilken förtjänar anmärkas, och var en af de Lagar som jag hade äran insända med Herr Kentel. Eljes finnes den också i 6te Tomen, pagina 379, af John B. Colvins uplaga af "Laws of the United States of America", tryckt i Washington City år 1822, hvilket verk troligen är tillgängligt någorstädes i den Europæiska Norden.

Slutligen torde det intressera att mottaga inneslutna sednaste Pris Courant och "Shipping List" ifrån denna ort, hvarest en förfärlig reaction också nu inträffat i enskildta Handels-och Finance-angelägenheter.

NEW YORK den 24de November 1825.

ödmjukast

HENRY GAHN

[*Postscript*] I sidsta stunden inlämnas hos följande bref till Elias Eliasen Tasted i Stavanger, ifrån en af de omskrefne, hitkomne, Passagerare, hvilket jag förmodar kan recommenderas till K. Regeringens beskydd.

[*Addressed*] Till Kongl. Norrska Regeringens Finance-Handels och Tull Departement i Christiania.

[*Enclosures. Shipping and Commercial List (New York). Wednesday, November 23, 1825; clipping from the New York Gazette, November 24, 1825.*]

[*Translation*]

RESPECTFULLY SUBMITTED:

By the departing packet ship "William Thompson," bound for Liverpool, I had the honor, on October 15, last, of reporting the arrival of the Norwegian sloop "Restoration" with forty-five passengers from Stavanger. This vessel, the owner of which, Johannes Steen by name, was himself one of the arrivals, carrying passengers who have now left for the interior parts of the state of New York, has now been released by the government of the United States from the sequestration about which I had the honor to inform you, with the remission of all obligations and major expenses, giving the owner entire freedom to dispose of it as he sees fit.[22] Nevertheless, with respect to the only flag legally recognized for the sloop at this place, it under no circumstances

[22] *Den norske rigstidende* of Christiania took due notice, on January 23, 1826, of the release of the "Restoration." Its report was as follows: "The vessel that arrived in New York in America from Stavanger, which had carried more passengers in proportion to its tonnage than it had permission to under regulations there in force, and which as a consequence was subjected to confiscation, has nevertheless been freed, and without costs, by the American government — presumably because it was understood that the immigrants had violated the law solely because of innocence and ignorance. The public has also shown these inexperienced people much sympathy by giving them considerable gifts, both of money and of clothing, before their departure for the interior of New York, where they will establish themselves." Earlier notices of the "Restoration" appear in the same newspaper for July 25 and December 1, 1825.

has the right to navigate these remote waters under the protection of the Royal Swedish and Norwegian Union Government. I fear that the sloop finds itself in the category stipulated in the Royal Proclamation of July 17, 1821, the Royal Letter-Patent of January 23, 1822, and the Circular of the Royal Swedish *Commerce Collegium* of February 4, 1822, the contents of which are summarized in article 6, chapter 16, paragraph 2, page 431, of Assessor G. M. Danckwardt's edition of existing statutes, published in Stockholm in 1823 and presumably included in the Royal Norwegian Government's collection of documents received from Sweden. I have given formal warning of this to a party interested in the sloop who is still here and have supplied him with a Danish translation of the paragraph in question. I am not certain how far the jurisdiction of the consuls under the laws of Norway extends with reference to taking over inadequate ship's papers which neither are fraudulent nor seem otherwise irregular. These immigrants had in their possession passports and evidence of good character which in any event entitle them to my special favor and assistance; even as public sympathy for them has expressed itself in substantial gifts of money and clothing to equip them for their departure from the city into the country.[23]

On later inquiry at the customhouse, I have learned that the tonnage of the sloop "Restoration" has been increased to 60 2/95; but even this figure would not prevent sequestration. This tonnage entitled her to carry only twenty-four passengers, according to the act of Congress of March 2, 1819, entitled "An Act regulating passenger ships and vessels," which deserves attention and was one of the laws which I had the honor of transmitting with Mr. Kentel. It may also be found in volume 6, page 379, of John B. Colvin's edition of the *Laws of the United States of America,* published in Washington City in the year 1822, a work that is probably accessible some place in the European North.

Finally, it may be of interest to receive the enclosed latest Price Current and "Shipping List" from this place, where there

[23] The sympathetic interest of Americans in the sloop folk was widespread. "The Norwegians are an honest and industrious people, and we sincerely hope that these strangers will do well," said the *Niles' Weekly Register* on October 22, 1825. "It is not often that they leave their own country to make their home in another." Gahn, as has been noted, did take over the official papers of the "Restoration." See *ante,* p. 608 n.

is a tremendous reaction in certain private commercial and financial affairs.

NEW YORK, November 24, 1825.

Respectfully,
HENRY GAHN

[*Postscript*] At the last moment is enclosed a letter to Elias Eliasen Tasted in Stavanger from one of the previously mentioned passengers who arrived here, which I presume may be entrusted to the care of the Royal Government.[24]

[*Addressed*] To the Royal Norwegian Finance, Trade, and Customs Department in Christiania.

EXTRACT FROM A LETTER OF HENRY GAHN TO THE FINANCE, TRADE, AND CUSTOMS DEPARTMENT OF THE NORWEGIAN GOVERNMENT, December 16, 1825

[Riksarkiv, Oslo: Finans og Tolddepartementet, Kontor F, Journalsager, 1826/33 — A.L.S.]

Som jag, enligt Förordningarne, förklarat mig obefogad att vidare befatta mig med den omskrefna, hitkomna Slupen Restauration, såsom icke nu förande någon Laglig Flagga, så lära Intressenterne icke kunnat draga någon serdeles fördel af dess frigifvelse ifrån det anmälta Beslaget. Ett löst rykte har äfven kommit till min kunnskap om de hitkomna emigranternes redan yttrade missnöje öfver sitt företag, såsom icke realiserande de fördelar man lär innan afresan ifrån Norrige, hafva förestält dem såsom en osvikelig följd af denna besynnerliga utflyttning.

NEW YORK den 16 December 1825.

ödmjukast

HENRY GAHN

[*Postscript*] Min vördsammast åberopade jednaste Berättelse af d. 24 sidstl. November, befordrades härifrån med Paket-skeppet *Manhattan* till Liverpool, under adresse till K. Svänska och Norska General Consuln i London.

[*Translation*]

In view of the fact, as previously explained, that I have no legal authority to interest myself in behalf of the sloop "Restora-

[24] On Tasted, or Tastad, the leader of the Stavanger Quakers, see *Norwegian Migration*, 27 ff. The present writer made a search in the archives of the Society of Friends for the letter here referred to, but without success.

tion," which arrived here and has been written of earlier, since at present she flies no legally recognized flags, the interested parties have been unable to gain any considerable advantage by her release from sequestration.[25] An unverified rumor has reached me that the immigrants have expressed dissatisfaction with their undertaking; that they have not realized the advantages which, before their departure from Norway, had been represented to them as certain to result from this strange emigration.[26]

NEW YORK, December 16, 1825.

Respectfully,

HENRY GAHN

[*Postscript*] My most respectful last preceding report, of November 24, last, to which I have referred, was sent from here by the packet ship "Manhattan" to Liverpool, addressed to the Royal Swedish and Norwegian Consul General in London.[27]

[25] Rynning reported that the sloop was sold for not more than four hundred dollars. The purchase price, according to the same source, was eighteen hundred *speciedaler,* or about $1,370. *True Account of America,* 72.

[26] The Gahn report echoed the initial disappointments of the immigrants. Though they ultimately realized many of the promises that America seemed to hold out to them, their success came slowly. Rynning wrote, "They often suffered great need and wished themselves back in Norway; but they saw no possibility of getting there without giving up the last mite of their property, and they would not return as beggars." *True Account of America,* 73. One of the sloop folk, in a letter written many years later, said, "We were all poor, and none of us could speak English. When we arrived in Kendall the most of us became sick and discouraged. The timber was heavy and it took a long time before we could raise enough to support us." H. Hervig, in *Fædrelandet og emigranten,* February 9, 1871, reprinted in Anderson, *First Chapter,* 79.

[27] I am grateful to the staff of the National Archives in Washington, and particularly to Dr. Philip M. Hamer and Miss Edna Vosper, for generous and resourceful aid given me in my search for "Restoration" documents. After making the initial finds in Washington, I went to New York to search in the archives of the federal district court for additional materials. This proved to be a slow and difficult task in which Dr. Carlton C. Qualey of Bard College very generously came to my aid. To him I extend my most cordial thanks. He succeeded in finding the libel and bonding documents of October 13, 1825, and the formal notice of the hearing on November 1; while I turned up the original of the petition of the sloop folk. We were both accorded many courtesies by the officials of the district court and I desire to record my special appreciation of the interest and help given us by the custodian of the archives, Mr. Jack Edwards. Professor Cadbury of Harvard University kindly read the manuscript of the present appendix and gave me several helpful suggestions.

INDEX

INDEX

For the convenience of users the characters æ and ø, which occur frequently in names cited, are alphabeted respectively as ae and o.